Iran's Military Forces in Transition

Iran's Military Forces in Transition

Conventional Threats and Weapons of Mass Destruction

ANTHONY H. CORDESMAN

Westport, Connecticut
London

Library of Congress Cataloging-in-Publication Data

Cordesman, Anthony H.
    Iran's military forces in transition : conventional threats and weapons of mass destruction / Anthony H. Cordesman.
    p. cm.
    Includes bibliographical references and index.
    ISBN 0–275–96529–5 (alk. paper)
    1. Iran—Military policy. 2. National security—Iran. 3. Iran—Armed Forces—Weapons systems. 4. Weapons of mass destruction—Iran. 5. Iran—Politics and government—1979– 6. Iran—Strategic aspects. I. Title.
    UA853.I7 C62 1999
    355'.033555—dc21   98–41448

British Library Cataloguing in Publication Data is available.

Copyright © 1999 by Anthony H. Cordesman

All rights reserved. No portion of this book may be reproduced, by any process or technique, without the express written consent of the publisher.

Library of Congress Catalog Card Number: 98–41448
ISBN: 0–275–96529–5

First published in 1999

Praeger Publishers, 88 Post Road West, Westport, CT 06881
An imprint of Greenwood Publishing Group, Inc.

Printed in the United States of America

The paper used in this book complies with the Permanent Paper Standard issued by the National Information Standards Organization (Z39.48–1984).

10 9 8 7 6 5 4 3 2 1

To the men and women of the US defense intelligence community

Contents

	Acknowledgments	xi
1.	INTRODUCTION	1
	Iran's Threatening Actions	2
	President Khatami and the Hope for Change	4
	Other Military Developments	13
	"Demonization" versus "Sanctification"	16
2.	IRAN'S STRATEGIC PERSPECTIVE	20
	The Constant Threat of Outside Intervention	21
	The Shah After Mussadiq	22
	The Iran-Iraq War and the Tanker War	23
	The Situation Since the Iran-Iraq War	24
3.	THE CONTROL AND LEADERSHIP OF IRAN'S MILITARY FORCES	31
	The Khomeini Era	32
	Post-Khomeini Changes	33
	Partial Reform of the Command Structure	35
	Improving Revolutionary Forces	36
	Internal Security Command Structure	38
	The Competence and Cohesion of Command	39
	Iranian Military Expenditures	40
	Different Estimates of Total Military Expenditures	41

	The Burden of Military Expenditures	45
	Recent Increases in Military Expenditures	49
4.	IRANIAN CONVENTIONAL ARMS TRANSFERS AND MILITARY INDUSTRY	55
	The Quantity of Iran's Arms Transfers	55
	Patterns in New Agreements	62
	The Quality of Iran's Arms Transfers	63
	The Problem of Iran's Aging Weapons Inventory	69
	Iran's Military Industries	73
	Strengths and Weaknesses	79
5.	IRAN'S MILITARY MANPOWER	85
	Numbers versus Force Cohesion	86
	Allocation of Manpower by Service	91
6.	IRANIAN LAND FORCES	93
	Regular Army Organization and Major Combat Formations	94
	Iranian Armored Forces	99
	Iranian Artillery	114
	Anti-Aircraft Weapons	123
	Helicopter and Army Aviation Forces	124
	Communications and Battle Management Systems	126
	The Islamic Revolutionary Guards Corps (Pasdaran)	126
	Iran's Paramilitary Forces: The Basij	135
	Other Paramilitary Forces	136
	The War-Fighting Capabilities of Iranian Land Forces	137
7.	THE IRANIAN AIR FORCE	151
	Strength and Organization	152
	Readiness and Force Quality	161
	The Modernization of Iranian Air Forces	163
	The War-Fighting Capabilities of Iranian Air Forces	167
8.	IRANIAN GROUND-BASED AIR DEFENSES	176
	Strength and Organization	177
	Deployments and Capabilities	177
	Modernization Efforts	179
	The War-Fighting Capabilities of Iranian Land-Based Air Defense Forces	180

9.	IRAN'S NAVAL FORCES	186
	Iran's Surface Navy	187
	Iranian Mine Warfare Capabilities	196
	Iranian Amphibious Warfare Capabilities	198
	Iranian Naval Air Capabilities	199
	Iranian Anti-Ship Missile Forces	199
	Iran's Submarine Forces	202
	The Naval Branch of the Revolutionary Guards	207
	Iranian Naval War-Fighting Capabilities	208
10.	IRAN'S CONVENTIONAL WAR-FIGHTING OPTIONS	217
	Major Contingency Capabilities	217
	Other War-Fighting Options	219
	Key Caveats and Uncertainties	221
11.	IRAN AND WEAPONS OF MASS DESTRUCTION	222
12.	IRANIAN REASONS FOR PURSUING WEAPONS OF MASS DESTRUCTION	265
	Iran's Reasons for Denying Proliferation	267
	Iran's Current Tactical and Strategic Reasons for Proliferating	268
13.	PLANS, DOCTRINE, AND WAR-FIGHTING OPTIONS	271
	Acquisition Plans or Non-Plans	271
	The Technology of Uncertainty	272
	War-Fighting Options and the Inability to Predict Contingency Requirements	273
	Plans as the First Casualty of War	274
	"Command" and "Control"	275
14.	DEALING WITH UNCERTAINTY	279
15.	IRAN'S DELIVERY SYSTEMS AND LONG-RANGE MISSILE PROGRAMS	284
	Iranian Artillery	284
	Iranian Rockets	286
	Iranian Aircraft	288
	Iran's Ballistic Missiles	291
	Possible Cruise Missiles	318

16.	IRANIAN TERRORISM, UNCONVENTIONAL WARFARE, AND WEAPONS OF MASS DESTRUCTION	329
17.	IRANIAN DELIVERY SYSTEMS AND WAR-FIGHTING CAPABILITIES USING WEAPONS OF MASS DESTRUCTION	334
18.	IRANIAN CHEMICAL WEAPONS	337

The Impact of the Iran-Iraq War 337
Iran Responds by Developing Its Own Production Capabilities 341
Iranian Capabilities in the Late 1990s 343
Potential War-Fighting Capabilities 346
Iran and the Chemical Weapons Convention 349

19.	IRANIAN BIOLOGICAL WEAPONS	355
20.	IRANIAN NUCLEAR WEAPONS	362

Iranian Statements and Denials Regarding Nuclear Weapons 363
Nuclear Weapons Efforts under the Shah 365
The Revitalization of Iran's Nuclear Weapons Effort 367
Creeping Proliferation under Rafsanjani 369
Proliferation and the Nuclear Non-Proliferation Treaty 378
Possible Dates for Iran's Acquisition of Nuclear Weapons 385
Iran's Nuclear War-Fighting Doctrine and Capabilities 387

21.	THE UNCERTAIN IMPLICATIONS OF IRAN'S WEAPONS OF MASS DESTRUCTION	399
22.	IRAN'S MILITARY FUTURE AND THE PROPER RESPONSE	405

The Limits to Scenario-Driven Analysis 405
Iran's Uncertain Force Development 407
Predicting the "Unpredictable" 408
The Value of Containment and Deterrence 414

Sources and Methods 417
Selected Bibliography 421
Index 427

Acknowledgments

The author would like to thank the Smith-Richardson Foundation for a grant that funded part of the research for this book.

Iran's Military Forces in Transition

Chapter 1

Introduction

Iran is a nation that is still deeply in the process of revolutionary change, and which is deeply divided between "moderates" who have broad public support and "conservatives" who control the military, security system, and most other governmental institutions. The "moderates" now seem to be the strongest faction, and change may take a peaceful and positive course. Iran's regime has become steadily more pragmatic under President Ali Akbar Hashemi Rafsanjani and President Mohammad Khatami, and more concerned with Iran's national interests and economic development in the Gulf than with the export of revolution. Since the election of President Khatami, there are growing signs that Iran may evolve a more tolerant approach to defining an Islamic state, one that emphasizes the humanitarian and moral strength of Islam, rather than the effort to force other nations into accepting its concept of a repressive and an outdated theological rule and social customs.

Revolutions, however, can become more extreme as well as more moderate. Iran's pragmatists and moderates still face strong radical opposition. Iran's revolution may yet become the captive of ambitious leaders or elites. Conservative or extremist reaction can suppress the positive trends in political and social development, and nationalism and regional ambition can turn ideology into an excuse for aggression. Economic failure can also become an excuse for aggression, as can the need to justify authoritarian rule and social repression.

Iran did not attempt a massive rebuilding of its military forces after its defeat in the Iran-Iraq War, and it cut its military spending sharply after Iraq's defeat in the Gulf War. It may eventually limit its military build-up to creating a strong defense and set strategic goals that defend its own interests without threatening other nations. At the same time, Iran continues to proliferate and build up its capabilities to threaten shipping in the Gulf and the Gulf of Oman. An economically stronger Iran might import much larger numbers of arms, and Iran is creating military industries with the potential to greatly strengthen its forces.

It may be a decade or more before Iran's ultimate course is clear, and it is difficult for many observers to face the fact that it will take time and patience to observe the outcome. In the interim, Iran has developed many critics and apologists. There are those who "demonize" every Iranian action and event, even when such action appears positive or largely defensive. There are those who "sanctify" Iran's worst mistakes, just as there have been those who have excused or glorified every authoritarian and repressive regime in the history of the twentieth century.

Until recently, US policy makers and analysts have tended to demonize Iran. They have viewed Iran largely in terms of the threat its revolutionary regime has posed to Western interests since the fall of the Shah in 1979. For example, a 1995 report on US security strategy for the Middle East by the Office of the Secretary of Defense referred to Iran's regional intentions as follows: "Iran harbors ambitions of establishing Iranian hegemony over the Persian Gulf and expanding its influence over radical Islamist forces. . . . It is obvious that Iran is assertively flexing its muscles vis-à-vis its smaller Gulf neighbors."[1]

At the same time, Europe and many Arab states have seen more of an opportunity for better relations and dialogue. European and Arab governments and analysts felt that the Iranian regime was moderating and that its ambitions were far more modest and defensive than regional hegemony. Some believed Iran had already shifted to a focus on defense, accommodation with its neighbors, and internal development. Others believed that it could be persuaded to do so over time.

The election of President Khatami as Iran's new president on May 24, 1997, has led to more convergence on these issues. His election was a clear sign that Iran's people were deeply concerned with their own cultural freedoms and economic development. During his first year in office, President Khatami took dramatic new initiatives to improve Iran's relations with its neighbors at the Organization of Islamic Countries Conference in Tehran in the fall of 1997. He made a dramatic effort to improve relations with the United States in a television interview in early 1998. What Rafsanjani signaled through actions like offering CONOCO an oil deal, Khatami put into words and began an informal dialogue between Iran and the United States.

IRAN'S THREATENING ACTIONS

It is far too soon, however, to ignore the other aspects of Iran's behavior. The news is filled with signs of internal debates within Iran that could still bring a set of "hard-liners" to power. Iran has scarcely rejected the kind of revolutionary ideology and political rhetoric that have attacked Western secular values and the regimes of many Arab states since the Iranian revolution began.

President Khatami does not control the security structure, military forces, justice system and police, or even the radio and television. All these elements of power are under the direct control of the more conservative exemplified by Supreme Religious Leader Ayatollah Khamenei. Khatami must also deal with other centers of power. The most important of these centers include:

- The 270-member Majlis (Consultative Assembly), in which conservatives hold about one-third of the seats, moderates another third, independents about one-fourth, and religious minorities the remainder;
- The former President Rafsanjani, who now heads the powerful Expediency Council; and
- The hard-liners and extremists in Iranian Revolutionary Guards Corps, the Basij, and Iran's intelligence and security services.

Since Khatami's election there have been many signs that Iran has a complex political structure that is in the midst of an uncertain transition. Virtually every day there are new signs that the Iranian government is divided between "hard-liners" and "moderates." This struggle makes it very difficult to know how moderate Iran's moderates really are, and to determine whether a given speech attacking the United States or the West is really directed at its target or Iran's internal politics. It is scarcely surprising, therefore, that Iran's present political rhetoric is divided between initiatives that promise better relations and dialogue and repetitions of past hostility. Moderates must talk like hard-liners to survive, and this helps explain why one day's new moderate initiative may be followed by the next day's hard-line speech.

It also is too soon to forget the recent past. While the Iran-Iraq War began with Iraqi aggression, Iran's refusal to accept a cease-fire after 1982 needlessly extended the war by nearly half a decade and cost more than 100,000 lives. Iran deployed combat aircraft into Kuwaiti and Saudi air space during the Iran-Iraq War, sailed combat ships into Omani waters, and initiated a "tanker war" against the Southern Gulf states that led to a major military confrontation with the United States.

Iran's attempts to sponsor a coup in Bahrain in the early 1980s seem to have been followed by the ongoing support of Shi'ite extremists in both Bahrain and Saudi Arabia. Iran's seizure of all of Abu Musa and the Tunbs created a new source of confrontation following the Gulf War. Iran has continued to support extremist movements in the Sudan, Egypt, and Algeria. It has continued to oppose the Arab-Israeli peace process and has joined Syria in using the Hezbollah to conduct a proxy war against Israel in Lebanon.

Iran extended its struggle with hostile Iranian opposition movements to the point where it has conducted a systematic campaign of assassinations in Europe which have killed between 40 and 60 people. While these acts of state terrorism have often been taken against members of movements which are themselves terrorist in character, Iran has also murdered peaceful members of its opposition.

It has sponsored other terrorist movements and given them training and sanctuary as well.

Iran has further compensated for the overall weakness of its conventional weapons in three ways which pose a potential threat to its neighbors and the West:

- It has built up elite special forces, and large forces for unconventional warfare—many of which are trained for operations in the Gulf area.
- It has created a mix of anti-ship missile deployments, submarines, and mine warfare capabilities that cannot seriously threaten US naval power, but which can threaten commercial tanker and cargo traffic in the Gulf and which can be used as a tool to put pressure on the Southern Gulf states.
- It has acquired new long-range missiles from North Korea, built up significant stocks of chemical weapons, and pursued a nuclear weapons program. It has developed biological weapons, although US experts do not believe that it has yet begun to deploy them.

PRESIDENT KHATAMI AND THE HOPE FOR CHANGE

The past, however, may well not be a prologue to the future. The election of Mohammad Khatami as Iran's new president revealed deep fracture lines between Iran's more conservative clerics and the Iranian people. Khatami campaigned by calling for social liberalization and economic reform in Iran. He stressed themes he had raised throughout his career, calling for a dialogue between civilizations, cultures, and religions.

While Khatami broadly endorsed Iran's hard-line policies towards the United States, he had little other choice. No candidate would have been allowed to run who did not openly support Iran's existing policies, and Khatami was by far the most liberal of the four candidates out of 238 applicants that the conservative Council of Guardians allowed to run. As it stood, the Council of Guardians clearly expected Ali Akbar Nateq Nouri, the conservative speaker of the Majlis, to win.

In spite of the political constraints he faced, Khatami became a symbol of domestic political reform to Iran's youth, women, and most of its men. He promised economic reform and growth, an easing of the religious constraints on social and cultural life, and an emphasis on human rights and the rule of law. As a result, he received nearly 70% of the vote in an election involving 94% of Iran's 32 million eligible voters.[2] Iran's voters decisively rejected Ali Akbar Nateq Nouri.

In the months that have followed, Khatami has spoken repeatedly about his belief that there should be no clash of cultures and that Islam and other cultures had much to teach each other. Iran made efforts to improve its relations with the Arab Gulf states and the Arab world. It began a dialogue with Iraq at the ministerial level, improved its relations with Turkey, and took new steps to improve its relations with the European Union.

On December 9, 1997, at the meeting of the Organization of Islamic Conference (OIC) in Tehran, President Khatami gave an opening speech that stated that Islamic civil society and its Western counterpart were "not necessarily in conflict and contradiction in all their manifestations and consequences.... This is why we should never be oblivious to judicious acquisition of the positive accomplishments of the Western civil society."[3]

Khatami condemned terrorism and called for peaceful relations between all Islamic states, including Iran and the Southern Gulf states, stating that

Living in peace and security can be realized only when one fully understands not only the culture and thinking but also the concerns as well as the ways and manners of others. ... In our view, a new order based on pluralism is taking shape in the world that, God willing, will not be the monopoly of any single power... (Islam and the West) are not necessarily in conflict and contradiction in all their manifestations and consequences. This is exactly why we should never be oblivious to judicious acquisition of the positive accomplishments of Western civil society.

Khatami clearly emphasized tolerance and democracy, arguing that, "In the civil society that we espouse, although centered around the axis of Islamic thinking and culture... personal or group dictatorship or even the tyranny of the majority and the elimination of the minority has no place." He urged all Islamic nations to "strengthen confidence, reduce security concerns, and... render ineffective the wrong inculcation by the enemies of Islam."[4]

Khatami's remarks made a sharp contrast to those of Iran's religious leader, the Ayatollah Ali Khamenei, who gave an opening address stating that

Western materialistic civilization is directing everyone towards materialism while money, gluttony and carnal desires are made the greatest aspirations. Sincerity, truthfulness, altruism and self-sacrifice have been replaced in many parts of the world by deception, conspiracy, avarice, jealousy and other indecent features.... Most nations are deprived of scientific progress while a group have used their science and knowledge as a means to mete out oppression on others.... Western liberalism, communism, socialism and all other-"isms" have gone through their tests and proved their debility. As in the past, so today, Islam is the only remedial, curative and savior angel.... The Zionists, the notorious global Zionist media and the agents of arrogance, in particular the Americans— namely those who have sustained the greatest losses due to the (Iranian) revolution— have been and are most active and vocal in slandering the Islamic republic.[5]

In spite of the obvious divisions within Iran, these developments led to an important change in US policy. The United States eased its rhetoric regarding Iran and declared violent Iranian opposition movements like the People's Mujahideen terrorist organizations. United States President Bill Clinton made new overtures to Iran and offered a dialogue without asking Tehran to drop its opposition to peace agreements with the Israelis. Clinton defended past US efforts to isolate Iran. "On our embargo, I think it is the right thing to do. And it will have varying degrees of effectiveness." He also stated, however, that "It [Iran] is a country with a great history that at various times has been quite close to the United States.... Americans have been greatly enriched by Persian culture."

Clinton went on to state that the United States was taking a new approach to assessing US policy, and that no decisions had been taken. He indicated that the United States had been encouraged by the conciliatory remarks of President Khatami and believed that the presidential elections showed that Iranians wanted a more open society.

We would not expect any Islamic state ... to say it had no opinions on issues involving what it would take to have a just and lasting peace settlement in the Middle East.... We would never ask any country to give up its opinions on that. But we would ask every country to give up the support, the training, the army, the financing of terrorism.

The President cited the US dialogue with China:

I think we have to be able to discuss those things in order to have an honest dialogue, just like we have an honest dialogue with China now. We don't have to agree on everything. But people have to be able to have an honest discussion even when they disagree.[6]

Less than a month later, President Khatami gave an interview on the Cable News Network (CNN) on January 8, 1998. He called for a "crack in the wall of mistrust" between Iran and the United States. He made no direct proposal for talks between governments, but he did suggest a dialogue between the two academics, writers, artists, and journalists in the two countries. He also stated that terrorism "should be condemned ... and we condemn every form of it in the world," and "denied categorically" that Iranian intelligence maintained surveillance on US officials and military presence in the Gulf.[7]

Iran's religious leader, the Ayatollah Ali Khamenei, seemed far less forthcoming. He gave a speech shortly after Khatami in which he stated that, "Talks and relations with America would be detrimental to the Iranian nation and to the world Moslem movement.... The American regime is the enemy of [Iran's] Islamic government and our revolution.... It is the enemy of your revolution, your Islam, and your resistance to American bullying."[8]

Khatami was also careful to qualify his remarks in later speeches. Nevertheless, even his most negative comments about the United States were interesting because they were anything but aggressive:

Today we do not need to have the United States at our side. We can go ahead without the help of the United States.... Those who put coercive pressure on others and resort to force, and world powers that try to make oppressive pressure the basis of their relations with other nations ... they cannot expect anything from the Iranian nation.... We have suffered the greatest harm from the unjust policies of America.... Before the revolution, as you know, after the revolution, and even today, American politicians behave like the masters of the world. They impose sanctions on any place that does not bow to their interests and want to impose their sanctions by force on the world, not just on us.... The United States feels it can talk to Iran in whatever form it likes, and do whatever it feels like.... It not only puts pressure on Iran, it puts pressure on Europe, Asia, Japan, saying, for example, "If you want to invest in Iran more than such an amount, we will impose sanctions on you." It tries to impose its own domestic laws on the world. That is its domineering way. The fruit of our revolution is that we have freed ourselves from the yoke of our masters, and we will never submit to any new one. Today we are building our country ourselves. If we have shortcomings, they belong to us and we can remove them.[9]

Iran's Uncertain Future under Khatami

The United States has improved its rhetoric regarding Iran and has reached an agreement with the European Union that seems likely to waive the application of economic sanctions. Nevertheless, it is far too soon to state that Khatami's election means good relations between Iran, its neighbors, and the West. There also are few signs of radical changes in Iran's national security policy. Iran continues its efforts to acquire long-range missiles and weapons of mass destruction. It continues its support of the Hezbollah and ties to extremist movements like the Palestinian Islamic Jihad. It continues its military build-up in the lower Gulf and its intelligence surveillance of US facilities and military operations in Saudi Arabia and other countries in the Gulf.

Iran's most powerful political figure is still the Leader of the Islamic Revolution, the Ayatollah Ali Hoseini Khamenei, and not Iran's new president. Khamenei is the formal commander of the armed forces and has ultimate authority over Iran's intelligence and security services.

This includes the Supreme Council for National Security, whose members include the President, the speaker of the Majlis, head of the judiciary, Chief of the General Staff, Minister of Foreign Affairs, Minister of Intelligence and Security, Minister of the Interior, and the head of the Plan and Budget Organization. Khamenei and his hard-line supporters seem to dominate bodies like the Special Operations (Coordinating) Committee, which includes the President, Supreme Leader's representative, Chief of the General Staff, Minister of Foreign Affairs, Minister of Intelligence and Security, head of the IRGC, and others and which some experts feel manages Iran's overseas operations and support of extremist groups.

Khamenei has an effective veto over the actions of the other branches of Iran's government, and Iran's government has many centers of power, many of which are still under conservative control.

President Khatami seems to have firm control only over the Ministry of Islamic Guidance, the Ministry of the Interior (which does not control the police in Iran), and the Foreign Ministry. The Majlis remains under the leadership of

Khatami's rival, Ali Akbar Nateq Nouri, and about two-thirds of its members seem to be "conservative" in most of their votes. A largely religious Council of Guardians can veto the actions of the president and Majlis and arbitrate many types of issues. Khatami's predecessor, Ali Akbar Hashemi Rafsanjani, now heads a much strengthened Expediency Council, which is generally more liberal than the Council of Guardians and serves as a rival body of review. The Iranian Revolutionary Guards Corps (IRGC) represents conservative military force that is closely linked to the Leader of the Islamic Revolution, and conservative clerics still have de facto control of key popular security forces like the Basij.

At the same time, Khatami's new cabinet, which the Majlis subsequently endorsed, is the most moderate since the fall of the Shah. Kamal Kharrazi, Iran's ambassador to the UN, became the new foreign minister, replacing Ali Akbar Velayati. Kharrazi was scarcely a liberal, had been a spokesman for the revolution in the past, and had rejected the possibility of a dialogue with the United States as recently as November, 1996. At the same time, he received part of his education in the United States, taught there from 1972 to 1979, and was once a member of the American Association of University Professors. He helped negotiate the end of the Lebanese hostage crisis in the early 1990s. He was generally regarded as being much more pragmatic and moderate than Velayati, far better educated in the practical realities of foreign affairs, and much more experienced in dealing with other nations and the West.

Kharrazi's statements promised a more moderate attitude towards Iran's neighbors and the West. He called for "a dialogue among civilizations, rather than a clash among civilizations," and the "expansion of relations with all nations on the basis of mutual respect." Kharrazi talked about opening a dialogue with the United States "in principle," although he stated that, "the policies of the United States towards Iran have not changed. The same hostility towards Iran is going on. The sanctions policy is still in place, and the USA does not miss any opportunity to make problems for Iran, to make obstacles in the efforts by Iran for peace and security in the region.... The ball is in the court of the Americans."[10] Kharrazi was also quite clear in stating that, "We don't recognize Israel ... I can't imagine Iran could recognize Israel as a country."[11]

The Ataollah Mohajerani, who became the Minister of Culture and Islamic Guidance, had advocated direct dialogue with the United States as early as 1990. He was a 43-year-old historian whose public views have long been much more liberal than those of most of Iran's ruling clerics. The Minister of Culture and Islamic Guidance has no formal role in national security policy but is a powerful voice in shaping the extent to which the revolution propagandizes Iranian society and interferes in its cultural life. Both Kharrazi's and Mohajerani's appointment came in the face of significant conservative opposition.

Abdoullah Nouri, who became Minister of the Interior, had held the same position during the period 1990–1994. He had become progressively more moderate, however, and was seen as a powerful voice for political reform. Hossein

Namazi, the new minister for the economy and finance, was a doctor of economics who had studied in Austria. He had held a similar post during the period 1982–1986 and was expected to take the lead in emphasizing economic reform of a kind that required better relations with Iran's neighbors and the West. Many other posts—including agriculture, industry, justice, labor, and oil—went to ministers who were seen as pragmatic moderates by Iranian standards, and as officials that would emphasize Iran's economic development over ideology and efforts to export the revolution.

Khatami's Key National Security Appointments

Iran's military leadership is changing. On September 15, 1997, Khatami called for the depoliticization of Iran's armed forces and urged them to stay out of Iran's politics. "The armed forces have to abstain from factional politics and do their utmost to serve ... (the) pillars of the revolution."[12]

While most of Khatami's key national security appointments were less reassuring than his civil appointments, others offered a hope of increased moderation. Rear Admiral Ali Shamkani left the navy and became the new Minister of Defense. Shamkani had long been regarded as a close associate of the Ayatollah Ali Hoseini Khamenei, and the Ministry of Defense remained closely tied to the Leader of the Islamic Revolution. At the time, Shamkani had never been regarded as a revolutionary fanatic or hard-liner and was viewed as one of the most apolitical and professional of Iran's senior officers. He had been a leader in Iran's military modernization and the development of its military industries, seeking to strengthen its forces and capabilities rather than engage in military adventures.

Some observers felt it was significant that Khatami did not appoint a direct replacement for Shamkani, who had commanded both the regular navy and the naval branch of the IRGC. Instead, Rear Admiral Abbas Mohtaj became commander of the regular navy, and Brigadier General Ali Akbar Ahmadian became commander of the naval branch of the IRGC. This led to speculation that Khatami had divided the command to prevent any member of the military from having too much power, although other analysts felt that Khamenei might have intervened to ensure the independence of the IRGC.

Khatami fired Ali Fallahiyan from his position as the Minister of the Ministry of Intelligence (information) and Security (MOIS). Fallahiyan had strongly opposed Khatami during the election and had become something of an embarrassment to Iran after the Mykonos trial of Iranian assassins in Germany. Qorban'ail Dorri Najafabadi became the new minister. Najafabadi was a relatively obscure figure with no intelligence background. Although Najafabadi was considered relatively moderate and had backed Khatami during the election, it seems likely that Khatami would have preferred to appoint a closer associate like Mohammad Musavi Ko'einiha, and that Najafabadi's appointment was a concession to Khamenei and the hard-line clerics. Najafabadi, however, was regarded as part of the more moderate wing of the conservative faction and as less likely to engage in terrorism and aggressive efforts to export the revolution than his predecessor, Ali Fallahiyan.

Khatami replaced Reza Amrollahi, the head of the Atomic Energy Organization of Iran, with Gholamreza Aghazadeh, Iran's former oil minister. The reasons for this appointment were not clear. Some sources argued that it represented an effort to improve the administration of Iran's nuclear programs (Amrollahi had developed a reputation as an awful administrator and manager). Some felt it might be part of an effort to make Iran's nuclear power program more efficient, while others saw it as part of an effort to review whether such a program was cost-effective at all. A few suggested it might represent a downplaying of Iran's nuclear weapons program.

There is no way to predict Iran's future intentions regarding nuclear weapons. Aghazadeh did, however, reaffirm Iran's commitment to a massive nuclear power program on October 3, 1997. At a meeting with Hans Blix, the head of the International Atomic Energy Agency (IAEA), Aghazadeh indicated that Iran planned to add a second 1,000 megawatt generating unit to its existing efforts to build a 1,000 megawatt unit in Bushehr, and eventually to produce 20% of Iran's electric power needs from nuclear units. He indicated that Iran had approached Russia to buy two more 440 megawatt reactors and was seeking an eventual total of six, and that it was still seeking two 300 megawatt nuclear reactors from China.[13] Since that time, Iran has experienced continuing problems with the first reactor in Bushehr, although it has converted some of the more difficult Iranian-led construction activity to programs managed by Russia.

On September 9, 1997, Khamenei replaced Major General Mohsen Rezaei (Rezai), the head of the IRGC, with his former deputy, Major General Yahya Rahim Safavi. Rezaei was then the longest-serving senior military official in Iran and had been commander for 16 years. Rezaei had previously threatened to turn the Gulf into a "slaughterhouse" if the United States attacked Iran in June, 1997. He had supported Nateq-Nouri and had openly criticized Khatami during the election campaign. He had called for a Syrian-Iranian alliance against Israel and the West just days before the change in command—a sharp contrast with Khatami's continuing calls for dialogue.[14]

This change in command was greeted in Iran as a sign of moderation, and even led to rumors that Rezaei's family had fled Iran and/or that Rezaei was being set aside for his failure to get the IRGC and Basij to support Nateq-Nouri in the election.[15] Rezaei, however, made a point of declaring, in an interview on September 12, that while the Revolutionary Guards needed a strong ideological motivation, they "had to maintain a neutral stance in matters related to the existing factions in the country."[16]

The Supreme Leader, Ali Khamenei, made Rezaei the deputy head of the Expediency Council, potentially one of the most powerful political bodies in Iran. Rezaei's appointment also gave Khamenei a potential hard-line balance to ex-President Rafsanjani, the more "moderate" head of the Council.[17] Furthermore, Brigadier-General Safavi scarcely emerged as a moderate. Iran's official news agency, IRNA, quoted him on May 2, 1998, as saying that some of the new publications allowed President Khatami to "threaten national security." He went on to say that, "We seek to tear out the roots of counter-revolution wherever they may be. We should cut the neck of some of them. We will cut the tongues of others.... Our sword is our tongue. We will expose ... these cowards." Safavi also criticized President Khatami's call in January for cultural exchanges with Americans in January, 1998 by saying, "Can we counter the threat posed by America, which seeks to dominate the world, through a dialogue between cultures and civilizations?"

Furthermore, Major General Safavi has scarcely been a moderate or a loyal supporter of Khatami. He has talked about cutting off the heads of the opposition, and on June 3, 1998, he gave a speech that seemed to clearly align him with Khamenei and against Khatami. He said his forces would bide their time before moving against reform-minded opponents who thrived under moderate President Mohammad Khatami.

The Guards ... have identified many of the elements of these groups.... They have at this time left them free to set up their groups and newspapers, but we will go after them when the time is ripe.... The fruit has to be picked when it is ripe. That fruit is unripe now. We will pick it ... when it turns ripe.... We have thrown a stone inside the nest of snakes which have received blows from our revolution, and are giving them time to stick their heads out.

Safavi referred to this part of the opposition as "the third group," which most observers felt were the liberals and dissidents outside of the mainstream moderate and conservative Islamic factions which share power in Iran.

This speech came only weeks after Safavi stated that the revolution should "cut the necks and tongues" of opponents.

We do not interfere in politics but if we see that the foundations of our system of government and our revolution is threatened ... we get involved.... When I see that a [political] current has hatched a cultural plot, I consider it my right to defend the revolution against this current. My commander is the exalted leader and he has not banned me [from doing this].

Khatami's Defeats and Victories

Khatami has not won every battle. He has seen one of his strongest supporters, Gholamhoession Karbaschi, the mayor of Tehran, brought up on charges of corruption. These charges were raised in late 1997, and Karbaschi was only allowed out on bail before his trial after political intervention. He was sentenced to five years in jail, given a 20-year ban on holding office, and fined $333,000. A sentence of 60 lashes was suspended. Karbaschi faced a show trial, which was broadcast on the state radio and television network, which is controlled by Iran's conservatives. The judge simultaneously acted as prosecutor, and took responsibility for gathering the evidence. He stated after the trial that he had "considered God and doomsday in issuing my verdict." Karbaschi is still free awaiting the outcome of his appeal, but the same day he was sentenced, conservatives succeeded in shutting down *Jameeah* for publishing "insults and lies." *Jameeah* is one of Iran's most liberal and pro-Khatami newspapers. While a successor paper soon began publishing, it too was shut down in September, 1998, along with several magazines.

The Majlis impeached Khatami's liberal Interior Minister, Abdullah Nouri, on June 21, 1998. Nouri was widely recognized as one of Karbaschi's strongest defenders, and the Majlis charged him with putting the country's security at risk, arrogance, dismissing 1,700 officials with more conservative politics, and weakening the stability of the economy. The vote was 137 to 111, with 13 abstentions, although Khatami had defended Nouri and called him "one of the strongest ministers in the cabinet." The vote came only three days after US Secretary of State Madeleine Albright had praised Khatami for leading Iran in a more moderate direction.

The conservatives were winning rounds, however, and not the fight. Khatami was able to give Nouri the position of one of Iran's vice presidents, the Vice President for Development and Social Affairs. He promptly appointed Mostafa Tajzadeh as acting minister. Tajzadeh has been one of Nouri's deputies and a close supporter. In July, Khatami made Abdolvahed Mousavi-Lavi the Minister of Interior. Mousavi-Lavi had served as Khatami's Vice President for Development and Social Affairs, and had been Khatami's Deputy of Ministry of Culture and Islamic Guidance when Khatami served as minister in the 1980s.

The Supreme Leader named three conservatives to the Council of Guardians in July, including the Ayatollah Mohammad Jannati, a strong and highly vocal hard-line critic of Khatami. This event may have helped lead Mousavi-Lavi to give a speech on August 12, 1998, calling upon the Council of Guardians to allow moderate candidates to run for the election to the Assembly of Experts. The election takes place on October 23, 1998. The Assembly has the power to appoint and dismiss the Supreme Leader, and the election occurs every eight years. The Council of Guardians must screen all candidates for the Assembly of Experts and has rejected moderate candidates in the past.

Khatami was able, however, to persuade the Ayatollah Khamenei to appoint Mousavi-Lavi as the acting commander of the police services on August 1, 1998. Nouri had never been given the post and the appointment did seem to strengthen Khatami. Further, Khamenei immediately endorsed the liberal and free-market-oriented economic reform plan that a Khatami-appointed committee presented to him in mid-August.

It is clear that a major political struggle is taking place. There have been other judicial excesses, including the arrest of several pro-Khatami deputy mayors of Teheran. Thugs in the hard-line Ansar-e Hezbollah (Helpers of God) have been allowed to attack peaceful pro-Khatami demonstrations while the police and security services stood by.

Nevertheless, it is far from clear that this power struggle will lead to open civil conflict. Khatami has public opinion and the street and Khamenei has the security forces and military power. At the same time, some students and youth groups, like the Basij support Khamenei, while the military forces and Revolutionary Guards are 70% conscript and are filled with young men who voted for Khatami. Some observers feel that both sides are too frightened to use force on a large scale. They feel that a new political structure is emerging where Khatami tries to maneuver around Khamenei, Khamenei tries to isolate or undercut Khatami, and key players like Rafsanjani shift their direction according to the winds of power and act as opportunists.

OTHER MILITARY DEVELOPMENTS

Few dramatic changes took place in Iran's military behavior during President Khatami's first year in office. On September 22, 1997, the seventeenth anniversary of the beginning of the Iran-Iraq War, Khatami repeated the kind of speech calling for strong Iranian forces that Rafsanjani had given for years. He referred to foreign navies in the Gulf (United States and British) as a major threat, and he singled out US-Israeli-Turkish joint naval exercises in the Mediterranean as a threat to Iran.[18]

At the conference of the Organization of Islamic Conference (OIC), President Khatami stated that there should be a pact to enable Gulf nations to defend themselves without relying on "foreign forces."

Iran . . . considers the conclusion of collective defense-security arrangements in the Persian Gulf an assured step towards the establishment of lasting security in the region. . . . In the sensitive and strategic region of the Persian Gulf, the regional states themselves should undertake to preserve security and peace. . . . The presence of foreign forces and armada . . . serves not only as a source of tension and insecurity but also of tragic environmental consequences.

The Ayatollah Ali Khamenei used harsher language when he said:

Right now, the presence of foreign warships and more importantly the US military muscle flexing in the Persian Gulf, which is an Islamic sea and an important source of energy for the entire world, is faced with insecurity. He referred to the "poisonous breath" of the United States, and called on the OIC to "force the aliens to dispense with this intervention and on the other hand eliminate the pretexts for this improper presence.[19]

Iran has continued to seek new technology and supplies to produce chemical and nuclear weapons, long-range missiles, and advanced conventional weapons. It has continued its intelligence surveillance of US facilities in Saudi Arabia.[20]

It bombed the bases of the People's Mujahideen, a violent opposition group based in Iraq, on September 29, 1997.[21]

Although Secretary of Defense William Cohen made a point of stating that the sudden deployment of the carrier *Nimitz* to the Gulf in late September, 1997 was a reaction to Iraqi flights in the "no fly zone," and that the "deployment order only cited Iraq and did not mention Iran," Iran reacted with a new flood of rhetoric.[22] Key Iranian military officers like Rear Admiral Abbas Mohtaj, the new commander of Iran's navy, have continued to issue statements like,

The aim of the US presence in the Gulf is to create a crisis and to sell billions and billions of dollars worth of weapons to the Arab countries in the region.... The presence of foreign countries, including the USA, in the Gulf is illegitimate and contrary to the security of the region.[23]

Defense Minister Shamkani has picked up the same old themes, stating that the United States was seeking to pursue a strategy of "distinctive control" in dealing with the Gulf states and defending Iran's right to attack People's Mujahideen bases in Iraq, even if this meant flying through the UN no-fly zones.[24] Admiral Mohammed Razi Hadayeq, the commander of Iran's missile forces, stated that Iran was the region's "strongest missile power."[25] Mohammed Sadr, Iran's new Deputy Foreign Minister, visited Damascus on September 9, 1997, to discuss the security situation in Lebanon and to pledge continued military aid to the Hezbollah. Iran supplied the Hezbollah with new, longer-range rockets, although these seem to have been shipped before the election.[26]

Iran held massive military exercises in September, 1997 to commemorate the start of the Iran-Iraq War. Khamenei attended the final week of the exercises, which Iran claimed involved 200,000 men, air units, and several heavy divisions operating in an 1,800 square kilometer area north of Qom. As usual, the exercises were rationalized as defensive, but taught just as many lessons in offensive warfare.[27]

Iraq held naval war games in mid-October, which it claimed involved 100 ships operating over a 15,000 square mile area. These exercises began almost at the same time the *Nimitz* entered the Gulf. Iran issued claims that it had sent a new, small "stealth" remotely piloted reconnaissance system to spy on the US task force. Somewhat ironically, it then accused a US destroyer and reconnaissance plane of spying on its maneuvers. The US destroyer it named, the *USS Kinkaid*, was sitting in port in Bahrain at the time Iran claimed it was doing the spying.[28]

Another low point in Iran's relations with other nations occurred in mid-October, 1997, when Iran's Agriculture Minister, Issa Kalantari, charged that the United States was conspiring to keep Iran's pistachios out of European markets. In fact, the European Union had limited imports because it had found up to 200 times the permitted level of Aflatoxin B1, a substance found in food mold, which causes cancer of the liver.[29]

If there is any irony in Iran's military rhetoric, it lies in the fact that Iran's Majlis has continued to indulge in the same kind of hostile posturing as the US Congress. On January 25, 1998, it approved a fund for countering US "plots" against the Islamic republic for the third consecutive year. Deputies voted to allocate half of the fund to the Intelligence (internal security) Ministry and to give President Mohammad Khatami control over the rest of the budget, which is to be used to "uncover and neutralize the American government's plots and interference in Islamic Iran's internal affairs." The amount set aside for the fund was not announced, but a parliamentary debate broadcast on the radio indicated that it would be about the same as the current year's 25 billion Rials ($14.3 million).

One deputy claimed that 10 billion Rials had already been used to set up Iran's satellite television channel which was launched last month and covers Europe and parts of Asia and the Middle East. "If today our dear president talks to the American people for one hour on CNN, with this budget we can launch a network through which we could address the Americans every day and bring them the message of the Islamic revolution and tell them about our just stands." The debate also indicated that some of the money would be used to bring suits against Washington at international bodies and to fight a "US cultural invasion," and that some of the money would also go to the Islamic Propagation Organization, a state-affiliated body which sends Shi'ite Moslem clerics to other countries.

Iranian Foreign Minister Kamal Kharrazi followed up with a speech on April 22, 1998, that condemned the US plan to beam radio broadcasts to Iran by stating that, "A wall of mistrust still stands between Tehran and Washington. . . . America's policies prove that, as in the past, one cannot trust what American officials say." He stated that the United States' plans to set up a Persian-language radio station aimed to wage a "psychological war" against Iran and constituted US interference in the internal affairs of the country. A war of words is not a war of weapons, however, and the Majlis only began this effort after US media reports revealed that the US Congress had set up a similar fund for covert action against Tehran.

Furthermore, there are some indications that military tensions have begun to diminish. President Khatami's speech on Armed Forces Day on April 18, 1998, stressed defensive nationalist themes: "Our army is strong and sovereign; our armed forces are strong and powerful, but neither our revolution nor our nation or armed forces are expansionist," he said in a speech at a military parade to mark Iran's Armed Forces Day. "We want a sovereign country and nation that seeks independence and honor and could act as a model for all the nations and countries of the region."

The main focus of the Armed Forces Day parade in 1998 was also largely defensive. It was to remember the casualties of Iran's war with Iraq, which Iran referred to as "the imposed war" and "the sacred defense," and to celebrate the recent repatriation of Iran's POWs under the supervision of the International

Committee of the Red Cross. The exchange included 5,584 Iraqis and 316 Iranians, most of which had been held captive for more than 15 years. Some of the freed Iranian POWs watched the parade and were honored by Khatami, who hung laurels around their necks.

The equipment used in the parade was also not particularly threatening. It included a flypast of MiG-27 and Sukhoi 24 fighters, but it also included a flypast of 25-year-old F-4 Phantom fighters. It included British Chieftain and Scorpion tanks and US Hawk surface-to-air missiles, which were acquired before the 1979 Islamic revolution that toppled the pro-Western shah. If there was any ominous element it was the march of nuclear, biological, and chemical warfare decontamination units, but these were displayed to recall the deaths of many Iranians from Iraqi chemical weapons, and no reference was made to any present Iranian capability.

Iran did hold the usual exercises following Armed Forces Day. They involved some 15,000 naval and air force personnel and all three of Iran's Russian-built Kilo-class diesel submarines. They produced the usual rhetoric about Iran's strength and served as a tangible demonstration of the threat it could pose to shipping through the Strait of Hormuz and the Gulf. At the same time, the official rhetoric surrounding the exercises was less strident than in the past, and the exercises did not involve any offensive operations. Like all previous Iranian exercises, no attempt was made to practice extensive amphibious operations involving significant movements of armor or over-the-beach operations.

Even a worst-case interpretation of Iran's military actions and intentions indicates that the end result may be a period of confrontation and hostility, with occasional low-level clashes and acts of terrorism. This would be far short of war, or the aggressive ambitions of Iraq, and would still allow the region to evolve towards peace. If Iran's revolutionary regime does become steadily more pragmatic and moderate with time, the problem Iran's military forces raise for its neighbors and the United States may be transformed to one of creating a new and stable balance of regional security and deterrence, one where Iran may gradually become a partner rather than a potential threat.

"DEMONIZATION" VERSUS "SANCTIFICATION"

The key problem in dealing with Iran is that there is no way to predict the ultimate balance of power between Iran's moderates and conservatives. No week went by during President Khatami's first year in office in which some conflict did not surface between the two sides. The jailing of Tehran's moderate mayor, Gholamhossein Karabachi, on April 4, 1998, was a clear conservative attempt to put pressure on Khatami by attacking one of his closest allies on trumped-up charges of corruption. Every initiative Khatami took to improve relations with the United States was counterbalanced by hard-line rhetoric from leaders like Khamenei.

As a result, it is as dangerous to "sanctify" Iran as it is to "demonize" it.

Khatami has repeatedly criticized the United States and its role in the Gulf, although his criticism has not involved extremism or threats of violence. His words in a speech in April, 1998 indicate that the United States and Iran have a long way to go before they can have friendly relations, although they also indicate that a modus vivendi based on mutual compromise may well be possible:

Today we do not need to have the United States at our side. We can go ahead without the help of the United States.... Those who put coercive pressure on others and resort to force, and world powers that try to make oppressive pressure the basis of their relations with other nations... they cannot expect anything from the Iranian nation.... We have suffered the greatest harm from the unjust policies of America.... Before the revolution, as you know, after the revolution, and even today, American politicians behave like the masters of the world. They impose sanctions on any place that does not bow to their interests and want to impose their sanctions by force on the world, not just on us. [The United States feels it can talk to Iran] in whatever form it likes, and do whatever it feels like.... It not only puts pressure on Iran, it puts pressure on Europe, Asia, Japan, saying, for example, "If you want to invest in Iran more than such an amount, we will impose sanctions on you." It tries to impose its own domestic laws on the world. That is its domineering way. The fruit of our revolution is that we have freed ourselves from the yoke of our masters, and we will never submit to any new one. Today we are building our country ourselves. If we have shortcomings, they belong to us, and we can remove them.

At this moment in the Iranian revolution, Iran does seem likely to become more "moderate" and "pragmatic" than to become more extreme. However, a "moderate" and "pragmatic" Iranian regime is unlikely to mean an Iran whose strategic interests coincide with those of the United States, its Southern Gulf neighbors, or any other state in the region. Actions that a "moderate" and "pragmatic" Iran regards as defensive and as serving its vital national interests will often be seen as threatening by some of its neighbors, Israel, and the West.

The key word is patience. It may be half a decade before it is possible to determine how Iran's military capabilities are evolving, what will happen to its support of extremist movements, and how it will deal with proliferation. These risks and uncertainties mean Iran's military forces must be analyzed in terms of capabilities and possible contingencies, rather than on the basis of some prediction of its intentions.

Even if Iran never tries to initiate a conflict, it is impossible to dismiss the risk that some incident or clash could escalate into a much more serious conflict. Iraq will continue to present a "wild card" in two important ways: First, in terms of the risk of another major military encounter with Iran, and second, in terms of some kind of opportunistic alliance between Iran and Iraq.

As a result, the analysis that follows makes no attempt to either "demonize" or "sanctify" Iran. It focuses on Iran's current military strength and its future military capabilities. It addresses Iran's military expenditures and arms imports, and its military demographics. It examines Iran's war-fighting capabilities in major regional contingencies, its capacity to intimidate other Gulf states, its efforts to acquire weapons of mass destruction, and its ability to conduct more limited and less conventional forms of war.

One lesson of this analysis is that there is a strong case for continuing the kind of military containment that will limit potential threats without blocking Iran's development or affecting its security. While such efforts cannot halt proliferation, they probably delay it and sharply limit it in scope. The same is true of efforts to block large, destabilizing deliveries of advanced conventional weapons.

At the same time, the results of this analysis do not support the need for economic sanctions, even when considered solely in the context of Iran's defense efforts. It is also clear that there is a need for the kind of a dialogue where both sides can explore the extent to which the West and Iran can resolve their differences. In the process, nations like the United States will almost certainly have to compromise, as well as Iran, and there may be areas where both sides will have to agree to disagree. This seems far more positive, however, than open hostility, Iranian treatment of the United States as the "great Satan," and failed US efforts to sanction Iran's economy and energy exports.

NOTES

1. Office of the Assistant Secretary of Defense for International Security Affairs (Middle East and African Affairs), "United States Security Strategy for the Middle East," Washington, Department of Defense, May, 1995, pp. 16–17.

2. Iran has a very young electorate. The voting age is 15, and half of Iran's population is 18 or younger.

3. The Islamic summit was the eighth in a series begun in Rabat in 1969. Some 25 heads of state took part and vowed to liberate from Israel the holy city of Jerusalem, site of Islam's third most sacred shrine, the al-Aqsa Mosque. The meeting established the Organization of Islamic Countries (OIC) and based its secretariat in Jeddah, Saudi Arabia. Since then, Islamic summits have convened in Lahore in 1974, the Saudi city of Taif in 1981, Casablanca in 1984, Kuwait in 1987, Dakar in 1991, and Casablanca in 1994. The OIC comprises 55 members representing the world's 1.2 billion Moslems. The members are: Afghanistan, Albania, Algeria, Azerbaijan, Bahrain, Bangladesh, Benin, Brunei, Burkina Faso, Cameroon, Chad, Comoros, Djibouti, Egypt, Gabon, Gambia, Guinea, Guinea-Bissau, Indonesia, Iran, Iraq, Jordan, Kazakhstan, Kuwait, Kyrgyzstan, Lebanon, Libya, Malaysia, Maldives, Mali, Mauritania, Morocco, Mozambique, Niger, Nigeria, Oman, Pakistan, Palestinian territories, Qatar, Saudi Arabia, Senegal, Sierra Leone, Somalia, Sudan, Surinam, Syria, Tajikistan, Togo, Tunisia, Turkey, Turkmenistan, Uganda, United Arab Emirates, Uzbekistan, and Yemen. Bosnia, the Central African Republic, Guyana, and the Ivory Coast have observer status, along with the Turkish Cypriots and the Moro National Liberation Front of the Philippines.

4. Associated Press, December 9, 1997, 0614.

5. Associated Press, December 9, 1997, 0614.

6. Reuters, December 16, 1997, 2209.

7. CNN, Internet Home Page, January 8, 1998.
8. January 16, 1998, 2331.
9. Reuters, January 20, 1998, 0048.
10. *Los Angeles Times*, September 28, 1997, p. M3. The author listened to the Foreign Minister make the same points during his initial speech at the UN and at a private dinner. Also see the interview with Kharrazi in the *Washington Post*, October 5, 1997, p. C-4.
11. *Los Angeles Times*, September 28, 1997, p. M-3.
12. *Iran Focus*, October, 1997, p. 7; *Middle East Economic Digest*, October 3, 1997, p. 10.
13. *Middle East Economic Digest*, October 17, 1997, p. 10.
14. *The Estimate*, September 12, 1997, p. 4; *Policywatch*, October 1, 1997, No. 269; *Jane's Defense Weekly*, November 12, 1998, p. 30.
15. *Iran Focus*, October, 1997, pp. 7, 9.
16. *Iran Focus*, October, 1997, pp. 7, 9.
17. Reuters, September 10, 1997, 1250; *Washington Times*, September 10, 1997, p. A-13.
18. *Middle East Economic Digest*, October 3, 1997, p. 10.
19. Associated Press, December 9, 1997, 0741.
20. *Los Angeles Times*, October 15, 1997, p. A-1.
21. *Jane's Defense Weekly*, October 8, 1997, p. 4; *Philadelphia Inquirer*, September 20, 1997, p. A-17.
22. Reuters, October 7, 1997, 0639.
23. *USA Today*, October 6, 1997, p. 10A; *The Estimate*, October 10, 1997, p. 1.
24. Reuters, October 7, 1997, 0639.
25. Associated Press, NY, October 18, 1997, 1731 EDT.
26. Reuters, September 9, 1997, Damascus; *Washington Times*, August 22, 1997.
27. Reuters, September 28, 1997, 0417; *Washington Post*, October 13, 1997, p. A-24.
28. *Washington Post*, October 13, 1997, p. A-24; *Washington Times*, October 11, 1997, p. A-6, October 16, 1997, p. A-11; Associated Press, October 14, 1997, 1113, October 16, 1997, 0624; *Jane's Defense Weekly*, October 22, 1997, p. 3.
29. Associated Press, NY, October 19, 1996, 1136EDT; *New York Times*, October 19, 1997, p. A-10.

Chapter 2

Iran's Strategic Perspective

Iran's strategic literature is deeply divided. Some of it consists of hard-line speeches and writings that imply a national strategy that focuses on driving the West out of the Gulf and radical efforts to export Iran's revolution. Iranian writings are filled with extremist rhetoric and nationalist boasts, and some Iranian speeches and Iranian media reporting can be paranoid in character when it deals with the risk of US military attacks and criticism by other states.[1]

For example, Moshen Rezaei, then commander of the Revolutionary Guards, stated in April, 1997 that Iran was capable of closing the Strait of Hormuz to tanker traffic, and that Iran's military exercises during the spring of 1997 were designed to demonstrate this capability and Iran's ability to destroy any American invasion. "Iran will never start any war, but if the Americans one day decide to attack us, then they would have committed suicide. We will turn the region into a slaughterhouse for them. There is no place better than the Persian Gulf to destroy America's might."[2] Rezaei also repeatedly stated that, "The Persian Gulf belongs to the regional countries and the Americans should leave it. . . . The Persian Gulf is our region; they have to leave our region."[3]

Rezaei, however, is a voice of the past, and it is possible to find other speeches that are much more pragmatic, which is certainly true of the speeches and writings of Iran's new president and foreign minister. Much of Iran's military literature is highly pragmatic, and it is clear that Iran actively learns from the strategic literature and military experience of other states—including the United States. In fact, most of Iran's military and strategic literature has gotten steadily more professional in character since the end of the Iran-Iraq War, and even more so since the end of the Gulf War.[4]

Iranian speeches, articles, and press releases do reveal obvious divisions between ideologues and professionals, and some conceptual divisions between the regular military and the Islamic Revolutionary Guards Corps (IRGC). Iranian officials continue to make unrealistic boasts about self-sufficiency, and simultaneously brag about their missile programs and deny that they are proliferating.

At the same time, a great deal of Iranian writing at the professional level now reveals a good understanding of the lessons of the Gulf, the real-world problems Iran faces in dealing with US military forces, the rapid advances in tactics and military technology, and the problems posed by proliferation. Iran tends to publicly deny some aspects of its interest in unconventional warfare, but there are many indications that it now understands the need for proper professionalism, training, and equipment and is much more cautious about substituting ideological fervor for good planning and execution. Similarly, while Iran's public rhetoric about its acquisition of submarines and anti-ship missiles may fluctuate between boasting and defensiveness, its methods of training and deployment often reveal a high degree of professionalism.

It is far too soon to determine how Khatami's election will change Iran's strategic perspective, if it does so at all. Much can be learned, however, by looking beyond the words of Iran's current revolutionary regime and considering the historical background that shapes Iran's strategic perspective.

THE CONSTANT THREAT OF OUTSIDE INTERVENTION

Iran has legitimate security concerns and a history that helps explain much of its current ambitions, rhetoric, and hostility toward the West. During most of the latter part of the nineteenth century, Iran's history consisted of efforts to defend itself against British and Russian efforts to dominate the country as part of the "Great Game."[5] Russia's impact on Iran declined after the fall of the czar in 1917, but it was Britain and Russia which helped end Iran's democratic revolution during the period 1907–1912. British imperialism played a major role in exploiting the Iranian economy after the Anglo-Persian agreement of 1919. It was Reza Khan, an illiterate former NCO of a Russian Cossack regiment, who subverted Iran's second attempt at democratic revolution in 1921, and who had strong British support when he took the title of shah and founded the Pahlavi dynasty in 1925.[6]

When Reza Shah began to challenge Britain's exploitation of Iran's oil resources and the dominance of the Anglo-Persian oil company in 1932, it became brutally clear that Britain still dominated Iran and was willing to use force when necessary. This led Reza Shah to tilt towards the Axis powers after 1939, but the end result was an Anglo-French ultimatum on August 16, 1941, that he halt all ties to the Axis. When Reza Shah did not comply, Britain and Russia invaded Iran and occupied the country. They deposed Reza Shah in favor of his son, Mohammed Reza Pahlavi—the shah who was eventually overthrown in 1979.

Britain and Russia used martial law and their occupation of Iran to help supply Russia during World War II. In 1943 and 1944, the British went so far as to seize a substantial part of the Iranian harvest to help feed Russia. The end result was near starvation, popular riots in Tehran, and eventually a crisis where British commanders forced Iranian units to machine-gun a massive protest group moving towards government buildings from the Bazaar in Tehran.[7] While British troops largely withdrew in 1945, the Union of Soviet Socialist Republics (USSR) attempted to create a new pro-Soviet state composed of parts of Iranian Kurdistan and Azerbaijan. The Soviet Union only withdrew its forces from Iran in 1946—after substantial Iranian concessions. Russia's de facto control of much of northern Iran only ended in 1947—after US pressure on Russia convinced the Majlis that it was secure enough to revoke the concessions.

Nothing about this experience left Iran with reason to show confidence in the West, although it often attempted to turn to the United States to act as a counterweight to Britain and Russia between the 1890s and 1949. Beginning in 1949, however, the United States became increasingly involved in Cold War efforts to secure Iranian oil against Russia, and in complex negotiations with Britain and various Iranian political factions—many of which came to be seen as tools of the West. In 1951, the resulting political turmoil led to the rise of Mohammed Mussadiq and a major confrontation between the US and Iranian nationalist movement. This eventually led to the Anglo-US coup that began in February, 1953, and which resulted in the Shah's return and the suppression of the Majlis and democratic opposition in August, 1953.

THE SHAH AFTER MUSSADIQ

The end result was a de facto secular dictatorship, in which Mohammed Reza Pahlavi ruled with the support of the Iranian military. It was also a dictatorship whose claims of a "white revolution" and land reform were almost totally spurious. The Shah's Pahlavi foundation effectively seized the assets of the mosques and former land-owning class and kept them—alienating many of Iran's conservatives as well as its socialists and moderates. While the Shah was only moderately repressive, he was seen as having strong US and British backing and as serving US interests in the Cold War.

The dictatorial nature of the Shah's regime did not lead to broad popular resentment during Iran's oil boom—which lasted from roughly 1972 to 1976. However, the end result among Iran's political elite was to transform the image of the United States from a counterweight to British and Russian imperialism to the role of a new "imperialist" who backed a dictator and dominated Iran. Coupled with the major recession that began in 1977, this laid the background for Khomenei's political attacks on the United States as the "Great Satan" in the late 1970s. More generally, it created a political climate among Iran's religious conservatives, socialists, and Marxists that eventually helped trigger the US embassy hostage crisis.

Iran faced other problems in dealing with its neighbors. Britain's creation of Iraq following World War I placed a new power on Iran's western border that was often hostile, had a disputed border with Iran, and occasionally claimed part of Iran's oil-rich Southwest and rights to the whole of the Shatt al-Arab—the main Gulf shipping channel to both Iranian and Iraqi ports. The fall of the Hashemite dynasty in Iraq on July 14, 1958, then created a series of radical military and socialist regimes which triggered a major Iranian-Iraqi arms race and then a low-level border war which began in the late 1960s. Iran effectively won the border war in 1975 and dominated the arms race until the Shah's fall in 1979. However, Iraq then attempted to exploit the chaos caused by the fall of the Shah and the revolution by invading Iran and "liberating" much of Iran's oil reserves—which it claimed were part of an Arab-dominated region. The result was the Iran-Iraq War, which lasted until 1988.

THE IRAN-IRAQ WAR AND THE TANKER WAR

Although Iraq invaded Iran, it gained little sympathy from the world community. The US embassy hostage crisis cut off Iran's new regime from any major resupply from the West. Iran's aggressive ideology, its efforts to export its Islamic revolution, and its refusal to negotiate a cease-fire once it had liberated its territory led most outside powers to support Iraq. The United States, Russia, other Western powers, and all of the Southern Gulf states supported Iraq once the possibility emerged that an Islamic Iran might win the war and dominate part or all of Iraq.

From an Iranian perspective, however, the West was supporting an aggressor nation that had unleashed an all-out struggle between Iran and Iraq. There was little outside protest when Iraq escalated to the use of chemical weapons and strategic attacks on Iran's civilian targets. France equipped Iraq to conduct long-range strategic attacks on Iran's oil export facilities, and the United States led a tanker reflagging effort during the period 1987–1988 that led to a low-level naval war between the United States and Iran. This outside support was critical to Iran's military defeat in 1987–1988, when it might otherwise have won, and to its forced agreement to a cease-fire in August, 1988. This defeat cost Iran some 45–60% of its heavy land-force equipment, and came after Iraq had repeatedly struck at Iranian military cities and made massive new use of chemical weapons. It ended a war that cost Iran hundreds of thousands of casualties.

Iraq's invasion of Kuwait and the Gulf War that followed did not greatly improve Iran's relations with its Gulf neighbors or with the West. From an outside perspective, this was because Iran opposed Iraq to serve its own self-interest and because Iran did not change the other threatening aspects of its behavior. Iran's regime remained revolutionary in character and often launched ideological attacks on its neighbors and the West. Iran's seizure of complete control of Abu Musa and the Tunbs alienated the United Arab Emirates (UAE) and the rest of the Gulf states, as did its steady build-up of its capabilities to threaten Gulf tanker traffic, acquisition of new long-range ballistic missiles, and efforts to acquire weapons of mass destruction.

Once again, the situation looked different when seen with Iranian eyes. A

US-dominated coalition ignored Iran's actions in supporting the UN and efforts to improve its relations with the United States and its neighbors. When the war ended, Iran confronted a hostile, US-dominated coalition that was far stronger than existed before the Gulf War, and a regional security structure in the form of the Gulf Cooperation Council (GCC) from which it was excluded. While Iraq had been weakened, its conventional forces remained stronger than those of Iran. Further, the breakup of the Soviet Union and the Warsaw Pact meant that the United States had emerged as the world's sole superpower. Iran then faced the challenge of the US policy of "dual containment," and even those Southern Gulf nations that appeared to maintain good relations clearly structured their forces to deal with a potential Iranian threat.

Under the circumstances, it is not surprising that Iran began to refer to the US presence as an "alien power destabilizing regional security" and to consistently demand the departure of its "intruding forces." It is also understandable that Iran demanded that the GCC should be expanded to include all regional countries, and that Iranian officials like Major-General Mohsen Rezaei, the commander of the IRGC, should state that, "It is time the Arabs realized that their security can best be protected through peaceful coexistence with Iran, and this is not possible without cooperation."[8]

THE SITUATION SINCE THE IRAN-IRAQ WAR

Few changes have taken place in Iran's basic strategic perspective since the Iran-Iraq War. The US policy of "dual containment" is seen as yet another outside threat from the West. The Southern Gulf states are seen as both a potential threat and as lacking in religious and political legitimacy. The alliance between the United States, Britain, and the Southern Gulf states is seen as a conspiracy against Iran, and every new moment of tension between the United States and Iran creates internal fears that the United States may attack or invade Iran.

Iran still sees the Arab-Israeli peace process as a threat to Islamic justice, and Israel's occupation of Lebanon is seen as an effort to suppress Shi'ites in a country that once provided the Mullahs that converted Iran to the Shi'ite sect. Israel is seen as a Western-backed foreign intervention in the Middle East.

In spite of occasional talks, Iran and Iraq only moved towards a full cease-fire in 1998. Iran continued to hold well over 100 Iraqi combat aircraft that flew to Iran for sanctuary during the Gulf War. Iraq claimed that Iran was still holding 18,229 prisoners of war, and Iran claimed that Iraq was still holding 5,000–10,000. It was only in the spring of 1998 that the two nations finally exchanged their prisoners of war, some of which had been held captive for 17 years.

There have, however, been important changes in the way Iran acts upon its strategic perspective, largely due to the leadership of President Khatami. As has been touched upon earlier, President Khatami set a new tone for Iran in his speech on Iran's Armed Forces Day on April 18, 1998. He made it clear that Iran had no regional ambitions:

Our army is strong and sovereign, our armed forces are strong and powerful, but neither our revolution or Armed forces are expansionist.... We want a sovereign country and nation that seeks independence and honor and which could act as a model for all nations and countries of the region.

Khatami did, however, go on to state that the United States should leave the Gulf. He also warned that

we are prepared to defend, with all our being, our revolution, country, homeland, and nation against the malice of ill-wishers and plots of conspirators.... Today, the most spiritually powerful armed forces are the Iranian armed forces.... All the martyrs and war-disabled sing of the invincibility and the enemy's disappointment with aggression against this country.

There have been particularly significant developments in the Gulf. Iraq opened its border with Iran in September, 1997, for the first time in 17 years. It claimed it did so to allow Iranians to visit the shrines in Najaf and Karbala in Southern Iraq, but it seems to have been attempted to ease relations with Iran in order to obtain support against UN sanctions.

Iran initially rejected the initiative, and less than a month later the nations clashed over a raid that the People's Mujahideen e-Khalq (MEK), a violent Iraqi-based Iranian opposition group, launched into Iran. Iran retaliated on September 29, 1997, by bombing the two MEK military bases near the border area, and Iraq responded by sending up sortie after sortie of Iraqi fighters to patrol the area. The end result of the clash did more to present problems for the United States in enforcing the southern "no-fly zone" than lead to actual conflict, but it was scarcely a signal that Iraq or Iran were moving towards peace.[9]

The clash did not halt a visit to Tehran, however, by the Iraqi Foreign Minister Mohammed Said al-Sahhaf, which took place on January 18, 1998. Khatami, Kharazi, and Shamkani indirectly defended Iraq's position in February, 1998, when it seemed the United States might use force to make Iraq allow the UN Special Commission (UNSCOM) to carry out inspections in Iraq. Khatami called upon Iraq to comply with the UN, but stated that, "The presence of dozens of warships in the Persian Gulf gives offense to the peoples of the region. The people of the region should defend themselves." Shamkani "urged Islamic states, especially countries of the Persian Gulf region, to resist new American military moves."[10] The first Iranian pilgrims in 18 years crossed the Iraqi border in mid-August, 1998.[11]

There is always a risk of some kind of "devil's bargain" between Iraq and Iran. So far, however, the fear of Iraq is a consistent aspect of Iran's strategic perspective. It is also a fear colored by the fact that Saddam is still in power, by the fact that Iraq used chemical weapons against Iran, and by the fear that it might use even more lethal weapons in the future. The Iranian-Iraqi arms race and proliferation remain a key factor that shapes Iran's force planning and view of future military threats.

Iran has made more progress in improving relations with other countries. During the Organization of the Islamic Conference (OIC) in December, 1997, Iranian President Khatami met twice with Saudi Crown Prince Abdullah, the first such high-level meetings between Iranian and Saudi leaders since the 1979 Iranian Revolution. The meetings led to steadily better relations between the two countries in spite of the fact that the Ayatollah Khomeini had once stated that the Saudi regime was even worse than that of the United States. In February, 1998, former President Rafsanjani visited Saudi Arabia for 10 days for talks on boosting bilateral ties and formulating a "security and economic strategy" for boosting security in the region. Rafsanjani was the most senior Iranian to visit Saudi Arabia since the 1979 Iranian Revolution.

The end result has been steadily better relations. The two countries have cooperated on some aspects of oil policy, and have minimized their differences over the way the Haj is conducted in Saudi Arabia and the Saudi treatment of Shi'ites. On May 29, 1998, the Saudi Minister of the Interior, Prince Nayef bin Abdul-Aziz, made a public statement that the bombing at Al Khobar "took place at Saudi hands. No foreign party had any role in it."[12] This statement effectively absolved Iran, and symbolized the change in Iranian and Saudi relations.

Iran has steadily strengthened its relations with Kuwait, Oman, and Qatar. It seems to have reduced any support of Bahrain's Shi'ite opposition to the point where Bahrain has reestablished friendly relations.

Negotiations have taken place with the UAE over Abu Musa and Tunb Islands. Iran had seized the Greater and Lesser Tunbs from Ras al-Khaimah in 1971. In 1992, Iran claimed sovereignty over Abu Musa despite a 1971 agreement between the two countries. Joint control of Abu Musa was maintained until 1994, at which time Iran forcibly took the island. In March 1996, Iran rejected a proposal by the Gulf Cooperation Council which advocated that the International Court of Justice resolve the dispute, an option supported by the UAE. This rejection was preceded in December, 1995 by an Iranian Foreign Ministry statement declaring that the islands are "an inseparable part of Iran." Iran also took further moves to strengthen its hold on the disputed islands. These moves included starting up a power plant on Greater Tunb, opening an airport on Abu Musa, and planning the construction of a new port on Abu Musa.

The UAE has received strong support in the dispute from the GCC, but from the UN and the United States. In December, 1997, the UAE called for talks with Iran over the islands, and Iran called for closer ties with its "Arab neighbors." In early March, 1998, the GCC, while praising Iran's President Khatami, issued a statement supporting the UAE in its dispute with Iran over Abu Musa and the Tunbs. Since that time, Iran has shown that it is at least willing to discuss the issue with the UAE, and the foreign ministers of the two countries have exchanged visits.

On August 5, 1998, Khatami gave a speech stating that

Thankfully, with each passing day, our relations with the countries of the region are getting better and today we have much better relations than in the past. These improved relations are important because it improves security for the Persian Gulf region and the Strait of Hormuz.... Our goal is to achieve peace and security in the region.

Khatami spoke following a visit by Prince Turki Bin Abdullah, the son of Crown Prince Abdullah, and Brigadier General Mohammed bin Sadd al-Arezi, the Commander of the Omani Air Force. Prince Turki and General al-Arezi both stated that they were not concerned with recent missile tests, although their sincerity was far from clear.[13]

Iran has continued to reach out to the Caspian and Central Asian states, and to try to create a new "silk road" that would lead to pipelines through Iran, oil and gas swaps, and the Central Asian use of Iranian ports. Iran's relations with Turkey are correct, and it has tried to improve the situation in Afghanistan, largely because of its concern over the future of Afghani Shi'ites and desire to return some 2 million Afghan refugees to their homes.

Iran has also improved its relations with Europe. In November, 1997, European Union (EU) ambassadors returned to Iran. In April, 1997, all 15 EU member nations recalled their ambassadors from Tehran following a German court ruling that the Iranian government was responsible for the 1992 killings of four opposition émigrés in Germany. Besides recalling its ambassadors, the EU had stated its intention to break-off its "critical dialogue" with Iran.

Iran seems to have learned that it has nothing to gain from violent attacks on its legitimate opposition, and some aspects of its terrorist activities already seem to be sharply reduced in scope. While Iran does continue to support the Hezbollah and some extremist movements like the Palestinian Islamic Jihad, it seems to have less interest in operations in the Southern Gulf and the rest of the Arab world.

At the same time, no Iranian regime is likely to remain passive when it is under violent attack by its extreme opposition. This is particularly true in the case of the People's Mujahideen, which is itself a terrorist group. The People's Mujahideen lost a bloody civil war in Iran in the early 1980s in which it made widespread use of bombings and assassinations. It killed Westerners long before the fall of the Shah, and supported the student seizure of the US embassy and hostages. The People's Mujahideen has since maintained an Iraqi-supported military force near Iran's border, and gone on with its terrorist attacks inside Iran. Similarly, Iran is unlikely to tolerate the Kurdish groups that supported a Kurdish uprising in Iran in 1980–1983, and which also has elements that threaten to attack Iran. Violence in Iranian politics is almost certain to be met with violence, and "terrorism with terrorism."

Ironically, Iran has also become far more hostile towards another radical religious regime in the region. The Sunni-Pushtan–dominated Taliban movement that took control over most of Afghanistan in the summer of 1998 has presented Iran with many problems. One is a massive flow of narcotics across Iran's borders, sometimes smuggled in by tribes using captured armored vehicles left over from the Soviet occupation. Another is a massive refugee problem. Iran now has well over 1 million Afghan refugees, and some estimates go as high as 2 million.

The Taliban's harsh treatment of Afghanistan's Shi'ites ensures that few Afghan refugees would return from Iran. The Taliban has harassed Iranian diplomats, and nine were killed in what may have been a Taliban-sponsored attack on the Iranian Consulate in Mazar e-Sharif, a heavily Shi'ite area in Northwest Afghanistan.

The tensions between the two Islamic regimes are so serious that Iran's Foreign Minister Kharrazi accused Afghanistan of "genocide" in August, 1998. He attacked the Taliban for the way it treats Shi'ites and ethnic minorities, and stated that, "The Taleban . . . are a danger to the stability of the entire region and promote a false image of Islam, and repeatedly violate human rights, particularly those of women."[14]

Religious differences explain part of the differences between Iran, which is predominantly Shi'ite, and the Taliban, which is Sunni. Although Iran and the Taliban both claim to govern according to Islamic law, many Iranians feel the Taliban has perverted Islamic law to support its extremist position. For example, women cannot appear in public in Iran without robes and head scarves, but they are well represented in government, teaching, and other professions—something the Taliban prohibits, along with music and most other activity. With the moderate Khatami trying to open Iranian society, Iranians worry about what some call the "medieval" Islamic values being propagated next door.

Iran also feels that the Taliban forces have been killing Shi'ite Muslims in Afghanistan, and may be seeking to exterminate some groups of Shi'ites. The Hazaras are a predominantly Shi'ite ethnic group, and have been systematically persecuted by the Taliban. Unconfirmed reports from the Hazaras' traditional stronghold in Bamian indicate that large numbers of residents were summarily executed when the Taliban captured the city in September, 1998.

These developments led Iran to hold a massive military exercise near the Afghan border called Ashura 3 in September, 1998. Iran initially announced that Iran's totaled 35,000–40,000 Revolutionary Guard troops, some 25 attack aircraft, two SA-6 batteries, and forces of T-72S tanks. It later announced that its forces included 70,000 Revolutionary Guards and some 2,000 Afghan "volunteers" loyal to the former governor of Herat, the capital of the main Shi'ite province in Afghanistan. Major General Yahya Rahim Safavi, the commander of the IRGC forces heading the exercise, stated that Iranian forces would not leave the area after the exercise, and that "Tehran will not tolerate mischievous acts and disturbances at its borders by any country." The exercise led some analysts to believe Iran might cross the border to "liberate" the Shi'ite areas around Herat.[15]

Later in September, Iran claimed to have 270,000 troops along its border with Afghanistan. Defense Minister Rear Admiral Ali Shamkhani stated on September 26 that Iran would soon begin the Zulfaqar-2 exercise, and had mobilized 200,000 regular troops with tanks, artillery, and other weapons in the border area, in addition to the 70,000 Revolutionary Guards that had staged exercises earlier in the month. Taliban retaliated by threatening to attack Iranian cities.

Iran faced the risk of fighting a guerilla war with few conventional military targets against its Eastern neighbor. While the Taliban only had around 50,000–75,000 troops, many of which were engaged in fighting other ethnic factions in Afghanistan, it had a much larger pool of militia and paramilitary forces. It also had the potential advantage of fighting in some of the most difficult mountain terrain in the world, and could draw on a pool of military equipment that it captured from earlier governments. This equipment included some 600–870 main battle tanks, 400–860 armored fighting vehicles, 700–1,100 armored personnel carriers, 600–1,000 towed artillery weapons, and 100–200 multiple rocket launchers. The Taliban also had captured some 150–190 jet fighters, 40–80 armed helicopters, 150–225 SA-2 and SA-3 surface-to-air missile launchers, and an unknown number of Scud missiles.

President Khatami and other Iranian moderates made it clear that they would try to avoid a conflict. At the same time, Iran's hard-liners began to use the Afghan crisis as an excuse to crack down on moderates, using the excuse that they were disloyal. They also began to talk about using a combination of Iranian forces and Afghan refugee forces to carve out a secure Shi'ite enclave in Western Afghanistan.

NOTES

1. A review of Iranian statements and articles over the last five years in the US Information Agency's Foreign Broadcast Information Service—Near East Summary (FBIS-NES) provides countless examples of such statements and rhetoric. For example, Brigadier General Ahmad Dadbin, then commander of Iran's land forces, stated in the June 23, 1996, edition of *Kayhan Havai* that, "The Americans should think twice before attacking us. . . . I believe no country in the world would dare to attack us." He went on to warn about Abu Musa and the Tunbs that, "These islands are ours, and we're entirely prepared to defend them. . . . Any threat against an inch of Iranian territory will be met with a response by our strong army."

2. Reuters, July 3, 1997, 0452; IRNA, July 2, 1997.

3. Associated Press, June 30, 1997, 0629; *Washington Post*, June 30, 1997, p. A-20.

4. Most unclassified Iranian military literature is available only in excerpt form, or it has limited distribution. However, *The Iranian Journal of International Affairs*, and the other publications of the Institute for Political and International Studies in Tehran, are good examples of such pragmatism and professionalism in Iran's strategic publications.

5. For a good summary, see Peter Hopkirk, *The Great Game*, New York, Kodansha Press, 1991.

6. These events are described in a large number of books. For early background, see David Fromkin, *A Peace to End All Peace*, New York, Henry Holt, 1989. For more recent summaries of events, see the author's *The Gulf and the Search for Strategic Stability*, Boulder, Westview, 1984, and Richard W. Cottam, *Iran and the United States*, Pittsburgh, University of Pittsburgh Press, 1988.

7. The author served in the US embassy in Tehran and interviewed a wide range of Iranian officers in the early 1970s, including many in the Shah's Imperial Guard. Many raised their memories—or family histories—of events during World War II as a reason for never trusting outside states.

8. A review of the FBIS-NES for the period 1994–1997 shows that these themes have been repeated by Iranian officials like Khamenei, Rafsanjani, and Velayati since the Gulf War. The specific quotes used here are drawn from statements made in April, 1997 in preparation for the Tariq-ol Qods amphibious exercises. See the *Tehran Times*, April 21, 1997; IRNA, April 21, 1997; Reuters, April 22, 1997, 07:09.

9. *New York Times*, October 8, 1997, p. A-6; *Philadelphia Inquirer*, September 30, 1997, p. A-17; Reuters, September 27, 1997, 0244.

10. *Washington Times*, February 4, 1998, p. A-12.

11. Associated Press, August 13, 1998, 0928.

12. *Washington Post*, May 23, 1998, p. A-21; *New York Times*, May 22, 1998, p. A-11.

13. Reuters, August 5, 1998, 0846.

14. *Washington Post*, September 5, 1998, p. A-22.

15. *Washington Post*, September 5, 1998, p. A-22.

Chapter 3

The Control and Leadership of Iran's Military Forces

Many aspects of the control and leadership of Iran's military politics are unclear, and the present structure may change significantly as a result of Khatami's election. The limited literature that is available on Iran's strategic policies has often been heavily influenced by information obtained from unreliable opposition sources. It is far easier to make authoritative claims about the way in which Iran's national security policy and national command authority functions than it is to find real evidence to support those claims.

It does seem likely that there have been debates between "pragmatists/moderates" and "ideologues/extremists" over the amount of resources to devote to military forces, the level of modernization and professionalism Iran's forces require, and how provocative Iran should be in dealing with its neighbors and the United States. However, it is far from clear that such debates have represented any major and consistent split within the Iranian leadership over the resources to be allocated to defense, the size and character of Iran's military build-up, its acquisition of weapons of mass destruction, and its use of unconventional and proxy warfare outside of Iran. Further, there is remarkably little public evidence that major internal debates took place over the cuts Iran made in its military spending and arms imports after the end of the Iran-Iraq War.

There was a debate at the beginning of the revolution over the value of Western-style regular military forces using advanced weapons and popular military forces relying on mass and revolutionary fervor. This debate was largely resolved by the painful lessons of Iran's defeat in the Iran-Iraq War and the lessons of the Gulf War. Popular forces could produce some victories, but could not exploit them and created massive casualties. Iraq's superior equipment and firepower was of obvious importance in defending against Iran during the period 1984–1987 and in defeating it in 1988. The UN coalition's technological superiority over Iraq was equally decisive in 1991. There are still important divisions between the regular forces and the Revolutionary Guards, but there is clearly a broad agreement within Iran's national security structure that Iran needs well-structured, professional military forces and modern military technology.

Similarly, there are important continuities in Iran's military development that could not occur without the support of Iran's leaders. Iran has been consistent in its efforts to build up its special forces and forces for unconventional warfare; to acquire anti-ship missiles, submarines, and mine warfare capabilities; and to acquire new long-range missiles and weapons of mass destruction. It has been equally consistent in attempting to expand the capabilities of its military industries, improve its defensive capabilities in the Northern Gulf, and acquire more modern air and land systems when available. If there are serious debates over these issues within the Iranian leadership, they are among the few debates that remain largely invisible to the outside world.

THE KHOMEINI ERA

Iran's present leadership has inherited a difficult military situation. Iran emerged from the Iran-Iraq War as a defeated nation which had lost most of its major weapons in the climactic battles of 1988, and which had not had significant resupply from the West in nearly a decade. There were long-standing divisions between Iran's regular and revolutionary forces, and much of Iran's force structure consisted of units dominated by massive call-ups of "volunteers" whose revolutionary fervor and a willingness to accept "martyrdom" in human wave attacks were supposed to make up for their lack of training and modern weapons.

Ali Akbar Hashemi Rafsanjani recognized these weaknesses when he was appointed commander-in-chief toward the end of the Iran-Iraq War. Under his leadership, Iran adopted a broad military reform plan that called for the creation of a single chain of command; a rationalization of the complex and unwieldy command system that had grown up around various subdivisions of the regular armed forces and Islamic Revolutionary Guards Corps; the development of national defense industries; and the acquisition of modern arms. Command of all of the armed forces was placed under a unified General Command or General Staff in 1988, which seemed to indicate that control of the regular forces and the IRGC had been unified at the highest level of command—at least at the very top.

At the same time, the Ayatollah Ruhollah Khomeini blocked Rafsanjani's efforts to merge the Islamic Revolutionary Guards with the Iranian regular army from June, 1988 to August, 1989. Khomeini put a hard-line mullah in a position where he had authority nearly equal to that of Rafsanjani and gave him supervisory authority over IRGC Minister Ali Shamkhani and IRGC Commander Mohsen Rezaei. These actions reinforced the feuding between Iran's regular forces and the IRGC that helped contribute to Iran's defeat at the hands of Iraq.[1]

POST-KHOMEINI CHANGES

Khomeini's death in June, 1989 freed Iran's leadership to carry out reforms that were clearly necessary by the mid-1980s. The Ayatollah Ali Hoseini Khamenei became Leader of the Islamic Revolution (supreme religious leader) following Khomeini's death on June 4, 1989. Rafsanjani became president on August 3, 1989. Rafsanjani and Khamenei seem to have quickly reached a working accord over the control of the armed forces. Khamenei became the formal commander of the armed forces on September 2, 1989. At the same time, Rafsanjani retained effective practical command as head of the Supreme Council for National Security. There does not seem to have been any major debate within the Iranian leadership over the need to change senior appointments to ease the tensions between the military factions.

When Rafsanjani formed his own cabinet on August 19, 1989, he purged some extremists—such as Interior Minister Ali Akbar Mohtashemi and Intelligence Minister Mohammad Reyshahri. He also appointed a number of leading technocrats to offices within the Ministry of Defense.[2] It is hard to determine which changes represented the result of jockeying for personal power and which changes were designed to achieve other goals. Certainly, they did little to affect the repressive activities of the Ministry of the Interior or the various adventures of Iranian intelligence.[3]

At the end of the Iran-Iraq War, Brigadier General Ismail Sohrabi was dismissed as chief of staff for the failure of Iranian forces to hold at Faw. A number of other Iranian regular army officers were also dismissed or arrested, and some may have been executed.[4] The Minister of the Revolutionary Guard, Mohsen Rafiqdust, was removed for incompetence in September, 1988—although he was then made military advisor to Rafsanjani and later held a critical position in the government as head of the Foundation for the Oppressed.[5]

These changes do not seem to have punished those who were really guilty of causing Iran's defeat. In most cases, the need to find a scapegoat and personal politics shaped the decisions. A number of the Ayatollah Ruhollah Khomeini's supporters and hard-line revolutionaries remained in senior positions. Iran's Islamic Revolutionary Guards Corps continued to remain under the command of Mohsen Rezaei, a strong revolutionary. It remained subordinate to Khamenei and retained considerable independence from Rafsanjani and his supporters. The clergy remained virtual "commissars" down to the small-unit level in both the regular forces and the IRGC.

Rafsanjani did, however, preside over a number of command changes that eased the divisions within the military, improved efficiency, and mixed the guard and regular military leadership to reduce the friction between the IRGC and regular forces. Two of these changes were especially important:

- The first was the abolition of the Ministry for the Revolutionary Guard in the fall of 1989 and the creation of a Ministry of Defense and Armed Forces Logistics

(MODAFL) under Akbar Torkan, a close supporter of Rafsanjani. Ali Shamkhani was moved from the position of Minister of the Revolutionary Guard to commander of the navy in October, 1989, and Torkan was given a portfolio that combined the administrative apparatus of the regular forces and the IRGC. Torkan was a civilian with no clear ties to either the regular armed forces or the Guards and, therefore, was in a good position to be seen as relatively neutral.[6] This appointment marked the first meaningful attempt since the beginning of the revolution to set up a unified ministry of defense.

- The second change was the transformation of the Supreme Defense Council into the Supreme Council for National Security in the period 1990–1991. Rafsanjani is the Secretary General or "Chairman" of the Supreme Council for National Security, and has ensured that several of his loyalists play an important role in the Council. Until Khatami's election, these loyalists included Iran's Foreign Minister, Ali Akbar Velayati. The Council included Ayatollah Ali Hoseini Khamenei, who remained the commander-in-chief of the armed forces. It included a wide range of Iranian officials, including the Speaker of the Majlis, the head of the judiciary, two representatives of Khamenei, the Minister of Foreign Affairs, the Minister of the Interior, the head of the Plan and Budget Organization, the Minister for Intelligence and Security, and the Chief of the General Staff. This membership gave Khamenei and a number of hard-liners, like the ol-Eslam Ali Akbar Nateq-Nuri, strong representation. Furthermore, all of the Council's decisions required the approval of Khamenei as the Leader of the Islamic Revolution.[7]

What is less clear is how Iran has organized other aspects of its high command structure. The Supreme Council for National Security seems to be too large a forum for some critical aspects of policy formation, particularly decisions relating to Iran's weapons of mass destruction and unconventional ("terrorist") operations against other states. It seems likely that both are compartmented, with decisions restricted to a smaller cadre of members of the Supreme Council for National Security.

This compartmentation seems particularly likely for overseas operations by the IRGC, its Quds (Qods) force, and its foreign operations branch of the Iranian Ministry of Intelligence and Security (variously referred to as the MOIS, VEVAK, and Vezarat e-Ettela'at). Information released during the Mykonos trial in April, 1997 indicates that such operations have been managed by a ministerial committee called the "Special Operations Council," which includes the president, supreme religious leader, minister of intelligence and a limited number of other members of the Supreme Council for National Defense.[8]

Abol Hassan Bani Sadr—an ex-president of Iran—has charged that the control of Iran's foreign intelligence and operations has been under the direct command of its president since 1987. Bani Sadr is closely associated with the People's Mujahideen, and his credibility is uncertain. Nevertheless, he has stated to a German court that,

In 1987, President Rafsanjani issued the order to create a special council for affairs which should remain absolutely secret and not subject to the decisions of the Majlis. These secret affairs included confidential contracts with foreign countries, arms purchases, the country's nuclear programs, and the manhunt of opponents, both domestic and foreign. ... The members of the council include Khamenei, Rafsanjani, Ali Akbar Velayati (then Foreign Minister), Ali Mohammed Basharati-Jahromi (Interior Minister), Ali Fallahian (Intelligence Minister), Moshen Rezaei (Commander of the Revolutionary Guards), Reyshari (former head of the secret intelligence services and now head of Khamenei's Special Bureau), and Hijazi (head of intelligence in Khamenei's special bureau).[9]

Although some experts feel that the IRGC and VEVAK may have conducted independent operations which are not approved by the more "moderate" or "pragmatic" members of the Supreme Council for National Defense, this seems unlikely. The history of Iranian operations overseas—including the investigations into the Mykonos assassinations and the bombing at Al Khobar—provides strong indications that all elements of Iran's leadership coordinate in the direction of such operations, including the Leader of the Islamic Revolution, President, Foreign Minister, and Leader of the Majlis.[10]

PARTIAL REFORM OF THE COMMAND STRUCTURE

The changes in Iran's high command structure still left separate regular and IRGC joint staffs, as well as the separate military branches of the regular and IRGC forces intact. The IRGC had enough political power to persuade Khamenei to reestablish the IRGC's Central Headquarters Staff under Rezaei in 1989. The joint staff was originally formed in late 1984 and includes the commanders of the land, air, and naval branches of the IRGC, chiefs for the workers units and for military industry. There also are representatives of the Qods Force and Basij, and liaison officers from the regular services, Ministry of Intelligence and Security, and Ministry of the Interior.[11]

As a result, the creation of a single Office of the General Staff of the Armed Forces had limited practical meaning. A joint staff had been created at the top of the armed forces which combined elements from the three regular military services, the three military services of the IRGC, and the Basij Resistance Force. Yet, the regular armed forces and the IRGC retained their own headquarters with separate joint staffs under separate Chiefs of Staff. The political leadership of the IRGC could continue to report independently to the Leader of the Islamic Revolution and the Supreme Council for National Security. As a result, the Office of the General Staff/General Command seems to have been far more effective in controlling the regular forces than the IRGC.[12]

Relations between the regular forces and the IRGC do seem to have improved—at least at the highest level of command. Pragmatic professionals were appointed to some senior positions. These included Brigadier General Ali Shahbazi's appointment as Chief of the Regular Forces Joint Staff. Rafsanjani and Khamenei retained professionals like Brigadier General Mansoor Sattari as regular Air Force Commander and Brigadier General Hussein Hansani-Sadi as

Commander of the regular land force. This emphasis on professionalism gave the regular forces the first effective and stable command they had enjoyed since 1979, although Hansani-Sadi has since been replaced.

Further, the role of the General Staff/General Command was strengthened in 1992. Hassan Firouzabadi, a civilian associated with the Guards, was made commander of the Office. The strengthening of this office and Firouzabadi's appointment marked another attempt to mix regular force and IRGC commanders at the senior staff level. Firouzabadi announced the creation of a Supreme Council for Military Policy to help implement the creation of clear roles and missions and command structures for the armed forces.

At the same time, this growing professionalism did not result in any clear trend in favor of moderates or the regular armed forces. Many regular army appointments are influenced by the IRGC. Supporters of the revolution dominate every aspect of the leadership of all the armed forces. These include Firouzabadi, who was made Chief of Staff of the armed forces in May, 1995. He holds the rank of Major-General and outranks the two most senior officers in the Iranian armed forces, the commander of the IRGC and the chief of staff of the regular army.[13]

After Rafsanjani's reelection in 1993, Akbar Torkan was replaced as Minister of Defense by Mohammad Foruzandeh—a member of the IRGC. Other senior revolutionaries in critical security positions included Hojatolislam Ali Fallahiyan, head of the internal security services, Mohammad Gharazi, Minister of Telecommunications, and Ali Larinjani, Minister of Culture and Islamic Guidance. Some sources include Mohammed Ali Besharati, Minister of the Interior, and a protégé of the Ayatollah Khamenei in this group.

IMPROVING REVOLUTIONARY FORCES

There have been changes within the organization of the Islamic Revolutionary Guards Corps which have marginally diminished the impact of any splits and rivalries with the regular forces. The IRGC has come a long way since its formation in the early 1980s, when it was little more than a disorganized militia which was only effective because it was engaged in desperate defensive operations driven by patriotism and ideological fervor. The course of the Iran-Iraq War gave many of its members the military experience they needed to transform the IRGC into a more professional and effective force. Like many other defeated forces, the IRGC was also forced to learn from its shattering losses in 1987 and 1988.

Mohammed Baqer-Zolqadr was made Chief of Staff of the IRGC Central Headquarters (now referred to as the IRGC Joint Staff) in 1989 and given special responsibility for enforcing discipline and requiring the IRGC to implement orders. Mustafa Izadi was appointed head of the IRGC Ground Forces in 1989 and Alireza Afshar was appointed commander of the Basij or volunteer forces in January, 1990.[14] Hussein Dehqan, the former commander of the IRGC contingent in Lebanon, was appointed the first head of the IRGC Air Forces in April, 1990.

The IRGC adopted military ranks and uniforms similar to those of the regular military in 1991. At the same time, its commander stipulated that promotion within the IRGC would be based on the following traditional military criteria: (1) military skills and knowledge attained during the war with Iraq; (2) the level of education of the IRGC member—the higher the level of one's education, the greater the prospects for promotion; (3) organizational, administrative, and managerial skills and level of experience in these areas. Ideological and spiritual fervor were no longer sufficient qualifications on their own.

The IRGC created a relatively modern command structure within its headquarters and each of its branches. Further, the IRGC expanded its technical staffs and role in Iran's military industries, and seems to have been given a dominant role in operating Iran's long-range missiles and controlling most of the military aspects of the development and deployment of weapons of mass destruction.

Hussein Rehqan was replaced by Brigadier General Hosein Jalali in early 1992, in what seems to have been an effort to give the air branch more professional leadership.[15] Hussein Alai was replaced in 1990 as head of the IRGC naval forces by Ali Shamkhani, who headed both the regular navy and the IRGC naval forces until Khatami appointed him Minister of Defense in August, 1997. Brigadier General Hossein Mantequei became the commander of the IRGC's missile forces and seems to have been in command of both Iran's long-range missiles and its weapons of mass destruction.[16]

It is too soon to know how Major General Yahya Rahim Safavi's replacement of Major General Mohsen Rezaei as the head of the IRGC in September, 1997 will affect this situation. Major General Safavi is Rezaei's former deputy and presumably shares many of Rezaei's political views and Khamenei's trust. It seems probable, however, that Rezaei's replacement will put a less political and independent figure in charge of the IRGC and ease the problems in modernizing its command and coordination with the regular forces. Rezaei had been in place for sixteen years, and he had become a major force in Iranian politics and a personal source of at least some of the friction between the IRGC and the regular forces.

The end result is that the IRGC is now closer to a regular military force, although major shortcomings remain. There continues to be serious rivalry between the IRGC and regular forces, although the political importance of such splits is diminished. The regular forces are no longer the forces shaped by the Shah. It has been more than a decade and a half since the Shah's fall. Most of Iran's current military manpower consists of young conscripts who have had no Western training and who have no history of loyalty to the former monarch. Iran's officers and non-commissioned officers (NCOs) have largely grown to adulthood since the revolution, and the IRGC and regular forces owe far more to their common heritage of combat during the Iran-Iraq War than any vestigial memories of the Shah's regime.[17]

Certainly, the IRGC is far stronger than its token opposition. The only meaningful opposition movement with paramilitary capability is the People's Mujahideen or Mujahideen e-Kalq (MEK). The MEK continues the war of assassination against Iranian officials it has conducted since the early days of the revolution and carries out occasional bombings and terrorist incidents. Its conduct led Secretary of State Madeleine K. Albright to formally declare it a terrorist organization on October 8, 1997.[18]

The MEK continues to launch raids with small groups of infiltrators. For example, it was linked to a group of 11 personnel that the Iranians successfully ambushed near Mehran on September 11, 1997.[19] However, its claims to have up to 30,000 troops in its Iraqi-supplied bases near the Iranian border are false, and its military exercises and training activities are little more than a hollow facade. It was decisively defeated in its one real clash with Iranian forces in 1988, and it has never been more than an Iraqi propaganda tool since that time. Other Iranian opposition groups, however, have little military power, and the regime does not seem to face any major ethnic challenges—although it has some low-level problems with Kurdish nationalists.

INTERNAL SECURITY COMMAND STRUCTURE

Iran has improved the command and control of its paramilitary forces. Most of the internal security services—police, Gendarmerie, and Islamic Revolutionary Committees (*komitehs*)—were merged in 1991 and renamed the Law Enforcement Forces of the Islamic Republic (*entezamat*). They were placed under Brigadier-General Reza Seyfollahi, who was appointed by the Leader of the Islamic Revolution, the Ayatollah Khamenei. Seyfollahi, since replaced by Brigadier General Heydayat Lffian in early 1997, reported to the Minister of the Interior, Ali Mohammad Besharati. There are at least two coordinating committees that affect intelligence and internal security operations, one high enough in level to include the president, foreign minister, head of the VEVAK, and other top-level Iranian officials.

These developments may have improved the government's ability to control Iran's internal security—in spite of Iran's growing economic and social problems. The regular forces are more closely aligned with the government. The IRGC and internal security forces are better disciplined and better organized than before, although they still have not reached the standard of the regular forces.

These mergers have not, however, created a truly unified internal security structure or made day-to-day life easier or less repressive for many Iranians. Several agencies share responsibility for internal security, including the Ministry of Intelligence and Security, the Ministry of Interior, and the Revolutionary Guards, a military force established after the revolution. Paramilitary volunteer forces known as Basijis, and gangs of street thugs, known as the Ansar-e Hezbollah (Helpers of the Party of God), who are often aligned with specific conservative members of the clergy, act as vigilantes.

All of these security elements and police forces are still under the control of the Supreme Leader, the conservatives, and the traditionalists, along with various clerical groups. Iran also keeps its foreign intelligence and internal security functions under one Ministry, the Ministry of Intelligence and Security (MOIS). This combination of functions is not unusual in the developing world, but it is rarely efficient and can be repressive.

Quite aside from the fact that the MOIS is under the Supreme Leader while the Foreign Ministry is under President Khatami, Iran's intelligence and security structure makes it difficult to separate the development of objective intelligence collection and analysis from conducting covert and "revolutionary" operations. These problems are compounded by the fact that the current structure of Iranian intelligence owes its origins to the Revolutionary Guards and is so closely linked with Iran's hard-liners. As a result, intelligence analysis tends to become tied to the security of the regime, as well as being more ideological and parochial. The regime's domestic opponents are confused with its foreign enemies, and attacks on opposition groups outside of the country become a routine part of foreign intelligence operations.

THE COMPETENCE AND COHESION OF COMMAND

It is difficult to generalize about the current trends in the control and leadership of Iran's military forces, and these may change in any case as a result of Khatami's election. In broad terms, Iran seems to have evolved a workable mix of command relationships, an effective leadership structure, and a pattern of organization that is as effective as that of most military and intelligence systems in the developing world. Iran's management of its military expenditures and modernization programs, and the individual developments within its armed forces, also has had considerable competence and consistency.

The Iranian system does retain serious divisions between its regular and revolutionary forces that may prove to be major drawbacks, although Soviet Russia and Nazi Germany managed to develop effective military forces in spite of splits and rivalries between their regular and political armed forces. Ironically, these divisions within Iran's command structure may also give some of its more extreme actions a "plausible deniability" that Iran's leadership could not otherwise achieve.

Some experts have argued that Iran has had growing problems with internal unrest in the regular armed forces and the IRGC since 1994. However, there have been few signs of overt problems with the loyalty of either the regular armed forces or the IRGC. If anything, the growing tension between Iran and the United States over "dual containment" and the leadership's use of the "threat" of an American attack, seems to have improved the loyalty of the armed forces since 1995, as have higher oil revenues and improvements in the management of Iran's economy. It seems likely that Khatami's election has also had a unifying impact. If the new Khatami government can make good on its promise, the resulting economic reforms should steadily improve the life of ordinary Iranians, and the loyalty of the armed forces should not be a problem.

IRANIAN MILITARY EXPENDITURES

The trends in Iran's military expenditures provide an important measure of the threat Iran can pose to the region. It is important to note in this context that US advocates of dual containment have been careful to avoid accusing Iran of a massive military build-up, and have focused on Iran's threatening actions rather than on the size of its expenditures. In 1995, a report on US security strategy for the Middle East by the Office of the Secretary of Defense referred to military developments in Iran as follows:

While Iran's conventional military capability will remain limited throughout the 1990s, recent purchases such as submarines, attack aircraft, and anti-shipping missiles, and the build-up of Iranian forces on several disputed islands near the Strait of Hormuz suggested that it is actively seeking the capability to menace merchant ships moving in and out of the Gulf. It is obvious that Iran is assertively flexing its muscles vis-à-vis its smaller Gulf neighbors.[20]

Joseph S. Nye, then Assistant Secretary of Defense for International Security Affairs, provided a similar description of the Iranian conventional military threat:

Iran's ... recent purchases demonstrate its desire to develop an offensive capability in specific mission areas that endanger US interests.... We are especially concerned about the recent sales of Russian Kilo submarines and tactical aircraft and Chinese and North Korean missiles to an Iranian government that makes no secret of its desire to dominate maritime traffic in and out of the Persian Gulf. In this regard, we are also closely watching the Iranian military build-up on several islands whose ownership is disputed between Iran and the UAE—Abu Musa and Greater and Lesser Tunbs. Whatever the specific Iranian motivation for fortifying the islands, the creation by a hostile power of bases sitting aside the western approaches to the Strait of Hormuz is obviously a matter of serious concern for commercial traffic, our own naval presence, and the security of our Arab friends.[21]

Little is known about the way in which Iran makes military resource allocation decisions, or about its long-term spending plans. The Supreme National Security Council seems likely to review key decisions, but little has emerged on how it does so. There have been some debates over military spending in the Majlis, but none with sufficient depth to shed great light on the issues. Like most Middle

Eastern countries, Iran does not publish reliable data on its military budget or anything approaching a meaningful long-term program or five-year plan. It is particularly difficult to estimate the true cost of Iran's research and procurement plans and paramilitary forces.

While there have been reports of ambitious Iranian military build-up and spending plans, most seem to come from unreliable opposition sources or to be little more than inflated rumors. It is also very difficult to determine how Iran allocates resources by military service, divides resources between the regular forces and the IRGC, and manages its investments in military production and weapons of mass destruction. While some hints are available in unclassified reports and Iranian speeches, they cannot be translated into meaningful estimates.

The best data that currently are available on Iran's military expenditures and arms transfers are the unclassified data available from reporting by the US Arms Control and Disarmament Agency (ACDA). These data are shown in Table 3.1, and the trends are summarized in Figures 3.1 to 3.4. It is important to note that these data still have significant uncertainties, largely because they involve estimates that attempt to convert some aspects of Iranian military expenditures—like manpower costs and arms transfers—to a specific dollar value.

DIFFERENT ESTIMATES OF TOTAL MILITARY EXPENDITURES

The data in Table 3.1 indicate that Iran's real defense spending is now less than one-half of the level it reached during the Iran-Iraq War, but that Iranian military expenditures still total over $4 billion a year. Measured in constant 1995 dollars, Iran's military expenditures peaked in 1986, at a cost of $14.8 billion. They dropped from $10.9 billion to $8.9 billion immediately after the cease-fire in the Iran-Iraq War, and then dropped from $8.6 billion to $5.4 billion after the UN Coalition destroyed much of Iraq's military capability in the Gulf War. They then dropped to $4.2 billion in 1995, the most recent year for which the ACDA has released unclassified figures.[22]

To put such spending levels in context, the ACDA estimates that Egypt's total spending during the period 1990–1995 averaged around $1.7 to $2.7 billion. Iraq's expenditures averaged around $10 billion during the period 1988–1991, but no firm recent figures are available. Kuwait's spending reached peaks of $15 billion a year during the period 1990–1992, but dropped to $3.2 to 3.6 billion from 1993 to 1995. Turkey has recently spent between $6 billion and $7 billion. The UAE spends around $1.8–2.2 billion annually, and Saudi Arabia spends $17.2–$20 billion.[23]

There are wide differences of opinion within the US government over the size of Iranian military expenditures. For example, US intelligence experts felt in 1994 that Iran had spent up to $8 billion on military forces in 1993, while

Table 3.1
Iranian Annual Military Expenditures and Arms Imports

	Military Expenditures ($ Millions)		Arms Imports ($ Millions)	
	$ Current	$ 95 Constant	$ Current	$ 95 Constant
1983	5,264	7,290	875	1,446
1984	6,559	8,986	2,700	3,737
1985	8,523	11,680	2,000	2,741
1986	11,120	14,840	2,400	3,203
1987	9,416	12,190	1,700	2,200
1988	8,696	10,860	2,600	3,246
1989	7,422	8,893	1,800	2,157
1990	8,098	9,307	1,900	2,184
1991	7,831	8,654	1,600	1,768
1992	5,029	5,410	850	914
1993	6,041	6,333	1,100	1,153
1994	5,449	5,586	390	400
1995	4,191	4,191	270	270
1996	*4,050*	*3,995*	*565*	*505*
1997	*4,230*	*4,130*	*800*	*736*
1998	*4,700*	*3,890*	*750*	*695*

Sources: Adapted by Anthony H. Cordesman from ACDA, *World Military Expenditures and Arms Transfers,* tables I and II; Richard F. Grimmett, *Conventional Arms Transfers to the Third World*, various editions. Data in italics estimated by Anthony H. Cordesman.

the ACDA estimated only $4.9 billion. The CIA issued revised estimates in 1995 that stated it could not make accurate conversions of expenditures in Iranian rials to dollars, but indicated that Iran had reported it had spent 1,785 billion rials on defense in 1992, including $808 million in hard currency, and 2,507 billion rials in 1993, including $850 million in hard currency.[24]

The International Monetary Fund (IMF) has also produced its own figures, which are shown in Figure 3.2. The IMF's figures are much lower than those of the United States, but evidently exclude many Iranian military activities which Iran does not report as such to the IMF. The International Institute of Strategic Studies (IISS) has produced a third set of figures. It estimates that Iran's economic problems and defeat in 1988 reduced Iran's defense spending from $9.9 billion in 1987–1988, to $5.8 billion in 1989–1990, $3.2 billion in 1990, $5.8 billion in 1991, $1.8–$2.3 billion in 1992, $4.86 billion in 1993, $2.3 billion in 1994, $2.5 billion in 1995, and $3.6 billion in 1996.[25] These IISS estimates, however, do not seem to include some procurement expenses and most of Iran's

Figure 3.1
Iranian Military Expenditures and Arms Transfers: 1984–1995 (Constant $95 millions)

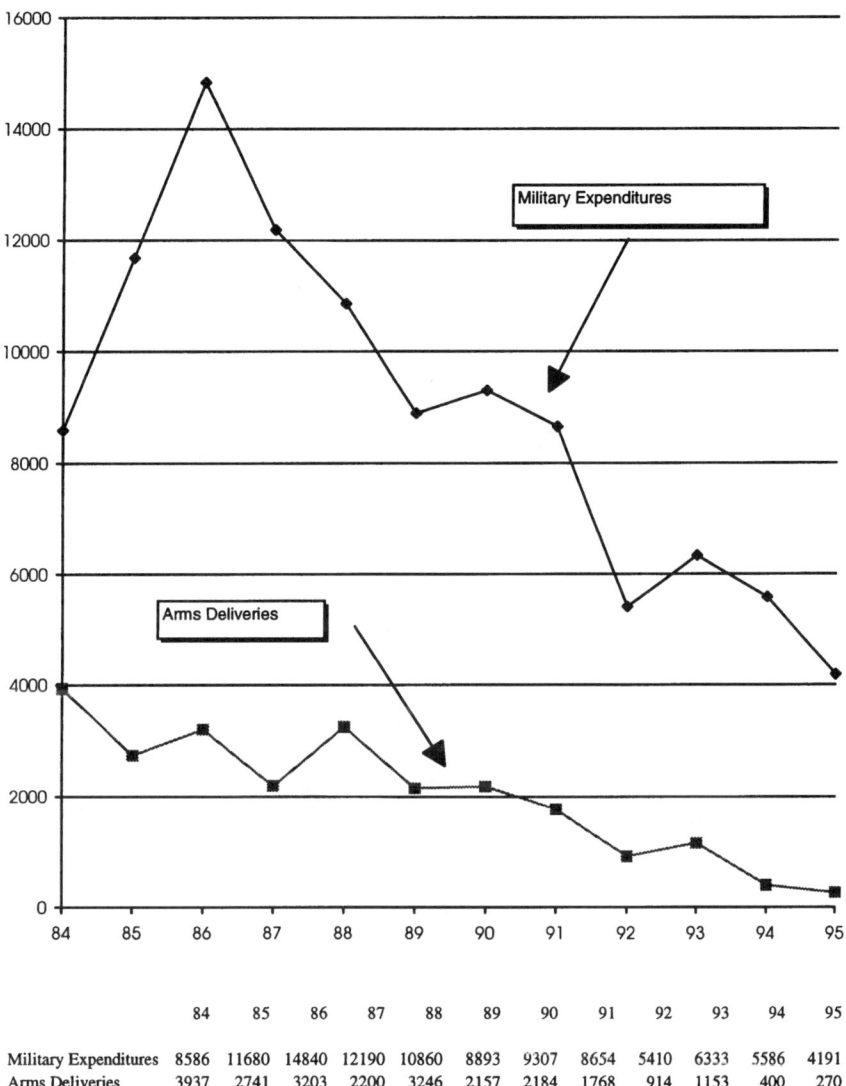

	84	85	86	87	88	89	90	91	92	93	94	95
Military Expenditures	8586	11680	14840	12190	10860	8893	9307	8654	5410	6333	5586	4191
Arms Deliveries	3937	2741	3203	2200	3246	2157	2184	1768	914	1153	400	270

Source: Adapted by Anthony H. Cordesman from ACDA, *World Military Expenditures and Arms Transfers*, various editions.

Figure 3.2
IMF Estimate of Iranian Military Expenditures by Type (Current $US Billions)

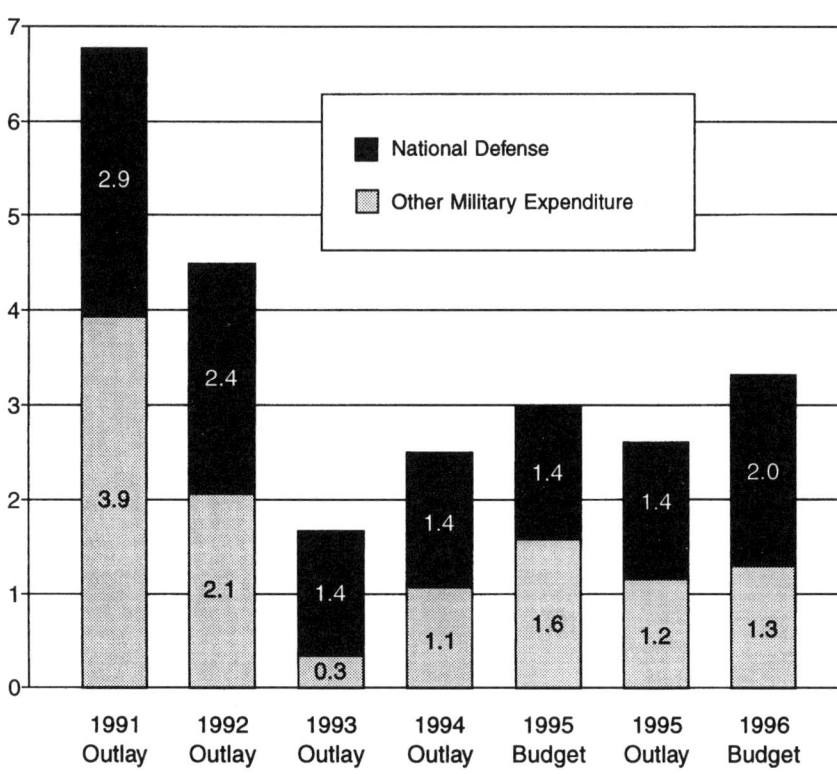

Source: Adapted by Anthony H. Cordesman from IISS, *Military Balance, 1997/1998*, p. 116.

expenditures on weapons of mass destruction. The IISS estimates that Iran spent only $1.3 billion on procurement in both 1995 and 1996.[26]

There is little debate, however, that Iranian defense spending has dropped sharply since the end of the Iran-Iraq War. Figure 3.1 shows that this drop has occurred in stages. At some point in the mid-1980s, Iran chose to make major cuts in its total military spending in spite of the fact that it was still fighting the Iran-Iraq War. The most likely explanation is that it no longer felt that Iraq could succeed in winning the war, but it may also have been unable to sustain the peak level of spending it reached in 1986.

Spending was cut again after Iran's defeat in the Iran-Iraq War, in spite of Iran's massive equipment losses and its need to rebuild its forces. It then remained relatively level during the period 1989–1991. Iran may have felt it could not make further cuts, given Iraq's victory and massive military superiority. It may also have feared a new confrontation with the United States. Iran then made further massive cuts in military spending in 1992, however, after Iraq's massive defeat during the UN Coalition's liberation of Kuwait. This seems to have been both the result of the drop in the threat from Iraq, and Iran's growing economic problems.

THE BURDEN OF MILITARY EXPENDITURES

Estimates of the burden military expenditures have placed on Iran's economy and total government budget are even more uncertain than estimates of military expenditure. Figures 3.3 and 3.4 provide an estimate of the trends in this burden based on unclassified US intelligence estimates.

- Figure 3.3 shows the trends in Iran's military spending as a percentage of its GNP and central government expenditures, in arms imports as a percent of total imports, and in the amount of Iran's total manpower assigned to its military forces. All of these trends reveal a consistent emphasis on civil development over military forces. All of them long precede any US sanctions legislation and the policy of "dual containment."
- Figure 3.4 provides a comparison of the trend in the Iranian GDP and the trend in military expenditures, based on data from the IISS. The data are very different from US government estimates, but it is clear that Iranian military spending has placed a steadily diminishing burden on the Iranian national budget.
- Figure 3.5 shows the trends in Iran's military expenditures and arms imports relative to its total central government expenditures based on IMF data. It again illustrates the extent to which the Iranian government has emphasized civil spending relative to military spending, and that Iran's arms imports have declined sharply relative to its export earnings. It is important to note that these decisions long predate US efforts at sanctioning Iran.
- Figure 3.6 provides further perspective. It shows the trend in the Iranian per capita income in constant dollars. The decline since the revolution and the beginning of the Iran-Iraq War is precipitous. It indicates that the Iranian government has strong domestic political reasons to emphasize domestic spending over military expenditures.
- Figure 3.7 makes this point a different way. It shows that Iranian central government expenditures are growing much more quickly than Iran's export earnings—a major problem for a country whose economy and government are so dependent on oil and gas exports.

What is striking about the mix of trends shown in Figures 3.1–3.7 is that all of these charts reflect estimates of Iran's military expenditures that do not indicate any military build-up since 1988. In fact, all indicate that Iran is spending too little to maintain its present force structure to "recapitalize" it to replace the equipment lost to combat, age, and war, or to modernize its current force structure.

These trends do not mean that Iran has abandoned its search for regional power and influence. Iranian spending levels have been high enough to allow Iran to remain a major regional military power. Iran has also concentrated its

Figure 3.3
Iranian Military Efforts as a Percentage of GNP, Government Expenditures, Imports, and Total Population: 1984–1994 (All percentages are measured in absolute manpower and in constant 1994 US dollars)

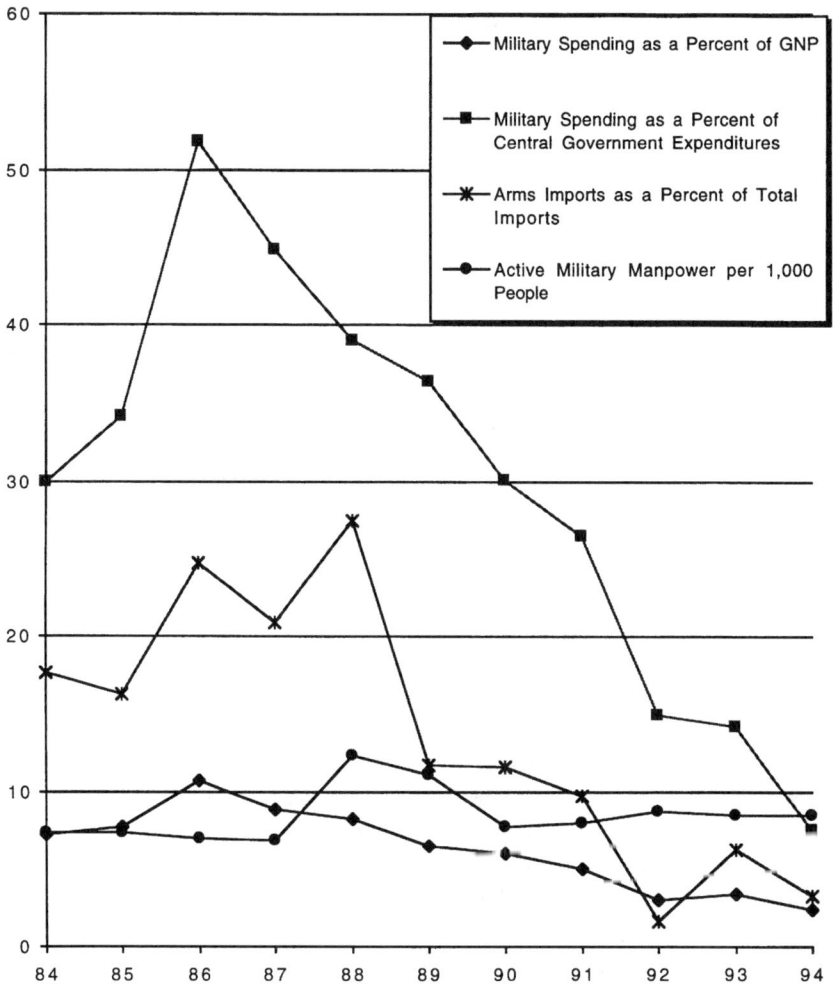

Source: Adapted by Anthony H. Cordesman from ACDA, *World Military Expenditures and Arms Transfers, 1995.*

resources in areas that pose a serious threat to its neighbors and the West. It has steadily built up its ability to threaten Gulf shipping and to acquire and deliver weapons of mass destruction.

Nevertheless, the trends in Iranian military spending do suggest that Iran's leaders may have decided that they face a long window of opportunity in which they can rebuild and modernize Iran's forces without having to fear an Iraqi

Figure 3.4
IISS Estimate of Recent Iranian and Iraqi GDP and Military Expenditures (Current $US Billions)

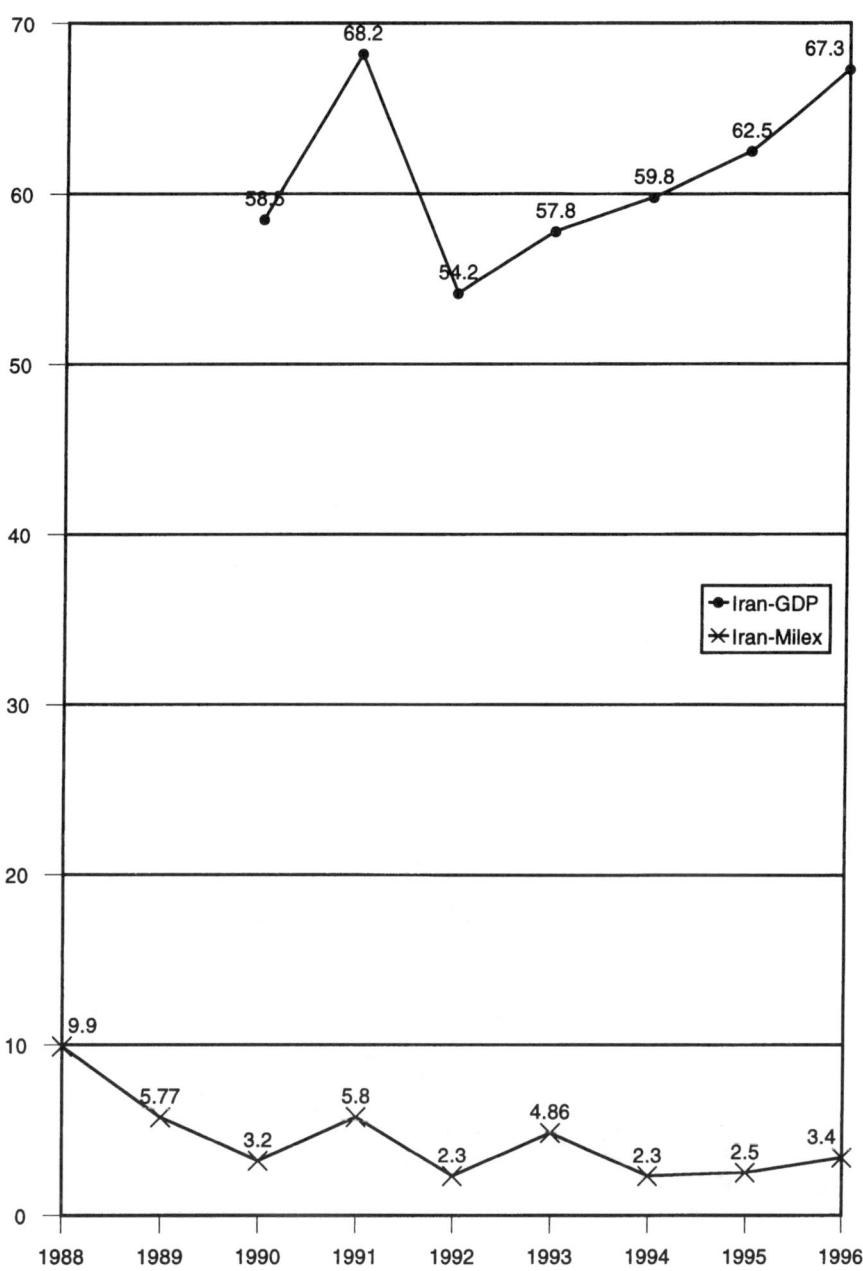

Source: Adapted by Anthony H. Cordesman from IISS, *Military Balance*, various editions.

Figure 3.5
IMF Estimate of Iranian Central Government Expenditures and Military Expenditures (Current $US Billions)

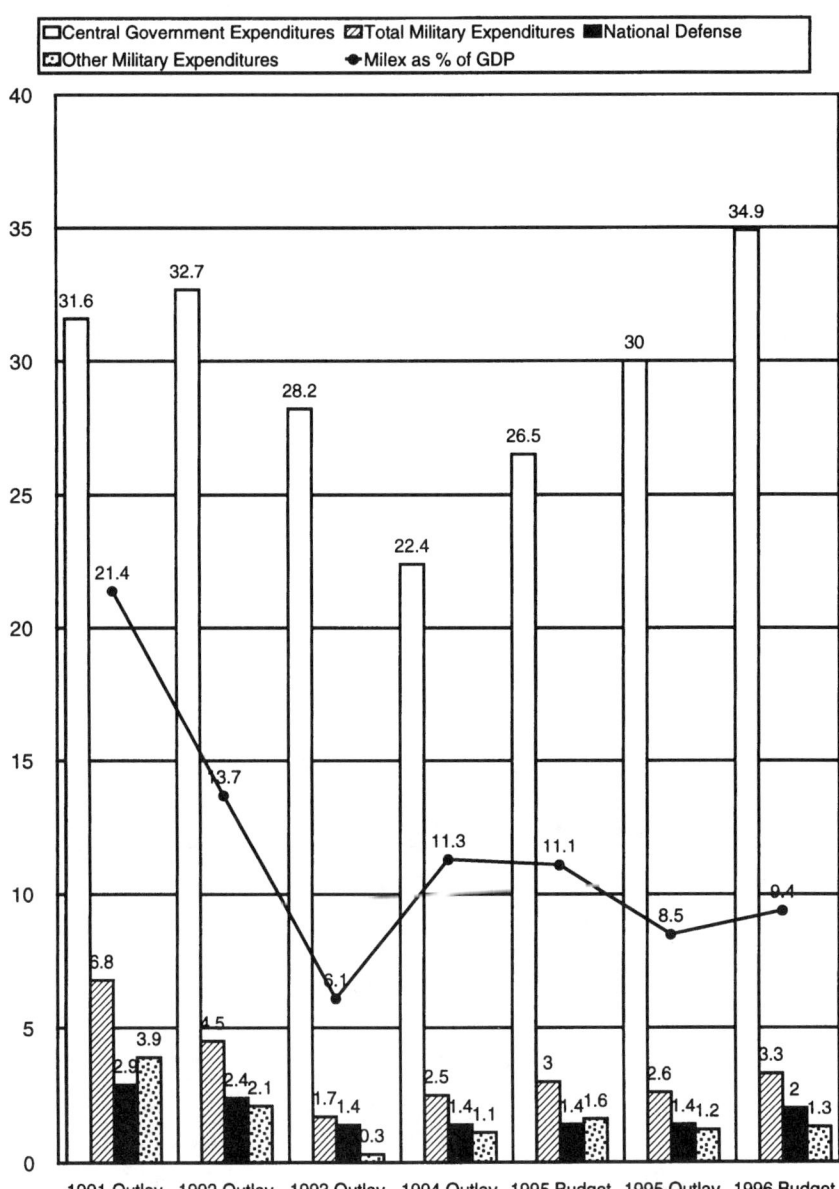

Source: Adapted by Anthony H. Cordesman from IISS, *Military Balance, 1997/1998*, p. 116.

Figure 3.6
Iranian Per Capita Income in Constant 1987 US Dollars

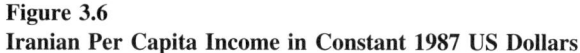

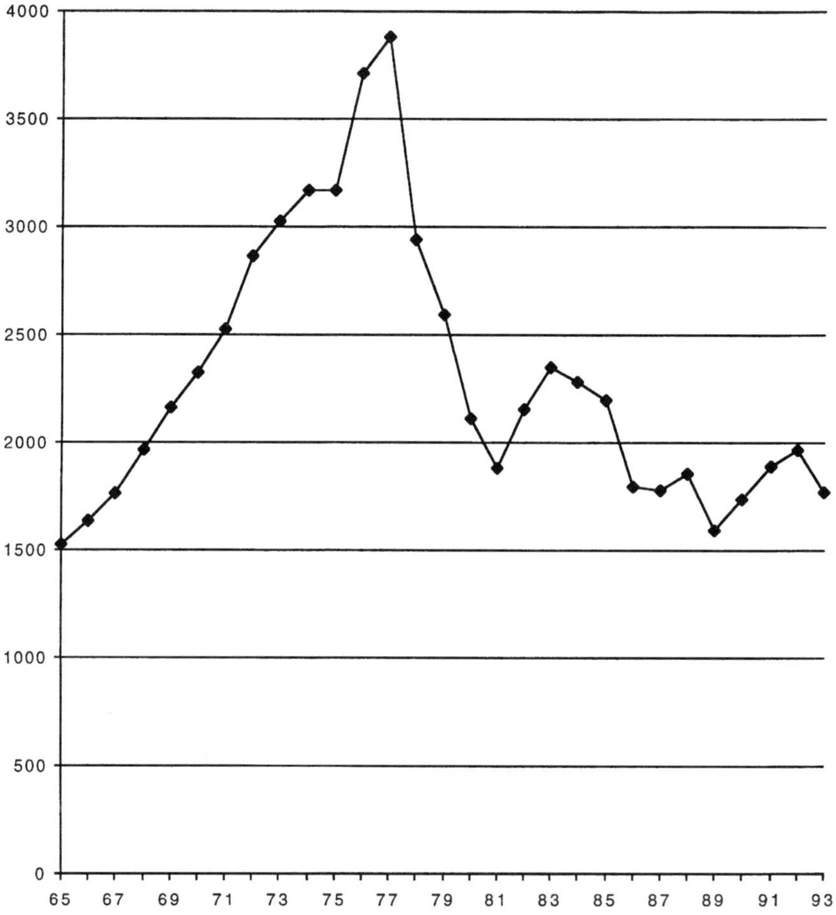

Sources: Adapted by Anthony H. Cordesman from International Energy Agency (IEA), *Middle East Oil and Gas*, pp. 227–228; International Monetary Fund, *International Financial Statistics*; OECD, *Main Economic Indicators*.

attack, while they have no chance of creating the kind of forces that can compete directly with the conventional military capabilities of the United States. The outcome of Iran's presidential election in 1997 has also made it clear that Iran's leaders face growing domestic political pressure to focus on economic development and social programs.

RECENT INCREASES IN MILITARY EXPENDITURES

Unfortunately, the data the Iranian government reports on military spending have little reliability, and there is no way to draw a meaningful correlation

Figure 3.7
Iranian Central Government Expenditures, Military Expenditures, Total Exports, and Arms Import Deliveries: 1985–1995 (Constant $95 millions)

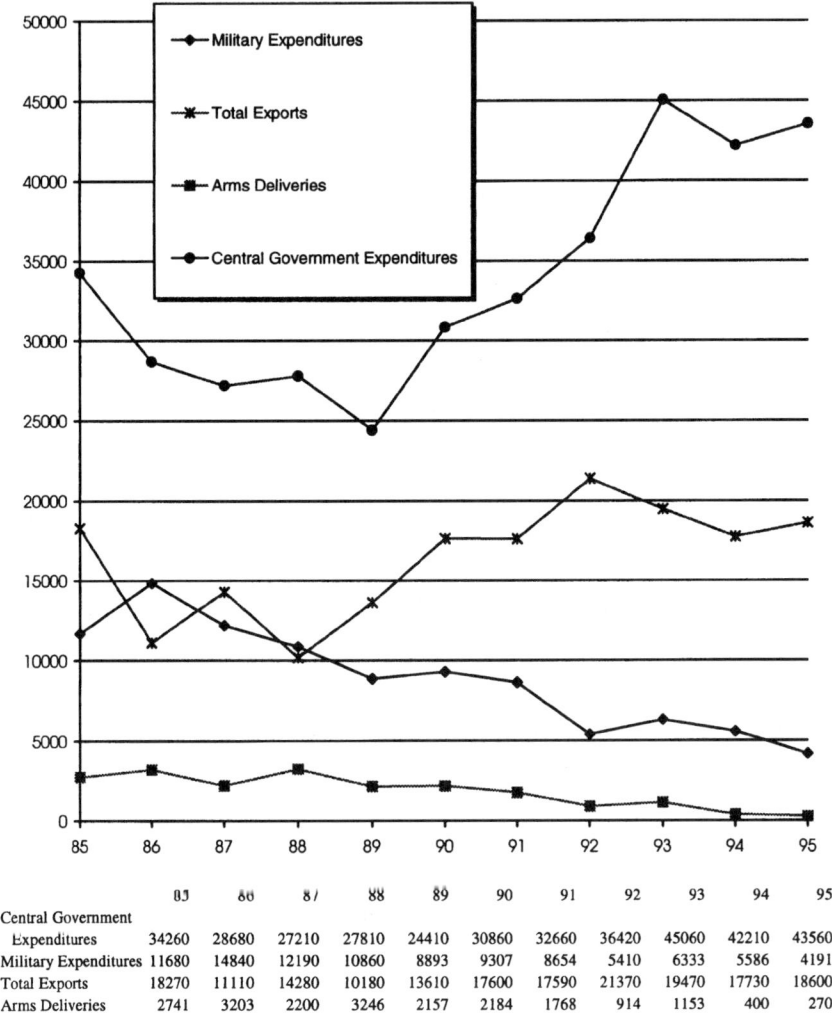

	85	86	87	88	89	90	91	92	93	94	95
Central Government Expenditures	34260	28680	27210	27810	24410	30860	32660	36420	45060	42210	43560
Military Expenditures	11680	14840	12190	10860	8893	9307	8654	5410	6333	5586	4191
Total Exports	18270	11110	14280	10180	13610	17600	17590	21370	19470	17730	18600
Arms Deliveries	2741	3203	2200	3246	2157	2184	1768	914	1153	400	270

Sources: Adapted by Anthony H. Cordesman from ACDA, *World Military Expenditures and Arms Transfers*, various editions; CIA data.

between Iranian and US estimates. For example, Iran reported total military expenditures of only $1.8 billion in 1992 and $1.2 billion in 1993, while it estimated its GNP at $71 billion for 1992. Such estimates are far too low to reflect the true cost of military forces as large as those of Iran, and what is known about Iranian arms imports.[27]

Iran spending claims may, however, be valuable as an indication of the trends in spending. Rafsanjani's military spending request for the 1996–1997 budget totaled 5.9 billion rials (roughly $3.9 billion in January, 1996 $US). This request seems to have been funded. To the extent that it was a real increase in spending, rather than a reflection of the impact of inflation, it marked a significant increase over Iran's 1994–1995 budget ($2.3 billion) and a 31% increase over its 1995–1996 budget request ($2.46 billion). Further, Rafsanjani made his request in the context of a civil budget that called for new sacrifices for Iran's future, speeches which condemned American "aggressiveness" in the Gulf, and estimates of oil revenues that only totaled 51.5% of Iran's revenues—the lowest percentage in recent history.

Rafsanjani proposed another increase in military spending for the period 1997–1998. In a speech to the Majlis on November 24, 1996, Rafsanjani noted that Iran had received a major increase in export revenues due to high oil prices, and could afford to increase its budget and still keep it balanced. He called for a 35% increase in the total budget over the previous year's budget and a 44% increase in the defense budget. However, it is again impossible to distinguish how much of the increase was intended to pay for inflation and how much was an increase in constant rials, and whether the increase reflected any shift in the government's overall policy or simply the fact that Iran was receiving higher oil revenues.[28]

The level of confusion involved is indicated by the fact that President Mohammad Khatami said the total defense allocations he was seeking for the period 1998–1999 amounted to 10.1 trillion rials when he presented the draft national budget in November, 1997. This would have been a 22% rise in rials over the current year's total military budget, and it was not clear if additional sums were set aside for defense purposes in other parts of the budget. On January 18, 1998, however, the Majlis allocated 2.89 trillion rials to the Defense Ministry in the budget for the 1998–1999 budget year. These expenditures could scarcely equal Iran's total military budget. The dollar value of such an allocation could range from $1.65 billion, if calculated at the official exchange rate used for essential state accounts, and to $963 million at Iran's other official rate, which the government has increasingly been using.[29] Iran's near-term spending has become even more uncertain since the collapse of oil prices in 1998.

In practice, Iran's future oil revenues and its success in economic reform may be much more important in determining the actual shape of its military capabilities than its military plans and strategy. If oil prices are high, and exports remain high, Iran may spend more. If prices and revenues drop, as they have since late 1997, it may cut its spending. Iran is now in the midst of an economic crisis because of low oil prices. Its oil revenues are running at about only 60% of the level projected for the fiscal year 1998–1999. While President Khatami gave a speech of economic reform on June 15, 1998, and presented the broad outlines of a reform plan in August, his proposals will have little effect for at least two years. Things could be much worse in 1999–2000.

Much will depend on the degree to which Iran's neighbors maintain or increase their production, and Iraq is allowed to resume its oil exports. Mere reports that Iraq would resume exports of even 1.5 million barrels a day put significant downward pressure on oil prices in the early winter of 1993. Further price cuts took place in late 1996, after Iraq agreed to resume oil exports under the terms of UN Security Council Resolution 986.

Iran will also have to choose between trying to work with its neighbors to keep oil prices high and threatening them to make them limit their production. Iran is currently choosing cooperation and is working with Saudi Arabia and other OPEC states in an attempt to stabilize oil prices and set production quotas, but it is unclear what policy it will choose in the future. Iran has also talked about raising production capacity to 4.5 million barrels per day by 1994 and 5 million barrels per day by 1995, and investing $5 billion in on-shore and offshore oil drilling, exploration, and development. It is uncertain whether Iran can actually produce at these levels, and it is equally uncertain what oil price it will receive if it does.[30]

NOTES

1. *Jane's Defense Weekly*, June 30, 1990, pp. 1301–1302.
2. *Washington Post*, August 20, 1989, p. A-1.
3. Much of this analysis is based on work by Kenneth Katzman in *The Warriors of Islam: Iran's Revolutionary Guard*, Boulder, Westview, 1993; Mark J. Roberts, *Khomeini's Incorporation of the Iranian Military*, Washington, Institute for National Security Studies, National Defense University, January, 1996; Ahmed Hashim, "The Crisis of the Iranian State," Adelphi Paper 296, London, IISS, Oxford, July, 1995, pp. 7–30 and 50–70; Andrew Rathmell, *The Changing Military Balance in the Gulf*, London, RUSI, Whitehall Papers 38, 1996, pp. 9–23; Michael Eisenstadt, *Iranian Military Power, Capabilities, and Intentions*, Washington, Washington Institute, 1996, pp. 9–65; and Anoushiravan Enreshami, "Iran Strives to Regain Military Might," *International Defense Review*, 7/1996, pp. 22–26.
4. These purges continued in March and April of 1989. *Washington Times*, April 20, 1989, p. A-2.
5. Tehran domestic radio, English service, September 12, 1988.
6. *New York Times*, September 3, 1989, p. A-4; *Washington Post*, September 3, 1989, p. A-25.
7. CIA, LDA, 94–10142, March, 1994; USCENTCOM, *Atlas, 1996*, MacDill Air Force Base, USCENTCOM, 1997, pp. 14–15.
8. *New York Times*, April 11, 1997, p. A-1; *Washington Post*, April 11, 1997, p. A-1; *Time*, March 21, 1994, pp. 50–54, November 11, 1996, p. 82; *The Guardian*, October 30, 1993, p. 13, August 24, 1996, p. 16, April 16, 1997, p. 10; Jane's Sentinel, *Pointer*, June, 1997, p. 7; *Washington Times*, July 10, 1997, p. A-15.
9. *Jane's Intelligence Review*, November, 1997, p. 512.
10. The details of this involvement are uncertain, and a great deal of the literature involved adds charges that cannot be confirmed. For a good press summary of the evidence relating to key trials and terrorist incidents, see *Time*, March 21, 1994, pp. 50–54,

November 11, 1996, pp. 78–82. Also see *Washington Post*, November 21, 1993, p. A-1, August 22, 1994, p. A-17, October 28, 1994, p. A-17, November 27, 1994, p. A-30, April 11, 1997, p. A-1, April 14, 1997, p. A-1; *Los Angeles Times*, November 3, 1994, pp. A-1, A-12; *Deutsche Presse-Agentur*, April 17, 1997, 11:02; Reuters, April 16, 1997, BC cycle, April 17, 1997, BC cycle; *The European*, April 17, 1997, p. 13; *The Guardian*, October 30, 1993, p. 13, August 24, 1996, p. 16, April 16, 1997, p. 10; *New York Times*, April 11, 1997, p. A1; Associated Press, April 14, 1997, 18:37; *Jane's Defense Weekly*, June 5, 1996, p. 15; Agence France Press, April 15, 1997, 15:13; BBC, April 14, 1997, ME/D2892/MED; Deustcher Depeschen via ADN, April 12, 1997, 0743; *Washington Times*, April 11, 1997, p. A22.

11. Iran domestic radio service, May 11, 1986, November 15, 1987, and March 2, 1988; interviews, *Jane's Sentinel: The Gulf States, 1997*.

12. CIA, LDA 94–10142, March, 1994; interviews, *Jane's Sentinel: The Gulf States, 1997*.

13. *Jane's Defense Weekly*, May 20, 1995, p. 3.

14. Afshar was Deputy Chief of Staff at the armed forces headquarters when Rafsanjani had command over the military.

15. FBIS, July 25, 1990, pp. 60–62.

16. *Jane's Defense Weekly*, June 30, 1990, pp. 1301–1302; March 18, 1989, p. 428; *Baltimore Sun*, February 28, 1989, p. 2A; *Washington Times*, March 23, 1989, p. A-7, April 20, 1989, p. A-2; *Jane's Intelligence Monthly*, July, 1993, pp. 311–312.

17. *Jane's Defense Weekly*, March 18, 1989, p. 428; *Baltimore Sun*, February 28, 1989, p. 2A; *Washington Times*, March 23, 1989, p. A-7, May 26, 1992, p. A-2, June 9, 1992, p. A-2, June 16, 1992, p. A-2, July 8, 1992, p. A-7; *The Estimate*, October 13–16, 1989, p. 1; *Washington Post*, April 28, 1992, p. A-1, July 16, 1992, p. A-18; *Wall Street Journal*, May 5, 1992, p. A-1.

18. Fact sheet released by the Office of the Coordinator for Counterterrorism, US Department of State, October 8, 1997.

19. Associated Press, NY, November 1, 1997, 0759EST.

20. Office of the Assistant Secretary of Defense for International Security Affairs (Middle East and African Affairs), "United States Security Strategy for the Middle East," Washington, Department of Defense, May, 1995, pp. 16–17.

21. Testimony before the Senate Foreign Relations Committee Subcommittee on Near Eastern and South Asian Affairs, March 2, 1995.

22. Arms Control and Disarmament Agency (ACDA), *World Military Expenditures and Arms Transfers, 1996*, Washington, GPO, 1997, table one.

23. ACDA, *World Military Expenditures and Arms Transfers, 1993–1994*, Washington, GPO, 1995, table one; ACDA, *World Military Expenditures and Arms Transfers, 1995*, Washington, GPO, 1996, table one; and ACDA, *World Military Expenditures and Arms Transfers, 1996*, Washington, GPO, 1997, table one.

24. British sources quoted in *Jane's Defense Weekly*, February 1, 1992, p. 158. *The Egyptian Gazette* projected expenditures of $5 billion per year in 1992, 1993, and 1994 in its January 29, 1992, issue. The Jaffee Center estimated expenditures of $8.5 billion in 1989 and $8.6 billion in 1990. Andrew Duncan of the IISS estimated expenditures of $10 billion annually in 1992, 1993, and 1994 in *Defense News*, January 27, 1992. The CIA estimate is taken from CIA, *World Factbook, 1992*, "Iran"; CIA, *World Factbook, 1993*, "Iran"; CIA, *World Factbook, 1994*, "Iran"; and CIA, *World Factbook, 1995*, "Iran." It is extremely difficult to relate any Iranian statistics to dollar figures because

Iran uses multiple exchange rates and often reports inaccurate statistics. See Patrick Clawson, *Iran's Challenge to the West: How, When, and Why?* Washington, The Washington Institute Policy Papers, Number Thirty-Three, 1993, p. 58.

25. IISS, *Military Balance*, various editions.

26. IISS, *Military Balance, 1997–1998*, p. 132. Other IISS estimates indicate that Iran's expenditures in constant 1995 US dollars totaled $19.4 million in 1985, $3 billion in 1995, and $3.3 billion in 1996. *Middle East Economic Digest*, October 24, 1997, p. 16.

27. Author's guesstimate. Iran claimed in February, 1992 that it was spending only 1.3% of its GNP on defense. *Washington Times*, February 20, 1992, p. A-9.

28. *Middle East Economic Digest*, December 6, 1996, p. 17.

29. Reuters, January 19, 1998, 1923. ($1–1,750 rials was then the official rate used for essential state budget accounts such as oil and major national projects. $1–3,000 rials was the official rate used in other cases.)

30. *New York Times*, November 2, 1992, p. A-4.

Chapter 4

Iranian Conventional Arms Transfers and Military Industry

Iran faces major problems in modernizing and expanding its forces, and continues to have problems with interoperability, standardization, and quality. As a result of the Iran hostage crisis and the Iran-Iraq War, Iran has not received any major resupply of Western-made weapons, parts, and munitions since the early 1980s.

Iran faced serious difficulties during the eight years of the Iran-Iraq War because it could not get resupply from the West, and it was unwilling to deal with the Soviet Union on the kind of terms that might have led the Soviet Union to favor Iran over Iraq. The Former Soviet Union did attempt to use arms exports to expand its influence several times during the Iran-Iraq War, but Khomeini never gave the "little Satan" much more support than he did the United States, and it was Iraq that received most Russian exports to the region.

As a result, Iran became heavily dependent on the People's Republic of China, North Korea, and Eastern Europe throughout the Iran-Iraq War. This, however, meant that it could only obtain low-to-moderate quality systems which were not standardized or interoperable with Western-supplied arms it had received before the Shah's fall. This had a devastating qualitative and quantitative impact on Iran's weapons holdings, particularly after it lost 40–60% of its total mix of major land force equipment during the final battles of the Iran-Iraq War.[1]

THE QUANTITY OF IRAN'S ARMS TRANSFERS

This situation has not improved since the Iran-Iraq War in terms of the quantities of arms Iran has been able to obtain. The previous figures have already shown that Iran's imports have dropped steadily since 1986. Table 4.1 and

Table 4.1
Iranian Arms Transfers by Major Supplier: 1983–1997 (in millions of current US dollars)

Agreements	1983-1986	1987-1990	1991-1994	1994-1997
Soviet Union/Russia	10	2,500	1,200	200
China	1,845	3,400	400	900
United States[a]	0	0	0	0
Major West European	865	200	100	100
All Other European	3,835	2,100	100	100
All Others	2,385	2,000	900	300
TOTAL	**8,940**	**10,200**	**2,700**	**1,600**
Deliveries	1983-1986	1987-1990	1991-1994	1993-1996
Soviet Union/Russia	100	1,100	2,400	700
China	1,165	2,500	1,100	800
United States[a]	0	0	0	100
Major West European	460	500	100	100
All Other European	3,285	1,900	0	1,200
All Others	2,250	1,800	300	300
TOTAL	**7,260**	**7,800**	**3,900**	**3,200**

a. Values of covert US sales to Iran in 1985–1986 are not included.
0 = data less than $50 million or nil. All data are rounded to the nearest $100 million. Major West European includes Britain, France, Germany, and Italy.

Sources: Adapted by Anthony H. Cordesman from material provided by the US government and Richard F. Grimmett, *Conventional Arms Transfers to the Third World, 1983–1990*, Washington, Congressional Research Service, CRS-91–578F, August 2, 1991; *Conventional Arms Transfers to the Third World, 1984–1991*, CRS-92–577F, July 20, 1991; *Conventional Arms Transfers to the Third World, 1987–1994*, CRS-95–862F, August 4, 1995; *Conventional Arms Transfers to the Third World, 1988–1995*, CRS-97–778F, August 13, 1997; and *Conventional Arms Transfers to the Third World, 1989–1996*, CRS-96–667F, August 15, 1996.

Figures 4.1–4.4 provide further data on both Iran's recent arms orders and deliveries.

- Table 4.1 shows Iran's new arms orders and deliveries by major supplier in four-year increments, from 1983 to 1996, and contrasts the trends at the end of the Iran-Iraq War and after the Gulf War.
- Figure 4.1 shows recent deliveries by major supplier countries since the end of the Iran-Iraq War.
- Figure 4.2 shows the cumulative volume of transfers from given supplier countries.

Figure 4.1
Iranian New Arms Agreements and Deliveries by Major Supplier (Current $US millions)

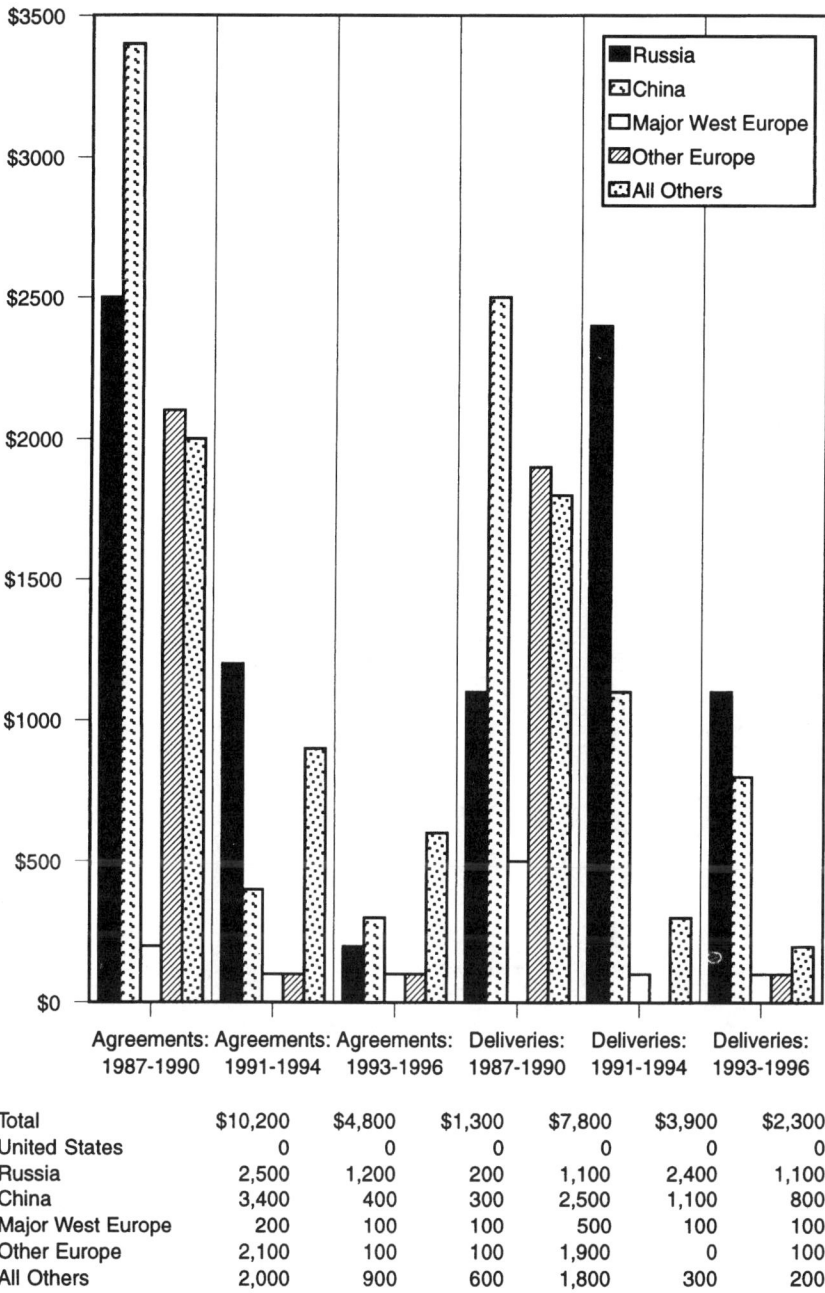

	Agreements: 1987-1990	Agreements: 1991-1994	Agreements: 1993-1996	Deliveries: 1987-1990	Deliveries: 1991-1994	Deliveries: 1993-1996
Total	$10,200	$4,800	$1,300	$7,800	$3,900	$2,300
United States	0	0	0	0	0	0
Russia	2,500	1,200	200	1,100	2,400	1,100
China	3,400	400	300	2,500	1,100	800
Major West Europe	200	100	100	500	100	100
Other Europe	2,100	100	100	1,900	0	100
All Others	2,000	900	600	1,800	300	200

0 = less than $50 million or nil, and all data rounded to the nearest $100 million
Source: Richard F. Grimmett, *Conventional Arms Transfers to the Developing Nations*, Congressional Research Service, various editions.

Figure 4.2
Arms Deliveries to Iran by Supplier Country: 1993–1996 (Current $US millions)

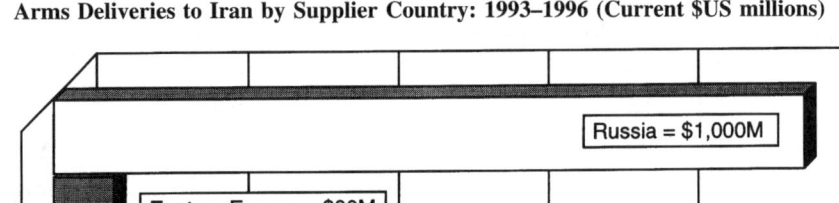

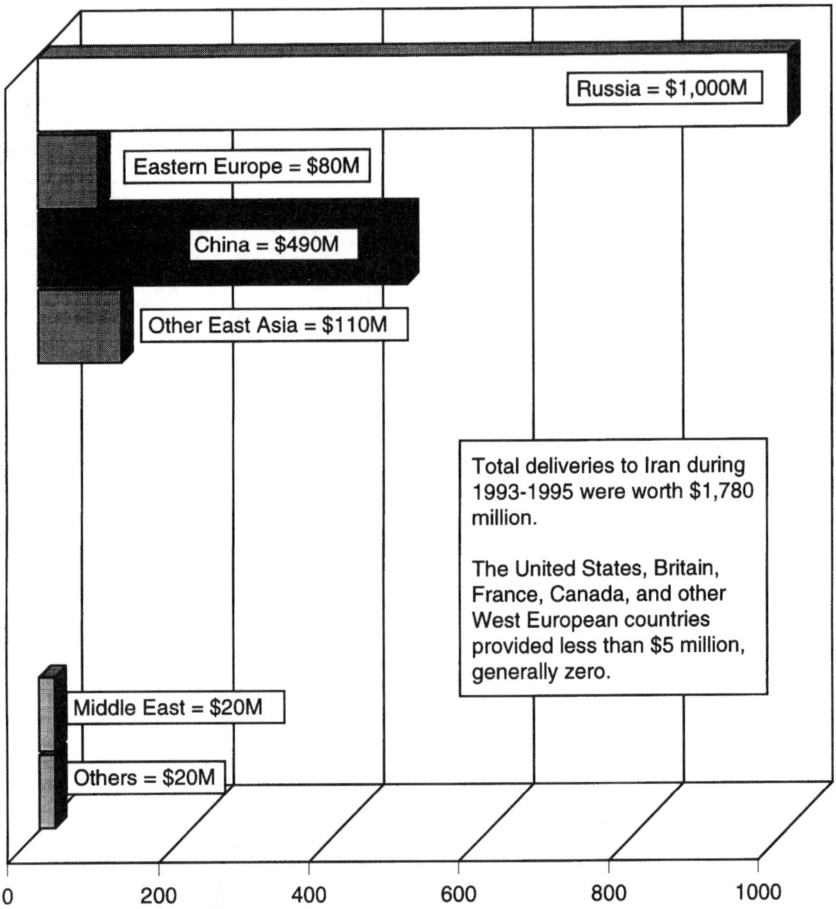

Source: Adapted by Anthony H. Cordesman from ACDA, *World Military Expenditures and Arms Transfers, 1996.*

- Figure 4.3 shows the trend in deliveries by major supplier countries since 1973.
- Figure 4.4 shows the trend in new agreements by major supplier countries since 1987.

These charts reflect the major decline in the size of Iran's arms imports since the Gulf War and show that Iranian new orders have dropped more quickly than deliveries. They also show the shifting patterns in Iran's suppliers and the continuing difficulty Iran has experienced in finding a reliable source of modern arms.

Figure 4.3
Trend in Deliveries to Iran by Supplier Country: 1973–1994 (In $US Current Millions)

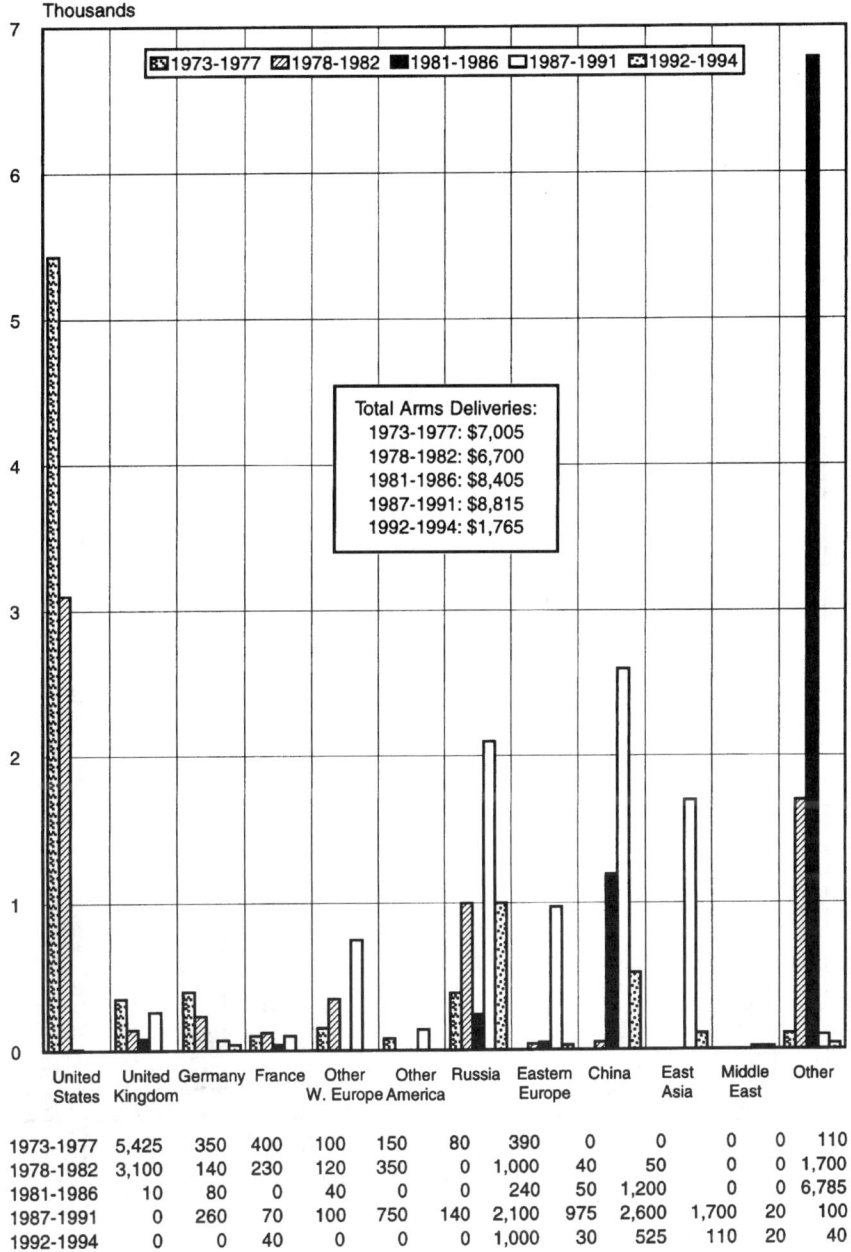

	United States	United Kingdom	Germany	France	Other W. Europe	Other America	Russia	Eastern Europe	China	East Asia	Middle East	Other
1973-1977	5,425	350	400	100	150	80	390	0	0	0	0	110
1978-1982	3,100	140	230	120	350	0	1,000	40	50	0	0	1,700
1981-1986	10	80	0	40	0	0	240	50	1,200	0	0	6,785
1987-1991	0	260	70	100	750	140	2,100	975	2,600	1,700	20	100
1992-1994	0	0	40	0	0	0	1,000	30	525	110	20	40

Total Arms Deliveries:
1973-1977: $7,005
1978-1982: $6,700
1981-1986: $8,405
1987-1991: $8,815
1992-1994: $1,765

Source: Adapted by Anthony H. Cordesman from ACDA, *World Military Expenditures and Arms Transfers*, various editions.

Figure 4.4
Trend in New Iranian Arms Sales Agreements by Supplier Country: 1987–1996 (Current $US millions)

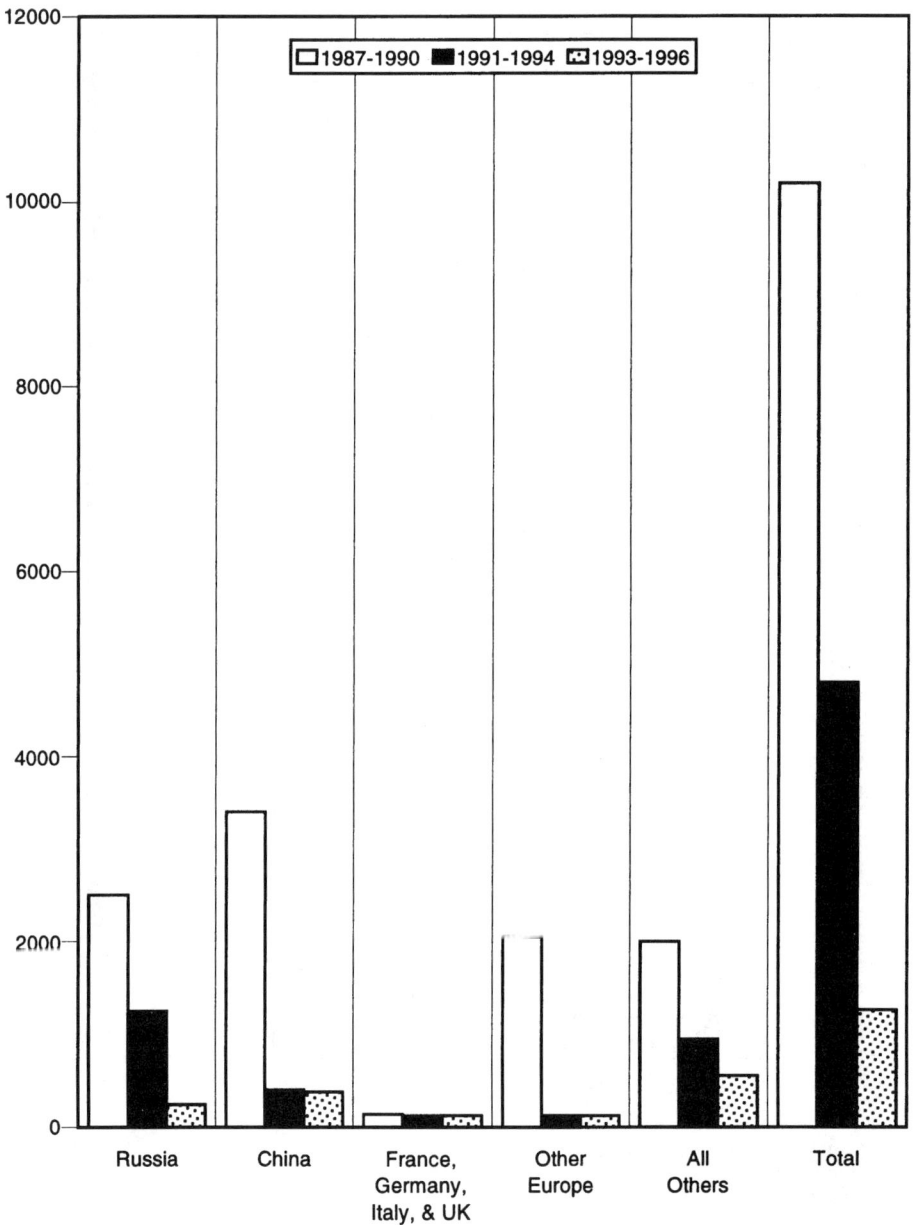

0 = less than $50 million or nil, and all data rounded to the nearest $100 million.
Source: Richard F. Grimmett, *Conventional Arms Transfers to the Developing Nations*, various editions.

Patterns in Recent Deliveries

Deliveries are the easiest aspect of Iran's arms imports to quantify, since the estimate can be based on declassified intelligence coverage of actual holdings and changes in Iranian forces. These deliveries are shown by year in Table 4.1 and reflect the following trends:

- *Iran took delivery on $10.2 billion worth of arms during the four-year period 1987–1990—the time between the final years of the Iran-Iraq War and the Gulf War.* It did not receive any significant military imports from the United States and only received $500 million from its major Western European suppliers. In contrast, Iran received $1.1 billion in deliveries from Russia, $2.5 billion from China, $1.9 billion from other European states (mostly Eastern Europe), and $1.8 billion from other countries (mostly North Korea). Virtually all of these deliveries were the product of agreements that had been signed during the first four years of the Iran-Iraq War.

  While some deliveries helped compensate for Iran's losses during the last year of the Iran-Iraq War, most were low-quality systems and many were land weapons whose value was restricted to the kind of grinding war of attrition that Iran was fighting with Iraq, and not modern maneuver warfare. The deliveries from Russia, China, East Europe, and North Korea not only lacked standardization and were interoperable with Iran's holdings of Western weapons, they often differed enough in design and caliber so that they were not fully standardized and/or interoperable with each other.[2]

- *The volume of arms deliveries to Iran dropped sharply during the four-year period 1991–1994, and Iran took delivery on only $3.9 billion worth of arms.*[3] Despite some reports of a massive Iranian military build-up during the 1990s, the total volume of arms deliveries during the period 1991–1994 was only worth one-quarter of the values of the deliveries that were received during the previous four years, even measured in current dollars. Iran still could not obtain any military imports from the United States and only received $100 million worth from Western Europe.

  Many of Iran's deliveries were still the result of orders it had placed during the Iran-Iraq War. However, Iran had been able to shift its limited resources to concentrate them on the higher quality arms it obtained from Russia. Iran received a total of $1.2 billion in deliveries from Russia, $400 million from China, $100 million from other European states (mostly Eastern Europe), and $900 million from other countries (mostly North Korea).[4]

- *Iran only received $2.3 billion during the period 1993–1996, an era that reflects deliveries of orders placed after the Gulf War.* These deliveries included $1,100 million from Russia, $800 million from China, $100 million from other European states (mostly Eastern Europe), and $200 million from other countries (mostly North Korea).

- Once again, Iran received no deliveries from the United States and $100 million worth from Western Europe. This meant it had had no major replacements or modernization of most of its Western-supplied weapons for nearly two decades. Even in current dollars, Iran's deliveries were worth only about one-ninth of the value of the arms it had imported during a similar period in the Iran-Iraq War. They were only worth about one-fifth of Iran's imports during the four-year period before the Gulf War.[5]

PATTERNS IN NEW AGREEMENTS

The US estimates of the trends in Iran's new arms agreements summarized in Table 4.1 and Figures 4.1–4.4 indicate that these agreements dropped from $10.2 billion during the period 1987–1990 to $4.8 billion during the period 1991–1994—a decline of 53%. They then dropped to $1.3 billion during the period 1993–1996, a drop of 73% relative to 1987–1990.[6] This precipitous decline in new orders was even sharper than the decline in new deliveries, and scarcely indicated that Iran's intentions were "aggressive," although many of these reductions were probably more the result of Iran's growing economic crisis than of its desires.[7]

The patterns in Iranian agreements may be summarized as follows:

- *According to the estimates in Table 4.1, Iran signed new agreements worth $10.2 billion during the four-year period between 1987 and 1990—the time between the final years of the Iran-Iraq War and the Gulf War.* It signed $2.5 billion worth of agreements with Russia, $3.4 billion with China, $200 million with Western Europe, $2.1 billion with other European states (mostly Eastern Europe), and $2.1 billion with other countries (mostly North Korea).

  Once again, it is clear that Iran began to concentrate its limited resources on higher quality arms following the end of the Iran-Iraq War, and cut back on the purchases of large amounts of towed artillery, munitions, and low-quality weapons it had needed for a war of attrition with Iraq.[8]

- *Iran's new arms agreements again dropped sharply during the four-year period following the Gulf War, and totaled only $4.8 billion during the period 1991–1994.*[9] Despite some reports of a massive Iranian military build-up—new agreements during the 1991–1994 period totaled only one-quarter of the value of the agreements that Iran had signed during the previous four years. It signed $1.2 billion in new agreements with Russia, but only $400 million with China, $100 million from other European states (mostly Eastern Europe), and $900 million from other countries (mostly North Korea). It got no new orders from the United States and only $100 million from Western Europe.[10]

- *Iran signed only $1.3 billion worth of new arms agreements during the period 1993–1996—a period heavily influenced by an economic crisis inside Iran, low oil revenues, and problems in repaying foreign debt.* Iran ordered $200 million from Russia, $300 million from China, $100 million from other European states (mostly Eastern Europe), and $600 million from other countries (mostly North Korea).[11] The drop in agreements with Russia reflected both Iran's financial problems and the result of US pressure that had led President Yeltsin to not make major new arms sales to Russia. Iran's new agreements with China and North Korea heavily emphasized missiles and missile production technology.

Iran's level of new orders during the period 1993–1996 was so low that it is virtually certain to rise in the future, probably to levels of at least $1 billion a year. Iran has underinvested in its overall force structure for so long that it must either maintain this level of spending or make major cuts in the size and quality of its forces. It is also reaching the point where some of its Western-supplied equipment is so old that it must be replaced.

THE QUALITY OF IRAN'S ARMS TRANSFERS

There have been important changes in the sources of Iran's arms transfers. Some have benefited Iran, by giving it access to higher-quality arms. This new access to arms is summarized in Table 4.2, which provides an estimate by service and type of weapon. Iran has not, however, found a reliable supplier of high-quality arms, and it remains reliant on suppliers that cannot compete with the West in technology and military effectiveness.

Purchases from China and Asia

The end of the Iran-Iraq War allowed Iran to reduce orders for wartime replacements and munitions, and to concentrate on acquiring more advanced Chinese weapons and technology, such as anti-ship missiles, ballistic missile production capability, and anti-aircraft missiles. Iran cut its new arms orders from China from $3.4 billion during the four-year period 1987–1990 to $400 million during 1991–1994, the four-year period following the Gulf War. It placed a total of $300 million in new orders during the period 1993–1996.[12]

Chinese deliveries to Iran dropped from $2.4 billion during the period 1987–1990 to only $100 million during 1991–1994. They rose back to $800 million during 1993–1996 because China was delivering orders dating back to the 1980s, and because Iran shifted its procurements from China away from the mass purchase of land weapons it needed to fight Iraq to the more sophisticated systems it needed to deal with the United States and its Southern Gulf neighbors.[13]

According to some reports, Iran received up to 150 CSS-8 (B-601 surface-to-surface versions of the SA-2) missiles from China, plus stocks of C-801s and C-802s. It took delivery on 10 Hudong missile patrol boats, 4 HQ-2B surface-to-air missile batteries and 48 missiles, and 12 Type 69-II tanks. Iran may also have negotiated technology transfer agreements to obtain the technology it needed to produce relatively advanced anti-ship missiles.[14] Some reports indicate that Iran signed agreements with China in late 1996 that could eventually be worth up to $4.5 billion, although such reports seem likely to be highly exaggerated.[15]

Russia as a Supplier

Iran turned to Russia after the Iran-Iraq War as a potential supplier of the kind of advanced arms it could not get from the West. As a result, Russian deliveries increased from $1.1 billion during the period 1987–1990 to $2.4 bil-

Table 4.2
Key Iranian Equipment Developments

Land

- Russian and Polish T-72 exports. Reports indicate Iran has procured about 120 T-72Ss from Russia and 100 T-72M1s from Poland since 1990. Inventory of about 220 T-72s of various types in mid-1996.
- Russian sources indicate Iran has ordered a total of 1,000 T-72s.
- Claims to be producing the Iranian-made Zolfaqar MBT, and M-48/M-60-like tank.
- Has an upgraded T-54/T-55 called Safir-74. Claims to have upgraded Iraqi T-54s captured in Iran-Iraq War.
- Purchased Russian BMPs. Inventory of 300 BMP-1s and 100 BMP-2s in mid-1996.
- Russian sources indicate Iran has ordered a total of 1,200 other armored fighting vehicles.
- Russia may be licensing Iranian production of T-72 and BMP-2.
- Domestic production of a Chinese version of the BMP called the Boragh.
- Domestic production of an APC called the BMT-2 or Cobra.
- Possible purchase of 100 M-46 and 300 D-30 artillery weapons from Russia.
- Testing prototype of 122 mm self-propelled gun called Thunder.
- Has shown a modified heavy equipment transporter called the "Babr 400."
- Russian and Asian AT-2s, AT-3s, and AT-4s. Does not seem to include 100 Chinese Red Arrows.
- Chinese and 15+ North Korean 146 mm self-propelled weapons.
- Has 60 Russian 2S1 122 mm self-propelled howitzers in inventory.
- Growing numbers of BM-24 240 mm, BM-21 122 mm, and Chinese Type 63 107 mm MRLs.
- Iranian Hadid 122 mm, 40 round MRL.
- Manufacturing Iranian Arash and Noor rockets (variants of Chinese and Russian 122 mm rockets).
- Manufacturing Iranian Haseb rockets (variants of Chinese 107 mm rocket).
- Manufacturing Iranian Shahin 1 and 2, Oghab, Nazeat 5 and 10 (may be additional versions), and Fajr battlefield rockets.

Air/Air Defense

- Keeping up to 115 combat aircraft that Iraq sent to Iran during Gulf War. Seems to include 24 Su-24s and four MiG-29s.
- Has 30 MiG-29s with refueling in inventory, may be receiving 15–20 more from Russia.
- Has 30 Su-24s in inventory (probably Su-24D version), may be receiving 6–9 more from Russia.
- May be negotiating purchase of AS-10, AS-11, AS-12, AS-14/16s from Russia.

Table 4.2 (continued)

- Has Su-25s (formerly Iraqi), although has not deployed.
- May be trying to purchase more Su-25s, as well as MiG-31s, Su-27s and Tu-22Ms.
- Considering imports of Chinese F-8 fighter and Jian Hong bomber.
- Has 25 Chinese F-7M fighters with PL-2, PL2A, and PL-7 AAMs.
- Has purchased 25 Brazilian Tucano trainers and 25 Pakistani MiG-17 trainers. Uncertain report has bought 12 MiG-29UB trainers from Russia.
- Has bought 12 Italian AB-212, 20 German BK-117A-3, and 12 Russian Mi-17 support and utility helicopters.
- Iran claims to have fitted F-14s with I-Hawk missiles adapted to the air-to-air role.
- Claims to produce advanced electronic warfare systems.
- IRGC claims to be ready to mass produce gliders.

Land-Based Air Defense

- May be negotiating purchase of SA-10, SA-12, SA-14/16s from Russia.
- Reported to have acquired four HQ-23/2B (CSA-1) launchers and 45–48 missiles, plus 25 SA-6 and 10–15 SA-5 launchers.
- Has acquired Chinese FM-80 launchers and a few RBS-70s.
- More SA-7s and HN-5s man-portable missiles; may have acquired 100–200 Strelas.
- Reported to be seeking to modernize Rapier and 10–15 Tigercat fire units.
- May be modifying and/or producing ZSU-23–4 radar-guided anti-aircraft guns.
- Claims to produce advanced electronic warfare systems.

Sea

- Claims it will soon start producing 6 multi-purpose destroyers.
- Has taken delivery on three Russian Type 877EKM Kilo-class submarines, possibly with 1,000 modern magnetic, acoustic, and pressure-sensitive mines.
- Reported to have North Korean midget submarines (never confirmed).
- Has obtained 10 Hudong-class Chinese missile patrol boats.
- US Mark 65 and Russian AND 500, AMAG-1, KRAB anti-ship mines.
- Reported to be negotiating to buy Chinese EM-52 rocket-propelled mine.
- Iran claims to be developing non-magnetic, acoustic, free-floating, and remote-controlled mines. It may have also acquired non-magnetic mines, influence mines, and mines with sophisticated timing devices.
- Wake-homing and wire-guided Russian torpedoes.
- Seersucker (HY-2) sites with 50–60 missiles—Iran is working to extend range to 400 km.
- Iran has 60–100 Chinese CS-801 (Ying Jai-1 SY-2) and CS-802 (YF-6) SSMs.
- Iran is developing FL-10 anti-ship cruise missile, a copy of Chinese FL-2 or FL-7.
- Boghammer fast interceptor craft.

Table 4.2 (continued)

Missiles
- Has obtained up to 250–300 Scud Bs with 8–15 launchers.
- Has obtained up to 150 Chinese CSS-8 surface-to-surface missiles with 25–30 launchers.
- Reports that China is giving Iran technology to produce long-range solid fuel missile.
- Iran-130 missile(?).
- Has bought North Korean Scud Cs with 5–14 launchers.
- South Korea reports that Iran has bought total of 100 Scud Bs and 100 Scud Cs from North Korea.
- May be developing the Zelzal-3 missile with a range of 900 kilometers with Chinese and North Korean support.
- May be planning to purchase North Korean No-Dong 1/2s.
- Also interested in North Korea's developmental Tapeo Dong 1 or Tapeo Dong 2.
- Claims it will launch its first experimental satellite by 2000 with Russian aid.
- Reports of tunnels for hardened deployment of Scuds and SAMs.

CBW
- Chemical weapons (sulfur mustard gas, hydrogen cyanide, phosgene, and/or chlorine; possibly Sarin and Tabun).
- Biological weapons (possibly Anthrax, hoof and mouth disease, and other biotoxins).
- Nuclear weapons development (Russian and Chinese reactors).

Sources: Based on interviews, reporting in various defense journals, and IISS, *Military Balance*, various editions.

lion during 1991–1994. Iran was able to import first line tanks like the T-72 and aircraft like the MiG-29 and Su-24 from the Russian Republic.

During the longer period 1991–1997, Iran was able to obtain nearly $3.4 billion worth of deliveries from Russia, including two Kilo submarines, about 120 T-72S tanks, up to 48 MiG-29 fighters, and 200 Strela 3 man-portable surface-to-air missiles. One estimate also indicates that Iran received extensive artillery deliveries from Russia, including 100 M-46s and 300 D-30s.[16]

Iran's shift to arms imports from Russia has, however, had disadvantages as well as advantages. Russian imports have meant that Iran has had to convert to a third major supplier of arms in the course of about 15 years. They have potentially forced Iran to move from dependence on the West to dependence on Asia, and simultaneously to dependence on Russia, creating serious problems in conversion and standardization.

Iran's force structure is still heavily based on Western-supplied equipment, which is not interoperable with Russian and Asian equipment. While much of Iran's military equipment from China and North Korea is based on older Soviet designs, many parts, detailed maintenance procedures, training, and some aspects of tactical operations are not standardized with the newer Russian designs that Iran has imported directly from Russia and Eastern Europe. This sharply increases Iran's problems in interoperability, sustainability, training, and operations.

Further, Iran's ability to obtain arms from Russia has proved highly uncertain. Russia has a strong economic incentive to sell to Iran, but only if it can obtain oil or hard currency. As a result, Iran's economic problems seem to have been a key reason why new arms agreements with Russia dropped from $2.5 billion during the period 1987–1990 to $1.2 billion during 1991–1994, and only $200 million during 1993–1996.

The United States has put strong pressure on Russia to not make major arms sales to Iran ever since, and Russia has to consider the impact of every sale to Iran on its relations with the United States. Russia agreed not to make major or destabilizing sales to Iran in a meeting between Clinton and Yeltsin in September, 1994. This agreement was formalized during a meeting between Vice President Gore and Viktor Chernomyrdin on June 29, 1995. Russia agreed to strengthen its controls on the transfer of "dual-use" technology to Iran during the Clinton-Yeltsin summit meeting in Moscow in May, 1995, and this issue has been a continuing subject of high-level dialogue between the United States and Russia ever since.

This has scarcely meant that Russia has cut off all sales. Although Iran only placed a total of $200 million in new orders in Russia during the period 1993–1996, it did take delivery on $1.1 billion worth of new Russian weapons.[17] There also does not seem to be any formal Russian-US agreement over exactly what kind of items Russia will or will not export to Iran, and there is considerable evidence that some Russian military institutes have sold Iran critical technology for systems like long-range missiles.[18]

Russia has stated that any cutoff of exports will only apply to new orders. Since Russia has never defined the nature of Iran's existing orders, this leaves considerable leeway about what Russia may or may not deliver in the future. For example, there have been repeated reports that Russia has actively discussed the sale of such advanced technology as an SA-10/SA-12-based air defense system, and Russia and Iran have discussed the sale of up to 1,000 T-72 Exports and a similar number of BMPs. Senior Russian sources indicated in June, 1998 that Iran had placed an order worth over $590 million before Russia reached an agreement with the United States, and that this did include a total of 1,000 T-72s and 1,200 other armored vehicles.

There are important figures in Russia that advocate much larger sales to Iran. These have included some of Yeltsin's hard-line supporters like Oleg Soskovets, the chairman of Yeltsin's reelection campaign, and a number of Yeltsin's opponents. According to some reports, a number of experts in Russia's Foreign and Defense Ministries have advocated the use of arms sales to Iran as a way of reasserting Russian influence in the Gulf, as well as of earning hard currency.[19]

On a visit to Tehran in October, 1995, Russian Defense Minister Pavel Grachev announced, "Russia will allow no country to decide partners for Russia." A Russian Ministry of Foreign Trade official announced in February, 1996 that Iran was planning to buy $1 billion worth of military-related equipment during the next two years, and that Iran had accounted for more than 85% of Russian sales to the Gulf in recent years. The spokesman indicated that Iran had bought $437 million worth of exports in 1994, with $104 million in military technology and arms and $330 million in equipment and services. She indicated that Russian military-related sales might total $4 billion over the next decade. There are also many reports that Russian military firms and institutes have sold highly sensitive nuclear and missile technology, although possibly without the central government's permission.[20]

Russia has since indicated that Iran is seeking a long-term cooperation agreement on arms and paid $380 million on its past debts to Russia in 1995—$250 million in oil and $150 million in cash. At the same time, President Yeltsin agreed to continue the limitations on Russian sales in 1996 and 1997. He has done so at summit meetings with President Clinton, and the Russian government reiterated its agreement at the meeting between Vice Presidents Gore and Chernomyrdin in September, 1996, and between Secretary of State Albright and Foreign Minister Primakov in July, 1997.[21]

Other Sources of Arms

Iran has sought advanced arms from a number of other sources—including India, Belarus, and Poland—and has even attempted to smuggle in arms from the United States and Canada.[22] In its 1994 declaration to the UN arms register, it stated that it had imported 20 export versions of the T-72 tank from Russia in 1994 and 100 T-72M1s from Poland. Iran has kept up the smuggling system it developed during the Iran-Iraq War to buy arms illegally, and it has obtained arms and technology from a number of West European countries. Iran also has sought Latin American arms and technology.[23]

Iran has been able to import equipment and supplies for its biological and chemical weapons efforts, and has received increased—if still limited—imports of high technology for its nuclear weapons program.[24] At the same time, Iran continues to have serious difficulties obtaining equipment, munitions, and spare parts from the West and Eastern Europe. Iran cut its total orders from Western and Eastern European sources from $2.3 billion during the period 1987–1990 to $200 million during 1991–1994, and deliveries dropped from $2.3 billion during the period 1987–1990 to $1,100 million during 1990–1993 and $200 million during 1992–1995.

Iran placed only $100 million worth of new orders with the major Western European powers during the period 1993–1996, and only $100 million with the rest of Europe. It received only $100 million worth of deliveries from the major

Western European powers during the period 1993–1996, and only $100 million in deliveries from the rest of Europe. Iran had no arms trade with the United States. This left Iran without the parts and munitions necessary to support and modernize the Western-supplied equipment obtained during the Shah's reign—although most of this inventory is now over 20 years old and has had so many modifications and updates that many major subsystems and parts are no longer compatible with the equipment in Iranian inventory.[25]

THE PROBLEM OF IRAN'S AGING WEAPONS INVENTORY

Iran's efforts to import arms must also be evaluated in terms of (1) Iran's losses during the Iran-Iraq War; (2) the fact that most of its weapons are either low-grade PRC or North Korean exports, or Western-supplied systems that have seen hard service in combat and are now 15–25 years old; and (3) Iran has limited access to the spare parts and technical support required to maintain, repair, and modernize such systems.

The problems Iran faces because of its continuing dependence on major Western-supplied systems are summarized in Table 4.3. Iran has shown it can buy some Western spares, upgrades, weapons systems, and dual use technologies on the black market. It has built upon the complex mix of overt and covert purchasing offices it established during the Iran-Iraq War. Among these are the State Procurement Organization, Aviation Technology Affairs (ATA), Foreign Procurement Management Center, Defense Support Organization (Saziman Poshtiban Defa), Qods Research Centre, Lavson Ltd., National Iranian Oil Company (NIOC), and various fronts and subsidiaries. These organizations are particularly important components of Iran's covert purchasing system. Iran has had some success in using them to buy older US equipment, which it can use to obtain spare parts for the repair of its US weapons.

Iran has used such organizations to get high technology components like radar testing devices, navigation and avionics equipment, fiber optics, logic analyzers, high speed computers, high speed switches, precision machinery, jet engines, tank engines, and remote sensors. It has aggressively sought out chemical protection and detection gear, refueling technology, early warning radar technology, and avionics conversion equipment—although it is not clear if it has been able to deploy such equipment in its forces.

Despite these procurement efforts, Iran has achieved only limited overall progress in keeping its more sophisticated Western-supplied weapons fully operational, and in giving them sustainability in extended combat. Iran's purchasing efforts have encountered steadily improving Western efforts to control exports, and Iranian success has been highly erratic. The end result is that Iran often cannot get all of the key parts it needs to make equipment mission-effective, and it can no longer cannibalize many systems to obtain parts because it has already been forced to draw down its inventory to critical levels. Further, un-

Table 4.3
Iranian Dependence on Decaying Western-Supplied Major Weapons

Military Service	Weapon Type	Number	Comments
Land Forces	Chieftain tank	240-260	Worn, underarmored, underarmed, and underpowered. Fire control and sighting systems now obsolete. Cooling problems.
	M-47/M-48	150-260	Worn, underarmored, underarmed, and underpowered. Fire control and sighting systems now obsolete.
	M-60A1	150-160	Worn, underarmored, underarmed, and underpowered. Fire control and sighting systems now obsolete.
	Scorpion AFV	70-80	Worn, light armor, underarmed, and underpowered.
	M-114s	70-80	Worn, light armor, underarmed, and underpowered.
	M-109 155 mm SP	150-160	Worn, fire control system now obsolete. Growing reliability problems due to lack of updates and parts.
	M-107 175 mm SP	20-30	Worn, fire control system now obsolete. Growing reliability problems due to lack of parts.
	M-110 203 mm SP	25-35	Worn, fire control system now obsolete. Growing reliability problems due to lack of parts.
	AH-1J Attack heli.	100	Worn, avionics and weapons suite now obsolete. Growing reliability problems due to lack of updates and parts.
	CH-47 Trans. heli.	35-45	Worn, avionics now obsolete. Growing reliability problems due to lack of updates and parts
	Bell, Hughes, Boeing, Agusta, Sikorsky helis.	350-445	Worn, growing reliability problems due to lack of updates and parts.
Air Force	F-4D/E FGA	55-60	Worn, avionics now obsolete. Critical problems due to lack of updates and parts.
	60 F-5E/FII FGA	60	Worn, avionics now obsolete. Serious problems due to lack of updates and parts.
	F-5A/B	10	Worn, avionics now obsolete. Serious problems due to lack of updates and parts.
	RF-4E	8	Worn, avionics now obsolete. Serious problems due to lack of updates and parts.

Table 4.3 (continued)

Military Service	Weapon Type	Number	Comments
Air Force (cont.)	RF-5E	5-10	Worn, avionics now obsolete. Serious problems due to lack of updates and parts. (May be in storage)
	F-14 AWX	60	Worn, avionics now obsolete. Critical problems due to lack of updates and parts. Cannot operate some radars at long ranges. Phoenix missile capability cannot be used.
	P-3F MPA	5	Worn, avionics and sensors now obsolete. Many sensors and weapons cannot be used. Critical problems due to lack of updates and parts.
	Key PGMs	-	Remaining Mavericks, Aim-7s, Aim-9s, and Aim-54s are all long past rated shelf life. Many or most are unreliable or inoperable.
	I-Hawk SAM	150-175	Worn, electronics, software, and some aspects of sensors now obsolete. Critical problems due to lack of updates and parts.
	Rapier SAM	30	Worn, electronics, software, and some aspects of sensors now obsolete. Critical problems due to lack of updates and parts.
Navy	Babr DE	1	Worn, weapons and electronics suite obsolete, many systems inoperable or partly dysfunctional because of critical problems due to lack of updates and parts.
	Samavand DDG	5	Worn, weapons and electronics suite obsolete, many systems inoperable or partly dysfunctional because of critical problems due to lack of updates and parts.
	Alvand FFG	3	Worn, weapons and electronics suite obsolete, many systems inoperable or partly dysfunctional because of critical problems due to lack of updates and parts.
	Bayandor FF	2	Obsolete. Critical problems due to lack of updates and parts.
	Hengeman LST	4	Worn, needs full-scale refit.

Sources: Estimate made by Anthony H. Cordesman based on the equipment counts in IISS, *Military Balance, 1997–1998*, "Iran," and discussions with US experts. Note that different equipment estimates are used later in the text.

predictable successes in importing some of the parts Iran needs make it almost impossible to plan effective maintenance schedules or plan for efficient Iranian efforts to produce substitutes.

Many key parts for Iran's Western-supplied equipment are no longer in supply because the original manufacturer has either halted production, or has modified the system so much since the 1960s and 1970s that the equipment must be extensively modified or rebuilt to use the new or available parts and sub-assembly. At the same time, the parts available on the black and gray markets from other users of Western-supplied equipment are worn, dated, and/or of uncertain quality. The end result is that Iran has been unable to upgrade or modernize most of its Western-supplied systems to anything approaching Western standards for 10–20 years.

Interviews indicate that Iran's military maintenance efforts have a less than impressive record. Under the Shah, Iranian maintenance standards were poor to mediocre, and each service relied heavily on foreign contractors and on extensive foreign resupply of major sub-assemblies as a substitute for effective preventive and ongoing in-country maintenance activity.

Iran has had to become more effective and self-dependent since the fall of the Shah. However, the improvements taking place in some aspects of Iran's maintenance efforts seem to have been largely offset by the cumulative effect of the revolution, the Iran-Iraq War, a lack of adequate technical training, the low technical standards of some elements of the regular forces and Revolutionary Guards, a growing lack of standardization and interoperability, and growing shortages of some critical spare parts. This has led to steady equipment losses through age, wear, and attrition, or the long-term deadlining of equipment which appears in inventory and the order of battle, but is not really operational.

As a result, sustainability remains low and unpredictable. Even where parts and modifications have kept equipment operating, it is often uncertain how long the equipment will hold up in combat, and the maintenance burden has been increased. Many units do not have standard tables of organization and equipment (TO&Es), or unit equipment sets (UEs), and must design their maintenance and sustainability efforts to support a mix of aging, Western-supplied equipment with a wide mix of equipment from non-Western sources, most of which is inferior and not interoperable. This lack of standardization within Iranian forces has also created additional training, battle management, and logistic support problems.

It is unlikely that these problems will grow easier with time. The Bush and Clinton administrations have made steadily more serious efforts to persuade European states, Russia, and China to limit arms transfers to Iran. The United States has put heavy pressure on Russia, Poland, the Czech Republic, Slovakia, and Germany to limit their arms transfers of dual-use items, and has been joined in such efforts by Britain. The European Community steadily strengthened its controls in June, 1993 and began to examine additional sanctions as a result of the Mykonos trial in April, 1997. China agreed to stop sending anti-ship missiles and nuclear technology to Iran in October, 1997 as part of a deal between President Clinton and President Jiang Zemin that gave China access to US nuclear reactor technology. These efforts have led Iran to turn to new sources for parts and support, such as Belarus and India, but it is unclear how successful such efforts will be.[26]

IRAN'S MILITARY INDUSTRIES

Iran is also attempting to deal with its modernization and sustainability problems by expanding its military industries. While there is no way to estimate the size of this Iranian effort with any precision, some experts believe that Iran may be spending as much as several hundred million dollars a year in manufacturing conventional arms domestically, and an even larger amount on missiles and weapons of mass destruction.[27] According to Akbar Torkan, a former Minister of Defense and Armed Forces Logistics, Iran has merged its plans for the Iranian regular army and the IRGC forces into one system to make them more efficient, and has tripled its output of arms since 1979. However, there are still distinct regular and IRGC programs, and the Khatami administration does not seem to be any more successful in rationalizing Iran's production efforts than the Rafsanjani administration.[28]

Claims to Self-Sufficiency

These claims are difficult to put into perspective. Like many developing states, Iran has made exaggerated claims about its self-sufficiency, its ability to modify equipment, and its ability to produce its own or foreign weapons designs. Some of these claims are patently absurd, although they have sometimes been used by the regime's enemies as "evidence" of a large-scale Iranian build-up.[29]

For example, Iranian officials have claimed to be able to mass-produce Scud missiles and tanks. They have even gone so far as to assert that Iran no longer needs major arms imports. For example, Ali Akbar Nateq-Nuri, the speaker of the Majlis, proclaimed on January 1, 1995,

Thanks to God, we stand today in such a position that we have reached self-sufficiency within the defense industries. This issue has caused fear and concern for the global powers, especially the USA.... It is a great honor for the armed forces that we do not depend on outside countries for military purchases.[30]

Similarly, Iran's former Minister of Defense and Armed Forces Logistics, Mohammed Forouzandeh, declared,

Iran has reached self-sufficiency in arms ... and ammunition production and can be the best source for supplying other states.... We are today exporting arms and ammunition to 14 other countries, and even transferring technology for making some weapons.[31]

These claims have been repeated since Khatami came to office, but they make little sense due to the size and nature of Iran's arms imports and the limitations of its military industries. This is particularly true given the fact that Iran has been found to conduct systematic clandestine efforts to obtain parts for key systems like its US-made aircraft using sources in Europe, Canada, and Asia.[32] Nevertheless, such statements reflect interesting insights into the current character of Iran's regime, and its possible hopes for the future.

Major Plants and Facilities

In the late 1980s, Iran claimed to have at least 240 state-owned arms plants under the control of the Ministry of Defense and Armed Forces Logistics, Defense Industries Organization, the IRGC, and the Reconstruction Jihad Ministry during the Iran-Iraq War. Iran also claimed to have some 12,000 privately owned workshops, which employed a total of about 45,000 people, and that it planned to expand their operations to a level that would employ 60,000 people within the coming five years. These claims may or may not be accurate, but a review of Iran's order of battle and exercise performance during the period 1986–1991 indicates that they had little impact in modernizing Iran's overall order of battle and could not meet any of Iran's needs for sophisticated weapons and support systems.

However, the investment in plant and capital for Iran's military R&D and production efforts has improved steadily since 1991. Each of the three main organizations—the Ministry of Defense, Islamic Revolutionary Guards Corps, and (Re)Construction Jihad—have been expanded and given more advanced capabilities. As a result, Iran is slowly shifting away from a procurement strategy based on imports, and military industries dependent on foreign parts and technical support, to one that seeks to emphasize self-sufficiency.

Iran has obtained technical support from China and North Korea, and Iran has had at least some help from Russian, Pakistani, Argentine, Brazilian, Indian, Taiwanese, and German nationals in expanding these facilities. In addition, Iran has created a more effective organization for managing its military industries, called the Defense Industries Organization (DIO). This organization supervises the Iran Aircraft Industry, the Iran Helicopter Industry, and some aspects of the Iran Electronics Industry. Iran also has plants and facilities and some parallel weapons development and production efforts under the control of its Revolutionary Guards.[33]

Some estimates indicate that Iran's plants have doubled their output of basic weapons since the end of the Iran-Iraq War. They can now manufacture ammunition, mortars, light anti-tank weapons, small arms, and automatic weapons. According to some estimates, they can now produce nearly 50 types of munitions, including tank rounds, artillery shells, and rockets. They can probably meet between 50% and 75% of Iran's needs in a major regional contingency, and their output is steadily building up Iran's reserves. They make most of Iran's assault rifles, mortars up to 120 mm in caliber, and anti-tank rocket launchers.

Iranian plants can rebuild the armor and engines for Iran's armored weapons and a number of other Western, former Soviet bloc, North Korean, and Chinese weapons systems. They have the capability to make spare parts for Iran's Western-supplied tanks and other armored vehicles, and limited production of a light-wheeled APC. Iran is also working on reactive armor, and it may be able to modify its tanks with improved armor at some point in the next few years.

Iran has upgraded some of its F-4s, F-14s, and C-130s—with mixed success. It can manufacture long-range rockets, and it has successfully adapted a number of Chinese-supplied anti-ship missile systems for use on patrol craft and Western-supplied ships. Iran claimed to have launched an Iranian-manufactured anti-ship missile, the Tondar, on May 13, 1996. Iran has also launched at least one Iranian-made landing craft.

Capabilities and Major Programs

The key question, however, is whether Iran's military industries can produce more advanced weapons and move towards real self-sufficiency. Iran has made claims to far more ambitious production efforts, which are listed in Table 4.4. These efforts now include a wide range of relatively advanced armored weapons, artillery systems, anti-tank weapons, aircraft, missiles, and ships.

In many cases, there are prototypes to back some aspects of these claims. For example, Iran first exhibited the Iranian-made prototype of a main battle tank called the Zulfiqar (Zolfaqar) in 1994. Reports differ about the Zulfiqar's production status. One report indicates that Iran announced on July 8, 1997, that President Rafsanjani opened the "first phase" of a plant to produce the tank in Dorud, some 300 kilometers southwest of Tehran. Another report indicates that it will be produced at the Shahdid Industrial Complex in southeastern Tehran. Some 60 Iranian firms are reported to have cooperated in setting up the plant.[34]

It is unclear what components Iran can and cannot produce for a modern tank, and whether it can really mass-produce a world-class main battle tank. Few Third World countries have mastered the required skills in large-scale systems integration and in effectively managing the extremely complex production and quality control efforts necessary to produce sophisticated first-line military equipment. It is unclear whether Iran is yet capable of carrying out reliable and sustainable rebuilds of advanced engines, transmissions, and turret drive systems, much less building entire new components. Iran also seems to be unable to produce sophisticated military electronics and fire control systems, although it may be able to modify existing systems. However, there is little doubt that Iran could produce or assemble tanks if it could import the more complex components, acquire production lines for such components from another country, or acquire whole turn-key plants from a nation like Russia.[35]

Table 4.4
Can Iran Mass Produce Major New Weapons Systems?

Land

- Can produce nearly 50 types of munitions, including tank rounds, artillery shells, and rockets. Probably meets between 50% and 75% of Iran's needs in a major regional contingency and their output is steadily building up Iran's reserves.

- Manufactures most of Iran's assault rifles, mortars up to 120 mm in caliber, and anti-tank rocket launchers.

- Showed prototype of a main battle tank called the Zulfiqar (Zolfaqar) in 1994. Tank has undergone field trials ever since the Velayat military exercises of May, 1996. Its drive train and suspension seems to be modeled on the US-designed M-48A5 and M-60A1 series of tanks and to have either a 105 mm or 125 mm rifled gun. Reports differ as to the Zulfiquar's production status. One report indicates that Iran announced on July 8, 1997, that President Rafsanjani opened the "first phase" of a plant to produce the tank in Dorud, some 300 kilometers southwest of Tehran. Another report indicates that it will be produced at the Shahdid Industrial Complex.

- T-72S (Shilden) tanks being assembled under license.

- Upgrading T-54s, T-55s, and T-59s with 105 mm gun made in Iran and new fire control system.

- Claims ready to produce light tank for "unconventional warfare" called the Towan (Wild Horse or Fury) with 90 mm gun.

- Developed Iranian-made modification of the Chinese Type WZ 501/503 armored infantry fighting vehicle which Iran calls the Boragh. The WZ 501/503 is itself a Chinese copy of the Russian BMP, and is a 30-year-old technology.

- Displayed APC called the Cobra or BMT2, which seems to be an indigenous design armed with a 30 mm gun or the ZU-23-2 anti-aircraft gun, a light automatic weapons system that Iran has been manufacturing for some years. Like the Zulfiqar, the Cobra has been undergoing field trials in Iranian military exercises since May, 1996.

- Iran now makes a number of anti-tank weapons. These include an improved version of the manportable RPG-7 anti-tank rocket with an 80 mm tandem HEAT warhead instead of the standard 30 mm design, the NAFEZ anti-tank rocket, and a copy of the Soviet SPG-9 73 mm recoilless anti-tank gun. Iran also makes a copy of the Russian AT-3 9M14M (Sagger or Ra'ad) anti-tank guided missile.

- Claimed in May, 1996 to have produced a self-propelled version of a Russian 122 mm gun that it called the Thunder-1, with a firing range of 15,200 meters and a road speed of 65 kilometers per hour.[1] It may use the Boragh chassis for this weapon. It also claimed to have tested a "rapid fire" 155 mm self-propelled weapon in September, 1997, called the Thunder 2.

- Makes military radios and low-technology RPVs like the 22006, Baz, and Shahin.

Air/Air Defense

- Necessary technical sophistication to rebuild the jet engines for many of its American fighters and helicopters.

Table 4.4 (continued)

- Produce parts and modifications for some of its radars, missile systems, avionics, ships, and armored personnel carriers.
- Reported the test of an Iranian-built fighter called the Azarazkhsh (Lightning), similar to the F-4 in September, 1997, and the development of another indigenous fighter design called the Owj (Zenith).
- Claims to have built its first Iranian-designed helicopter, and to have tested a locally built fighter plane. Brigadier General Arasteh, a deputy head of the General Staff of the Armed Forces (serving under Major General Ali Shahbazi, the joint chief of staff), stated in April, 1997 that the "production line of this aircraft will begin work in the near future."
- Chinese F-7 assembled in Iran.
- Defense Industries Organization claimed that Iran was soon going to start producing two trainers, a jet-powered Dorna (Lark) and propeller-driven Partsu (Swallow). There had been reports in 1996 that Iran had obtained Ukrainian aid in producing the Antonov An-140 at a factory in Isfahan. In September, 1997, Iran indicated that it had signed a contract to buy 10 Antonov An-74 transport jets, and reports surfaced that it might coproduce the An-T74T-200.
- Iran has upgraded some of its F-4s, F-14s, and C-130s.

Land-Based Air Defense

- President Rafsanjani announced on October 11, 1997, that Iran had test-launched a major new surface-to-air missile system with a range of 250 kilometers, although he gave no further details. The description of the missile sounded vaguely like the Russian SA-5, which is deployed in Iran. Reports that Iran has acquired four HQ-23/2B (CSA-1) launchers and 45–48 missiles, plus 25 SA-6 and 10–15 SA-5 launchers.
- May be modifying and/or producing ZSU-23-4 radar-guided anti-aircraft guns.
- Claims to produce advanced electronic warfare systems.

Sea

- Claims will soon start producing six multi-purpose destroyers, with an initial production run of three.
- Constructing small submarine (?).
- Iran claims to be developing non-magnetic, acoustic, free-floating, and remote-controlled mines. It may have also acquired non-magnetic mines, influence mines, and mines with sophisticated timing devices.
- Wake-homing and wire-guided Russian torpedoes.
- Iran is developing FL-10 anti-ship cruise missile which is copy of Chinese FL-2 or FL-7.
- Boghammer fast interceptor craft.
- Iran claimed to have launched an Iranian-manufactured anti-ship missile, the Tondar, on May 13, 1996.
- Iran has launched at least one Iranian-made landing craft.

Table 4.4 (continued)

Missiles

- Iranian-made IRAN 130 rocket with 150+ kilometers range.
- Iranian Oghab (Eagle) rocket with 40+ kilometers range.
- New SSM with 125-mile range may be in production, but could be modified FROG.
- May be developing the Zelzal-3 missile with a range of 900 kilometers with Chinese and North Korean support.
- Claims that Russia is helping Iran develop four missiles. These missiles include: Shihab 3, a liquid fueled missile with a range of 810 miles (1,200–1,500 kilometers) and a payload of 1550 pounds. Israel claims the Shihab might be ready for deployment as early as 1999; Shihab 4, with a range of 1,250 miles and a payload in excess of one ton; other two missiles are longer-range systems with maximum ranges of 4,500 and 10,000 kilometers.
- Claims will launch its first experimental satellite by the year 2000 with Russian aid.
- Reports of tunnels for hardened deployment of Scuds and SAMs.
- Experimenting with cruise missile development, although no links as yet to the employment of such missiles with warheads using the weapons of mass destruction.

CBW

- Chemical weapons (sulfur mustard gas, hydrogen cyanide, phosgene, and/or chlorine; possibly Sarin and Tabun).
- Biological weapons (possibly Anthrax, hoof and mouth disease, and other biotoxins).
- Nuclear weapons development (Russian and Chinese technology).

1. *Jane's Defense Weekly*, June 5, 1996, p. 15.
Sources: Based on interviews, reporting in various defense journals, and IISS, *Military Balance*, various editions.

Iran claims to be ready to produce a light tank called the Towan, with a 90 mm gun, for unconventional warfare. It is also clear that it has developed an Iranian-made modification of the Chinese Type WZ 501/503 armored infantry fighting vehicle, which Iran calls the Boragh, and an APC called the Cobra or BMT-2.[36] Iran makes a number of anti-tank weapons, which include an improved version of the manportable RPG-7 anti-tank rocket, the NAFEZ anti-tank rocket, and a copy of the Soviet SPG-9 73 mm recoilless anti-tank gun. Iran also makes a copy of the Russian AT-3 9M14M (Sagger or Ra'ad) anti-tank guided missile.[37] Iran has not made heavy tube artillery weapons in the past, but it has long been able to recondition and repair such weapons and manufacture or remanufacture artillery barrels. It claimed in May, 1996 to have produced a self-propelled version of a Russian 122 mm gun, called the Thunder-1, and to have tested a "rapid fire" 155 mm self-propelled weapon in September, 1997 called the Thunder 2.[38]

Although Iran is scarcely competitive with the West and with Russia in military electronics, it has a growing capability to produce moderate technology military electronics, and it makes military radios and low-technology RPVs like the 22006, Baz, and Shahin. Some of its claims to be manufacturing or modifying electronic warfare and fire control systems now seem to be correct, although these lag significantly behind the more advanced Western and Russian systems.

Iran now has the necessary technical sophistication to rebuild the jet engines for many of its American fighters and helicopters, as well as to produce parts and modifications for some of its radars, missile systems, avionics, ships, and armored personnel carriers. It also claims to have built its first Iranian-designed helicopter, and it plans to make its own destroyers and small submarines.

Iran's most ambitious claim is that it has tested a locally built fighter plane called the Azarakhsh (Lightning) and has developed a new design called the Owj (Zenith).[39] This announcement is only one of several that Iran plans to establish a major aviation industry. Officials in the Defense Industries Organization claimed that Iran was soon going to start producing two trainers, a jet-powered Dorna (Lark) and a propeller-driven Partsu (Swallow). There were reports in 1996 that Iran had obtained Ukrainian aid in producing the Antonov An-140 at a factory in Isfahan. In September, 1997, Iran indicated that it had signed a contract to buy 10 Antonov An-74 transport jets, and reports surfaced that it might coproduce the An-T74T-200. The An-74 can carry 10 tons of cargo for ranges over 1,500 kilometers, and it is used by the Russian military to operate from unimproved runways.[40]

Ex-President Rafsanjani announced on October 11, 1997, that Iran had test-launched a major new surface-to-air missile system with a range of 250 kilometers, although he gave no further details. The description of the missile sounded vaguely like the Russian SA-5, which is deployed in Iran.[41]

Iran may well have the capability to assemble advanced weapons or to build a basic combat aircraft and tactical missile system, but many of its recent claims seem likely to prove more ambitious than real. No developing country has yet succeeded in designing and manufacturing a fighter that can compete with Western and Russian designs.[42] There have also been many cases where such production efforts simply ended in diverting massive resources of skilled personnel and large amounts of hard currency to projects that never went beyond the prototype of the limited production stage.

STRENGTHS AND WEAKNESSES

Iran has made impressive progress in several aspects of its military production efforts, which are giving Iran growing capability relative to Third World threats like Iraq. At the same time, Iran faces nations with advanced weapons and equipment, like the United States, and similarly equipped, Western-supplied nations, like Saudi Arabia. As a result, Iran's successes are severely limited by the fact that Iran cannot currently sustain or modernize its major Western-supplied weapons systems. In spite of claims to be ready to manufacture tanks, fighters, and various guided missiles, there is still no evidence that Iran can as yet mass-produce any of these systems.[43] Further, it is doubtful that it can mass-produce any type of advanced conventional weapon, unless it imports the major parts it needs and at least some of the production designs and equipment.

In short, Iran not only does not approach self-sufficiency in arms and military technology, it has no prospect of doing so in the foreseeable future. Iran may, however, be able to acquire significant additional capabilities in several key areas. Iran is giving the funding of long-range missile and weapons of mass destruction plants high priority, and it is obtaining significant support from North Korea and China.[44] Iran would be able to produce tanks if it acquired the necessary plant designs and equipment, and it may also be able to improve significantly its ability to manufacture sophisticated avionics, missile control systems, and other advanced military electronics.

NOTES

1. Richard F. Grimmett, *Conventional Arms Transfers to the Third World, 1986–1993*, Washington, Congressional Research Service, CRS-94–612F, July 29, 1994, p. 57, and Richard F. Grimmett, *Conventional Arms Transfers to the Third World, 1987–1995*, Washington, Congressional Research Service, CRS-95–862F, August 4, 1995, pp. 57–58, 67–69; Kenneth Katzman, "Iran: Arms and Technology Acquisitions," Library of Congress, CRS-97–474F, October 1, 1997; Kenneth Katzman, "Iran: Military Relations with China," Library of Congress, CRS-967–572F, June 26, 1996; Shirley A. Kan, "Chinese Proliferation of Weapons of Mass Destruction, Background and Analysis," Library of Congress, CRS-96–767F, September 13, 1996.

2. Richard F. Grimmett, *Conventional Arms Transfers to the Third World, 1986–1993*, Washington, Congressional Research Service, CRS-94–612F, July 29, 1994, p. 57, and Richard F. Grimmett, *Conventional Arms Transfers to the Third World, 1987–1995*, Washington, Congressional Research Service, CRS-95–862F, August 4, 1995, pp. 57–58, 67–69.

3. Richard F. Grimmett, *Conventional Arms Transfers to the Third World, 1987–1995*, Washington, Congressional Research Service, CRS-95–862F, August 4, 1995, pp. 57–58, 67–69.

4. Richard F. Grimmett, *Conventional Arms Transfers to the Third World, 1986–1993*, Washington, Congressional Research Service, CRS-94–612F, July 29, 1994, p. 57, and Richard F. Grimmett, *Conventional Arms Transfers to the Third World, 1987–1995*, Washington, Congressional Research Service, CRS-95–862F, August 4, 1995, pp. 57–58, 67–69.

5. Richard F. Grimmett, *Conventional Arms Transfers to the Third World, 1986–1993*, Washington, Congressional Research Service, CRS-94–612F, July 29, 1994, p. 57, and Richard F. Grimmett, *Conventional Arms Transfers to the Third World, 1988–1995*, Washington, Congressional Research Service, CRS-96–667F, August 15, 1996. 0 = data less than $50 million or nil. All data are rounded to the nearest $100 million. Major West European includes Britain, France, Germany, and Italy.

6. The reader who is not familiar with the US methodology in estimating the value of arms transfers should be aware of the fact that the estimated cost of transfers from non-market economies like China, the FSU, etc. are based on the estimated price of producing the equipment in the West. This methodology ensures a rough comparability in the value of arms transfers from different sources, but means that such figures cannot be used to provide more than gross estimates of the amount of a nation's military budget going to arms imports.

7. Richard F. Grimmett, *Conventional Arms Transfers to the Third World, 1986–1993*, Washington, Congressional Research Service, CRS-94–612F, July 29, 1994, p. 57, Richard F. Grimmett, *Conventional Arms Transfers to the Third World, 1987–1994*, Washington, Congressional Research Service, CRS-95–862F, August 4, 1995, pp. 57–58, 67–69, and Richard F. Grimmett, *Conventional Arms Transfers to the Third World, 1988–1995*, Washington, Congressional Research Service, CRS-96–667F, August 15, 1996. 0 = data less than $50 million or nil. All data are rounded to the nearest $100 million. Major West European includes Britain, France, Germany, and Italy.

8. Richard F. Grimmett, *Conventional Arms Transfers to the Third World, 1986–1993*, Washington, Congressional Research Service, CRS-94–612F, July 29, 1994, p. 57, and Richard F. Grimmett, *Conventional Arms Transfers to the Third World, 1987–1995*, Washington, Congressional Research Service, CRS-95–862F, August 4, 1995, pp. 57–58, 67–69.

9. Richard F. Grimmett, *Conventional Arms Transfers to the Third World, 1987–1995*, Washington, Congressional Research Service, CRS-95–862F, August 4, 1995, pp. 57–58, 67–69.

10. Richard F. Grimmett, *Conventional Arms Transfers to the Third World, 1986–1993*, Washington, Congressional Research Service, CRS-94–612F, July 29, 1994, p. 57, and Richard F. Grimmett, *Conventional Arms Transfers to the Third World, 1987–1995*, Washington, Congressional Research Service, CRS-95–862F, August 4, 1995, pp. 57–58, 67–69.

11. Richard F. Grimmett, *Conventional Arms Transfers to the Third World, 1983–1990*, Washington, Congressional Research Service, CRS-91–578F, August 2, 1991, *Conventional Arms Transfers to the Third World, 1984–1991*, Washington, Congressional Research Service, CRS-92–577F, July 20, 1991, *Conventional Arms Transfers to the Third World, 1987–1994*, Washington, Congressional Research Service, CRS-95-862F, August 4, 1995; *Conventional Arms Transfers to the Third World, 1988–1996*, Washington, Congressional Research Service, CRS-96–667F, August 15, 1996; and *Conventional Arms Transfers to the Third World, 1989–1996*, Washington, Congressional Research Service, CRS-97–778F, August 13, 1997. 0 = data less than $50 million or nil. All data are rounded to the nearest $100 million. Major West European includes Britain, France, Germany, and Italy.

12. Richard F. Grimmett, *Conventional Arms Transfers to the Third World, 1983–1990*, Washington, Congressional Research Service, CRS-91–578F, August 2, 1991, *Conventional Arms Transfers to the Third World, 1984–1991*, Washington, Congressional Research Service, CRS-92–577F, July 20, 1991, *Conventional Arms Transfers to the Third World, 1987–1994*, Washington, Congressional Research Service, CRS-95-862F, August 4, 1995; *Conventional Arms Transfers to the Third World, 1989–1996*, Washington, Congressional Research Service, CRS-96–667F, August 15, 1996; and *Conventional Arms Transfers to the Third World, 1989–1996*, Washington, Congressional Research Service, CRS-97–778F, August 13, 1997.

13. Richard F. Grimmett, *Conventional Arms Transfers to the Third World, 1983–1990*, Washington, Congressional Research Service, CRS-91–578F, August 2, 1991, *Conventional Arms Transfers to the Third World, 1984–1991*, Washington, Congressional Research Service, CRS-92–577F, July 20, 1991, *Conventional Arms Transfers to the Third World, 1987–1994*, Washington, Congressional Research Service, CRS-95-862F, August 4, 1995; *Conventional Arms Transfers to the Third World, 1988–1996*, Washington, Congressional Research Service, CRS-96–667F, August 15, 1996; and *Conventional Arms Transfers to the Third World, 1989–1996*, Washington, Congressional Research Service, CRS-97–778F, August 13, 1997.

14. Reports of the transfer of 100 Red Arrow 8 anti-tank missile launchers do not seem to be correct. *Jane's Defense Weekly*, July 17, 1996, p. 13, September 11, 1996, p. 3; Kenneth Katzman, "Iran's Regional Strategy," DIA Symposium, August 27, 1996; Richard F. Grimmett, *Conventional Arms Transfers to the Third World, 1987–1994*, Washington, Congressional Research Service, CRS-95–862F, August 4, 1995, pp. 57–58, 67–69; *Conventional Arms Transfers to the Third World, 1989–1996*, Washington, Congressional Research Service, CRS-96–667F, August 15, 1996; and *Conventional Arms Transfers to the Third World, 1988–1996*, Washington, Congressional Research Service, CRS-97–778F, August 13, 1997. 0 = data less than $50 million or nil. All data are rounded to the nearest $100 million. Major West European includes Britain, France, Germany, and Italy.

15. *Jane's Defense Weekly*, September 11, 1996, p. 3; *Washington Times*, November 21, 1996, p. A-1.

16. *Jane's Sentinel: The Gulf States*, 1997, *Jane's International Defense Review*, 7/1996, pp. 23–25.

17. Richard F. Grimmett, *Conventional Arms Transfers to the Third World, 1983–1990*, Washington, Congressional Research Service, CRS-91–578F, August 2, 1991, *Conventional Arms Transfers to the Third World, 1984–1991*, Washington, Congressional Research Service, CRS-92–577F, July 20, 1991; *Conventional Arms Transfers to the Third World, 1987–1994*, Washington, Congressional Research Service, CRS-95-862F, August 4, 1995; *Conventional Arms Transfers to the Third World, 1988–1996*, Washington, Congressional Research Service, CRS-96–667F, August 15, 1996; and *Conventional Arms Transfers to the Third World, 1989–1996*, Washington, Congressional Research Service, CRS-97–778F, August 13, 1997.

18. *New York Times*, August 22, 1997, p. A-1; Associated Press, August 25, 1998, 1548.

19. *Jane's Defense Weekly*, November 4, 1995, p. 4, February 7, 1996, p. 15, March 27, 1996, p. 14; Reuters, October 17, 1995, 0617, February 14, 1996, 1054; *Defense News*, January 29, 1996, pp. 1, 29.

20. *New York Times*, August 22, 1997, p. A-1; Associated Press, August 25, 1998, 1548; *Jane's Defense Weekly*, November 4, 1995, p. 4, February 7, 1996, p. 15; Reuters, October 17, 1995, 0617, February 14, 1996, 1054; *Defense News*, January 29, 1996, pp. 1, 29.

21. *Jane's Defense Weekly*, February 7, 1996, p. 15; *New York Times*, August 22, 1997, p. A-1; Associated Press, August 25, 1998, 1548, 0617, February 14, 1996, 1054; *Defense News*, January 29, 1996, pp. 1, 29.

22. Associated Press, May 15, 1998, 0848; *The Globe and Mail*, May 15, 1998, Internet edition; *New York Times*, May 16, 1998, p. A-7.

23. *Jane's Defense Weekly*, May 20, 1995, p. 6, November 4, 1995, p. 4, February 7,

1996, p. 15; *Washington Times*, June 21, 1995, p. A-17, July 15, 1995, p. A-8; Reuters, July 14, 1995, 0940; Executive News Service, August 6, 1995, 1342; Reuters, October 17, 1995, 0617, February 14, 1996, 1054; *Defense News*, January 29, 1996, pp. 1, 29.

24. See Anthony H. Cordesman, *Iran and Weapons of Mass Destruction*, Washington, CSIS, 1997.

25. Richard F. Grimmett, *Conventional Arms Transfers to the Third World, 1983–1990*, Washington, Congressional Research Service, CRS-91–578F, August 2, 1991; *Conventional Arms Transfers to the Third World, 1984–1991*, Washington, Congressional Research Service, CRS-92–577F, July 20, 1991; *Conventional Arms Transfers to the Third World, 1987–1994*, Washington, Congressional Research Service, CRS-95-862F, August 4, 1995; *Conventional Arms Transfers to the Third World, 1988–1996*, Washington, Congressional Research Service, CRS-96–667F, August 15, 1996; and *Conventional Arms Transfers to the Third World, 1989–1996*, Washington, Congressional Research Service, CRS-97–778F, August 13, 1997.

26. *Washington Post*, November 10, 1992, pp. A-1 and A-30, May 23, 1993, p. A-26, June 10, 1993, p. A-27; *New York Times*, November 18, 1992, p. A-5, October 18, 1997, p. A-1; *Defense News*, March 8, 1993, p. 4; *Business Week*, June 14, 1993, p. 31; *Los Angeles Times*, June 10, 1993, p. A-3; *Washington Times*, June 10, 1993, p. A-1, June 21, 1995, p. A-17, July 15, 1995, p. A-8; *Philadelphia Inquirer*, November 21, 1993, p. A-2.

27. *Jane's Defense Weekly*, June 30, 1989, pp. 1299–1301.

28. Iran has long been making light arms and ammunition. The Shah set up the Import Substitute Industrialization (ISI) program in 1970 with the goal of making Iran self-sufficient in arms. See Kenneth Katzman, "Iran: Arms and Technology Acquisitions," Library of Congress, CRS-97–474F, October 1, 1997; Kenneth Katzman, "Iran: Military Relations With China," Library of Congress, CRS-967–572F, June 26, 1996; Shirley A. Kan, "Chinese Proliferation of Weapons of Mass Destruction, Background and Analysis," Library of Congress, CRS-96–767F, September 13, 1996.

29. A review of Iranian claims in the FBIS-NES for the period 1990–1997 proved to be largely a waste of time. Iranian officials repeatedly made claims to self-sufficiency which were absurd, given the fact that so few Iranian-produced and modified systems had entered Iran's order of battle.

30. BBC, Middle East, ME/2191/MED, January 3, 1995.

31. Executive News Service, September 9, 1995, 0902.

32. *Washington Times*, September 27, 1997, p. A-4.

33. *International Defense Review*, 4/1994, pp. 72–73; *International Defense Review*, 7/1996, pp. 24–27; *Washington Times*, November 21, 1996, p. A-1; *Jane's Sentinel, The Gulf States*, 1997.

34. *Tehran Times*, "Velayat Military Exercises No Threat," May 30, 1996; *Jane's Defense Weekly*, April 30, 1997, p. 33, July 30, 1995, p. 3, December 10, 1997, p. 20, January 14, 1998, pp. 23–25; *Middle East Economic Digest*, July 18, 1997, p. 23.

35. *Tehran Times*, "Velayat Military Exercises No Threat," May 30, 1996; *Jane's Defense Weekly*, April 30, 1997, p. 33, July 30, 1995, p. 3.

36. *International Defense Review*, 7/1996, pp. 24–27; *Tehran Times*, "Velayat Military Exercises No Threat," May 30, 1996, *Jane's Defense Weekly*, December 10, 1997, p. 20, January 14, 1998, pp. 23–25.

37. *Jane's Defense Weekly*, April 30, 1997, p. 33; *Jane's Intelligence Review*, September, 1997, pp. 419–421.

38. Reports that one of these systems, the Fadjr 3—with a range of 40 kilometers—has seen extensive service with the Hezbollah forces in Lebanon are not correct. *Jane's Defense Weekly*, November 6, 1996, p. 23, September 17, 1997, p. 5, December 10, 1997, p. 20, January 14, 1998, pp. 23–25; *International Defense Review*, 7/1996, pp. 24–27; *Jane's Intelligence Review*, September, 1997, pp. 419–421.

39. *Jane's Defense Weekly*, October 8, 1997, p. 30; *Iran Focus*, October, 1997, p. 5.

40. *Jane's Defense Weekly*, October 8, 1997, p. 30; *Iran Focus*, October, 1997, p. 5.

41. IRNA, October 12, 1997.

42. *International Defense Review*, 4/1994, pp. 72–73.

43. *Jane's Defense Weekly*, June 12, 1996, p. 27.

44. See *Middle East Defense News*, March 1, 1993, and *JINSA Security Affairs*, June–July 1993, p. 7; Anoushiravan Ehteshami, "Iran Boosts Domestic Arms Industry," *International Defense Review*, 4/1994, pp. 72–73.

Chapter 5

Iran's Military Manpower

The trends in Iran's total military manpower, and comparisons of this manpower with the manpower of other Gulf forces, are shown in Figures 5.1 and 5.2. Figure 5.1 shows the trend in total active military manpower since 1967. Figure 5.2 uses a different source to show manpower trends by service. Figure 5.3 compares the trends in Iranian and other Gulf military manpower, showing the post Iran-Iraq War decline in Iranian manpower, but also showing the sharper decline in Iraqi manpower. Figure 5.4 shows the difference in total Gulf military manpower in the year of the Gulf War versus 1998, and Figure 5.5 shows total Gulf active military manpower by individual military service.

Iran's current military capabilities are heavily influenced by its demographics and by the size of its total military manpower. Iran is by far the most heavily populated Gulf state, giving it a major potential advantage in building up its military forces. Iran's total population was well over 66 million in 1997, and its pool of military manpower reached 15,200,000, counting the male population from ages 15 to 49. The CIA estimated that 9,010,000 males were fit for military service.[1] The IISS estimated that there were 3,993,000 males between the ages of 13 and 17, another 3,293,000 between the ages of 18 and 22, and a total of 5,017,000 males between the ages of 23 and 32.[2]

To put Iran's manpower potential in perspective, some 633,000 Iranian males reached military age in 1997, and nearly 45% of Iran's population is 14 years or younger, which means that Iran's manpower pool will grow rapidly for at least the next decade. In comparison, Iraq had 238,000 males reach military age, Kuwait had 17,544, Qatar had 4,115, Saudi Arabia had 265,010, and the UAE had 21,250.[3]

Figure 5.1
Trends in Iranian Military Manpower: 1967–1997 (in 1,000s)

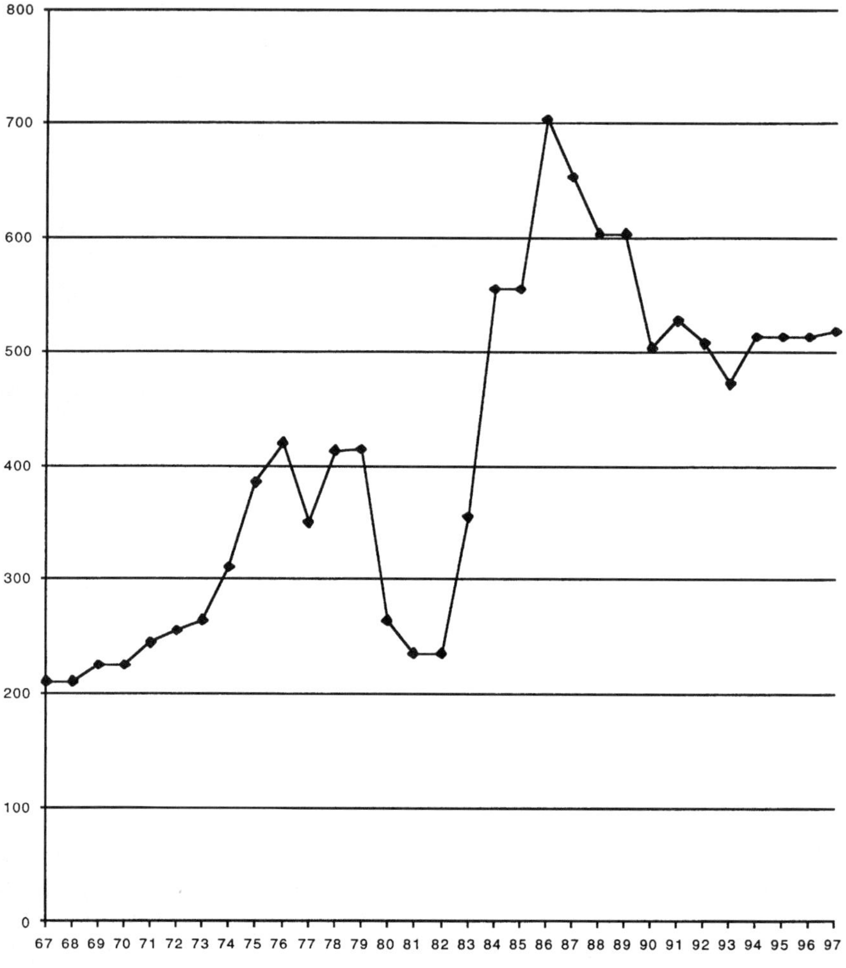

Sources. Adapted by Anthony H. Cordesman from ACDA, *World Military Expenditures and Arms Transfers*, table 11, and IISS, *Military Balance*, with adjustments by US experts.

NUMBERS VERSUS FORCE COHESION

At the same time, sheer manpower numbers have little importance in modern warfare, and Iran cannot rely on the kind of revolutionary and patriotic fervor that existed during the early years of the Iran-Iraq War. Iran's ability to transform its manpower numbers into military power is limited by its economic problems and access to arms imports. Its manpower base also has deep ethnic, religious, and linguistic divisions.

Figure 5.2
Trends in Iranian Military Manpower: 1978–1997 (in 1,000s)

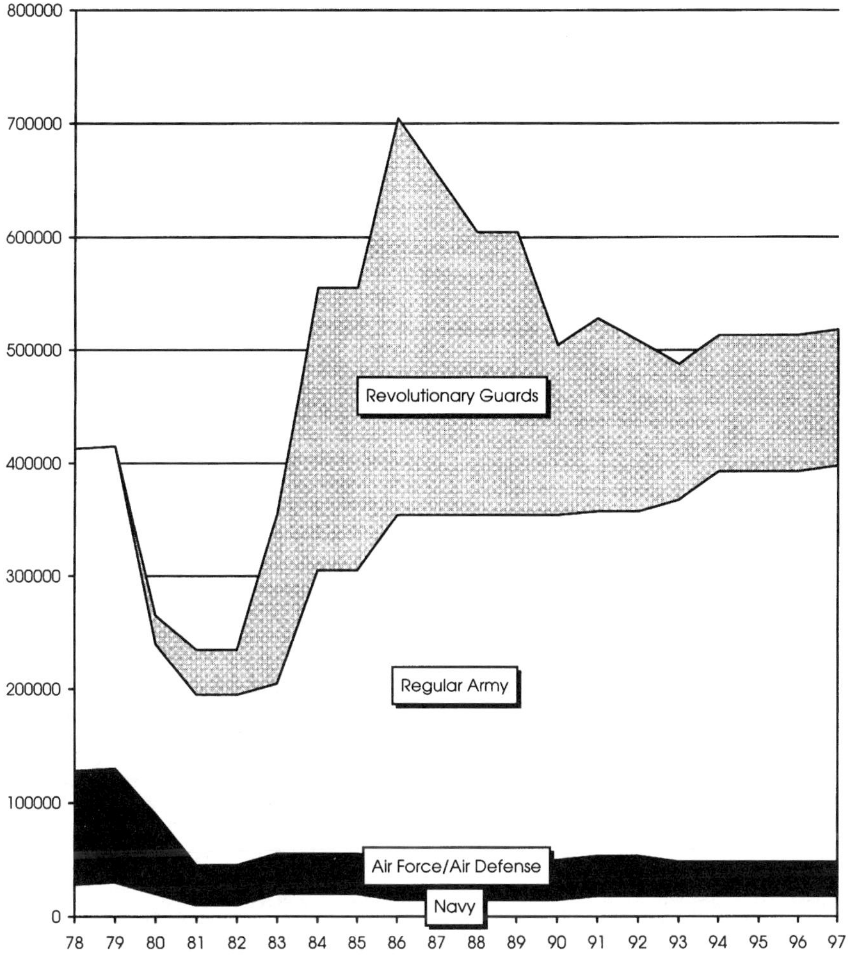

Source: Adapted by Anthony H. Cordesman from various editions of IISS, *Military Balance*.

While 51% of Iran's population is Persian, about 24% is Azerbaijani, 8% is Gilaki and Mazandarani, 7% is Kurdish, 3% is Arab, and the remaining 7% is composed of Lurs, Balochi, Torkomens, and other minorities.[4] Iran's population is 89% Shi'a Muslim, 10% Sunni Muslim, and 1% Zoroastrian, Jewish, Christian, and Baha'i. About 58% of the population speaks Persian and Persian dialects, 26% speaks Turkic and Turkic dialects, and 9% speaks Kurdish. Iran's smaller linguistic groups include Luri (2%), Baloch (1%), Arabic (1%), Turkish (1%), and other (2%).[5]

Visitors to both regular and IRGC forces indicate that training levels tend to

Figure 5.3
Total Active Military Manpower in All Gulf Forces: 1979–1998

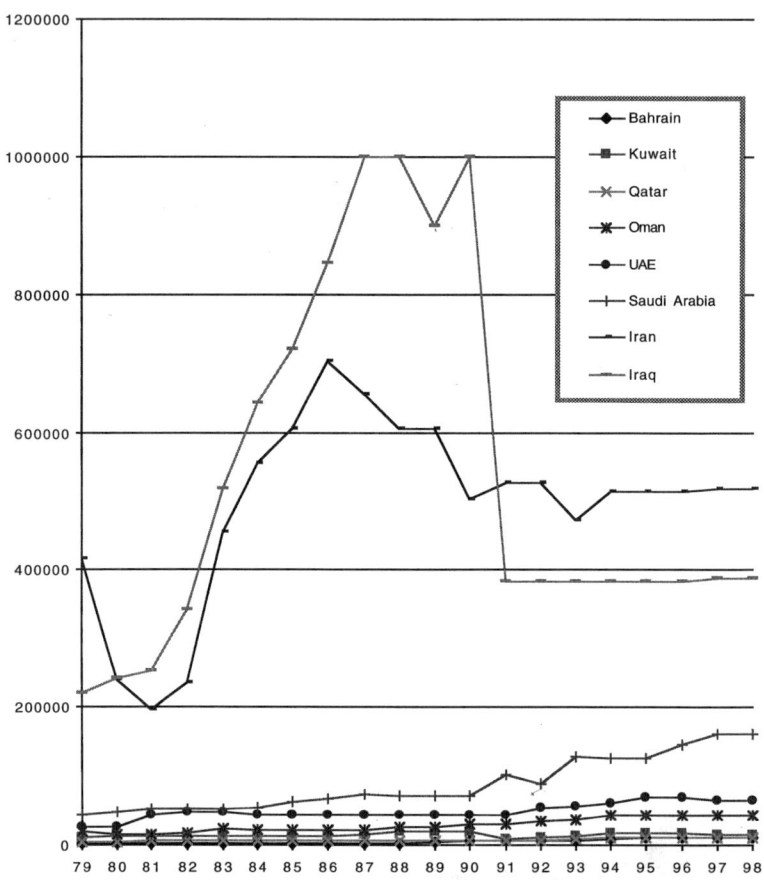

Note: Iran includes active forces in the Revolutionary Guards. Saudi Arabia includes active forces in the National Guard.
Sources: Adapted by Anthony H. Cordesman from various sources, and IISS, *Military Balance.*

be low and that language and technical training are inadequate for both operations and maintenance when Iranian forces must use sophisticated foreign equipment. Conscript manpower is poorly trained and lacks motivation. NCO training and manpower management is poor. Junior officers receive inadequate tactical and technical training and are not trained to show sufficient initiative in exercises and field training.

The idea that developing countries can take advantage of their total manpower base is usually a military myth. Manpower without modern equipment and specialized training and skills can be of great value in guerrilla and infantry combat, and in some forms of unconventional warfare, but it has little application to

Figure 5.4
Total Active Military Manpower in All Gulf Forces—Gulf War in 1990 versus 1998

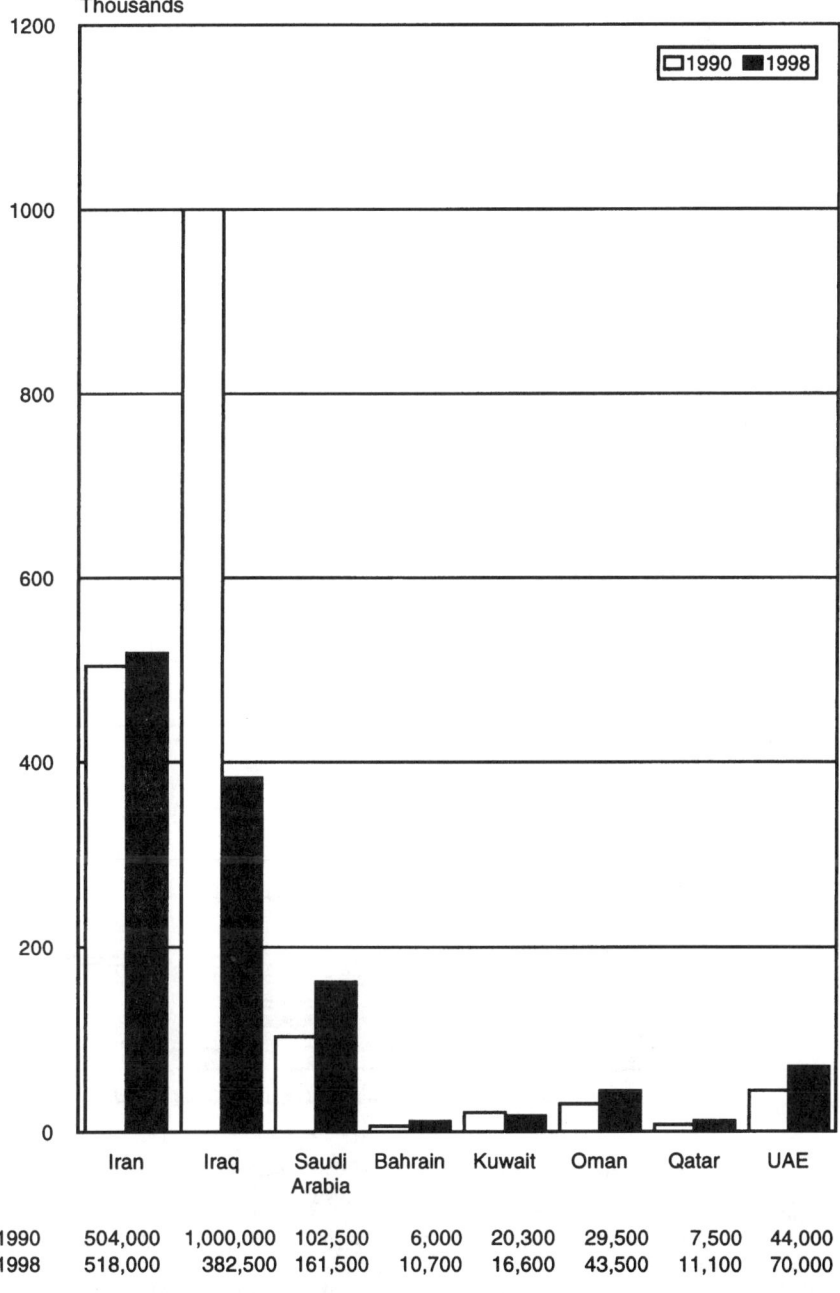

Note: Iran includes active forces in the Revolutionary Guards. Saudi Arabia includes active forces in the National Guard.
Sources: Adapted by Anthony H. Cordesman from various sources, and IISS, *Military Balance*.

Figure 5.5
Total Gulf Military Manpower by Service: 1998

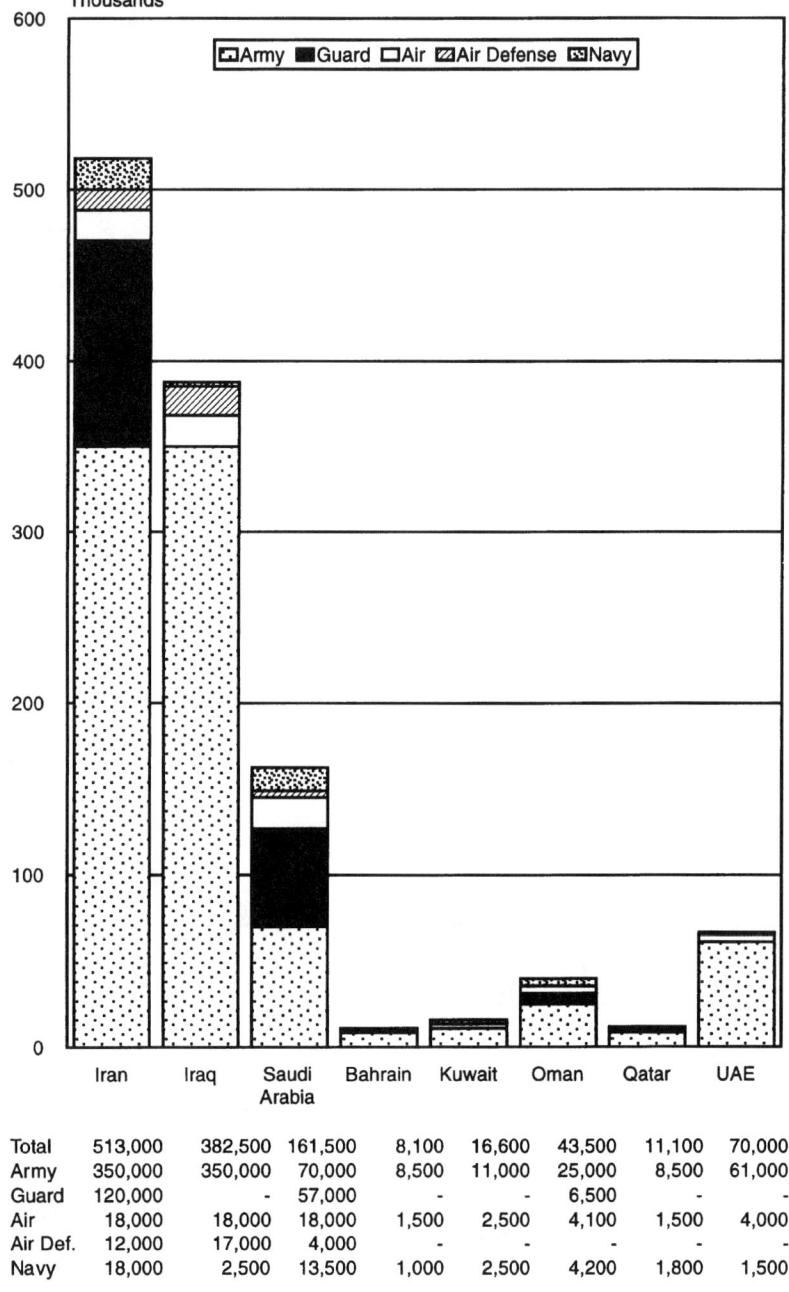

	Iran	Iraq	Saudi Arabia	Bahrain	Kuwait	Oman	Qatar	UAE
Total	513,000	382,500	161,500	8,100	16,600	43,500	11,100	70,000
Army	350,000	350,000	70,000	8,500	11,000	25,000	8,500	61,000
Guard	120,000	-	57,000	-	-	6,500	-	-
Air	18,000	18,000	18,000	1,500	2,500	4,100	1,500	4,000
Air Def.	12,000	17,000	4,000	-	-	-	-	-
Navy	18,000	2,500	13,500	1,000	2,500	4,200	1,800	1,500

Source: Adapted by Anthony H. Cordesman from IISS, *Military Balance*.

sophisticated military operations. Skilled manpower is costly to train, retain, and employ effectively, and countries like Iran are poorly organized to carry out effective manpower management. While salaries may be low, the overhead costs of military productivity in Third World forces usually raise the cost of performing technically skilled and military leadership tasks above those of developed countries. This makes it difficult or impossible to use military manpower effectively in demanding technical tasks and complex military operations, and Iran faces particularly serious problems because its forces are divided into regular and revolutionary units.

These factors help explain why Iran currently does not currently maintain an active military manpower base proportionate to its total population. The most accurate total is probably around 330,000–345,000, with about 220,000–230,000 full time actives in the regular forces and 120,000 Revolutionary Guards. At least 70% of this manpower consists of low-grade, short-term conscripts. US experts feel that these figures are a much more accurate estimate of the size of Iranian military manpower as of early 1998 than some competing estimates, which they feel may reflect some double counting of elements of the regular forces and Revolutionary Guards.

US Central Command (USCENTCOM), however, provides different totals. The regular forces are estimated to have around 300,000 actives and the Revolutionary Guards a total strength of around 170,000. This gives Iran's total land forces a strength of 470,000 actives. According to the IISS, Iran's active strength is around 518,000.[6] These totals compare with estimates of around 387,500 men for Iraq—which has less than one-third of Iran's total population, and 161,500 regular and National Guard actives for Saudi Arabia. Regardless of which total is correct, it is clear that Iran has difficulty in fully exploiting its manpower potential because of some combination of the cost of added manpower, the problems in mobilizing public support after the losses of the Iran-Iraq War, the divisions within Iran's forces, and Iran's equipment and sustainability limitations.

ALLOCATION OF MANPOWER BY SERVICE

Iran's allocation of military manpower clearly reflects the division of its forces into a number of rival elements, but estimates again differ about how Iran allocates its manpower. US experts feel that the regular Iranian land forces have around 175,000–180,000 men, the air and air defense forces have 30,000–35,000, and the navy has around 18,000. They estimate that the Revolutionary Guards have around 120,000 men, with a naval branch of 18,000–20,000. Iran also has around 300,000 men in various militia, paramilitary, and national police forces. These figures seem likely to provide the most accurate picture of Iran's manning levels.

USCENTCOM provides different figures. The regular army is estimated to have around 300,000 actives, the Revolutionary Guards to have a total strength of around 170,000, the air force and air defense force to have 35,500, and the navy to have 18,000. This gives Iran's total land forces a strength of 470,000 actives versus a strength of 518,000 in the IISS estimate.[7]

The IISS estimates that the regular army has about 350,000 actives, including 250,000 conscripts. The Revolutionary Guards have a total strength of around 120,000, roughly 100,000 of which are assigned to the land branch. The Iranian air force and air defense force have around 37,000, and the IISS reports strength of the air branch of the Revolutionary Guards as part of the land branch. The regular Iranian Navy is estimated to have 18,000 men, and the Iranian Naval Guards to total about 20,000 (including 2,000 in the IRGC naval air and marine forces). The IISS also estimates that Iran has roughly 200,000 personnel in the Basij (Population Mobilization Army), with about 90,000 full-time actives. The law-enforcement forces include a total of around 150,000, with more than 45,000 paramilitary Gendarmerie and border guards.[8]

NOTES

1. *Washington Post*, May 8, 1992, p. A-17; CIA, *World Factbook, 1996*, "Iran."
2. IISS, *Military Balance, 1997–1998*, "Iran."
3. *Washington Post*, May 8, 1992, p. A-17; CIA, *World Factbook, 1996*, "Iran."
4. *Washington Post*, May 8, 1992, p. A-17; CIA, *World Factbook, 1996*, "Iran."
5. CIA, *World Factbook, 1996*, "Iran."
6. IISS, *Military Balance, 1997–1998*, "Iran."
7. Interviews and USCENTCOM, *Atlas, 1996*, MacDill Air Force Base, USCENTCOM, 1997, pp. 14–15.
8. IISS, *Military Balance, 1997–1998*, "Iran."

Chapter 6

Iranian Land Forces

Military expenditures, arms imports, and total military manpower are useful measures of Iran's military potential, but they are not measures of its warfighting and contingency capabilities. It is the strength, organization, equipment, training, sustainability, and readiness of Iran's military services which largely determine the kinds of threats Iran can pose in the region and whether these threats will increase in the future.[1]

Iran's land forces have been in a constant state of change since the end of the Iran-Iraq War, and it is difficult to make accurate estimates of their strength. Iran's army and Revolutionary Guards units have suffered from the combined impact of revolution, a Western embargo on arms transfers, and the Iran-Iraq War. Iran's ground forces also took far greater losses during the Iran-Iraq War than the Iranian air force or navy, particularly during the war's final battles. Iran's defeats in the land battles of 1988 were so severe that they led to the disintegration of some elements of the IRGC and even Iran's main regular army units. These defeats also caused a massive loss of weapons and equipment.

While Iran's exact losses are disputed, it is clear that it lost over half of its operational armor between February and July, 1988. Iraq seems to be correct in claiming to have captured some 1,298 Iranian tanks and heavy armored fighting vehicles, 155 other armored fighting vehicles, 512 armored personnel carriers, large amounts of artillery, 6,196 mortars, 8,050 RPGs and recoilless rifles, 60,694 rifles, 322 pistols, 501 pieces of heavy engineering equipment, 6,156 pieces of communications gear, 16,863 items of chemical warfare defense equipment, and 24,257 caskets.[2] The degree of disintegration in Iran's land forces at the end of the Iran-Iraq War is reflected in the fact that much of this captured equipment showed no sign of combat damage or wear. Much was abandoned in the field, either out of panic or because of supply problems.

REGULAR ARMY ORGANIZATION AND MAJOR COMBAT FORMATIONS

Since that time, Iran has rebuilt many of the capabilities of its land forces, and it has made them considerably more professional and effective. US experts estimate that Iran's regular army now has some 220,000–225,000 actives, including 200,000 conscripts. Its reserves have a strength of roughly 300,000–350,000 men, but most of these men have little call-up training and no clear mobilization assignment. There are roughly 100,000 men in the land forces of the IRGC. Other sources put the total somewhat higher, and the IISS estimates that the Iranian land forces have a total of 350,000 men, including the IRGC.[3] A comparison of the strength of Iranian and other Gulf land forces is shown in Table 6.1 and Figure 6.1.

Major Combat Formations

The Iranian regular army had a strength of 12 division equivalents in 1998, and around 42–45 maneuver brigades. These formations included four "armored" divisions (two with three brigades and two with four brigades), and seven infantry divisions:[4]

- The nominal table of organization and equipment (TO&E) of an Iranian armored division includes three armored brigades, one mechanized brigade, one reconnaissance battalion, a self-propelled artillery battalion, a towed artillery battalion, an engineer battalion, a supply battalion, a transport battalion, an army aviation group, and an air defense group.
- The nominal TO&E of an infantry division includes one armored brigade, three mechanized brigades, one reconnaissance battalion, a self-propelled artillery battalion, a towed artillery battalion, an engineer battalion, a supply battalion, a transport battalion, an army aviation group, and an air defense group.

In practice, each Iranian division tends to have a slightly different organization. For example, only one Iranian division (the 92nd) is equipped well enough in practice to be a true armored division, and two of the armored divisions are notably larger than the others. Two of the infantry divisions (28th and 84th) are more heavily mechanized than the others.[5]

The lighter and smaller formations in the regular army include the 23rd Special Forces Division, which was formed during the period 1993–1994, and the 55th paratroop division. According to one source, the 23rd Special Forces Division has 5,000 full-time regulars and one of the few fully professional units in the Iranian Army. The airborne and special forces are trained at a facility in Shiraz.[6]

The regular army also has a number of independent brigades and groups. These include some small armored units, one infantry brigade, one airborne and

Table 6.1
Gulf Military Forces in 1998

	Iran	Iraq	Bahrain	Kuwait	Oman	Qatar	Saudi Arabia	UAE	Yemen
Manpower									
Total Active	518,000	387,500	11,000	15,300	43,500	11,800	161,500	64,500	66,300
Regular	398,000	387,500	11,000	15,300	37,000	11,800	105,500	64,500	66,300
National Guard and Other	120,000	0	0	0	6,500	0	57,000	0	0
Reserve	350,000	650,000	0	23,700	0	0	20,000	0	40,000
Paramilitary	135,000	55,400	9,850	5,000	4,400	0	15,500	2,700	80,000
Army and Revolutionary Guard									
Manpower	450,000*	350,000	8,500	11,000	31,500	8,500	127,000	59,000	61,000
Regular Army Manpower	350,000	350,000	8,500	11,000	25,000	8,500	70,000	59,000	61,000
Reserve	350,000	450,000	0	0	0	0	20,000	0	40,000
Active Main Battle Tanks	1,390	2,700	106	249	117	34	710-910	231	1,125
Total Main Battle Tanks***	1,410	2,700	106	341	135	34	1,055	231	1,125
AIFV/Recce, Lt. Tanks	515	1,600	55-71	283	37	76	1,205	558	620
APCs	550	2,200	340	100	73	172	3,030	570	560
Self-Propelled Artillery	289	150	13	41	18	28	200	175	36
Towed Artillery	1,995	1,800	36	0	91	12	260-318	82	512-548
MRLs	659	150	9	27	0	4	60	42-66	220
Mortars	6,500	2,000+	18	50	74	39	510+	135	500
SSM Launchers	46	36?	0	52	0	0	10	6	18
Light SAM Launchers	700	3,000	65	48	62	58	650	100	700
AA Guns	1,700	5,500	0	0	18	12	10	62	362
Air Force Manpower	18,000	18,000	1,500	2,500	4,100	1,500	18,000	4,000	3,500
Air Defense Manpower	12,000	17,000	0	0	0	0	4,000	0	0

Table 6.1 (continued)

	Iran	Iraq	Bahrain	Kuwait	Oman	Qatar	Saudi Arabia	UAE	Yemen
Total Combat Aircraft	297	353	24	76	47	11	336	108	69
Bombers	0	6?	0	0	0	0	0	0	0
Fighter/Attack	150	130	12	40	19	11	128	52	27
Fighter/Interceptor	114	180	12	8	0	1	139	22	28
Recce/FGA Recce	8	8	0	0	12	0	10	8	0
AEW C4I/BM	0	0	0	0	0	0	5	0	0
MR/MPA**	6	0	0	0	0	0	0	0	0
OCU/COIN/CCT	0	18	0	28	16	0	23	26	0
Other Combat Trainers	30	155	0	0	0	0	38	0	6
Transport Aircraft****	71	34	3	4	11	6	51	22	20
Tanker Aircraft	5	2	0	0	0	0	15	0	0
Total Helicopters	609	500	29	32	31	25	171	98	22
Armed Helicopters****	100	120	22	20	0	20	24	42	6
Other Helicopters****	509	380	7	12	31	5	147	56	16
Major SAM Launchers	204	340	12	40	0	0	128	36	87
Light SAM Launchers	45	200	0	12	28	45	181-249	34	200
AA Guns	-	-	24	12	-	-	234(+150)	-	-
Total Naval Manpower	18,000*	2,500	1,000	1,800	4,200	1,800	13,500	1,500	1,800
Major Surface Combatants									
Missile	4	0	3	0	2	0	8	2	0
Other	0	1-2	0	0	0	0	0	0	0

Patrol Craft									
Missile	20	1	4	2	4	3	9	8	7
Other	26	5	6	5	9	4	21	9	7
Submarines	3	0	0	0	0	0	0	0	0
Mine Vessels	7	4	0	0	0	0	6	0	5
Amphibious Ships	8	(3)	1	0	2	0	0	0	2
Landing Craft	17	-	4	6	4	1	8	4	1
Marines	(1,200)		0	0	0	0	(3,000)	0	0
Naval Guards	18,000		0	0	0	0	0	0	0
Naval Air	2,000		-	-	-	-	-	-	-
Naval Aircraft									
Fixed Wing Combat	0	0	0	0	0	0	0	0	0
MR/MPA	(6)	0	0	0	(7)	0	0	0	0
Armed Helicopters/SAR	9	-	-	-	-	-	24	6	-
Other Helicopters	-	-	-	-	-	-	-	-	-

Notes: Equipment in storage shown as higher figure in range. Air Force totals include all helicopters, and all heavy surface-to-air missile launchers.

*Iranian total includes roughly 100,000 Revolutionary Guard actives in land forces and 20,000 in naval forces.

**Saudi totals include 60,000 reserves which are National Guard Tribal Levies. The total for land forces includes active National Guard equipment. These additions total 262 AIFVs, 1,165 APCs, and 70 towed artillery weapons.

***Total tanks include tanks in storage or conversion.

****Includes navy, army, national guard, and royal flights, but not paramilitary.

Sources: Adapted by Anthony H. Cordesman from interviews; IISS, *Military Balance*; various data available from *Jane's*, *Military Technology*, *World Defense Almanac*; and Jaffee Center for Strategic Studies, *The Military Balance in the Middle East* (Tel Aviv, JCSS).

Figure 6.1
Total Active Military Manpower in Gulf Armies in 1998

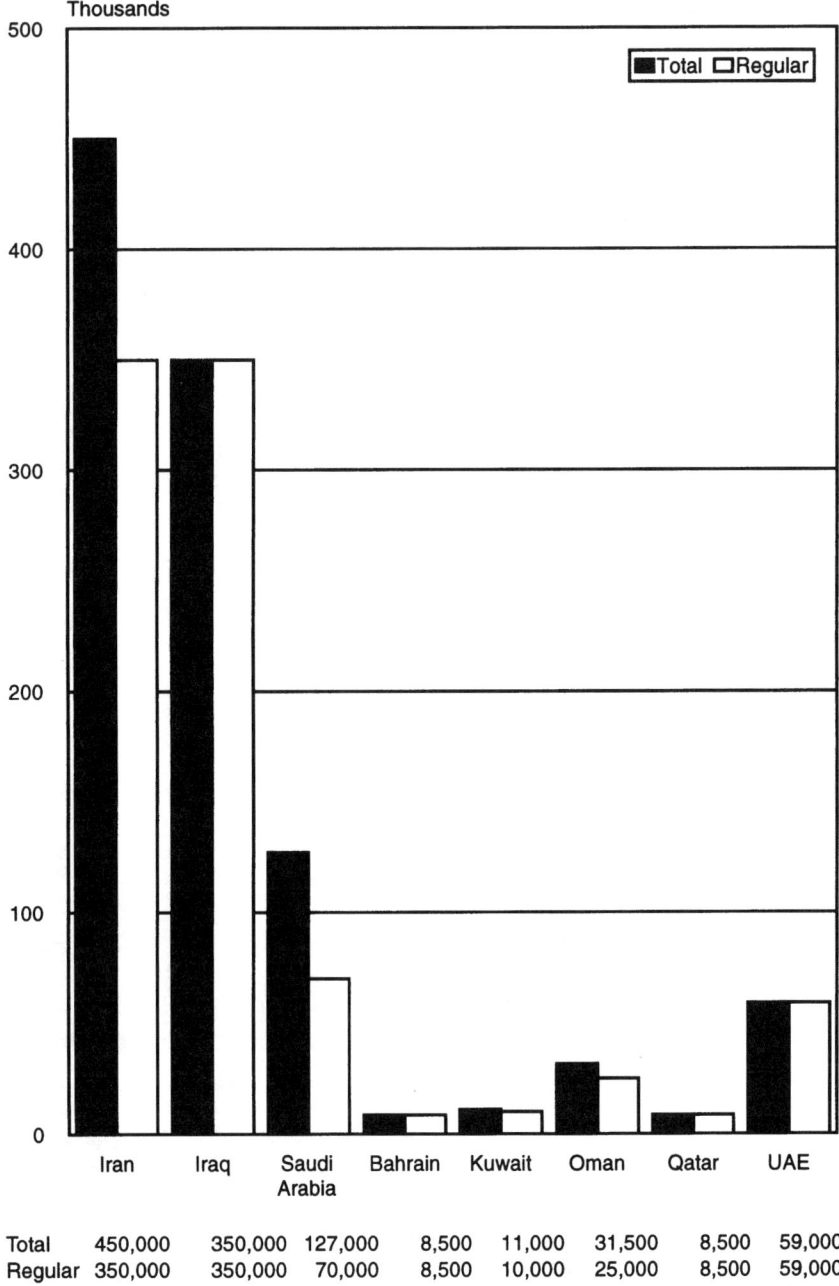

	Iran	Iraq	Saudi Arabia	Bahrain	Kuwait	Oman	Qatar	UAE
Total	450,000	350,000	127,000	8,500	11,000	31,500	8,500	59,000
Regular	350,000	350,000	70,000	8,500	10,000	25,000	8,500	59,000

Sources: Estimated by Anthony H. Cordesman from various sources, and IISS, *Military Balance*. The IISS estimates Iran's total land force manpower at 350,000, with over 100,000 men in the IRGC forces.

2–3 special forces brigades, coastal defense units, a growing number of air defense groups, five artillery brigades/regiments, 4–6 army aviation units, and a growing number of logistic and supply formations. The land forces have six major garrisons and 13 major casernes. There is a military academy at Tehran and a signal training center in Shiraz.[7]

Command Structure and Major Deployments

According to the IISS, Jane's, and various US experts, the Commander of the Iranian regular army reports through its Commander to the Armed Forces Joint Staff. The Army General Staff and Ideological-Political Directorate report to the commander of the Army. A surface-to-surface missile brigade and an air mobile forces group report directly to the high command. The rest of the army's organization is largely regional, with a heavy emphasis on the defense of Iran's western border with Iraq.

The largest regional command is the Western Area Command, which has four field headquarters for the Northern Sector (Mahabad), North-Central Sector (Hamadan), Central Sector (Dezful), and Southern Sector (Awaz). It controls some 60–75% of the regular army forces. The Southern Area Command is being expanded because of Iran's fear of US military action, but it still has only two field headquarters. The Eastern Area Command has three field headquarters. The IRGC officers are present in most of these headquarters.

Most of the combat forces of the Iranian army are normally deployed in three army-sized formations and a smaller corps-sized formation located north to south along the border with Iraq. Iran seems to have been able to move some units away from the south-western border since 1991, as Iraq has concentrated its forces to deal with the domestic threat posed by its Shi'ites in the South and Kurds in the North, but tensions between the Iranian government and the Kurds have forced Iran to maintain strong forces in the Northwest.

Many of the army's major facilities and casernes are the same as during the time of the Shah. They include Zahedan in the Southeast; Mashhad and Gorgan in the Northeast; Tehran, Qazvin, and Sarab in the north-central region; Kharramabad, Isfahan, and Shiraz in central Iran; Orimiyah, Maragheh, and Sanandaj in the Northeast; Kermanshah in west-central Iran; and Ahwaz and Shushtar in the Southeast. Army aviation is headquartered at Tehran, Mashhad, Isfahan, and Shiraz.[8]

IRANIAN ARMORED FORCES

Estimates of the current equipment holdings of Iran's land forces are uncertain, and it is not possible to distinguish the holdings of the Iranian regular army from those of the Islamic Revolutionary Guards Corps. Figure 6.2 provides an indication of the trends in Iranian armored weapons strength, and Figures 6.3– 6.10 show how Iran's armored weapons strength ranks relative to other Gulf

Figure 6.2
Trends in Iranian Armored Weapons: 1979–1998

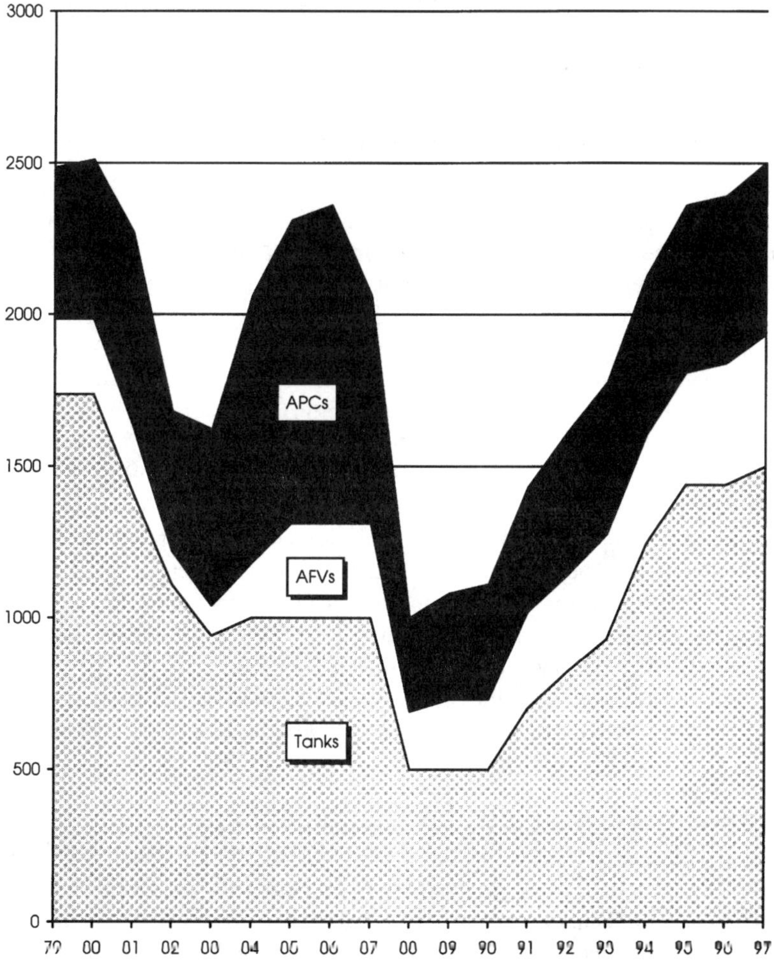

Source: Adapted by Anthony H. Cordesman from various editions of IISS, *Military Balance*.

powers. These figures provide separate comparisons of the trends in all types of armored vehicles, main battle tanks, operational and modern tanks, armored personnel carriers and other armored fighting vehicles, modern infantry fighting vehicles, and armored personnel carriers.

It is clear from these figures that Iran has still not fully recovered its maximum holdings at the time of the Shah, but that it has recovered from most of its losses during the end of the Iran-Iraq War. Iran has also benefited from Iraq's losses during the period 1990–1991 and the sanctions that followed, and Iranian and Iraqi forces are now much closer to parity.

Figure 6.3
Total Gulf Operational Armored Fighting Vehicles: 1998

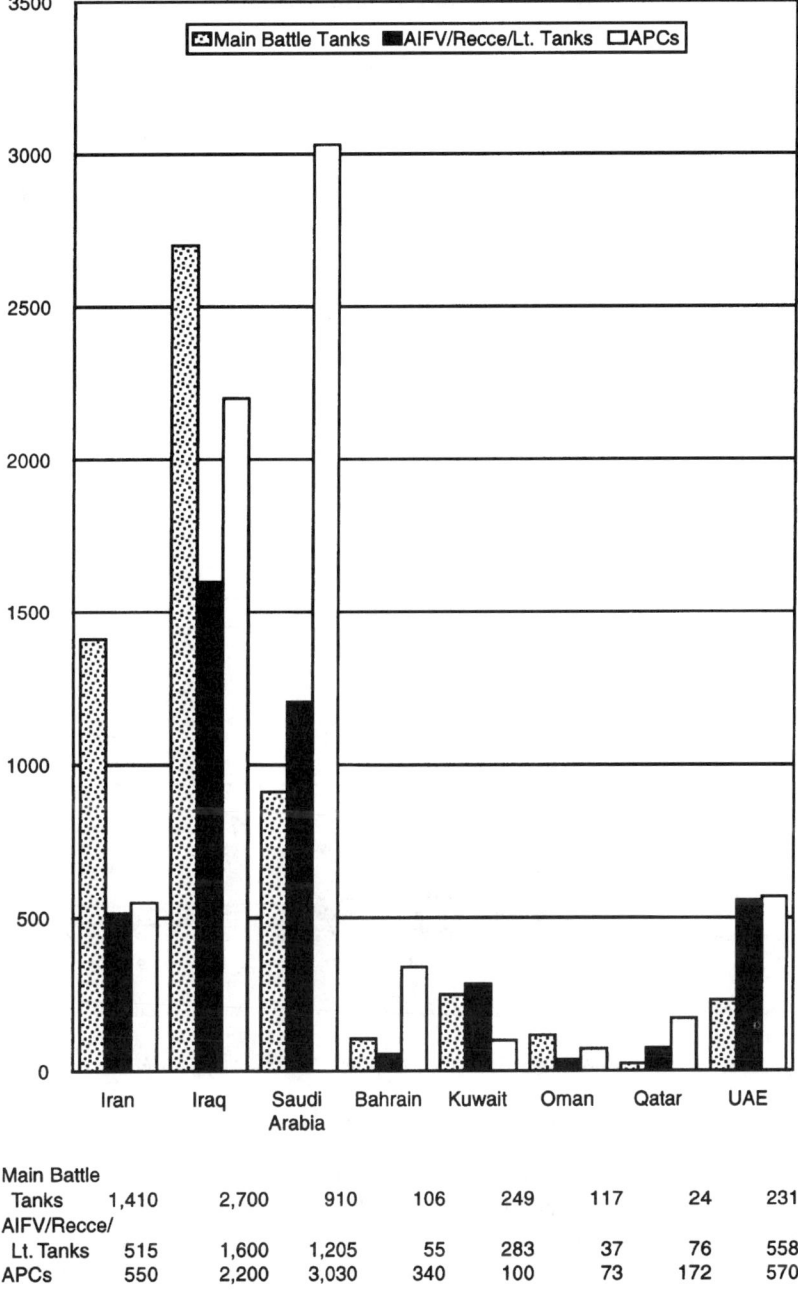

	Iran	Iraq	Saudi Arabia	Bahrain	Kuwait	Oman	Qatar	UAE
Main Battle Tanks	1,410	2,700	910	106	249	117	24	231
AIFV/Recce/Lt. Tanks	515	1,600	1,205	55	283	37	76	558
APCs	550	2,200	3,030	340	100	73	172	570

Sources: Adapted by Anthony H. Cordesman from various sources, and IISS, *Military Balance*.

Figure 6.4
Total Tanks in Gulf Forces: 1979–1998

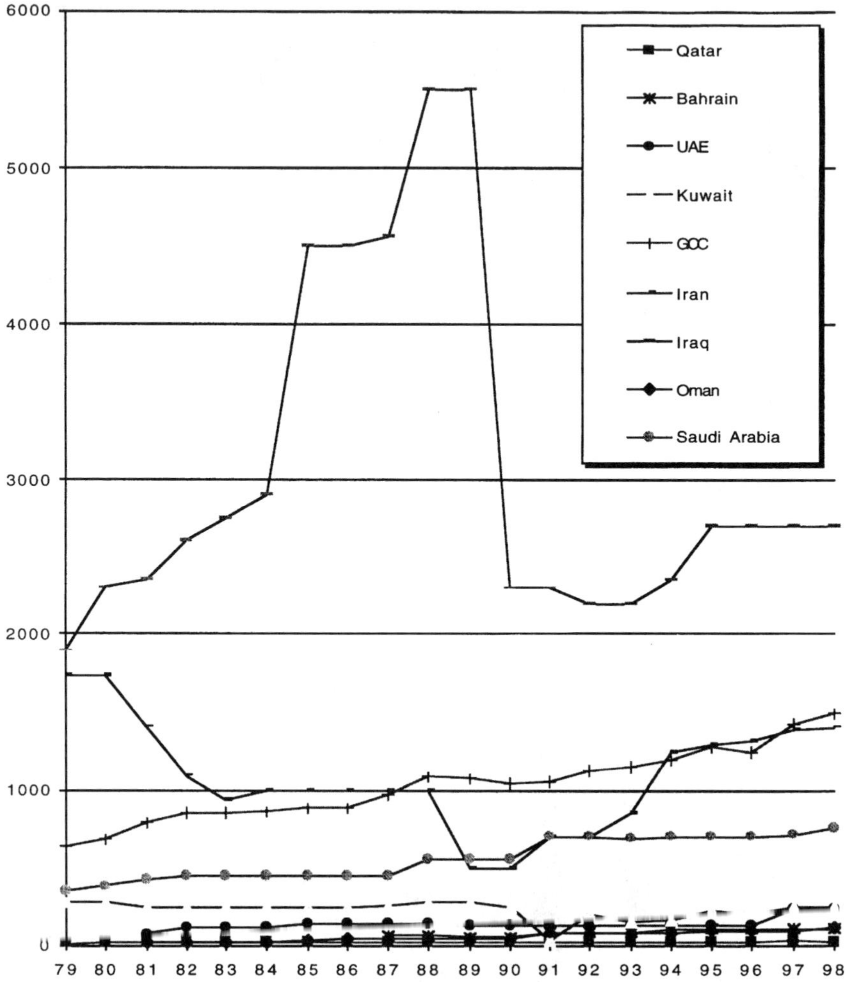

Note: Iran includes active forces in the Revolutionary Guards. Saudi Arabia includes active forces in the National Guard.
Sources: Adapted by Anthony H. Cordesman from various sources, and IISS, *Military Balance*, various editions.

Figure 6.3 shows that Saudi Arabia is one of the few Gulf forces to fully mechanize its land forces, and that Iran and Iraq both have a much lower ratio of other armored vehicles to tanks than US or Saudi Arabian heavy combat units. Figure 6.4 shows that Iran and Iraq have a lower proportion of modern tanks to total tanks than Saudi Arabia, but that both have a larger proportion of

Figure 6.5
Gulf Tanks in 1998

Total Main Battle Tanks in Inventory

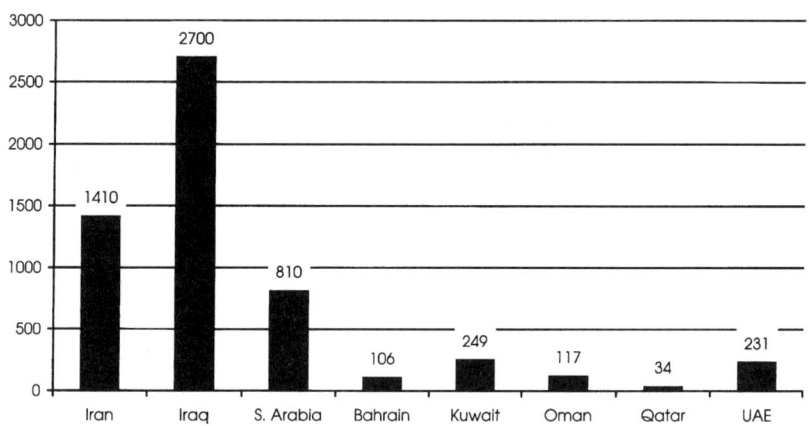

Operational Holdings of Advanced Modern Tanks: T-72, M-84, M-60A2/A3, M-1A1/2, Challenger, Le Clerc

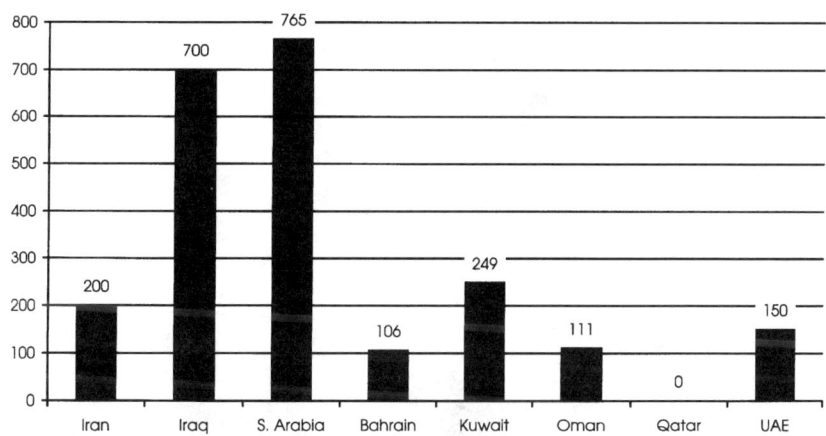

Source: Adapted by Anthony H. Cordesman from IISS, *Military Balance*.

armored fighting vehicles to armored personnel carriers. This may reflect the fact that Iranian and Iraqi forces are now modeled more on Soviet/Chinese models than Western models, although most developing nations tend to emphasize tanks over other armored vehicles.

Main Battle Tanks

Iran has steadily rebuilt its armor since the Iran-Iraq War. As Figures 6.3–6.6 show, Iran may have had as few as 500 operational main battle tanks after

Figure 6.6
Gulf Modern Tanks in 1998

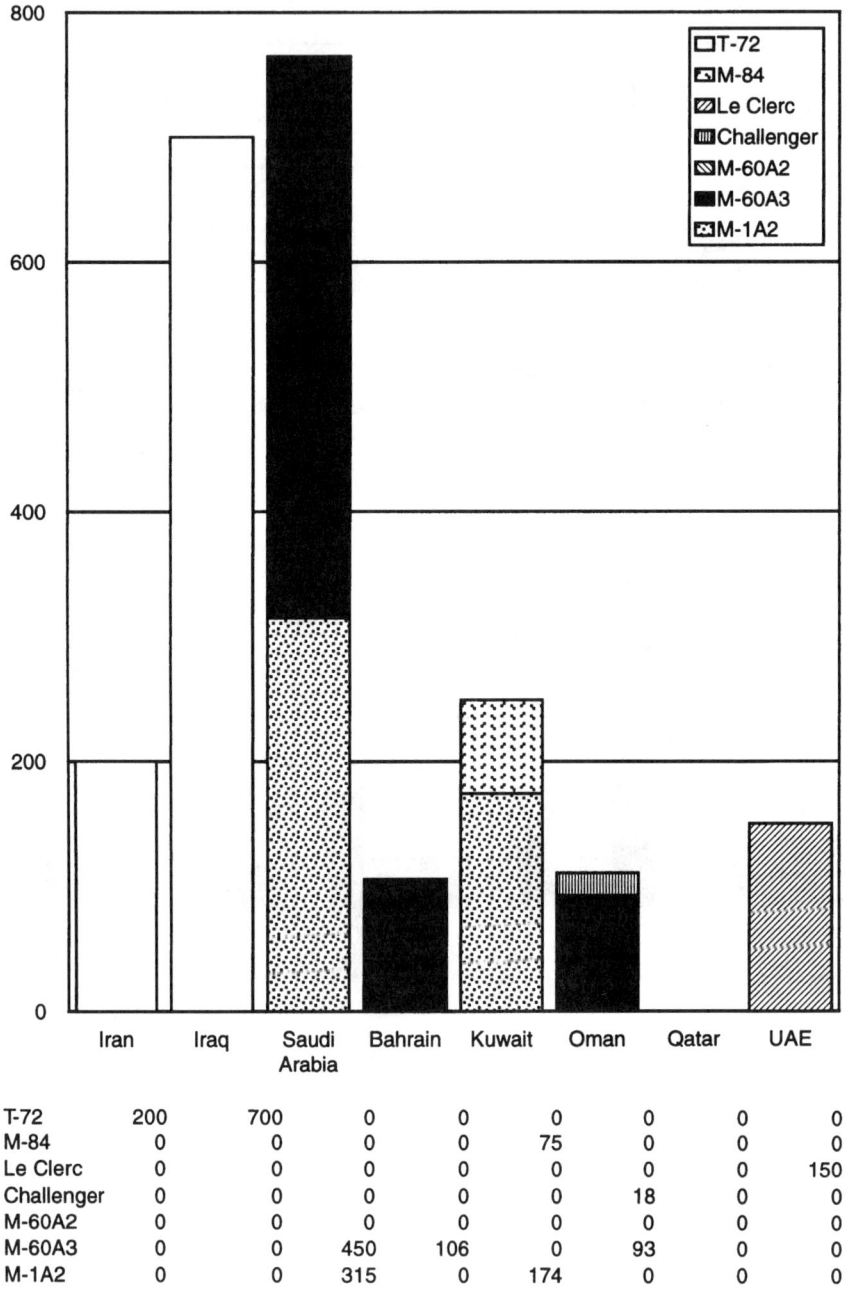

	Iran	Iraq	Saudi Arabia	Bahrain	Kuwait	Oman	Qatar	UAE
T-72	200	700	0	0	0	0	0	0
M-84	0	0	0	0	75	0	0	0
Le Clerc	0	0	0	0	0	0	0	150
Challenger	0	0	0	0	0	18	0	0
M-60A2	0	0	0	0	0	0	0	0
M-60A3	0	0	450	106	0	93	0	0
M-1A2	0	0	315	0	174	0	0	0

Source: Adapted by Anthony H. Cordesman from IISS, *Military Balance*.

Figure 6.7
Total Gulf Other Armored Fighting Vehicles (OAFVs): 1990–1998

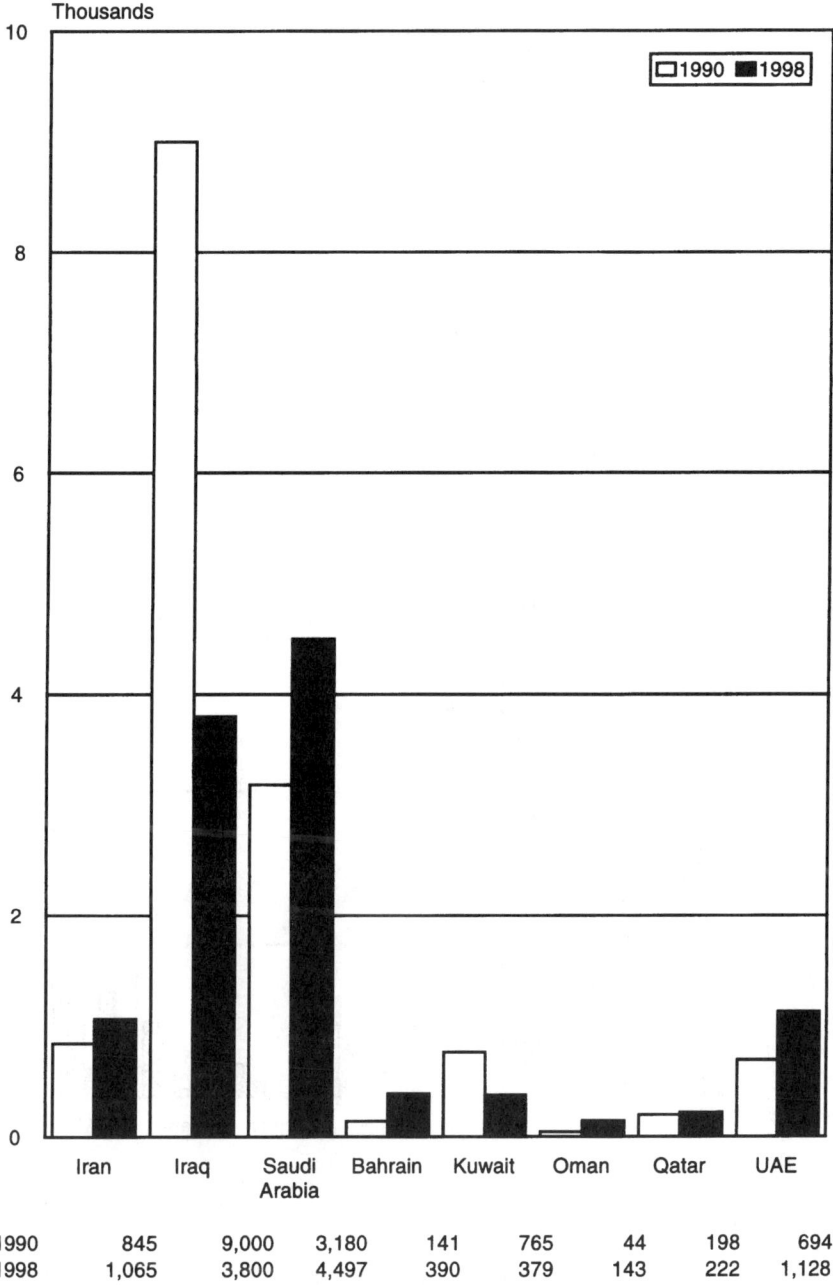

	Iran	Iraq	Saudi Arabia	Bahrain	Kuwait	Oman	Qatar	UAE
1990	845	9,000	3,180	141	765	44	198	694
1998	1,065	3,800	4,497	390	379	143	222	1,128

Note: Iran includes active forces in the Revolutionary Guards. Saudi Arabia includes active forces in the National Guard.
Sources: Adapted by Anthony H. Cordesman from various sources, and IISS, *Military Balance*.

Figure 6.8
Gulf Other Armored Fighting Vehicles by Major Category in 1998

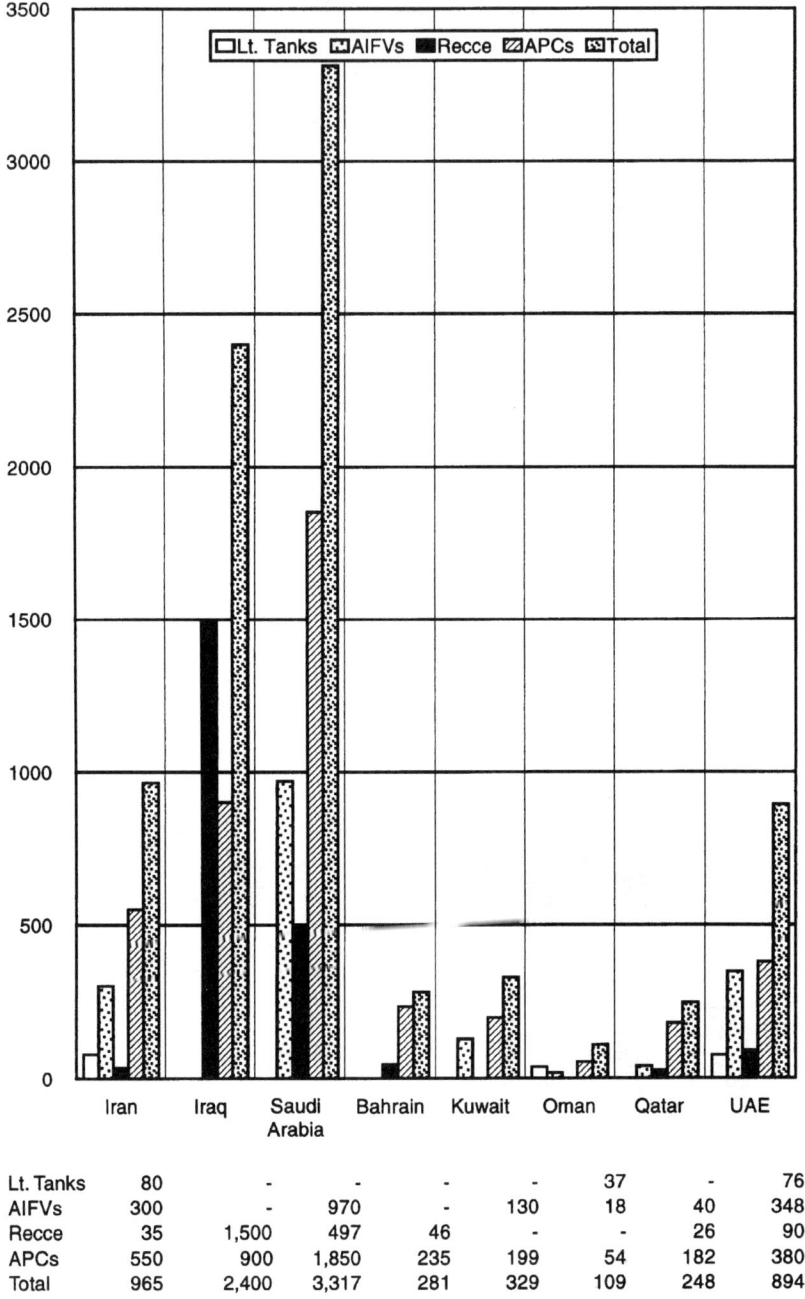

	Iran	Iraq	Saudi Arabia	Bahrain	Kuwait	Oman	Qatar	UAE
Lt. Tanks	80	-	-	-	-	37	-	76
AIFVs	300	-	970	-	130	18	40	348
Recce	35	1,500	497	46	-	-	26	90
APCs	550	900	1,850	235	199	54	182	380
Total	965	2,400	3,317	281	329	109	248	894

Sources: Estimated by Anthony H. Cordesman from various sources, and IISS, *Military Balance*.

Figure 6.9
Gulf Armored Infantry Fighting Vehicles, Reconnaissance Vehicles, Scout Vehicles, and Light Tanks in 1998

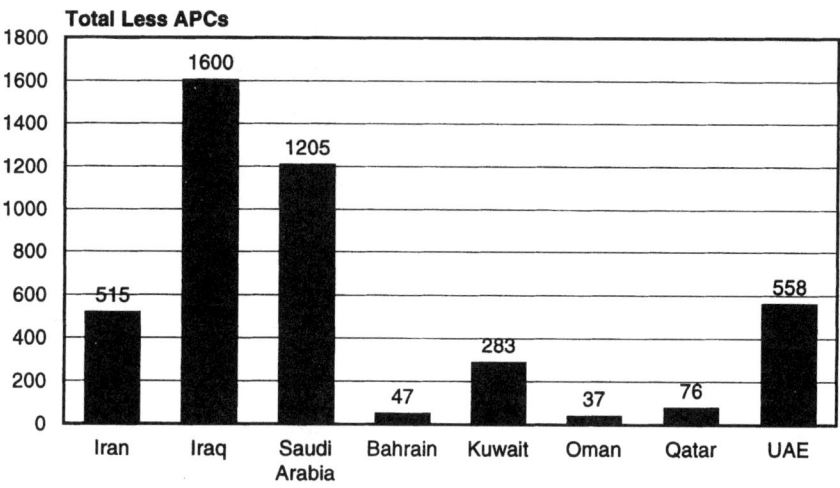

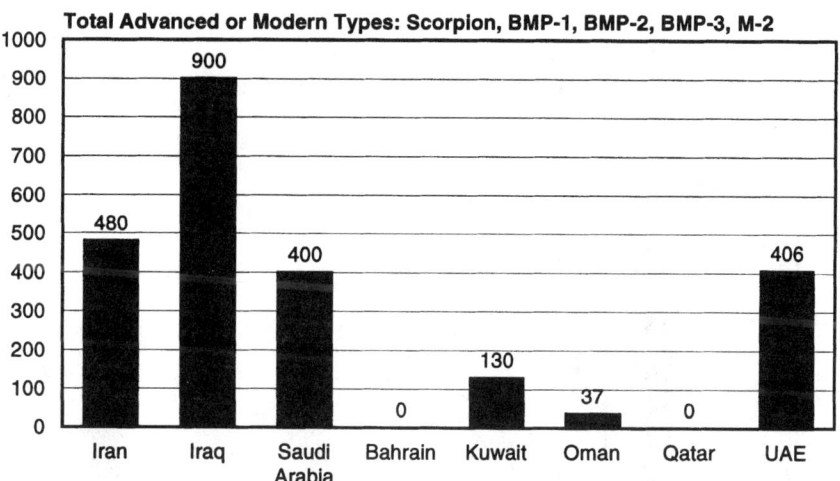

Sources: Estimated by Anthony H. Cordesman from various sources, and IISS, *Military Balance*.

its defeats in 1988. It seems to have rebuilt to an inventory of 1,250 main battle tanks in early 1995. It received enough deliveries to raise this total to over 1,300–1,360 operational tanks by January, 1996, and then to around 1,390 tanks by early 1998. This total compares with around 2,700 tanks for Iraq and 710–1,055 for Saudi Arabia.[9]

In early 1998, Iran's inventory of main battle tanks seems to have consisted

Figure 6.10
Armored Personnel Carriers (APCs) in Gulf Armies: 1998

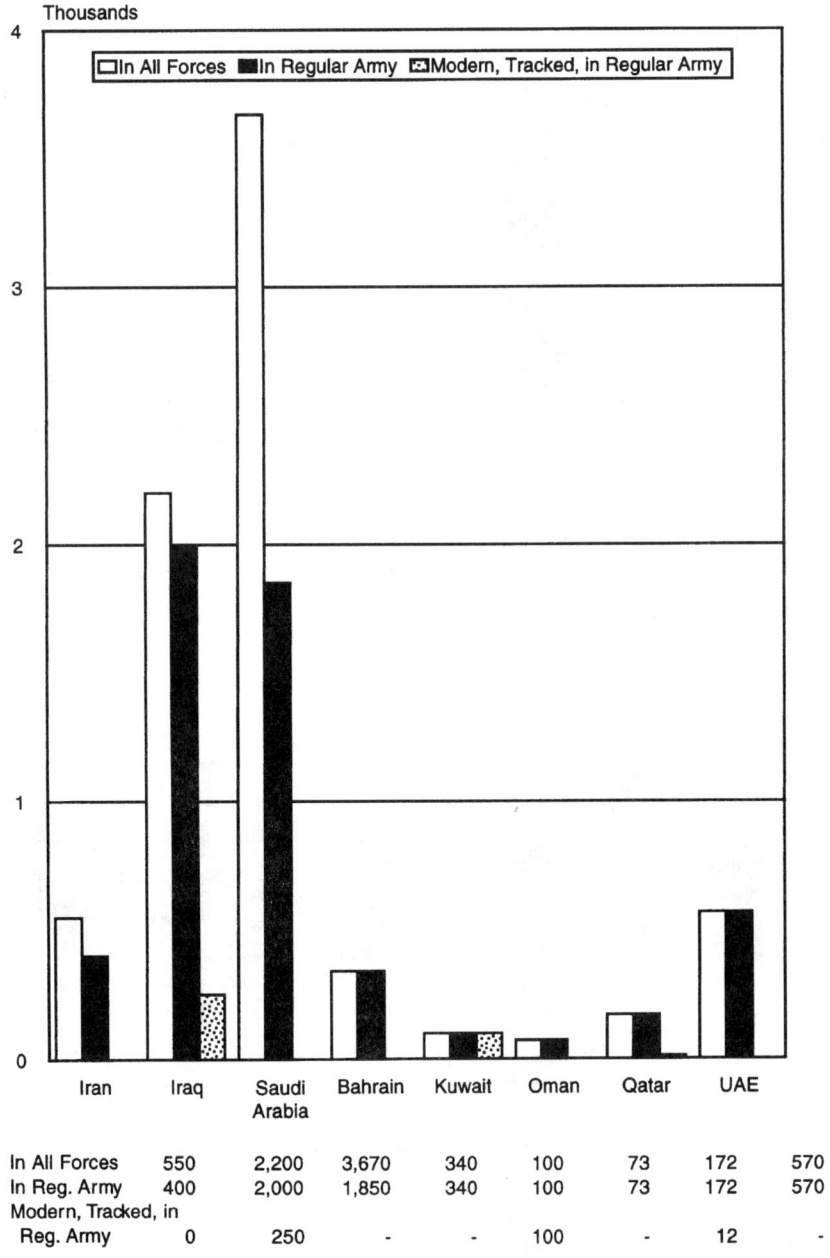

Note: Iran includes active land forces in the Revolutionary Guards. Saudi Arabia includes active forces in the National Guard.

Sources: Estimated by Anthony H. Cordesman from various sources, and IISS, *Military Balance*.

of about 150 M-47/M-48s and 150–160 M-60A1s, 250 Chieftain Mark 3/5s, 75 T-62s, 225–275 T-72/T-72Ss, 250 T-54/T-55s, 150–250 T-59s, 50 T-62s, and 150–250 T-69IIs.[10] Another estimate indicates, however, that Iran had roughly 1,430 main battle tanks, including about 150 M-47/M-48s, 160 M-60A1s, 200 Chieftain Mark 3/5s, 200 T-62s, 200 T-72/T-72Ss, 100 T-54/T-55s, 220 T-59s, and 200 T-69s. Iran originally had 460 M-60A1s, at least 240 M-48s, and 160 M-47s.[11]

These totals include the remainder of 187 improved FV4030/1 versions of the Mark 5 delivered to Iran before the fall of the Shah. They also include Iran's surviving upgraded M-47Ms. These M-47s were upgraded by the American firm of Bowen-McLaughlin York, during the period 1970–1972, which also built a vehicle manufacturing plant in Iran. They have many of the components of the M-60A1, including the diesel engine, automatic transmission, suspension, and gun and fire control components. The conversion extended the operating range of the M-47 from 130 to 600 kilometers, and increased space to hold 79 rounds by eliminating the bow mounted machine gun and reducing the crew to four. A total of about 150 conversions seem to have been delivered to Iran.[12]

Iran has extended the life of its T-54s, T-55s, and T-59s by arming them with an Iranian-made M-68 rifled 105 mm gun, similar to the one used on the M-60A1. This weapon seems to be made by the Armament Industries Division of the Iranian Defense Industries Organization. The Revolutionary Guard is reported to have a special conversion of the T-54, called the Safir-74, and Iran is experimenting with conversions of all of its tanks to use a reactive armor package manufactured by the Shahid Kolah Dooz Industrial Complex. This package is designed to be rapid fitted and to defeat both chemical energy and kinetic energy rounds. Some of these tanks may have upgraded engines and protective skirts.[13]

Iran's T-72Ss are export versions of the Soviet T-72B design built at the Uralvagonzavod factory in Nizhny Tagil. Some have been built under license in Iran, and are armed with a 125 mm 2A46M smoothbore gun. They have a relatively modern IA40–1 fire control system and computer, a laser range finder, and a night and day image intensifying sighting system. There are some reports that they can fire the Svir 9M119 (AT-11 "Sniper") laser beam riding missile with ranges of up to 4,000 meters, but this is uncertain. Some versions of the 9M119 are claimed to have a tandem HEAT warhead that can defeat and penetrate reactive armor. The T-72S is powered by an 840 horsepower V-84MS diesel engine, it has an upgraded suspension and a mine protection, a combat weight of 44.5 tons, and a power-to-weight ratio of 18.9 horsepower per ton.[14] Russian sources indicate that Iran has ordered a total of 1,000 T-72Ss from Russia.

Only part of Iran's tank inventory is fully operational, however, and it is uncertain how many Chieftains and M-47/M-48s are operational. Some experts estimate that Iran's sustainable *operational* tank strength may be fewer than 1,000 tanks. Further, its Chieftains and M-60s are at least 16 to 20 years old, and the T-72S is Iran's only tank with advanced fire control systems, sights, and anti-armor ammunition.

As has been touched upon earlier, Iran has claimed to have developed a world-class main battle tank. It announced in late December, 1994 that it had spent a total of $10 billion on military forces in the preceding five years, and it claimed to have begun production of a new main battle tank called the Zulfiqar, after two and one-half years of development. Prototypes of this tank were first shown in April, 1994. At least four such tanks seemed to be in service in Iranian armored units and were undergoing field trials in late 1997.[15]

Some confusion has arisen over this new tank because it is sometimes called the T-72Z. This name, however, seems to refer to the tank's original production date in the Iranian calendar, and not to the Russian design for the T-72S. At least two prototypes of the tank have been seen, differing largely in the commander's cupola. Its main armament may be a rifled 105 mm gun, but some reports claim that it has a 125 mm gun with a fume extractor and possibly an automatic loader. One report indicates that the 125 mm gun is in a narrow mantlet and does not have a coaxial machine gun. This makes the turret somewhat similar to that of the Brazilian Osorio MBT. Pictures of these prototypes show a chassis design closer to the M-48/M-60. The technical analysis of these photos indicates that the Zulfiqar uses welded steel construction for its hull and turret, has a box-shaped hull, and that its suspension is similar to that of the M-60.

According to one report, the Zulfiqar is powered by a V-46–6-12 V-12 diesel engine with 780 horsepower and uses a SPAT 1200 automatic transmission. This engine is used in the Soviet T-72S. Its combat weight is reported to be 36 tons, and it is reported to have a maximum speed of 65 kilometers per hour and a power-to-weight ratio of 21.7 horsepower per ton. It has a 7.62 mm coaxial and a 12.7 mm roof mounted machine gun. It uses a modern Slovenian Fontana EFCS-3 computerized fire control system to provide a fully stabilized fire on the move capability. It may have a roof-mounted laser warning device. It could use the same reactive armor system discussed earlier.

Iran claims to be beginning large-scale production of the Zulfiqar, but it has not yet entered Iran's order of battle in any numbers. There is no current evidence that Iran can mass-produce the advanced armor, engines, suspensions, or guns for a first-line main battle tank of any type, and many other nations, including India and Egypt, have failed in such efforts.[16] In any case, Iran currently remains dependent on its holdings of the Soviet designed-T-72S for anything approaching a new, advanced tank. The export versions of the T-72S performed badly in Iraqi hands during the Gulf War. They proved to be highly vulnerable to modern anti-tank rounds and missiles and to have poor long-range engagement capability. They lacked the thermal sights, night vision systems, fire control systems, and advanced armor to compete with first-line Western tanks like the M-1A1/2, Challenger, Le Clerc, or Leopard 2.

Iran's total main battle tank holdings are only sufficient to fully equip five to seven of its divisions by Western standards, and Iran could only sustain about half of this force for any period of extended maneuver warfare. At present, however, they are dispersed in relatively small lots among all of its regular Army and some of its IRGC combat units—all of the IRGC units generally only have small tank force cadres, and it is unclear how heavy these forces will really be in the future. The 92nd Armored Division is the only Iranian division that has enough tanks to be considered a true armored division, even by regional standards.

Armored Fighting Vehicles and Armored Personnel Carriers

Iran seems to have about 1,000–1,360 armored infantry fighting vehicles (AIFVs) and armored personnel carriers (APCs) in its operational inventory, although counts are contradictory and it is difficult to estimate which parts of Iran's holdings are fully operational and/or sustainable for any length of time in combat. The IISS, for example, estimates 515 light tanks and armored infantry fighting vehicles and 500 APCs. Virtually all estimates indicate, however, that Iran only has about half of the total holdings it would need to fully mechanize its forces.[17] This total compares with around 3,800 such weapons for Iraq and 3,000–3,600 for Saudi Arabia.

Iran appears to retain 70–80 British-supplied Scorpions out of the 250 it received before the fall of the Shah.[18] This is the only Western-supplied system Iran has that approaches a modern armored fighting vehicle, and is a tracked weapon equipped with a 76 mm gun. However, the Scorpion is more than 20 years old, and as few as 30 Scorpions may be operational. Iran may also have some 100 PT-76 light tanks in inventory, but this is a Korean War vintage design with an obsolete fire control system, main weapon, armor, and drive train. The PT-76 is little more than a death trap in modern combat, and it is not clear whether Iran would actually deploy it.

These problems may explain why Iran has recently claimed to have developed a new light tank called the Tosan ("Wild Horse" or "Fury") with a 90 mm gun. Brigadier General Mohammed Ali Jafari, the Commander of the IRGC, announced the tank in December, 1997, and said that the Tosan was specially designed for unconventional warfare. He also stated that it would be made at an IRGC factory at Khorramambad, about 125 kilometers northwest of Tehran. Iran may also be considering upgrading its Scorpions and equipping them with 90 mm guns.[19]

Iran does, however, have more than 300 BMP-1s and 100 BMP-2 equivalents. They are Iran's only modern AIFVs and they comprise only about 20% of Iran's total holdings of other armored vehicles. The BMPs are Soviet-designed systems, but they have serious ergonomic and weapons suite problems. They are hard to fight from, hard to exit, and too slow to keep pace with modern tanks. They lack thermal vision systems and modern long-range fire control systems, and their main weapons are hard to operate in combat, even from static positions.

Nevertheless, many have smoothbore anti-tank guns and anti-tank guided missiles. They are well enough armored to operate against infantry and fast enough to keep pace with most of Iran's armor. Russian sources indicate that Iran has ordered a total of 1,200 other armored vehicles from Russia, but they would not discuss the precise types.

Iran also has at least 35 EE-9 Cascavel armored reconnaissance vehicles, and one estimate indicates that number is 100. The Cascavel is an acceptable design for Third World combat, although it lacks modern sensors and weapons.

Iranian forces have some 230–240 M-113s and other Western APCs, and a mix of 300–320 BTR-40s, BTR-50s, and BTR-60s. One count credits Iran with 150–200 BTR-40s, 50 BTR-50s, and 230–240 BTR-60s. As few as 100 of Iran's M-113s and 200 of its 320 BTR-40s, BTR-50s, and BTR-60s may be operational in sustained combat, but Iran may bring more of its M-113s, BTR-50s, and BTR-60s to combat readiness.[20]

As has been discussed previously, Iran has claimed to be producing an armored fighting vehicle called the Boragh (Boraq) and a lighter APC called the Cobra, or BMT-2. The Boragh seems to be a copy of a Chinese version of the BMP. It is amphibious and has a combat weight of 13 tons. It can carry 8–12 people, plus two crew members. Reports differ as to its armament—perhaps reflecting different variants. Initial reports indicated that it has a turret armed with a 73 mm smoothbore gun and an anti-tank guided missile launcher. It seems more likely that it does not have the commander's position that exists in the BMP-1, and that it is armed only with a 12.7 mm machine gun—although a 50 mm gun is possible. It has two fewer ports, which could present problems in exiting the vehicle, and the kind of side firing ports common in older Soviet vehicle designs, but which have proved to have little value in modern combat. It seems to use road wheels and tracks similar to those of the M-113. Iran has been manufacturing such replacements for its own M-113s for some years, and this seems to be a logical adaptation. The chassis may be used for variants that carry anti-tank weapons, mortars, and anti-aircraft weapons, and possibly a 122 mm self-propelled gun.[21] Iran claimed that at least 40 Boraghs were in service in the IRGC by July, 1997.

The Cobra or BMT-2 is largely a troop carrier, which can hold seven personnel. It may, however, have a ZU-23-2 or 30 mm gun. It has a low profile, and its engine is in the front, which seems to be an indigenous design armed with a 30 mm gun or the ZU-23-2 anti-aircraft gun—a light automatic weapons system that Iran has been manufacturing for some years. Like the Zulfiqar, the Cobra has been undergoing field trials in Iranian military exercises since May, 1996. It is said to carry seven men, and it too is reported to be in production at the Shahdid Industrial Complex in southeastern Tehran. There is no firm evidence as yet of mass production of the Boragh and Cobra, but Iran claimed to have begun mass production in July, 1997. Such production would strengthen Iranian forces, particularly in combat against a force like Iraq, which is also equipped with dated armor and anti-armor weapons.[22]

Armored Doctrine and Proficiency

It is difficult to interpret the unclassified data available on Iranian armored operations, but Iran's armored warfare doctrine seems to be borrowed from US, British, and Russian sources without achieving any coherent concept of operations. Even so, Iran's armored doctrine is improving more quickly than its organization and exercise performance. Iran's armored forces are very poorly structured, and its equipment pool is dissipated among far too many regular and IRGC units. Iran has only one armored division—the 92nd—with enough tanks and other armor to be considered a true armored unit.

Iran seems to practice the kind of armored combat that might be effective against Iraq, but even in late 1997, its exercises were slow moving and emphasized day combat and short-to-medium-ranged engagements. Many are highly notional and do not involve large-scale actual movements. The movements that do take place have a preplanned, set-piece character. The tactics Iran does practice seem to be far more effective in relatively static defensive operations and limited, local, counter-attack modes than in training for longer-range defensive maneuvers or offensive operations. Only a few of Iran's heavy combat brigades seem to have made real efforts to improve their combined arms operations and joint operations with airborne and air units. Nevertheless, Iran's armor does seem to be recovering from the Iran-Iraq War, and its doctrine has become steadily more realistic and contemporary with Western and Russian doctrine. The emphasis on massed infantry, "popular armies," and "revolutionary forces" that crippled Iran's armored development during the Iran-Iraq War seems to have sharply diminished.[23]

Iran has an unknown number of British Chieftain bridging-tanks and a wide range of specialized armored vehicles, and some heavy equipment transporters. It is steadily improving its ability to support armored operations in the field and to provide recovery and field repair capability. However, its exercises reveal that these capabilities are still limited, relative to those of US forces, and that a lack of recovery and field repair capability, coupled with poor interoperability, will probably seriously limit the cohesion, speed, and sustainability of Iranian armored operations.[24]

Anti-Armored Weapons

Iran has large holdings of anti-tank guided weapons, and it has been manufacturing copies of Soviet systems while buying missiles from China, Russia, and the Ukraine. It has approximately 80–100 TOW and 20–30 Dragon anti-tank guided missile launchers that were originally supplied by the United States, although the operational status of such systems is uncertain. It has introduced Soviet and Asian versions of the AT-2, AT-3, and the AT-4 into its forces.

Iran seems to have at least 100–200 AT-4 (9K111) launchers, but it is impossible to make an accurate estimate because it is producing its own copies of the similar AT-3.[25] Iran also has roughly 750 RPG-7Vs, RPG-11, and 3.5 inch rocket launchers, and roughly 150 M-18 57 mm, 200 M-20 75 mm, and B-10 82 mm, and 200 M-40 106 mm and B-11 107 mm recoilless guns.[26]

Iran now makes a number of anti-tank weapons. These include an improved version of the manportable RPG-7 anti-tank rocket with an 80 mm tandem HEAT warhead instead of the standard 30 mm design, the NAFEZ anti-tank rocket, and a copy of the Soviet SPG-9 73 mm recoilless anti-tank gun. Iran also makes a copy of the Russian AT-3 9M14M (Sagger or Ra'ad) anti-tank guided missile. This system is a crew-operable system with a guidance system that can be linked to a launcher holding up to four missiles. It has a maximum range of 3,000 meters, a minimum range of 500 meters, and a flight speed of 120 meters per second.[27]

The Iranian copy of the AT-3 is made by the Shahid Shah Abaday Industrial Group in Tehran, and it seems to be an early version of the missile which lacks semi-automatic guidance that allows the operator to simply sight the target, rather than to use a joystick to guide the missile to the target by using the light from the missile to track it. The Iranian version also seems to have a maximum armored penetration capability of 500 mm, which is not enough to penetrate the forward armor of the latest Western and Russian main battle tanks. Russia has, however, refitted most of its systems to a semi-automatic line of sight guidance and warheads capable of penetrating 800 mm. Iran may have or may be acquiring such capability, and it would significantly improve the lethality of its anti-armor forces.[28]

Interviews and reports on Iran's exercise performance seem to indicate that its performance in using anti-tank weapons is improving, but that it remains oriented toward daylight and line-of-sight operations. There are indications that Iran tends to locate portable crew-operated weapons in predictable sites with a maximum range that makes them vulnerable to artillery suppression, and that its use of vehicle-mounted weapons tends to be largely defensive.[29]

IRANIAN ARTILLERY

Iran had some 3,000–3,400 operational medium and heavy artillery weapons and multiple rocket launchers in early 1998. This total compares with around 2,000 weapons for Iraq and 500 for Saudi Arabia, and reflects Iran's continuing effort to build up artillery strength that began during the Iran-Iraq War, when Iran used artillery to support its infantry and Islamic Revolutionary Guards Corps in their attacks on Iraqi forces. Figure 6.11 shows the trends in Iranian artillery strength from 1979 to 1988, and what has become a massive build-up in towed artillery strength. Figures 6.12–6.15 show how Iran's artillery strength ranks relative to other Gulf powers. Figure 6.12 compares the total artillery in each country at the time of the Gulf War with current holdings. Figure 6.13 shows total operational strength in 1998. Figure 6.14 compares holdings of

Figure 6.11
Trends in Iranian Artillery Weapons: 1983–1996

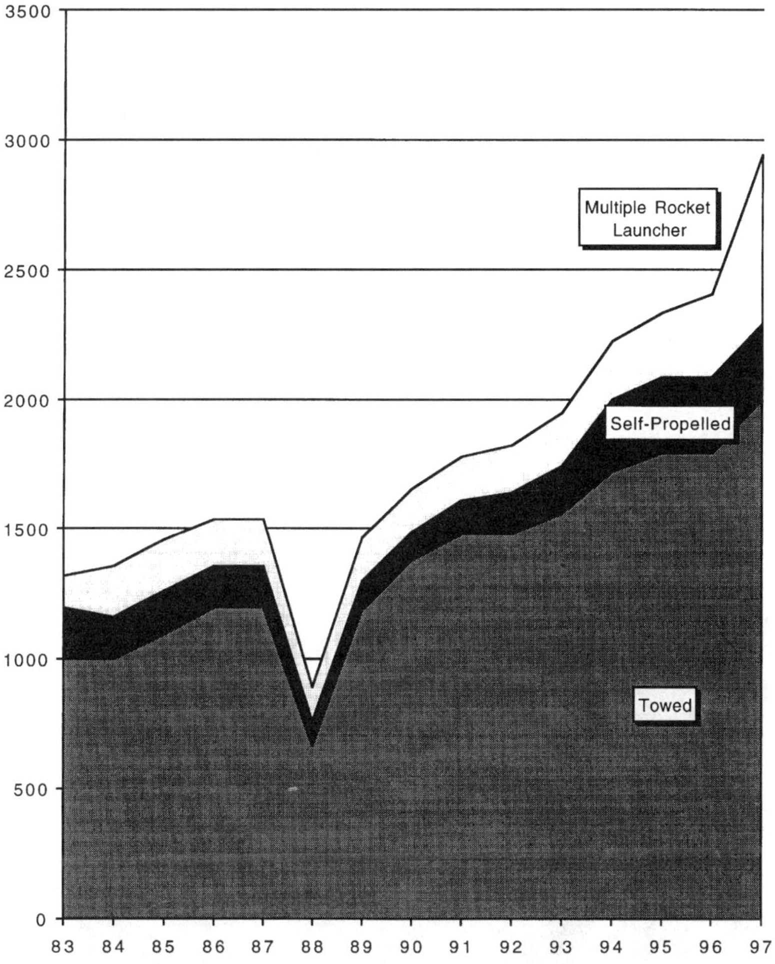

Sources: Adapted by Anthony H. Cordesman from various sources, and IISS, *Military Balance*, various editions.

towed and self-propelled tube artillery, and Figure 6.15 shows holdings of multiple rocket launchers.

Iran had to use artillery as a substitute for armor and air power during much of the Iran-Iraq War, and generally used relatively static massed fires. While some regular army units used artillery more flexibly, Iran artillery tended to pound away at area targets and often with little success. Iranian forces showed little skill at targeting and often missed Iraqi concentrations or continued to fire at heavily sheltered Iraqi forces. Iran's artillery fire control system had serious

Figure 6.12
Total Operational Self-Propelled and Towed Tube Artillery and Multiple Rocket Launchers in Gulf Forces: 1990 and 1998

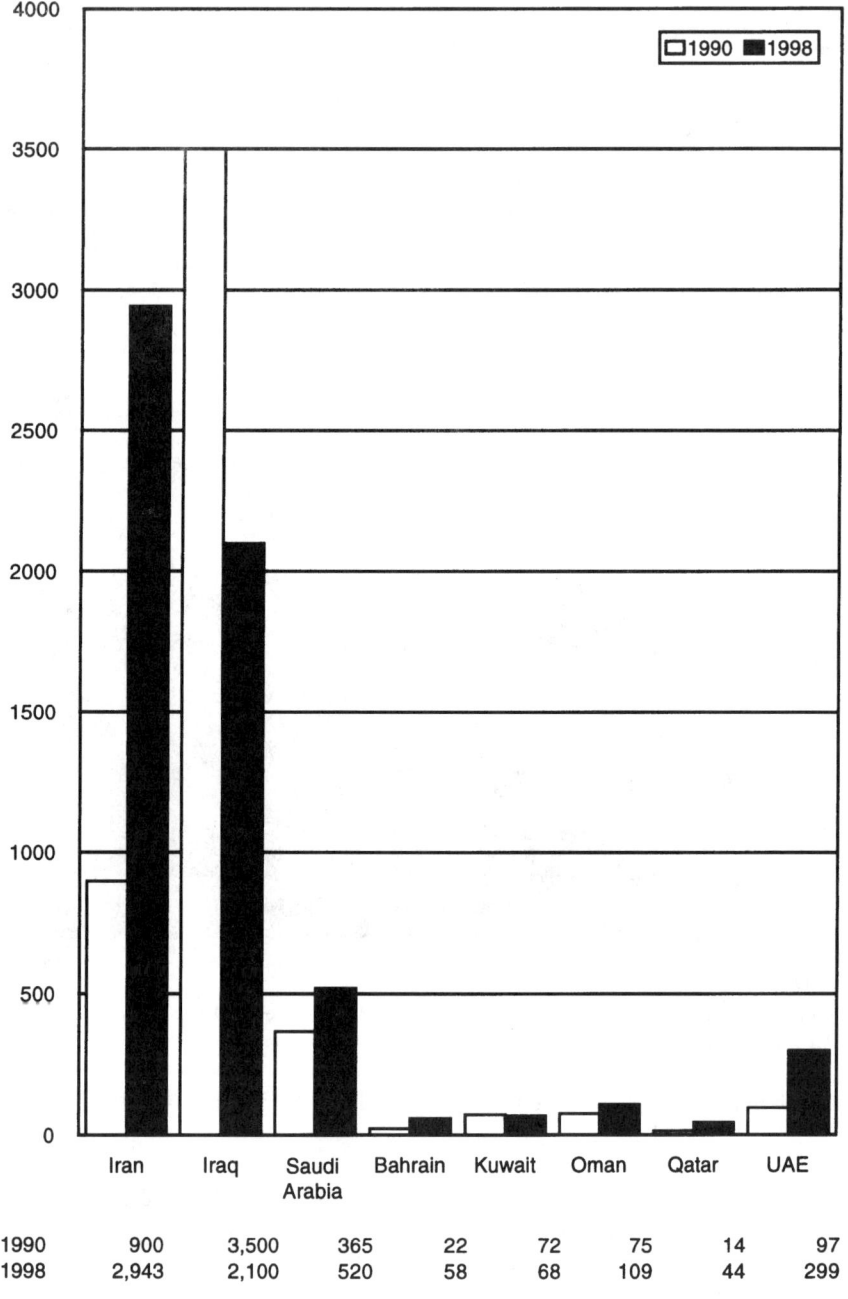

Note: Iran includes active forces in the Revolutionary Guards. Saudi Arabia includes active forces in the National Guard.
Sources: Adapted by Anthony H. Cordesman from various sources, and IISS, *Military Balance*.

Figure 6.13
Total Operational Gulf Artillery Weapons: 1998

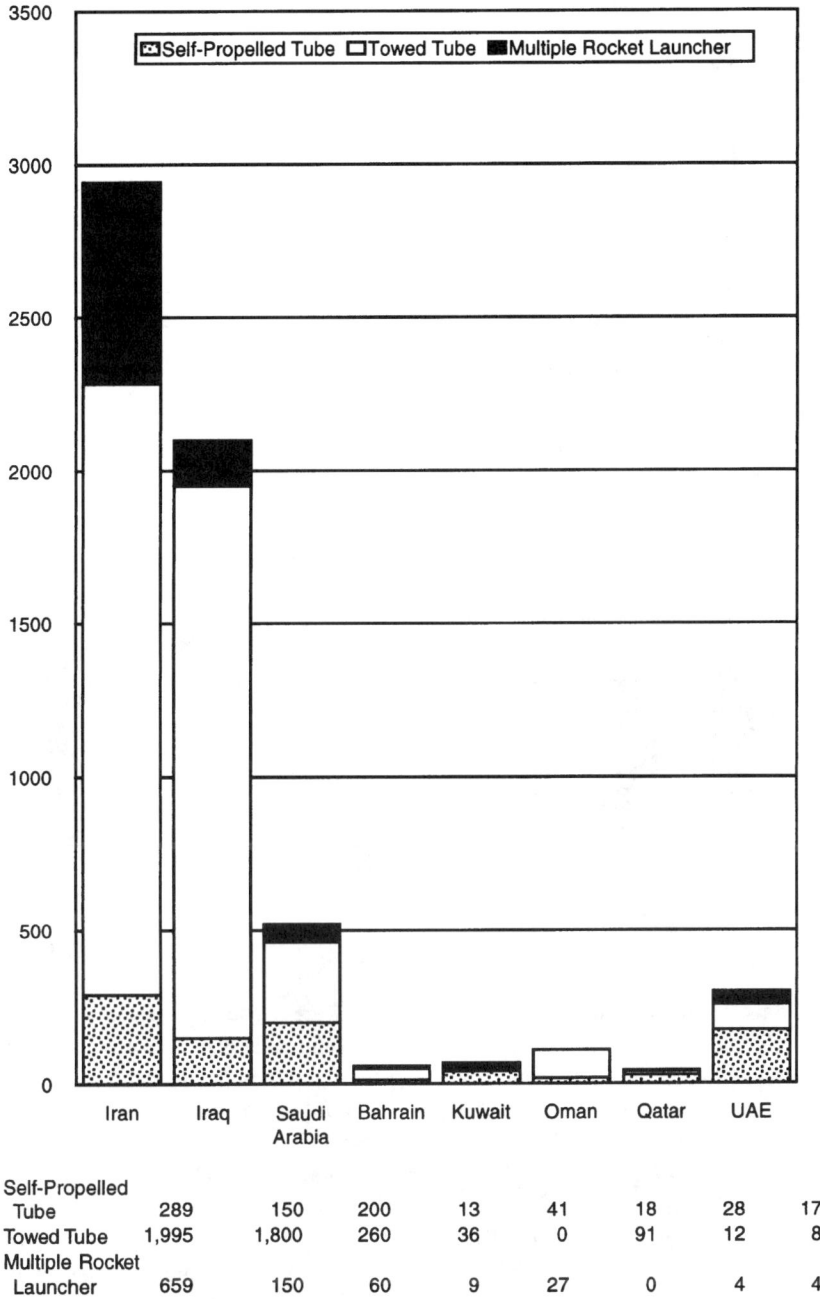

	Iran	Iraq	Saudi Arabia	Bahrain	Kuwait	Oman	Qatar	UAE
Self-Propelled Tube	289	150	200	13	41	18	28	175
Towed Tube	1,995	1,800	260	36	0	91	12	82
Multiple Rocket Launcher	659	150	60	9	27	0	4	42

Sources: Estimated by Anthony H. Cordesman from various sources, and IISS, *Military Balance*.

Figure 6.14
Gulf Tube Artillery Weapons in 1998

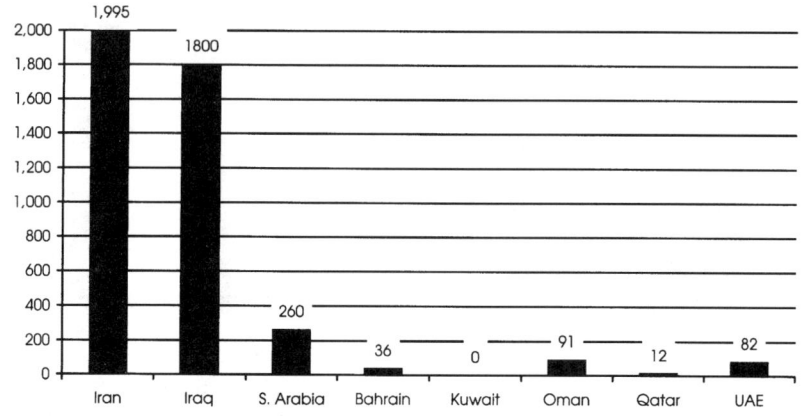

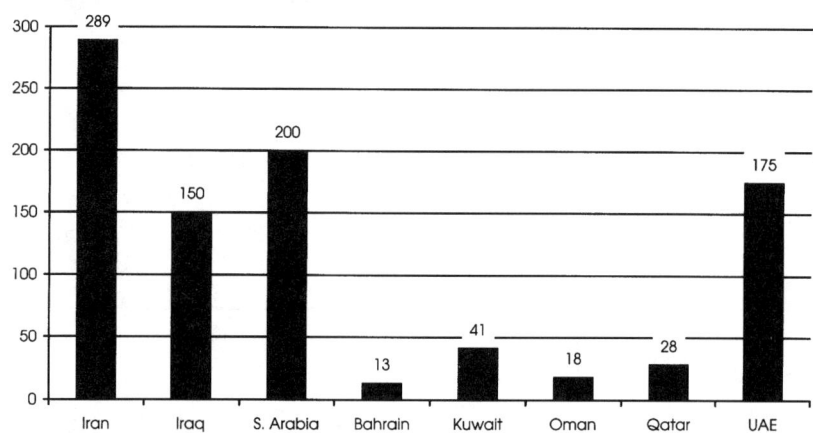

Sources: Estimated by Anthony H. Cordesman from various sources, and IISS, *Military Balance*.

problems in massing fires suddenly against an area, and in altering range to properly support even slow-moving infantry advances. This problem was further complicated by poor coordination between the regular forces and the IRGC.

Iran's reliance on towed artillery limited Iran's combined arms maneuver capabilities, and Iran failed to develop effective night and beyond-visual-range targeting capability. Iranian artillery did a consistently miserable job of targeting and striking Iraqi rear areas—although it often inflicted serious damage on settled areas and towns—and could not effectively engage once Iranian and Iraqi forces came into close proximity. It was also highly vulnerable to suppression by Iraqi chemical weapons. As a result, much of Iran's artillery fire was rela-

Figure 6.15
Total Operational Gulf Multiple Rocket Launchers: 1998

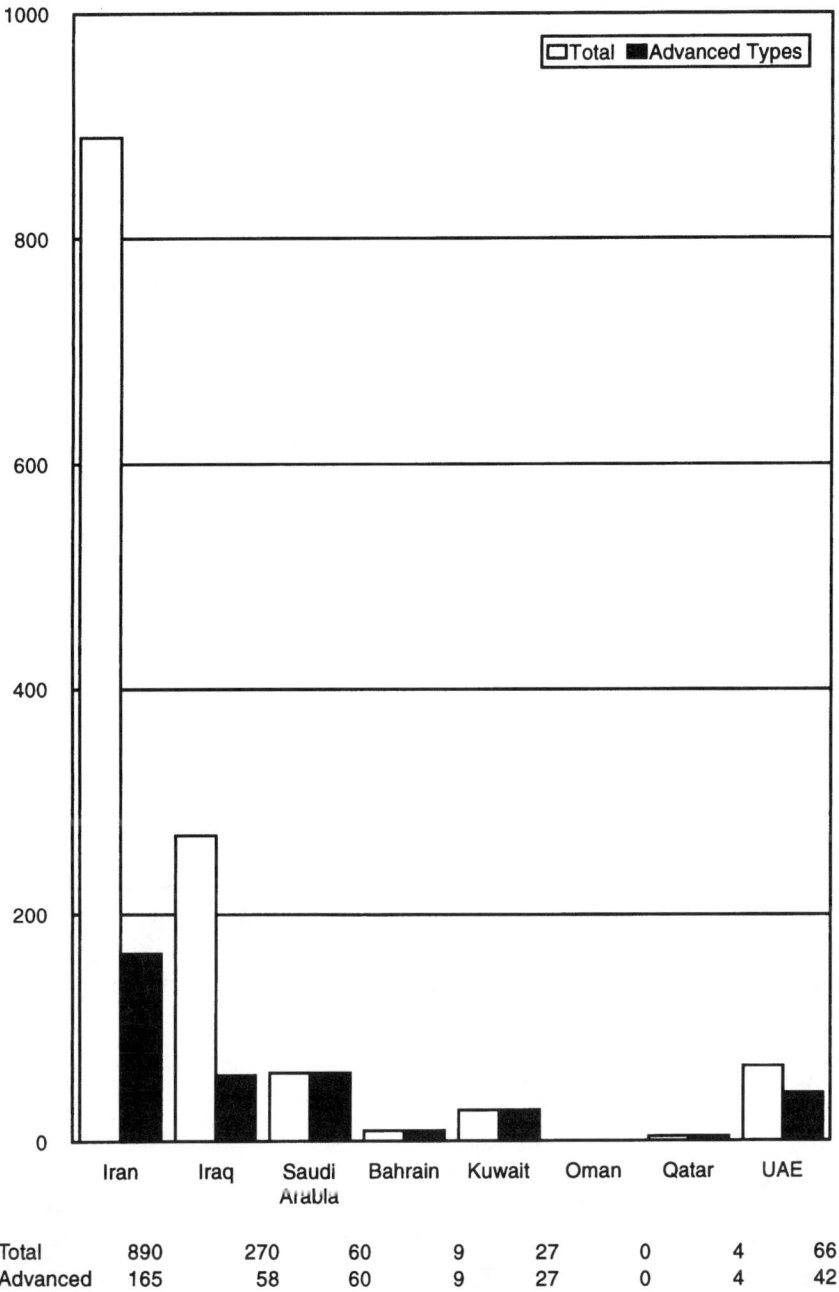

Sources: Estimated by Anthony H. Cordesman from various sources, and IISS, *Military Balance*.

tively ineffective and/or had a harassment and interdiction impact that inflicted few casualties.

Iran has improved, however, since the war. It has emphasized more modern concepts of combined operations, and it has sought to give its artillery more maneuver capability. Its artillery doctrine is more modern and comparable to that of modern Western and Russian forces, although it still has serious conceptual problems in dealing with the need for more precise targeting, the rapid massing of fires, fighting night combat, and dealing with targets in rear areas. The limited data available also indicate that Iran may sharply overestimate the lethality of artillery against most types of targets.

The exercise performance of Iran's forces has steadily improved since 1988, both in dealing with maneuver warfare threats like Iraq and the potential defense of Iran's coastline. At the same time, Iran is scarcely capable of the rapid fluid support of armored maneuver operations, and much of its exercise activity has a set piece character that constantly announces unearned and untested successes, rather than realistically stressing and testing combat unit performance. Counter-battery capabilities also seem to continue to lag, and either lack adequate targeting or fire control systems, or depend on systems that may be relatively easy to target or counter. Iran's performance may be adequate by the generally low standards of Iraq and most Southern Gulf forces, but it lags far behind the level of US and the better Western artillery forces.

Tube Artillery and Mortars

Iran's holdings of self-propelled weapons still appear to include a substantial number of US-supplied systems, including 25–35 M-110 203 mm howitzers, 20–30 M-107 175 mm guns, and 150–160 M-109 155 mm howitzers. These US-supplied weapons are badly worn, have not been modernized in over 15 years, and lack modern fire control systems and artillery radars. Many lack sustainability, and a number may not be operational.

Iran appears to have up to 20–25 M-115 towed 203 mm howitzers and 130–140 M-101A1 towed 105 mm howitzers surviving from the arms that Iran imported from the United States during the time of the Shah—although some observers feel substantial numbers of these weapons are no longer in active Iranian units. Iran also has 80–90 Austrian GHN-45 155 mm towed gun/howitzers, and 1,000–1,150 North Korean, Chinese, and Soviet M-46 and Type 59–1 towed 130 mm guns; and 550 Soviet, North Korean, Polish, and Czech D-30 122 mm gun-howitzers. Its holdings include 30–35 D-20 towed 152 mm howitzers, 100 People's Republic of China 122 mm towed howitzers, and other former Soviet bloc, PRC, and North Korean towed weapons.[30]

Iran seems to understand that it has less than a quarter of the self-propelled artillery it needs to properly support its present force structure, and that maneuverable artillery is critical to success in dealing with Iraqi and other maneuver forces. It is attempting to compensate for the resulting lack of modern artillery and artillery mobility by replacing its US self-propelled weapons with other self-propelled systems. Iran already has 60–80 Soviet 2S1 122 mm self-propelled howitzers, and 9–12 M-1978 170 mm self-propelled guns.

Iran has exhibited an Iranian-made design called the Thunder 1. Some reports indicate that this 122 mm weapon is mounted on a high-profile, fully tracked chassis, although one report indicates that Iran may use the Boragh chassis for this weapon. The driver and engine compartment are in the front, and the turret is fully enclosed at the rear. The turret is somewhat similar in design to the Soviet 122 mm 2S1 self-propelled howitzer, a design dating back to 1971. Some sources indicate that Iran has taken delivery on up to 60 2S1s since 1990, and the Thunder 1 may use imported turrets or copy the Soviet design. It has a maximum range of 15,200 meters, and it can fire five rounds per minute. If Iran has access to rocket-assisted projectiles, the range would be extended to 21,000 meters. The weapon may use some form of automatic loading device or aid to achieve this high rate of fire. The vehicle has a maximum speed of 65 kilometers per hour (kmph), and it supposedly is fully amphibious.[31]

Iran claimed to have tested a "rapid fire" 155 mm self-propelled weapon in September, 1997, which it called the Thunder 2. This weapon is similar to the US M-109A1, and Iran received 440 M-109A1s before the fall of the Shah. If the Thunder 2 uses US 155 mm rounds, it has a maximum range of 18,100 meters, which it could extend to around 34,000 meters with rocket-assisted projectiles. Like the Thunder 1, it can fire five rounds per minute and may use some form of automatic loading device or aid. The vehicle has a maximum speed of 700 kmph, and is claimed to have a maximum range of 300 kilometers.[32]

Both the Thunder 1 and Thunder 2 seem to be made by the Armament Industries Division of the Defense Industry Organization, and their ammunition by the Ammunition Industries Division. These divisions have extensive experience in making gun barrels and ammunition and copies of Soviet-designed 122 mm towed howitzers.[33]

Iran bought large numbers of mortars during the Iran-Iraq War for the same reasons it bought large numbers of towed tube artillery weapons. Iran had some 3,500 weapons in 1998, of which approximately 800 were 107 mm and 120 mm heavy mortars, and 800–900 were 81 mm and 82 mm mortars. Iran had mounted at least several hundred of its heavy mortars in armored vehicles.[34]

Multiple Rocket Launchers

Iran's emphasis on massed, static area fire is also indicated by the fact it has 700–900 multiple rocket launchers, although a number may no longer be in service or may be assigned to low-grade IRGC forces.[35] It is difficult to estimate Iran's inventory, but its holdings include roughly 10 M-1989 240 mm multiple rocket launchers, 500–700 Chinese Type 63 107 mm multiple rocket launchers, 50–100 Soviet BM-21s, and five Soviet BM-11 122 mm launchers. Iranian exercises indicate that Iran understands such weapons are useful largely in the suppression, harassment, and interdiction roles unless an enemy chooses to expose infantry forces in predictable and vulnerable areas.[36]

Iran has also produced at least 50 of its own multiple rocket launchers. These include the 122 mm 40 round Hadid rocket launcher system, which mounts the launcher on a 6 × 6 truck, and the entire load can be salvo-fired in 20 seconds. Its maximum range is about 20.4 kilometers, and a hydraulic crane is fitted so the launcher can be reloaded in about 8–10 minutes. It is not clear how many Hadid launchers are currently deployed among Iranian forces.

Iran has also exhibited a 240 mm artillery rocket with a range of up to 40–43 kilometers, called the Fadjr 3. This system has been used against Israel by the Hezbollah, and it seems to be adapted from a North Korean design. Iran has shown the system mounted in a 12 rocket launcher on a Japanese Isuzu 6 × 6 truck. It has wrap-around fins at the rear, which unfold after launch. It is 5.2 meters long and weighs 408 kilograms. The warhead weighs 90 kilograms, of which 45 kilograms is high explosive.[37]

In addition, Iran is producing variants of Chinese and Russian 122 mm rockets, called the Arash and Noor, as well as variants of the Chinese 107 mm rocket, called the Fajer and Haseb. Some of these rockets have chemical warheads.

Battlefield Rocket Launchers

Iran's land forces also operate a number of long-range unguided rockets, including the Shahin 1 and 2, Oghab, and Nazeat:[38]

- The Shahin 1 is a trailer-launched 333 mm caliber unguided artillery rocket with a solid propelled rocket motor, a maximum range of 13 kilometers, and a 190 kilogram conventional or chemical warhead. The Shahin 2 is an improved version of the Shahin 1 with a maximum range of 20 kilometers and a 190 kilogram warhead. The Shahin evidently can be equipped with three types of warheads: a 180 kilogram high explosive warhead, a warhead using high explosive submunitions, and a warhead that uses chemical weapons.

- The Oghab is a 320 mm caliber unguided artillery rocket which is spin stabilized in flight, has a maximum range of 34 kilometers, and a 70 kilogram high explosive (HE) fragmentation warhead—although chemical warheads may be available. While it may have a chemical warhead, it lacks the range and/or accuracy to hit anything smaller than large area targets like assembly areas and cities. It has a circular error of probability (CEP) that has proved to be in excess of 500 meters at maximum range.[39] Further, Iran has no way to target accurately the Oghab or any other long-range missile against mobile or point targets at long ranges, other than a limited ability to use RPVs.[40]

- The Nazeat is a TEL-launched system with conventional and possibly chemical and biological warheads. The full details of this system remain unclear, but it seems to be based on Chinese technology and uses a solid fuel rocket, with a simple inertial guidance system. Nazeat units are equipped with communications vans, meteorological vans, and a global positioning system for surveying the launch site. There are two variants of the Nazeat solid-fueled rocket system—a 355.6 mm caliber rocket with 105 kilometers range and a 150 kilogram warhead, and a 450 mm caliber rocket with a reported range of 130–150 kilometers and a 250 kilogram warhead. Both systems have maximum closing velocities of Mach 4–5, but both also appear to suffer from poor reliability and accuracy.[41]

All of these long-range rocket systems lack the accuracy and long-range targeting capability to be used against anything other than populated areas and static rear area targets. All would have to use chemical or biological weapons to achieve significant lethality, although all could inhibit operations in the target area and potentially force an enemy to don protective gear and take chemical-biological defense measures. Iranian exercises indicate, however, that they may offer Iran a relatively survivable way to strike at US forces invading an island or a shore area, and could also counter Iraqi attacks on Iranian towns and rear areas.[42]

Artillery Doctrine and Proficiency

Iran's artillery forces have considerable ability to mass fire against relatively static area targets, but towed artillery is an anachronism in modern maneuver warfare operations, and most of its artillery units are only effective against slow-moving mass targets at ranges of less than 10–15 kilometers, or for harassment and interdiction fire. Iran clearly needs more self-propelled artillery.

Iran also has only limited artillery fire control and battle management systems, counterbattery radar capability, and long-range target acquisition capability (although it does have some RPVs) to support its self-propelled weapons. It has actively sought more modern fire control and targeting systems since the mid-1980s. It has had some success in deploying and testing RPVs as targeting systems, and it has obtained some additional counterbattery radars, but it is unclear about how many it obtained or put into service.

ANTI-AIRCRAFT WEAPONS

The Iranian land forces have a total of some 1,700 anti-aircraft guns, including 14.5 mm ZPU-2/4s, 23 mm ZSU-23-4s and ZU-23s, 35 mm M-1939s, 37 mm Type 55s, and 57 mm ZSU-57-2s.[43] Iran also has 100–180 Bofors L/70 40 mm guns and moderate numbers of Skyguard 35 mm twin anti-aircraft guns (many of which may not be operational). Its largest holdings consist of unguided ZU-23-2s (which it can manufacture) and M-1939s.

It is unclear how many of these systems are really operational as air defense weapons. Most would have to be used to provide very short-range "curtain fire" defense of small point targets. They would not be lethal against a modern aircraft using an air-to-ground missile or laser guided weapon. The only notable exception is the ZSU-23–4 radar guided anti-aircraft gun. Iran has 50–100 fully operational ZSU-23–4s. The weapon is short ranged and vulnerable to electronic countermeasures (ECM), but is far more lethal than Iran's unguided guns.

Iran also has large numbers of SA-7 (Strela 2M) manportable surface-to-air missiles and a growing number of SA-14 (Strela) manportable surface-to-air missiles. It has some RBS-70 low-level surface-to-air missiles and many HN-5 manportable surface-to-air missiles. Iran has some US-made Stinger manportable surface-to-air missiles it bought from Afghan rebels, but the numbers seem limited and were probably bought so Iran could attempt to reverse engineer the production of some features of the Stinger system. Iran seems to be producing some version of the SA-7, perhaps with Chinese assistance. It is not clear whether it can do this in any numbers. Iran's land-based air defense forces are also acquiring growing numbers of Chinese FM-80s, a Chinese variant of the French-designed Crotale.

As is the case with its anti-aircraft guns, Iran's shorter-range air defense missiles present significant operational problems. The SA-7 and HN-5 are now so dated that they are valuable largely as a method of forcing aircraft to fly at higher altitudes. The SA-14 and SA-16 are more effective, but they lack the range to be lethal against a modern aircraft which is aware such weapons are in the area and which is using an air-to-ground missile or laser guided weapon. They could be effective in forcing a local air force to operate at stand-off ranges from a well defended point target or small land unit, which would inhibit the operations of an air force like Iraq's. The US Air Force, however, could suppress them, use countermeasures, or use air-to-surface missiles from positions outside of their range. As a result, Iran's lack of adequate short-range air defense systems (SHORADS) is a significant limitation.

HELICOPTER AND ARMY AVIATION FORCES

Iran pioneered the use of army aviation and attack helicopters during the time of the Shah, but built up its holdings of helicopters far more quickly than it expanded its training and maintenance capability. As a result, it had a vast hollow force at the time the Shah fell which had very poor overall performance and little capability for combined operations, and which was almost totally dependent on foreign contractors. This situation was further complicated by corruption and mismanagement within the army and a procurement system which bought equipment with uncertain operational capability and reliability at high temperatures and altitudes, and by the purchase of an early generation of assault helicopters whose weapons and fire control systems required the helicopter to combat close enough to their targets to be highly vulnerable, and then to hover in vulnerable positions while they guided their missiles to their targets.

Iranian helicopter holdings are uncertain. USCENTCOM reports a total of about 300 helicopters.[44] According to the IISS and Jane's, the Iranian Army retains 100–110 AH-1J Sea Cobra attack helicopters, and 36–40 CH-47Cs, 110–130 Bell-214As, 30–35 AB-214Cs, 35–40 AB-205As, 80–90 AB-206s, 12 AB-212s, 27–30 Bell 204s, 5 Hughes 300Cs, 9RH-53Ds, 10 SH-53Ds, 10 SA-319s, and 40–45 UH-1H transport and support helicopters supplied by the West. Many experts agree, however, that Iran probably only retains about 80–100 of its AH-1s, that Iran's Western-supplied transport and support helicopters have low operational readiness—perhaps as low as 35–65% of inventory—and they have little sustained sortie capability.

Iran is seeking to remedy this situation by building its own helicopters and by acquiring variants of the Soviet Mi-8 and Mi-17 support helicopters. There have also been reports that Iran is interested in, or is acquiring, the Mi-24, Mi-28, and KA-50 attack helicopters and the Mi-26TM heavy transport helicopter. Iran also seems to have experimented with arming helicopters with the AT-3 (9M-14M Sagger) anti-tank missile.

Iran also announced plans to build a light attack helicopter, called the Seyedo Shohada Zafar 300, in 1989, which was based on the Bell Jet Ranger and had tandem cockpits.[45] This helicopter has never appeared in Iran's inventory, and there is no evidence of such production activity, although Iran claimed to have begun production of some form of helicopter in mid-1996.

The IISS and Jane's have issued estimates that the Iranian ground forces' fixed wing aircraft included 20–40 Cessna 185, 310, and O-2A aircraft, 2–19 F-27 Series 200, 2–8 Falcon 20/50, 15 Pilatus PC-16B STOL light transports, and 4–5 Strike Commanders in 1998.[46] It is unclear what Iran's holdings are, however, and what fixed wing aircraft are actually operational.

What is clear is that Iran's land forces have placed growing emphasis on attack helicopters and air assault capabilities since the end of the Iran-Iraq War, and have improved their combined operations training. Both the regular army and the IRGC have made major efforts to improve their airmobile doctrine and capability since the late 1980s, and the regular army special forces units and at least four IRGC units now have integrated attack and support helicopters. Iran's army aviation facilities at Isfahan, Mashhad, and Tehran/Mehrabad have been improved, and Iran has shown that it can do a better job of supporting its helicopters in remote deployments and field operations.

The doctrine taught at Iran's aviation school in Isfahan seems to exhibit a good understanding of Western, Russian, and Chinese concepts.[47] Iran's exercises reveal a steady improvement in the conceptual and tactical skill with which Iran used helicopters in small-to-mid-sized tactical encounters, although Iran so far has exhibited little ability to make widespread and sustained use of air assault and air mobile forces, and seems to be equipment-limited in making major further improvements of its capabilities. It either needs new attack helicopters or it needs to rebuild and modernize its AH-1s, and it also needs to make a major increase in its heliborne lift capability.[48]

Iran is also seeking to create a significant RPV force which borrows in many ways from Israeli technical developments and doctrine. It has produced some such RPVs, and several exercise reports refer to their use. However, insufficient data are available to assess this aspect of Iranian capabilities.

COMMUNICATIONS AND BATTLE MANAGEMENT SYSTEMS

Iran has steadily improved its organization, doctrine, training, and equipment for land force operations. It ended the Iran-Iraq War with a slow-moving and largely manual/relay-oriented battle management system and poor communications density and operational proficiency at virtually every level. It could plan and execute the initial phases of offensive operations against static Iraqi forces, but its battle management and communications began to fail the moment Iranian operations did not go as planned, or scored initial breakthroughs. Similarly, Iran's battle management system and communications were incapable of properly characterizing any major Iraqi success and reacting in time. These problems were compounded by the lack of coordination between regular and revolutionary forces and the various branches of combat arms, by major equipment and/or processing problems at the small unit to field command level, and by rivalries and "end-running" at the command level.

Iranian army communications have since improved, as have Iranian battle management and communications exercises. They are now capable of better coordination between branches, the density of communications equipment has improved, and the functional lines of communication and command now place more emphasis on maneuver, quick reaction, and combined arms.

However, Iranian battle management and communications capabilities seem to remain relatively limited. Iran's holdings still consist largely of aging VHF radio with some HF and UHF capability. This equipment cannot handle high traffic densities, and secure communications are poor. Only Iranian landlines offer reasonable levels of security. Iran still relies heavily on analogue data handling and manually switched telephone systems. It is, however, acquiring a steadily growing number of Chinese and Western encryption systems and some digital voice, fax, and telex encryption capability

THE ISLAMIC REVOLUTIONARY GUARDS CORPS (PASDARAN)

The Islamic Revolutionary Guards Corps (IRGC)[49] presents a serious problem in analyzing Iran's military forces. It is primarily a land force, but it can be treated as an independent force with naval and air branches. There is a great deal of conflicting data on the size, mission, and future of the IRGC, and there is no reliable source of unclassified information which allows an analyst to distinguish between its equipment holdings and those of the Iranian regular army.

The IRGC has a complex structure which is both political and military. It has separate organizational elements for its land, naval, and air units, which include both military and paramilitary units. The Basij and the tribal units of the Pasdaran are subordinated to its land unit command, although the commander of the Basij often seems to report directly to the commander-in-chief and Minister of the Pasdaran, and through him to the Leader of the Islamic Revolution. A number of cases have taken place where the high command of the IRGC has acted without fully consulting the President. There are also eleven regional commands which report to the commander-in-chief and the Minister of the Pasdaran. The IRGC also has separate organizational elements for worker units (which control a network of local committees) and defense industries.

The IRGC has close ties to the foreign operations branch of the Iranian Ministry of Intelligence and Security (MOIS), particularly through the IRGC's Qods force. The Ministry of Intelligence and Security was established in 1983 and has an extensive network of offices in Iranian embassies. It is often difficult to separate the activities of the IRGC, VEVAK, and Foreign Ministry, and many seem to be integrated operations managed by a ministerial committee called the "Special Operations Council," which includes the Leader of the Islamic Revolution, the President, the Minister of Intelligence and Security, and other members of the Supreme Council for National Defense.[50]

All of these organizations have played some role in what the West calls "terrorism," although many such Iranian actions have been addressed against terrorist opposition organizations like the People's Mujahideen, with a long history of murdering Iranian officials in Iran. Iran's new Foreign Minister, Kamal Kharrazi, has stated that, "As long as terrorist groups are committing terrorist acts against our country, we have the right to defend ourselves."[51]

The IRGC plays a major role in internal security. It has close ties to the Savama—the internal security force and secret police that replaced the Savak—and cooperates with the rest of Iran's internal security forces in surveillance and gathering technical intelligence on opposition movements and dissidents, and in attempting to suppress violent and underground opposition movements like the Peoples Mujahideen/National Liberation Army/Mujahideen e-Khalq, the Babak Khoramidin Organization (BKO), and Kurdish groups like the Democratic Party of Iranian Kurdistan (DPIK), Kurdish Communist Party of Iran (KOMALA), and Kurdish People's Party (PKK). Pasdaran forces maintain bases outside of virtually every Iranian city and often set up customs posts to control movement within Iran. They sometimes operate independently and sometimes cooperate with the Gendarmerie, National Police, and highway police. It is often difficult to distinguish the activities of the IRGC from those of the security forces under the Ministry of the Interior.

Nevertheless, it seems best to treat the IRGC primarily as a military land force which parallels the Iranian regular army, and which would operate with it in most contingencies. As has been discussed earlier, the IRGC has been placed under an integrated command with Iran's regular armed forces at the General

Staff level. It retains an independent command chain below this level, however, and generally continues to exercise as an independent force. It rarely exercises with the regular Iranian army—and then usually in large, set piece exercises which do not require close cooperation.[52]

There is little evidence to date that the land elements of the IRGC and the Iranian army can operate effectively in relatively sophisticated joint operations. Further, the rivalries between the regular forces and the IRGC do seem to involve less of the extreme ideological and doctrinal rivalries that existed during much of the Iran-Iraq War. Virtually all of the regular military personnel who served under the Shah, and continued to serve during the Iran-Iraq War, have now left the Iranian armed forces. Most of the military personnel who remain are "children of the revolution."[53]

As has been noted previously, more is involved than the typical interservice rivalries in other countries. The IRGC remains the ideological arm of the regime than the regular armed forces, and it retains an independent Central Staff Headquarters and many aspects of an independent chain of command. The structure of this chain of command is somewhat unclear, but the commander-in-chief of the IRGC and Minister for the IRGC both seem to report directly to Khamenei.

The Minister for the IRGC also reports to the Supreme Council for National Defense, and the commander-in-chief of the IRGC reports to the Chief of the General Staff of the Armed Forces. However, many experts believe that this does not prevent the IRGC from conducting independent operations—particularly by the Al Quds force, which will be described shortly. The IRGC's growing role in internal security since the Iran-Iraq War is also the result of the fact that the regular army proved uncooperative in dealing with riots and civil unrest, and there is still suspicion within the IRGC that the regular army cannot be fully trusted to protect the revolution. It is not clear that the civil operations of the IRGC are fully coordinated with the General Staff.

IRGC Strength and Combat Units

The IRGC made up the largest element of Iran's military forces during the Iran-Iraq War. It reached a strength of roughly 300,000 in the mid-1980s, and a peak strength of 700,000–750,000 by the end of the war. During the Iran-Iraq War, it emphasized mass infantry operations using poorly trained mass conscripts armed with relatively light weapons. It used human wave attacks on Iraqi forces, and while these attacks were often initially successful, they led to massive casualties. The IRGC's weak organization, and lack of mechanization and sustainability, then usually led to a failure to successfully exploit any initial success and even greater losses. The end result was that IRGC operations closely paralleled those of the Chinese army in the Korean War, with similar results.[54]

The IRGC had a "popular army" structure during the Iran-Iraq War, without regular military ranks, and a large number of small combat units. On paper, it reached a peak wartime strength of 21 infantry divisions, 15 independent infantry brigades, 40 artillery/missile/chemical defense brigades, 20 air defense brigades, and three engineer divisions. In practice, many of its divisions/brigades were little more than reinforced regiments or battalions. Its forces lacked anything approaching a standard TO&E. While the IRGC gradually developed a cadre of highly capable infantry forces, the bulk of its forces consisted of little more than loosely organized groups of conscripts with impressive unit names.[55]

Iran's defeat in the Iran-Iraq War and Iraq's devastating defeat in the Gulf War have since led to the steady evolution of the military elements of the IRGC into a better organized and professionally trained force. Rafsanjani's efforts to integrate the IRGC and regular forces into a combined command, while not entirely successful, helped lead to a major reorganization of the IRGC after the cease-fire in the Iran-Iraq War, and the rapid cuts in the IRGC to a force of under 200,000 men allowed it to be restructured in ways that kept its best trained and most experienced personnel. The IRGC carried out another major shift towards professionalism in September, 1991, probably as a result of the lessons of the Gulf War. It adopted a system of formal military ranks, roughly paralleling those of the regular forces, and began to create a truly professional officer and NCO corps.

The IRGC's growing involvement in Iran's military industries, and its lead role in Iran's efforts to acquire surface-to-surface missiles and weapons of mass destruction, also gave it growing experience with advanced military technology. As a result, the IRGC is believed to be the branch of Iran's forces which plays the largest role in Iran's military industries.[56] It also operates all of Iran's Scuds, controls most its chemical and biological weapons, and provides the military leadership for missile production and the production of all weapons of mass destruction.

US experts believe that the IRGC had a total manning of around 120,000 in 1998, of which roughly 100,000 men were in the land forces. Sources like the IISS estimate a higher figure of around 150,000 for the entire IRGC, of which 18,000 men are assigned to the naval branch.[57] Another source states the strength is 175,000. All sources indicate that this manpower overwhelmingly consists of conscripts chosen from the same pool as all other conscripts without special selection as to education or ideological loyalty. It is not surprising, therefore, that over 70% of the IRGC voted for Khatami—although important elements within the IRGC are largely career professionals, and some units with internal security functions are screened for ideology and loyalty.

Unlike the regular army, which is organized as a national force, the IRGC is organized primarily along territorial lines. The IRGC was organized into eleven Internal security regions, with most of its military/paramilitary forces assigned to conventional military and internal security missions. Some reports credited the IRGC with very high numbers of major units. One source quotes a strength of 15–20 "divisions" in early 1998.[58] Another source refers to a build-up that was completed in 1993, and a strength of 11 regional headquarters (fully manned), two mobilizable armored divisions, and 24 cadre strength infantry divisions.[59]

The most probable estimate of major units is that these units included 13 infantry "divisions," two armored "divisions," and a large number of independent infantry, airborne, special forces, armored, surface-to-surface missile, artillery, engineer, border, and air defense units—many of which were called brigades. This ambitious order of battle, however, would require over 250,000 men to fully man and sustain divisions as small as 10,000 full-time actives. In practice, the IRGC should be regarded as having a total force of about 15 small brigade equivalents, only a few of which are armed well enough to be regarded as anything other than light infantry, plus a number of independent formations. The IRGC's 15 independent "brigades" normally have a total manning equivalent to large battalions in Iran's regular forces.[60]

The full order of battle of the IRGC is not available, but some sources indicate that it includes the Karbala-25, Imam Hussein 14, Holy Prophet 27, Vali-ye-Asr 7, and Ashura 31 divisions, and seems to include the 10th Special Forces Division, 8th Najaf-e Ashraf Unit, and 41st Saraollah Unit. The IRGC does not have any armored formations larger than brigade size, and even these units seem to be far less heavily armored than Iranian regular army armored brigades.

Rezaei and other leaders of the IRGC have called for more armored forces, including large numbers of T-72s. Most IRGC land forces remain light infantry forces, however, and the IRGC is only slowly being upgraded. The IRGC has set the goal of creating mechanized "divisions," but none have yet emerged, and experts have different views regarding the extent to which the IRGC will or will not establish heavy formations that parallel those of the regular army. It is unclear how Rezaei's replacement, Major General Yahya Rahim Safavi, feels about this issue.

The Iranian regular army still received most of Iran's new heavy weapons until recent years. During the last few years, the IRGC has gotten nearly 50% of Iran's imports of advanced land weapons, including such key systems as T-72s and BMPs. These deliveries have been limited, however, and the IRGC tends to disperse them in small, ineffective lots throughout the IRGC's main combat units. As a result, it will be some years before even the best IRGC units can rival the regular forces in firepower and maneuver capability, unless radical changes are made in the allocation of Iran's weapons.

The Quds (Qods) Forces

The IRGC has a large component for intelligence operations and unconventional warfare. Roughly 5,000 of the men in the IRGC are assigned to the unconventional warfare mission. The IRGC has the equivalent of one special forces "division," plus additional smaller formations, and these forces are given special priority in terms of training and equipment. In addition, the IRGC has a special Quds force which plays a major role in giving Iran the ability to conduct unconventional warfare overseas, using various foreign movements as proxies. This force is under the command of General Ahmad Vahidi (Wahidi), who used to head the information department in the IRGC General Command and had the mission of exporting the revolution.[61]

The Quds force evolved out of the efforts to spread Iran's revolution, which began in 1979, such as the Liberation Movements Bureau, Islamic Information Organization, and Martyr's Bureau. It seems to have been created in the mid-1980s, after these efforts proved to do more to embarrass Iran than to spread the revolution. According to some reports, it was created by then-President Khamenei, to work in cooperation with the Ministry of Foreign Affairs, Information, and Culture and Islamic Guidance.

The budget for this part of the IRGC is a classified budget directly controlled by Khamenei, which is not reflected in the Iranian general budget. It operates primarily outside of Iran's borders, although it has bases inside and outside of Iran. The Quds troops are divided into specific groups or "corps" for each country or area in which they operate. For example, there is a corps for Lebanon, Sudan, and Africa. There are also Directorates for Iraq; Lebanon, Palestine, and Jordan; Afghanistan, Pakistan, and India; Turkey, the Arabian Peninsula; the Asiatic republics of the former Soviet Union (FSU), Western Nations (Europe and North America) and North Africa (Egypt, Tunisia, Algeria, Sudan, and Morocco).

The Quds have offices or "sections" in many Iranian embassies, which operate as closed sections. It is not clear whether these are integrated with Iranian intelligence operations, or that the ambassador in such embassies has control of, or detailed knowledge of, operations by the Quds staff. However, there are indications that most operations are coordinated between the IRGC and offices within the Iranian Foreign Ministry and Ministry of Intelligence and Security (MOIS). There are separate operational organizations in Lebanon, Turkey, Pakistan, and several North African countries. There are also indications that such elements may have participated in the bombings of the Israeli Embassy in Argentina in 1992 and the Jewish Community Center in Buenos Aires in 1994—although Iran has strongly denied this.[62] Similarly, hard-line elements of the IRGC may be cooperating with the MOIS in operations in the Southern Gulf, although Saudi Arabia has denied that Iran played a significant role in the Al Khobar bombings in June, 1996.[63]

The Quds force seems to control many of Iran's training camps for unconventional warfare, extremists, and terrorists in Iran and countries like the Sudan and Lebanon. It has at least four major training facilities in Iran. The Quds forces have a main training center at Imam Ali University, which is based in the Sa'dabad Palace in Northern Tehran. Troops are trained to carry out military and terrorist operations, and they are indoctrinated in ideology. The University is chaired by Mohammed Shams, a general in the Iranian Army. The Imam Ali University trains Egyptian, Saudi, and Lebanese as well as Iranians.

There are other training camps in the Qom, Tabriz, and Mashhad governates, and in Lebanon and the Sudan. These include the Al Nasr camp for training Iraqi Shi'ites and Iraqi and Turkish Kurds in northwest Iran, and a camp near Mashhad for training Afghan and Tajik revolutionaries. The Quds seem to help operate the Manzariyah training center near Qom, which recruits from foreign students in the religious seminary and which seems to have trained some Bahraini extremists. Some foreigners are reported to have received training in demolition and sabotage at an IRGC facility near Isfahan, in airport infiltration at facilities near Mashad and Shiraz, and in underwater warfare at an IRGC facility at Bandar Abbas.[64]

It is not clear how the Quds, or Iran's other organizations supporting various revolutionary and extremist groups, will evolve in the future. Iran has made an obvious effort to reduce the visibility of its support of foreign extremist movements since the Mykonos trial in Germany and the Al Khobar bombings in Saudi Arabia. At the same time, Iran has always denied that it supports terrorism while it has justified its support of revolutionary and Islamic movements. Iran's new Foreign Minister, Kamal Kharrazi, repeated Iran's claims that it was firmly opposed to "terrorism" shortly after President Khatami's election. He stated that, "Iran has not been involved in or associated with this incident (Al Khobar) in any way, form, or fashion."[65] He also stated in a message to Russian Foreign Minister Yevgeny Primakov that Iran was ready to consult with Russia and other "anti-terrorism countries" to implement a comprehensive program to fight all kinds of terrorist activities.[66]

The practical problem is that one man's "terrorist" is another man's "freedom fighter," and it is still far from clear that Iran's new regime can or will make major changes in the role of the Al Quds forces or the role of Iranian intelligence in supporting violent extremist movements. The recent reduction in Iran's support of opposition movements in the Gulf may be more tactical opportunism than the result of any change in fundamental beliefs or strategy, and the same may be true of its lower rate of attacks on members of the Iranian opposition in Europe. At the same time, the hard-liners in the IRGC and Quads force may act independently, or deliberately attempt to end any rapproachment between Iran's moderates and the outside world by launching new acts of terrorism.

Iran also has shown few signs of reducing its support to the Hezbollah and Islamic extremist groups like the Palestinian Islamic Jihad.[67] As Kharrazi put it,

Our support for Hamas and Jihad in Palestine is on moral and intellectual ground. In the case of the Hezbollah and the Lebanese people who are under occupation and massive daily attacks, we believe the government and Lebanese people are quite justified and deserve the support of the international community to fight occupation of their land. . . . Since the beginning we did not endorse this so-called peace process, because it was the rights of the Palestinian people in terms of their self-determination, return of refugees and the liberation of all occupied territories, including the Al Quds, Al Sharif, Southern

Lebanon, and the Syrian Golan will not be ensured. The developments of the last few years clearly show that any process that disregards these realities on the ground is bound to fail.[68]

Iran's rhetoric is less strident and moderation may come, but it has scarcely arrived.

Major Weapons and Equipment

As has been noted earlier, there is no way to separate the equipment holdings of the regular army and the IRGC. It is clear, however, that it is the regular army which operates most of Iran's heavy weaponry, although the armored elements of the IRGC are slowly expanding and some have T-72s and armored fighting vehicles. Other IRGC units, with T-54 tanks, are reported to be upgrading their tanks with T-72 engines and laser range finders.

This conversion is called the Safir-74 (Messenger 74) and supposedly upgrades tanks captured from Iraq with what Rezaei has stated are "major changes in engine power, transmission, firepower, and internal fire extinguishing system." It is supposed to have better target acquisition capability against mobile and static targets and better armor. Iran has claimed that the components for this conversion are manufactured in Iran, but it is unclear whether this is true, how many of Iran's 190 T-54s and T-55s are in the IRGC, and how many have been converted.[69]

Like the Iranian Army, the IRGC possesses numerous anti-tank weapons, including the Dragon, TOW, and AT-3 ATGMs, 3.5" rockets, and RPG-7s. It also has about 1,500 air defense guns, large numbers of small and manportable surface-to-air missiles, and increasing numbers of the HN-5 light surface-to-air missiles. Iran's holdings of such weapons are uncertain, but it seems to be importing both Chinese and Russian short-range air defense missiles.[70]

The IRGC seems to be the principal operator of Iran's land-based surface-to-surface missile forces. Both the Iranian regular army and the IRGC have offensive and defensive chemical warfare capabilities, but the IRGC seems to have custody of most of these weapons and to provide the military supervision for related research, development, and production activities. Such activities cannot be separated, however, from the IRGC role in other military industry and development activities. It is not clear how Iran would coordinate or conduct chemical and biological operations and long-range missile strikes.

IRGC Exercises and Proficiency

The IRGC land forces have a total active strength equivalent to at least one-third of that of the Iranian army and form a potentially critical part of Iran's total land forces. While the IRGC is still largely a light infantry force, it is large enough to provide holding rear area security operations for Iranian land operations against Iraq, and it has a powerful special force component that can play a major role in unconventional warfare against the United States and Southern Gulf states.

It is extremely difficult to estimate the proficiency of the IRGC units. It seems likely, however, that they vary sharply by unit and that only a portion of the IRGC land forces are intended to participate in joint operations with the regular army in regular combat. These forces seem to have improved steadily in their training, organization, and discipline since the early 1990s, and have also expanded their joint training with the regular army, navy, and air force. Exercises in 1996 and 1997 have shown that the IRGC can support the army and navy in exercises designed to demonstrate Iran's ability to threaten shipping traffic and combat ships in the Gulf, defend Iran's offshore islands and facilities, deal with surprise attacks by the United States, defend the border with Iraq, and close the Afghan border.[71]

At the same time, it has been more than a decade since the end of the Iran-Iraq War, and the IRGC is largely a conscript force. Even the cadres of junior to mid-level career personnel generally have no combat experience. Further, the literature that Iran issues on its military exercises indicates that most involve preplanned operations that invariably end in Iranian success, rather than stress the participating forces with realistic exercises that confront them with superior enemy capabilities and defeat. This kind of training is not unusual for armies in the developing world, but it rarely produces high levels of proficiency.

Iran has conducted a number of recent "urban warfare" exercises that indicate that the IRGC is receiving more training for internal security missions. The "Ashura" exercise in June, 1995 involved elements from a wide range of Revolutionary Guards units, and involved operations in a nearly 400 square kilometer area in the Neinava Region southwest of Tehran, although Iranian claims that the exercise involved 450,000 men were grossly exaggerated.

It is interesting to note that such exercises are often presented to the Iranian people as being defensive and in preparation for a possible US invasion. Moshen Rezaei, the former commander of the Revolutionary Guards, stated in 1995 that Iranian exercises,

will convey a clear message to our enemies, that is our ability to defend the liberty and independence of Iran. . . . [They will] also assure the friends of the Islamic Republic that Iran possesses the most reliable defensive power to maintain peace and security in the region and that it could exploit its capabilities to consolidate friendly relations in the region and the world.[72]

Rezaei stated repeatedly in 1997 that Iran was capable of closing the Strait of Hormuz to tanker traffic, and that Iran had the ability to destroy any American invasion of Iran.[73] Rezaei's replacement, Major General Safavi, is his former deputy and often uses extreme rhetoric, which indicates that he may share many of Rezaei's attitudes.

The IRGC's internal security mission may be less popular than its other missions, and this might affect its effectiveness in such mission. Over 70% of the manpower of the IRGC consists of conscripts which are not selected on the basis of ideology or loyalty, and the vast majority of this manpower voted for President Khatami.

There are also indications that both regular army and IRGC officers have reservations about the use of military forces in internal security missions. At least one source argues that both regular army and IRGC officers have protested such a role ever since a series of urban demonstrations in Tehran, Shiraz, Qom, and Tabriz in the spring of 1991. Some reports claim that up to 138 NCOs were executed for failing to obey orders to fire on crowds in Mashad in May, 1991, although such sources seem extremely dubious. There are similar reports that the regular forces and the IRGC presented problems in internal security operations during urban demonstrations in 1992.

The case for which there is the most evidence is a popular riot in Qazvin in August, 1994, which took place when the Majlis refused to create a separate Persian province out of Qazvin and separate it from the Turkish-speaking province of Zanjan. According to such reports, the regular forces refused to act. This led to arrests and to the deployment of a division of the IRGC which consisted largely of regulars and which had special urban warfare training. Even the use of this IRGC unit, however, is reported to have led to letters of protest from some of the IRGC personnel involved, and to resulting arrests. As a result, there are reports that the regime has been forced to create special elite units of the IRGC. One report claims that a Special Guards Unit of the Islamic Revolution (Yekan-e Vijeh Pasdaran-e Engheleb-e Eslami) was created that reported to the Supreme Leader. This unit is said to be composed of four brigades, with a strength of 8,000–9,000 men, and to be under the command of Brigadier General Abdollah Oghabae'i.[74]

There are also reports that the government has had to shift some of the internal security role to the Basij. The difficulty with such reports is that many seem to come from opposition sources with a long track record of exaggeration and false reports, and there is no way to confirm whether a few scattered incidents are being blown out of proportion, or if such incidents represent a significant trend.

Most US experts feel that the high command of the IRGC would execute any orders to carry out internal security missions and that most units would obey orders, particularly if the claim was made that such missions were needed to deal with foreign-sponsored conspiracies.[75] The fact remains, however, that most of the IRGC did vote for Khatami and might not follow Khamenei or conservative leaders in any civil action that favored Iran's conservatives over its moderates.

IRAN'S PARAMILITARY FORCES: THE BASIJ

The rest of Iran's paramilitary and internal security forces seems to have relatively little war-fighting capability. The Basij (Mobilization of the Oppressed) is a popular reserve force of about 90,000 men with an active and a reserve strength of up to 300,000 men and a mobilization capacity of nearly 1,000,000 men. It is controlled by the Islamic Revolutionary Guards Corps and consists largely of youths, men who have completed military service, and the elderly. During the Iran-Iraq War, the Basij was organized into poorly trained and equipped infantry units which were often used in Iran's human wave assaults.

Since the war, the Basij has been restructured into a pool of men that can be called up during wartime. This pool consists of up to 740 regional battalions, with about 300–350 men each, composed of three companies or four platoons, plus support. These include the former tribal levies and are largely regional in character. Many have little or no real military training and active full-time active manning, although Iran has used the Basij to provide local security since the popular riots of 1994. It called up over 100,000 men in 19 regions in September, 1994, and it began far more extensive training for riot control and internal security missions. It also introduced a formal rank structure and a more conventional system of command and discipline, and it created specialized Ashura battalions for internal security missions. Some reports indicate that 36 of these battalions were established in 1994.[76]

The Basij does continue to hold large-scale exercises, including exercises which began on November 26, 1997, and which were supposed to demonstrate its capability to defend against a US invasion. In practice, however, the Basij remained poorly trained and organized, and would be valuable largely as a source of replacements for other combat units.[77]

The primary mission of the Basij now seems to be internal security, and monitoring the activities of Iranian citizens. The Basij help the other security forces, and the Ansar-e Hezbollah monitor the social activities of citizens. The Basij's actions also vary with the political climate and jurisdiction, and it is difficult to generalize about a force that is so large on paper and comparatively limited in practice. The Basij units with meaningful paramilitary training and full time cadres are equipped with small arms and can act as a force to secure rear areas or to deal with ethnic forces or popular riots. Further, they provide a potential base for the expansion of the IRGC in times of crisis and war. The Basij is also used for civil projects or activities where the regime seeks to mobilize youth for a single task or propaganda purposes. The Basij includes a large home guard force which serves some of the same purposes, but which is a static militia force tied to local defense missions.

OTHER PARAMILITARY FORCES

Iran claimed to have integrated many of its other internal security forces in 1991 and placed them under the Ministry of Interior. These forces totaled about 300,000 men in 1998, of which 45,000–60,000 had some value as paramilitary forces. These forces were comprised of the former Gendarmerie, other police elements, and border guards.

The border guards are organized as a paramilitary police force with light utility vehicles, light patrol aircraft (Cessna 185/310 and AB-205 and AB-206s), 90 coastal patrol craft, and 40 harbor patrol craft. They keep order throughout the rural areas of Iran and deal with ethnic and tribal security problems. The border guards have a regional organization and some military training and equipment. This equipment includes automatic weapons, mortars, and light, anti-tank weapons. A tribal force drawn largely from the Khorasan tribes and clans has existed for many years, which now seems to be part of the Basij element of the IRGC.[78]

These paramilitary forces seem unlikely to offer Iran much advantage in wars against its neighbors, and Iran seems to have experienced some problems with the loyalty of some of these forces in late 1993—leading to the arrests of a number of officers in October.[79] Iran also lacks the equipment to waste it on such untrained and low-quality forces in other combat roles. Such forces can, however, provide rear area security and a manpower pool to draw upon in an extended conflict. They offer Iran improved internal security and should be adequate to deal with most ethnic threats, although the best-trained forces of the Iraqi-backed People's Mujahideen may be a possible exception.

The situation is different in the case of Iran's intelligence forces, which may pose a significant threat to Iran's neighbors and other states. In addition to Iran's main intelligence service—the VEVAK—Iran has other intelligence elements within the Foreign Ministry, the IRGC, and the Iranian armed forces. Iran supports other states and extremist movements in a number of unconventional warfare and terrorist roles, and US experts believe that there is considerable evidence that they have done so with the direct knowledge of Iran's foreign minister and senior leadership operating within the "Special Operations Council" and Supreme Council for National Defense.[80]

THE WAR-FIGHTING CAPABILITIES OF IRANIAN LAND FORCES

Iran's overall capabilities for land warfare seem likely to improve during the coming decade. In spite of Iran's economic problems, a combination of regular army and IRGC forces seems likely to give Iran about 400,000–500,000 full-time actives—and Iran has the capacity to develop significant reserves. Iran's current equipment holdings are also likely to increase. Iran is likely to acquire an inventory of around 1,700–1,900 tanks by the period 2000–2005. It is likely to have about 1,800–2,100 operational armored personnel carriers and armored infantry fighting vehicles and 2,500–3,000 medium and heavy artillery weapons and multiple rocket launchers. At the same time, much will depend on Iran's ability to pay for arms imports, the future structure of Iran's land forces, Iran's strength relative to Iraq, and whether Iran can develop a significant capability to project power across the Gulf.

Proficiency and Exercises

Many of the qualitative strengths and weaknesses of Iran's regular army and the IRGC land forces have already been discussed. Iran has recognized the need for combined arms and joint operations training, but the regular army and the IRGC land forces have only cooperated in large, set-piece exercises in recent years. There is little evidence even within the separate exercises of the regular army and the IRGC that they can employ armor effectively by the standards of the United States, or a US led-coalition, use artillery effectively in maneuver warfare or precision fire/counter-battery roles, fight mechanized maneuver warfare at night, conduct effective combined arms or joint operations, and sustain mechanized maneuver warfare in offensive attacks. Iranian forces train in largely defensive or small unit operations, and generally only train for slow-moving counterattacks, rather than for the kind of operations that would be effective against Western-led operations. Regular army and the IRGC exercises involving the Iranian Air Force consist largely of preplanned "flybys," rather than effective joint training.

Iranian military exercises do, however, reflect some improvements by regional standards. The regular army and the IRGC have increased the size and tempo of their armored warfare and biological and chemical warfare defense exercises, as well as their land-air and land-air-naval exercises. For example, Iran held large joint exercises in 1996 and a major series of amphibious exercises in April, 1997. These exercises involved some joint regular-IRGC operations of considerable sophistication, and the IRGC demonstrated that it could use anti-ship guided missiles in amphibious exercises.[81]

The Victory 4 exercise in the spring of 1993 marked the beginning of a series of major multiservice exercises involving amphibious and heliborne assaults of the kind that would give Iran the capability to project power across the Gulf, although Iran's performance was not particularly impressive. While there were follow-on exercises during the period 1994–1997, these exercises lacked the scale and content that would indicate Iran has the ability to do much more than launch limited raids or attack small islands and oil facilities in the Gulf.

Many of Iran's recent exercises also seem to have a political character that limits their serious military content, which hampers Iran's progress in improving the realism of many aspects of their exercises and their ability to teach actual war-fighting skills. Some Iranian exercises seem designed as much to intimidate neighboring states—particularly Iraq and the UAE—as to improve military effectiveness. For example, the Beyt-ol-Muqaddas (Jerusalem) series in August, 1995 and the Zafar (Victory) series in March, 1996 had a political character, although they involved more demanding training than Iran's showpiece exercises of the early 1990s.

Iran held one of the largest military exercises in its peacetime history during May 23–24, 1996. It claimed that the exercise involved 200,000 men, 10 full divisions, six full brigades, 100 army helicopters, 1,700 field guns and tanks, and more than 700 armored and tracked vehicles. The air force commander of the exercise stated that it was designed to "create fear in the hearts of enemies and increase the combat readiness of the armed forces." Iran also claimed that the exercise involved Iranian-made Zulfiqar tanks and Cobra APCs. In fact, the exercise did not actually involve all of the forces that Iran claimed, and many aspects were poorly structured.

The exercise does, however, seem to have involved over 60,000 men and was a joint exercise involving all of Iran's military services. It involved extensive exercises near the Iraqi border, and over a large area in the Koush-e Nosrat Desert, south of Qom. Like many of Iran's other recent exercises, the exercise indicated that there is less political tension between the regular forces and the IRGC, in part because most personnel who served under the Shah left the regular forces and in part because of the influence the leaders of the Revolutionary Guard had on senior regular army appointments.[82]

Iran held another major series of exercises in April, June, and July, 1997, to show the "firm resolve of the armed forces to defend the precious heritage of our Martyrs," and "the defensive power of the IRGC in the event of a threat to Iran." The exercise was designed to show that (1) Iran was preparing to deal with any attack by the United States, and (2) could deploy a major threat in the lower Gulf and near the Strait of Hormuz. The exercise also had the usual political trappings: Exaggerated claims were made about amphibious exercises involving 200,000 men and the employment of a fleet of 180 IRGC boats near the Straits. Khamenei made a highly publicized visit, Major General Mohsen Rezaei made an appearance, and Iran made new claims about its missile capabilities.[83]

These exercises were primarily IRGC and militia exercises and did involve meaningful joint activity with the regular army and the air force. They also involved a mix of land, air, naval, amphibious, and unconventional warfare exercises, and limited firings of surface-to-air, surface-to-surface missiles, as well as notional firings of CS-802 anti-ship missiles. Like many of Iran's other exercises in the 1990s, they can be summarized as having demonstrated progress, but not success.

Iran held additional exercises in September and October, 1997. The Zulfiqar series of land-air exercises were held to celebrate the beginning of the Iran-Iraq War, north of Qom. Iran claimed that they involved some 200,000 men from the regular army and the IRGC, operating in an 1,800 square kilometer area, while the IRGC held another series of exercises in the Southern Gulf. The exercises involved heavy divisions, paratroops, and air force operations—some of which took place over the Strait of Hormuz. Iran claimed that 150 aircraft from eight bases were involved, and it showed pictures of C-130s air dropping armor as well as troops.[84] Similar exercises have continued since Khatami's election, and were held in both late 1997 and the spring of 1998.

Iran's Modernization Needs

In fairness to Iran, it is impossible to organize, train, and exercise capabilities one does not have. Many of Iran's problems reflect its lack of overall modernization, its lack of standardization and interoperability, and a host of other problems that limit the capabilities of its land forces. As the previous analysis has shown, the mix of equipment in Iran's land forces is likely to retain so many different types and generations that it will be difficult to support and maintain for the next decade.

Iran has no way to standardize its equipment, ammunition, and missiles rapidly. Even if it has a well-structured plan to create modern and standardized armored, mechanized, and artillery forces, it still lacks a reliable supplier and/or the funds to make the massive integrated purchases it needs. Iran's purchase of the T-72s are a case in point. It marks an important step in modernizing Iran's armored forces, but Iran would need deliveries of around 1,500–2,000 T-72s to meet its requirements.

Iran needs to acquire modern armored infantry fighting vehicles for its first-line units and to standardize on a given type. This would entail a total of 2,000 relatively modern armored vehicles. In addition, Iran needs much larger inventories of self-propelled artillery, improved anti-tank weapons and short-range air defenses, and a much stronger support and logistic training system to sustain mobile armored warfare and fast-moving offensive operations.

Iran faces other major challenges in improving the quality of its land forces. It disperses its armor and heavy weapons among far too many regular and IRGC units, and most of its combat units lack the critical mass of armor and artillery necessary to fight effectively in modern maneuver warfare.

Most of its tanks lack modern fire control systems, armor, night and thermal vision devices, and guns and ammunition equal to those of the most advanced neighboring states. Sustainability and power projection capabilities are limited, as are battlefield recovery and repair capabilities. Overall night warfare capabilities are limited, and Iran has only limited ability to move artillery rapidly, mass and shift fires, and acquire beyond-visual-range targets. Communications, command, and control systems are obsolete and unreliable. Helicopter and combined operations training with fixed wing aircraft is of limited quality at best.

Virtually all of Iran's land force equipment holdings must be modernized or reconditioned to recover from the combined impact of a cutoff of Western weapons and equipment, the wear of eight years of war, and the massive losses of 1988. Iran needs improved tank and artillery rounds, remotely piloted vehicles (RPVs) that are integrated into division or brigade level operations, improved mobile short range air defense systems (SHORADS) and manportable surface-to-air missiles, tank transporters, secure communications, night vision and improved sights, modern fire control systems, and tracked support equipment. It would also greatly benefit from advanced training and simulation technology.

The Iranian regular army almost certainly understands these requirements. It has learned from the Iran-Iraq War and the Gulf War that a reliance on mass, rather than quality, is ineffective. It has sought to provide its existing units with more armor and artillery, strengthen the firepower and mobility of selected specialized independent brigades, and give its infantry divisions added artillery strength and armored infantry fighting vehicles. Even so, the preceding analysis has shown that it will be well beyond the year 2000 before Iran's land forces can acquire anything like the full mix of modern equipment they need.

Iran's Need for Qualitative Improvements

Iran's regular army has other improvements to make before most of its forces are properly prepared for combined operations, high-tempo combined arms operations, power projection, and amphibious warfare missions.[85] Its conscript training, junior officer, and noncommissioned officer training is mediocre, and its medium-to-large-scale unit training is also poor. Regular army formations differ sharply in size, force mix, and equipment, and they are difficult to supply and support.

Many units are badly under strength, and some combat and support units only have about 65%–80% of the strength needed to fully man them. The land forces' logistic system is compartmented and ineffective. Many Iranian combat units have low overall manpower strength, and some of Iran's units lack the manpower and equipment to be employed in anything other than static defensive battles. Logistics, combat engineering, and support capabilities are limited and dependent on reinforcement from the civil sector for any sustained operations.

Contingency Capabilities

It is difficult to translate this mix of strengths and weaknesses into estimates of Iran's regional war-fighting capabilities, because so much depends on Iran's future access to more advanced arms and technology, the extent to which the Southern Gulf states acquire serious military capabilities, and the strength of Western power projection forces.

Iran's ground forces are now much more capable of conducting successful defensive operations against Iraq today than they were after their defeats in 1988. Given Iraq's diminished strength, it is unlikely that even an all-out Iraqi attack on Iran, led by all of the Iraqi Republican Guards, could achieve more than limited initial gains. Iran may also be strong enough to conduct successful limited offensives in the Iran-Iraq border area.

Iran still, however, lacks effective air support and faces severe problems in conducting large-scale joint maneuver warfare and sustained offensive operations. It is doubtful that Iran could take and hold significant amounts of Iraqi territory, or could seize a significant part of the Shi'ite areas in southeastern Iraq unless it was supported by a massive—and highly unlikely—popular uprising. Much would depend, however, on how well Iraqi forces fought and on their loyalty to Saddam Hussein. Iran does not seem capable of defeating Iraq, but Iraq could defeat itself.

Much of Iran's future contingency capability against Iraq depends on how rapidly Iraq can recover from the impact of the Gulf War and the sanctions that have followed, and the rate at which it can then begin to rebuild and modernize its land forces. Iraq should be able to preserve enough strength and capability to be able to defend against a major Iranian invasion through 2000, but this defense will be heavily dependent on Iraqi unity and the willingness of Iraqi Shi'ites to fight for the central government. Iraq is also likely to become significantly more vulnerable to an Iranian invasion after 2000, if it does not begin to receive significant supplies of parts, munitions, and new arms.

Iran's land forces could play a significant role in low-intensity combat in Iran's northern and eastern border areas, although they are no match for a major military power like Turkey. They are just beginning to acquire significant offensive power projection capabilities. They can currently support the seizure of islands and off-shore oil facilities in the Gulf and defeat any Kurdish uprising. They also have impressive capabilities for unconventional warfare. However, Iran's land forces lack the lift capability and air support to sustain large-scale armored thrusts deep into the territory of a Southern Gulf state, and they are not capable of significant amphibious operations in the face of opposition by a power like the United States.

If there is a "worst case" scenario affecting the Southern Gulf, it seems to be successful Iranian support of a popular coup attempt in an exposed country like Bahrain. It is impossible to rule out a sudden or surprise Iranian attack in support of an uprising against a Southern Gulf regime that might produce success out of all proportion to the size and effectiveness of the Iranian forces deployed. Iran has a number of land units that should perform well in unconventional warfare missions in support of any popular uprising. It could deploy lightly armed, brigade-sized forces relatively rapidly across the Gulf, if it were allowed to make an unopposed amphibious and air assault. Iran has yet to demonstrate that it can use heavy weapons in its amphibious exercises, or has a significant "over-the-shore" capability to employ armor and artillery. However, Iran could intervene in a civil war in smaller Gulf states under highly permissive conditions.

Iran could not hope, however, to defend such gains against serious US naval or air action. Iran might have serious difficulty in responding quickly to a US air or amphibious assault against positions it was not defending at the time of attack, and it would probably find it difficult to maneuver in the face of US naval and air operations. Further, Iran's land forces seem likely to continue to present only a limited threat to the Southern Gulf states, unless a radical change in a Southern Gulf regime should produce a friendly regime that would allow Iran to build up a significant military presence in the Southern Gulf. Iran's conventional military build-up is so slow that there is no near to mid-term prospect of Iranian success as long as the United States and Southern Gulf states cooperate, the United States maintains an effective forward presence and power projection capability, and the United States and its regional allies are firm in their resolve.

Iran may already, however, be able to inflict considerable casualties on any US amphibious or land operation that directly attacked a well-positioned Iranian land unit on Iran's islands or southern coast. Iran could probably conduct a costly war of attrition in the face of a more serious US attack and effort to occupy part of Iran. The problem with this contingency is that it is about as likely as a deliberate US effort to engage in a land war in Asia. The United States could conduct limited operations along the Iranian coast to deter Iran, or punish it for aggressive actions. Any major US land action in Iran is so unlikely, however, that this contingency is only a serious possibility in the minds of Iran's more xenophobic planners. Invading a nation of more than 60 million people with no clear strategic purpose is not an American goal.

Iranian land forces could easily defeat the Iranian Kurds or any other internal opposition force. They are also capable of intervening at the brigade and division levels in a conflict like the war between Azerbaijan and Armenia, and in Afghanistan. They have very limited capability, however, against Turkey's first-line forces.

Iranian future conventional land warfare capabilities will only improve to the extent that Iran's build-up outpaces that of its neighbors. In addition, Iran's freedom of action in the Gulf will be heavily dependent on the reaction of US naval and air forces and the position taken by Iraq. It is far from clear that Iran's conventional land warfare capabilities will improve faster than those of its neighbors, particularly if its land forces remain split between the regular forces and those of the Revolutionary Guards.

As a result, Iran may pose more of an indirect threat to its neighbors and to the West than it does in terms of threatening a major regional conflict. Iranian land forces, particularly the IRGC, already play a significant role in training, equipping, and supporting guerrilla and terrorist forces in countries like Lebanon, the Sudan, and Bosnia. They can also covertly project power in terms of supporting radical or extremist movements in other states. All of these capabilities will improve as Iran builds up and modernizes its land forces.[86]

NOTES

1. In addition to the general sources on Iranian force strength referenced at the beginning of this section, this analysis draws on Andrew Rathmell, *The Changing Military Balance in the Gulf*, London, Royal United Services Institute, Whitehall Papers 38, 1996; Edward B. Atkenson, *The Powder Keg*, Falls Church, NOVA Publications, 1996; Geoffery Kemp and Robert E. Harkavy, *Strategic Geography and the Changing Middle East*, Washington, Carnegie Endowment/Brookings, 1997; USCENTCOM, *Atlas, 1996*, MacDill Air Force Base, USCENTCOM, 1997; *Armed Forces Journal*, March, 1992, pp. 26–27; *Defense Electronics*, March, 1992, p. 16; *Inside the Air Force*, February 28,

1992, p. 1; Dr. Andrew Rathmell, "Iran's Rearmament: How Great a Threat?" *Jane's Intelligence Review*, July, 1994, pp. 317–322; Armed Forces (UK), May, 1989, pp. 206–209; Jane's *Sentinel: The Gulf States, 1997*; London, Jane's Publishing, 1997; Michael Eisenstadt, *Iranian Military Power*, Washington, Washington Institute, 1996; *Jane's Helicopter Markets and Systems* (CD-ROM); *Jane's All the World's Armies* (CD-ROM); *Jane's Armor and Artillery* (CD-ROM); *Jane's Land-Based Air Defense* (CD-ROM); *Jane's Military Vehicles and Logistics* (CD-ROM).

2. The author visited this display in August after a substantial amount of the equipment had been moved to Jordan and to other areas. Even then, there were immense stocks of heavy weapons, almost all of which had been abandoned without any combat damage. It should be noted, however, that Iraq made claims about capturing tanks that seem to have included all light tanks and BMP-1s.

3. IISS, *The Military Balance, 1997–1998; Jane's Sentinel: The Gulf States, 1997*.

4. USCENTCOM, *Atlas, 1996*, MacDill Air Force Base, USCENTCOM, 1997, pp. 14–15; IISS, *Military Balance, 1997–1998*.

5. IISS, *The Military Balance, 1997–1998; Jane's Sentinel: The Gulf States, 1997*, p. 24.

6. There are reports that the lighter and smaller formations in the regular army include an Airmobile Forces group created since the Iran-Iraq War, which includes the 29th Special Forces Division, formed during the period 1993–1994, and the 55th paratroop division. There are also reports that the regular army and the IRGC commando forces are loosely integrated into a corps of up to 30,000 men, with integrated helicopter lift and air assault capabilities. The airborne and special forces are trained at a facility in Shiraz. These reports are not correct. Note that detailed unit identifications for Iranian forces differ sharply from source to source. It is unclear that such identifications are accurate, and now dated wartime titles and numbers are often published, sometimes confusing brigade numbers with division numbers.

7. No reliable data exist on the size and number of Iran's smaller, independent formations.

8. Dr. Anoushiravan Ehteshami, "The Armed Forces of the Islamic Republic of Iran," *Jane's Intelligence Review*, February, 1993, pp. 76–79; IISS, *The Military Balance, 1997–1998; Jane's Sentinel: The Gulf States, 1997*.

9. IISS, *Military Balance, 1997–1998*, "Iran"; *Jane's Sentinel: The Gulf States, 1997*, "Iran"; *New York Times*, May 17, 1995, p. A-3; *Los Angeles Times*, May 18, 1995, p. 8. USCENTCOM reports only 1,000 tanks, but this may represent a rounding of the number for security purposes or a different way of estimating operational strength. USCENTCOM, *Atlas, 1996*, MacDill Air Force Base, USCENTCOM, 1997, pp. 14–15.

10. IISS, *Military Balance, 1997–1998*, "Iran"; *Jane's Sentinel: The Gulf States, 1997*, "Iran"; *New York Times*, May 17, 1995, p. A-3; *Los Angeles Times*, May 18, 1995, p. 8. USCENTCOM reports only 1,000 tanks, but this may represent a rounding of the number for security purposes or a different way of estimating operational strength. USCENTCOM, *Atlas, 1996*, MacDill Air Force Base, USCENTCOM, 1997, pp. 14–15.

11. *Jane's Defense Weekly*, January 14, 1998, pp. 23–25.

12. *Jane's Defense Weekly*, January 14, 1998, pp. 23–25.

13. *Jane's Defense Weekly*, January 14, 1998, pp. 23–25.

14. *Jane's Defense Weekly*, January 14, 1998, pp. 23–25.

15. *Jane's Defense Weekly*, January 7, 1995, p. 4; February 25, 1995, p. 4, November

25, 1995, January 31, 1996, p. 18, July 30, 1997, p. 3, December 10, 1997, p. 20, January 14, 1998, pp. 23–25.

16. *Jane's Defense Weekly*, January 7, 1995, p. 4; February 25, 1995, p. 4, November 25, 1995, January 31, 1996, p. 18, July 30, 1997, p. 3; *Middle East Economic Digest*, July 18, 1997, p. 23, December 10, 1997, p. 20, January 14, 1998, pp. 23–25.

17. The low estimate of Iran's AFV and APC strength is based on interviews with Israeli, British, and US civilian experts, and the IISS, *Military Balance, 1997–1998*, "Iran"; *Jane's Sentinel: The Gulf States, 1997*, "Iran." USCENTCOM reports a total of 1,360 other armored vehicles. USCENTCOM, *Atlas, 1996*, MacDill Air Force Base, USCENTCOM, 1997, pp. 14–15.

18. USCENTCOM reports 50 as being operational. USCENTCOM, *Atlas, 1996*, MacDill Air Force Base, USCENTCOM, 1997, pp. 14–15.

19. *Jane's Defense Weekly*, December 17, 1997, p. 14; January 14, 1998, pp. 23–25.

20. *International Defense Review*, 7/1996, p. 24, *Jane's Defense Weekly*, January 7, 1995, p. 4; February 25, 1995, p. 4; *Tehran Times*, May 30, 1996.

21. *Jane's Intelligence Review*, September, 1997, pp. 419–421.

22. *Jane's Defense Weekly*, January 7, 1995, p. 4; February 25, 1995, p. 4, July 30, 1997, p. 3, December 10, 1997, p. 20, January 14, 1998, pp. 23–25; *Tehran Times*, May 30, 1996.

23. Based largely on interviews. For typical recent reporting on Iranian exercises, see *Washington Times*, May 12, 1997, p. A-13, October 11, 1997, p. A-6; *Jane's Defense Weekly*, June 25, 1997, p. 14, October 1, 1997, p. 19; Reuters, July 3, 1997, 0452, July 9, 1997, 1655, September 28, 1997, 0417, October 6, 1997, 1600.

24. Based on estimates by Israeli, British, and US civilian experts, and IISS, *Military Balance, 1997–1998*, "Iran"; *Jane's Sentinel: The Gulf States, 1997*, "Iran." Also see *Washington Times*, May 12, 1997, p. A-13, October 11, 1997, p. A-6; *Jane's Defense Weekly*, June 25, 1997, p. 14, October 1, 1997, p. 19; Reuters, July 3, 1997, 0452, July 9, 1997, 1655, September 28, 1997, 0417, October 6, 1997, 1600.

25. *Jane's Defense Weekly*, April 30, 1997, p. 33.

26. *Jane's Defense Weekly*, April 30, 1997, p. 33.

27. *Jane's Defense Weekly*, April 30, 1997, p. 33; *Jane's Intelligence Review*, September, 1997, pp. 419–421.

28. *Jane's Defense Weekly*, April 30, 1997, p. 33.

29. Based on estimates by Israeli, British, and US civilian experts, and IISS, *Military Balance, 1997–1998*, "Iran"; *Jane's Sentinel: The Gulf States, 1997*, "Iran."

30. These counts are very uncertain and mix interview and IISS data.

31. *Jane's Defense Weekly*, June 5, 1996, p. 15.

32. *Jane's Defense Weekly*, June 5, 1996, p. 15.

33. *Jane's Defense Weekly*, June 5, 1996, p. 15.

34. USCENTCOM reports a total of 3,600 artillery weapons, SSM launchers, MRLs, and mortars, but this total seems too low. USCENTCOM, *Atlas, 1996*, MacDill Air Force Base, USCENTCOM, 1997, pp. 14–15.

35. Reports that one of these systems, the Fadjr 3—with a range of 40 kilometers—has seen extensive service with the Hezbollah forces in Lebanon are not correct. *Jane's Defense Weekly*, November 6, 1996, p. 23, September 17, 1997, p. 5, December 10, 1997, p. 20, January 14, 1998, pp. 23–25; *International Defense Review*, 7/1996, pp. 24–27; *Jane's Intelligence Review*, September, 1997, pp. 419–421.

36. Based largely on interviews. For typical recent reporting on Iranian exercises, see

Washington Times, May 12, 1997, p. A-13, October 11, 1997, p. A-6; *Jane's Defense Weekly*, June 25, 1997, p. 14, October 1, 1997, p. 19; Reuters, July 3, 1997, 0452, July 9, 1997, 1655, September 28, 1997, 0417, October 6, 1997, 1600.

37. *Jane's Defense Weekly*, November 6, 1996, p. 23.

38. *International Defense Review*, 7/1996, pp. 23–26; Anthony H. Cordesman, *Iran's Weapons of Mass Destruction*, CSIS, 1997.

39. Iran publicly displayed the Oghab at a military show in Libreville in 1989. It is 230 mm in diameter, 4,820 mm long, and weighs 320 kilograms, with a 70 kilogram warhead. Iran also displayed another rocket called the Nazeat, which is 355 mm in diameter, 5,900 mm long, weighs 950 kilograms, and has a 180 kilogram warhead. *Jane's Defense Weekly*, February 11, 1989, p. 219; Lora Lumpe, Lisbeth Gronlund, and David C. Wright, "Third World Missiles Fall Short," *The Bulletin of the Atomic Scientists*, March, 1992, pp. 30–36.

40. *Jane's Defense Weekly*, June 20, 1987, p. 1289; Lora Lumpe, Lisbeth Gronlund, and David C. Wright, "Third World Missiles Fall Short," *The Bulletin of the Atomic Scientists*, March, 1992, pp. 30–36.

41. Some estimates indicate a range of up to 200 kilometers. For background on the system, see *Financial Times*, June 8, 1988, p. 20, and *The Middle East*, April, 1988, pp. 1 and 18.

42. *Washington Times*, May 12, 1997, p. A-13, October 11, 1997, p. A-6; *Jane's Defense Weekly*, April 30, 1997, p. 6, June 25, 1997, p. 14, October 1, 1997, p. 19; Reuters, July 3, 1997, 0452, July 9, 1997, 1655, September 28, 1997, 0417, October 6, 1997, 1600.

43. USCENTCOM reports a total of 1,500 guns. USCENTCOM, *Atlas, 1996*, MacDill Air Force Base, USCENTCOM, 1997, pp. 14–15.

44. USCENTCOM, *Atlas, 1996*, MacDill Air Force Base, USCENTCOM, 1997, pp. 14–15.

45. *Jane's Sentinel: The Gulf States*, "Iran," 1997.

46. IISS, *The Military Balance, 1997–1998*, London, IISS, 1996, "Iran"; *Jane's Sentinel: The Gulf States*, "Iran," 1997.

47. Some reports place the aviation school in Tabriz. Tabriz is used for training in combat support.

48. Based largely on interviews. Also see *Washington Times*, May 12, 1997, p. A-13, October 11, 1997, p. A-6; *Jane's Defense Weekly*, June 25, 1997, p. 14, October 1, 1997, p. 19; Reuters, July 3, 1997, 0452, July 9, 1997, 1655, September 28, 1997, 0417, October 6, 1997, 1600.

49 This analysis draws on Anthony H. Cordesman, *Iran and Iraq: The Threat from the Northern Gulf*, Boulder, Westview, 1994; Anthony H. Cordesman and Ahmed S. Hashim, *Iran: Dilemmas of Dual Containment*, Boulder, Westview, 1997; *Jane's Sentinel: The Gulf States*, "Iran"; Mark J. Roberts, *Khomeini's Incorporation of the Iranian Military*, Washington, Institute for National Security Studies, National Defense University, January, 1996; Ahmed Hashim, "The Crisis of the Iranian State," Adelphi Paper 296, London, IISS, Oxford, July, 1995, pp. 7–30 and 50–70; Andrew Rathmell, *The Changing Military Balance in the Gulf*, London, RUSI, Whitehall Papers 38, 1996, pp. 9–23; Michael Eisenstadt, *Iranian Military Power, Capabilities and Intentions*, Washington, Washington Institute, 1996, pp. 9–65; Anoushiravan Ehteshami, "Iran Strives to Regain Military Might," *International Defense Review*, 7/1996, pp. 22–26; the *Washington Times*, May 2, 1989, p. A-9, June 23, 1989, p. A-9; March 1, 1992, p. B-3, March 22,

1989, p. A-8, January 17, 1992, p. A-1, February 20, 1992, p. 9; *Armed Forces Journal*, March, 1992, pp. 26–27; *Defense Electronics*, March, 1992, p. 16; *Inside the Air Force*, February 28, 1992, p. 1; *Jane's Defense Weekly*, November 19, 1988, pp. 1252–1253, June 3, 1988, p. 1057, February 11, 1989, p. 219, June 30, 1990, pp. 1299–1302, February 11, 1992, p. 158–159; Dr. Andrew Rathmell, "Iran's Rearmament: How Great a Threat?" *Jane's Intelligence Review*, July, 1994, pp. 317–322; *Armed Forces (UK)*, May, 1989, pp. 206–209; *Washington Post*, June 23, 1989, p. A-1; August 18, 1989, p. A-25; August 20, 1989, p. A-1, September 3, 1989, p. A-25, February 1, 1992, p. A-1, February 2, 1992, p. A-1, February 5, 1992, p. A-19; *New York Times*, September 3, 1989, p. A-4; *The Estimate*, October 13–26, 1989, p. 1; *Christian Science Monitor*, February 6, 1992, p. 19; *Philadelphia Inquirer*, February 6, 1992, p. A-6; *Los Angeles Times*, January 7, 1992, p. A-1; *Baltimore Sun*, January 25, 1992, p. 4A; *Defense News*, January 27, 1922, p. 45, February 17, 1992, p. 1; *Chicago Tribune*, January 19, 1992, p. 1.

50. See *Time*, March 21, 1994, pp. 50–54, November 11, 1996, pp. 78–82. Also see *Washington Post*, November 21, 1993, p. A-1, August 22, 1994, p. A-17; October 28, 1994, p. A-17, November 27, 1994, p. A-30, April 11, 1997, p. A-1, April 14, 1997, p. A-1; *Los Angeles Times*, November 3, 1994, pp. A-1, A-12; Deutsche Presse-Agentur, April 17, 1997, 11:02; Reuters, April 16, 1997, BC cycle, April 17, 1997, BC cycle; *The European*, April 17, 1997, p. 13; *The Guardian*, October 30, 1993, p. 13, August 24, 1996, p. 16, April 16, 1997, p. 10; *New York Times*, April 11, 1997, p. A1; Associated Press, April 14, 1997, 18:37; *Jane's Defense Weekly*, June 5, 1996, p. 15; Agence France Press, April 15, 1997, 15:13; BBC, April 14, 1997, ME/D2892/MED; Deustcher Depeschen via ADN, April 12, 1997, 0743; *Washington Times*, April 11, 1997, p. A22.

51. *USA Today*, October 6, 1997, p. 10A.

52. Interviews and *Washington Times*, May 12, 1997, p. A-13, October 11, 1997, p. A-6; *Jane's Defense Weekly*, June 25, 1997, p. 14, October 1, 1997, p. 19; Reuters, July 3, 1997, 0452, July 9, 1997, 1655, September 28, 1997, 0417, October 6, 1997, 1600.

53. Based largely on interviews. For typical recent reporting on Iranian exercises, see *Washington Times*, May 12, 1997, p. A-13; *Jane's Defense Weekly*, November 6, 1996, p. 23, June 25, 1997, p. 14; Reuters, July 3, 1997, 0452, July 9, 1997, 1655.

54. See Anthony H. Cordesman and Abraham R. Wagner, *The Lessons of Modern War, Volume II, The Iran-Iraq War*, Boulder, Westview, 1991; A. J. Venter, "Iran Still Exporting Terrorism," *Jane's Intelligence Review*, November, 1997, pp. 511–516.

55. *Jane's Sentinel: The Gulf States*, "Iran."

56. For typical reporting by officers of the IRGC on this issue, see the comments of its acting Commander-in-Chief Brigadier General Seyyed Rahim Safavi, speaking to reporters during the IRGC week (December 20–26, 1995), FBIS-NES-95–250, December 25, 1995, IRNA 1406 GMT.

57. IISS, *Military Balance, 1997–1998*.

58. A review of Iranian media reporting and unclassified Iranian military literature does not clarify this situation. The Iranian media issue conflicting reports, and Iran's military literature does not seem to provide a definitive picture of the IRGC's military organization and actual command structure. This analysis is based largely on the views of US experts, but there may be more than 15 "brigades."

59. A. J. Venter, "Iran Still Exporting Terrorism," *Jane's Intelligence Review*, November, 1997, pp. 511–516.

60. Interviews with US experts. Division, brigade, regiment, and battalion are Western

terms which do not really apply to the IRGC formations. Actual unit strengths and organization often have nothing to do with the titles applied in Western reporting.

61. The reader should be aware that much of the information relating to the Quds is highly uncertain and drawn from Israeli sources. Also, however, see the article from the Jordanian publication *Al-Hadath* in FBIS-NES-96-108, May 27, 1996, p. 9, and in *Al-Sharq Al-Awsat*, FBIS-NES-96-110, June 5, 1996, pp. 1, 4; A. J. Venter, "Iran Still Exporting Terrorism," *Jane's Intelligence Review*, November, 1997, pp. 511–516.

62. *New York Times*, May 17, 1998, p. A-15; *Washington Times*, May 17, 1998, p. A-13; *Washington Post*, May 21, 1998, p. A-29.

63. *New York Times*, May 22, 1998, p. A-11; *Washington Post*, May 23, 1998, p. A-26.

64. A. J. Venter, "Iran Still Exporting Terrorism," *Jane's Intelligence Review*, November, 1997, pp. 511–516.

65. *Washington Post*, October 5, 1997, p. C-4.

66. Reuters, September 17, 1997, 0231.

67. For a pro-Israeli view with interesting detail, see Hillary Mann, "Iranian Links to International Terrorism—The Khatami Era," *Policywatch*, No. 296, January 28, 1998. Also see A. J. Venter, "Iran Still Exporting Terrorism," *Jane's Intelligence Review*, November, 1997, pp. 511–516.

68. *Washington Post*, October 5, 1997, p. C-4.

69. Dr. Andrew Rathmell, "Iran's Rearmament: How Great a Threat?" *Jane's Intelligence Review*, July, 1994, pp. 317–322; *Defense and Foreign Affairs*, No. 1, 1994, pp. 4–7; Kenneth Katzman and Scott Modell, "Terrorism: Middle Eastern Groups and State Sponsors, 1997," Library of Congress, CRS-97–6924F, July 10, 1997; *Jane's Defense Weekly*, January 31, 1996, p. 18.

70. Adapted from interviews with US, British, and Israeli experts, Iranian exiles, Anthony H. Cordesman, *Iran and Iraq: The Threat from the Northern Gulf*, Boulder, Westview, 1994; Anthony H. Cordesman and Ahmed S. Hashim, *Iran: Dilemmas of Dual Containment*, Boulder, Westview, 1997; John W. R. Taylor and Kenneth Munson, "Gallery of Middle East Air Power," *Air Force*, October, 1994, pp. 59–70; the IISS, *The Military Balance, 1997–1998*, IISS, London, 1996, "Iran," *Jane's Sentinel: The Gulf States*, "Iran," London, Jane's Information Group, 1997; Ahmed Hashim, "The Crisis of the Iranian State," Adelphi Paper 296, London, IISS, Oxford, July, 1995, pp. 7–30 and 50–70; Andrew Rathmell, *The Changing Military Balance in the Gulf*, London, RUSI, Whitehall Papers 38, 1996, pp. 9–23; Michael Eisenstadt, *Iranian Military Power, Capabilities and Intentions*, Washington, Washington Institute, 1996, pp. 9–65; Anoushiravan Ehteshami, "Iran Strives to Regain Military Might," *International Defense Review*, 7/1996, pp. 22–26; USNI Data Base, *Military Technology, World Defense Almanac: The Balance of Military Power*, Vol. XVII, Issue 1–1933, ISSN 0722–3226, pp. 139–142; Anoushiravan Ehteshami "Iran's National Strategy," *International Defense Review*, 4/1994, pp. 29–37; and working data from the Jaffee Center for Strategic Studies and the *Washington Times*, January 16, 1992, p. G-4; *Washington Post*, February 1, 1992, p. A1, February 2, 1992, pp. A1 and A25, February 5, p. A-19; *Financial Times*, February 6, 1992, p. 4; *Christian Science Monitor*, February 6, 1992, p. 19; *Defense News*, February 17, 1992, p. 1; Kenneth Katzman and Scott Modell, "Terrorism: Middle Eastern Groups and State Sponsors, 1997," Library of Congress, CRS-97–6924F, July 10, 1997.

71. For example, see *Jane's Defense Weekly*, June 24, 1995, p. 5, November 6, 1996, p. 23, June 25, 1997, p. 14; *Washington Times*, May 4, 1997, p. A7; May 12, 1997, p. A-

13, Reuters, July 3, 1997, 0452, July 9, 1997, 1655; *Washington Post*, June 30, 1997, p. A-20; Associated Press, June 30, 1996, 0629.

72. *Jane's Defense Weekly*, June 24, 1995, p. 5; *Washington Post*, June 30, 1997, p. A-20; Associated Press, June 30, 1996, 0629.

73. IRNA, May 2, 1997; Iranian TV, April 26, 1997; *Jane's Defense Weekly*, June 24, 1995, p. 5, November 6, 1996, p. 23, June 25, 1997, p. 14; *Washington Times*, May 4, 1997, p. A7; May 12, 1997, p. A-13, Reuters, May 7, 1997, 0452, July 3, 1997, 0452, July 9, 1997, 1655; *Washington Post*, June 30, 1997, p. A-20; Associated Press, June 30, 1996, 0629.

74. Based on work by Kenneth Timmerman, *The Iran Brief*, June 1, 1995, and Tehran Domestic Service, November 14, 1989, *FBIS-NES*, November, 15, 1989.

75. For an excellent summary of the issues involved, see Michael Eisenstadt, *Iranian Military Power, Capabilities, and Intentions*, Washington, Washington Institute, 1996, pp. 41–42. Also see the *Independent*, September 9, 1994, p. 11; FBIS-NES, September 28, 1994, p. 40, November 18, 1994, p. 54; Edward G. Shirley, "Is Iran's Present Algeria's Future," *Foreign Affairs*, 74, No. 3, May–June 1995, pp. 36–37.

76. *Jane's Sentinel: The Gulf States*, "Iran," London, Jane's Information Group, 1997; Ahmed Hashim, "The Crisis of the Iranian State," Adelphi Paper 296, London, IISS, Oxford, July, 1995, pp. 7–30 and 50–70; Michael Eisenstadt, *Iranian Military Power, Capabilities, and Intentions*, Washington, Washington Institute, 1996, pp. 41–42.

77. *Jane's Defense Weekly*, December 10, 1997, p. 18.

78. Based on various interviews. Strength data are estimated on the basis of reports in IISS, *Military Balance, 1997–1998*, "Iran"; *Jane's Sentinel: The Gulf States, 1997*, "Iran"; USNI Data Base; *Military Technology, World Defense Almanac: The Balance of Military Power*; and working data from the Jaffee Center for Strategic Studies.

79. Amnesty International, *Report 1994*, New York, Amnesty International, 1994, pp. 163–166.

80. As noted earlier, the details of this involvement are uncertain, and a great deal of the literature involved adds charges that cannot be confirmed. For a good press summary of the evidence relating to key trials and terrorist incidents, see *Time*, March 21, 1994, pp. 50–54, November 11, 1996, pp. 78–82. Also see *Washington Post*, November 21, 1993, p. A-1, August 22, 1994, p. A-17; October 28, 1994, p. A-17, November 27, 1994, p. A-30, April 11, 1997, p. A-1, April 11, 1997, p. A-1, April 14, 1997, p. A-1; *Los Angeles Times*, November 3, 1994, pp. A-1, A-12; Deutsche Presse-Agentur, April 17, 1997, 11:02; Reuters, April 16, 1997, BC cycle, April 17, 1997, BC cycle; *The European*, April 17, 1997, p. 13; *The Guardian*, October 30, 1993, p. 13, August 24, 1996, p. 16 April 16, 1997, p. 10; *New York Times*, April 11, 1997, p. A1; Associated Press, April 14, 1997, 18:37; Jane's Sentinel, *Pointer*, June, 1997, p. 7; *Washington Times*, July 10, 1997, p. A-15.

81. *Tehran Times*, April 21, 1997; IRNA April 21, 1997, May 2, 1997; Iranian TV, April 26, 1997; *Jane's Defense Weekly*, June 24, 1995, p. 5, November 6, 1996, p. 23, June 25, 1997, p. 14; *Washington Times*, May 4, 1997, p. A7; May 12, 1997, p. A-13; Reuters, May 7, 1997, 0452, July 3, 1997, 0452, July 9, 1997, 1655; *Washington Post*, June 30, 1997, p. A-20; Associated Press, June 30, 1996, 0629; May 7, 1997, 0452, July 3, 1997, 0452, July 9, 1997, 1655; *Washington Post*, June 30, 1997, p. A-20; Associated Press, June 30, 1996, 0629.

82. *Jane's Defense Weekly*, June 5, 1996, p. 15, June 12, 1996, p. 27, April 23, 1997, p. 19; Agence France Press, April 15, 1997, 15:13; BBC, April 14, 1997, ME/D2892/

MED; Deustcher Depeschen via ADN, April 12, 1997, 0743; IRNA, English, May 25, 1996, 14:29; *Tehran Times*, May 30, 1996.

83. IRNA April 21, 1997, May 2, 1997; Iranian TV, April 26, 1997; *Jane's Defense Weekly*, April 23, 1997, p. 19, April 30, 1997, p. 6, June 24, 1995, p. 5, November 6, 1996, p. 23, June 25, 1997, p. 14; *Washington Times*, May 4, 1997, p. A7; May 12, 1997, p. A-13; Reuters, April 23, 1997, 0818, May 7, 1997, 0452, July 3, 1997, 0452, July 9, 1997, 1655; *Washington Post*, June 30, 1997, p. A-20; Associated Press, June 30, 1996, 0629; May 7, 1997, 0452, July 3, 1997, 0452, July 9, 1997, 1655.

84. *Washington Times*, October 11, 1997, p. A-6; *Jane's Defense Weekly*, October 1, 1997, p. 19; Reuters, September 28, 1997, 0417, October 6, 1997, 1600.

85. *Defense and Foreign Affairs*, No. 1, 1994, pp. 4–7.

86. See James P. Wootten, "Terrorism: US Policy Options, Congressional Research Service, IB92074, October 6, 1994, pp. 6–7; Kenneth Katzman, Iran: Current Developments and US Policy, Congressional Research Service, IB93033, September 9, 1994, pp. 5–7; *Christian Science Monitor*, March 22, 1994, p. 6, June 28, 1994, p. A-1; *Time*, March 21, 1994, pp. 50–54; *Washington Times*, December 19, 1993, p. A-3, February 19, 1994, p. A-8, March 9, 1994, June 22, 1994, p. A-14, June 24, 1994, p. A-1, June 27, 1994, p. A-22; *Washington Post*, January 1, 1994, p. A-15, February 4, 1994, p. A-14.

Chapter 7

The Iranian Air Force

Iran's air force has gone through a decade and a half of revolution and war, and its current operational strength is as hard to estimate as the operational strength of Iran's ground forces. While Iran had 85,000 men and 447 combat aircraft in its air force at the time the Shah fell from power, it steadily lost air strength from 1980 to 1988. As Figure 7.1 shows, the air force suffered major combat losses in the early years of the Iran-Iraq War, and many aircraft gradually ceased to be operational once Iran was cut off from its US suppliers. In addition, the Iranian air force has lacked effective foreign technical support for fifteen years. The air force was also purged of some of the pilots, technical personnel, and other officers that served under the Shah, during the first few years of the Khomeini regime.[1]

Figure 7.1 also shows, however, that Iran's air strength has improved since 1988, and Figure 7.2 shows that it now has limited holdings of modern Russian combat aircraft. The commanders of Iran's air force have been some of Iran's most professional and effective officers. Both Brigadier Mansour Sattari (who was killed in an aircraft accident on January 6, 1995) and his successor, Habib Baqai, have sought to create a more modern force, and the Iranian air staff seems to be aware of the lessons of the Gulf War, and the changes in tactics, training, organization, and technology that are being imposed on air power by the revolution in military affairs.

The air force also seems to face a very different political environment from the purges and uncertainties of revolution during the early years of the Iran-Iraq War. Iran's present leadership seems to understand the need for modern air power and to have firmly rejected any effort to rely on popular warfare. The air force also had had an orthodox command structure since the early 1990s, which follows the broad pattern that exists in most other countries. The commander of the Iranian air force reports to the Chief of Staff of the armed forces, and the Air Force Central Staff reports to the General Staff of the Armed Forces, and through him to the Supreme Leader.

STRENGTH AND ORGANIZATION

By 1998, the Iranian air force and air defense force had built back to a total inventory of around 260–300 combat aircraft. The air force also had an independent, surface-to-surface missile brigade. The air force and air defense force had a strength of about 30,000–37,000 men, with 17,000–18,000 men in the air force plus 12,000–15,000 more in the land-based air defense forces. However, the Iranian air force was scarcely the dominant regional force that the Shah sought to create before his fall.

Iran's air strength is shown in Figures 7.1 and 7.2. It is compared to that of its neighbors in Table 7.1, and in Figures 7.3 to 7.6. Figure 7.3 shows comparative air force manpower. Figure 7.4 shows comparative fixed wing combat aircraft strength. Figure 7.5 and Table 7.1 compare relative holdings of attack and armed helicopters.

Saudi Arabia is clearly the major air power in the Gulf, and Iraq remains a rival. It is clear that the air forces of the Southern Gulf are modernizing and expanding faster than Iran's forces, while Iraq has remained static since its massive losses in the Gulf War. It is also clear that any major US air reinforcements will tip the balance decisively in favor of the Southern Gulf states.

The Iranian air force is headquartered in Tehran with training, administration, and logistics branches, and a major central Air Defense Operations Center. It has a political directorate and a small naval coordination staff. It has three major regional headquarters: Northern Zone (Badl Sar), Central Zone (Hamaden), and Southern Zone (Bushehr). Each regional zone seems to control a major air defense sector with subordinate air bases and facilities. The key air defense subzones and related bases in the Northern Zone are at Badl Sar, Mashhad, and Shahabad Kord. The subzones and bases in the Central Zone are at Hamadan and Dezful, and the subzones and bases in the Southern Zone are at Bushehr, Bandar Abbas, and Jask. The air force has given high priority to the modernization and improvement of the Southern Zone in recent years because of the fear of US attack, and the air force has strengthened its liaison with the Navy and the IRGC.[2]

As is the case with most aspects of Iranian military forces, estimates differ by source. USCENTCOM does not break aircraft out by type in its unclassified estimates, but indicates that Iran has 35 fighter-bombers, 45 fighters, 10 fighter interceptors, 8 reconnaissance aircraft, 17 tanker-transports, 41 transports, 81 trainers, 76 helicopters, and 1,025 surface-to-air missiles. USCENTCOM indicates that Iran had a total of 10 fighter bases. These USCENTCOM estimates indicate that Iran had a total of 98 combat aircraft, but the USCENTCOM estimates do not include any Russian/Soviet combat aircraft.[3]

Figure 7.1
Trends in Iranian Operational Major Combat Aircraft: 1979–1998

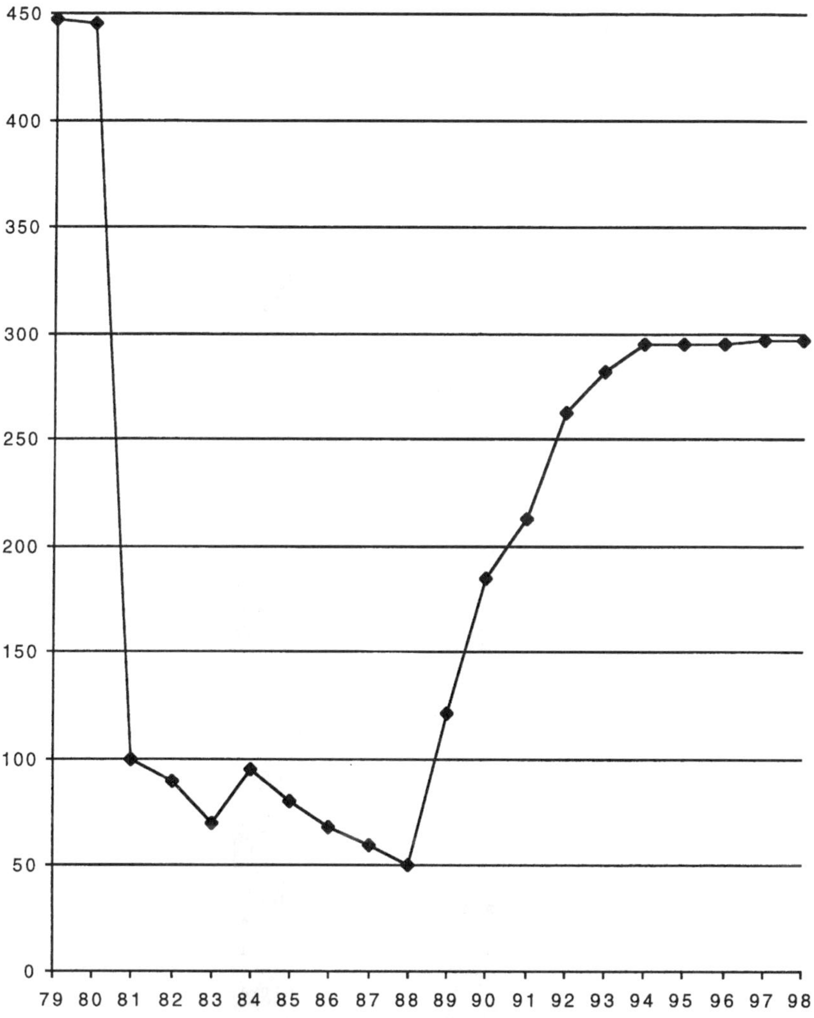

Sources: Adapted by Anthony H. Cordesman from various sources, and IISS, *Military Balance*. No useful estimate is possible of armed helicopter strength. Armed helicopters are operated by the land forces.

A comparison of estimates by the IISS and other sources indicates that the air force had 18 main combat squadrons in early 1998. These included nine fighter ground-attack squadrons, with 4/50–60 US-supplied F-4D/Es and 4/55–65 F-5E/FIIs, and 1/27–30 Soviet-supplied Su-24s. Iran had seven air defense squadrons, with 4/30–60 US-supplied F-14s, 2/30–35 Russian/Iraqi-supplied MiG-29s, and 1/25–35 Chinese-supplied F-7Ms.[4] According to some reports,

Figure 7.2
**Iranian High-Quality Gulf Fixed Wing Fighter Combat Aircraft by Type: 1998
(Includes Mirage F-1, Mirage 2000, F-15, F-16, F-18, Tornado, Su-20/22, Su-24,
MiG 25/25R, MiG-29)**

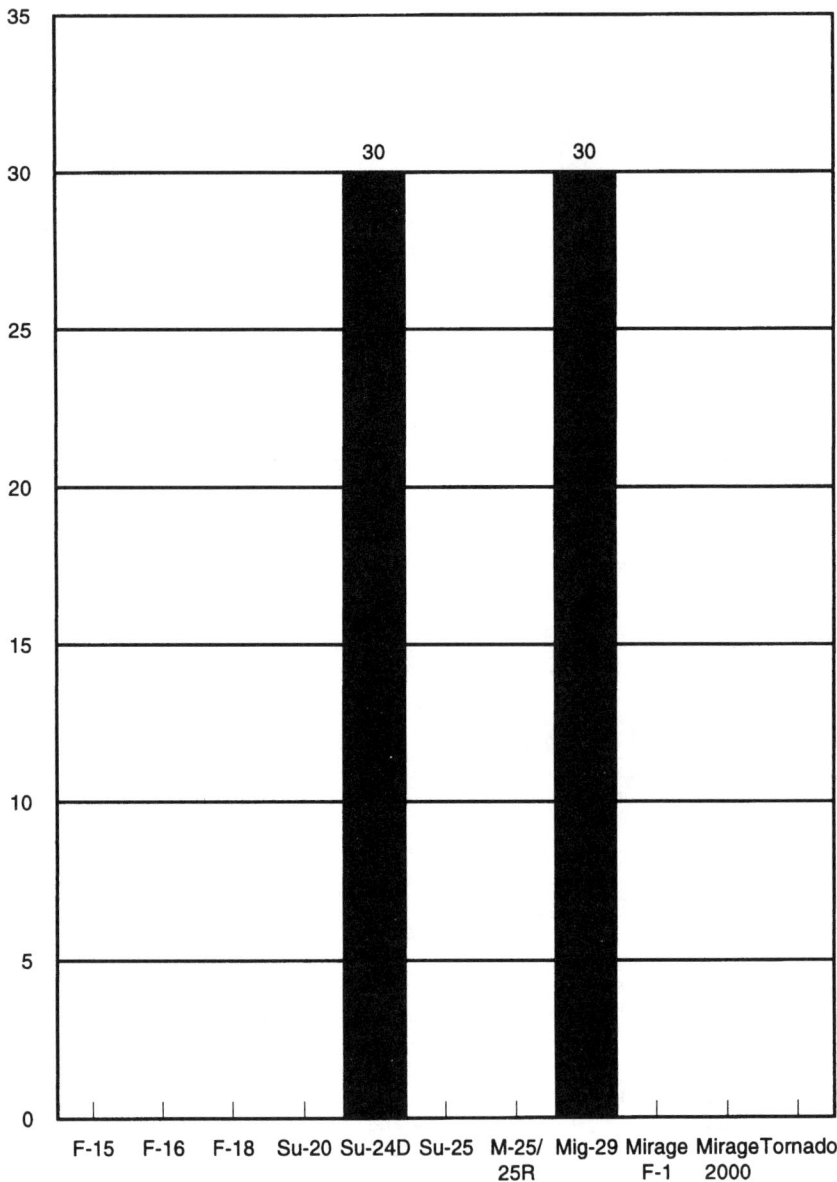

Sources: Estimated by Anthony H. Cordesman from various sources, and IISS, *Military Balance*.

Table 7.1
Advanced Combat Aircraft by Type in Gulf Forces in 1998

	Number	Type
Bahrain	24	Total Fixed Wing Combat
	12	F-16C/D
Iran	297	Total Fixed Wing Combat
	60	Modern Combat Aircraft
	30	Su-24D
	30	MiG-29
Iraq	353	Total Fixed Wing Combat
	81	Modern Combat Aircraft
	30	Su-20
	1	Su-24D
	12	Su-25
	38	Mirage F-1EQ5/200
	12	MiG-29
	15	MiG-25
	4	MiG-25R
Kuwait	76	Total Fixed Wing Combat
	40	F/A-18C/D
Oman	46	Total Fixed Wing Combat
	(17)	Jaguar (SO) Mark 1, T-2
Qatar	11	Total Fixed Wing Combat
	5	Mirage F-1EDA/DDA
	(12)	Mirage 2000-5 in delivery
Saudi Arabia	336	Total Fixed Wing Combat
	197	Modern Combat Aircraft
	58	Tornado IDS
	24	Tornado ADV
	95	F-15C/D
	15	F-15S
	5	E-3A
United Arab Emirates	108	Total Fixed Wing Combat
	45	Modern Combat Aircraft
	9	Mirage 2000E
	22	Mirage 2000EAD
	6	Mirage 2000DAD
	8	Mirage 2000RAD
	(72)	F-16C/D Block 60 on order

Note: Older aircraft with inferior avionics are not included. Supersonic flight performance is not regarded as more than a marginal measure of combat performance.
Source: Adapted by Anthony H. Cordesman from IISS, *Military Balance*.

Figure 7.3
Total Gulf Air Force and Air Defense Manpower: 1998

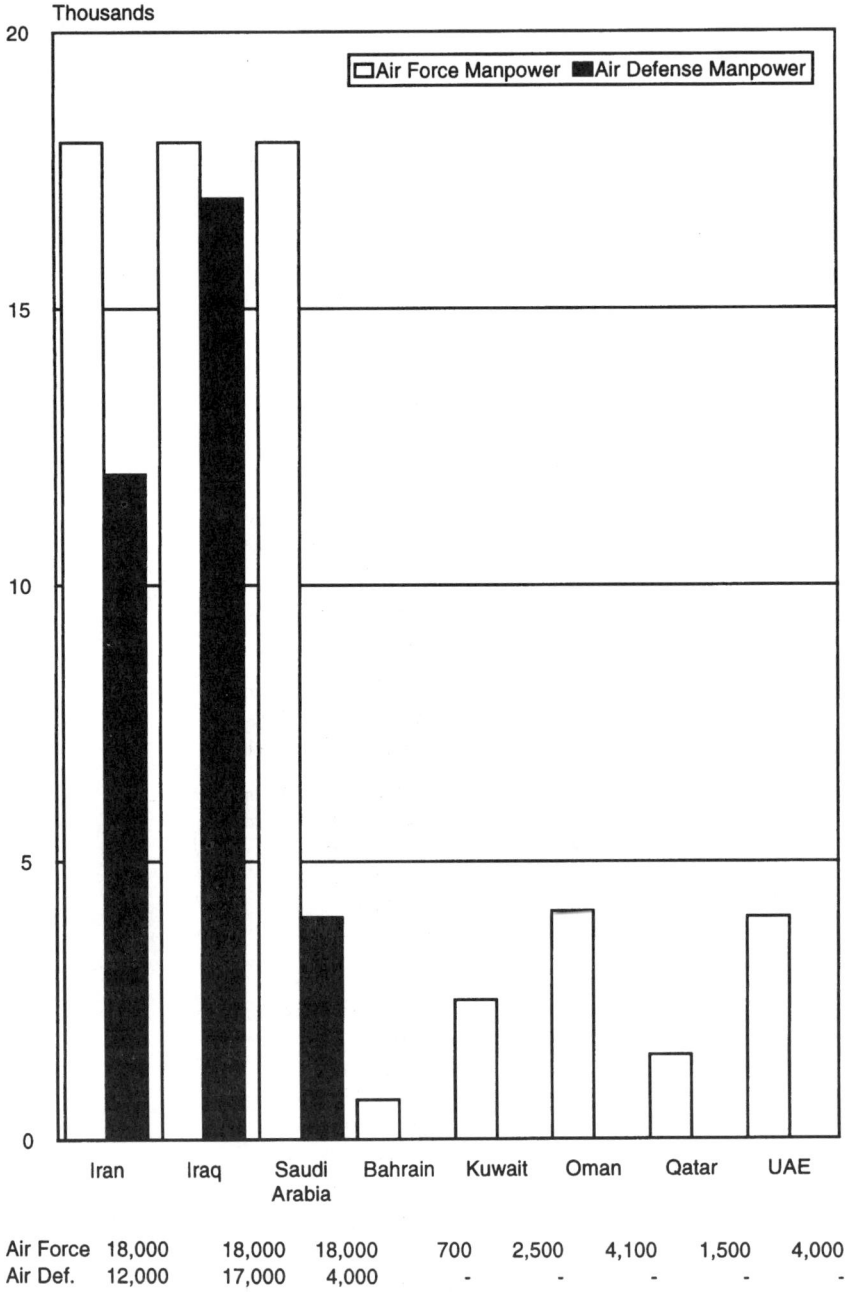

Sources: Estimated by Anthony H. Cordesman from various sources, and IISS, *Military Balance*.

Figure 7.4
Total Operational Combat Aircraft in Gulf Forces in 1990 versus 1998

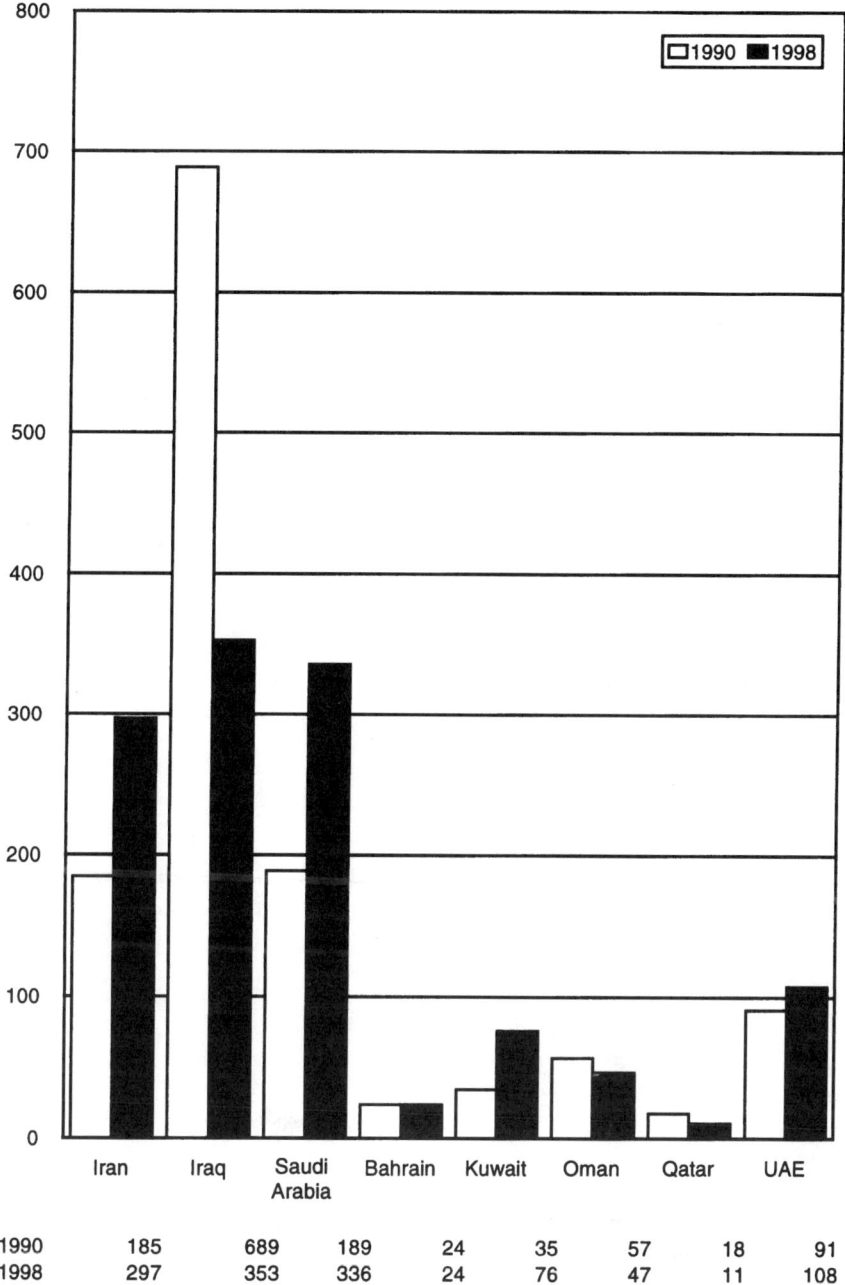

	Iran	Iraq	Saudi Arabia	Bahrain	Kuwait	Oman	Qatar	UAE
1990	185	689	189	24	35	57	18	91
1998	297	353	336	24	76	47	11	108

Note: Iran includes active forces in the Revolutionary Guards. Saudi Arabia includes active forces in the National Guard.

Sources: Adapted by Anthony H. Cordesman from various sources, and IISS, *Military Balance*.

Figure 7.5
High-Quality Combat Aircraft in Gulf Military Forces: 1998
(Includes Mirage F-1, Mirage 2000, F-15, F-16, F-18, Tornado, Su-20/22, Su-24, MiG 25/25R, MiG-29)

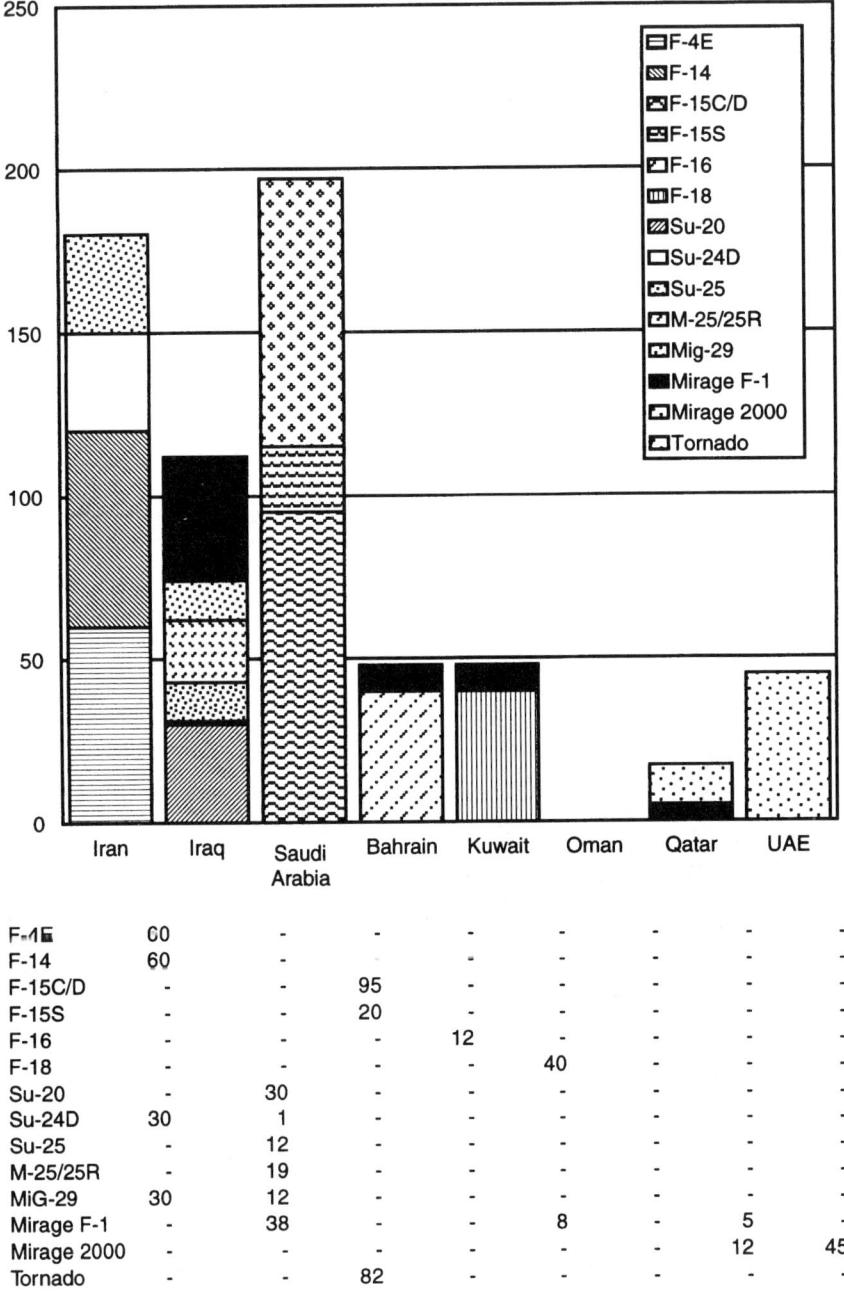

	Iran	Iraq	Saudi Arabia	Bahrain	Kuwait	Oman	Qatar	UAE
F-4E	60	-	-	-	-	-	-	-
F-14	60	-	-	-	-	-	-	-
F-15C/D	-	-	95	-	-	-	-	-
F-15S	-	-	20	-	-	-	-	-
F-16	-	-	-	12	-	-	-	-
F-18	-	-	-	-	40	-	-	-
Su-20	-	30	-	-	-	-	-	-
Su-24D	30	1	-	-	-	-	-	-
Su-25	-	12	-	-	-	-	-	-
M-25/25R	-	19	-	-	-	-	-	-
MiG-29	30	12	-	-	-	-	-	-
Mirage F-1	-	38	-	-	8	-	5	-
Mirage 2000	-	-	-	-	-	-	12	45
Tornado	-	-	82	-	-	-	-	-

Sources: Estimated by Anthony H. Cordesman from various sources, and IISS, *Military Balance*.

Figure 7.6
Gulf Attack Helicopters in 1998

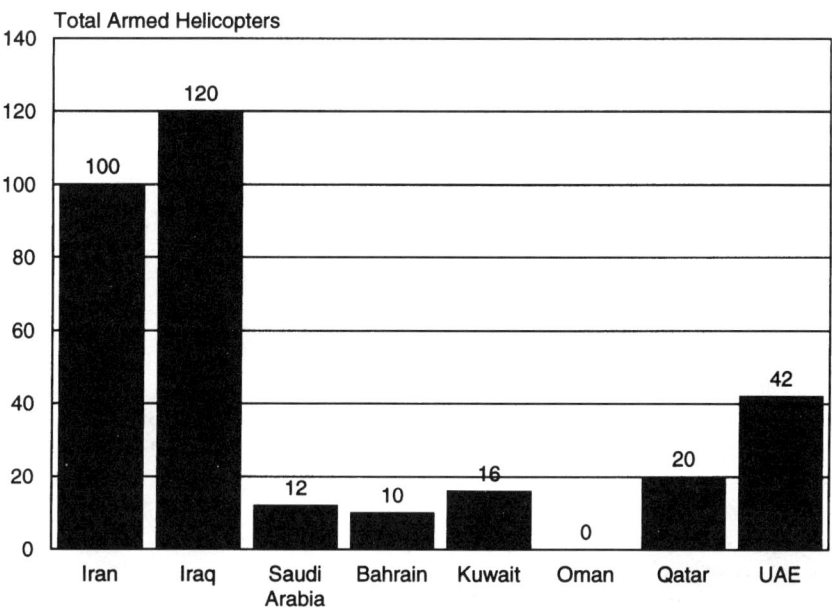

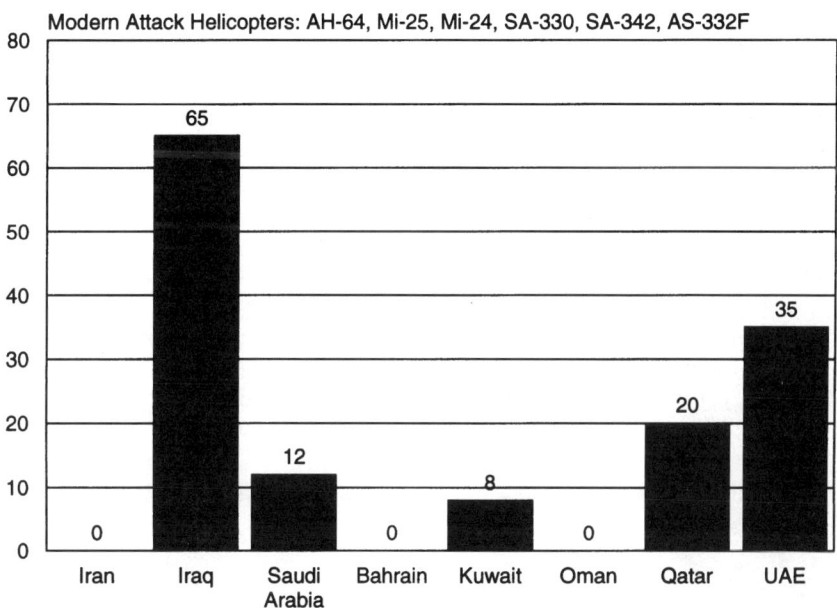

Source: Adapted by Anthony H. Cordesman from IISS, *Military Balance*.

Iran has modified its Standard SM-1 anti-ship missiles so that they can be delivered by its F-4Es.[5]

Most Iranian squadrons could perform both air defense and attack missions, regardless of their principal mission—although this was not true of Iran's F-14 (air defense) and Su-24 (strike/attack) units. Iran's F-14s have not been able to use their Phoenix air-to-air missiles since the early 1980s. Iran has claimed that it is modernizing its F-14s by equipping them with I-Hawk missiles adapted to the air-to-air role, but it is far from clear that this is the case or that such adaptations can have more than limited effectiveness.[6]

The Iranian air force had a small reconnaissance squadron with 3–8 RF-4Es, and possibly 5–10 additional RF-5EIIs. It operated five P-3Fs; maritime reconnaissance aircraft, one RC-130, and other intelligence/reconnaissance aircraft, along with large numbers of transports and helicopters. Iran also had five MiG-29s, 20–25 F-5Bs and F-5FIIs, five FT-7s, seven T-33s, and 26 Beech F-33A/Cs. Many were combat-capable, although the operational status of these aircraft is unclear.[7]

Iran has moderate airlift capabilities for a regional power. The Iranian air force's air transport assets included one tanker/transport squadron with 4 B-707s, and five transport squadrons with eight B-747Fs, 10 B-707s, one B-727, 18–19 C-130E/Hs, three Commander 690s, 12–15 F-27s, and 3–5 Falcon 20As. Its helicopter strength includes two AB-206As, 34–39 Bell 214Cs, and 3–5 CH-47 transport helicopters. As has been discussed earlier, the bulk of Iran's rotary wing assets were assigned to the land forces.

The IRGC also has some air elements, and its air branch has had an independent commander since 1992.[8] This commander originally was Brigadier General Mohammad Hossein Jalalai, who had served as Minister of Defense from 1985 to 1989. Jalalai became Deputy Chief of Staff of the entire armed forces for logistics, research, and industry on October 30, 1997, perhaps because he had played a major role in the development of Iran's indigenously made fighter and training aircraft. Jalalai was replaced by Brigadier General Mohammed Baqr Ghalibaf.[9]

It is not clear what combat formations exist within the IRGC, but the IRGC seems to operate Iran's 10 EMB-312 Tucanos.[10] It seems to operate many of Iran's 45 PC-7 trainers, as well as some Pakistani-made trainers at a training school near Mushhak, but this school may be run by the regular air force. It has also claimed to manufacture gliders for use in unconventional warfare. The IRGC has not recently expanded its combat air capabilities.[11]

Iran has large combat air bases at Mehrabad, Tabriz, Hamadan, Dezful, Bushehr, Shiraz, Isfahan, and Bandar Abbas. It has smaller bases in at least eleven other locations. Shiraz provides interceptor training and is the main base for transport aircraft.[12]

READINESS AND FORCE QUALITY

In spite of Iran's efforts, readiness and force quality remain major issues. The Iranian air force still has many qualitative weaknesses, and it is far from clear that its current rate of modernization can offset the aging of its Western-supplied aircraft and the qualitative improvements in US and Southern Gulf forces. The air force also faces serious problems in terms of sustainment, command and control, and training.

Problems in Maintaining and Sustaining US-Supplied Aircraft

Brigadier General Mansour Sattari, then Chief of Staff of the Iranian Air Force, claimed in 1994 that the air force had "reached self-sufficiency in all fields, including pilot training, missiles, radar, air defenses, maintenance and repair, manufacture of parts and basic repair of facilities.... We constantly patrol the international waters and have a watchful eye on the moves of foreign warships there.... If the foreigners pose any threat, we will meet them with all our might."[13]

These claims were little more than whistling in the dark. Many of Iran's operational aircraft have only limited operational capability. As few as 50% of Iran's US-supplied combat aircraft may be operational, and few of Iran's operational US-equipped squadrons can support sustained sortie rates higher than one per aircraft every three to four days.

An estimate by the US Office of Naval Intelligence indicated that Iran had only 175 operational combat aircraft in 1996. Roughly 44% of these aircraft were "second generation" aircraft like the Chinese F-7 and US F-5, 22% were "third generation" aircraft like the F-4 and F-14, and 34% were "fourth generation" aircraft like the Su-24 and MiG-29. The same estimate indicated that Iran's operational strength had only increased from 150 aircraft in 1985 to 175 in 1995, and that Iran's strength would drop to 125 aircraft in 2005.[14]

Furthermore, some US-supplied aircraft seem to lack the operational avionics necessary to fire air-to-air and air-to-surface missiles properly. For example, Iran has lost the capability to make use of most of the long-range air defense capabilities of the F-14. It has kept the plane flying by reverse-engineering critical parts, but its Phoenix missiles have not been operational since 1980, and efforts to adapt it to use other missiles have apparently failed.

Iran's overall track record in obtaining parts and spares for its US-supplied aircraft has been limited. Iran has had some successes, but failed in covert efforts, such as attempting to buy compressor blades for the F-5's engines in the UK and surplus F-5s from Vietnam.[15] In 1993, these problems led Defense Minister Akbar Torkan to state that,

Our equipment is mostly American: F-4, F-5, F-14 fighter jets. Our transport aircraft are also American: C-130s, Boeing 747s, and 707s. We have a very good fleet: 14 707s, 12

747s, and 53 C-130s. This should be enough to see us through the next 30 years.... We have 72 F-14s.... For closer support we have F-5 fighters and for deep strikes we have F-4 fighters. This is a very good configuration. We have 750 helicopters.... Unfortunately, because our fleet is mainly made up of American products, providing spares is very difficult.[16]

Pilot and Manpower Quality Problems

Iran has a severe pilot quality problem. Many of its US-trained pilots were purged at some point during the revolution. Its other US-trained pilots and ground-crew technicians are aging to the point where many should soon retire from service, and they have not had advanced air-to-air combat and air attack training for more than 15 years. While Iran practices more realistic individual intercept training using its US-supplied aircraft than Iraq, it fails to practice effective unit or force-wide tactics and has shown only limited capability to fly large numbers of sorties with its US-supplied aircraft on even a surge basis.

Ground crew training and proficiency generally seem mediocre—although the layout of Iranian air bases, aircraft storage and parking, the deployment of equipment for maintenance cycles, and the other physical signs of air unit activity is generally better organized than those of most Middle Eastern air forces.

Iran's Russian-made aircraft do not require radically different training methods, but there are major differences between the way in which the US and Russian air forces carry out pilot training, organize unit leadership and tactics, and deal with the problems of command, control, communications, computers, and intelligence (C^4I). Iran has almost certainly found it difficult to "deconflict" two such very different systems. The United States and Russia also have quite different maintenance systems, and most of the developing countries using Russian aircraft have encountered major problems in obtaining spare parts.

Dealing with the American "Revolution in Military Affairs"

The Iranian air force must also deal with the fact that its primary challenge now consists of the US and Saudi air forces, rather than a typical Third World air force like Iraq's. The US and Saudi air forces are high technology air forces that operate the AWACS airborne control system, have some of the most advanced electronic warfare and targeting systems in the world, and have full refueling capability. They use sophisticated, computer-aided aggressor training and have all of the range and training facilities for beyond-visual-range combat and stand-off attacks with air-to-surface munitions.

Iran has no airborne control system, although it may be able to use the radars on its F-14s to support other aircraft from the rear. Its overall C^4I system is a totally inadequate mix of different sensors, communications, and data processing systems. It has limited electronic warfare capabilities by US standards, although it may be seeking to acquire two Beriev A-50 Mainstay AEW aircraft, and it has converted some aircraft to provide a limited ELINT/SIGINT capability. It has limited refueling capabilities—although it has four B-707 tanker/transports and may have converted other transports. The Iranian air force lacks advanced training facilities and has only limited capability to conduct realistic training for beyond-visual-range combat and stand-off attacks with air-to-surface munitions.

THE MODERNIZATION OF IRANIAN AIR FORCES

There is considerable debate over exactly how many new aircraft Iran is obtaining from the People's Republic of China, from the former Soviet Union, and from other sources. There have been many reports that Iran plans large purchases of highly advanced combat aircraft and support systems, but few signs of such plans going forward. At the same time, the delivery of Russian-made aircraft is modernizing important aspects of Iran's combat air capabilities.

Chinese Aircraft

According to many experts, Iran imported 30 Xian F-7M fighters from the Chinese by mid-1993, out of a possible total order of 50–72, but it did not take further deliveries. As was the case in Pakistan, Iran found the F-7M to be inferior in performance and extremely difficult to maintain. The People's Republic of China also sold Iran PL-2 and PL-2A air-to-air missiles (Chinese copies of the Sidewinder) and PL-7 air-to-air missiles (Chinese copies of the Matra Magic R-550) with these aircraft.

A few experts believe that Iran made larger purchases of Chinese fighters, and that it took delivery of over 50 Chinese-made F-6 fighters between 1987 and mid-1992. These experts also believe that Iran had nearly 70 Chinese-made F-7s in operation by mid-1994. US experts believe that these estimates are incorrect and that the Iranian air force does not have the F-6 operational in combat units, although the IRGC may operate such.

Some other experts have reported that Iran is interested in buying up to 24 JH-7 (B-7) strike aircraft, for delivery of the CS-801K or CS-802 anti-ship missiles. Such a purchase would give Iran improved naval strike capability, but the WS9 turbofans in the JH-7 are said to be as difficult to maintain as those in the F-7, which require constant maintenance. This has led Xian to consider producing an engine licensed from Russia, such as the AL31F. It seems more likely that Iran will import the necessary missiles and avionics and modify its existing aircraft.[17]

Regardless of which estimate is correct, purchases of the F-7M will do little to affect the regional balance if it faces the modern, Western-supplied aircraft in the Gulf or US air units. The F-7M is a marginal copy of the MiG-21, with poor ground attack performance and limited air-to-air combat capability against first-line fighters of any potential opponent. It is also difficult to upgrade and overhaul.[18] What could be more significant are reports that Iran is considering major imports of the more advanced F-7 attack variant, F-8 fighter, Jian Hong 7 bomber, and/or F-10. The F-10 is a developmental fighter derived from the Israeli Lavi; if it is successful, it will be the first truly modern Chinese-made fighter.[19]

The MiG-29

Iran's new MiG-29s and Su-24s are far superior in quality to the aircraft it has obtained from the Chinese, and Iran's most important source of new aircraft has been Russia. Iran now has 30–35 MiG-29s, which are late-model MiG-29As or MiG-29Bs, and Iran has claimed to have given them refueling capability.[20] These aircraft are designed for forward area air superiority and escort missions, including deep penetration air-to-air combat. Their flight performance and flying qualities are excellent and are roughly equivalent to that of the best Western fighters.[21] They have relatively modern avionics and weapons and an advanced coherent pulse-Doppler radar with look-down/shoot-down capabilities that can detect a fighter-sized (2 square meter) target at a range of 130 kilometers (70 nautical miles), and track it at 70 kilometers (38 nautical miles).

The MiG-29 also has a track-while-scan range of 80 kilometers (44 nautical miles) against a 5 square meter target and is designed to operate with the radar off or in the passive mode, using ground-controlled intercept.[22] It has an infrared search and track system collimated with a laser range finder, a helmet-mounted sight, an internal electronic countermeasure system, an SPO-15 radar warning receiver, a modern inertial navigation, and the modern Odds Rod IFF. The range of the infrared search and track system is 15 kilometers (8.2 nautical miles) against an F-16-sized target. The maximum slant range of the laser is 14 kilometers (7.7 nautical miles), and its normal operating range is 8 kilometers (4.4 nautical miles).

The MiG-29 can carry up to six air-to-air missiles, a 30 mm gun, a wide mix of bombs, and 57 mm, 84 mm, and 240 mm air-to-ground rockets. A typical air combat load would include 250 rounds of 30 mm gun ammunition, 335 gallons of external fuel, four AA-8 Aphid infrared guided missiles, and two AA-10 Alamo radar-guided medium-range air-to-air missiles. Iran may also have acquired AA-8, AA-10, and AA-11 Archer air-to-air missiles from Russia.

The MiG-29 does, however, have a number of ergonomic problems. The cockpit frames and high cockpit sills limit visibility. The cockpit display is fussy and uses outdated dials and indicators similar to those of the F-4. There is only a medium angle heads-up display and only a partial hands-on system control. The CRT display is dated, and the cockpit is cramped. The helmet mounted sight allows the pilot to slave the radar, IRST, and heads up display (HUD) together for intercepts and covert attacks using off-boresight cueing, but the weapons computer and software supporting all combat operations are several generations behind those in fighters like the F-15C.[23] This makes it doubtful that even a well-trained MiG-29 pilot has the air-to-air combat capability of a well-trained pilot flying an F-16C/D, F-15C, F/A-18D, or Mirage 2000 in long range missile or beyond visual range combat, or in any form of combat when only the other side has the support of an AWACS-type aircraft.

The Su-24

The Su-24 is a twin seat, swing wing strike-attack aircraft that is roughly equivalent in terms of weight to the F-111, although it has nearly twice the thrust loading and about one-third more wing loading. The Su-24 can carry payloads of up to 25,000 pounds and operate on missions with a 1,300-kilometer radius when carrying 6,600 pounds of fuel. With a more typical 8,818 pound (4,000 kilogram) combat load, it has a mission radius of about 790 kilometers in the Lo-Lo-Lo profile, and 1,600 kilometers in the Lo-Hi-Lo profile. With extended range fuel tanks and airborne refueling by an aircraft like the F-14, the Su-24 can reach virtually any target in Iraq and the Southern Gulf.[24]

Although it is not clear what variant of the SU-24 has gone to Iran, it seems likely to be the Su-24D, which includes a sophisticated radar warning receiver, an improved electronic warfare suite, an improved terrain avoidance radar, a beam, satellite communications, an aerial refueling probe, and the ability to deliver electro-optical, laser, and radar-guided bombs and missiles.[25]

The Su-24D is an excellent platform for delivering air-to-surface missiles and biological, chemical, and nuclear weapons. The air-to-ground missiles it can carry include up to three AS-7 Kerry radio command guided missiles (5 kilometers range), one AS-9 Kyle anti-radiation missile with passive radar guidance and an active radar fuse (90 kilometers range), three AS-10 Karen passive laser-guided missiles with an active laser fuse (10 kilometers range), three AS-11 Kilter anti-radiation missiles with passive radar guidance and an active radar fuse (50 kilometers range), three AS-12 Kegler anti-radiation missiles with passive radar guidance and an active radar fuse (35 kilometers range), three AS-13 Kingposts, and three AS-14 Kedge semi-active laser-guided missiles with an active laser fuse (12 kilometers range). It can also carry demolition bombs, retarded bombs, cluster bombs, fuel air bombs, and chemical bombs. Some experts believe that Russia has supplied Iran with AS-10, As-11, AS-12, and possibly AS-14/AS-16 air-to-surface missiles.

Iran's purchase of Russian aircraft has the major additional benefit of enabling the Iranian air force to use some of the Iraqi aircraft that fled to Iran during the Gulf War. There is some question about the exact number of aircraft involved, and how many are flyable. Some sources report as few as 106 combat aircraft, but Iraq has officially claimed that they total 139. The author's estimate, based on conversations with various experts, is 24 Mirage F-1s, 22 Su-24s, 40 Su-22s, four Su-17/20s, seven Su-25s, four MiG-29s, seven MiG-23Ls, four MiG-23BNs, one MiG-23UB, and one Adnan. This is a total of 112 combat aircraft—the total usually counted by the IISS.

Iran's transport and support aircraft include two B-747s, one B-707, one B-

727, two B-737s, 14 IL-76s, two Dassault Falcon 20s, three Dassault Falcon 50s, one Lockheed Jetstar, one A-300, and five A-310s. This is a total of 31 aircraft.[26] Reports surfaced in 1996 that Iran had obtained Ukrainian aid in producing the Antonov An-140 at a factory in Isfahan. In September, 1997, Iran indicated that it had signed a contract to buy 10 Antonov An-74 transport jets and that it might coproduce the An-T74T-200. This would greatly improve Iran's airlift, since the An-74 can carry 10 tons of cargo for ranges over 1,500 kilometers, and it is used by the Russian military to operate from unimproved runways.[27]

Future Modernization

Iran has already begun to fly its Russian-supplied MiG-29s and Su-24s, and it has obtained Russian support at training facilities in Iran. Iran may have signed agreements that would give it a total of 48–50 MiG-29s, 36 Su-24, and the necessary support equipment.[28] Such deliveries would greatly improve Iranian capabilities. They would give Iran up to 90 additional combat aircraft, if it can continue to obtain suitable support from Russia, and there have been reports that Iran is also seeking to buy at least 24 long-range MiG-31 Foxhounds.

Iran seems to be absorbing all of Iraq's flyable MiG-29s, Su-24s, and possibly its Su-20/Su-22s into its force structure.[29] Ex-Foreign Minister Velayati stated in November, 1995 that Iran would not return the combat aircraft even if the UN lifted its sanctions on Iraq, and discussed the possible return of only 22 of the 31 civil aircraft.[30] Iran later indicated that it might return the aircraft if asked to do so by the UN Security Council, but it also indicated that it regarded them as part of its reparations claims for the Iran-Iraq War. In September, 1997, Iraqi Foreign Minister Kofi Annan stated that Iran still had 115 military aircraft and 33 civilian airliners and cargo aircraft. He protested that Iran had painted the Iraqi military aircraft in Iranian colors and integrated them into its force structure, and that 27 of the Iraqi civilian aircraft were in use by Iran's civil aviation or military transport command.[31]

Iran's ability to use all of the combat aircraft it has obtained from Iraq is uncertain. It probably cannot operate Iraqi Mirage F-1s effectively without French technical assistance, which currently seems highly unlikely. The 8–12 Iraqi MiG-23s are sufficiently low in capability so that Iran may be unwilling to pay for the training and logistic burden of adding this type to its inventory. The seven Su-25s are a more attractive option, since they are specially equipped for the close air support mission, but it would be very expensive for Iran to operate a force of only seven aircraft.

Iran is reported to have discussed buying Tu-22M3 (Tu-26) Backfire C bombers from Russia and other states of the former Soviet Union, as well as buying Su-25 close support aircraft, MiG-31 fighters, and Su-27 attack aircraft. Reports of Iranian efforts to buy the Tu-22M seem to be correct, and Iran evidently sought 10–15 such bombers—although the exact configuration it wanted is unclear. Unlike the obsolete Soviet Tu-16 and Tu-22—or the even more obsolete Chinese H-5 and H-6—the Tu-22M is a modern bomber with a maximum range near 2,500 miles, a good-range payload, adequate avionics, and a reasonable low altitude flight performance. Any Russian sale of such aircraft would significantly improve Iranian offensive capability.

Iran is also seeking to improve its capabilities by acquiring more advanced air ordnance, and it seems to be examining options for improving the engines and avionics of its existing aircraft. Iranian F-4Es test fired the C-801K air-to-ship missile in June, 1997—potentially giving Iran an important new air attack capability.[32] Iran has sought Russian aid in improving its jet engine overhaul and maintenance capability, and possibly in up-engining some of its US-supplied aircraft—although the real-world feasibility of such an effort seems dubious. Iran is also attempting to develop its own electronic warfare design and manufacturing capability—although its success is highly uncertain.[33]

Iran stated in September, 1997 that it was testing its own jet fighter, the Azarakhsh (Lightning). Brigadier General Arasteh, a deputy head of the General Staff of the Armed Forces (serving under Major General Ali Shahbazi, the joint chief of staff), had first announced in April, 1997 that the "production line of this aircraft will begin work in the near future." Shahbazi then announced on September 28, 1997, that one of the jet fighters participated in maneuvers near the city of Qom. He said the aircraft was called the Azarakhsh (Lightning), and that the prototype had begun flights in June.

The aircraft was said to have participated in bombing missions during a weeklong exercise called Zulfiqar, and to have dropped two 113-kilogram napalm bombs. Shahbazi said the aircraft had taken 11 years to develop and cost one-eighth of "similar types," but gave no technical details.[34] Iran had previously announced in November, 1987 that it was flying a prototype jet fighter, which was later identified as a Chinese F-7 assembled in Iran. This time, however, Iran claimed that the aircraft was largely Iranian in design and that Khamenei had awarded medals to its designers, Morteza Sanai and Morteza Satari.[35]

Officials in the Defense Industries Organization claimed that same month that Iran was going to start producing another fighter called the Owj (Zenith) and two trainers—a jet-powered Dorna (Lark) and propeller-driven Partsu (Swallow).[36]

THE WAR-FIGHTING CAPABILITIES OF IRANIAN AIR FORCES

There is no way to determine exactly how Iran assesses the recent lessons of the Gulf War and the trends in the "revolution in military affairs." It is clear from Iran's imports of combat aircraft and other technology that it is seeking to obtain first-line air defense and long-range strike fighters. Iran has also shown an interest in a wide range of modern C⁴I and electronic warfare technology and in modern air munitions. These are strong indicators that it would like to build a high technology air force.

Iran is slowly improving its capability for joint land-air and air-sea operations. For example, its Zulfiqar series of exercises in September, 1997 involved some 200,000 men from the regular army and the IRGC operating in an 1,800-square kilometer area, while the IRGC held another series of exercises in the Southern Gulf. The exercises involved heavy divisions, paratroops, and air force operations—some of which took place over the Strait of Hormuz. Iran claimed that 150 aircraft from eight bases were involved, and showed pictures of C-130s air dropping armor as well as troops. Iran aircraft participated in naval exercises in mid-October, 1997. Iran claimed these exercises involved aircraft and some 100 ships operating in a 60,000-square kilometer area. It also claimed to be using new stealth reconnaissance drones, submarines, helicopters, and IRGC speed boats, and to have tested a new surface-to-air missile with a range of 156 kilometers.[37]

Iranian exercises and statements provide strong indications that Iran would like to develop an advanced air defense system, the ability to operate effectively in long-range maritime patrol and attack missions, effective joint warfare capabilities, and strike/attack forces, with the ability to penetrate deep into Iraq, the Southern Gulf states, and other neighboring powers.

Iran's exercises, military literature, and procurement efforts also make it clear that its air planners understand the value of airborne early warning and C⁴I systems, the value of airborne intelligence and electronic warfare platforms, the value of RPVs, and the value of airborne refueling. Iran has even sought to create its own satellite program.[38] Further, the air force's efforts at sheltering and dispersal indicate that it understands the vulnerability of modern air facilities and the stand-off attack capabilities of advanced air forces like those of the United States.

Improving an Equipment-Limited Force

At the same time, Iran clearly recognizes that many aspects of its air force modernization are equipment limited, and that it cannot move forward without access to new aircraft, critical weapons, and C⁴I systems. In spite of their occasional public denials, Iran's leaders also seem to fully understand that the Iranian air force currently has problems in obtaining enough modern aircraft to maintain even its current combat air strength.

Table 4.3 has shown that Iran faces serious problems in keeping its US-supplied aircraft operational much beyond the late 1990s, which may explain a growing list of crashes and accidents in recent years.[39] Iran also needs to either recondition and upgrade its RF-4Es and RC-130E/Hs, or acquire modern reconnaissance and intelligence aircraft. Furthermore, it needs to recondition and improve the sensors and weapons on the army's AB-206B and AH-1J attack helicopters, as well as recondition its force of transport helicopters. It needs spares, support organization, and training to achieve dramatic improvements in sortie rates and sustainability. Additional air bases, for the purpose of reducing the air force's vulnerability through greater aircraft dispersal are also necessary. Iran may well find it difficult to convert to Russian fighters fast enough to offset its losses of US aircraft.

Building Iranian fighters is a high-risk proposition that may simply end in wasting resources, and even if Iran imports more modern fighters—like MiG-29s, Su-24s, Su-27s, Su-25s, and MiG-31s—there is a wide range of other areas where it needs to improve its equipment and technology. These areas include acquiring some form of airborne warning and air control system (AWACS), modern air-to-air and air-to-surface missiles, remotely piloted vehicles (RPVs), improved electronic countermeasure systems, and airborne refueling technology. Iran also needs support in repairing and reconditioning some of its captured Iraqi fighters, and in finding the technology and software to integrate its fighters into an effective air control and warning system and integrating their operations with those of its ground-based air defense system.

Going Beyond the "Glitter Factor"

What is less clear is how far the Iranian air force planners look beyond the "glitter factor" of modern weapons and technology and properly understand the other aspects of the "revolution in military affairs." Most air forces in the developing world can read a catalog and develop a shopping list. Few give advanced training and sustainability the priority it deserves. Few understand the problems inherent in scaling up from planning and executing individual sorties and small air unit operations to the effective force-wide use of air power. It is much easier to talk about integrating fighter and land-based air defense with survivable C^4I links in the face of a sophisticated air defense suppression capability than it is to achieve the necessary operational capabilities, and no developing nation to date has shown the force management and systems integration capabilities necessary to do so.

Like all other Gulf air forces—and most Third World air forces—the Iranian air force is still a collection of small individual formations, rather than a unified force. It lacks cohesive air battle tactics, mission planning, and C^4I/BM organization. It trains on a formation level, and it rarely operates even as integrated squadrons. It does conduct joint training with the other services, but in the form of limited sorties in set-piece exercises. In many of these exercises, the Iranian air force has indicated it lacks the force cohesion and training to operate in the air defense mode or attack mode, even in local operations.

The Iranian air force's maintenance and conversion problems are likely to seriously limit its combat endurance and ability to effectively mass its forces. There is little evidence that Iran can currently sustain high sortie rates for more than one-third to one-half of its combat aircraft for more than a matter of days.

More generally, the Iranian air force is still organized to fight at the squadron level. In spite of recent exercises, the Air force only seems to be making slow progress in organizing to fight effectively on a force-wide basis, and to use mass and technology effectively in air defense, close air support, or interdiction missions. Iran also lacks the training, advanced training facilities, and sensors to compete with the West in beyond-visual-range and dog-fight combat.

Current Contingency Capabilities

At the same time, the Iranian air force has strengths which give it a moderate war-fighting capability against most of its neighbors. For all of its problems, the Iranian air force is not limited to the highly individualized "knights of the air," or World War I type training, characteristic of some Southern Gulf air forces. It has more effective force-on-force capabilities than any Gulf air force except the Royal Saudi Air Force, and it has steadily improved its air combat and exercise training since the end of the Gulf War. These exercises include the Raad or Thunder series, the ninth version of which was held in September, 1997. It has conducted increasingly larger and more realistic joint exercises with land forces, land-based air defense forces, and naval forces. Its annual Pirouzi series of air-naval exercises also indicate that the Iranian air force would now be considerably more effective in supporting naval and amphibious operations than in the early 1990s, as do the recent naval warfare exercises of the IRGC like the Tariq-o Qods exercise of April, 1997.[40]

Unless the Southern Gulf air forces were on alert and operated under the central coordination of US and/or Saudi command, the Iranian air force might be able to dominate the northern coast of the Gulf, and most of the waters of the lower Gulf. Unless it met major US or Saudi resistance, the Iranian air force could selectively attack shipping in the Gulf and assist Iranian naval forces in their operations.

The Iranian air force is strong enough to deter offensive strikes from any Southern Gulf air force, except for the Saudi air force. It can strike using precision-guided weapons, chemical weapons, and possibly biological weapons. It can probably penetrate the air space of all Southern Gulf countries, except Saudi Arabia, at least to the extent of conducting selective slash-and-run attacks on key military depots or bases. It might well be able to execute at least one successful mass surprise attack on a key Saudi target before the Saudi air force could fully organize its air defenses, although much would depend on the activity of the Saudi E-3A force and the readiness of Saudi F-15Cs.

The Iranian air force has no foreseeable near to mid-term hope of challenging a combination of US, British, and Saudi air power. The Iranian Air Force could, however, deploy quickly to a friendly air base in the Southern Gulf—in the event of a coup or other change in the political posture of that state—although it would take several weeks for Iran to deploy enough support equipment and stocks to support more than limited squadron-sized operations from such a base.

It could also assist Iran's land forces in any new fighting with Iraq. Iran might not be able to win air superiority over the Iranian border area, but it could probably provide significant air cover and air support capability in selected sectors of the front in spite of Iraqi resistance. It could do a much better job of defending Iranian territory than it did during the Iran-Iraq War, and it could inflict significant damage on the camps and bases of the People's Mujahideen and hostile Kurdish movements.

Iran could not dominate the skies along the Turkish border, or sustain more than a limited number of long-range strikes against Turkey before the Turkish air force won air superiority. While the Iranian air force could not compete with the Turkish or Pakistani air forces, it might be able to fly combat support and offensive missions over the territory of Azerbaijan, or the other former Soviet republics near the Iranian border. Such operations would, however, have to be squadron sized, and Iran could only fly relatively low sortie rates. The Iranian air force could operate successfully against the air forces of the other FSU states, and would face little meaningful opposition from the remnants of the Afghan air force.

Future Capabilities

The future capabilities of the Iranian air force are difficult to estimate, and much will depend on the rate of improvement in Southern Gulf forces—particularly Saudi Arabia, on the size and availability of US air capabilities, and on the relative rate of build-up by the Iraqi air force. The Iranian air force and land-based air defense force are likely to expand to around 35,000 men by the years 2000–2005, but it is unclear whether the air force will increase its total inventory much above 300 aircraft. At some point in the near future, Iran must make a clear decision between trying to maintain a hybrid air force and standardizing on Russian aircraft. Continued reliance on aging US aircraft presents obvious risks, and there are no near-term prospects that the United States will relax its constraints on the sale of parts and new equipment.

The Iranian air force is going to need to replace its 4/55–60 F-4D/Es (four squadrons/55–60 aircraft), 4/60 F-5E/FIIs, 4/60–65 F-14s, and 1/25–30 F-7Ms no later than 2010, and there is little prospect that Iran could rebuild its US-supplied fighters without direct US support. It also needs to replace its 5–10 RF-5EIIs, 3–8 RF-4Es, and probably its five P-3Fs, and its RC-130s, with more modern intelligence and reconnaissance aircraft.

The most logical replacements of these US aircraft would be to seek something like 150 MiG-29s, or some more advanced Russian dual-role fighters, and over 100 Su-24s, or some other advanced Russian strike aircraft. Iran has already shown an interest in such purchases and it attempted to buy some 21 surplus MiG-29s from Moldova in the summer of 1997.[41] This purchase was preempted by the United States, but would have included one MiG-29B, six MiG-29As, and 14 new-model MiG-29Cs, plus some 100 modern AA-11 Archer air-to-air missiles, and AA-2s, AA-8s, and AA-10s.[42]

At the same time, Iran has reason to examine other types of Russian aircraft like the Su-25 close support aircraft, MiG-31 fighters, and Su-27 attack aircraft, and to seek advanced Russian reconnaissance and intelligence aircraft. An Iranian air force based on Russian attack aircraft like the Su-24 and Su-27, close support aircraft like the Su-25, Tu-22M bombers, advanced Russian air-to-surface weapons like the AS-9, AS-10, and AS-14, air defense aircraft like the MiG-29 and MiG-31, and air-to-air missiles like the AA-8, AA-10, and AA-11 would have the weaponry and technology to become a major air power by Gulf standards.

However, it would take Iran 5–8 years to obtain such aircraft and convert them into an effective force. Such a program would be extremely costly, and it would require a major change in Russian arms sales policies. Iran cannot turn to states like China because they cannot supply the necessary advanced fighters and other equipment and technology. Unless Iran's regime changes radically in character, it is unlikely to get significant sales from Britain, France, and Germany—the only European states capable of selling it the systems it needs.

It also will not be enough for Iran to simply purchase the appropriate advanced fighters, attack aircraft, and reconnaissance aircraft. If the Iranian air force is to compete with the US and Saudi air forces, it must develop the C^{4}I capabilities and battle management systems to fight effectively on a force-wide basis in large-scale battle. It must develop all of the major capabilities that now shape modern air power, and this means AWACS-like aircraft, advanced beyond-visual-range missiles and combat capabilities, advanced stand-off air attack ordnance, a new C^{4}I/battle management system, much more advanced electronic warfare capabilities, and all the related training, sustainment, and maintenance capabilities. Russia could still prove to be a problem, even if it did change its arms sales policies. As nations like India have learned to their cost, Russia has so far failed to provide any client with the associated equipment, training, and technical support to fight effectively as a coherent modern air force or adequate aid in advanced air combat and air-to-ground training.

NOTES

1. In addition to the general sources on Iranian force strength referenced in this section, this analysis draws on the following: Andrew Rathmell, *The Changing Military Balance in the Gulf*, London, Royal United Services Institute, Whitehall Papers 38, 1996; Edward B. Atkenson, *The Powder Keg*, Falls Church, NOVA Publications, 1996; Geoffery Kemp and Robert E. Harkavy, *Strategic Geography and the Changing Middle East*, Washington, Carnegie Endowment/Brookings, 1997; USCENTCOM, *Atlas, 1996*, MacDill Air Force Base, USCENTCOM, 1997; *Armed Forces Journal*, March, 1992, pp. 26–27; *Defense Electronics*, March, 1992, p. 16; *Inside the Air Force*, February 28, 1992, p. 1; Dr. Andrew Rathmell, "Iran's Rearmament: How Great a Threat?" *Jane's Intelligence Review*, July, 1994, pp. 317–322; Armed Forces (UK), May, 1989, pp. 206–209; *Jane's Sentinel: The Gulf States, 1997*; London, Jane's Publishing 1997; Michael Eisenstadt, *Iranian Military Power*, Washington, Washington Institute, 1996; *Jane's Air-Launched Weapons* (CD-ROM); *Jane's Aircraft Upgrades* (1997–1998); *Jane's Avionics*

(1997–1998); *Jane's All the World's Aircraft* (1997–1998); *Jane's World Air Forces* (binder, April, 1997); *Jane's Land-Based Air Defense, 1997–1998* (CD-ROM); *Jane's Air-Launched Weapons* (binder); *Jane's Radar and Electronic Warfare Systems* (CD-ROM); *Jane's Military Communications, 1997–98*; *Jane's Unmanned Aerial Vehicles and Targets* (binder).

2. Dr. Anoushiravan Ehteshami, "The Armed Forces of the Islamic Republic of Iran," *Jane's Intelligence Review*, February, 1993, pp. 76–79; ISSN, *Military Balance, 1997–1998*, "Iran"; *Jane's Sentinel: The Gulf States, 1997*, "Iran." Another source indicates that the Iranian air force is based principally at Bandar Abbas, Bushehr, Dezful, Doshan, Tehran (Tapeh, Ghaleh Morghi, Mehrabad), Hamadan, Isfahan, Shiraz, Tabriz, and Zahedan. Its fighter attack units are based at Bandar Abbas, Bushehr, Dezful, Mehrabad, Hamadan, and Tabriz. Its air defense units are based at Doshan, Tapeh, Mehrabad, and Shiraz.

3. Interviews and USCENTCOM, *Atlas, 1996*, MacDill Air Force Base, USCENTCOM, 1997, pp. 14–15.

4. The range of aircraft numbers shown reflects the broad uncertainties affecting the number of Iran's aircraft, which are operational in any realistic sense. Many aircraft counted, however, cannot engage in sustained combat sorties in an extended air campaign. The numbers are drawn largely from interviews; *Jane's Intelligence Review*, Special Report No. 6, May, 1995; *Jane's Sentinel: The Gulf States, 1997*, "Iran," the IISS, *Military Balance, 1997–1998*, "Iran"; Andrew Rathmell, *The Changing Military Balance in the Gulf*, London, Royal United Services Institute, Whitehall Papers 38, 1996; Dr. Andrew Rathmell, "Iran's Rearmament: How Great a Threat?" *Jane's Intelligence Review*, July, 1994, pp. 317–322; *Jane's World Air Forces* (CD-ROM).

5. *Jane's Defense Weekly*, April 29, 1998, p. 17.

6. *Wall Street Journal*, February 10, 1995, p. 19; *Washington Times*, February 10, 1995, p. A-19.

7. Reports that Iran has some Chinese F-6 trainers in inventory are not correct. Based on interviews with British, Israeli, and US experts, and Anthony H. Cordesman, *Iran and Iraq: The Threat from the Northern Gulf*, Boulder, Westview, 1994; Anthony H. Cordesman and Ahmed S. Hashim, *Iran: Dilemmas of Dual Containment*, Boulder, Westview, 1997; IISS, *Military Balance, 1997–1998*, "Iran"; *Jane's Sentinel: The Gulf States, 1997*, "Iran"; USNI Data Base; Military Technology, *World Defense Almanac: The Balance of Military Power*, Vol. XVII, Issue 1–1993, ISSN 0722–3226, pp. 139–142; Ahmed Hashim, "The Crisis of the Iranian State," Adelphi Paper 296, London, IISS, Oxford, July, 1995, pp. 7–30 and 50–70; Andrew Rathmell, *The Changing Military Balance in the Gulf*, London, RUSI, Whitehall Papers 38, 1996, pp. 9–23; Michael Eisenstadt, *Iranian Military Power, Capabilities, and Intentions*, Washington, Washington Institute, 1996, pp. 9–65; Anoushiravan Ehteshami, "Iran Strives to Regain Military Might," *International Defense Review*, 7/1996, pp. 22–26; Anoushiravan Ehteshami, "Iran's National Strategy," *International Defense Review*, 4/1994, pp. 29–37; and working data from the Jaffee Center for Strategic Studies. US and Israeli experts do not confirm reports that Iran has ordered and taken delivery on 12 TU-22M Backfire bombers. There are some indications that it may have discussed such orders with the USSR.

8. *Jane's Sentinel: The Gulf States, 1997*, "Iran."

9. *Jane's Defense Weekly*, November 12, 1997, p. 30.

10. Reports that the IRGC is operating F-7 fighters do not seem to be correct.

11. Reuters, June 12, 1996, 17:33.

12. Dr. Anoushiravan Ehteshami, "The Armed Forces of the Islamic Republic of Iran," *Jane's Intelligence Review*, February, 1993, pp. 76–79; IISS, *Military Balance, 1997–1998*, "Iran"; *Jane's Sentinel: The Gulf States, 1997*, "Iran." Another source indicates that the Iranian air force is based principally at Bandar Abbas, Bushehr, Dezful, Doshan, Tehran (Tapeh, Ghaleh Morghi, Mehrabad), Hamadan, Isfahan, Shiraz, Tabriz, and Zahedan. Its fighter attack units are based at Bandar Abbas, Bushehr, Dezful, Mehrabad, Hamadan, and Tabriz. Its air defense units are based at Doshan, Tapeh, Mehrabad, and Shiraz.

13. *Philadelphia Inquirer*, February 5, 1994, p. A-18.

14. Office of Naval Intelligence, *Worldwide Challenges to Naval Strike Warfare*, Washington, Department of the Navy, January, 1996, p. 31.

15. Based on interviews with British, Israeli, and US experts. *Washington Times*, January 16, 1992, p. G-4; *Washington Post*, February 1, 1992, p. A1, February 2, 1992, pp. A1 and A25, February 5, p. A-19; *Financial Times*, February 6, 1992, p. 4; *Christian Science Monitor*, February 6, 1992, p. 19; *Defense News*, February 17, 1992, p. 1; *Flight International*, February 17–23, 1992, p. 4.

16. See *London Financial Times*, February 8, 1993, p. 4. Northrop helped Iran set up an Iran Aircraft Industries in 1970, but this virtually ceased operation in 1979.

17. *International Defense Review*, 6/1997, p. 17.

18. One source indicates that Iran is modifying its F-7M fighters to use Western avionics at the old Iranian Aircraft Industries facility, but such modification efforts have had little value in other countries.

19. *Defense News*, March 28, 1994, p. 38.

20. Executive News Service, August 8, 1995, 0826; Associated Press, August 8, 1995, 1456.

21. Richard Pawloski, *Changes in Threat Air Combat Doctrine and Force Structure, 24th Edition*, General Dynamics DWIC-91, Fort Worth Division, February, 1992, pp. I-85 to I-117.

22. Rostislav Belyakov and Nikolai Buntin, "The MiG 29M Light Multi-role Fighter," *Military Technology*, 8/94, pp. 41–44; Richard Pawloski, *Changes in Threat Air Combat Doctrine and Force Structure, 24th Edition*, General Dynamics DWIC-91, Fort Worth Division, February, 1992, pp. I-85 to I-117.

23. Richard Pawloski, *Changes in Threat Air Combat Doctrine and Force Structure, 24th Edition*, General Dynamics DWIC-91, Fort Worth Division, February, 1992, pp. I-85 to I-117.

24. *Aviation Week and Space Technology*, April 10, 1989, pp. 19–20; *New York Times*, April 5, 1989, September 7, 1989; *Washington Times*, January 16, 1989; *FBIS/NES*, April 10, 1989.

25. The Su-24 has a wing area of 575 square feet, an empty weight of 41,845 pounds, carries 3,385 gallons or 22,000 pounds of fuel, has a takeoff weight of 871,570 pounds, with bombs and two external fuel tanks, carries 2,800 gallons or 18,200 pounds of external fuel, has a combat thrust-to-weight ratio of 1.02, a combat wing loading of 96 pounds per square foot, and a maximum load factor of 7.5G. *Jane's Soviet Intelligence Review*, July, 1990, pp. 298–300; *Jane's Defense Weekly*, June 25, 1985, pp. 1226–1227; and Richard Pawloski, *Changes in Threat Air Combat Doctrine and Force Structure, 24th Edition*, General Dynamics DWIC-91, Fort Worth Division, February, 1992, pp. I-65 and I-110 to 1–117.

26. Based on interviews with British, Israeli, and US experts, and Anthony H. Cor-

desman, *Iran and Iraq: The Threat from the Northern Gulf*, Boulder, Westview, 1994; IISS, Anthony H. Cordesman and Ahmed S. Hashim, *Iran: Dilemmas of Dual Containment*, Boulder, Westview, 1997; *Military Balance, 1997–1998*, "Iran"; *Jane's Sentinel: The Gulf States, 1997*, "Iran"; USNI Data Base, Military Technology, *World Defense Almanac: The Balance of Military Power*, Vol. XVII, Issue 1–1993, ISSN 0722–3226, pp. 139–142; and working data from the Jaffee Center for Strategic Studies; *Jane's Defense Weekly*, November 18, 1995, p. 16; Ahmed Hashim, "The Crisis of the Iranian State," Adelphi Paper 296, London, IISS, Oxford, July, 1995, pp. 7–30 and 50–70; Andrew Rathmell, *The Changing Military Balance in the Gulf*, London, RUSI, Whitehall Papers 38, 1996, pp. 9–23; Michael Eisenstadt, *Iranian Military Power, Capabilities, and Intentions*, Washington, Washington Institute, 1996, pp. 9–65; Anoushiravan Ehteshami, "Iran Strives to Regain Military Might," *International Defense Review*, 7/1996, pp. 22–26.

27. *Jane's Defense Weekly*, October 8, 1997, p. 30; *Iran Focus*, October, 1997, p. 5.

28. *Jane's Intelligence Review*, Special Report No. 6, May, 1995, p. 23; *Washington Times*, January 16, 1992, p. G-4; *Washington Post*, February 1, 1992, p. A1, February 2, 1992, pp. A1 and A25, February 5, p. A-19; *Financial Times*, February 6, 1992, p. 4; *Christian Science Monitor*, February 6, 1992, p. 19; *Defense News*, February 17, 1992, p. 1; *Jane's Defense Weekly*, February 1, 1992, p. 159.

29. *Jane's Intelligence Review*, Special Report No. 6, May, 1995, p. 23.

30. *Jane's Defense Weekly*, November 18, 1995, p. 16.

31. *The Estimate*, September 26, 1997, p. 4.

32. *Jane's Defense Weekly*, June 25, 1997, p. 3; Associated Press, June 17, 1997, 1751; United Press, June 17, 1997, 0428; *International Defense Review*, 6/1996, p. 17.

33. *Defense News*, June 2, 1997, pp. 3, 35.

34. *Jane's Defense Weekly*, October 8, 1997, p. 30, November 12, 1997, p. 30; *Iran Focus*, October, 1997, p. 5.

35. *Jane's Defense Weekly*, October 8, 1997, p. 30, *Iran Focus*, October, 1997, p. 5.

36. *Jane's Defense Weekly*, October 8, 1997, p. 30; *Iran Focus*, October, 1997, p. 5.

37. *Washington Times*, October 11, 1997, p. A-6; *Jane's Defense Weekly*, October 1, 1997, p. 19; Reuters, September 28, 1997, 0417, October 6, 1997, 1600.

38. *Jane's Defense Weekly*, September 4, 1996, p. 4.

39. *Jane's Defense Weekly*, March 26, 1997, p. 15.

40. IRNA, April 21, 1997, May 2, 1997; Iranian TV, April 26, 1997; *Jane's Defense Weekly*, April 23, 1997, p. 19, April 30, 1997, p. 6, June 24, 1995, p. 5, November 6, 1996, p. 23, June 25, 1997, p. 14; *Washington Times*, May 4, 1997, p. A7; May 12, 1997, p. A-13; Reuters, April 23, 1997, 0818, May 7, 1997, 0452, July 3, 1997, 0452, July 9, 1997, 1655; *Washington Post*, April 30, 1997, p. 6; April 23, 1997, p. 19, April 30, 1997, p. 6, June 30, 1997, p. A-20; Associated Press, June 30, 1996, 0629; May 7, 1997, 0452, July 3, 1997, 0452, July 9, 1997, 1655.

41. Moldova had inherited the MiG-29s, which formerly equipped the 86th Fighter Regiment of the Soviet Navy and which were located at Makuleshty Air Base. Moldova was attempting to sell its fighters and use the earnings to buy helicopters.

42. Department of Defense, *Fact Sheet*, November 4, 1997; *Washington Post*, November 5, 1997, p. A-23; *Jane's Defense Weekly*, November 12, 1997, p. 18.

Chapter 8

Iranian Ground-Based Air Defenses

Iran's ground-based air defenses play a critical role in shaping Iran's ability to defend against the kind of air offensive the UN Coalition conducted against Iraq during Desert Storm, and to defend its navy, off-shore facilities, islands, and coastline. Iran has recognized this, and it has steadily attempted to improve its overall air defense system and coverage of its Gulf coast ever since the "tanker war" of 1987–1988.

It has intensified these efforts since the mid-1990s, as part of its growing fear of US attack. Iran's efforts to improve its ground-based defenses have probably been further reinforced by the fact that Iran has no near-term prospect of acquiring an airborne defense platform similar to the E-3A airborne warning and air control system (AWACS) operated by the Saudi and US air forces, or matching the West in airborne electronic warfare capabilities.[1]

So far, Iran has had only limited success. It has acquired older Soviet and Chinese surface-to-air missiles and some better radar and C^{4}I equipment, and it has improved its electronic warfare systems. These advances have improved its deterrent and defense capabilities against Iraq and the Southern Gulf states.

Such improvements, however, have done little to give it the capability to defend key targets against US cruise missiles and stealth strike aircraft, or to defend against a US air defense suppression attack that made full use of such American assets as modern electronic warfare systems, anti-radiation missiles, and stand-off missiles. Iran's land-based air defenses are unlikely to give its military planners and political leaders much confidence that they could deter or defend against modern air power.

STRENGTH AND ORGANIZATION

Iran seemed to have assigned about 12,000–15,000 men to land-based air defense functions in 1998, including at least 8,000 regulars and 4,000 IRGC personnel. It is not possible to distinguish clearly between the major air defense weapons holdings of the regular air force and the IRGC, but the air force appeared to operate most major surface-to-air missile systems. The relative strength of Iran's land-based air defenses is shown in Table 8.1, and total holdings seem to have included 30 Improved Hawk fire units (12 battalions/150+ launchers), 45–55 SA-2 and HQ-2J/23 (CSA-1) launchers (Chinese-made equivalents of the SA-2), and possibly 25 SA-6 launchers. The air force also had three Soviet-made long-range SA-5 units with a total of 10–15 launchers—enough for six sites.

Iran's holdings of lighter air defense weapons included five Rapier squadrons with 30 Rapier fire units, 5–10 Chinese FM-80 launchers, 10–15 Tigercat fire units, and a few RBS-70s. Iran also holds large numbers of manportable SA-7s, HN-5s, and SA-14s, plus about 2,000 anti-aircraft guns—including some Vulcans and 50–60 radar-guided and self-propelled ZSU-23-4 weapons.[2] Reports that Iran also has SA-10s or SA-12s are not correct.

It is not clear which of these lighter air defense weapons were operated by the army, the IRGC, or the air force. The IRGC clearly had larger numbers of manportable surface-to-air launchers, including some Stingers, which it had obtained from Afghanistan. It almost certainly had a number of other light air defense guns as well.

DEPLOYMENTS AND CAPABILITIES

During the Iran-Iraq War, Iran's major surface-to-air missiles were redeployed to cover the Iraqi border, its major cities, and its ports in the Gulf. There are no authoritative data on how Iran deployed these air defenses, but Iran seems to have deployed its new SA-5s to cover its major ports, oil facilities, and Tehran. It seems to have concentrated its Improved Hawks and Soviet and Chinese-made SA-2s around Tehran, Isfahan, Shiraz, Bandar Abbas, Kharg Island, Bushehr, Bandar Khomeini, Ahwaz, Dezful, Kermanshah, Hamadan, and Tabriz, although some I-Hawks seem to have been deployed on Abu Musa and the Tunbs.

Since that time, Iran's air defense forces have steadily increased the number of surface-to-air missile sites along the Gulf coast and on islands in the Gulf. Iran had only three major (Hawk, SA-6, SA-5) missile sites in 1992. It had ten to twelve major sites in 1997, although these sites are still too widely spaced to provide more than limited air defense for key bases and facilities, and many lack the missile launcher strength to be fully effective. This is particularly true of Iran's SA-5 sites, which provide long-range medium-to-high altitude coverage

Table 8.1
Gulf Land-Based Air Defense Systems

Country	Major SAM	Light SAM	AA Guns
Bahrain	None	40+ RBS-70 18 Stinger 7 Crotale	12 Oerlikon 35 mm 12 L/70 40 mm
Iran	12/150 I Hawk 3/? SA-5 45 HQ-2J (SA-2) ? SA-2 15 Tigercat	SA-7 HN-5 30 Rapier FM-80 (Ch Crotale) Type 55	1,700 guns ZU-23, ZSU-23-4, ZSU-57-2, KS-19 ZPU-2/4, M-1939
Iraq	SA-2 SA-3 SA-6	Roland SA-7 SA-8 SA-9 SA-13 SA-14, SA-16	5,500 guns ZSU-23-4 23 mm, M-1939 37 mm, ZSU-57-2 SP, 57 mm 85 mm, 100 mm, 130 mm
Kuwait	4/24 I Hawk 4/16 Patriot	6/12 Aspede	6/2X35 mm Oerlikon
Oman	None	Blowpipe 34 SA-7 28 Javelin 28 Rapier	2 VAB/VD 20 mm 4 ZU-23-2 23 mm 12 L-60 40 mm
Qatar	None	Blowpipe 12 Stinger 9 Roland	?
Saudi Arabia	128 I Hawk ? Patriot	Crotale Stinger 500 Redeye 68 Shahine mobile 40 Crotale 73 Shahine static	92 M-163 Vulcan 20 mm 50 AMX-30SA 30 mm 128 35 mm guns 150 L-70 40 mm (in store)
United Arab Emirates	5 I Hawk Bty.	20+ Blowpipe 10 SA-16 12 Rapier 9 Crotale 13 RBS-70 100 Mistral	48 M-3VDA 20 mm SP 20 GCF-BM2 30 mm

Source: Estimated by Anthony H. Cordesman.

of key coastal installations. Too few launchers are scattered over too wide an area to prevent relatively rapid suppression.[3]

Iran also lacks the low altitude radar coverage, overall radar net, command and control assets, sensors, resistance to sophisticated jamming and electronic countermeasures, and systems integration capability necessary to create an effective air defense net. Its land-based air defenses must operate largely in the point defense mode, and Iran lacks the advanced battle management systems and data links to allow it to take maximum advantage of the overlapping coverage of some of its missile systems—a problem further complicated by the problems in trying to net different systems supplied by Britain, China, Russia, and the United States. Iran's missiles and sensors are most effective at high-to-medium altitudes against aircraft with limited penetrating and jamming capability.

MODERNIZATION EFFORTS

Iran faces serious problems in modernizing its land-based air defense system to correct these weaknesses—many of which date back to the time of the Shah. Although Iran bought modern US and British surface-to-air missiles at the time of the Shah, it never integrated these missiles into an effective land-based air defense system. It had not made its air control and warning system fully operational at the time the Shah fell, and had experienced serious problems in operating some of its largely British-supplied radars.

Once the Shah was deposed, Iran had no way of purchasing the equipment needed to improve or properly maintain its Western-supplied radars, communications system, and software. It also lost many of its Western-trained operators, technicians, and commanders during the purges following the revolution. This reduced its ability to use its Western-supplied equipment effectively. In spite of some limited deliveries as a result of the Iran-hostage deal, Iran has never been able to find a source of parts, equipment, and technical expertise that has allowed it to properly support its Western-supplied systems.[4] Many of the Western-supplied surface-to-air missiles in Iran's order of battle are not fully operational, and Iran is forced to rely on inadequate radars, data processing systems, and command and control links to support its missile units.[5]

Iran has responded by obtaining the SA-2, CSA-1/2, SA-6, and SA-5 from the PRC, Russia, and Central Europe. It has acquired some Soviet warning and battle management radars, command, and communications equipment. It has deployed the SA-5 to several of its bases on the Gulf coast, including Bandar Abbas, and it has obtained some new Soviet radars as part of the sale of SA-5 missiles. There are reports that Iran is seeking to import three more batteries of SA-5 missiles from the former Soviet Union, more CSA-1s, and further deliveries of Russian and Chinese radars. There are also reports that Iran may be paying North Korea for assistance in creating a network of underground command centers in 18 sites—although such reports are uncertain.[6]

These transfers of surface-to-air missiles and sensors from Russia and the People's Republic of China have helped improve Iran's land-based capabilities, but they have not been adequate to meet all of its needs. They have given Iran improved capability against regional air forces without sophisticated jammers and anti-radiation missiles, but they scarcely give Iran a modern integrated air defense system that can resist attack by a power like the United States.

THE WAR-FIGHTING CAPABILITIES OF IRANIAN LAND-BASED AIR DEFENSE FORCES

In the short term, Iran requires substantial deliveries of added equipment to make its Western-supplied weapons fully operational, much more advanced heavy surface-to-air missiles, and a considerably more advanced C^4I/BM system. Iran must also find a reliable source of Hawk parts to make its current missiles functional. It needs to rehabilitate and improve its radar-guided anti-aircraft guns and most of its short-range air defense systems. In addition, it is necessary for Iran to either modernize or replace its Rapiers, Tigercats, and FM-80s, and to replace its obsolescent mix of different systems of radar and command and control equipment.

Iran has boasted of its advanced electronic warfare and battle management capabilities. In fact, Khamenei has claimed,

Today, one of the most sophisticated military tools—to which the Americans would never even conceive Iran could have access—is being built in workshops of the Islamic Revolutionary Guards Corps and mass produced by Iranian experts ... [The US] with all its intelligence apparatus and spy networks is unaware of this.[7]

Iran has been able to improve some aspects of its electronic warfare capabilities using European and Russian equipment—some imported by its covert purchasing network—but it has shown no signs of having anything approaching an adequate electronic warfare capability for its air defense forces, any more than it has for its air forces, land forces, or navy. Further, US experts indicate that Iran's electronic warfare exercises are primitive, poorly structured, and poorly integrated.

Improving the capabilities of its Western systems and further purchases of SA-2 and SA-5 systems cannot give Iran the range of capabilities it needs. The SA-2, CSA-1, SA-6, and SA-5 are highly vulnerable to active and passive countermeasures. Even the latest versions of the Improved Hawk do not approach the Patriot in performance capability, and the Improved Hawks in Iranian hands are nearly 17 years old. Similarly, while President Rafsanjani announced on October 11, 1997, that Iran had test-launched a major new surface-to-air missile system with a range of 250 kilometers, such claims seem unlikely to result in a truly advanced surface-to-air missile. Rafsanjani's description of the missile sounded vaguely like the Russian SA-5, which is nearly a quarter of a century-old design.[8]

If Iran is to create the land-based elements of an air defense system capable of dealing with the retaliatory capabilities of Western air forces, it needs major improvements in its electronic warfare capabilities and a modern, heavy surface-to-air missile system that is part of a larger and better integrated air defense C^{4}I/battle management system.

Such a system will not be easy for Iran to obtain either. No European or Asian power can currently sell Iran either an advanced ground-based air defense system or an advanced heavy surface-to-air missile system. The United States and Russia are the only current suppliers of such systems, and the only surface-to-air missiles that can meet Iran's needs are the Patriot and S-300 (also called the SA-10, SA-12a, and SA-12b).

Iran has no hope of getting the Patriot system from the United States, making Russia the only potential source of the required land-based air defense technology. This explains why Iran has sought to buy the S-300 heavy surface-to-air missile/anti-tactical ballistic missile systems and a next generation warning, command, and control system from Russia. The S-300PMU-1 variant of the S-300 series (also named the Fakel 5300PMU or Grumble) is a highly advanced system with sophisticated warning radar, tracking radar, and terminal guidance system and warhead, and it has good electronic warfare capabilities. It is a far more advanced and capable system than the SA-2, SA-3, SA-5, or SA-6.[9]

There are at least four, possibly five, versions of the S-300: The known versions are the S-300P (5V55K), S-300PM (5V55R), S-300PMU (5V55RUD), and S-300PMU-1 (48N6). They are the product of successive improvements in the system. Development began in 1967, and the first missile entered service in 1980, with a maximum range of 47 kilometers, a maximum altitude of 27 kilometers, a minimum effective range of 25 kilometers, and a maximum target speed of 1,300 meters per second. The missile was 7.11 meters long and 450 millimeters in diameter. In 1982, the second version extended the system's maximum range to 75 kilometers, and in 1985, the third version extended the maximum range to 90 kilometers.[10]

There is no way to determine what version Russia would export to Iran, if any, but Iran would have a strong incentive to buy at least the fourth generation of the system. The S-300PMU-1 system entered service in 1995. It is a major advance over its predecessors and is far more competitive with the Patriot.

The missile is called the 48N6. Its length is increased to 7.5 meters, the diameter to 515 millimeters, and the warhead from 133 kilograms to 143 kilograms. It has a range of 5–150 kilometers, a maximum altitude of 27 kilometers, a minimum effective range of 10 kilometers, and a maximum target speed of 2,800 meters per second. It can stand up to 20 lateral Gs. A version with self-homing warhead capability is in development, and there seem to be naval variants of the older system which might be used on Iran's largest surface ships.[11]

A firing battery can deploy up to 48 48N6 missiles on its 12 self-propelled

5P8S 8X8 transporter-erector-launchers (TLEs), or on the 5P85T tractor-trailer. It can fire a missile every three seconds. There is a command post and vehicle-mounted engagement radar called the 36N85, with a slightly less sophisticated export version called the 30NE6E1. The engagement radar can guide up to 12 missiles at once against up to six different targets. The radar can be mounted on an extendable tower to improve coverage of cruise missiles and low-flying aircraft. A battery seems to sell for around $85–$95 million.

The S-300PMU is deployed with the first truly advanced mix of C^{4}I/battle management and surveillance systems that Russia has made operational at the tactical level. This system is called the Almuz, or 83M6, and is deployed in missile brigades that can be linked together to provide a coherent area defense, and which can also be linked to Iran's SA-5s to provide integrated fire control. The brigade-level set includes the 64N6 (Tombstone) long-range, three-dimensional, phased array surveillance radar, which is mounted on a semi-trailer; and the 54K6 command post, which is mounted on a MAZ-543 truck. The 54K6 can provide C^{4}I/battle management and surveillance for a battalion of up to eight batteries. The 64N6's detection range is 300 kilometers for targets of up to 2,780 kilometers per second and it can track up to 70–100 targets. A full brigade seems to sell for around $400–600 million.

The combination of the 83M6 and the S-300PMU give the S-300 the speed and C^{4}I features necessary to act as a short-range tactical ballistic missile defense system, and the electronic warfare capabilities of the system seem competitive with those of US and European design capabilities.

Much depends on Russian willingness to make an export sale of such a system in the face of US pressure. Reports surfaced in July, 1995 that Russia might have decided to sell Iran the SA-10. They surfaced again in April, 1997, although a spokesman for the US State Department then issued a denial that the United States had evidence of such a sale. These reports indicate that Russia would sell Iran the Baikal-1E air defense system along with the 83M6 and the S-300PMU.[12]

There are also reports that Iran attempted to buy SA-10s from Kazakhstan in early 1997. According to these reports, Kazak military intelligence officers—including Zhenis Raspayev, the director of military intelligence, and a former Kazak minister of defense—were involved in a $90 million deal to sell Russian-made systems to Iran. The deal was brokered by Colonel Oleg Sinkin, possibly with the knowledge of the current Minister of Defense, Mukhtar Altynbayev. The transfer was blocked by US concerns over the deal and by Chinese concerns that two proposed overflights of China from Taldygorghan in southeastern Kazakhstan to Iran would create new problems for China in dealing with the United States. US pressure may also have prevented a Kazak deal with a Russian arms broker that would have given Iran a total of three S-300 batteries and 36 missiles.[13]

If such a sale ever does take place, it would be a significant development, since Russia has the capability to provide the S-300 quickly and in large numbers, as well as support it with a greatly improved early warning sensor system and an advanced command and control system for both its fighters and land-based air defenses. Given the fact that the 83M6 can be linked to Iran's SA-5s, there is no other mix of systems that Iran could buy that would solve as many of its land-based air defense and command and control problems so quickly.

At the same time, the resulting system would still have important limits:

- Russia has not fully completed integration of the SA-300 into its own air defenses, still has significant limitations on its air defense computer technology, and relies heavily on redundant sensors and different, overlapping surface-to-air missiles to compensate for a lack of overall system efficiency.
- A combination of advanced Russian missiles and an advanced sensor and battle management system would still be vulnerable to active and passive attack by the United States.
- It could take three to five years for Iran to deploy and integrate such a system fully, once Russia agreed to the sale.
- Much of the system's effectiveness would also depend on Russia's ability to both provide suitable technical training and to adapt a Russian system to the specific topographical and operating conditions of Iran.
- A Russian system cannot simply be transferred to Iran as an equipment package. It would take a major effort in terms of software, radar deployment, and technology—and considerable adaptation of Russian tactics and siting concepts—to make such a system fully combat-effective.

As a result, full-scale modernization of the Iranian land-based air defense system is unlikely to occur before 2005 under the most optimistic conditions, and it will probably lag well beyond 2010.[14] An advanced land-based Russian air defense system would, however, give Iran far more capability to defend against retaliatory raids from Iraq or any Southern Gulf air force. It would allow Iran to allocate more fighter/attack aircraft to attack missions and use its interceptors to provide air cover for such attack missions. It would also greatly complicate the problem of using offensive US air power against Iran, require substantially more US forces to conduct a successful air campaign, and probably greatly increase US losses.

NOTES

1. Sources include *Defense Electronics*, March, 1992, p. 16; Dr. Andrew Rathmell, "Iran's Rearmament: How Great a Threat?" *Jane's Intelligence Review*, July, 1994, pp. 317–322; *Inside the Air Force*, February 28, 1992, p. 1; *The Estimate*, October 13–26, 1989, p. 1; Andrew Rathmell, *The Changing Military Balance in the Gulf*, London, Royal United Services Institute, Whitehall Papers 38, 1996; Edward B. Atkenson, *The Powder Keg*, Falls Church, NOVA Publications, 1996; USCENTCOM, *Atlas, 1996*, MacDill Air Force Base, USCENTCOM, 1997; *Armed Forces Journal*, March, 1992, pp. 26–27; *Jane's Sentinel: The Gulf States, 1997*; London, Jane's Publishing 1997; Mi-

chael Eisenstadt, *Iranian Military Power*: Washington, Washington Institute, 1996; *Jane's Land-Based Air Defense* (CD-ROM); *Jane's Military Vehicles and Logistics* (CD-ROM); *Jane's Radar and Electronic Warfare Systems* (1997–1998); *Jane's G⁴I Systems* (1997–1998).

2. Based on interviews with British, Israeli, and US experts, and Anthony H. Cordesman, *Iran and Iraq: The Threat from the Northern Gulf*, Boulder, Westview, 1994; Anthony H. Cordesman and Ahmed S. Hashim, *Iran: Dilemmas of Dual Containment*, Boulder, Westview, 1997; IISS, *Military Balance, 1997–1998*, "Iran"; *Jane's Sentinel: The Gulf States, 1997*, "Iran"; USNI Data Base; Anoushiravan Ehteshami, "Iran's National Strategy," *International Defense Review*, 4/1994, pp. 29–37; Military Technology, *World Defense Almanac: The Balance of Military Power*, Vol. XVII, Issue 1–1993, ISSN 0722-3226, pp. 139–142; and working data from the Jaffee Center for Strategic Studies; Dr. Andrew Rathmell, "Iran's Rearmament: How Great a Threat?" *Jane's Intelligence Review*, July, 1994, pp. 317–322; Ahmed Hashim, "The Crisis of the Iranian State," Adelphi Paper 296, London, IISS, Oxford, July, 1995, pp. 7–30 and 50–70; Andrew Rathmell, *The Changing Military Balance in the Gulf*, London, RUSI, Whitehall Papers 38, 1996, pp. 9–23; Michael Eisenstadt, *Iranian Military Power, Capabilities, and Intentions*, Washington, Washington Institute, 1996, pp. 9–65; and Anoushiravan Ehteshami "Iran Strives to Regain Military Might," *International Defense Review*, 7/1996, pp. 22–26.

3. *Jane's Defense Weekly*, February 7, 1996, p. 14, March 27, 1996, p. 14.

4. Based on interviews with British, Israeli, and US experts. Reports of MiG-31s do not seem to be correct. Adapted from the IISS, Annapolis, and JCSS databases, and the *Washington Times*, January 16, 1992, p. G-4; *Washington Post*, February 1, 1992, p. A1, February 2, 1992, pp. A1 and A25, February 5, p. A-19; *Financial Times*, February 6, 1992, p. 4; *Christian Science Monitor*, February 6, 1992, p. 19; *Defense News*, February 17, 1992, p. 1.

5. Adapted from the IISS, Annapolis, and JCSS databases, and the *Washington Times*, January 16, 1992, p. G-4; *Washington Post*, February 1, 1992, p. A1, February 2, 1992, pp. A1 and A25, February 5, p. A-19; *Financial Times*, February 6, 1992, p. 4; *Christian Science Monitor*, February 6, 1992, p. 19; *Defense News*, February 17, 1992, p. 1.

6. *Defense and Foreign Affairs*, No. 1, 1994, pp. 4–7. There were also reports that Czechoslovakia might sell Iran an advanced mobile air surveillance system called Tamara. The manufacturer of this system—Tesla Pardubice—has claimed that it is capable of tracking stealth aircraft. Tamara, however, seems to be a signals intelligence system with some air defense applications, and its claims to special advantages in detecting "stealth" aircraft seem to be nothing more than sales propaganda. *Defense News*, July 12, 1993, p. 1; *New York Times*, December 27, 1993, p. A-17.

7. *Jane's Defense Weekly*, October 28, 1995, p. 19.

8. IRNA, October 12, 1997.

9. *Flight International*, August 24, 1993, p. 12.

10. This analysis is based largely on the work of Steven J. Zaloga in analyzing the S-300 series. For example, see his work in *Jane's Intelligence Review*, April, 1997, pp. 153–156.

11. Michael Barletta, Erik Jorgensen, and Peter Saracino, "A Military and Technical Analysis: The Russian S-300PMU-1 TMD System," Monterey Institute of International Studies, Center for Non-Proliferation Studies, July, 1998.

12. *Washington Times*, April 16, 1997, p. A-1.
13. This report is unreliable. *Washington Times*, June 4, 1997, p. A-4.
14. Based on interviews with British, US, and Israel experts, and *Washington Times*, January 16, 1992, p. G-4; *Washington Post*, February 1, 1992, p. A1, February 2, 1992, pp. A1 and A25, February 5, p. A-19; *Financial Times*, February 6, 1992, p. 4; *Christian Science Monitor*, February 6, 1992, p. 19; *Defense News*, February 17, 1992, p. 1; and *Jane's Intelligence Review*, April, 1997, pp. 153–156.

Chapter 9

Iran's Naval Forces

Iran's naval forces are now under separate commanders for the regular and Revolutionary Guard naval forces. Both forces were under the command of Rear Admiral Ali Shamkani until he became Iran's Minister of Defense in August, 1997. The regular navy was then placed under the command of Rear Admiral Abbas Mohtaj, who had been Shamkani's deputy since October, 1990. The IRGC naval forces were placed under the command of Brigadier-General Ali Akbar Ahmadian.[1]

Iran's naval forces play a key role in shaping its capabilities to project power in the Gulf, to threaten Iraq's oil export capabilities, to attack or intimidate the Southern Gulf states, and to deter or limit US military action. Most of the Gulf nations have treated sea power as an afterthought, but the Iranian Navy and Naval Branch of the Islamic Revolutionary Guards Corps are likely to play a critical role in shaping Iran's military capabilities.

Any Iranian intervention in a Gulf state that does not involve the cooperation of a Southern Gulf government and free access to ports and air fields would require some kind of amphibious operation. Naval forces are equally essential to a wide spectrum of other possible conflicts that affect the islands in the Gulf, control of the Strait of Hormuz, unconventional warfare using naval forces, attacks on coastal targets in Iraq and the Southern Gulf, and Western and Southern Gulf naval operations in the Gulf.[2]

As a result, it is not surprising that Iran has given the modernization of its naval forces high priority. Since the end of the Iran-Iraq War, Iran has obtained new anti-ship missiles and missile patrol craft from China, midget submarines from North Korea, submarines from Russia, and modern mines. It has expanded the capabilities of the naval branch of the IRGC, acquired additional mine warfare capability, and upgraded some of its older surface ships.

The Iranian navy has stepped up its training and exercise activity, most notably in the Victory, Lightning 3, Val Fajr 1 and 2, Fatah 3, Naser, and Tariq ol-Qods series of exercises. In October, 1997, Iran held naval exercises which it claimed involved some 100 ships operating in a 60,000-square-kilometer area. It claimed to be using new stealth reconnaissance drones, all three of its new Russian submarines, helicopters, and IRGC speed boats, as well as the larger ships of the Iranian navy.[3]

Iran's exercises have included a growing number of joint and combined arms exercises with the land forces and air force.[4] Iran has also improved its ports and strengthened its air defenses, while obtaining some logistic and technical support from nations like India and Pakistan.[5]

These Iranian efforts have steadily improved Iran's capabilities to threaten Gulf shipping and offshore oil facilities, its capability to support unconventional warfare, and its ability to defend Iran's offshore facilities, islands, and coastline. They have not, however, done much to help Iran act as an effective "blue water" navy. Iranian naval forces still have many limitations, but the military capability of Iranian naval forces should not be measured in terms of the ability to win a battle for sea control against US and British naval forces, or any combination of Southern Gulf states supported by US and British forces. For the foreseeable future, Iran's forces are likely to lose any such battle in a matter of days. As a result, it is Iran's ability to conduct limited or unconventional warfare, or to threaten traffic through the Gulf, which gives it the potential ability to threaten or intimidate its neighbors.

IRAN'S SURFACE NAVY

Iran's regular navy, the naval elements of the Islamic Revolutionary Guards Corps, and the Iranian marines totaled around 38,000 men in 1998—with about 18,000 regulars and 17,000–20,000 men in the Iranian Naval Revolutionary Guard forces. These forces were organized into two fleets.[6] While some sources list Iran as having three Marine Brigades, USCENTCOM estimates a total strength of only three Marine battalions. It is not clear how these marine units are structured, trained, or equipped.[7]

The relative strength of Iran's navy is shown in Figures 9.1–9.3. While most Iranian major surface ships have limited operational capability by Western standards, the numerical strength of the Iranian navy is impressive by Gulf standards. It is clear from these charts that Iran retains a large naval order of battle, while Iraq's naval capabilities are almost nonexistent. At the same time, these charts show that several Southern Gulf states are beginning to acquire significant ship strength, much of which is more modern than that of Iran. The Southern Gulf navies have much less operational experience than Iran, but they are improving and cannot be totally discounted.

There are significant differences among experts as to how to classify given ships and count Iran's naval order of battle. US experts dropped Iran's destroyers

Figure 9.1
Iranian Naval Ships by Category in 1998

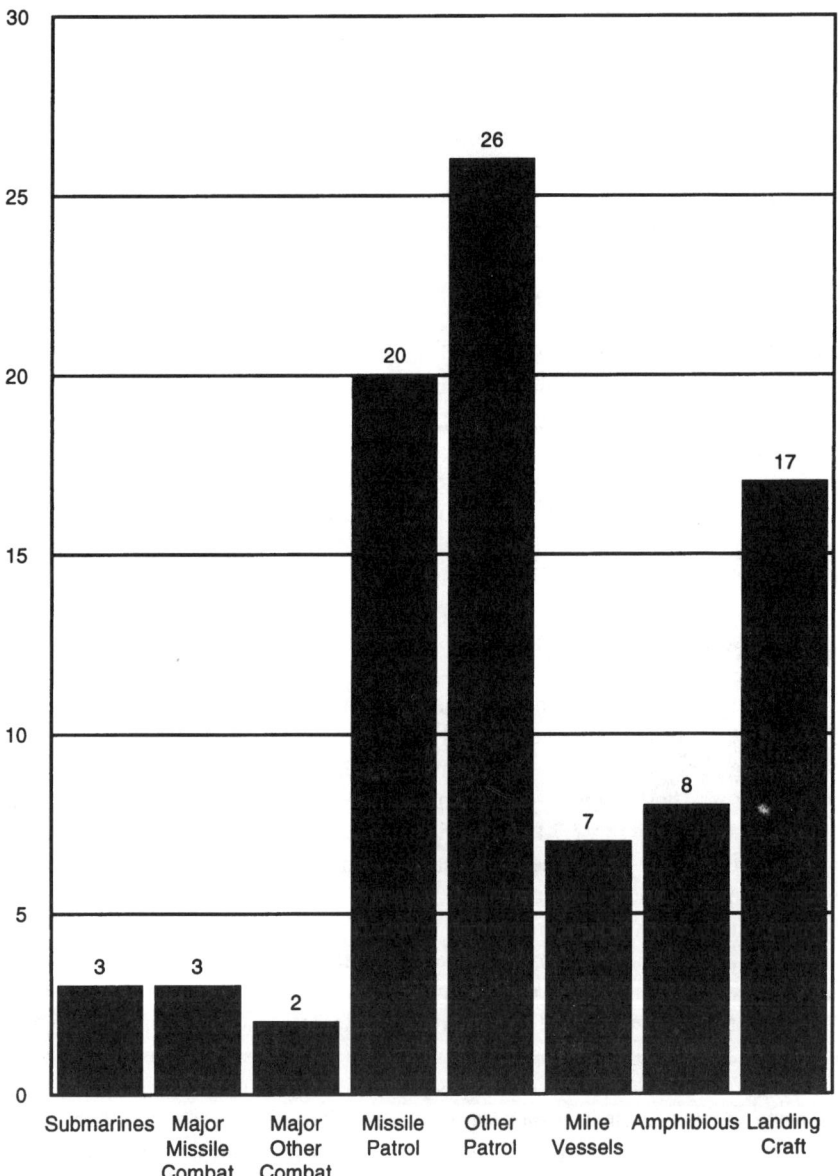

Source: Adapted from Anthony S. Cordesman from IISS, *Military Balance*.

Figure 9.2
Total Gulf Naval Manpower: 1998 (in 1,000s)

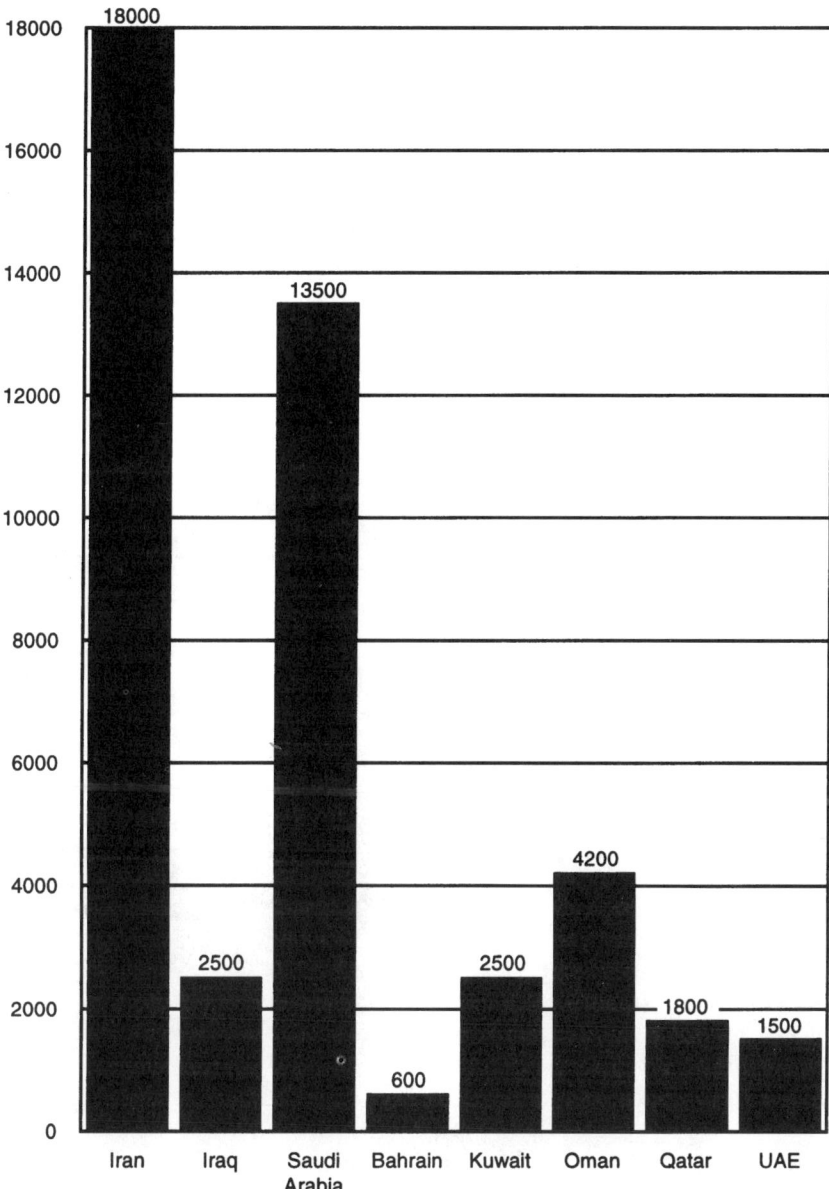

Source: Adapted by Anthony H. Cordesman from IISS, *Military Balance*.

Figure 9.3
Gulf Naval Ships by Category in 1998

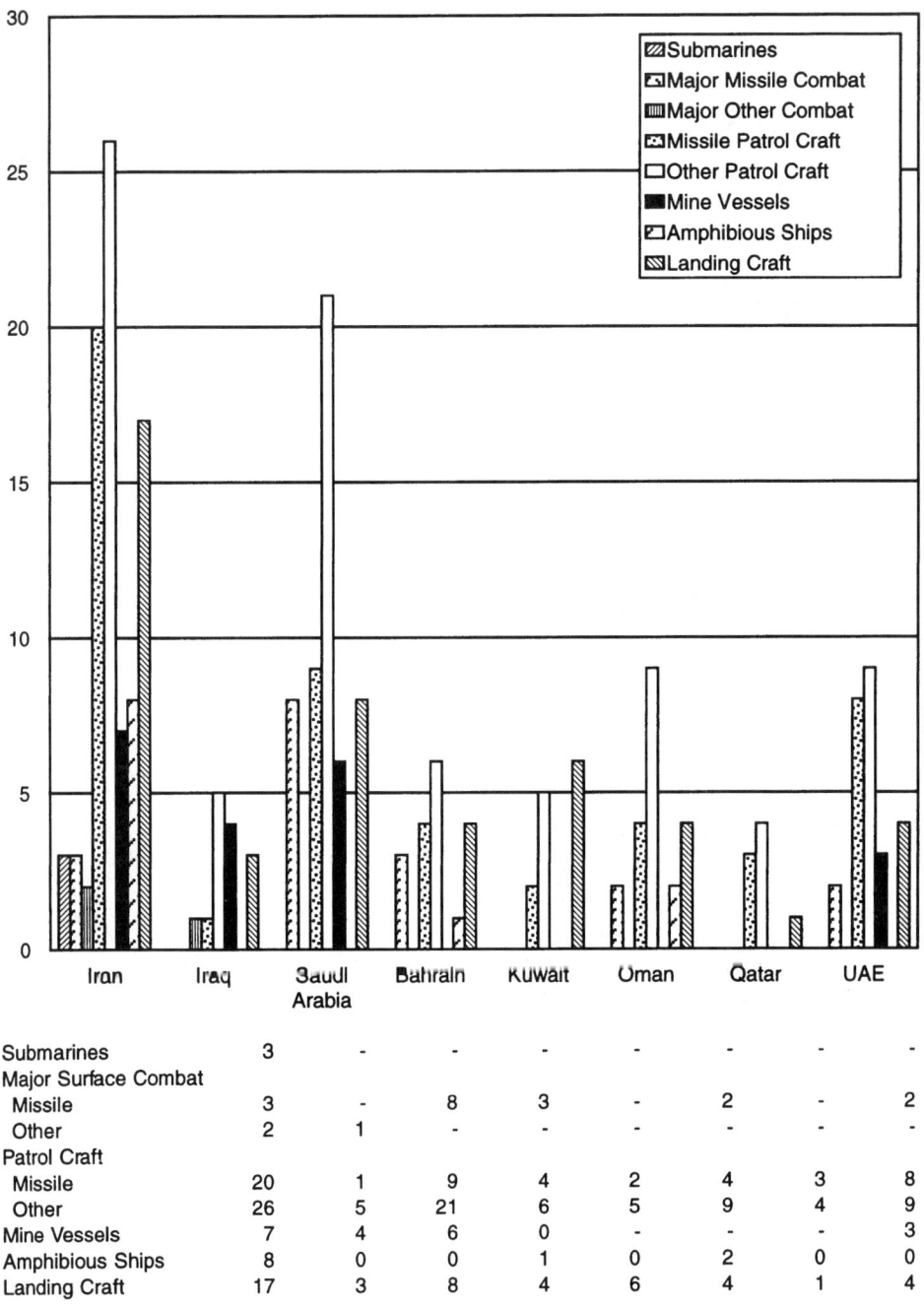

	Iran	Iraq	Saudi Arabia	Bahrain	Kuwait	Oman	Qatar	UAE
Submarines	3	-	-	-	-	-	-	-
Major Surface Combat								
Missile	3	-	8	3	-	2	-	2
Other	2	1	-	-	-	-	-	-
Patrol Craft								
Missile	20	1	9	4	2	4	3	8
Other	26	5	21	6	5	9	4	9
Mine Vessels	7	4	6	0	-	-	-	3
Amphibious Ships	8	0	0	1	0	2	0	0
Landing Craft	17	3	8	4	6	4	1	4

Sources: Adapted by Anthony H. Cordesman from IISS, *Military Balance*, and material provided by US experts.

from its operational order of battle and felt that only five of Iran's Combattante II (Karman-class) fast attack boats have been modernized to carry Chinese anti-ship missiles in late 1997. They indicated that Iran had a total of about 20 missile patrol craft. These estimates gave Iran a total of three frigates, 20 missile combatants, 10 large patrol ships, 32 medium coastal combatants, 5–7 mine warfare ships (including one training ship), 8–9 amphibious ships, 10 amphibious craft, 14 hovercraft, nine large auxiliary ships, and roughly 32 smaller auxiliary ships. They give Iran's naval air units roughly nine armed helicopters, nine fixed-wing transports, and an unknown number of support helicopters.

Other sources often counted more of these ships as operational, and some estimated that all of Iran's Combattante Is had been modernized to carry Chinese anti-ship missiles by the end of 1997. Unclassified USCENTCOM estimates show a total of three destroyers, three Kilo-class submarines, two PF-103 corvettes, eight fast patrol boats, seven large patrol boats, three minesweepers, 11 landing ships and craft, four logistical support ships, two BH-7 hovercraft, 11 fixed-wing aircraft, and 19 helicopters. The IISS and Jane's still indicate that Iran's destroyers are operational. According to other estimates, Iran's operational inventory includes three submarines, two destroyers, three frigates, two corvettes, and 25–30 missile combatants.[8]

Iran has large numbers of naval Revolutionary Guards. They operate the 5–7 Seersucker (HY-2) anti-ship missile sites Iran used to defend its ports and cover the Strait of Hormuz, plus a large number of smaller anti-ship missile sites on its coast and islands, and a number of shelters and dispersal sites to which it could rapidly deploy missiles in a crisis. While it is impossible to distinguish precisely between the IRGC's holdings of small craft and those of the regular navy, the IRGC seemed to operate large numbers of Peterson PBI coastal patrol craft, at least six other inshore patrol craft, some 30 Boghammer patrol boats, several hovercraft, about 30 craft somewhat similar to the Boston Whaler, and large numbers of small boats similar to River Roadstead patrol craft.

Much of the regular navy is based at Bandar Abbas, the only large Iranian port far enough away from Iraq to be relatively secure from Iraqi air attack during the Iran-Iraq War. This port is the home of Iran's destroyers, frigates, and Kilo-class submarines. Iran does not conduct extensive patrols in the Gulf of Oman, but it does hold occasional exercises there, and it is expanding its base at Chah Bahar in the Gulf of Oman. Iran has another large naval base at Bushehr, where it deploys most of its guided missile patrol boats. It has operated hovercraft forces out of the oil port at Kharg Island since the time of the Shah, and it has a moderate force at its Western port of Bandar Kharg Khomeini, which covers the waters opposite Iraq and the entrance to the Shatt al-Arab. It has small bases at Bandar e-Anzali and Noshahr on the Caspian. Noshahr is used for training Islamic Revolutionary Guards Corps forces in unconventional warfare.[9]

Opinions differ as to how much of Iran's surface force is fully operational.

Iran is clearly able to operate some of its British-made Sa'am-class fast attack craft. According to some reports, it can also operate most of the weapons systems on at least one destroyer, two frigates, six to ten fast attack craft (FAC), seven large patrol boats, and 40 coastal patrol boats. Furthermore, these experts suggest an ability to operate a maximum of 14 Hovercraft and 57 amphibious assault ships, logistics ships, and small patrol boats. If these reports are true, Iran has a total operational force of more than 80 vessels, although it would lack adequate air defense and is still developing adequate anti-ship missile capabilities for its major surface ships.[10]

Iran's Destroyers

All of Iran's major surface vessels are obsolescent or obsolete, although they could theoretically be updated in Western shipyards. Iran's two largest ships are its Sumner-class (Babr-class) destroyers—the *Babr* and *Palang*. These ships were originally laid down in 1943 and 1944, have not been refitted since the period 1971–1972, and possess weapons systems, sensors, and equipment that are over twenty years old. These two ships are moored at Bandar Abbas, but it is unclear whether they can use their Western-supplied anti-ship and anti-aircraft missiles, and anti-submarine mortars effectively. One was decommissioned in 1996, and the other is likely to be fully decommissioned by 2000.

While such data now seem to be largely of historical interest, the ships require a complement of 290 men, displace 3,200 tons fully loaded, and were capable of speeds of 31 knots. Each was armed with four paired elevating Standard SM-1MR surface-to-surface missile launchers, two twin 5" gun mounts, six Mark 32 torpedo tubes, and an Agusta AB-204AS helicopter. The Standard is still a potentially effective missile, with command guidance and semiactive radar homing and a maximum range of 46 kilometers. Iran's missile suites, however, have not been modernized in over 20 years, and all of Iran's Standard missiles have now aged beyond their normal shelf life. The guns and torpedoes of the Sumner-class ships would have little value against modern US and British surface ships and air power, and they face a growing threat from the modern anti-ship missiles in Southern Gulf navies. As a result, the *Babr* or *Palang* might be put back into service to display an Iranian naval presence in peacetime and low-level conflicts, but would be little more than targets in war.

Similarly, Iran has one British-supplied 2,288-ton Battle-class ship called the *Damavand*. This ship, too, is effectively decommissioned, and its performance capabilities are largely of historical interest. The *Damavand* displaces 3,360 tons fully loaded, has a speed of 31 knots, and is armed with four paired elevating Standard SM-1MR surface-to-surface missile launchers, two twin 5" gun mounts, a single Contraves RTN-10X Sea Hunter fire control radar, and a quadruple Sea Cat ship-to-air missile launcher. The *Damavand* had relatively modern air and sea search radars and modern commercial grade ESM and EW gear when it was first transferred to Iran. However, its main refitting took place in

1966, and its Standard missiles were added in South Africa during the period 1974–1975. Its Sea Cats, Standards, and electronics no longer seem to be operational. The *Damavand* is no longer counted as part of Iran's operational strength.[11]

Iran's Frigates

The backbone of Iran's operational naval forces consists of three British-supplied Vosper Mark 5 Sa'am-class frigates—the *Alvand, Alborz,* and *Sabalan*—each an 1,100-ton frigate with a crew of 125–146 and maximum speeds of 39 knots. Each is armed with one five-missile Sea Killer Mark II surface-to-surface missile launcher and one Mark 8 4.5" gun mount. The Sea Killer has a relatively effective beam-riding missile with radio command or optical guidance, a maximum range of 25 kilometers, and a 70-kilogram warhead. The *Sabalan* was extensively damaged in combat with the US Navy in 1988, during an engagement where the United States sank its sister ship. It was refloated and repaired, and it began to deploy occasionally in 1991. It is now considered combat operational.[12] The Alvand-class ships, however, were last fully refitted in 1977, and the operational readiness of their missiles and more sophisticated electronics is uncertain. It seems likely that the missiles have uncertain operational reliability and that their associated electronics are vulnerable to Western countermeasures.

There have been reports that Iran may have removed some of the missile launchers from these Sa'am-class frigates and replaced them with a BM-21 multiple rocket launcher to provide added fire support capability. Such modifications, however, have not taken place. Even if they did, they would only have value against land targets, very large off-shore targets, or possibly super tankers. They would not enhance the survivability of the ships against anti-ship missiles and air strikes.[13]

Iran's Corvettes

Iran has two US PF-103 (Bayandor-class) corvettes called the *Bayandor* and the *Naghdi*. These ships are 900-ton vessels, with crews of 140, two 76 mm guns, and a maximum speed of 18 knots. They were laid down in 1962 and delivered in 1964. The *Bayandor* and the *Naghdi* are probably the most active large surface ships in the Iranian navy. However, neither is equipped with anti-ship and anti-air missiles, sophisticated weapons systems, or advanced electronic warfare equipment and sensors. The only major modifications to the ships are that one was reengined in 1988 and given 20 mm guns (in place of a 23 mm gun) and depth charge racks.[14]

In broad terms, Iran's destroyers, frigates, and corvettes now have little overall value in a major regional contingency involving US forces, although they might have value in a contingency that did not involve US, British, and Saudi air and sea power. Reports that Iran is modifying some of its surface ships to use Russian SA-N-10 anti-air missiles and Chinese-supplied anti-ship missiles such as the HY-2 Seersucker have not proven correct, although Iran can equip them with the CS-801 anti-ship missile. Iran is also capable of modifying the radar suite on its major surface ships, improving some aspects of their electronic warfare capability and providing a limited amount of improvement in the capability of their overall fire control/battle management capabilities to integrate the use of Russian and Chinese-supplied missiles. As a result, it is not possible to totally discount their survivability and combat capability in a major regional contingency.

Iran's Missile Patrol Boats

The rest of Iran's major surface vessels consist of missile patrol boats. These include 10 68-ton Chinese Hudong-class fast attack craft or missile patrol boats. The Hudong-class fast attack craft are equipped with I-band search and navigation radars, but do not have a major anti-air missile system. Iran ordered these ships for the naval branch of its Iranian Revolutionary Guards Corps in 1992, and they are an improved Chinese version of the Russian Osa II missile boat. All 10 were delivered to Iran by March, 1996. The vessels have a crew of 28. They are 27 meters in length, carry four anti-ship missiles, and have two twin 25 mm guns. The vessels are armed with the CS-801s and the more capable CS-802 missile. Iran now has at least 100 CS-801s and CS-802s.

Iran publicly fired its first CS-802 in November, 1996.[15] The CS-802 is a relatively modern anti-ship missile design which China first made public in 1989. It has a 0.36 meter diameter and a weight of around 715 kilograms. It is a turbofan-powered missile with a range of 70–75 miles (120 kilometers), cruises at an altitude of around 20–30 meters, and can carry warheads of up to 363 pounds (165 kilograms). It has an over-the-horizon capability because it can be remotely targeted with a separate tracking and targeting radar.[16]

The Hudong-class vessels also have a significant long-range strike capability. They have been used in exercises for the defense of islands like Abu Musa and Iran's oil facilities in the Gulf. They have also been used to simulate attacks on US style surface ships. Unlike Iran's larger surface ships, they are relatively easy to disperse and conceal. They would be much more survivable than Iran's destroyers, frigates, and corvettes in contingencies which could be used to threaten commercial traffic through the Strait of Hormuz. They seem to have been transferred to the naval branch of the IRGC, which has used them in exercises. However, reports that Iran has deployed them to Sirri and Abu Musa were not correct as of early 1998.[17]

Iran's missile patrol boats also include 10 French-made Combattante II (Kaman-class) fast attack boats, out of an original total of twelve. Two were sunk during the "tanker war." These boats are relatively large and displace 275 tons. They are armed with anti-ship missiles, one 76 mm gun, and have maximum speeds of 37.5 knots. These Combattante II (Kaman-class) fast attack boats were delivered during the period 1974–1981 and are Iran's most modern Western-supplied combat ships. They are equipped with Signaal I/J band search and fire control radars and electronic countermeasures. They were originally armed with four US Harpoon missiles, but their Harpoons are probably no longer operational. At least five had been successfully converted with launchers that can carry four CS-801/CS-802s, each by late 1997, although reports that all ten might be converted during 1997 did not prove correct. They also are armed with SA-7 and SA-14 manportable surface-to-air missiles.[18]

Iran's Patrol and Fast Attack Craft

Iran also has a number of large patrol craft and fast attack craft. The operational ships of this type include:

- one Iraqi 245-ton Bogomol, armed with a 76 mm gun and equipped with search and fire control radars. This boat was seized when it fled to Iran in 1991 and has had limited use
- three North Korean-supplied Zafar-class (Chaho-class) fast attack craft. They displace 82 tons, have I-band search radars, and are armed with 23 mm guns and a BM-21 multiple rocket launcher
- three Kavian-class (US Cape-class) large patrol craft. These displace 148 tons fully loaded and are armed with 40 mm and 23 mm guns. They are part of a delivery of four US Coast Guard ships. One was sunk during the "tanker war," and two were damaged and repaired
- three Improved PGM-71 Parvin-class large patrol craft supplied by Peterson Builders in the late 1960s. These are 98-ton boats armed with 40 mm and 20 mm guns and are equipped with sonar and search radars
- several hundred small boats operated by the IRGC

Most of these craft are operational and can be effective in patrol missions. They lack, however, sophisticated weapons systems or air defenses, other than machine guns and SA-7s and SA-14s.

Iran's Hovercraft and Coastal Patrol Craft

Iran has 5–6 BH-7 and 7–8 SRN-6 Hovercraft. About half of these Hovercraft may be operational. They are capable of speeds of up to 60–70 knots, although their normal cruising speed is about half that. The BH-7 can carry 53.8 tons of cargo, and the SRN-6 can carry 10 tons. They are lightly armed and vulnerable, but their high speed makes them useful for many reconnaissance and unconventional warfare missions, and they can rapidly land troops on suitable beaches. In addition, Iran has up to 70 PBI coastal patrol craft. It is not possible to determine exactly which ships/boats are operated by the navy and which are operated by the IRGC. Iranian forces have hundreds of small boats.

Iran's Expansion Plans

Iran reported in July, 1997 that it would soon start building six multipurpose destroyers. It gave no details, but Rear Admiral Abbas Mohtai, the deputy commander of the navy, indicated that such efforts might still be largely on the drawing board. He stated, "Planning and design of the vessels will start soon, once approval is issued by the command headquarters of the armed forces." Interesting enough, Rear Admiral Mohammad Karim Tavakoli, the Commander of the First Naval Zone headquartered in Bandar Abbas, announced in late 1997 that Iran was going to manufacture three multirole destroyers, without any reference to Mohtai's earlier announcement.[19]

Iran is building five MIG-2–1800 60-ton coastal patrol craft with 20 mm guns and an I-band search radar. It has six US-supplied Mark II 22-ton coastal patrol craft and 14 Mark III 41.6-ton coastal patrol craft. Iran is building six copies of the Mark II, which it calls the MIG-G-1900. It has also claimed to have completed the design of a small submarine.[20]

IRANIAN MINE WARFARE CAPABILITIES

Mine warfare, amphibious warfare, anti-ship missiles, and unconventional warfare offer Iran other potential ways of compensating for the weakness of its conventional air and naval forces. Iran's mine warfare vessels include two to three Shahrock-class MSC-292/268 coastal minesweepers (One used for training in the Caspian Sea). Two of these three ships, the *Shahrock* and the *Karkas*, are known to be operational. They are 378-ton sweepers that can be used to lay mines as well as sweep, but their radars and sonars date back to the late 1950s and are obsolete in sweeping and countermeasure activity against modern mines.

Iran has 1–2 Cape-class (Riazzi-class) 239-ton inshore minesweepers and seems to have converted two of its Iran Ajar-class LSTs for mine warfare purposes. Many of its small boats and craft can also lay mines.

Both the Iranian navy and the naval branch of the IRGC are expanding their capability for mine warfare. While Iran has only a limited number of specialized mine vessels, it can also use small craft, LSTs, Boghammers, helicopters, and submarines to lay mines. As a result, it is impossible to determine how many ships Iran would employ to plant or lay mines in a given contingency, and some of its mines might be air dropped or laid by commercial vessels, including dhows.

Iran has a wide range of Soviet, Western, and Iranian-made moored and drifting contact mines, and US experts estimate that Iran has at least 2,000 mines. Iran has significant stocks of anti-ship mines, and it has bought Chinese-made and North Korean-made versions of the Soviet mines. It has claimed to be making its own nonmagnetic, acoustic, free-floating, and remote-controlled mines, and it has had Chinese assistance in developing the production facilities for such mines. It may have acquired significant stocks of nonmagnetic mines, influence mines, and mines with sophisticated timing devices from other countries.[21]

Even obsolete moored mines have proven difficult to detect and sweep when intelligence does not detect the original laying and size of the minefield, and free-floating mines can be used to present a constant hazard to shipping. Bottom-influence mines can use acoustic, magnetic, or pressure sensors to detect ships passing overhead. They can use multiple types of sensor/actuators to make it hard to deceive the mines and force them to release, can be set to release only after a given number of ships pass, and some can be set to attack only ships of a given size or noise profile. Such mines are extremely difficult to detect and sweep, particularly when they are spaced at wide intervals in shipping lanes.

There also are reports that Iran has negotiated with China to buy the EM-52 or MN-52 rocket-propelled mine. The EM-52 is a mine that rests on the bottom until it senses a ship passing over it, and then uses a rocket to hit the target. It can be set to fire only after it has sensed a given number of ships passing over it, and some reports claim it can operate to depths of 110 meters (363 feet). The maximum depth of the Strait of Hormuz is 80 meters (264 feet), although currents are strong enough to displace all but firmly moored mines.[22] Combined with modern submarine laid mines and anti-ship missile systems like the CS-801/802 and SS-N-22, the EM-52 would give Iran considerable capability to harass Gulf shipping and even the potential capability to close the Gulf until US naval and air power could clear the mines and destroy the missile launchers and submarines.

Mines can be used throughout the Gulf, and in parts of the Gulf of Oman. Iran has both moored and bottom influence mines, and it can place such mines in tanker routes—as it did during the Iran-Iraq War. Mines can be located near the Strait of Hormuz to deter commercial traffic, in narrow zones of operation to threaten warships, or in the Gulf of Oman—where sweeping and defensive coverage would be even more difficult than in the Persian Gulf. While mine activity would do more to harass Gulf shipping than halt it, and cannot provide a serious war-fighting capability against the US Navy, it could be combined with the use of land-based anti-ship missiles, commando raids, and submarine deployments. This might give Iran leverage in creating a meaningful cumulative threat to tanker and other shipping in the Gulf, one that would be difficult to entirely target, counter, and destroy.

The Southern Gulf states may develop effective mine sweeping capabilities to clear concentrated fields in limited areas, but Iran could use such mines throughout the Gulf, and tanker companies and captains are unlikely to take their ships into harm's way in the face of even limited risks. It is also difficult for even the most advanced Western mine countermeasure systems to detect and sweep modern mines. The US ships damaged by mines during the Gulf War were all operating in waters that had supposedly been swept, and even the best trained and equipped mine-sweeping teams have serious problems in sweeping nonmagnetic mines, large areas with loose mines, and bottom mines or other mines which are timed to activate only after several ships have passed, or at fixed intervals.

IRANIAN AMPHIBIOUS WARFARE CAPABILITIES

Iran has significant amphibious assets by Gulf standards, and the regular navy and naval branch of the IRGC have independent marine forces. These assets are large enough to move a battalion-sized force relatively rapidly, and include:

- four Hengam-class (Larak-class) LST amphibious support ships (displacement of 2,940-tons loaded). Each can carry up to six tanks, 600 tons of cargo, and 227 troops. They can embark a Sikorsky RH-53D helicopter and have 40 mm guns.
- three Iran Hormuz-class (South Korean) LSTs (2,014-tons loaded). Each can carry up to nine tanks and berth 140 troops.
- two Iran Ajar-class LST (2,274-tons loaded). These ships may now be dedicated to the mine laying mission, but one was scuttled by the US Navy in 1987 and may not be fully operational.
- three Hormuz-class 1,400-ton LCTs, each with 600 tons lift
- one 250 ton LSL
- at least six—and possibly more than 12—nine-ton Rotork 421-class LCUs
- many smaller amphibious assault vehicles

Iran's amphibious ships give Iran the capability to deploy about 1,000 troops and, theoretically, about 30–40 tanks in an amphibious assault—although Iran has not practiced amphibious operations using heavy weapons and has never demonstrated that it has an effective over-the-shore capability. Iran might use commercial ferries and on-roll off ships if it felt they could survive. Iran has also built up its capability to hide or shelter small ships in facilities on its islands and coastline along the Gulf and the ability to provide them with defensive cover from anti-air and anti-ship missiles. However, all of Iran's training to date has focused on amphibious raiding and not on operations using heavy weapons or larger operations.

Iran has held several amphibious warfare exercises every year since 1992. These include exercises like the Great Khaibar in September, 1995, which were centered on the Strait of Hormuz and Hengam Island, and which involved the IRGC naval and marine units and navy commands operating from Iranian navy landing ships. They also included large-scale exercises in 1996 and 1997.[23] Iran clearly, however, lacks the air and surface power to move its amphibious forces across the Gulf in the face of significant air/sea defenses, or to support a landing in a defended area.

Iran has support ships, but these are generally insufficient to sustain "blue water" operations and to support an amphibious task force. It has one Kharg-class 33,014-ton replenishment ship, two Bandar Abbas-class 4,673-ton fleet supply ships and oilers, one 14,410-ton repair ship, two 12,000-ton water tankers, seven 1,300-ton Delva-class support ships, 5–6 Hendijan-class support vessels, two floating dry-docks and 20 tugs, tenders, and utility craft to help support a large naval or an amphibious operation.

IRANIAN NAVAL AIR CAPABILITIES

The Iranian navy's air capability consists of two to three operational P-3F Orion maritime patrol aircraft out of an original inventory of five. According to reports from the Gulf, none of the surviving P-3Fs have fully operational radars, and their crews often use binoculars. It also has up to 12 Sikorsky SH-3D ASW helicopters, two RH-53D mine-laying helicopters, and seven Agusta-Bell AB-212 helicopters. It uses air force AH-1J attack helicopters, equipped with French AS.12 missiles, in naval missions, and has adapted Hercules C-130 and Fokker Friendship aircraft for mine-laying and patrol missions.[24]

The most significant recent development in Iran's capabilities to use airpower to attack naval targets has been the acquisition of the CS-801K for its regular air force.

IRANIAN ANTI-SHIP MISSILE FORCES

Iran's lack of a modern long-range anti-ship missile, suitable targeting capability, and competitive electronic warfare capability has been a major weakness in its war-fighting capability. Iran seems to have expended virtually all of its Harpoon missiles during the Iran-Iraq War. Further, its Standards and the rest of its remaining US-supplied naval, air-to-air, and air-to-surface missiles have now aged well beyond their normal life cycle. Iran does not have a single reliable US-supplied missile in its naval or air inventory, and all of Iran's Western-supplied systems are so unreliable that some experts feel they can no longer be rated as operational in any form.

These problems explain why Iran obtained the Seersucker, CS-801, and CS-802 anti-ship missiles, and the C-801K air-launched anti-ship missile. They also explain its interest in producing such missiles, and in obtaining upgraded versions of the Chinese CS-802, the Russian SS-N-22, and the Russian TU-22M bombers, equipped with long-range anti-ship missiles. All of these purchases are ways of compensating for its current lack of an advanced sea-based anti-ship missile capability.[25]

Iranian forces are now operating all four of the new systems that Iran has obtained from China:

- *The Seersucker* is a long-range, mobile anti-ship missile, which is designated the HY-2 or Sea Eagle-2 by the People's Republic of China. It is a copy of the Soviet CSS-N-2 "Styx" missile, and it is made by the China Precision Machinery Import and Export Corporation (CPMIEC). It is a very large missile with a 0.76 meter diameter and a weight of 3,000 kilograms. It has an 80–90 kilometer range and a 450 kilogram warhead.[26] It climbs to 145 meters (600') after launch and then drops to a cruise profile at 30 meters (100'). There are two variants. One uses radar active homing at ranges from the target of eight kilometers (4.5 nautical miles). The other is set to use passive IR homing and a radar altimeter to keep it at a constant height over the water.[27] While the Seersucker can be launched from large ships, the Seersuckers in Iranian hands all seem to be land based. Iran fired at least eight Seersuckers against targets in Kuwait during the Iran-Iraq War, three of which were hits.

- *The CS-801* anti-ship missile, also called the Yinji (Hawk) missile, is a solid-fueled missile that began test flights in 1986. It is roughly equivalent to the French Exocet, and it can be launched from land and ships. It has a range of approximately 74 kilometers in the surface-to-surface mode, and it uses J-Band active radar guidance. It has a 512-kilogram warhead and cruises at an altitude of 20–30 meters.

- *The CS-802* is an upgraded CS-801 that was first exhibited in 1988. It has many characteristics similar to the CS-801, but it uses a turbojet propulsion system with a rocket booster instead of the solid-fueled booster in the CS-801. As has been discussed earlier, it has a range of 70–75 miles, a warhead of up to 363 pounds, and it can be targeted by a radar deployed on a smaller ship or aircraft operating over the radar horizon of the launching vessel.[28]

- *The CS-801K* is a Chinese-supplied, air-launched anti-ship missile which Iran first tested on June 3 and 6, 1997. The CS-081K is a variant of the CS-801. It too is a sea-skimming, high-subsonic cruise missile and has a range in excess of 20 nautical miles (some reports indicate a range of 15–120 kilometers). It has been test-fired by Iran's F-4Es, but Iran may be able to use other launch aircraft. This air delivery capability gives Iran what some analysts have called a "360 degree" attack capability, since aircraft can rapidly maneuver to far less predictable launch points than Iranian combat ships.[29]

The naval branch of the Revolutionary Guards plays a major role in operating these new anti-ship missile systems. The Guards have operated Iran's Chinese-supplied Seersucker surface-to-ship missiles, since they were first delivered during the Iran-Iraq War, although these IRGC units may have had support from the Iranian navy. The Guards also operate Iran's ten new 68-ton Chinese Hudong (Hudong)-class fast attack craft, which are equipped with CS-802 missiles.

Many of the systems are land based and are deployed in shelters or tunneled facilities. Iran has established fixed and presurveyed launch sites near the Strait of Hormuz and in a number of other locations—including positions near Iraq and Kuwait. The number of sites is also increasing. There was one known Seersucker launch site in 1990.[30] The IRGC had a total of 12 Seersucker launchers in three operational land-based anti-ship missile batteries in early 1998, with four launchers each. These units were deployed near Iran's naval base at Chah

Bahar, Bandar Abbas, Qeshem Island, and at Khuestak and Sirri Island near the Strait of Hormuz, to cover the entrance to the Gulf. Iran had at least 50–60 Seersucker missiles, and a total of less than 100.[31]

The IRGC has also steadily increased its number of presurveyed dispersal sites and mobile missile launchers. Vice Admiral John Scott Redd, then the commander of the US Fifth Fleet, indicated in July, 1996 that Iran had tripled the number of missiles deployed on its Gulf coast since 1994. He indicated that Iran was fitting anti-ship missiles on 25 boats, and that Iran's acquisition of the CS-802 was a "new dimension in the regional naval threat." Redd later stated that the Iranian navy and the IRGC's missile capabilities were creating a "360 degree threat that can come from basically anywhere at sea in the Gulf or in the Gulf of Oman."[32]

The CS-802 missile was fired at a "sea target" from a Hudong near the Iranian naval base at Jask on November 28, 1996, as part of the Victory III exercise. Jask is on Iran's southeast coast near the Strait of Hormuz, and the Iranian press release announcing the firing referred to it as the first operational testing of "advanced missile systems" by the Iranian navy. US sources then indicated that Iran had taken delivery on 40 such missiles.[33] Iran carried out another test in January, 1997. By then, it may have had as many as 100 CS-802s in inventory. US experts estimate that Iran had a total of 100–200 CS-801s and CS-802s in January, 1988.[34]

Iran has sought to buy even more advanced anti-ship missiles from Russia, North Korea, and China, to buy anti-ship missile production facilities, and possibly even Chinese-made missile armed frigates. As a result, there is no way to know how many Iranian ships will acquire effective new anti-ship and anti-air missiles, or when any new types of missiles and ships might be delivered. Iran will have to make some such order by the late 1990s to keep up its present strength, however, its major Western-supplied ships can be made fully modern and operational without a comprehensive refit, which can be accomplished in Iranian shipyards. Iran has also announced that it will build its own "frigates."[35]

Some sources have claimed that Iran has bought eight Soviet-made SS-N-22 "Sunburn" or "Sunburst" anti-ship missile launch units from Ukraine and has deployed them near the Strait of Hormuz. However, US experts have seen no evidence of such a purchase and doubt that Iran has any operational holdings of such systems. The "SS-N-22" is a title that actually applies to two different modern long-range supersonic sea-skimming systems—the P-270 Moskit (also called the Kh-15 or 3M80) and the P80 or P-100 Zubi/Onika.

Although the performance of these systems is not as advanced as some descriptions in the Western press might indicate, the deployed versions have a maximum range of up to 100–120 kilometers. They have relatively sophisticated guidance systems, are harder to intercept than the CS-801/802 or HY-2, and are more resistant to countermeasures. If Iran should have such systems, they would be the only systems in the Gulf designed to defeat the defense on US Aegis ships.[36]

There are unverified reports that Iran is working on a version of the Seersucker with a range of up to 400 kilometers. US experts do not believe this, and it is unclear how Iran could target such a system without remote surveillance and a targeting platform. It is also unclear whether Iran is attempting to build a longer-range anti-ship system, or is using this development effort to build a land attack system. Furthermore, it is important to note that China is developing two follow-on supersonic missiles with cruise speeds of Mach 2.0 that could directly replace the HY-2 with little or no warning. The missiles are the HY-3 and C-101 and use ramjet propulsion and active radar terminal homing.[37]

Finally, Iran announced in May, 1996 that it had fired a new missile, called the Tondar, during naval exercises. This seems to have been an Iranian-assembled Chinese CS-802 missile rather than a completely new system. It was clear, however, that the Revolutionary Guards had strengthened their anti-ship missile deployments to cover the Northern Gulf as well as the lower Gulf. Further, in 1997, the IRGC announced that it had conducted a four-day exercise involving some 200,000 personnel with some 200 vessels, involving extensive exercises with anti-ship missiles, and that the Hudong-class boats would fire the Tondar. Iran also stated that the range of the Tondar was 120 kilometers, but it is unclear whether Iran's claims were more than rhetoric. Radar cannot look over the horizon—which is a distance of about 26 nautical miles at sea level— and no land or ship-based sensor system can fire at such ranges without remote designation of the target by an airborne platform or another vessel with tracking radar.[38]

There were also indications from other sources that Iran might be seeking to produce the CS-801, CS-802, or some variant of the Chinese FL-2 or FL-7, called the FL-10. The FL-2 is a subsonic missile with a range of 50 kilometers. The FL-7 is supersonic and has a range of 30 kilometers. Both missiles are made by the China Precision Machinery Import and Export Corporation.[39]

These deals, however, seem increasingly unlikely. China agreed to stop sending anti-ship missiles and nuclear technology to Iran in October, 1997 as part of a deal between President Clinton and President Jiang Zemin that gave China access to US nuclear reactor technology. US Secretary of Defense William Cohen stated on January 20, 1998, that he had received further assurances from President Jiang Zemin and Chinese Minister of Defense Chi Haotian during his visit to China: "I think these two assurances will go a long way to building upon the very cooperative relationship that we are developing." It was the clear message that no sales will go forward, no transfers—period—to Iran that would include those missiles that have been contracted for before. If these assurances prove valid, Iran could face serious problems in further modernizing the capability of both its regular naval forces and the naval branch of the IRGC.[40]

IRAN'S SUBMARINE FORCES

Iran has also attempted to offset the weakness of its major surface forces by emphasizing unconventional forms of naval warfare, although some Iranian capabilities have been exaggerated. For example, reports that Iran purchased or assembled up to nine 27-ton midget submarines from North Korea, beginning in 1988, seem to be incorrect. These reports claimed that the midget submarines could dive to 300 feet, had a compartment for divers, and carried two side cargoes of five tons, or enough for 14 limpet mines. However, Iran has not conducted any exercises to show it operates midget submarines, and the deliveries probably never took place. Rear Admiral Mohammad Karim Tavakoli, the Commander of the First Naval Zone, headquartered in Bandar Abbas, also announced in late 1997 that Iran was going to manufacture its own midget submarine without any reference to existing ships.[41]

In contrast, Iran has obtained three Type 877 EKM Kilo-class submarines. It signed an agreement in early 1992 to buy these three submarines from the United Admiralty Sudomeh shipyard in St. Petersburg, at a cost of $600 million each. It subsequently sent crews for training to a Russian-controlled naval base in Latvia.

The first Kilo was transferred to Iran in November, 1992, and it was commissioned as the *Tareq-901*. The ship completed its work-up exercise in the Gulf of Oman in the winter of 1992–1993. The United States reacted by sending the nuclear attack submarine *Topeka* into the Gulf as a show of strength. The *Topeka* was the first US nuclear submarine deployment into the Gulf, and it demonstrated the seriousness of US concern regarding Iran's acquisition of the Kilo.[42]

Despite this US response, the second Kilo was delivered to Iran in late July, 1993, and it was commissioned as the *Noor*.[43] The commander of the Iranian navy, Rear Admiral Ali Shamkani, announced in November, 1995 that he expected a third submarine to be delivered in 1996. However, the delivery of the third submarine was delayed by financing problems, and by the need to upgrade the submarine's batteries and air conditioning systems to operate efficiently in the Gulf's high water temperatures. It was only delivered to Iran in mid-January 1997, and only began to actively deploy in July of that year.[44] All of these submarines participated in an extensive naval exercise in the spring of 1988 which was supposed to demonstrate Iran's ability to close the Gulf. This Ettihad (Unity) series involved two destroyers, two amphibious ships, F-4Es and other aircraft, and a wide range of other ships, as well as the three submarines.[45]

The Kilo is a relatively modern and quiet submarine which first became operational in 1980. The Iranian Kilos are Type 877EKM export versions that are about 10 meters longer than the original Kilos and are equipped with advanced command and control systems. Each Type 877EKM has a teardrop hull coated with anechoic tiles to reduce noise. It displaces approximately 3,076 tons when submerged and 2,325 tons when surfaced. It is 72.6 meters long, 9.9 meters in beam, has a draught of 6.6 meters, and is powered by three 1,895 HP generator sets, one 5,900 SHP electric motor, and one six-bladed propeller. It has a complement of 52 men and an endurance of 45 days. Its maximum submerged speed is 17 knots, and its maximum surface speed is 10 knots.

Each Kilo has six 530 mm torpedo tubes, including two wired guided torpedo tubes. Only one torpedo can be wire guided at a time. The Kilo can carry a mix of 18 homing and wire-guided torpedoes or 24 mines. Russian torpedoes are available with ranges of 15–19 kilometers, speeds of 29–40 knots, and warheads with 100-, 205-, and 305-kilogram weights. Their guidance systems include active sonar homing, passive homing, wire guidance, and active homing. Some reports indicate that Iran bought over 1,000 modern Soviet mines with the Kilos, and that the mines were equipped with modern magnetic, acoustic, and pressure sensors. Russia is developing both improved torpedoes and anti-ship missiles for deployment in the 503 mm torpedo tube, but these do not seem to be operational.

The Kilo has a remote anti-aircraft launcher with one pre-loaded missile in the sail, and Soviet versions have six SA-N-5 (Igla/SA-16) surface-to-air missiles stored inside. However, Russia only supplied Iran with the SA-14 (Strela).

The Kilo has a maximum surface speed of 10 knots, a maximum submerged speed of about 17 knots, a minimum submerged operating depth of about 30 meters, an operational diving depth of 240 meters, and a maximum diving depth of 300 meters. The submarine also has a surface cruise range of 3,000–6,000 nautical miles and a submerged cruise range of 400 nautical miles—depending on speed and combat conditions.[46]

The Iranian submarines do not seem to have any of the newer systems in the Project 636 version of the Kilo. The Project 636 is a considerably more advanced submarine than the 877 EKM, with an improved teardrop-shaped double hull, advanced watertight compartments, and a motor eight decibels quieter than that of the 877 EKM. It also has a slightly greater length (73.8 meters), more power and speed, a maximum range of 7,500 nautical miles, and a maximum diving depth of 350 meters. It has an advanced MGK-400EM sonar that Russia claims can detect a low-noise submarine at ranges up to 20 kilometers. It has a new 490 sonar array with three times the area of the array used on previous Russian diesel submarines, which can use multiple digital beams and has far more advanced data processing and displays than earlier Russian systems. It can track up to five targets and has improved shallow water and reload control capability. The MGK-400EM could be fitted or retrofitted to the 877 EKM, although Iran's submarines do not have it.

Iran's purchase of the Kilos thus give it the capability to operate in the Gulf and in the Gulf of Oman in a way that reduces the vulnerability of its naval forces to air and surface attack. At the same time, Iran can use its minisubmarines to hide in the shallow depths and currents near the Strait, or to support covert operations. Both types of submarines can be used to fire torpedoes against slow-moving tankers and launch mines near ports. Iran has shown that it can use helicopters with dipping sonars to communicate with its submarines, and that it can provide its submarines with targeting information from its shore-based radars and patrol aircraft.[47]

Iran announced that it had conducted full-scale naval maneuvers, which included its Kilo submarines for the first time, beginning on March 5, 1995. It also indicated that it had test fired advanced wake-homing and wire-guided Russian torpedoes.[48] Iran's submarines have been used in exercises in the shallow waters near Iran's ports and islands in the Northern Gulf, and in independent operations near the Strait of Hormuz and in the Gulf of Oman.[49] They also fired ammunition at mock targets during the Ettihad (Unity) series of exercises in April, 1998.[50] However, US experts are not particularly impressed by the performance of Iranian crews, particularly in using their torpedoes.[51]

Iran's ability to use its submarines to deliver mines and fire long-range, wake-homing torpedoes gives it an important capability to strike in ways that make it difficult to detect or attack the submarine. Mines can be laid covertly in critical areas before a conflict, and the mines can be set to activate and deactivate at predetermined intervals in ways that make mining difficult to detect and sweep. Long-range homing torpedoes can be used against tanker-sized targets at ranges in excess of 10 kilometers, and to attack slow-moving combat ships which are not on alert and/or which lack sonars and countermeasures. Many Southern Gulf navies have ships with sonar, but none have highly advanced detection gear, countermeasure capability, or the training and equipment to be more than moderately effective in ASW missions. Saudi Arabia is seeking to upgrade the limited ASW sensors on its Al Madinah-class frigates, and Bahrain and the UAE are considering improving their ASW assets, but even such upgrades would leave Southern Gulf forces with only limited real-world capability to protect the Gulf's shipping lanes.[52]

At the same time, many Third World countries have found submarines difficult to operate. For example, Russia delivered the first two Kilos with two 120-cell batteries designed for rapid power surges, rather than power over long periods. They proved to last only 1–2 years in warm waters versus 5–7 years for similar batteries from India and the UK. Iran had to turn to India for help in developing batteries that were reliable in the warm waters of the Gulf.

These imports seem to have solved Iran's initial problems in operating its submarines, and Iran may have obtained continuing technical support from India. Russia may also have corrected the battery problems in the third Kilo delivered to Iran in the spring of 1997.[53] Nevertheless, even nations as advanced as Egypt and Syria have not been able to make their submarines highly effective or to keep them fully combat operational.

Iran also faces significant problems in using its submarines in local waters. Many areas of the Gulf do not favor submarine operations. The Gulf is about 241,000 square kilometers in area, and it stretches 990 kilometers from the Shatt al-Arab to the Strait of Hormuz. It is about 340 kilometers wide at its maximum width, and about 225 kilometers wide for most of its length. While heat patterns disturb surface sonars, they also disturb submarine sonars, and the advantage seems to be slightly in favor of sophisticated surface ships and maritime patrol aircraft.

The deeper parts of the Gulf are noisy enough to make ASW operations difficult, but large parts of the Gulf—including much of the Southern Gulf on a line from Al Jubail across the tip of Qatar to about halfway up the UAE—are less than 20 meters deep. The water is deeper on the Iranian side, but the maximum depth of the Gulf—located about 30 kilometers south of Qeys Island—is still only 88 meters. This means that no point in the Gulf is deeper than the length of an SN-688 nuclear submarine. The keel-to-tower height of such a submarine alone is 16 meters. Even smaller coastal submarines have maneuver and bottom suction problems and cannot hide in thermoclines, or take advantage of diving for concealment or self-protection.

The Strait of Hormuz is about 180 kilometers long, but has a minimum width of 39 kilometers, and only the two deep water channels are suitable for major surface ship or submarine operations. Each of these channels is only about 2 kilometers wide. Further, a limited flow of fresh water and high evaporation makes the Gulf extremely saline. This creates complex underwater currents in the main channels at the Strait of Hormuz and complicates both submarine operations and submarine detection. There are some areas with considerable noise, but not of a type that masks submarine noise from sophisticated ASW detection systems of the kind operated by the United States and UK. Further, the minimum operating depth of the Kilo is 45 meters, and the limited depth of the area around the Strait can make submarine operations difficult.

Submarines are easier to operate in the Gulf of Oman, which is noisy enough to make ASW operations difficult, but such deployments would expose the Kilos to operations by US and British nuclear attack submarines. It is unlikely that Iran's Kilos could survive for any length of time if hunted by a US or British navy air-surface-SSN hunter-killer team.[54]

Iran might be able to complicate the US and British search problem if it could base its submarines where their deployment patterns and range would be less predictable. There have been reports that Iran made arrangements to base Iranian ships, including submarines, in Mozambique's ports as a way of reducing its vulnerability and need to operate in Gulf waters. The port of Ncala is a deep water port that would be particularly useful for Kilo operations in the Indian Ocean and Mozambique Channel. Mozambique, however, has denied that any such arrangements exist.[55]

In any case, the effectiveness of Iran's submarines is likely to depend heavily on the degree of Western involvement in any ASW operation. If the Kilos did not face the US or British ASW forces, the Iranian Kilos could operate in or near the Gulf with considerable impunity. If they did face US and British forces, they might be able to attack a few tankers or conduct some mining efforts, but are unlikely to survive extended combat. This makes the Kilos a weapon that may be more effective in threatening Gulf shipping, or as a remote minelayer, than in naval combat. Certainly, Iran's purchase of the Kilos has already received close attention from the Southern Gulf states and convinced them that they must take Iran more seriously.

THE NAVAL BRANCH OF THE REVOLUTIONARY GUARDS

The relative role of the IRGC and regular navy is unclear, although the IRGC seems to concentrate on coastal defense and unconventional warfare, while the regular navy plays a more conventional "blue water" role. Some experts believed the naval branch of the IRGC would be merged with the regular navy when Admiral Ali Shamkani was made commander of both forces in 1989. However, they were still an independent force in 1998, with their own island bases and a facility at Noshahr Naval Academy on the Caspian Sea.

The naval branch of the Islamic Revolutionary Guards Corps operates Iran's land-based anti-ship missiles and coastal defense artillery. The manpower of the naval branch of the IRGC is sometimes estimated at 20,000 men, but the actual total could be as low as 12,000–15,000. It has training facilities and five bases in the Gulf, including the islands of Sirri, Abu Musa, Al Farisyah, and Larak, and the Halul oil platform—with a main base at Bandar Abbas. Most IRGC facilities are relatively small, although the IRGC has established more extensive positions. For example, it has increased its troop presence on Abu Musa from 150 to several hundred men, created Seersucker anti-ship missile launch sites, and dug in tanks and artillery to support its fortifications.

The naval branch of the IRGC also operates Iran's 10 new 68-ton Chinese Hudong-class fast attack craft fast patrol boats and a number of other surface vessels, and many of Iran's CS-802 anti-ship missiles.[56] In addition, the naval branch operates some of Iran's 11 US Mark III-class (41.6 ton), 6–20 US Swift Mark II-class (22.9 ton), 20 operational PBI type (20.1 ton), three Sewart type (9.1 ton), and 12 Enforcer type (4.7 ton) coastal patrol craft.[57] The PBI-type vessel has been sighted with crude installations of unguided Tigercats, which have a maximum range of 6 kilometers.

The naval branch has some of the largest unconventional warfare capabilities in the world.[58] It currently operates several hovercraft, Iran's 32–36 up-engined Boghammer craft (6.4 tons), 35 or more craft roughly similar to the Boston Whaler (1.3 tons), numerous River Roadsted patrol craft, and large numbers of river craft. The Boghammer fast interceptor craft is a 41-foot craft which is particularly important to IRGC exercises and operations.[59] It is built by Boghammer Marine of Sweden, can reach speeds of up to 69 knots, has a range of up to 926 kilometers, and has a 1,000-pound equipment load. The craft, which are similar to Boston Whalers, are only about 22 feet long.

The Boghammers and other fast patrol boats are largely unarmed, but crews can be equipped with heavy machine guns, grenade launchers, anti-tank guided weapons, manportable surface-to-air missiles, and 106 mm recoilless rifles. The IRGC also uses small launches and at least 30 Zodiak rubber dinghies to practice rocket, small arms, and recoilless rifle attacks. Its other small craft were armed with a mix of machine guns, recoilless rifles, and man and crew-portable anti-tank guided missiles.

The Boghammers, the other smaller fast patrol boats, and light craft like Iran's Zodiacs, are extremely difficult to detect by radar in anything but the calmest sea state. Iran bases them at a number of offshore islands and oil platforms, and they can strike quickly and with limited warning. The naval branch of the IRGC also has naval artillery, divers, and minelaying units. It had extensive stocks of scuba equipment and an underwater combat center at Bandar Abbas.[60] Iran is also improving the defenses and port capabilities of its islands in the Gulf, adding covered moorings, more advanced sensors, and better air defenses.

The naval branch of the IRGC is also steadily improving its survivability and capability to conduct sustained low-intensity naval combat in the face of US air and naval attacks. It has the ability to widely disperse its vessels into small, unimproved ports and moorings where they will be difficult to detect and strike. Many of its small craft are difficult to detect at long ranges in anything other than a quiet sea, and they are too small to attack with missiles. Its troops can be widely dispersed as light infantry, using light anti-ship, anti-air, and anti-land missiles and weapons to defend a given area or facility without presenting lucrative targets for air, missile, and artillery fire.[61]

Its exercises are anything but models of military efficiency, but its exercises in late 1997 showed a growing capability to use anti-ship and surface-to-air missiles. Admiral Ali Akbar Ahmadian, the new commander of the naval branch of the IRGC, announced that the IRGC had begun construction of its own missile craft and had upgraded anti-ship missiles. "So far, our speedboats and missiles sites have been a distinct feature of the Guards navy.... Now we're adding an aspect which will make us all the more powerful... the situation of a real missile war was acted out during various stages of the maneuvers."[62]

Iran can use IRGC forces to conduct the kind of low-intensity/guerrilla warfare that can only be defeated by direct engagement with land forces, and filter substantial reinforcements into a coastal area on foot or with light vehicles, making such reinforcement difficult to attack. It can use virtually any surviving small craft to lay mines and to place unmoored mines in shipping lanes. Its IRGC forces can use small craft to attack offshore facilities and raid coastal targets. Finally, the United States did not successfully destroy a single land-based Iraqi anti-ship missile launcher during the Gulf War, and the IRGC now has many dispersal launch sites and storage areas over a much longer coast. It also has a growing number of caves, shelters, and small hardened facilities. Such targets are sometimes difficult to detect until they are used, and they present added problems because they usually are too small and too numerous to attack with high cost ordnance until it is clear that they have valuable enough contents to merit such attack.

IRANIAN NAVAL WAR-FIGHTING CAPABILITIES

Iran's surface *forces* cannot hope to challenge the combined power of US naval and air forces on a sustained basis. Iran can, however, use systems like anti-ship missiles, mines, and submarines to threaten US freedom of action and ability to deploy vulnerable high-value targets, like carriers, in Gulf waters. As a result, it might take several weeks to defeat Iran's ability to attack Gulf shipping decisively, once the United States deployed major naval and air forces, although much of Iran's naval power might be destroyed in a matter of days.

Threatening Traffic through the Gulf

Iran's new forms of sea power also offer Iran the ability to tacitly and actively threaten the flow of oil through the Gulf, and thereby the economic lifeblood of Iraq and its Southern Gulf neighbors. Consequently, Iran can threaten or attack shipping near the Strait until decisive action is taken to destroy Iran's anti-ship missile units, mine warfare capabilities, submarines, and ability to use smaller ships.

Iran can take advantage of the long shipping routes through the Gulf. It has the ability to launch mines, naval or air strikes, and anti-ship missile strikes from positions along the entire length of the Gulf and the Gulf of Oman and to threaten or harass Gulf shipping. While strategists sometimes focus on "closing the Strait," a bottle does not have to be broken at the neck, and low-level mine and unconventional warfare strikes on shipping that are designed to harass and intimidate may allow Iran to achieve its objectives much more safely than escalating to all-out attacks on the flow of oil.

Supporting Amphibious Operations and Power Projection

As for power projection, Iran cannot project power by land without crossing Iraq, but it can carry out small amphibious operations. This allows Iran to pose a tacit or an active threat to the Southern Gulf states, particularly small vulnerable states like Bahrain and the UAE—although Iran's capability to conduct such operations is currently limited. Unless the Southern Gulf states and the United States permit Iran to use ferries or commercial ships to conduct unopposed landings or transfers of troops, the Iranian navy and the IRGC are very limited in capability. While they can conduct small landing operations, these operations would be highly vulnerable unless they achieved total surprise. There is no way Iran could sustain them once US naval and air counterattacks began.

If Iran was to strike across the Gulf in force, the Iranian navy and Naval Guards would need much more effective air cover, a stronger surface fleet, and better night vision and targeting systems for their small craft, additional amphibious ships, and hovercraft. Large-scale assaults would also require Iran to use commercial ships with roll-on, roll-off capability, and to practice over-the-beach operations using heavy equipment and armor—training that is now totally lacking. At the same time, Iran can already use small elements of its naval forces to deploy mines and other unconventional warfare forces covertly, to supply arms to radical movements in the Southern Gulf, to seize undefended islands, and to threaten or attack offshore oil operations, ports, and desalinization facilities.

Exercises, Training, and Proficiency

The Iranian navy is scarcely equal to Western navies in training and proficiency, but it is the only Gulf navy—aside from Oman—to conduct extensive and meaningful training. It operates jointly with the naval arm of the IRGC, and it has steadily increased its number of exercises in recent years. It conducted 36 exercises in 1993, 49 exercises in 1994, 57 exercises in 1995, and numerous exercises in 1996 and 1997. It has slowly improved its amphibious, missile deployment, combined arms, interdiction, mine warfare, electronic warfare, and underwater warfare training.[63]

In addition to the limits imposed by Iran's ships and weaponry, these training efforts still have many tactical limitations. Nevertheless, such training efforts give Iran a much higher overall level of proficiency than most Southern Gulf navies. While some Southern Gulf navies have more modern ships and more advanced Western-supplied equipment, they fail to train effectively. The Southern Gulf navies are more showpiece forces than fighting forces. In spite of additional exercises with the US and British navies, most have shown little improvement in real-world war-fighting proficiency since their virtual nonperformance in the Gulf War.

Contingency Capabilities

As a result, Iran can use its navy to threaten and intimidate, and to cause significant initial or short-term damage to shipping in the Gulf, as well as offshore and coastal facilities in the Southern Gulf. Iran can use both its navy and the naval branch of the IRGC to conduct extensive campaigns using unconventional warfare, can mine Gulf waters, and can harass and attack Gulf shipping using anti-ship missiles and long-range homing torpedoes. Iran can also probably disperse enough of its IRGC forces, smaller ships, and missiles so that some of its capabilities will survive anything other than an all-out US air attack.

Iran cannot, however, hope to succeed in sustained naval warfare as long as the United States commits major naval and air forces, and the Southern Gulf states are willing to provide bases and facilities to resist Iranian pressure. Iran's regular navy and air force is simply too vulnerable to survive a combination of US naval and air power for more than a matter of days—although many of Iran's land-based anti-ship missiles and the IRGC's boats and small craft could be dispersed, hid, and small "slash and run" attacks and minelaying continue to be conducted almost indefinitely. Iran would have to build up a very different mix of naval capabilities to directly challenge a coalition of US, Britain, and the Southern Gulf states directly—or US air and naval power acting with little or no Southern Gulf support.

If Iran is ever to compete directly with US sea power, it must rebuild its navy as a modern "blue water" force and create an effective overall war-fighting capability. To do this, it would need to replace or rebuild most of its surface fleet and develop adequate training and joint warfare tactics and doctrine. It would need to obtain anti-ship missiles that are competitive with those of Southern Gulf, US, and British naval forces. Iran also needs more advanced torpedoes, better minelaying capability, and more advanced mines like bottom and moored influence and smart mines.

In addition, Iran would need to modernize and expand the coverage of its shore-based missiles and deploy them in enough locations and in a mobile enough form to make them more survivable. Further, Iran would require improved C^4I/BM and electronic warfare systems, advanced land-based and surface ship-based sensor systems, rebuilt and modernized P-3s or the purchase of a suitable replacement, new or modified air defense and anti-ship missiles, and suitable electronics for its surface forces. Finally, Iran would need better, or modified, naval helicopters and advanced exercise and training technology. Iran has announced programs to build three multirole destroyers, advanced anti-ship missiles, and other naval systems, but it has failed to produce any such systems to date. It is currently unlikely that Iran can obtain such capabilities before 2010, and there are few clear indications that Iran is seeking them.

NOTES

1. Reuters, August 27, 1997, 0838; *Jane's Defense Weekly*, November 12, 1997, p. 30.

2. This analysis draws on Anthony H. Cordesman, *Iran and Iraq: The Threat from the Northern Gulf*, Boulder, Westview, 1994; Anthony H. Cordesman and Ahmed S. Hashim, *Iran: Dilemmas of Dual Containment*, Boulder, Westview, 1997; IISS, *Military Balance, 1997–1998*, "Iran"; *Jane's Sentinel: The Gulf States, 1997*, "Iran"; Dr. Andrew Rathmell, "Iran's Rearmament: How Great a Threat?" *Jane's Intelligence Review*, July, 1994, pp. 317–322; US Naval Institute, *The Naval Institute Guide to the Combat Fleets of the World, 1993: Their Ships, Aircraft, and Armament*, Annapolis, Naval Institute, 1993; John Jordan, "The Iranian Navy," *Jane's Intelligence Review*, May, 1992, pp. 213–216; Anoushiravan Ehteshami, "Iran's National Strategy," *International Defense Review*, 4/1994, pp. 29–37; Ahmed Hashim, "The Crisis of the Iranian State," Adelphi Paper 296, London, IISS, Oxford, July, 1995, pp. 7–30 and 50–70; Andrew Rathmell, *The Changing Military Balance in the Gulf*, London, RUSI, Whitehall Papers 38, 1996, pp. 9–23; Michael Eisenstadt, *Iranian Military Power, Capabilities, and Intentions*, Washington, Washington Institute, 1996, pp. 9–65; Anoushiravan Ehteshami, "Iran Strives to Regain Military Might," *International Defense Review*, 7/1996, pp. 22–26; *Washington Times*, May 2, 1989, p. A-9, June 23, 1989, p. A-9; March 1, 1992, p. B-3, March 22, 1989, p. A-8, January 17, 1992, p. A-1, February 20, 1992, p. 9; *Armed Forces Journal*, March, 1992, pp. 26–27; *Defense Electronics*, March, 1992, p. 16; *Inside the Air Force*, February 28, 1992, p. 1; *Jane's Defense Weekly*, November 19, 1988, pp. 1252–1253, June 3, 1988, p. 1057, February 11, 1989, p. 219, June 30, 1990,

pp. 1299–1302, February 11, 1992, p. 158–159; *Armed Forces (UK)*, May 1989, pp. 206–209; *Washington Post*, June 23, 1989, p. A-1; August 18, 1989, p. A-25; August 20, 1989, p. A-1, September 3, 1989, p. A-25, February 1, 1992, p. A-1, February 2, 1992, p. A-1, February 5, 1992, p. A-19; *New York Times*, September 3, 1989, p. A-4; *The Estimate*, October 13–26, 1989, p. 1; *Christian Science Monitor*, February 6, 1992, p. 19; *Philadelphia Inquirer*, February 6, 1992, p. A-6; *Los Angeles Times*, January 7, 1992, p. A-1; *Baltimore Sun*, January 25, 1992, p. 4A; *Defense News*, January 27, 1922, p. 45, February 17, 1992, p. 1; *Chicago Tribune*, January 19, 1992, p. 1.

3. *Washington Times*, October 11, 1997, p. A-6; *Jane's Defense Weekly*, October 1, 1997, p. 19, October 29, 1997, p. 4; Reuters, September 28, 1997, 0417, October 6, 1997, 1600.

4. *Defense and Foreign Affairs*, No. 1, 1994, pp. 4–7; *Navy News and Undersea Technology*, April 11, 1994, p. 4; *Defense News*, January 17, 1994, p. 1; *Jane's Defense Weekly*, April 30, 1997, p. 6, October 29, 1997, p. 4.

5. FBIS-NES-89-144, July 28, 1989, p. 51; FBIS-NES-89-191, October 4, 1989, p. 66, FBIS-NES-89-206, October 26, 1989, p. 66, FBIS-NES-89-214, November 7, 1989, p. 73; *International Defense Review*, June, 1990, pp. 51–52; IRNA, April 21, 1997, May 2, 1997; Iranian TV, April 26, 1997; *Jane's Defense Weekly*, April 23, 1997, p. 19, April 30, 1997, p. 6, June 24, 1995, p. 5, November 6, 1996, p. 23, June 25, 1997, p. 14; *Washington Times*, May 4, 1997, p. A7; May 12, 1997, p. A-13; Reuters, April 23, 1997, 0818, May 7, 1997, 0452, July 3, 1997, 0452, July 9, 1997, 1655; *Washington Post*, April 30, 1997, p. 6; April 23, 1997, p. 19, April 30, 1997, p. 6, June 30, 1997, p. A-20; Associated Press, June 30, 1996, 0629; May 7, 1997, 0452, July 3, 1997, 0452, July 9, 1997, 1655.

6. This analysis draws heavily on *Jane's Fighting Ships, 1992–1993, 1995–1996*, and *1996–1997*; US Naval Institute, *The Naval Institute Guide to the Combat Fleets of the World, 1993: Their Ships, Aircraft, and Armament*, Annapolis, Naval Institute, 1996; Anthony H. Cordesman, *Iran and Iraq: The Threat from the Northern Gulf*, Boulder, Westview, 1994; Anthony H. Cordesman and Ahmed S. Hashim, *Iran: Dilemmas of Dual Containment*, Boulder, Westview, 1997; Anoushiravan Ehteshami, "Iran's National Strategy," *International Defense Review*, 4/1994, pp. 29–37; Andrew Rathmell, *The Changing Military Balance in the Gulf*, London, RUSI, Whitehall Papers 38, 1996, pp. 9–23; Michael Eisenstadt, *Iranian Military Power, Capabilities, and Intentions*, Washington, Washington Institute, 1996, pp. 9–65; Anoushiravan Ehteshami, "Iran Strives to Regain Military Might," *International Defense Review*, 7/1996, pp. 22–26; IISS, *Military Balance, 1997–1998*, "Iran"; *Jane's Sentinel: The Gulf States, 1997*, "Iran"; USNI Data Base, *Military Technology, World Defense Almanac: The Balance of Military Power*, Vol. XVII, Issue 1–1993, ISSN 0722-3226, pp. 139–142, USNI Data Base; *Jane's Underwater Technology, 1997–1998; Jane's Underwater Warfare Systems, 1997–1998; Jane's Fighting Ships, 1997–1998; Jane's Naval Weapons Systems, 1997–1998*.

7. Interviews and USCENTCOM, *Atlas, 1996*, MacDill Air Force Base, USCENTCOM, 1997, pp. 14–15.

8. Interviews and USCENTCOM, *Atlas, 1996*, MacDill Air Force Base, USCENTCOM, 1997, pp. 14–15; *Jane's Sentinel: The Gulf States, 1997*, "Iran"; IISS, *Military Balance, 1997–1998*.

9. IRNA, April 21, 1997, May 2, 1997; Iranian TV, April 26, 1997; *Jane's Defense Weekly*, April 23, 1997, p. 19, April 30, 1997, p. 6, June 24, 1995, p. 5, November 6, 1996, p. 23, June 25, 1997, p. 14; *Washington Times*, May 4, 1997, p. A7; May 12, 1997,

p. A-13; Reuters, April 23, 1997, 0818, May 7, 1997, 0452, July 3, 1997, 0452, July 9, 1997, 1655; *Washington Post*, April 30, 1997, p. 6; April 23, 1997, p. 19, April 30, 1997, p. 6, June 30, 1997, p. A-20; Associated Press, June 30, 1996, 0629; May 7, 1997, 0452, July 3, 1997, 0452, July 9, 1997, 1655.

10. Adapted from the IISS, Annapolis, and JCSS databases, and the *Washington Times*, January 16, 1992, p. G-4; *Washington Post*, February 1, 1992, p. A1, February 2, 1992, pp. A1 and A25, February 5, p. A-19; *Financial Times*, February 6, 1992, p. 4; *Christian Science Monitor*, February 6, 1992, p. 19; *Defense News*, February 17, 1992, p. 1; *Jane's Defense Weekly*, October 29, 1997, p. 4.

11. *Jane's Fighting Ships, 1992–1993, 1995–1996,* and *1996–1997.*

12. *Jane's Fighting Ships, 1992–1993, 1995–1996,* and *1996–1997.*

13. *Jane's Fighting Ships, 1992–1993, 1995–1996,* and *1996–1997.*

14. *Jane's Fighting Ships, 1992–1993, 1995–1996,* and *1996–1997.*

15. Reuters, December 9, 1996, 02:41.

16. *Washington Times*, March 27, 1996, p. A-1.

17. *Jane's Defense Weekly*, October 1, 1994, p. 6, March 11, 1995, p. 2, March 18, 1995, p. 5; *Sea Power*, November, 1994, p. 21; *Jane's Armor and Artillery, 1995–1996*, pp. 759–762.

18. *Jane's Fighting Ships, 1992–1993* and *1996–1997.*

19. The submarines are based on World War II designs. They can lay mines, have a five-man crew, a maximum range of 1,200 miles, and a speed of 6 knots. Iran claims to have made one of the submarines. The first underwent trials in 1987. The second was delivered in 1988. These ships are difficult to use in mine laying and often require frogmen to place the mines. It is not surprising if Iran abandoned them as lacking effectiveness once the Iran-Iraq War was over. *Jane's Fighting Ships, 1992–1993*, London, Jane's Publishing; Naval Institute database; IISS, *Military Balance, 1997–1998*, "Iran"; *Jane's Sentinel: The Gulf States, 1997*, "Iran"; *Jane's Defense Weekly*, July 30, 1997, p. 3, December 17, 1997, p. 14; Reuters, November 26, 1997, 0746.

20. *Jane's Defense Weekly*, July 30, 1997, p. 3.

21. *Washington Times*, March 27, 1996, p. A-1.

22. *Defense News*, January 17, 1994, pp. 1, 29.

23. IRNA, April 21, 1997, May 2, 1997; Iranian TV, April 26, 1997; *Jane's Defense Weekly*, October 7, 1995, p. 22, April 23, 1997, p. 19, April 30, 1997, p. 6, June 24, 1995, p. 5, November 6, 1996, p. 23, June 25, 1997, p. 14, October 29, 1997, p. 4; *Washington Times*, May 4, 1997, p. A7; May 12, 1997, p. A-13; Reuters, April 23, 1997, 0818, May 7, 1997, 0452, July 3, 1997, 0452, July 9, 1997, 1655; *Washington Post*, April 30, 1997, p. 6; April 23, 1997, p. 19, April 30, 1997, p. 6, June 30, 1997, p. A-20; Associated Press, June 30, 1996, 0629; May 7, 1997, 0452, July 3, 1997, 0452, July 9, 1997, 1655.

24. Anthony H. Cordesman, *Iran and Iraq: The Threat from the Northern Gulf*, Boulder, Westview, 1994; Anthony H. Cordesman and Ahmed S. Hashim, *Iran: Dilemmas of Dual Containment*, Boulder, Westview, 1997; IISS, *The Military Balance, 1993–1994*, IISS, London, 1993, pp. 115–117; IISS, *Military Balance, 1997–1998*, "Iran"; *Jane's Sentinel: The Gulf States, 1997*, "Iran"; USNI Data Base, Military Technology,*World Defense Almanac: The Balance of Military Power*, Vol. XVII, Issue 1–1993, ISSN 0722-3226, pp. 139–142; and working data from the Jaffee Center for Strategic Studies; Ahmed Hashim, "The Crisis of the Iranian State," Adelphi Paper 296, London, IISS, Oxford, July, 1995, pp. 7–30 and 50–70; Andrew Rathmell, *The Changing Military Balance in*

the Gulf, London, RUSI, Whitehall Papers 38, 1996, pp. 9–23; Michael Eisenstadt, *Iranian Military Power, Capabilities, and Intentions,* Washington, Washington Institute, 1996, pp. 9–65; Anoushiravan Ehteshami, "Iran Strives to Regain Military Might," *International Defense Review,* 7/1996, pp. 22–26.

25. *Inside the Navy,* January 8, 1994, p. 1; *Defense and Foreign Affairs,* No. 1, 1994, pp. 4–7; *Navy News and Undersea Technology,* April 11, 1994, p. 4; *Defense News,* January 17, 1994, p. 1.

26. Estimates that the HY-2 has a range of 95–100 kilometer range and a 513 kilogram warhead seem to slightly exaggerate the capability of this system, but could be correct.

27. *Jane's Defense Weekly,* June 6, 1987, p. 1113; Richard Palowski, *Changes in Threat Air Combat Doctrine and Force Structure, 24th Edition,* Fort Worth Division, General Dynamics DWIC-91, February, 1992, pp. 11–275 to 11–277.

28. *World Missiles Briefing,* Teal Group Corporation.

29. *Jane's Defense Weekly,* June 25, 1997, p. 3; Associated Press, June 17, 1997, 1751; United Press, June 17, 1997, 0428; *International Defense Review,* 6/1996, p. 17.

30. *Jane's Defense Weekly,* December 9, 1995, p. 3, February 7, 1996, p. 14.

31. *Jane's Defense Weekly,* May 1, 1996, p. 20; April 30, 1997, p. 6.

32. There are reports that the Guards have formed at least one new unit using Chinese-supplied CS-801 anti-ship and ship-to-ship missiles, and there are reports that Iran is seeking to acquire much longer range anti-ship cruise missiles either from the People's Republic of China or the former Soviet Union. Iran has at least 60 to 100 CS-801 (YF-6) anti-ship missiles from the Chinese and may be using these to refit its surface fleet as well as to equip some shore-based facilities and the naval branch of the IRGC. US experts do not believe that these reports are correct. *Jane's Defense Weekly,* December 9, 1995, p. 3, February 7, 1996, p. 14; *Baltimore Sun,* July 16, 1996, p. 7A; *Jane's Defense Weekly,* May 1, 1996, p. 20; April 30, 1997, p. 6.

33. *World Missiles Briefing,* Teal Group Corporation.

34. *Jane's Defense Weekly,* December 9, 1995, p. 3, February 7, 1996, p. 14, March 27, 1996, p. 14, January 8, 1997, p. 13; *Washington Times,* March 27, 1996, p. A-1; *New York Times,* January 31, 1996, p. A-5; *Washington Post,* January 31, p. A-10; *The Estimate,* February 2, 1996, p. 4; Reuters, November 11, 1995, 0954, February 2, 1996, 0345; Reuters, December 9, 1996, 02:41.

35. *Jane's Defense Weekly,* July 17, 1996, p. 13; Dr. Anoushiravan Ehteshami, "The Armed Forces of the Islamic Republic of Iran," *Jane's Intelligence Review,* February, 1993, pp. 76–79; Gordon Jacobs and Tim McCarthy, "China Missile Sales—Few Changes for the Future," *Jane's Intelligence Review,* December, 1992, pp. 559–563.

36. *Naval Forces,* Vol. 15, No. 3, 1994, p. 62; *World Missiles Briefing,* Teal Group Corporation; *Defense and Foreign Affairs,* No. 1, 1994, pp. 4–7; *Defense News,* January 17, 1994, pp. 1, 29; *Inside the Navy,* January 10, 1994, p. 1; *Navy News and Undersea Technology,* April 1, 1994, p. 4; *Washington Times,* March 9, 1989, p. A-1, May 11, 1993, p. A-7; *Los Angeles Times,* February 14, 1989, p. 5; *Inside the Navy,* January 8, 1994, p. 1; *Defense and Foreign Affairs,* No. 1, 1994, pp. 4–7; *Navy News and Undersea Technology,* April 11, 1994, p. 4; *Defense News,* January 17, 1994, p. 1, *Jane's Defense Weekly,* May 1, 1996, p. 20.

37. *Jane's Intelligence Review,* November, 1992, pp. 512–513; *Time,* April 25, 1994, p. 39.

38. *Jane's Defense Weekly,* May 1, 1996, p. 20, June 6, 1996, p. 13, June 12, 1996,

p. 27; January 8, 1997, p. 13, April 30, 1997, p. 6; Reuters, December 9, 1996, 02:41; April 22, 1997, 07:09, April 23, 1997, 08:18, October 29, 1997, p. 4; *Tehran Times*, May 30, 1996; *Kayan Havai*, June 2, 1996; Agence France Presse, April 24, 1997, 24: 12.

39. *Jane's Defense Weekly*, December 17, 1998, pp. 18–19.

40. *New York Times*, October 18, 1997, p. A-1; Reuters, January 19, 1998, 2230; January 20, 1998, 0213; Associated Press, January 20, 1998, 0730EST.

41. *Jane's Fighting Ships, 1992–1993*, London, Jane's Publishing; Naval Institute database; IISS, *Military Balance, 1997–1998*, "Iran"; *Jane's Sentinel: The Gulf States, 1997*, "Iran"; *Jane's Defense Weekly*, July 30, 1997, p. 3, December 17, 1997, p. 14.

42. *Washington Times*, January 16, 1992, p. G-4; *Washington Post*, February 1, 1992, p. A-1, February 2, 1992, pp. A-1 and A-25, February 5, p. A-19, September 26, 1992, p. A-15, October 2, 1992, p. A-40, October 30, 1992, p. A-1, November 5, 1992, p. A-3; *Financial Times*, February 6, 1992, p. 4; *Christian Science Monitor*, February 6, 1992, p. 19; *Defense News*, February 17, 1992, p. 1; *Defense News*, February 17, 1992, p. 1, March 1, 1993, p. 1; *Time*, December 7, 1992, p. 26; *Wall Street Journal*, November 16, 1992, p. A-4; *Jane's Defense Weekly*, October 3, 1992, p. 12, November 21, 1992, p. 9, February 27, 1992, p. 9; *London Times*, October 5, 1992, p. 9.

43. *Washington Post*, August 4, 1993, p. A-12; *Washington Times*, June 12, 1993, p. A-2.

44. Reuters, November 11, 1995, 0954, February 2, 1996, 0345; *Jane's Defense Weekly*, October 28, 1995, p. 19, August 28, 1996, p. 10, July 9, 1997, p. 4.

45. *Jane's Defense Weekly*, April 22, 1998, p. 21.

46. Only two torpedo tubes can fire wire-guided torpedoes. *Defense News*, January 17, 1994, pp. 1, 29.

47. *Defense News*, December 6, 1993, p. 1.

48. *Jane's Defense Weekly*, October 8, 1994, p. 4, March 11, 1995, p. 2, March 18, 1995, p. 5; *The Estimate*, May 5, 1994, p. 4; *International Defense Review*, 12/1994, p. 9; *Washington Times*, January 17, 1995, p. A-11, March 8, 1995, p. A-10; *Sea Power*, November, 1994, p. 21.

49. Reuters, November 11, 1995, 0954, February 2, 1996, 0345; *Jane's Defense Weekly*, October 28, 1995, p. 19, August 28, 1996, p. 10.

50. Reuters, April 14, 1998, 1159; *Jane's Defense Weekly*, April 22, 1998, p. 21.

51. *Defense News*, December 6, 1993, p. 1.

52. See David Miller, "Submarines in the Gulf," *Military Technology*, 6/93, pp. 42–45; David Markov, "More Details Surface of Rubin's 'Kilo' Plans," *Jane's Intelligence Review*, May, 1997, pp. 209–215.

53. Interviews at USCENTCOM; *Jane's Defense Weekly*, July 9, 1997, p. 4; *Defense News*, June 9, 1997, p. 36.

54. See David Miller, "Submarines in the Gulf," *Military Technology*, 6/93, pp. 42–45; David Markov, "More Details Surface of Rubin's 'Kilo' Plans," *Jane's Intelligence Review*, May, 1997, pp. 209–215.

55. Reuters, February 11, 1997, 09:53; *Jane's Defense Weekly*, February 5, 1997, p. 5.

56. There have been unconfirmed reports that Iran is seeking to modify the Seersucker to extend its range and use it to deliver weapons of mass destruction.

57. Counts of these vessels differ sharply. Some estimates of the number of operational PBI types exceed 60. There are some reports that Iran is building its own version of the Boghammer.

58. IISS, *Military Balance, 1998–1999*, "Iran."

59. Although some reports refer to these craft as Boston Whalers, Iran has no Boston Whalers as such.

60. In addition to the sources listed at the start of this section, these assessments are based on various interviews, prior editions of IISS, *Military Balance*; the *Jaffee Center Middle East Military Balance; Jane's Sentinel: The Gulf States*, "Iran", and *Jane's Defense Weekly*, July 11, 1987, p. 15.

61. *Jane's Defense Weekly*, October 29, 1997, p. 4.

62. *Jane's Defense Weekly*, October 29, 1997, p. 4.

63. *Jane's Defense Weekly*, October 7, 1995, p. 22, October 28, 1995, p. 19, June 12, 1996, p. 27, August 28, 1996, p. 10; January 8, 1997, p. 13, May 7, 1997, p. 18, June 25, 1997, p. 14; Reuters, October 17, 1995, 13:31, February 1, 1996, 03:45, April 22, 1997, 07:09, April 23, 1997, 08:18, April 24, 1997, 0427, July 3, 1997, 0452, October 29, 1997, p. 4; FBIS-NES-95–250, December 25, 1995; *Tehran Times*, May 30, 1996; *Washington Times*, May 4, 1997, p. A-7, May 12, 1997, p. A-13; Associated Press, June 30, 1997, 0629.

Chapter 10

Iran's Conventional War-Fighting Options

Iran's conventional war-fighting options involve a complex mix of strengths and weaknesses which can be used in a wide range of different contingencies, ranging from acts of intimidation to a major war. Further, Iran is emphasizing an unusual mix of anti-ship missiles, submarines, mines, and unconventional warfare capabilities which do not lend themselves to a simple order of battle comparisons with the forces of other states, or to an emphasis on major regional conflicts. As a result, this analysis has emphasized the individual aspects of Iran's war-fighting capabilities, rather than using a scenario-driven approach.

It is possible, however, to summarize Iran's capabilities in a number of war-fighting options that illustrate the strengths and weaknesses of its conventional forces. These options are based on Iran's capabilities rather than on its intentions and are scarcely predictions of the future. They cannot anticipate Iran's future rate of modernization or that of its neighbors, or the future nature of the US and British presence in the Gulf. History is filled with examples of the fact that experts do as badly as nations in accurately anticipating the consequences of initiating military conflict and the impact of taking a new step on the "escalation ladder." Nevertheless, they provide at least a rough picture of the range of options that Iran's current military capabilities make possible.

MAJOR CONTINGENCY CAPABILITIES

In broad terms, Iran's conventional war-fighting options can be divided into four major contingencies: conflict in the Gulf, conflict with Iraq, conflict with the United States or a US-led coalition, and conflict with the Southern Gulf states. A conflict with Turkey or Pakistan currently seems so unlikely that it is not worth addressing. Iran has so far shown little interest in conventional military involvement in Afghanistan. Iran has little incentive to become involved in any kind of conflict with Armenia, Azerbaijan, or any of the states in Central Asia.

Iran's current capabilities in these four contingencies may be summarized as follows:

- Iranian forces are becoming steadily more professional, better organized, and better trained, are aware of outside studies of the lessons of the Gulf War, and are examining the implications of the "revolution in military affairs"—although there is no way to determine how well these lessons have been absorbed. Iran is also reducing, although scarcely eliminating, the friction between its regular and IRGC forces. Iran's forces are, however, severely equipment limited and cannot realistically practice capabilities they do not have.
- Iran is dealing with this situation by improving a number of important aspects of its military capabilities in each military service, by importing limited numbers of key arms and technologies where it can obtain them, and by expanding its military industries. Iran is not, however, in the process of a major build-up in conventional war-fighting capability by the standards of its build-up from the period 1971–1980, or the Iran-Iraq War. This is partly because of a lack of access to advanced arms and technology, and partly the result of Iran's economic problems. At the same time, it is not clear that Iran's top leadership really has plans to conduct such a build-up.
- Iran faces severe modernization problems in every service that it is as yet unable to address, and the aging of its existing equipment heavily offsets the modernization it has so far been able to achieve. A carefully focused arms import effort could, however, correct for some of these problems in 3–5 years if Iran could obtain free access to the systems it wants, and Iran can gradually improve its domestic military industries to manufacture more advanced systems. Buying more Russian fighters, more T-72s, and a land-based air defense system built around the S-300 are possible key priorities.
- Iran is attempting to cope with the overall weaknesses of its conventional forces by focusing on the development of weapons of mass destruction, by building up unconventional warfare capabilities in the Gulf, and by creating a growing capability to use mines, anti-ship missiles, and submarines to threaten tanker and shipping traffic through the Gulf. It is having at least moderate success in implementing these plans.

    Iran has sufficient land-air power to defend itself against most Iraqi offensives, and to make limited gains in the border area. It is too close to parity with Iraq, however, to make any definitive prediction about the outcome of any fighting. Iran's capabilities will improve steadily relative to Iraq, until Iraq can free itself of sanctions and resume major arms imports. The improvement in Iran's capabilities will be slow enough, however, so that a rough balance of power will remain into the 2005 time frame—provided that Iraq does not fragment internally and its military force remains unified.
- Iran is slowly expanding its naval capabilities in the Gulf and in the Gulf of Oman. It currently has little ability to survive a major engagement with US sea and airpower, however, and its submarines, major surface vessels, and air capabilities in the Gulf region probably would not survive more than a few days of determined US attack. Iran can disperse enough of its IRGC naval branch, mine warfare capabilities, and anti-ship

missiles to conduct a sustained series of low-level attacks and raids, even in the face of large-scale US attacks.
- Geography limits the Iranian threat to most Southern Gulf states. Iran can only launch a massive land attack by crossing through Iraq, making it much more dependent on naval, air, and power projection forces in exerting power in the Gulf. It will be years before Iran can become a major conventional military threat to its Southern Gulf neighbors, and Iran has no near-term prospect of being able to directly challenge the combined conventional war-fighting capabilities of the US, Britain, and the Southern Gulf states as long as the United States is willing to project power and act to ensure the security of the Gulf. Geography alone makes Iran different from Iraq.
- Iran can currently match any combination of Southern Gulf navies because their operational proficiency is dismal, although they often have superior equipment. However, Iran's mix of air and naval capabilities is probably too limited to engage Saudi Arabia in its own waters and airspace.
- Iran has limited power projection capabilities—probably confined to air-amphibious operations of battalion size. It could, however, transport larger forces relatively rapidly if it could move unopposed to a Southern Gulf country like Bahrain.

OTHER WAR-FIGHTING OPTIONS

Iran can pose other kinds of conventional war-fighting threats to the Southern Gulf, and it is not possible to dismiss the risk of other kinds of fighting between Iran and Iraq. Iran can use a wide range of combinations of conventional military force, unconventional military force, terrorism, and proxies to attack, threaten, or intimidate its neighbors. Iran seems to recognize that it has no near-to-midterm prospect of challenging the United States directly in a conventional war and that it has little incentive to directly confront the United States in the kind of conflict it is most likely to lose. It understands that it must find countervailing forms of strategy rather than attempt to exploit the political and military weaknesses in other aspects of US and Coalition solidarity and war-fighting capability.

In broad terms, Iran has the capabilities to threaten or actively use military force in the following contingencies:

- To provide extensive covert or overt support of a coup in Bahrain, support a Shi'ite uprising in Saudi Arabia, and training and weapons to an extremist movement in any other Gulf state or state in the region.
- To carry out threatening military exercises and actions in the Gulf, Gulf of Oman, Iran's islands and offshore facilities, and northern Iran to try to influence the behavior of other Gulf states, for example, in response to a major crisis in oil prices, and/or a struggle over oil quotas. This could include escalation to the deployment of submarines and the use of anti-ship missiles and mines.
- To intervene openly or covertly with IRGC forces to support the Shi'ites in Lebanon in more intense conflict against Israel.

- To systematically expand the ongoing military training, arms, and funding for Hamas in the West Bank and Gaza, and assassination and bombing attacks on Israeli embassies and citizens.
- To support a religious coup in an accessible neighboring state, or conflict between an "Islamic" force and peacekeeping or secular forces.
- To respond to any military challenge to Iranian control of the Tunbs and Abu Musa.
- To carry out a sustained low-level guerrilla war or low-intensity conflict on the other Iranian islands in the Gulf and along the Iranian coast, and to sustain a low-to-mid-intensity conflict in defense of Iran's cities.
- To fight an air or a naval clash in the Gulf over oil rights or shipping lanes.
- To force to assert Iran's claims to offshore gas fields claimed by Qatar, or to stage an "energy grab" to attack other offshore or onshore oil and gas fields or facilities or seize them as hostages.
- To intervene in a civil war or military upheaval in Iraq involving religious issues, or in a situation where Iraq appears vulnerable.
- To respond to Iraqi incursions into Iran, or to conduct attacks on People's Mujahideen forces and camps based in Iraq.
- To intervene in a Kurdish uprising in Iraq, suppression of a Kurdish uprising in Iran, or a military response to the slipover of the Kurdish conflicts in Turkey or Iraq.
- To defeat an Armenian or Azerbaijani military incursion into Iran, and to suppress any Armenian or Azerbaijani movement that attempted to use Iran as a base. To intervene to prevent an Armenian defeat of Azerbaijan of the kind which threatened Azerbaijan's existence or in a war between the two states which took on a religious character.
- To support ethnic/religious conflicts with secular governments in the Islamic republics of the former Soviet Union, such as Tajikistan.
- To intervene in a major clash between Israel and the Palestinians and/or Syria after the failure of the current peace settlement.
- To attack US citizens or forces in the Middle East to eliminate the US presence in the Gulf and region, or to weaken US support of Israel.
- To respond to a crisis over the transfer of chemical, biological, or nuclear weapons material and technology to Iran, or the transfer of long-range missile systems.

Capabilities, however, are not intentions, and Iran seems unlikely to take military risks without good cause—particularly if the moderates under Khatami continue to gain power. At the same time, Iran seems likely to react with considerable unity if military action seems provoked. The current Iranian regime is a relatively popular government, and Iran's strategic and political history has also given it a high degree of nationalism.

Iran would have great difficulty in repeating the offensive "human wave" attacks of the Iran-Iraq War, but even this might be possible under the right conditions. Certainly, Iran has considerable capability to wage popular warfare against any invasion. This capability is particularly important in view of the large size of Iran's paramilitary forces, its long distances and strategic depth, and the fact that its holdings of arms and weapons are well dispersed throughout the country, and infantry forces can move and resupply evenly across its deserts and mountain barriers.

KEY CAVEATS AND UNCERTAINTIES

As the following analysis will show, some aspects of this contingency analysis need additional caveats. It is impossible to dismiss the possibility that Iran could use chemical and biological weapons in any major near-term conflict, obtain enough fissile material to build nuclear weapons within the next few years, or develop and deploy biological weapons with near-nuclear lethalities—if it does not already have them. The use of any weapon of mass destruction in an act of terrorism or unconventional war could radically change the outcome—although not necessarily in Iran's favor.

Iran may be becoming more moderate, but the apparent near-term stability in Iran's military capabilities is anything but certain. As the following analysis shows, weapons of mass destruction are "wild cards" that could suddenly and unpredictably change the balance of perceived risk in Iran's favor—or change all of the rules and constraints applying to the escalation of more orthodox forms of military force. Further, Iran's steadily improving chemical warfare capabilities, coupled to the near dismantling of Iraq's capabilities, might change the balance in any further major conflict between Iran and Iraq.

Finally, the preceding analysis of Iran's war-fighting options makes two other uncertain assumptions. The first is that no major arms supplier will rush massive arms deliveries to Iran to further its own strategic interests in the region. Such an action seems highly unlikely, given the end of the Cold War, and Russia and China's interest in hard currency, but it must at least be considered. The second assumption is that Iran and Iraq will *not* cooperate seriously in military terms. Once again, such an assumption seems by far the most probable case, but history has created enough partnerships between previously hostile states so that the possibility can never be totally discounted.

Chapter 11

Iran and Weapons of Mass Destruction

Iran has long sought weapons of mass destruction, and the means to deliver them—although its efforts have never compared in scale to those of Iraq. Iran has lacked the resources to finance such a massive worldwide purchasing effort, its radical regime has restricted its access to foreign technology, and its poor management of its economy has limited the efficiency of its industrial base. Iran has still, however, obtained long-range missiles, produced chemical weapons, developed biological weapons, and made continuing efforts to acquire nuclear weapons.

Given the limitations of Iran's conventional forces, these efforts to acquire weapons of mass destruction are probably the most threatening aspect of Iran's present and future military capabilities. This conclusion has been reflected in many recent US statements about the threat from Iran. For example, Joseph S. Nye, then Assistant Secretary of Defense for International Security Affairs, stated in 1995 that

Iran is . . . clearly dedicated to developing weapons of mass destruction, including chemical, biological, and nuclear weapons, a prospect that would have serious repercussions for regional stability and perhaps for our ability to protect our interests in the area. In another forum, I would be prepared to discuss the details. . . . I would merely note that we learned in Iraq that a country can pursue a clandestine program in violation of its commitments and international norms. This experience makes us skeptical about the ability of normal inspections to detect similar programs in Iran.[1]

The current status of these Iranian efforts to acquire long-range delivery systems and chemical, biological, and nuclear weapons are summarized in Table 11.1, along with the status of similar efforts of Iraq, Israel, and Syria. These

Table 11.1
Iranian, Iraqi, Israeli, and Syrian Weapons of Mass Destruction Programs and Related Delivery Systems

Iran's Search for Weapons of Mass Destruction

Delivery Systems

- The Soviet-designed Scud B (17E) guided missile currently forms the core of Iran's ballistic missile forces,—largely as a result of the Iran-Iraq War.

    - Iran only acquired its Scuds in response to Iraq's invasion. It obtained a limited number from Libya and then obtained larger numbers from North Korea. It deployed these units with a special Khatam ol-Anbya force attached to the air element of the Pasdaran. Iran fired its first Scuds in March, 1985. It fired as many as 14 Scuds in 1985, 8 in 1986, 18 in 1987, and 77 in 1988. Iran fired 77 Scud missiles during a 52-day period in 1988, during what came to be known as the "war of the cities." Sixty-one were fired at Baghdad, nine at Mosul, five at Kirkuk, one at Takrit, and one at Kuwait. Iran fired as many as five missiles on a single day, and once fired three missiles within 30 minutes. This still, however, worked out to an average of only about one missile a day, and Iran was down to only 10–20 Scuds when the war of the cities ended.

    - Iran's missile attacks were initially more effective than Iraq's attacks. This was largely a matter of geography. Many of Iraq's major cities were comparatively close to its border with Iran, but Tehran and most of Iran's major cities that had not already been targets in the war were outside the range of Iraqi Scud attacks. Iran's missiles, in contrast, could hit key Iraqi cities like Baghdad. This advantage ended when Iraq deployed extended range Scuds.

    - The Scud B is a relatively old Soviet design which first became operational in 1967, designated as the R-17E or R-300E. The Scud B has a range of 290–300 kilometers with its normal conventional payload. The export version of the missile is about 11 meters long, 85–90 centimeters in diameter, and weighs 6,300 kilograms. It has a nominal CEP of 1,000 meters. The Russian versions can be equipped with conventional high explosive, fuel air explosive, runway penetrator, submunition, chemical, and nuclear warheads.

    - The export version of the Scud B comes with a conventional high explosive warhead weighing about 1,000 kilograms, of which 800 kilograms are the high explosive payload and 200 are the warhead structure and fusing system. It has a single stage storable liquid rocket engine and is usually deployed on the MAZ-543 eight wheel transporter-erector-launcher (TEL). It has a strap-down inertial guidance, using three gyros to correct its ballistic trajectory, and uses internal graphite jet vane steering. The warhead hits at a velocity above Mach 1.5.

    - Most estimates indicate that Iran now has 6–12 Scud launchers and up to 200 Scud B (R-17E) missiles with a range of 230–310 kilometers.

    - Some estimates give higher figures. They estimate that Iran bought 200–300 Scud Bs from North Korea between 1987 and 1992, and may have continued to buy such missiles after that time. Israeli experts estimate that Iran had at least 250–300 Scud B missiles, and at least 8–15 launchers on hand in 1997.

Table 11.1 (continued)

- US experts also believe that Iran can now manufacture virtually all of the Scud B, with the possible exception of the most sophisticated components of its guidance system and rocket motors. This makes it difficult to estimate how many missiles Iran has in inventory and can acquire over time, as well as to estimate the precise performance characteristics of Iran's missiles, since it can alter the weight of the warhead and adjust the burn time and improve the efficiency of the rocket motors.
- Iran has new long-range North Korean Scuds, with ranges near 500 kilometers.
  - The North Korean missile system is often referred to as a "Scud C." Typically, Iran formally denied the fact it had such systems long after the transfer of these missiles became a reality. Hassan Taherian, an Iranian foreign ministry official, stated in February, 1995, "There is no missile cooperation between Iran and North Korea whatsoever. We deny this."
  - In fact, a senior North Korean delegation traveled to Tehran to close the deal on November 29, 1990, and met with Mohsen Rezaei, the former commander of the IRGC. Iran either bought the missile then or placed its order shortly thereafter. North Korea then exported the missile through its Lyongaksan Import Corporation. Iran imported some of these North Korean missile assemblies using its B-747s, and seems to have used ships to import others.
  - Iran probably had more than 60 of the longer-range North Korean missiles by 1998, although other sources report 100, and one source reports 170.
  - Iran may have 5–10 Scud C launchers, each with several missiles. This total seems likely to include four new North Korean TELs received in 1995.
  - Iran seems to want enough missiles and launchers to make its missile force highly dispersible.
  - Iran may have begun to test its new North Korean missiles. There are reports it has fired them from mobile launchers at a test site near Qom about 310 miles (500 kilometers) to a target area south of Shahroud. There are also reports that units equipped with such missiles have been deployed as part of Iranian exercises like the Saeqer-3 (Thunderbolt 3) exercise in late October, 1993.
  - The missile is more advanced than the Scud B, although many aspects of its performance are unclear. North Korea seems to have completed development of the missile in 1987, after obtaining technical support from the People's Republic of China. While it is often called a "Scud C," it seems to differ substantially in detail from the original Soviet Scud B. It seems to be based more on the Chinese-made DF-61 than on a direct copy of the Soviet weapon.
  - Experts estimate that the North Korean missiles have a range of around 310 miles (500 kilometers), a warhead with a high explosive payload of 700 kilograms, and relatively good accuracy and reliability. While this payload is a bit limited for the effective delivery of chemical agents, Iran might modify the warhead to increase payload at the expense of range and restrict the using of chemical munitions to the most lethal agents, such as persistent nerve gas. It might also concentrate its development efforts on arming its Scud C forces with more lethal biological agents. In any case, such missiles are likely to have enough range-payload to give Iran the ability to strike all targets on the southern coast of the Gulf and all of the populated areas in Iraq, although not the West. Iran could also reach targets in part of eastern

Table 11.1 (continued)

Syria, the eastern third of Turkey, and cover targets in the border area of the former Soviet Union, western Afghanistan, and western Pakistan.

- Accuracy and reliability remain major uncertainties, as does operational CEP. Much would also depend on the precise level of technology Iran deployed in the warhead. Neither Russia nor the People's Republic of China seem to have transferred the warhead technology for biological and chemical weapons to Iran or Iraq when they sold them the Scud B missile and CSS-8. However, North Korea may have sold Iran such technology as part of the Scud C sale. If it did so, such a technology transfer would save Iran years of development and testing in obtaining highly lethal biological and chemical warheads. In fact, Iran would probably be able to deploy far more effective biological and chemical warheads than Iraq had at the time of the Gulf War.
- Iran may be working with Syria in such development efforts, although Middle Eastern nations rarely cooperate in such sensitive areas. Iran served as a transshipment point for North Korean missile deliveries during 1992 and 1993. Some of this transshipment took place using the same Iranian B-747s that brought missile parts to Iran. Others moved by sea. For example, a North Korean vessel called the *Des Hung Ho*, bringing missile parts for Syria, docked at Bandar Abbas in May, 1992. Iran then flew these parts to Syria. An Iranian ship coming from North Korea and a second North Korean ship followed, carrying missiles and machine tools for both Syria and Iran. At least 20 of the North Korean missiles have gone to Syria from Iran, and production equipment seems to have been transferred to Iran and to Syrian plants near Hama and Aleppo.
- Iran has created shelters and tunnels in its coastal areas which it could use to store Scud and other missiles in hardened sites and reduce their vulnerability to air attack.
- Iran can now assemble Scud and Scud C missiles using foreign-made components.
- Iran is developing an indigenous missile production capability with both solid and liquid fueled missiles. It seems to be seeking capability to produce MRBMs.
  - The present scale of Iran's production and assembly efforts is unclear. Iran seems to have a design center, at least two rocket and missile assembly plants, a missile test range and monitoring complex, and a wide range of smaller design and refit facilities.
  - The design center is said to be located at the Defense Technology and Science Research Center, which is a branch of Iran's Defense Industry Organization, and located outside Karaj—near Teheran. This center directs a number of other research efforts. Some experts believe it has support from Russian and Chinese scientists.
  - Iran's largest missile assembly and production plant is said to be a North Korean–built facility near Isfahan, although this plant may use Chinese equipment and technology. There are no confirmations of these reports, but this region is the center of much of Iran's advanced defense industry, including plants for munitions, tank overhaul, and helicopter and fixed wing aircraft maintenance. Some reports say the local industrial complex can produce liquid fuels and missile parts from a local steel mill.
  - A second missile plant is said to be located 175 kilometers east of Tehran, near Semnan. Some sources indicate this plant is Chinese-built and began rocket production as early as 1987. It is supposed to be able to build 600–1,000 Oghab rockets per year, if Iran can import key ingredients for solid fuel motors like ammonium perchlorate. The plant is also supposed to produce the Iran-130.

Table 11.1 (continued)
- Another facility may exist near Bandar Abbas for the assembly of the Seersucker. China is said to have built this facility in 1987, and is believed to be helping the naval branch of the Guards to modify the Seersucker to extend its range to 400 kilometers. It is possible that China is also helping Iran develop solid fuel rocket motors and produce or assemble missiles like the CS-801 and CS-802. There have, however, been reports that Iran is developing extended range Scuds with the support of Russian experts, and of a missile called the Tondar 68, with a range of 700 kilometers.
- Still other reports claim that Iran has split its manufacturing facilities into plants near Pairzan, Seman, Shiraz, Maghdad, and Islaker. These reports indicate that the companies involved in building the Scuds are also involved in Iran's production of poison gas and include Defense Industries, Shahid, Bagheri Industrial Group, and the Shahid Hemat Industrial Group.
- Iran's main missile test range is said to be further east, near Shahroud, along the Teheran-Mashhad railway. A telemetry station is supposed to be 350 kilometers to the south at Taba, along the Mashhad-Isfahan road. All of these facilities are reportedly under the control of the Islamic Revolutionary Guards Corps.
- There were many reports during the late 1980s and early 1990s that Iran had ordered the North Korean No-Dong missile, which was planned to have the capability to carry nuclear and biological missile ranges of up to 900 kilometers. This range would allow the missile to reach virtually any target in the Gulf, Turkey, and Israel. The status of the No-Dong program has since become increasingly uncertain, although North Korea deployed some developmental types at test facilities in 1997.
  - The No-Dong underwent flight tests at ranges of 310 miles (500 kilometers) on May 29, 1993. Some sources indicate that Iranians were present at these tests. Extensive further propulsion tests began in August, 1994, and some reports indicate operational training began for test crews in May, 1995. Missile storage facilities began to be built in July, 1995, and four launch sites were completed in October, 1995.
  - The progress of the program has been slow since that time and may reflect development problems. However, mobile launchers were seen deployed in northeast North Korea on March 24, 1997. According to some reports, a further seven launcher units were seen at a facility about 100 kilometers from Pyongyang.
  - The No Dong 1 is a single-stage liquid-fueled missile, with a range of up to 1,000 to 1,300 kilometers (810 miles), although longer ranges may be possible with a reduced warhead and maximum burn. There are also indications that there may be a No-Dong 2, using the same rocket motor, but with an improved fuel supply system that allows the fuel to burn for a longer period.
  - The missile is about 15.2 meters long—four meters longer than the Scud B—and 1.2 meters in diameter. The warhead is estimated to weigh 770 kilograms (1,200–1,750 pounds) and a warhead manufacturing facility exists near Pyongyang. The No-Dong has an estimated theoretical CEP of 700 meters at maximum range, versus 900 meters for the Scud B, although its practical accuracy could be as wide as 3,000–4,000 meters. It has an estimated terminal velocity of Mach 3.5, versus 2.5 for the Scud B, which presents added problems for tactical missile defense. The missile is transportable on a modified copy of the MAZ-543P TEL that has been

Table 11.1 (continued)

  lengthened with a fifth axle and which is roughly 40 meters long. The added support stand for the vertical launch modes brings the overall length to 60 meters, and some experts questioned whether a unit this big is practical.
- Other reports during the later 1980s and early 1990s indicated that Iran was also interested in two developmental North Korean IRBMs, called the Tapeo Dong 1 and Tapeo Dong 2.
  - The Tapeo Dong 1 missile has an estimated maximum range of 2,000 kilometers, and the Tapeo Dong 2 may have a range up to 3,500 kilometers.
  - Both Tapeo Dongs are liquid-fueled missiles which seem to have two stages. North Korea tested a two-stage missile body in late August, 1998, with a range of up to 1,200 kilometers.
  - Unlike the No-Dong, the Tapeo Dongs must be carried to a site in stages and then assembled at a fixed site. The No-Dong transporter may be able to carry both stages of the Tapeo Dong 1, but some experts believe that a special transporter is needed for the first stage of the Tapeo Dong 1 and for both stages of the Tapeo Dong 2.
- Since the early 1990s, the focus of reports on Iran's missile efforts has shifted, and it has become clear that Iran is developing its own longer-range variants of the No Dong for indigenous production with substantial Russian and some Chinese aid:
  - As early as 1992, one such missile was reported to have a range of 800–930 miles and a 1,650-pound warhead. Reports differ sharply on its size. Jane's estimates a launch weight of up to 16,000 kilograms, provided the system is derived from the No-Dong. It could have a launch weight of 15,000 kilograms, a payload of 600 kilograms, and a range of 1,700–1,800 kilometers if it is based on a system similar to the Chinese CSS-5 (DF-21) and CSS-N3 (JL-1). These systems entered service in 1983 and 1987.
  - A longer-range missile was said to have improved guidance components, a range of up to 1,240 miles, and a warhead of up to 2,200 pounds.
  - IOC dates were then estimated to be 1999–2001.
  - Russia agreed in 1994 that it would adhere to the terms of the Missile Technology Control Regime and would place suitable limits on the sale or transfer of rocket engines and technology. Nevertheless, the CIA has identified Russia as a leading source of Iranian missile technology, and the State Department has indicated that President Clinton expressed US concerns over this cooperation to President Yeltsin. This transfer is one reason the president appointed former Ambassador Frank Wisner, and then Robert Galluci, as his special representatives to try to persuade Russia to put a firm halt to aid support of Iran.
  - These programs are reported to have continuing support from North Korea and from Russian and Chinese firms and technicians. One such Chinese firm is Great Wall Industries. The Russian firms include the Russian Central Aerohydrodynamic Institute, which has provided Iran's Shahid Hemmat Industrial Group (SHIG) with wind tunnels for missile design, equipment for manufacturing missile models, and the software for testing launch and reentry performance. They may also include Rosvoorouzhenie, a major Russian arms-export agency; NPO Trud, a rocket motor manufacturer; a leading research center called the Bauman Institute; and Polyus (Northstar), a major laser test and manufacturing equipment firm.

Table 11.1 (continued)

- The CIA reported in June, 1997 that Iran obtained major new transfers of new long-range missile technology from Russian and Chinese firms during 1996. Since that time, there have been many additional reports of technology transfer from Russia.
- The reports on Chinese technology transfers involve the least detail:
  - There have been past reports that Iran placed orders for PRC-made M-9 (CSS-6/DF-15) missile (280–620 kilometer range, launch weight of 6,000 kilograms).
  - It is more likely, however, that PRC firms are giving assistance in developing indigenous missile R&D and production facilities for the production of an Iranian solid-fueled missile.
  - The United States offered to provide China with added missile technology if it would agree to fully implement an end of technology transfer to Iran and Pakistan during meetings in Beijing on March 25–26, 1998.
- Recent reports and tests have provided more detail on these systems:
  - Some US experts believe that Iran tested booster engines in 1997 capable of driving a missile 1,500 kilometers. Virtually all US experts believe that Iran is rapidly approaching the point where it will be able to manufacture missiles with much longer ranges than the Scud B. It is less clear when Iran will be able to bring such programs to the final development stage, carry out suitable test firings, develop effective warheads, and deploy actual units. Much still depends on the level of foreign assistance.
  - Eitan Ben Eliyahu, the commander of the Israeli Air Force, reported on April 14, 1997, that Iran had tested a missile capable of reaching Israel. The background briefings to his statement implied that Russia was assisting Iran in developing two missiles, with ranges of 620 and 780 miles. Follow-on intelligence briefings that Israel provided in September, 1997, indicated that Russia was helping Iran develop four missiles. US intelligence reports indicate that China has also been helping Iran with some aspects of these missile efforts.
  - These missiles included the Shihab (''meteor'') missiles, with performance similar to those previously identified with Iranian missiles adapted from North Korean designs.
  - The Israeli reports indicated that the Shihab 3 was liquid fueled missile with a range of 810 miles (1,200–1,500 kilometers) and a payload of 1,550 pounds (700 kilometers).
  - Israel claimed the Shihab might be ready for deployment as early as 1998.
  - Israel has also reported that Iran is developing the Shihab 4, with a range of 1,250 miles (some reports say up to 4,000 kilometers) and a payload in excess of one ton. It indicates that this system could be operational in two to five years. Martin Indyck, the US Assistant Secretary for Near East Affairs, testified on July 28, 1998, that the United States estimated that the system still needed added foreign assistance to improve its motors and guidance system.
  - Israel indicated that Iran might have two other missile programs, including

Table 11.1 (continued)

longer-range systems with a maximum range of up to 4,500–5,000 and 10,000 kilometers.

- Iran tested the Shihab 3 on July 21, 1998, claiming that it was a defensive action to deal with potential threats from Israel.
  - The missile flew for a distance of up to 620 miles before it exploded about 100 seconds after launch. US intelligence sources could not confirm whether the explosion was deliberate, but indicated that the final system might have a range of 800–940 miles (a maximum of 1,240 kilometers), depending on its payload. The test confirmed that the missile was a liquid-fueled system.
  - General Mohammad Bagher Qalibaf, head of the Islamic Revolutionary Guards Corps' air wing, publicly reported on August 2, 1998, that the Shihab-3 is 53-foot-long ballistic missile that can travel at 4,300 miles per hour and carry a one-ton warhead at an altitude of nearly 820,000 feet. He claimed that the weapon was guided by an Iranian-made system that gives it great accuracy: "The final test of every weapon is in a real war situation but, given its warhead and size, the Shihab-3 is a very accurate weapon."
  - Other Iranian sources reported that the missile had a range of 800 miles. President Mohammad Khatami stated on August 1, 1998, that Iran was determined to continue to strengthen its armed forces, regardless of international concerns: "Iran will not seek permission from anyone for strengthening its defense capability."
  - Assistant Secretary Indyck testified on July 28 that the United States estimated that the system needed further refinement but might be deployed in its initial operational form between September, 1998 and March, 1999.
- There have been other reports that Iran might be using Russian technology to develop a very long-range missile with a range of 3,500 to 6,250 kilometers.
  - It seems clear that Iran has obtained some of the technology and design details of the Russian SS-4. The SS-4 (also known as the R-12 or "Sandal") is an aging Russian liquid fuel design that first went into service in 1959, and which was supposedly destroyed as part of the IRBM Treaty. It is a very large missile, with technology dating back to the early 1950s, although it was evidently updated at least twice during the period between 1959 and 1980. It has a CEP of 2–4 kilometers and a maximum range of 2,000 kilometers, which means it can only be lethal with a nuclear warhead or a biological weapon with near-nuclear lethality.
  - At the same time, the SS-4's overall technology is relatively simple and it has a throwweight of nearly 1,400 kilograms (3,000 pounds). It is one of the few missile designs that a nation with a limited technology base could hope to manufacture or adapt, and its throwweight and range would allow Iran to use a relatively unsophisticated nuclear device or biological warhead. As a result, an updated version of the SS-4 might be a suitable design for a developing country.
- Russia has been a key supplier of missile technology.
  - Some sources have indicated that Russian military industries have signed contracts with Iran to help produce liquid-fueled missiles and provide specialized wind tunnels, manufacture model missiles, and develop specialized computer software. For example, these reports indicate that the Russian Central Aerohydrodynamic Institute is cooperating with Iran's Defense Industries Organization (DIO) and the DIO's Shahid

Table 11.1 (continued)

Hemmat Industrial Group (SHIG). The Russian State Corporation for Export and Import or Armament and Military Equipment (Rosvoorouzhenie) and Infor are also reported to be involved in deals with the SHIG. These deals are also said to include specialized laser equipment, mirrors, tungsten-coated graphite material, and maraging steel for missile development and production. They could play a major role in helping Iran develop long-range versions of the Scud B and C, and more accurate variations of a missile similar to the No-Dong.

- The Israeli press reported in August, 1997 that Israel had evidence that Iran was receiving Russian support. In September, 1997, Israel urged the United States to step up its pressure on Iran, and leaked reports indicating that private and state-owned Russian firms had provided gyroscopes, electronic components, wind tunnels, guidance and propulsion systems, and the components needed to build such systems to Iran.
- President Yeltsin and the Russian Foreign Ministry initially categorically denied that such charges were true. Following a meeting with Vice President Gore, President Yeltsin stated on September 26, 1997, that "We are being accused of supplying Iran with nuclear or ballistic missile technologies. There is nothing further from the truth. I again and again categorically deny such rumors."
- Russia agreed, however, that Ambassador Wisner and Yuri Koptyev, the head of the Russian space program, should jointly examine the US intelligence and draft a report on Russian transfers to Iran. This report reached a very different conclusion from President Yeltsin and concluded that Russia had provided such aid to Iran. Further, on October 1, 1997—roughly a week after Yeltsin issued his denial—the Russian security service issued a statement that it had "thwarted" an Iranian attempt to have parts for liquid fuel rocket motors manufactured in Russia, disguised as gas compressors and pumps.
- Russian firms said to be helping Iran included the Russian Central Aerohydrodynamic Institute which developed a special wind tunnel; Rosvoorouzhenie, a major Russian arms-export agency; Kutznetzov (formerly NPO Trud), a rocket motor manufacturer in Samara; a leading research center called the Bauman National Technical University in Moscow, involved in developing rocket propulsion systems; the Tsagi Research Institute for rocket propulsion development; and the Polyus (Northstar) Research Institute in Moscow, a major laser test and manufacturing equipment firm. Iranians were also found to be studying rocket engineering at the Baltic State University in St. Petersburg and the Bauman State University.
- Russia was also found to have sold Iran high-strength steel and special foil for its long-range missile program. The Russian Scientific and Production Center Inor concluded an agreement as late as September, 1997 to sell Iran a factory to produce four special metal alloys used in long-range missiles. Inor's director, L. P Chromova, worked out a deal with A. Asgharzadeh, the director of an Iranian factory, to sell 620 kilograms of special alloy called 21HKMT, and provide Iran with the capability to thermally treat the alloy for missile bodies. Iran had previously bought 240 kilograms of the alloy. Inor was also selling alloy foils called 49K2F, CUBE2, and 50N in sheets 0.2–0.4 millimeters thick for the outer body of missiles. The alloy 21HKMT was particularly interesting because North Korea also uses it in missile designs. Inor

Table 11.1 (continued)

had previously brokered deals with the Shahid Hemat Industrial Group in Iran to supply maraging steel for missile cases, composite graphite-tungsten material, laser equipment, and special mirrors used in missile tests.

- The result was a new and often tense set of conversations between the United States and Russia in January, 1998. The United States again sent Ambassador Frank Wisner to Moscow, Vice President Gore called Prime Minister Viktor Chernomyrdin, and Secretary of State Madeleine Albright made an indirect threat that the Congress might apply sanctions. Sergi Yastrzhembsky, a Kremlin spokesman, initially responded by denying that any transfer of technology had taken place.

- This Russian denial was too categorical to have much credibility. Russia had previously announced the arrest of an Iranian diplomat on November 14, 1997, that it caught attempting to buy missile technology. The Iranian was seeking to buy blueprints and recruit Russian scientists to go to Iran. Yuri Koptev, the head of the Russian Space Agency, explained this, however, by stating that "There have been several cases where some Russian organizations, desperately struggling to make ends meet and lacking responsibility, have embarked on some ambiguous projects... they were stopped long before they got to the point where any technology got out."

- The end result of these talks was an agreement by Gore and Chernomyrdin to strengthen controls over transfer technology, but it was scarcely clear that it put an end to the problem. As Koptev has said, "There have been several cases where some Russian organizations, desperately struggling to make ends meet and lacking responsibility, have embarked on some ambiguous projects." Conditions in Russia are getting worse, not better, and the desperation that drives sales has scarcely diminished.

- Chernomyrdin again promised to strengthen his efforts to restrict technology transfer to Iran in a meeting with Gore on March 12, 1998. The United States informed Russia of 13 cases of possible Russian aid to Iran at the meeting and offered to increase the number of Russian commercial satellite launches it would license for US firms as an incentive.

- New arrests of smugglers took place on April 9, 1998. The smugglers had attempted to ship 22 tons of specialized steel to Iran via Azerbaijan, using several Russian shell corporations as a cover.

- On April 16, 1998, the State Department declared that 20 Russian agencies and research facilities were ineligible to receive US aid because of their role in transferring missile technology to Iran.

- A US examination of Iran's dispersal, sheltering, and hardening programs for its anti-ship missiles and other missile systems indicates that Iran has developed effective programs to ensure that they would survive a limited number of air strikes and that Iran had reason to believe that the limited number of preemptive strikes Israel could conduct against targets in the lower Gulf could not be effective in denying Iran the capability to deploy its missiles.

- Iran has shorter missile range systems:
  - In 1990, Iran bought CSS-8 surface-to-surface missiles (converted SA-2s) from China with ranges of 130–150 kilometers.

Table 11.1 (continued)
- It has Chinese sea-and land-based anti-ship cruise missiles. Iran fired 10 such missiles at Kuwait during the Iran-Iraq War, hitting one US-flagged tanker.
- Iran has acquired much of the technology necessary to build long-range cruise missile systems from China:
  - Such missiles would cost only 10% to 25% as much as ballistic missiles of similar range, and both the HY-2 Seersucker and CS-802 could be modified relatively quickly for land attacks against area targets.
  - Iran reported in December, 1995 that it had already fired a domestically built anti-ship missile called the Saeqe-4 (Thunderbolt) during exercises in the Strait of Hormuz and Gulf of Oman. Other reports indicate that China is helping Iran build copies of the Chinese CS-801/CS-802 and the Chinese FL-2 or F-7 anti-ship cruise missiles. These missiles have relatively limited range. The range of the CS-801 is 8–40 kilometers, the range of the CS-802 is 15–120 kilometers, the maximum range of the F-7 is 30 kilometers, and the maximum range of the FL-10 is 50 kilometers. Even a range of 120 kilometers would barely cover targets in the Southern Gulf from launch points on Iran's Gulf coast. These missiles also have relatively small high explosive warheads. As a result, Iran may well be seeking anti-ship capabilities, rather than platforms for delivering weapons of mass destruction.
  - A platform like the CS-802 might, however, provide enough design data to develop a scaled-up, longer-range cruise missile for other purposes, and the Gulf is a relatively small area where most urban areas and critical facilities are near the coast. Aircraft or ships could launch cruise missiles with chemical or biological warheads from outside the normal defense perimeter of the Southern Gulf states, and it is at least possible that Iran might modify anti-ship missiles with chemical weapons to attack tankers—ships which are too large for most regular anti-ship missiles to be highly lethal.
  - Building an entire cruise missile would be more difficult. The technology for fusing chemical and biological warfare and cluster warheads would be within Iran's grasp. Navigation systems and jet engines, however, would still be a major potential problem. Current inertial navigation systems (INS) would introduce errors of at least several kilometers at ranges of 1,000 kilometers and would carry a severe risk of total guidance failure—probably exceeding two-thirds of the missiles fired. A differential global positioning system (GPS) integrated with the INS and a radar altimeter, however, might produce an accuracy of 15 meters. Some existing remotely piloted vehicles (RPVs), such as the South African Skua, claim such performance. Commercial technology is becoming available for differential global positioning system (GPS) guidance, with accuracies of 2 to 5 meters.
  - There are commercially available reciprocating and gas turbine engines that Iran could adapt for use in a cruise missile, although finding a reliable and an efficient turbofan engine for a specific design application might be difficult. An extremely efficient engine would have to be matched to a specific airframe. It is doubtful that Iran could design and build such an engine, but there are over 20 other countries with the necessary design and manufacturing skills.
  - While airframe-engine warhead integration and testing would present a challenge and might be beyond Iran's manufacturing skills, it is inherently easier to integrate and test a cruise missile than a long-range ballistic missile. Further, such developments

Table 11.1 (continued)

  would be far less detectable than developing a ballistic system if the program used coded or low-altitude directional telemetry.
- Iran could bypass much of the problems inherent in developing its own cruise missile by modifying the HY-2 Seersucker for use as a land attack weapon and extending its range beyond 80 kilometers, or by modifying and improving the CS-801 (Ying Jai-1) anti-ship missile. There are reports that the Revolutionary Guards are working on such developments at a facility near Bandar Abbas.
- Su-24 long-range strike fighter with range payloads roughly equivalent to US F-111 and superior to older Soviet medium bombers.
- F-4D/E fighter bombers with capability to carry extensive payloads to ranges of 450 miles.
- Can modify HY-2 Silkworm missiles and SA-2 surface-to-air missiles to deliver weapons of mass destruction.
- Iran has made several indigenous-long range rockets.
  - The Iran-130, or Nazeat, since the end of the Iran-Iraq War. The full details of this system remain unclear, but it seems to use commercially available components, a solid fuel rocket, and a simple inertial guidance system to reach ranges of about 90–120 kilometers. It is 355 mm in diameter, 5.9 meters long, weighs 950 kilograms, and has a 150-kilogram warhead. It seems to have poor reliability and accuracy, and its payload only seems to be several hundred kilograms.
  - The Shahin 2. It too has a 355 mm diameter, but is only 3.87 meters long and weighs only 580 kilograms. It evidently can be equipped with three types of warheads: A 180-kilogram high-explosive warhead, another warhead using high explosive submunitions, and a warhead that uses chemical weapons.
  - Iranian Oghab (Eagle) rocket with 40+ kilometers range.
  - New SSM with 125 mile range may be in production, but could be a modified FROG.
- Large numbers of multiple rocket launchers and tube artillery for short-range delivery of chemical weapons.

Chemical Weapons
- Iran purchased large amounts of chemical defense gear from the mid-1980s onwards. Iran also obtained stocks of nonlethal CS gas, although it quickly found such agents had very limited military impact since they could only be used effectively in closed areas or very small open areas.
- Acquiring poisonous chemical agents was more difficult. Iran did not have any internal capacity to manufacture poisonous chemical agents when Iraq first launched its attacks with such weapons. While Iran seems to have made limited use of chemical mortar and artillery rounds as early as 1985—and possibly as early as 1984—these rounds were almost certainly captured from Iraq.
- Iran had to covertly import the necessary equipment and supplies, and it took several years to get substantial amounts of production equipment and the necessary feedstocks. Iran sought aid from European firms like Lurgi to produce large "pesticide" plants, and began to try to obtain the needed feedstock from a wide range of sources, relying heavily on its embassy in Bonn to manage the necessary deals. While Lurgi did not

Table 11.1 (continued)

provide the pesticide plant Iran sought, Iran did obtain substantial support from other European firms and feedstocks from many other Western sources.

- By 1986–1987, Iran developed the capability to produce enough lethal agents to load its own weapons. The director of the CIA and informed observers in the Gulf made it clear that Iran could produce blood agents like hydrogen cyanide, phosgene gas, and/or chlorine gas. Iran was also able to weaponize limited quantities of blister (sulfur mustard) and blood (cyanide) agents beginning in 1987, and had some capability to weaponize phosgene gas and/or chlorine gas. These chemical agents were produced in small batches, and evidently under laboratory scale conditions, which enabled Iran to load small numbers of weapons before any of its new major production plants went into full operation.
- These gas agents were loaded into bombs and artillery shells and were used sporadically against Iraq in 1987 and 1988.
- Reports regarding Iran's production and research facilities are highly uncertain:
  - Iran seems to have completed a major poison gas plant at Qazvin, about 150 kilometers west of Teheran. This plant is reported to have been completed between November, 1987 and January, 1988. While supposedly a pesticide plant, the facility's true purpose seems to have been poison gas production using organophosphorous compounds.
  - It is impossible to trace all the sources of the major components and technology Iran used in its chemical weapons program during this period. Mujahideen sources claim Iran also set up a chemical bomb and warhead plant operated by the Zakaria Al-Razi chemical company near Mahshar in southern Iran, but it is unclear whether these reports are true.
  - Reports that Iran had chemical weapons plants at Damghan and Parchin that began operation as early as March, 1988 and may have begun to test fire Scuds with chemical warheads as early as 1988–1989 are equally uncertain.
  - Iran established at least one large research and development center, under the control of the Engineering Research Centre of the Construction Crusade (Jahad e-Sazandegi), which had established a significant chemical weapons production capability by mid-1989.
- Debates took place in the Iranian parliament of Majlis in late 1988 over the safety of Pasdaran gas plants located near Iranian towns. Rafsanjani described chemical weapons as follows. "Chemical and biological weapons are poor man's atomic bombs and can easily be produced. We should at least consider them for our defense. Although the use of such weapons is inhuman, the war taught us that international laws are only scraps of paper."
- Post–Iran-Iraq War estimates of Iran chemical weapons production are extremely uncertain:
  - US experts believe Iran was beginning to produce significant mustard gas and nerve gas by the time of the August, 1988 cease-fire in the Iran-Iraq War, although its use of chemical weapons remained limited and had little impact on the fighting.
  - Iran's efforts to equip plants to produce V-agent nerve gases seem to have been delayed by US, British, and German efforts to limit technology transfers to Iran, but

Table 11.1 (continued)

Iran may have acquired the capability to produce persistent nerve gas during the mid-1990s.

- Production of nerve gas weapons started no later than 1994.
- Iran began to stockpile cyanide (cyanogen chloride), phosgene, and mustard gas weapons after 1985. Recent CIA testimony indicates that production capacity may approach 1,000 tons annually.
- Weapons include bombs and artillery. Shells include 155 mm artillery and mortar rounds. Iran also has chemical bombs and mines. It may have developmental chemical warheads for its Scuds, and it may have a chemical package for its 22006 RPV (doubtful).
- There are reports that Iran has deployed chemical weapons on some of its ships.
- Iran has increased chemical defensive and offensive warfare training since 1993.
- Iran is seeking to buy more advanced chemical defense equipment, and has sought to buy specialized equipment on the world market to develop indigenous capability to produce advanced feedstocks for nerve weapons.
- CIA sources indicated in late 1996 that China might have supplied Iran with up to 400 tons of chemicals for the production of nerve gas.
- One report indicated in 1996 that Iran obtained 400 metric tons of chemicals for use in nerve gas weapons from China, including carbon sulfide.
- Another report indicated that China supplied Iran with roughly two tons of calcium-hypochlorate in 1996, and loaded another 40,000 barrels in January or February of 1997. Calcium-hypochlorate is used for decontamination in chemical warfare.
- Iran placed several significant orders from China that were not delivered. Razak Industries in Teheran and Chemical and Pharmaceutical Industries in Tabriz ordered 49 metric tons of alkyl dimethylamine, a chemical used in making detergents, and 17 tons of sodium sulfide, a chemical used in making mustard gas. The orders were never delivered, but they were brokered by Iran's International Movalled Industries Corporation (Imaco) and China's North Chemical Industries Co. (Nocinco). Both brokers have been linked to other transactions affecting Iran's chemical weapons program since early 1995, and Nocinco has supplied Iran with several hundred tons of carbon disulfide, a chemical used in nerve gas.
- Another Chinese firm, only publicly identified as Q. Chen, seems to have supplied glass vessels for chemical weapons.
- The United States imposed sanctions on seven Chinese firms in May, 1997 for selling precursors for nerve gas and equipment for making nerve gas—although the United States made it clear that it had "no evidence that the Chinese government was involved." The Chinese firms were the Nanjing Chemical Industries Group and the Jiangsu Yongli Chemical Engineering and Import/Export Corporation. Cheong Yee Ltd., a Hong Kong firm, was also involved. The precursors included tionyl chloride, dimethylamine, and ethylene chlorohydril. The equipment included special glass lined vessels, and the Nanjing Chemical and Industrial Group completed construction of a production plant to manufacture such vessels in Iran in June, 1997.
- Iran sought to obtain impregnated Alumina, which is used to make phosphorous-oxychloride—a major component of VX and GB—from the United States.

Table 11.1 (continued)
- It has obtained some equipment from Israel. Nahum Manbar, an Israeli national living in France, was convicted in an Israeli court in May, 1997 for providing Iran with $16 million worth of production equipment for mustard and nerve gas during the period from 1990 to 1995.
- The CIA reported in June, 1997 that Iran had obtained new chemical weapons equipment technology from China and India in 1996.
- India is assisting in the construction of a major new plant at Qazvim, near Tehran, to manufacture phosphorous pentasulfide, a major precursor for nerve gas. The plant is fronted by Meli Agrochemicals, and the program was negotiated by Dr. Mejid Tehrani Abbaspour, a chief security advisor to Rafsanjani.
- A recent report by German intelligence indicates that Iran has made major efforts to acquire the equipment necessary to produce Sarin and Tabun, using the same cover of purchasing equipment for pesticide plants that Iraq used for its Sa'ad 16 plants in the 1980s. German sources note that three Indian companies—Tata Consulting Engineering, Transpek, and Rallis India—have approached German pharmaceutical and engineering concerns for such equipment and technology under conditions where German intelligence was able to trace the end user to Iran.
- Iran ratified the Chemical Weapons Convention in June, 1997.
  - It submitted a statement in Farsi to the CWC secretariat in 1998, but this consisted only of questions in Farsi as to the nature of the required compliance.
  - It has not provided the CWC with any data on its chemical weapons program.

Biological Weapons
- Extensive laboratory and research capability.
- Weapons effort documented as early as 1982. Reports surfaced that Iran had imported suitable type cultures from Europe and was working on the production of Mycotoxins, a relatively simple family of biological agents that require only limited laboratory facilities for small scale production.
- US intelligence sources reported in August, 1989 that Iran was trying to buy two new strains of fungus from Canada and the Netherlands that can be used to produce Mycotoxins. German sources indicated that Iran had successfully purchased such cultures several years earlier.
- The Imam Reza Medical Center at Mashhad Medical Sciences University and the Iranian Research Organization for Science and Technology were identified as the end users for this purchasing effort, but it is likely that the true end user was an Iranian government agency specializing in biological warfare.
- Many experts believe that the Iranian biological weapons effort was placed under the control of the Islamic Revolutionary Guards Corps, which is known to have tried to purchase suitable production equipment for such weapons.
- Since the Iran-Iraq War, Iran has conducted research on more lethal active agents like Anthrax, hoof and mouth disease, and biotoxins. In addition, Iranian groups have repeatedly approached various European firms for the equipment and technology necessary to work with these diseases and toxins.
  - Unclassified sources of uncertain reliability have identified a facility at Damghan as working on both biological and chemical weapons research and production, and be-

Table 11.1 (continued)

  lieve that Iran may be producing biological weapons at a pesticide facility near Tehran.
- Some universities and research centers may be linked to the biological weapons program.
- Reports surfaced in the spring of 1993 that Iran had succeeded in obtaining advanced biological weapons technology in Switzerland and containment equipment and technology from Germany. According to these reports, this led to serious damage to computer facilities in a Swiss biological research facility by unidentified agents. Similar reports indicated that agents had destroyed German bio-containment equipment destined for Iran.
- More credible reports by US experts indicate that Iran has begun to stockpile Anthrax and botulinum in a facility near Tabriz, can now mass manufacture such agents, and has them in an aerosol form. None of these reports, however, can be verified.
- The CIA has reported that Iran has "sought dual-use biotech equipment from Europe and Asia, ostensibly for civilian use." It also reported in 1996 that Iran might be ready to deploy biological weapons. Beyond this point, little unclassified information exists regarding the details of Iran's effort to "weaponize" and produce biological weapons.
- Iran may have the production technology to make dry storable and aerosol weapons. This would allow it to develop suitable missile warheads and bombs and covert devices.
- Iran may have begun active weapons production in 1996, but probably only on a limited scale suitable for advanced testing and development.
- CIA testimony indicates that Iran is believed to have weaponized both live agents and toxins for artillery and bombs and may be pursuing biological warheads for its missiles. The CIA reported in 1996 that, "We believe that Iran holds some stocks of biological agents and weapons. Tehran probably has investigated both toxins and live organisms as biological warfare agents. Iran has the technical infrastructure to support a significant biological weapons program with little foreign assistance."
- The CIA reported in June, 1997 that Iran had obtained new dual use technology from China and India during 1996.
- Iran announced in June, 1997 that it would not produce or employ chemical weapons, including toxins.

Nuclear Weapons
- The Shah established the Atomic Energy Organization of Iran in 1974, and rapidly began to negotiate for nuclear power plants.
  - He concluded an extendable ten-year nuclear fuel contract with the United States in 1974, with Germany in 1976, and with France in 1977.
  - In 1975, he purchased a 10% share in a Eurodif uranium enrichment plant being built at Tricastin in France that was part of a French, Belgian, Spanish, and Italian consortium. Under the agreement the Shah signed, Iran was to have full access to the enrichment technology Eurodif developed, and agreed to buy a quota of enriched uranium from the new plant.
  - He created an ambitious plan calling for a network of 23 power reactors throughout

Table 11.1 (continued)

Iran that was to be operating by the mid-1990s, and sought to buy nuclear power plants from Germany and France.

- By the time the Shah fell in January, 1979, he had six reactors under contract and was attempting to purchase a total of 12 nuclear power plants from Germany, France, and the United States. Two 1,300-megawatt German nuclear power plants at Bushehr were already 60% and 75% completed, and site preparation work had begun on the first of two 935-megawatt French plants at Darkhouin that were to be supplied by Framatome.
- The Shah also started a nuclear weapons program in the early to mid-1970s, building upon his major reactor projects, investment in URENCO, and smuggling of nuclear enrichment and weapons-related technology from the United States and Europe.
- A 5-megawatt light-water research reactor operating in Tehran.
- A 27-kilowatt neutron-source reactor operating in Isfahan.
- Started two massive 1,300-megawatt reactor complexes.
- Attempted to covertly import controlled technology from the United States.
- US experts believe that the Shah began a low-level nuclear weapons research program, centered at the Amirabad Nuclear Research Center. This research effort included studies of weapons designs and plutonium recovery from spent reactor fuel.
  - It also involved a laser enrichment program which began in 1975 and led to a complex and highly illegal effort to obtain laser separation technology from the United States. This latter effort, which does not seem to have had any success, continued from 1976 until the Shah's fall, and four lasers operating in the critical 16 micron band were shipped to Iran in October, 1978.
  - At the same time, Iran worked on other ways to obtain plutonium, created a secret reprocessing research effort to use enriched uranium, and set up a small nuclear weapons design team.
  - In 1976, Iran signed a secret contract to buy $700 million worth of yellow cake from South Africa, and appears to have reached an agreement to buy up to 1,000 metric tons a year. It is unclear how much of this ore South Africa shipped before it agreed to adopt IAEA export restrictions in 1984, and whether South Africa really honored such export restrictions. Some sources indicate that South Africa still made major deliveries as late as 1988–1989.
  - Iran also tried to purchase 26.2 kilograms of highly enriched uranium; the application to the United States for this purchase was pending when the Shah fell.
  - The Shah did eventually accept full IAEA safeguards, but their value is uncertain.
- In 1984, Khomeini revived the nuclear weapons program begun under the Shah.
  - Received significant West German and Argentine corporate support in some aspects of nuclear technology during the Iran-Iraq War.
  - Limited transfers of centrifuge and other weapons related technology from PRC, possibly Pakistan.
  - Iran has a Chinese-supplied heavy-water, zero-power research reactor at Isfahan Nuclear Research Center, and two-Chinese supplied subcritical assemblies—a light water and graphite design.

Table 11.1 (continued)

- Iran has stockpiles of uranium and mines in the Yazd area. It may have had a uranium-ore concentration facility at the University of Tehran, but its status is unclear.
- Some experts feel that the IRGC moved experts and equipment from the Amirabad Nuclear Research Center to a new nuclear weapons research facility near Isfahan in the mid-1980s, and formed a new nuclear research center at the University of Isfahan in 1984 with French assistance. Unlike many Iranian facilities, the center at Isfahan was not declared to the IAEA until February, 1992, when the IAEA was allowed to make a cursory inspection of six sites that various reports had claimed were the location of Iran's nuclear weapons efforts.
- Bushehr I & II, on the Gulf Coast just southwest of Isfahan, were partially completed at the time of the Shah's fall. Iran attempted to revive the program and sought German and Argentine support, but the reactors were damaged by Iraqi air strikes in 1987 and 1988.
- Iran may also have opened a new uranium ore processing plant close to its Shagand uranium mine in March, 1990, and it seems to have extended its search for uranium ore into three additional areas. Iran may have also begun to exploit stocks of yellow cake that the Shah had obtained from South Africa in the late 1970s while obtaining uranium dioxide from Argentina by purchasing it through Algeria.
- Iran began to show a renewed interest in laser isotope separation (LIS) in the mid-1980s, and held a conference on LIS in September, 1987.
- Iran opened a new nuclear research center in Isfahan in 1984, located about 4 kilometers outside the city and between the villages of Shahrida and Fulashans. This facility was built at a scale far beyond the needs of peaceful research, and Iran sought French and Pakistani help for a new research reactor for this center.
- The Khomeini government may also have obtained several thousand pounds of uranium dioxide from Argentina by purchasing it through Algeria. Uranium dioxide is considerably more refined than yellow cake, and is easier to use in irradiating material in a reactor to produce plutonium.
- The status of Iran's nuclear program since the Iran-Iraq War is highly controversial, and Iran has denied the existence of such a program.
  - On February 7, 1990, the speaker of the Majlis publicly toured the Atomic Energy Organization of Iran and opened the new Jabir Ibn al Hayyan laboratory to train Iranian nuclear technicians. Reports then surfaced that Iran had at least 200 scientists and a workforce of about 2,000 devoted to nuclear research.
  - Iran's Deputy President Ayatollah Mohajerani stated in October, 1991 that Iran should work with other Islamic states to create an "Islamic bomb."
  - The Iranian government has repeatedly made proposals to create a nuclear-free zone in the Middle East. For example, President Rafsanjani was asked if Iran had a nuclear weapons program in an interview in the CBS program *60 Minutes* in February, 1997. He replied, "Definitely not. I hate this weapon."
  - Other senior Iranian leaders, including President Khatami, have made similar categorical denials. Iran's new Foreign Minister, Kamal Kharrazi, stated on October 5, 1997, that "We are certainly not developing an atomic bomb, because we do not believe in nuclear weapons. . . . We believe in and promote the idea of the Middle

Table 11.1 (continued)

East as a region free of nuclear weapons and other weapons of mass destruction. But why are we interested to develop nuclear technology? We need to diversify our energy sources. In a matter of a few decades, our oil and gas reserves would be finished, and therefore we need access to other sources of energy.... Furthermore, nuclear technology has many other utilities in medicine and agriculture. The case of the United States in terms of oil reserve is not different from Iran's. The United States also has large oil resources, but at the same time they have nuclear power plants. So there is nothing wrong with having access to nuclear technology if it is for peaceful purposes''

- The IAEA reports that Iran has fully complied with its present requirements, and that it has found no indications of nuclear weapons effort, but the IAEA only inspects Iran's small research reactors.
  - The IAEA's visits to other Iranian sites are not inspections, and do not use instruments, cameras, seals, etc. They are informal walk-throughs.
  - The IAEA visited five suspect Iranian facilities in 1992 and 1993 in this manner, but did not conduct full inspections.
  - Iran has not had any 93+2 inspections, and its position on improved inspections is that it will not be either the first or the last to have them.
  - Iranian officials have repeatedly complained that the West tolerated Iraqi use of chemical weapons and its nuclear and biological build-up during the Iran-Iraq War, and has a dual standard where it does not demand inspections of Israel or that Israel sign the Nuclear Non-Proliferation Treaty.
- These are reasons to assume that Iran still has a nuclear program:
  - Iran attempted to buy highly enriched fissile material from Khazakstan. The United States paid between $20 million and $30 million to buy 1,300 pounds of highly enriched uranium from the Ust-Kamenogorsk facility in Khazakstan that Iran may have sought to acquire in 1992. A total of 120 pounds of the material—enough for two bombs—cannot be fully accounted for.
  - Iran has imported maraging steel, sometimes used for centrifuges, by smuggling it in through dummy fronts. Britain intercepted 110 pound (50 kilo) shipment in August, 1996. Seems to have centrifuge research program at Sharif University of Technology in Tehran. The IAEA ''visit'' did not confirm.
  - Those aspects of Iran's program that are visible indicate that Iran has had only uncertain success. Argentina agreed to train Iranian technicians at its Jose Balaseiro Nuclear Institute, and sold Iran $5.5 million worth of uranium for its small Amirabad Nuclear Research Center reactor in May, 1987. A CENA team visited Iran in late 1987 and early 1988, and seems to have discussed selling Iran the technology necessary to operate its reactor with 20% enriched uranium as a substitute for the highly enriched core provided by the United States, and possibly uranium enrichment and plutonium reprocessing technology as well. Changes in Argentina's government, however, made it much less willing to support proliferation. The Argentine government announced in February, 1992 that it was canceling an $18 million nuclear technology sale to Iran because it had not signed a nuclear safeguards arrangement. Argentine press sources suggested, however, that Argentina was reacting to US pressure.

Table 11.1 (continued)

- In February, 1990, a Spanish newspaper reported that Associated Enterprises of Spain was negotiating the completion of the two nuclear power plants at Bushehr. Another Spanish firm called ENUSA (National Uranium Enterprises) was to provide the fuel, and Kraftwerke Union (KWU) would be involved. Later reports indicated that a 10-man delegation from Iran's Ministry of Industry was in Madrid negotiating with the director of Associated Enterprises, Adolofo Garcia Rodriguez.
- Iran negotiated with Kraftwerke Union and CENA of Germany in the late 1980s and early 1990s. It attempted to import reactor parts from Siemens in Germany and Skoda in Czechoslovakia. None of these efforts solved Iran's problems in rebuilding its reactor program, but all demonstrate the depth of its interest.
- Iran took other measures to strengthen its nuclear program during the early 1990s. It installed a cyclotron from Ion Beam Applications in Belgium at a facility in Karzaj in 1991.
- Iran conducted experiments in uranium enrichment and centrifuge technology at its Sharif University of Technology in Tehran. Sharif University was also linked to efforts to import cylinders of fluorine suitable for processing enriched material and attempts to import specialized magnets that can be used for centrifuges from Thyssen in Germany in 1991.
- It is clear from Iran's imports that it has sought centrifuge technology ever since. Although many of Iran's efforts have never been made public, British customs officials seized 110 pounds of maraging steel being shipped to Iran in July, 1996.
- Iran seems to have conducted research into plutonium separation, and Iranians published research on uses of tritium that had applications to nuclear weapons boosting. Iran also obtained a wide range of US and other nuclear literature with applications for weapons designs. Italian inspectors seized eight steam condensers bound for Iran that could be used in a covert reactor program in 1993 and high-technology ultrasound equipment suitable for reactor testing at the port of Bari in January, 1994.
- Other aspects of Iran's nuclear research effort had potential weapons applications. Iran continued to operate an Argentine-fueled five megawatt, light water, highly enriched uranium reactor at the University of Tehran. It is operated by a Chinese-supplied neutron source research reactor and subcritical assemblies with 900 grams of highly enriched uranium at its Isfahan Nuclear Research Center. This Center has experimented with a heavy water zero-power reactor, a light water sub-critical reactor, and a graphite sub-critical reactor. In addition, it may have experimented with some aspects of nuclear weapons design.
- The German Ministry of Economics has circulated a wide list of such Iranian fronts which are known to have imported or attempted to import controlled items. These fronts include the:
- Bonyad e-Mostazafan;
- Defense Industries Organization (Sazemane Sanaye Defa);
- Pars Garma Company, the Sadadja Industrial Group (Sadadja Sanaye Daryaee);
- Iran Telecommunications Industry (Sanaye Mokhaberet Iran);
- Shahid Hemat Industrial Group, the State Purchasing Organization, Education Research Institute (ERI);

Table 11.1 (continued)
- Iran Aircraft Manufacturing Industries (IAI);
- Iran Fair Deal Company, Iran Group of Surveyors;
- Iran Helicopter Support and Renewal Industries (IHI);
- Iran Navy Technical Supply Center;
- Iran Tehran Kohakd Daftar Nezarat, Industrial Development Group; and the
- Ministry of Defense (Vezerate Defa).
- Iran claims it eventually needs to build enough nuclear reactors to provide 20% of its electric power. This Iranian nuclear power program presents serious problems in terms of proliferation. Although the reactors are scarcely ideal for irradiating material to produce plutonium or cannibalizing the core, they do provide Iran with the technology base to make its own reactors, have involved other technology transfer helpful to Iran in proliferating, and can be used to produce weapons if Iran rejects IAEA safeguards.
- Russia has agreed to build up to four reactors—beginning with a complex at Bushehr—with two 1,000–1,200 megawatt reactors and two 465 megawatt reactors, and provide significant nuclear technology.
  - Russia has consistently claimed that the light water reactor designs for Bushehr cannot be used to produce weapons grade plutonium and are similar to the reactors the United States is providing to North Korea.
  - The United States has claimed, however, that Victor Mikhaliov, the head of Russia's Atomic Energy Ministry, proposed the sale of a centrifuge plant in April, 1995. The United States also indicated that it had persuaded Russia not to sell Iran centrifuge technology as part of the reactor deal during the summit meeting between Presidents Clinton and Yeltsin in May, 1995.
  - It was only after US pressure that Russia publicly stated that it never planned to sell centrifuge and advanced enrichment technology to Iran, and Iran denied that it had ever been interested in such technology. For example, the statement of Mohammed Sadegh Ayatollahi, Iran's representative to the IAEA, stated that, "We've had contracts before for the Bushehr plant in which we agreed that the spent fuel would go back to the supplier. For our contract with the Russians and Chinese, it is the same." According to some reports, Russia was to reprocess the fuel at its Mayak plant near Chelyabinsk in the Urals, and could store it at an existing facility, at Krasnoyarsk-26, in southern Siberia.
  - The CIA reported in June, 1997 that Iran had obtained new nuclear technology from Russia during 1996.
  - A nuclear accident at plant at Rasht, six miles north of Gilan, exposed about 50 people to radiation in July, 1996.
  - Russian Nuclear Energy Minister Yevgeny Adamov and Russian Deputy Prime Minister Vladimir Bulgak visited in March, 1998, and Iran dismissed US complaints about the risk the reactors would be used to proliferate.
    - Russia indicated that it would go ahead with selling two more reactors for construction at Bushehr within the next five years.
    - The first 1,000-megawatt reactor at Bushehr has experienced serious construction delays. In March, 1998, Russia and Iran agreed to turn the construction project into

Table 11.1 (continued)

a turn key plant because the Iranian firms working on infrastructure had fallen well behind schedule. In February, Iran had agreed to fund improved safety systems. The reactor is reported to be on a 30 month completion cycle.

- The United States persuaded the Ukraine not to sell Iran $45 million worth of turbines for its nuclear plant in early March, 1998, and to strengthen its controls on Ukrainian missile technology under the MTCR.
- China is reported to have agreed to provide significant nuclear technology transfer and the possible sale of two 300 megawatt pressurized water reactors in the early 1990s, but then to have agreed to halt nuclear assistance to Iran after pressure from the United States.
- Iran signed an agreement with China's Commission on Science, Technology, and Industry for National Defense on January 21, 1991, to build a small 27-kilowatt research reactor at Iran's nuclear weapons research facility at Isfahan. On November 4, 1991, China stated that it had signed commercial cooperation agreements with Iran in 1989 and 1991, and that it would transfer an electromagnetic isotope separator (Calutron) and a smaller nuclear reactor for "peaceful and commercial" purposes.
- The Chinese reactor and calutron were small research-scale systems and had no direct value in producing fissile material. They did, however, give Iran more knowledge of reactor and enrichment technology, and US experts believe that China provided Iran with additional data on chemical separation, other enrichment technology, the design for facilities to convert uranium to uranium hexaflouride to make reactor fuel, and help in processing yellow cake.
- The United States put intense pressure on China to halt such transfers. President Clinton and Chinese President Jiang Zemin reached an agreement at an October, 1997 summit. China strengthened this pledge in negotiations with the United States in February, 1998.
- In March, 1998, the United States found that the China Nuclear Energy Corporation was negotiating to sell Iran several hundred tons of anhydrous hydrogen flouride (AHF) to Isfahan Nuclear Research Corporation in central Iran, a site where some experts believe Iran is working on the development of nuclear weapons. AHF can be used to separate plutonium, help refine yellow cake into uranium hexaflouride to produce U-235, and as a feedstock for Sarin. It is on two nuclear control lists. China agreed to halt the sale.
- Iran denied that China had halted nuclear cooperation on March 15, 1998.
- Even so, the US Acting Under Secretary of State for Arms Control and International Security Affairs stated that China was keeping its pledge not to aid Iran on March 26, 1998.

- US estimates of Iran's progress in acquiring nuclear weapons have become more conservative with time.
  - In 1992, the CIA estimated that Iran would have the bomb by the year 2000. In 1995, John Holum testified that Iran could have the bomb by 2003.
  - In 1997, after two years in which Iran might have made progress, he testified that Iran could have the bomb by 2005–2007.
  - US experts increasingly refer to Iran's efforts as "creeping proliferation," and there

Table 11.1 (continued)

  is no way to tell when or if Iranian current efforts will produce a weapon, and unclassified lists of potential facilities have little credibility.
- Timing of weapons acquisition depends heavily on whether Iran can buy fissile material—if so it has the design capability and can produce weapons in 1–2 years—or must develop the capability to process plutonium or enriched uranium—in which case, it is likely to be 5–10 years.
- The control of fissile material in the FSU remains a major problem:
  - US estimates indicate the FSU left a legacy of some 1,485 tons of nuclear material. This includes 770 tons in some 27,000 weapons, including 816 strategic bombs, 5,434 missile warheads, and about 20,000 theater and tactical weapons. In addition, there were 715 tons of fissile or near-fissile material in eight countries of the FSU in over 50 sites, enough to make 35,000–40,000 bombs.
  - There are large numbers of experienced FSU technicians, including those at the Russian weapons design center at Arzamas, and at nuclear production complexes at Chelyabinsk, Krasnoyarsk, and Tomsk.
  - These factors led the United States to conduct Operation Sapphire in 1994, where the United States removed 600 kilograms of highly enriched uranium from the Ulba Metallurgy Plant in Kazakhstan at a time Iran was negotiating for the material.
  - They also led to Britain and the United States cooperating in Auburn Endeavor, and airlifting fissile material out of a nuclear research facility in Tiblisi, Georgia. There were 10 pounds of material at the institute, and 8.8 pounds were HEU. (It takes about 35 pounds to make a bomb.) This operation was reported in the *New York Times* on April 21, 1998. The British government confirmed it took place, but would not give the date.
- The *Jerusalem Post* reported on April 9, 1998, that Iran had purchased four tactical nuclear weapons from Russian smugglers for $25 million in the early 1990s, that the weapons had been obtained from Kazakhstan in 1991, and that Argentine technicians were helping to activate the weapon.
  - It quoted what it claimed was an Iranian report, dated December 26, 1991, of a meeting between Brigadier General Rahim Safavi, the deputy commander of the Revolutionary Guards, and Reza Amrohalli, then head of the Iranian atomic energy organization.
  - It also quoted a second document—dated January 2, 1992—saying the Iranians were awaiting the arrival of Russian technicians to show them how to disarm the protection systems that would otherwise inactivate the weapons if anyone attempted to use them.
  - The documents implied the weapons were flawed but did not indicate whether Iran had succeeded in activating them.
  - The US intelligence community denied any evidence that such a transfer had taken place.
- The most detailed reports of Iran's nuclear weapons program are the least reliable and come from the People's Mujahideen, a violent, anti-regime, terrorist group. Its claims are very doubtful, but the People's Mujahideen has reported that:

Table 11.1 (continued)

- Iran's facilities include a weapons site called Ma'allem Kelayah, near Qazvin on the Caspian. This is said to be an IRGC-run facility established in 1987, which has involved an Iranian investment of $300 million. Supposedly, the site was to house the 10 megawatt reactor Iran tried to buy from India.
- Two Soviet reactors were to be installed at a large site at Gorgan on the Caspian, under the direction of Russian physicists.
- The People's Republic of China provided uranium enrichment equipment and technicians for the site at Darkhouin, where Iran once planned to build a French reactor.
- A nuclear reactor was being constructed at Karaj, and another nuclear weapons facility exists in the south central part of Iran, near the Iraqi border.
- The ammonia and urea plant that the British firm M. W. Kellog was building at Borujerd in Khorassan province, near the border with Turkestan, might be adapted to produce heavy water.
- The Amir Kabar Technical University, the Atomic Energy Organization of Iran (AEOI) (also known as the Organization for Atomic Energy of Iran, or AEOI), Dor Argham Ltd., the Education and Research Institute, GAM Iranian Communications, Ghoods Research Center, Iran Argham Co., Iran Electronic Industries, Iranian Research Organization, Ministry of Sepah, Research and Development Group, Sezemane Sanaye Defa, the Sharif University of Technology, Taradis Iran Computer Company, and Zakaria Al-Razi Chemical Company are all participants in the Iranian nuclear weapons effort.
- Other sources based on opposition data have listed the Atomic Energy Organization of Iran, the Laser Research Center and Ibn-e Heysam Research and Laboratory Complex, the Bonab Atomic Energy Research Center (East Azerbaijan), the Imam Hussein University of the Revolutionary Guards, the Jabit bin al-Hayyan Laboratory, the Khoshomi uranium mine (Yazd), a possible site at Moallem Kalayeh, the Nuclear Research Center at Tehran University, the Nuclear Research Center for Agriculture and Medicine (Karaj), the Nuclear Research Center of Technology (Isfahan), the Saghand Uranium mine (Yazd), the Sharif University (Tehran) and its Physics Research Center.

Missile Defenses
- Seeking Russian S-300 surface-to-air missile system with limited anti-tactical ballistic missile capability.

Iraq's Search for Weapons of Mass Destruction

Delivery Systems
- Prior to the Gulf War, Iraq had extensive delivery systems incorporating long-range strike aircraft with refueling capabilities and several hundred regular and improved, longer-range Scud missiles, some with chemical warheads. These systems included:
  - Tu-16 and Tu-22 bombers.
  - MiG-29 fighters.
  - Mirage F-1, MiG-23BM, and Su-22 fighter attack aircraft.

Table 11.1 (continued)
- A Scud force with a minimum of 819 missiles.
- Extended range Al Husayn Scud variants (600 kilometer range) extensively deployed throughout Iraq, and at three fixed sites in northern, western, and southern Iraq.
- Developing Al-Abbas missiles (900 kilometer range), which could reach targets in Iran, the Persian Gulf, Israel, Turkey, and Cyprus.
- Long-range super guns with ranges of up to 600 kilometers.
- Iraq also engaged in efforts aimed at developing the Tamuz liquid fueled missile with a range of over 2,000 kilometers, and a solid-fueled missile with a similar range. Clear evidence indicates that at least one design was to have a nuclear warhead.
- Iraq attempted to conceal a plant making missile engines from the UN inspectors. It only admitted this plant existed in 1995, raising new questions about how many of its missiles have been destroyed.
- Iraq had design work underway for a nuclear warhead for its long-range missiles.
- The Gulf War deprived Iraq of some of its MiG-29s, Mirage F-1s, MiG-23BMs, and Su-22s.
- Since the end of the war, the UN inspection regime has also destroyed many of Iraq's long-range missiles:
  - UNSCOM has directly supervised the destruction of 48 Scud-type missiles.
  - It has verfied the Iraqi unilateral destruction of 83 more missiles and 9 mobile launchers.
- The UN still estimates, however, that it is able to account for 817 of the 819 long-range missiles that Iraq imported in the period ending in 1988:
  - Pre-1980 expenditures, such as training: 8
  - Expenditures during the Iran-Iraq War (1980–1981), including the war of the cities in February–April, 1988: 516
  - Testing activities for the development of Iraq's modifications of imported missiles and other experimental activities (1985–1990): 69
  - Expenditures during the Gulf War (January–March 1991): 93
  - Destruction under the supervision of UNSCOM: 48
  - Unilateral destruction by Iraq (mid-July and October, 1991: 83
  - UNSCOM's analysis has shown that Iraq had destroyed 83 of the 85 missiles it had claimed were destroyed. At the same time, it stated that Iraq had not given an adequate account of its proscribed missile assets, including launchers, warheads, and propellants.
  - UNSCOM also reports that it supervised the destruction of 10 mobile launchers, 30 chemical warheads, and 18 conventional warheads.
- Iraq maintains a significant delivery capability consisting of:
  - HY-2, SS-N-2, and C-601 cruise missiles, which are unaffected by UN cease-fire terms.
  - FROG-7 rockets with 70 kilometer ranges, also allowed under UN resolutions.

Table 11.1 (continued)
- Multiple rocket launchers and tube artillery.
- Experimental conversions such as the SA-2.
* Iraq claims to have manufactured only 80 missile assemblies, 53 of which were unusable. UNSCOM claims that 10 are unaccounted for.
  - US experts believe Iraq may still have components for several dozen extended-range Scud missiles.
  - They believe Iraq is concealing 5–12 missiles, which it has disassembled and scattered in various parts of the country.
  - Iraq is also lying about the production of parts for up to 85 missiles, which are also dispersed in many parts of the country. It is unclear how many can be rapidly assembled into entire missiles.
  - Iraq is concealing significant assets of liquid propellants for the missiles.
* In addition, Iraq has admitted to:
  - Hiding its capability to manufacture its own Scuds.
  - Developing an extended range variant of the FROG-7, called the Laith. The UN claims to have tagged all existing FROG-7s to prevent any extension of their range beyond the UN imposed limit of 150 kilometers for Iraqi missiles.
  - Experimenting with cruise missile technology and ballistic missile designs with ranges up to 3,000 kilometers.
  - Flight testing Al Husayn missiles with chemical warheads in April, 1990.
  - Developing biological warheads for the Al Husayn missile as part of Project 144 at Taji.
  - Initiating a research and development program for a nuclear warhead missile delivery system.
  - Successfully developing and testing a warhead separation system.
  - Indigenously developing, testing, and manufacturing advanced rocket engines to include liquid-propellant designs.
  - Conducting research into the development of Remotely Piloted Vehicles (RPVs) for the dissemination of biological agents.
  - Attempting to expand its Ababil-100 program designed to build surface-to-surface missiles with ranges beyond the permitted 100–150 kilometers.
  - Importing parts from Britain, Switzerland, and other countries for a 350 mm "super gun," as well as starting an indigenous 600 mm supergun design effort.
* Iraq initially claimed that it had 45 missile warheads filled with chemical weapons in 1992. It then stated that it had 20 chemical and 25 biological warheads in 1995. UNSCOM established that it had a minimum of 75 operational warheads and 5 used for trials. It has evidence of the existence of additional warheads. It can only verify that 16 warheads were filled with Sarin, and 34 with chemical warfare binary components, and that 30 were destroyed under its supervision—16 with Sarin and 14 with binary components.
  - Iraq may be concealing significant numbers of VX nerve gas-filled warheads.

Table 11.1 (continued)

- US and UN officials conclude further that:
  - Iraq is trying to rebuild its ballistic missile program using a clandestine network of front companies to obtain the necessary materials and technology from European and Russian firms.
  - This equipment is then concealed and stockpiled for assembly concomitant with the end of the UN inspection regime.
  - The equipment clandestinely sought by Iraq includes advanced missile guidance components, such as accelerometers and gyroscopes, specialty metals, special machine tools, and a high-tech, French-made, million-dollar furnace designed to fabricate engine parts for missiles.
- Recent major violations and smuggling efforts:
  - In November, 1995, Iraq was found to have concealed an SS-21 missile it had smuggled in from Yemen.
  - Jordan found that Iraq was smuggling missile components through Jordan in early December, 1995. These included 115 gyroscopes in 10 crates, and material for making chemical weapons. The shipment was worth an estimated $25 million. Iraq claimed the gyroscopes were for oil exploration but they are similar to those used in the Soviet SS-N-18 SLBM. UNSCOM also found some gyroscopes dumped in the Tigris.
- Iraq retains the technology it acquired before the war, and evidence clearly indicates an ongoing research and development effort, in spite of the UN sanctions regime.
- The fact the agreement allows Iraq to continue producing and testing short-range missiles (less than 150 kilometers range) means it can retain significant missile development effort.
  - The SA-2 is a possible test bed, but UNSCOM has tagged all missiles and monitors all high apogee tests.
  - Iraq's Al-Samoud and Ababil-100 programs are similar test beds. The Al-Samoud is a scaled-down Scud which Iraq seems to have tested.
  - Iraq continues to expand its missile production facility at Ibn Al Haytham, which has two new buildings large enough to make much longer-range missiles.
  - US satellite photographs reveal that Iraq has rebuilt its Al-Kindi missile research facility.
  - Ekeus reported on December 18, 1996, that Iraq retained missiles, rocket launchers, fuel, and command system to "make a missile force of significance." UNSCOM reporting as of October, 1997 is more optimistic, but notes that Iraq "continued to conceal documents describing its missile propellants, and the material evidence relating to its claims to have destroyed its indigenous missile production capabilities indicated in might have destroyed less than a tenth of what it claimed."

Chemical Weapons

- Iraq is the only major recent user of weapons of mass destruction. US intelligence sources report the following Iraqi uses of chemical weapons:

Table 11.1 (continued)

Date	Area	Type of Gas	Approximate Casualties	Target
August, 1983	Haij Umran	Mustard	Less than 100	Iranians/Kurds
October–November, 1983	Panjwin	Mustard	30,000	Iranians/Kurds
February–March, 1984	Majnoon Island	Mustard	2,500	Iranians
March, 1984	Al Basrah	Tabun	50–100	Iranians
March, 1985	Hawizah Marsh	Mustard/Tabun	3,000	Iranians
February, 1986	Al Faw	Mustard/Tabun	8,000–10,000	Iranians
December, 1986	Umm ar Rasas	Mustard	1,000s	Iranians
April, 1987	Al Basrah	Mustard/Tabun	5,000	Iranians
October, 1987	Sumar/Mehran	Mustard/Nerve Agents	3,000	Iranians
March, 1988	Halabjah	Mustard/Nerve Agents	Hundreds	Iranians/Kurds

Note: Iranians also used poison gas at Halabjah and may have caused some of the casualties.

- In revelations to the UN, Iraq admitted that, prior to the Gulf War, it:
  - Procured more than 1,000 key pieces of specialized production and support equipment for its chemical warfare program.
  - Maintained large stockpiles of mustard gas, and the nerve agents Sarin and Tabun.
  - Produced binary Sarin filled artillery shells, 122 mm rockets, and aerial bombs.
  - Manufactured enough precursors to produce 70 tons (70,000 kilograms) of the nerve agent VX. These precursors included 65 tons of choline and 200 tons of phosphorous pentasulfide and diisopropylamine.
  - Tested Ricin, a deadly toxin, for use in artillery shells.
  - Had three flight tests of long-range Scuds with chemical warheads.
  - Had a large VX production effort underway at the time of the Gulf War. The destruction of the related weapons and feedstocks has been claimed by Iraq, but not verified by UNSCOM. Iraq seems to have had at least 3,800 kilograms of V-agents by the time of the Gulf War, and 12–16 missile warheads.
- The majority of Iraq's chemical agents were manufactured at a supposed pesticide plant located at Muthanna. Various other production facilities were also used, including those at Salman Pak, Samara, and Habbiniyah. Though severely damaged during the war, the physical plant for many of these facilities has been rebuilt.
- Iraq possessed the technology to produce a variety of other persistent and non-persistent agents.
- The Gulf War and the subsequent UN inspection regime may have largely eliminated some of the stockpiles and reduced production capability.
- During 1991–1994, UNSCOM supervised the destruction of:

Table 11.1 (continued)
- 38,537 filled and unfilled chemical munitions.
- 690 tons of chemical warfare agents.
- More than 3,000 tons of precursor chemicals.
- Over 100 pieces of remaining production equipment at the Muthan State Establishment, Iraq's primary CW research, production, filling and storage site.
- Since that time, UNSCOM has forced new disclosures from Iraq that have led to:
  - The destruction of 325 newly identified production equipment, 120 of which were only disclosed in August, 1997.
  - The destruction of 275 tons of additional precursors.
  - The destruction of 125 analytic instruments.
  - The return of 91 analytic pieces of equipment to Kuwait.
- As of February, 1998, UNSCOM had supervised the destruction of a total of:
  - 40,000 munitions, 28,000 filled and 12,000 empty.
  - 480,000 liters of chemical munitions.
  - 1,800,000 liters of chemical precursors.
  - Eight types of delivery systems including missile warheads.
- US and UN experts believe Iraq has concealed significant stocks of precursors. Iraq also appears to retain significant amounts of production equipment dispersed before or during Desert Storm and not recovered by the UN.
- UNSCOM reports that Iraq has failed to account for
  - Special missile warheads intended for filling with chemical or biological warfare agents.
  - The material balance of some 550 155 mm mustard gas shells, the extent of VX programs, and the rationale for the acquisition of various types of chemical weapons.
  - 130 tons of chemical warfare agents.
  - Some 4,000 tons of declared precursors for chemical weapons.
  - The production of several hundred tons of additional chemical warfare agents and the consumption of chemical precursors.
  - 107,500 empty casings for chemical weapons.
  - Whether several thousand additional chemical weapons were filled with agents.
  - The unilateral destruction of 15,620 weapons, and the fate of 16,038 additional weapons Iraq claimed it had discarded. "The margin of error" in the accounting presented by Iraq is in the neighborhood of 200 munitions.
  - Systematically lying about the existence of its production facilities for VX gas until 1995 and making "significant efforts" to conceal its production capabilities after that date. Uncertainties affecting the destruction of its VX gas still affect some 750 tons of imported precursor chemicals and 55 tons of domestically produced precursors. Iraq has made unverifiable claims that 460 tons were destroyed by Coalition air

Table 11.1 (continued)

attacks, and that it unilaterally destroyed 212 tons. UNSCOM has only been able to verify the destruction of 155 tons by Iraq and to destroy a further 36 tons on its own.

- Developing basic chemical warhead designs for Scud missiles, rockets, bombs, and shells. Iraq also has spray dispersal systems.
- Maintaining extensive stocks of defensive equipment.
- The UN feels that Iraq is not currently producing chemical agents, but Iraq has offered no evidence that it has destroyed its VX production capability and/or stockpile. Further, Iraq retains the technology it acquired before the war and evidence clearly indicates an ongoing research and development effort, in spite of the UN sanctions regime.
- Recent UNSCOM work confirms that Iraq did deploy gas-filled 155 mm artillery and 122 mm multiple rocket rounds into the rear areas of the KTO during the Gulf War.
- Iraq's chemical weapons had no special visible markings, and were often stored in the same area as conventional weapons.
- Iraq has the technology to produce stable, highly lethal VX gas with long storage times.
- Iraq may have developed improved binary and more stable weapons since the Gulf War.
- Since 1992, Iraq attempted to covertly import precursors and production equipment for chemical weapons through Qatar, Saudi Arabia, and Jordan since the Gulf War.
- The current status of the Iraqi program is as follows (according to US intelligence as of February 19, 1998):

Agent	Declared	Potential Unaccounted for	Comments
Chemical Agents	(Metric Tons)	(Metric Tons)	
VX Nerve Gas	3	300	Iraq lied about the program until 1995.
G Agents (Sarin)	100–150	200	Figures include weaponized and bulk agents.
Mustard Gas	500–600	200	Figures include weaponized and bulk agents.
Delivery Systems	(Number)	(Number)	
Missile Warheads	75–100	45–70	UNSCOM supervised destruction of 30.
Rockets	100,000	15,000–25,000	UNSCOM supervised destruction of 40,000, 28,000 of which were filled.
Aerial Bombs	16,000	2,000	
Artillery Shells	30,000	15,000	
Aerial Spray Tanks	?	?	

Table 11.1 (continued)

Biological Weapons

- Had highly compartmented "black" program with far tighter security regulations than chemical program.

- Had 18 major sites for some aspect of biological weapons effort before the Gulf War. Most were non-descript and had no guards or visible indications that they were military facilities.

- The United States targeted only one site during the Gulf War. It struck two sites, one for other reasons. It also struck at least two targets with no biological facilities that it misidentified.

- Systematically lied about biological weapons effort until 1995. First stated that it had small defensive efforts, but no offensive effort. In July, 1995, admitted it had a major defensive effort. In October, 1995, finally admitted major weaponization effort.

- Continued to lie about its biological weapons effort since October, 1995. It has claimed that the effort was headed by Dr. Taha, a woman who only headed a subordinate effort. It has not admitted to any help by foreign personnel or contractors. It has claimed to have destroyed its weapons, but the one site UNSCOM inspectors visited showed no signs of such destruction and was later said to be the wrong site. It has claimed only 50 people were employed full time, but the scale of the effort would have required several hundred.

- Since July, 1995, Iraq has presented three versions of full, frank, and comprehensive disclosures (FFCDs) and four "drafts."

  - The most recent FFCD was presented by Iraq on September 11, 1997. This submission followed the UNSCOM's rejection, of the FFCD of June, 1996. In the period since receiving that report, UNSCOM conducted eight inspections in an attempt to investigate critical areas of Iraq's proscribed activities, such as warfare agent production and destruction, biological munitions manufacturing, filling and destruction, and military involvement in and support to the proscribed program. Those investigations confirmed the assessment that the June 1996 declaration was deeply deficient. The UNSCOM concluded that the new FFCD it received on September 11, 1997, contained no significant changes from the June, 1996 FFCD.

- Iraq has not admitted to the production of 8,500 liters of Anthrax, 19,000 liters of Botulinum toxin, and 2,200 liters of Aflatoxin.

- Reports indicate that Iraq tested at least seven principal biological agents for use against humans.

  - Anthrax, Botulinum, and Aflatoxin are known to be weaponized.

  - Looked at viruses, bacteria, and fungi. Examined the possibility of weaponizing gas gangrene and Mycotoxins. Some field trials were held of these agents.

  - Examined foot and mouth disease, hemorrhagic conjunctivitis virus, rotavirus, and camel pox virus.

  - Conducted research on a "wheat pathogen" and a Mycotoxin similar to "yellow rain" defoliant.

Table 11.1 (continued)

- The "wheat smut" was first produced at Al Salman and then put in major production during 1987–1988 at a plant near Mosul. Iraq claims the program was abandoned.
- The August, 1995 defection of Lieutenant General Husayn Kamel Majid, formerly in charge of Iraq's weapons of mass destruction, revealed the extent of this biological weapons program. Lt. General Kamel's defection prompted Iraq to admit that it:
  - Imported 39 tons of growth media (31,000 kilograms or 68,200 pounds) for biological agents obtained from three European firms. According to UNSCOM, 3,500 kilograms or 7,700 pounds remain unaccounted for. Some estimates go as high as 17 tons. Each ton can be used to produce 10 tons of bacteriological weapons.
  - Imported type cultures from the United States, which can be modified to develop biological weapons.
  - Had a laboratory- and industrial-scale capability to manufacture various biological agents including the bacteria which causes Anthrax and botulism; Aflatoxin, a naturally occurring carcinogen; clostridium perfringens, a gangrene-causing agent; the protein toxin Ricin; tricothecene Mycotoxins, such as T-2 and DAS; and an anti-wheat fungus known as wheat cover smut. Iraq also conducted research into the rotavirus, the camel pox virus, and the virus which causes hemorrhagic conjunctivitis.
  - Created at least seven primary production facilities, including the Sepp Institute at Muthanna, the Ghazi Research Institute at Amaria, the Daura Foot and Mouth Disease Institute, and facilities at Al-Hakim, Salman Pak Taji, and Fudaliyah. According to UNSCOM, weaponization occurred primarily at Muthanna through May, 1987 (largely Botulinum), and then moved to Al Salman. (Anthrax). In March, 1988 a plant was open at Al Hakim, and in 1989 an Aflatoxin plant was set up at Fudaliyah.
  - Had a test site about 200 kilometers west of Baghdad, used animals in cages, and tested artillery and rocket rounds against live targets at ranges up to 16 kilometers.
  - Took fermenters and other equipment from Kuwait to improve effort during the Gulf War.
  - Had at least 79 civilian facilities capable of playing some role in biological weapons production still in existence in 1997.
- The Iraqi program involving Aflatoxin leaves many questions unanswered.
  - Iraqi research on Aflatoxin began in May, 1988 at Al Salman, where the toxin was produced by the growth of fungus aspergilus in 5.3 quart flasks.
  - The motives behind Iraq's research on Aflatoxin remain one of the most speculative aspects of its program. Aflatoxin is associated with fungal-contaminated food grains, and is considered nonlethal. It normally can produce liver cancer, but only after a period of months to years, and in intense concentrations. There is speculation, however, that a weaponized form might cause death within days, and some speculation that it can be used as an incapacitating agent.
  - Iraq moved its production of Aflatoxin to Fudaliyah in 1989 and produced 481 gallons of toxin in solution between November, 1988 and May, 1990.
  - It developed 16 R-400 Aflatoxin bombs and two Scud warheads. It conducted trials with Aflatoxin in 122 mm rockets and R-400 bombs in November 1989 and May and August 1990. It produced a total of 572 gallons of toxin and loaded 410.8 gallons into munitions.

Table 11.1 (continued)

- UNSCOM concluded in October, 1997 that Iraq's accounting for its Aflatoxin production was not credible.
- Total Iraqi production of more orthodox biological weapons reached at least 19,000 liters of concentrated Botulinum (10,000 liters filled into munitions); 8,500 liters of concentrated Anthrax (6,500 liters filled into munitions); and 2,500 liters of concentrated Aflatoxin (1,850 liters filled into munitions).
- It manufactured 6,000 liters of concentrated Botulinum toxin and 8,425 liters of Anthrax at Al-Hakim during 1990; 5,400 liters of concentrated Botulinum toxin at the Daura Foot and Mouth Disease Institute from November, 1990 to January 15, 1991; 400 liters of concentrated Botulinum toxin at Taji; and 150 liters of concentrated Anthrax at Salman Pak.
- Iraq is also known to have produced at least:
  - 1,850 liters of Aflatoxin in solution at Fudaliyah.
  - 340 liters of concentrated clostridium perfringens, a gangrene-causing biological agent, beginning in August, 1990.
  - 10 liters of concentrated Ricin at Al Salam. It claimed to have abandoned work after tests failed.
- Iraq weaponized at least three biological agents for use in the Gulf War. The weaponization consisted of at least:
  - 100 bombs and 16 missile warheads loaded with Botulinum.
  - 50 R-400 air-delivered bombs and 5 missile warheads loaded with anthrax; and
  - 4 missile warheads and 7 R-400 bombs loaded with Aflatoxin, a natural carcinogen.
- The warheads were designed for operability with the Al Husayn Scud variant.
- Iraq had other weaponization activities:
  - It armed 155 mm artillery shells and 122 mm rockets with biological agents.
  - It conducted field trials, weaponization tests, and live firings of 122 mm rockets armed with Anthrax and Botulinum toxin from March, 1988 to May, 1990.
  - It tested Ricin, a deadly protein toxin, for use in artillery shells.
  - It produced at least 191 bombs and 25 missile warheads with biological agents.
  - It developed and deployed 250-pound aluminum bombs covered in fiberglass. Bombs were designed so they could be mounted on both Soviet and French-made aircraft. They were rigged with parachutes for low-altitude drops to allow efficient slow delivery and aircraft to fly under radar coverage. Some debate exists over whether bombs had cluster munitions or simply dispersed agents, like the LD-400 chemical bomb.
  - It deployed at least 166 R-400 bombs with 85 liters of biological agents each during the Gulf War, at two sites. One was near an abandoned runway where it could fly in aircraft, arm them quickly, and disperse with no prior indication of activity and no reason for the UN to target the runway.

Table 11.1 (continued)
- It filled at least 25 Scud missile warheads, and 157 bombs and aerial dispensers, with biological agents during the Gulf War.
- It developed and stored drop tanks ready for use for three aircraft or RPVs with the capability of dispersing 2,000 liters of Anthrax. Development took place in December, 1990. Iraq later claimed that tests showed the systems were ineffective.
  - The UN found, however, that Iraq equipped crop spraying helicopters for biological warfare and held exercises and tests simulating the spraying of Anthrax spores.
- Iraqi Mirages were given spray tanks to disperse biological agents.
  - Trials were held as late as January 13, 1991.
  - The Mirages were chosen because they have large 2,200 liter belly tanks and could be refueled by air, giving them a longer endurance and greater strike range.
  - The tanks had electric valves to allow the agent to be released, and the system was tested by releasing simulated agent into desert areas with scattered petri dishes to detect the biological agent. UNSCOM has video tapes of the aircraft.
- Project 144 at Taji produced at least 25 operational Al Husayn warheads. Ten of these were hidden deep in a railway tunnel and 15 in holes dug in an unmanned hide site along the Tigris.
- Biological weapons were only distinguished from regular weapons by a black stripe.
- The UN claims that Iraq had offered no evidence to corroborate its claims that it destroyed its stockpile of biological agents after the Gulf War. Further, Iraq retains the technology it acquired before the war and evidence clearly indicates an ongoing research and development effort, in spite of the UN sanctions regime.
- UNSCOM reported in October 1997 that:
  - Iraq has never provided a clear picture of the role of its military in its biological warfare program, and has claimed it only played a token role.
  - It has never accounted for its disposal of growth media. The unaccounted-for media is sufficient, in quantity, for the production of over three times more of the biological agent (Anthrax) Iraq claims to have been produced.
  - Bulk warfare agent production appears to be vastly understated by Iraq. Expert calculations of possible agent production quantities, either by equipment capacity or growth media amounts, far exceed Iraq's stated results.
  - Significant periods when Iraq claims its fermenters were not utilized are unexplained.
  - Biological warfare field trials are underreported and inadequately described.
  - Claims regarding field trials of chemical and biological weapons using R400 bombs are contradictory and indicate that "more munitions were destroyed than were produced."
  - The Commission is unable to verify that the unilateral destruction of the BW-filled Al Husayn warheads has taken place.[1]
  - There is no way to confirm whether Iraq destroyed 157 bombs of the R400 type, some of which were filled with Botulin or anthrax spores.[2]
  - "The September 1997 FFCD fails to give a remotely credible account of Iraq's

Table 11.1 (continued)

biological program. This opinion has been endorsed by an international panel of experts."[3]

- The current status of the Iraqi program is as follows (according to US intelligence as of February 19, 1998):

Agent	Declared Concentrated Amount		Declared Total Amount		Uncertainty
	Liters	Gallons	Liters	Gallons	
Anthrax	8,500	12,245	85,000	22,457	Could be 3–4 times declared amount.
Botulinum toxin	19,400	NA	380,000	NA	Probably twice declared amount. Some extremely concentratred.
Gas Gangrene Clostridium	340	90	3,400	900	Amounts could be higher.
Perfingens Alfatoxin	NA	NA	2,200	581	Major uncertainties.
Ricin	NA	NA	10	2.7	Major uncertainties.

- UNSCOM cannot confirm the unilateral destruction of 25 warheads. It can confirm the destruction of 23 out of at least 157 bombs. Iraq may have more aerosol tanks.
- The UN currently inspects 79 sites: 5 used to make weapons before war; 5 vaccine or pharmaceutical sites; 35 research and university sites, 13 breweries, distilleries, and dairies with dual-purpose capabilities; and 8 diagnostic laboratories.
- Iraq retains laboratory capability to manufacture various biological agents, including the bacteria which cause Anthrax, botulism, tularemia, and typhoid.
- Many additional civilian facilities are capable of playing some role in biological weapons production.

Nuclear Weapons

- Inspections by UN teams have found evidence of two successful weapons designs, a neutron initiator, explosives, and triggering technology needed for the production of bombs, plutonium processing technology, centrifuge technology, Calutron enrichment technology, and experiments with chemical separation technology. Iraq had some expert technical support, including at least one German scientist who provided the technical plans for the URENCO TC-11 centrifuge.
- Iraq's main nuclear weapons related facilities were:
  - Al Atheer—center of nuclear weapons program. Uranium metallurgy, production of shaped charges for bombs, remote controlled facilities for high explosives manufacture.
  - Al Tuwaitha—triggering systems, neutron initiators, uranium metallurgy, and hot cells for plutonium separation. Laboratory production of UO_2, UCL_4, UF_6, and fuel fabrication facility. Prototype-scale gas centrifuge, prototype EMIS facility, and testing of laser isotope separation technology.
  - Al Qa Qa—high explosives storage, testing of detonators for high explosive component of implosion nuclear weapons.

Table 11.1 (continued)

- Al Musaiyib/Al Hatteen—high explosive testing, hydrodynamic studies of bombs.
- Al Hadre—firing range for high explosive devices, including FAE.
- Ash Sharqat—designed for mass production of weapons grade material using EMIS.
- Al Furat—designed for mass production of weapons grade material using centrifuge method.
- Al Jesira (Mosul)—mass production of UCL_4.
- Al Qaim—phosphate plant for production of U308.
- Akashat uranium mine.
- Iraq had three reactor programs:
  - Osiraq/Tammuz I 40 megawatt light-water reactor destroyed by Israeli air attack in 1981.
  - Isis/Tammuz II 800 kilowatt light water reactor destroyed by Coalition air attack in 1991.
  - IRT-5000 5 megawatt light water reactor damaged by Coalition air attack in 1991.
- Iraq used Calutron (EMIS), centrifuges, plutonium processing, chemical defusion, and foreign purchases to create new production capability after Israel destroyed most of Osiraq.
- Iraq established a centrifuge enrichment system in Rashidya and conducted research into the nuclear fuel cycle to facilitate development of a nuclear device.
- After invading Kuwait, Iraq attempted to accelerate its program to develop a nuclear weapon by using radioactive fuel from French and Russian-built reactors. It made a crash effort in September, 1990 to recover enriched fuel from its supposedly safeguarded French and Russian reactors, with the goal of producing a nuclear weapon by April, 1991. The program was halted only after Coalition air raids destroyed key facilities on January 17, 1991.
- Iraq conducted research into the production of a radiological weapon which disperses lethal radioactive material without initiating a nuclear explosion.
  - Orders were given in 1987 to explore the use of radiological weapons for area denial in the Iran-Iraq War.
  - Three prototype bombs were detonated at test sites—one was a ground-level static test and two others were dropped from aircraft.
  - Iraq claims the results were disappointing, and the project was shelved, but it has no records or evidence to prove this.
- UN teams have found and destroyed, or secured, new stockpiles of illegal enriched material, major production and R&D facilities, and equipment—including Calutron enriching equipment.
- The IAEA believes that Iraq's nuclear program has been largely disabled and remains incapacitated, but warns that Iraq retains substantial technology and in 1990 established

Table 11.1 (continued)
a clandestine purchasing system that it has used to import forbidden components since the Gulf War.
- The major remaining uncertainties are:
  - Iraq still retains the technology developed before the Gulf War, and US experts believe an ongoing research and development effort continues, in spite of the UN sanctions regime.
  - Possible concealment and/or dispersal of all the components for 2–3 implosion-type nuclear devices, except the fissile material.
  - Possible concealment of an effective, high-speed centrifuge program.
  - Possible elements for radiological weapons.
  - Success in seeking to clandestinely buy components for nuclear weapons and examining the purchase of fissile material from outside Iraq. Iraq is known to be active in this effort.
  - The extent to which it is continuing with the development of a missile warhead suited to the use of a nuclear device.
  - A substantial number of declared nuclear weapons components and research equipment have never been recovered. There is no reason to assume that Iraqi declarations were comprehensive.

Israel's Search for Weapons of Mass Destruction

Delivery Systems
- New IRBM/ICBM range high payload booster developed with South Africa.
- A major missile test took place on September 14, 1989. It was either a missile test or failure of Ofeq-2 satellite.
- Israel has done technical work on a TERCOM-type smart warhead. It has examined cruise missile guidance developments using GPS navigation systems.
- Up to 50 "Jericho I" missiles deployed in shelters on mobile launchers, with a range of up to 400 miles and a 2,200 pound payload, and with possible nuclear warhead storage nearby.
- Jericho II missiles are now deployed, and some were brought to readiness for firing during the Gulf War.
- These missiles seem to include a single-stage follow-on to the Jericho I and a multi-stage, longer-range missile.
  - The missile seems to have a range of up to 900 miles with a 2,200 pound payload, and may be a cooperative development with South Africa. (Extensive reporting of such cooperation in press during October 25 and 26, 1989.)
  - Commercial satellite imaging indicates the missile may be 14 meters long and 1.5 meters wide. Its deployment configuration hints that it may have radar area guidance similar to the terminal guidance in the Pershing II.
- Jericho II missile production facility at Be'er Yakov.
- Unverified claims that up to 100 missiles are deployed west of Jerusalem.
- A missile base exists at Zachariah, several miles southeast of Tel Aviv.
  - Limestone region with caves, to shelter missiles, Transport-Erector-Launchers (TELs), and vehicles.

Table 11.1 (continued)

- TELs have been seen at this base on vehicles 16 meters long, 4 meters wide, and 3 meters high. May be road mobile for dispersal.
- They carry missiles 14 meters long and 1.5 meters wide.
- There seem to be 50 missiles deployed at the base.
- Each TEL has three support vehicles. One is a guidance programmer and power vehicle. Another seems to be a firing control vehicle, and the third seems to be a communications vehicle.
- The base is not hardened against nuclear attack, and would be vulnerable to chemical and biological attack.
- Israel's current review of its military doctrine seems to include a review of its missile basing options, and the study of possible hardening and dispersal systems. There are also reports that Israel will solve its survivability problems by deploying some form of nuclear-armed missile on its new submarines.
- F-15, F-16, F-4E, and Phantom 2000 fighter-bombers capable of long range refueling and of carrying nuclear and chemical bombs.
- Tel Nof may be the air base used to arm aircraft with nuclear weapons. Storage facilities may exist at Zachariah.
- Lance missile launchers and 160 Lance missiles with a range of 130 kilometers.
- Variant of the Popeye air-to-surface missile believed to have a nuclear warhead.
- MAR-290 rocket with a range of 30 kilometers is believed to be deployed.
- MAR-350 surface-to-surface missile with a range of 56 miles and a 735-pound payload is believed to have completed development or to be in early deployment.
- Israel is seeking super computers for Technion Institute (designing ballistic missile RVs), Hebrew University (may be engaged in hydrogen bomb research), and Israeli Military Industries (maker of "Jericho II" and Shavit booster).

Chemical Weapons

- Reports of mustard and nerve gas production facility established in 1982 in the restricted area in the Sinai near Dimona seem incorrect. May have additional facilities. May have capacity to produce other gases. Probable stocks of bombs, rockets, and artillery.
- Extensive laboratory research into gas warfare and defense.
- Development of defensive systems includes Shalon Chemical Industries protection gear, Elbit Computer gas detectors, and Bezal R&D air crew protection system.
- Extensive field exercises in chemical defense.
- Gas masks stockpiled and distributed to population with other civil defense instructions during Gulf War.
- Warhead delivery capability for bombs, rockets, and missiles, but none now believed to be equipped with chemical agents.

Table 11.1 (continued)

Biological Weapons

- Extensive research into weapons and defense.
- Ready to quickly produce biological weapons, but no reports of active production effort.

Nuclear Weapons

- Director of CIA indicated in May, 1989 that Israel may be seeking to construct a thermonuclear weapon.
- Has two significant reactor projects: the 5 megawatt HEU light-water IRR I reactor at Nahal Soreq; and the 40–150 megawatt heavy water, IRR-2 natural uranium reactor used for the production of fissile material at Dimona. Only the IRR-1 is under IAEA safeguards.
- Dimona has conducted experiments in pilot scale laser and centrifuge enrichment, purifies UO_2, converts UF_6, and fabricates fuel for weapons purpose.
- Uranium phosphate mining in Negev, near Beersheba, and yellow cake is produced at two plants in the Haifa area and one in southern Israel.
- Pilot-scale heavy water plant operating at Rehovot.
- Estimates of numbers and types of weapons differ sharply.
  - Stockpile of at least 60–80 plutonium weapons.
  - May have well over 100 nuclear weapons assemblies, with some weapons with yields over 100 Kilotons.
  - US experts believe Israel has highly advanced implosion weapons. Known to have produced Lithium-6, allowing production of both tritium and lithium deuteride at Dimona. Facility no longer believed to be operating.
  - Some weapons may be ER variants or have variable yields.
  - Stockpile of up to 200–300 weapons is possible.
- Major weapons facilities include production of weapons grade Plutonium at Dimona, nuclear weapons design facility at Nahal Soreq (south of Tel Aviv), missile test facility at Palmikim, nuclear armed missile storage facility at Kefar Zekharya, nuclear weapons assembly facility at Yodefat, and tactical nuclear weapons storage facility at Eilabun in eastern Galilee.

Missile Defenses

- Patriot missiles with future PAC-3 upgrade to reflect lessons of the Gulf War.
- Arrow 2 two-stage ATBM with slant intercept ranges at altitudes of 8–10 and 50 kilometers and speeds of up to Mach 9, plus possible development of the Rafale AB-10 close in defense missile with ranges of 10–20 kilometers and speeds of up to Mach 4.5 Taas rocket motor, Rafael warhead, and Tadiran BM/C41 system and "Music" phased array radar.
- Israel plans to deploy three batteries of the Arrow to cover Israel, each with four launchers, to protect up to 85% of its population. It seeks to deploy the system early in the 2000s.
- The program has progressed with considerable success since phase two tests, with

Table 11.1 (continued)

successful flights on August 20, 1996, and March 11, 1997. Development costs are estimated at $330 million, with Israel paying 28% and the United States paying 72%. Deployment will be jointly funded under a 1996 accord as a part of a $556 million, six-year program. Israel will pay 64% and the United States 36%. The total program cost is estimated at $1.6 billion.

- The Arrow will be deployed in batteries as a wide area defense system with intercepts normally at reentry or exoatmospheric altitudes. Capable of multitarget tracking and multiple intercepts.
- Israel is also examining the possibility of boost-phase defenses.

Advanced Intelligence Systems

- The Shavit I launched Israel's satellite payload on September 19, 1989. It used a three-stage booster system capable of launching a 4,000-pound payload over 1,200 miles or a 2,000-pound payload over 1,800 miles. It is doubtful that it had a payload capable of intelligence missions and seems to have been launched, in part, to offset the psychological impact of Iraq's missile launches.
- Ofeq 2 launched in April, 1990, one day after Saddam Hussein threatens to destroy Israel with chemical weapons if it should attack Baghdad.
- Launched first intelligence satellite on April 5, 1995, covering Syria, Iran, and Iraq in orbit every 90 minutes. The Ofeq 3 satellite is a 495-pound system launched using the Shavit launch rocket, and is believed to carry an imagery system. Its orbit passes over or near Damascus, Tehran, and Baghdad.[4]

Syria's Search for Weapons of Mass Destruction

Delivery Systems

- Four SSM brigades: 1 with FROG, 1 with Scud Bs, 1 with Scud Cs, and 1 with SS-21s.
- New long-range North Korean Scud Cs deployed.
  - Two brigades of 18 launchers each are said to be deployed in a horseshoe-shaped valley. This estimate of 36 launchers is based on the fact that there are 36 tunnels in the hillside. The launchers must be for the Scud Cs since the older Scud Bs would not be within range of most of Israel. Up to 50 missiles are stored in bunkers to north as possible reloads. There is a maintenance building and barracks.
  - Estimates indicate that Syria has 24–36 Scud launchers for a total of 120 missiles of all types. The normal ratio of launchers to missiles is 10:1, but Syria is focusing on both survivability and the capability to launch a large preemptive strike.
  - The Scud Cs have ranges of up to 550–600 kilometers.
  - Possible nerve gas warheads with cluster bomblets were reported in September, 1997.
  - CEP of 1,000–2,600 meters.
  - A training site exists about 6 kilometers south of Hama, with an underground facility where TELs and missiles are stored.
- There are up to 12 additional Scud B launchers and 200 Scud B missiles with a range of 310 kilometers. They are believed to have chemical warheads. Scud B warhead weighs 985 kilograms.

Table 11.1 (continued)

- There are 18 SS-21 launchers and at least 36 SS-21 missiles with a range of 80–100 kilometers. May be developing chemical warheads.
- Reports of Chinese deliveries of missiles do not seem correct:
  - Reports of PRC deliveries of missile components by China Precision Machinery Company, maker of the M-11, in July, 1996. The M-11 has a 186-mile range with a warhead of 1,100 pounds.
  - Some sources believe M-9 missile components, or M-9-like components, have been delivered to Syria. Missile is reported to have a CEP as low as 300 meters.
- Sheltered or underground missile production/assembly facilities at Aleppo and Hamas have been built with aid from Chinese, Iranian, and North Korean technicians, and possibly with some Russian technical aid.
- A missile test site exists 15 kilometers south of Homs where Syria has tested missile modifications and new chemical warheads. It has heavy-perimeter defenses, a storage area and bunkers, heavily sheltered bunkers, and a missile storage area just west of the site.
  - Syria has shorter-range systems:
  - Short range M-1B missiles (up to 60 miles range) seem to be in delivery from PRC.
  - SS-N-3, and SSC-1b cruise missiles.
- May be converting some long range surface-to-air and naval cruise missiles to use chemical warheads.
- 20 Su-24 long range strike fighters.
- 30–60 operational MiG-23BM Flogger F fighter ground attack aircraft.
- 20 Su-20 fighter ground attack aircraft.
- 60–70 Su-22 fighter ground attack aircraft.
- 18 FROG-7 launchers and rockets.
- Negotiations for PRC-made M-9 missile (185–375 mile range).
- Multiple rocket launchers and tube artillery.

Chemical Weapons

- First acquired small amounts of chemical weapons from Egypt in 1973.
- Began production of nonpersistent nerve gas in 1984. May have had chemical warheads for missiles as early as 1985.
- Experts believe Syria has stockpiled 500 to 1,000 metric tons of chemical agents.
- Syria is believed to have begun deploying VX in late 1996 or early 1997.
  - The CIA reported in June, 1997 that Syria had acquired new chemical weapons technology from Russia and Eastern Europe in 1996.
  - There are unconfirmed reports of sheltered Scud missiles with unitary Sarin or Tabun nerve gas warheads deployed in caves and shelters near Damascus.
  - Scuds were tested in a manner indicating possible chemical warheads in 1996.
  - Syria seems to have cluster warheads and bombs.

Table 11.1 (continued)

- Syria may have VX and Sarin in modified Soviet ZAB-incendiary bombs and PTAB-500 cluster bombs.
- Syria acquired the design for Soviet Scud warhead using VX in 1970s.
- There are major nerve gas and other possible chemical agent production facilities (2–3 plants) north of Damascus.
  - One facility is located near Homs, next to a major petrochemical plant. It reportedly produces several hundred tons of nerve gas a year.
  - There are reports that Syria is building new major plant near Aleppo.
  - There are reports that a facility co-located with the Center d'Etudes et de Recherche Scientifique (CERS) is developing a warhead with chemical bomblets for the Scud C.
- Many parts of the program are dispersed and compartmented. Missiles, rockets, bombs, and artillery shells are produced/modified and loaded in other facilities.
- There is a wide range of delivery systems:
  - Extensive testing of chemical warheads for Scud Bs; may have tested chemical warheads for Scud Cs.
  - Shells, bombs, and nerve gas warheads for multiple rocket launchers.
  - FROG warheads may be under development.
  - Reports of SS-21 capability to deliver chemical weapons are not believed by US or Israeli experts.
  - Israeli sources believe Syria has binary weapons and cluster bomb technology suitable for delivering chemical weapons.

Biological Weapons

- Signed, but did not ratify the 1972 Biological and Toxin Weapons Convention. Extensive research effort.
- ACDA report in August, 1996 indicated that "it is highly probable that Syria is developing an offensive biological capability."
- Extensive research effort. Reports of one underground facility and one near the coast.
- Probable production capability for Anthrax and botulism, and possibly other agents.
- Israeli sources claim Syria weaponized botulin and ricin toxin in early 1990s, and probably Anthrax.
- Limited indications may be developing or testing biological variations on ZAB-incendiary bombs and PTAB-500 cluster bombs and Scud warheads.

Nuclear Weapons

- Ongoing research effort.
- No evidence of major progress in development effort.
- Announced nuclear reactor purchase plans including 10 megawatt research reactor and six power reactors in 1980s, but never implemented.
- Has miniature 30 kilowatt neutron-source reactor, but unsuitable for weapons production.

Table 11.1 (continued)

Missile Defenses

- Seeking Russian S-300 surface-to-air missile system with limited anti-tactical ballistic missile capability.

1. Note by the Secretary General, "Report of the Secretary-General on the Activities of the Special Commission," S/1997/774, October 6, 1997, paragraphs 79–80.
2. Note by the Secretary General, "Report of the Secretary-General on the Activities of the Special Commission," S/1997/774, October 6, 1997, paragraphs 81–82.
3. Note by the Secretary General, "Report of the Secretary-General on the Activities of the Special Commission," S/1997/774, October 6, 1997, paragraph 83.
4. *Washington Post*, April 6, 1995, p. 1.

Source: Prepared by Anthony H. Cordesman.

efforts are leading the Middle East into a process of "creeping proliferation." At the same time, Iran's efforts are difficult to put into perspective. The fact that they threaten US and allied strategic interests does not necessarily mean that they are not "legitimate" in terms of Iranian strategic interests or are aggressive in character.

There are many important areas where it is impossible to be certain of Iran's goals in acquiring weapons of mass destruction, its probable command and control structure, and its likely strategy and doctrine. It is doubtful that Iran has any clear long force plans for deploying biological, chemical, and nuclear weapons, and for transforming them into specific war-fighting capabilities. Instead, it seems likely that many of Iran's present efforts are reactive to its history and its perception of the threats it faces, and that its future efforts will evolve largely on the basis of what it can afford and obtain in the face of US and other efforts to deny its supplies and technology.

In fact, the most important conclusions that can be drawn about Iran's approach to weapons of mass destruction are that it will be opportunistic and reactive. The form Iran's efforts take will be determined more by the course of events in the Gulf, Iran's success in acquiring nuclear weapons, and Iran's access to technology and critical materials for chemical and biological weapons than by Iran's present strategy and force plans. Iran has little real interest in arms control, and it is unlikely to react to sanctions and diplomatic incentives, except to the extent that they limit its capability to proliferate.

NOTE

1. Testimony before the Senate Foreign Relations Committee Subcommittee on Near Eastern and South Asian Affairs, March 2, 1995.

Chapter 12

Iranian Reasons for Pursuing Weapons of Mass Destruction

Iran's leaders have never provided statements indicating that Iran is acquiring weapons of mass destruction. While it is possible to find some Iranian statements regarding the desirability of weapons of mass destruction, they tend to be isolated examples in a sea of denials. The supposed ''leaks'' of Iran's plans to acquire biological, chemical, and nuclear weapons consist of extremely unreliable anti-regime propaganda by groups like the People's Mujahideen. The few instances where Iranian officials have talked about weapons of mass destruction are so isolated and limited in context that they cannot be taken credibly as being representative of Iranian plans and intentions. In fact, a review of the statements of Iranian leaders since the Shah shows that most such statements consist of denials that Iran is pursuing nuclear weapons.

The comments of Hoseyn Musavian, Iran's Ambassador to Germany, provide one of the most explicit examples of such denials.

The Americans have circulated extensive propaganda that we have nuclear arms. But we know very well that we do not have such arms . . . we condemn the existence of nuclear and chemical weapons. The truth is that since World War II, we have been the biggest victim of chemical weapons. And it was the Westerners who provided Iraq with this chemical technology that led to the death or maiming of thousands of human beings and inflicted heavy damage on us. In other words, to the same extent that they accuse us, we are truly worried about the West's sale of mass murder weapons to the region. . . . We should accept the fact that Iranians living abroad are living under a horrific propaganda empire that is churning out negative propaganda on Iran every second. We need some time to allow these Iranians to meet our officials, to learn about their intentions, and to realize that the West's propaganda is false.[1]

Iranian officials often issue similar statements about US and other reports that Iran is attempting to buy missile technology, chemical feedstocks, and biological equipment from nations outside of Iran. At the same time, Iranian military officials show little embarrassment about bragging about missile developments that involve weapons which would have to carry weapons of mass destruction to be lethal against even area targets. For example, Brigadier General Seyyed Rahim Safavi, stated in late 1995 that Iran "has made great progress in making surface-to-surface ballistic missiles with a firing range of 500 kilometers, as well as . . . missiles capable of hitting targets within a range of 200 kilometers."[2]

President Khatami, Foreign Minister Kamal Kharrazi, and the new head of Iran's Atomic Energy Organization have made many similar denials since President Khatami's election. These denials were particularly vehement during Iran's negotiations with Russia in May, 1998 and after India and Pakistan tested nuclear weapons that same month. Iranian Foreign Ministry officials routinely claimed in 1998 that International Atomic Energy Agency (IAEA) visits to Iranian facilities were "inspections" that were "targeted by the CIA" and showed Iran did not have a nuclear weapons program. They also indicated that Iran was prepared to join a much stronger IAEA inspection regime.

Iran took an ambiguous stand on Pakistan's nuclear tests in the spring of 1998. On June 1, 1998, Kharrazi was the first major world leader to praise Pakistan for its nuclear tests, saying that they were welcomed by Muslims worldwide. He spoke during a visit to Pakistan—the first by a foreign dignitary since Pakistan set off the blasts—and he spoke amid near-worldwide disapproval. He stated that Muslims in the Middle East had long worried about Israel's nuclear capability, and said,

Now, they feel confident, because a fellow Islamic nation possesses the know-how to build nuclear weapons. . . . As a matter of its national security and to create a balance in the region, Pakistan had to respond with its own nuclear tests. . . . Over the world, Muslims are happy that Pakistan has this capability.

Kharrazi did, however, dismiss suggestions that Iran was preparing to follow Pakistan with tests of its own. "We don't have any nuclear weapons program. What we have is for peaceful purposes." He also followed up his trip to Pakistan and India by calling for India and Pakistan to open a sweeping dialogue on key issues, including Kashmir and nuclear testing. In a speech to the UN Conference on Disarmament on June 4, 1998, Kharrazi criticized Israel's failure to join global arms control treaties and repeated Iran's call for a nuclear free zone in the Middle East.

The nuclear sword of Damocles is now hanging over the region by a slender thread. This was one genie that was much better . . . confined in the bottle. . . . Certainly we are very concerned about this arms race in our neighborhood, because it has direct impact on our national security. . . . The recent developments have underlined the necessity of ensuring the universality of the NPT. This imperative is not only of paramount importance in South Asia, but in fact in the Middle East, where the refusal by Israel to accede to the NPT and accept International Atomic Energy Agency (IAEA) safeguards has gravely endangered the security of the entire region.... It is thus necessary for all to accept the will of the international community to take practical steps for the establishment of a zone free from weapons of mass destruction in the Middle East.... The NPT cannot be said to be damaged. There are some breaks.... I think we all have to encourage India and Pakistan to eventually join the NPT.... I think we have to use single standards for everyone who proliferates nuclear weapons.

IRAN'S REASONS FOR DENYING PROLIFERATION

Iran's denial of its proliferation efforts is scarcely surprising. There are good strategic reasons for any Iranian regime to proliferate, while making every effort to conceal the nature of such efforts that Iran has every incentive to lie about its programs. The aftermath of the Gulf War has done little to remove Iran's incentive to proliferate. The work of the UN Special Commission has disclosed the massive scale of Iraq's pre-war effort to acquire weapons of mass destruction, and the failure of arms control regimes—particularly the IAEA and Geneva Protocol—to limit Iraq's efforts at proliferation. Iran has lacked funds and access to arms imports to massively rebuild its conventional forces. According to declassified US intelligence estimates, its arms imports have dropped from an annual average of around $3.5–$4 billion (in constant 1995 $US) during the last years of the Shah, and $3.5–$4 billion during the Iran-Iraq War, to an average of well under $1 billion since 1990.[3] At the same time, the United States has actively supported the military build-up of rival Southern Gulf states and has remained a strong supporter of Israel. Proliferation thus offers Iran a "bigger bang per rial," and a way of challenging its neighbors and the United States at a much lower cost for the same effect.

Iran's access to foreign technology is eased by such denials, as are its efforts to improve its relations with its neighbors. Iran has no incentive to provoke further efforts by Iraq or to justify Israeli and US claims that it is proliferating in view of Iran's history and the global and regional environment in which it operates. Iran's regime is anything but lovable, and its exaggerated political attacks on its neighbors and the West are anything but balanced and realistic.

Iran has a long tradition of lying or concealing facts from outside powers, and lies or deception to support moral or holy causes are permitted under the Shi'ite faith. This tradition is symbolized by the Farsi word *taqiyyah*, or "dissimulation," whose ultimate root is the Arabic word taqwa, or "piety." It is a term originally applied to the fact that it is acceptable to lie or dissimulate when one's life or faith is in danger. Similarly, one is allowed to lie, hide, or evade if the true faith of Islam, an Islamic cause, or the image and purity of Islam is threatened. Taqiyyah has long been practiced in response to persecution or in dealing with *dar al-Harb* ("outsiders")—principally during the Abbasid Caliphate, but also on many other occasions in Iranian history. The rhetoric of Iran's current regime and its constant attacks on the morality of its opponents clearly justifies the use of some form of *taqiyyah* in dealing with any aspect of Iran's activities, including weapons of mass destruction.

Such a cultural approach to interpreting Iran's actions may, however, do as much to mislead as to reveal. While it is easy to create a sophisticated cultural analysis of why Iran lies about its efforts, it is important to note that Iran is scarcely alone in denying or lying about actions it does not want to reveal. It is equally valid to ask what country does not engage in some version of *taqiyyah*.

Iran has strong incentives to hide its actions and intentions that have nothing to do with national culture and politics. Most small-and mid-sized proliferators in the Third World can only succeed by exploiting the gaps in Western and other arms and export control regimes. They must do everything possible to exploit "plausible deniability" if they are to be able to import the technology they need. Most such proliferators must treat arms control as a "game" in which they can only win by claiming that they are adhering to arms control regimes in order to minimize US and other outside interference, and to exploit the provisions of agreements like the Nuclear Non-Proliferation Treaty (NPT) that ease the transfer of critical technologies and materials to declared non-proliferators.

Iran has other reasons to exploit "plausible deniability." Like Iraq, Libya, and Syria, Iran must use every possible opportunity to challenge US efforts to call it a rogue state and obtain support for "dual containment." Iran also has no reason to make overt declarations that may stimulate regional rivals to step up their own efforts at proliferation, particularly since its undeclared acquisition efforts are clear enough to impress both such rivals and other regional states with the fact that Iran is actively acquiring such weapons. Ironically, the charges and criticisms of states like the United States do an excellent job of publicizing Iran's real and potential capabilities. Like Israel, Egypt, and most other Middle Eastern proliferators, the resulting ambiguity is adequate for domestic political and deterrent purposes.

IRAN'S CURRENT TACTICAL AND STRATEGIC REASONS FOR PROLIFERATING

Iran's official denials make it extraordinarily difficult to determine the exact motives of the current Iranian regime or any leading figure within it. At the same time, it is likely that if Iran's leadership did honestly and publicly articulate its reasons for proliferating, these reasons would not be limited to one or two dominant causes. Iran has a broad range of historical and strategic reasons to proliferate, and all probably act to motivate Iran's leaders. These reasons include:

- the historical pressures of an arms race with Iraq and Iran's Southern Gulf neighbors that date back to the late 1960s;

- the need to react to the lessons of the Iran-Iraq and Gulf wars and the fact that Iraq has used missiles and weapons of mass destruction against Iranian military and civilian targets;
- the prestige and regional superpower status given by possession of weapons of mass destruction: the "glitter factor";
- the unique value of weapons of mass destruction in intimidating other states, particularly states that do not have such weapons, and in creating an existential threat to hostile regional regimes;
- the unique deterrent value which only weapons of mass destruction can provide against Iraqi attacks and US pressure;
- the need for war-fighting capabilities to deal with Iraq and other regional states that possess weapons of mass destruction;
- the inability to predict the future scale of the proliferation by other regional states, the future expansion of their military forces, and their future intentions;
- finding a way of deterring, limiting, or attacking US and other Western power projection forces that offset the Western advantage in conventional forces;
- providing an alternative to expensive investments in conventional forces and a means of compensating for Iran's inability to modernize and expand its conventional forces since the Iran-Iraq War;
- the ability to react to the absence of meaningful arms control regimes or to help force regional arms control on acceptable terms; and
- furnishing weapons that can decisively enhance the lethality of state, proxy, or private forms of unconventional warfare and terrorism.

It is far from clear that Iran's acquisition of weapons of mass destruction was in any way inevitable. While Iran's efforts to acquire nuclear weapons date back to the Shah—possibly to the early 1970s—they never involved the kind of massive effort that took place in Iraq. Iran was never a regional leader in the effort to acquire biological and chemical weapons until the Iran-Iraq War, and the Khomeini regime showed far less initial interest in proliferation than the Shah. It largely dismantled the Iranian nuclear program and emphasized popular warfare and infantry forces. Iran only revitalized its nuclear program and gave its chemical and biological programs high priority after Iraq made extensive use of chemical warfare against Iranian troops, and after Iraq conducted extensive ballistic missile and attack aircraft strikes against civilian targets in Iran.

The fact is, however, that Iran has heavily institutionalized its proliferation program as a result of the Iran-Iraq War and is unlikely to end it as long as it feels threatened by Iraq. Further, having begun the program, it cannot ignore the strategic leverage it has obtained relative to its neighbors and the ability of weapons of mass destruction to offset its problems in strengthening its conventional forces. It may well see proliferation as the only possible counterbalance to US power—particularly after the Gulf War. Furthermore, Iran cannot ignore the fact that Israel possesses nuclear armed missiles that can target any population center or area target in Iran, or the implications of Israel's raid on Iraq's Osiraq reactor on June 7, 1981. While Israel has never directly threatened Iran, it seems highly probable that Iran will continue to develop weapons of mass destruction, even if its regime should change in character.

NOTES

1. FBIS-NES-96–015, January 11, 1996, Sourceline: NC2201121196, Tehran *Abrar*, January 11, 1996, p. 1. This report is typical of the denials found in a detailed review of the FBIS-NES over the period January, 1990 to March, 1997.

2. FBIS-NES-95–250, December 25, 1995, Sourceline: LD2512142195, Tehran *IRNA*, in English, 1406 GMT.

3. Based on various editions of ACDA, *World Military Expenditures and Arms Transfers*, Washington, GPO.

Chapter 13

Plans, Doctrine, and War-Fighting Options

It is clear that Iran is pursuing a broad strategy of acquiring long-range missiles and other delivery systems, and that it is simultaneously seeking biological, chemical, and nuclear weapons. At the same time, Iran's denial that it is acquiring weapons of mass destruction makes it impossible to use unclassified literature alone to determine the details of its acquisition plans, its doctrine for using such weapons, and the war-fighting options it is trying to create. It is possible to describe some aspects of these efforts by making a detailed examination of its programs to biological, chemical, and nuclear weapons, and suitable delivery systems. However, it is rarely possible to generalize without relying on informed guesswork.

ACQUISITION PLANS OR NON-PLANS

It seems highly unlikely that Iran's efforts to acquire weapons of mass destruction are the product of a consistent, detailed, overall strategy and plan. There is no doubt that Iran has steadily attempted to develop biological, chemical, and nuclear weapons capabilities since the mid-1980s, and that it has sought both long-range missiles and advanced attack aircraft. At the same time, each of these efforts has been vulnerable to outside interference, the uncertainties imposed by war and crisis, and the severe resource limitations imposed by Iran's economic problems. Many elements of these programs now seem to be more contingency-oriented than designed to lead to near-term production and weaponization. They lack the imperative of the Iran-Iraq War, and even a serious fear of the United States. Instead, they seem designed to give Iran the capability to deploy weapons over time, if it chooses to do so.

Iran cannot afford brute-force programs and expenditures of the kind which

Iraq attempted before the Gulf War. It simply does not have the money to maintain a high degree of consistency in major import-dependent programs in the face of US and other international opposition. Iran's procurement and acquisition efforts are highly reactive in character and shaped by the need to exploit targets of opportunity. Iran must import what it can and alter the pace of its programs to react to both what it can actually obtain and the impact of various efforts to deny Iran key technology and materials. It must accept the costs of concealment, pursue multiple approaches to proliferation as insurance against embargoes and discovery, and accept the cost of potentially relocating programs when this is necessary to give the appearance that Iran is complying with arms control agreements.

It is unlikely that Iran is developing and deploying weapons of mass destruction and delivery systems with a highly detailed national strategy for using them, and that it has sophisticated war plans and well-developed doctrine that go beyond the employment of chemical weapons in tactical land battles. Iran has had chemical and biological weapons long enough to begin some limited war planning and exercises, but it is a long way from being able to anticipate its mid-to long-term force mixes, whether it can obtain nuclear weapons, and what kind of broad crisis and war-fighting contingencies it must plan for.

THE TECHNOLOGY OF UNCERTAINTY

Iran is still a developing country with limited technical capability to develop and employ weapons of mass destruction. It faces major problems in measuring the potential effectiveness of its weapons, and it does not have advanced C^4I/BM systems, satellites, or effective long-range reconnaissance systems for targeting purposes and to characterize battle damage. In many cases, the problems Iran faces in developing effective weapons of mass destruction create large-scale uncertainties for war planning:

- *"Weaponizing" chemical, biological, and nuclear weapons.* Iran faces difficulties in developing the capability to load a biological or chemical agent, or nuclear device, into a bomb or warhead that will work safely, effectively, and reliably. Regardless of the theoretical lethality of a weapon of mass destruction, much depends on how well it can actually perform in combat.
- *"Weaponizing" different types of delivery systems.* It is relatively easy to fire chemical rounds at line-of-sight ranges. Artillery or multiple rocket launchers can fire enough of a chemical agent to be effective even if the warhead design is poor. However, firing chemical and other weapons of mass destruction at beyond-visual-range (BVR) targets requires sophisticated reconnaissance and intelligence systems, and effective warheads to produce highly lethal effects. Long-range attacks with aircraft and cruise missiles present challenges in terms of developing proven bomb and warhead designs that ensure safety, reliability, accurate targeting, and navigation. Even advanced industrial powers have problems designing warheads and bombs that achieve the proper height of burst conditions for the use of biological, chemical, and nuclear weapons.

- *Developing effective warheads for ballistic missile systems.* Although ballistic missiles have the advantage that they are harder to defend against than aircraft, they involve major challenges in terms of operational reliability, accuracy, and targeting. Warhead design is also far more difficult for ballistic missiles than for cruise missiles and aircraft. It is extremely difficult to disseminate biological and chemical agents effectively within the narrow time window allowed by the closing velocity of a ballistic missile, and the weapons package necessary to do so can use up much of the useful payload of such a missile.
- *Obtaining fissile material.* The design of a nuclear weapon is well within Iran's technical capabilities, and Iraq and Pakistan have shown that developing nations can manufacture the high explosive lenses, triggering devices, and neutron initiators necessary to make functional nuclear weapons. It is far more difficult, however, to enrich uranium or to process plutonium to weapons grade, which will present continuing problems for Iran unless highly enriched material can be purchased from another state.
- *Developing small nuclear devices with reliable fusing.* Nuclear weapons present challenges in weight reduction and ensuring precisely the correct height of burst to get the right effect. The cost and scarcity of nuclear fissile material create challenges in terms of the risk that a warhead package will fail to explode or a missile will not hit its intended target. Biological weapons require the safe storage of dry or wet agents and high technology fuses and agent dissemination systems.
- *Safety presents additional uncertainties, particularly with biological and nuclear devices.* The risk of accidents or misfires on friendly territory is very real. The technology to ensure the safety and arming of a warhead only after a missile has performed properly on launch is complex and involves further weight penalties. No technology currently exists that can reliably disarm a missile warhead by remote command, or on a fail-safe basis, once a missile has completed its initial boost phase and apogee.

WAR-FIGHTING OPTIONS AND THE INABILITY TO PREDICT CONTINGENCY REQUIREMENTS

Iran operates in a far more uncertain strategic environment than the United States. It can exercise some tactical aspects of using weapons of mass destruction, but it has little ability to predict the nature of future crises and contingencies. These uncertainties are compounded by the fact that there are many ways in which Iran might choose to use weapons of mass destruction for crises intervention and/or war fighting—almost all of which would almost certainly involve extensive improvisation in mid-crisis. These possible forms of war fighting include:

- using weapons of mass destruction in covert or proxy attacks, unconventional warfare, and/or "terrorism";
- using them to support conventional war fighting;
- avoiding conventional defeat through preemption or escalation;
- posing political threat—wars of intimidation;

- regional deterrence—threatened or illustrative use;
- attacking power projection facilities;
- counterproliferation attacks;
- attempting to enforce extended deterrence;
- controlled escalation ladders designed to limit counterattacks using such weapons by nations like Iraq;
- efforts to create asymmetric escalation or escalation dominance;
- efforts to establish "Firebreaks" to further attack or escalation;
- launch on warning/launch under attack;
- using such weapons to attempt to force conflict termination;
- destroying enemy as state—existential attacks on leaders and population centers;
- denying an enemy meaningful victory—martyrdom; and
- radically altering the strategic nature of conflict with the hope of creating a more favorable situation.

PLANS AS THE FIRST CASUALTY OF WAR

Even if Iran does have detailed war plans for using weapons of mass destruction, it is far from clear that they will survive contact with reality. It is an open question as to whether the battle plan or truth is the first casualty of war. In practice, however, doctrine and battle plans rarely survive peace. Once again, this is not a matter of nationality and culture. Today's US analysts either forget or never knew that the United States acquired chemical and biological weapons during the period 1945–1975 without clear or consistent strategic plans, and never evolved a doctrine and war-fighting concepts for using such weapons that extended beyond the tactical engagement level. The United States never institutionalized biological and chemical weapons into its war plans because it chose to rely on tactical nuclear weapons, and because—unlike the Soviet Union—it never treated chemical weapons as a special form of conventional weapons. After 1975, its doctrine became almost purely defensive—with very low priority even for defensive training and equipment—because of the Biological Weapons Convention and the decision to abolish US Army specialization in offensive chemical and biological warfare.

US nuclear plans and doctrine were slow to evolve during the period between 1945 and the early 1960s, and then emphasized mutual assured destruction rather than war fighting. While the United States evolved a highly detailed targeting and employment plan symbolized by the Single Integrated Operating Plan (SIOP), the SIOP never fully tracked with the US nuclear strategy approved by various presidents. Massive anomalies existed among US plans to use strategic nuclear weapons, US and NATO contingency plans to use theater nuclear weapons, a US emphasis on conventional war-fighting doctrine, and US contingency plans to react to the possible Warsaw Pact use of biological and chemical weapons.

What is clear is that the threat posed by Iran's weapons of mass destruction will become steadily more serious as the number and capability of Iran's weapons increase. So will regional perceptions of Iran. One does not need well structured acquisition plans, doctrine, and war plans to have a major impact on perceived power and actual conflict.

While much of the discussion of weapons of mass destruction focuses on the details of force postures and potential casualty and physical damage effects, their strategic impact may well depend on "intangibles." Weapons of mass destruction have major psychological, political, and nonlethal tactical effects like panic and area interdiction that may prove to be more important than lethality in a given contingency. Relative willingness to take risks and deal with the real-world outcome of uncertainty becomes critical, as do the relative value assigned to human life, the predictability of weapons effects, the nature of retaliation, and the protection of troops, civilians, and potential target areas. As a result, Iran might well change the perceived military balance in the Gulf simply by acquiring a few highly lethal biological or nuclear devices.

Similarly, weapons of mass destruction also produce unpredictable changes in the perceptions of both the attacker and defender in terms of political decisions and war fighting. The use of weapons of mass destruction can radically change crisis behavior, perceptions of the risks of escalation, acceptance of new levels of conflict, and acceptance of given kinds of conflict termination. They can do so in ways where decision makers and military commanders have at best a limited understanding of the technical capabilities and effectiveness of the weapons involved. They affect the transparency and predictability of war. This is particularly true in the case of the Gulf, since neither Iran nor Iraq have anything approaching the intelligence assets necessary to obtain near-real time data on the actual impact of such weapons. In addition, there is simply too little empirical data available for either side to predict short-term or long-term damage effects.

"COMMAND" AND "CONTROL"

Iran's command and control capabilities are likely to be just as unclear and unstable as its battle plans. US experts do seem to feel that its present peacetime command and control structure is highly centralized, in spite of reports of divisions within the Iranian leadership and that the Revolutionary Guards sometimes conduct independent or rogue operations. In broad terms, the Revolutionary Guards seem to be the branch of the military that supervises the development of weapons of mass destruction and the custodians of finished weapons. The Guards also operate some key delivery systems. For example, the Revolutionary Guards seem to operate and control Iran's ballistic missile systems. They also maintain a Land Force Missile and Artillery Training Center in Isfahan—which some reports indicate has Russian and Chinese instructors.[1]

There are indications, however, that chemical weapons are allocated to regular army and naval forces, and it is not clear that the Revolutionary Guards would control any major aspect of chemical operations once the decision was taken to allocate weapons to the regular army force during major land operations or would control the details of air operations using long-range strike aircraft. It is obvious that the use of weapons of mass destruction involves special command and control, planning, targeting, operational, and battle damage assessment tasks that need to be tightly integrated and managed in near-real time. However, there are no convincing unclassified reports that it has been possible to identify elite units whose function is to provide the Iranian leadership with specially trained forces for such battle management.

It is unclear whether Iran has fully assessed the real world problems in command and control that affect the chain of command and battle management in using weapons of mass destruction. The Iranian leadership may have examined the possible consequences of large-scale tactical chemical warfare against Iraq, or using chemical weapons to defend Iran's coast and islands. Iran has conducted so many large-scale exercises since 1990 that it seems highly likely that these involved some subexercises using chemical weapons, and that the results were briefed to the Iranian political leadership. Iran would only have the Iran-Iraq War as an empirical basis for planning and conducting such exercises, and this conflict was slow moving and relatively static until its final phases in 1988.[2]

Little about Iran's military experience and exercises to date indicates that it is likely to be capable of sophisticated battle management for long-range air and missile operations. The Iranian Supreme Council for National Security (Shura-ye Amniyat-e Jomhuri-e Islami-ye Iran) is chaired by the president and includes two representatives of the Leader of the Islamic Revolution, the head of the judiciary, the speaker of the Majlis, the Chief of the General Staff, the head of the Plan and Budget Organization, and the ministers of Foreign Affairs, Interior, Intelligence, and Security. The president's Diplomatic Foreign Affairs, Foreign Religious Affairs, and National Security Affairs advisors evidently sit in on some meetings. The Supreme Council for National Security is the possible equivalent of a national command authority, but there are no indications of how seriously it has discussed or debated any aspect of weapons of mass destruction.[3]

Similarly, it is far from clear how Iran's military command system actually operates. The general staff of the armed forces was created in June, 1988, but it is primarily an administrative body, and it is not clear that Iran really has anything approaching a true, unified joint staff for military planning and command purposes. The Chief of the General Staff is appointed by the Leader of the Islamic Revolution and is responsible to him, rather than to the president. This could lead to an uncertain chain of command in a crisis.

The supposed unification of the regular military forces and the Islamic Revolutionary Guards Corps (IRGC) in the late 1980s has never really been fully effective. There are duplicative commanders of the regular military forces and the IRGC for each service, plus a Chief of the Joint Staff for the regular forces, a Supreme Commander of the IRGC, a Chief of the Central Headquarters of the IRGC, and a Commander of the Basij Resistance Force. It seems likely that the IRGC has some sort of central authority for the control of weapons of mass destruction and long-range missiles, but the regular forces would probably handle the air delivery of such weapons and use short-range chemical and biological weapons.

The same uncertainties affect Iran's security arrangements for controlling weapons of mass destruction. The internal security forces were supposedly unified in April, 1991 and report to the Minister of the Interior. However, the Islamic Revolutionary Guards and Basij provide the manpower for some internal security units, and may well control security for Iran's weapons of mass destruction and long-range missiles. It is unclear whether they would provide custodial security for such weapons once transferred to the regular army, air force, or navy.

Iran has long had the capability to perform sophisticated target analysis of military, economic, and civil area targets in Iraq, the Southern Gulf, and US power projection forces, and the Iranian air force had targeting cells and planning staffs for such attacks in the early 1970s. The ability to target, however, is not the ability to assess and control, or to react to the rapid pattern of escalation likely to follow Iran's initial strikes. While Iran has studied the lessons of the Gulf War in detail, and routinely instructs its officers in Western and Soviet literature on the lessons of the war, its overall C^4I/battle management system remains relatively primitive and slow reacting, and it seems to follow the traditional Middle Eastern pattern of denying problems and failures while exaggerating successes.

Iran lacks effective long-range reconnaissance assets, and it would encounter severe survivability problems in attempting to penetrate US-defended airspace once US and Southern Gulf forces were alerted and deployed. It is far from clear how any Iranian C^4I/battle management system could produce more than the most crude estimates of battle damage for area strikes using any type of weapon of mass destruction, and how long an Iranian C^4I/battle management system would survive—or retain cohesive function—in the face of attacks by a US-led coalition. Even if an Iranian C^4I/battle management system survived the initial phases of a war using weapons of mass destruction, it would probably be highly degenerative and produce large amounts of misinformation. Past experience in the Middle East indicates that it could rapidly become highly politicized, and that the leadership could suddenly task command elements with impossible missions and little warning.

NOTES

1. *International Defense Review, Extra,* 2/1997, p. 5.
2. This assessment is based on interviews with US and French experts, and on a review of Iranian reports on Iranian exercises as provided in various editions of the Foreign

Broadcast Information Service (FBIS) reports during the period 1990–1997, and *Jane's Defense Weekly*.

3. CIA LDA 94–10142, March, 1994 as updated on the CIA web page as of March 3, 1997.

Chapter 14

Dealing with Uncertainty

Accepting the uncertainties, discussed in Chapter 13, makes the problem of analyzing Iran's efforts to acquire biological, chemical, and nuclear weapons exceptionally complex. It means that analysis must concentrate on exploring what is known about Iran's potential capabilities, rather than an estimate of Iranian intentions. It means dealing with the wide range of uncertainties and complexities surrounding each of Iran's major acquisition efforts, and recognizing that these efforts are constantly evolving. In practice, this means looking at what is known about every major aspect of Iran's pursuit of advanced delivery systems, its biological, chemical, and nuclear weapons, and examining the potential implications of Iran's procurement of very different types of war-fighting capabilities while recognizing that the consequences may be as unpredictable to Iran as to outside observers.

The potential range of war-fighting capabilities Iran is pursuing is illustrated in Table 14.1, which summarizes the different strengths and weaknesses of biological, chemical, and nuclear weapons. It is also illustrated in Table 14.2, which compares their possible casualty effects. There is no way to know what mix of biological, chemical, and nuclear weapons Iran is seeking to acquire. At the same time, it is obvious from these tables that each type of weapon has very different capabilities and could lead to a very different Iranian response in a given contingency.

The most important difference in war-fighting terms is in the low lethality of chemical weapons relative to biological and nuclear weapons. Iran's acquisition and steadily expanding stocks of chemical weapons do not give it anything approaching the capability of biological and nuclear weapons. At the same time, biological and nuclear weapons do have similar lethality, and there are broad potential strategic parallels between them. Nuclear weapons may confer more

Table 14.1
The Strengths and Weaknesses of Weapons of Mass Destruction

Chemical Weapons

Destructive Effects: Poisoning skin, lungs, nervous system, or blood. Contaminating areas, equipment, and protective gear for periods of hours to days. Forcing military units to don highly restrictive protection gear or use incapacitating antidotes. False alarms and panic. Misidentification of the agent, or confusion of chemical with biological agents (which may be mixed) leading to failure of defense measures. Military and popular panic and terror effects. Major medical burdens which may lead to mistreatment. Pressure to deploy high-cost air and missile defenses. Paralysis or disruption of civil life and economic activity in threatened or attacked areas.

Typical Military Targets: Infantry concentrations, air bases, ships, ports, staging areas, command centers, munitions depots, cities, key oil and electrical facilities, and desalinization plants.

Typical Military Missions: Killing military and civilian populations. Intimidation. Attack of civilian population or targets. Disruption of military operations by requiring protective measures or decontamination. Area or facility denial. Psychological warfare, production of panic, and terror.

Military Limitations: Large amounts of agents are required to achieve high lethality, and military and economic effects are not sufficiently greater than carefully targeted conventional strikes offering major war-fighting advantages. Most agents degrade quickly, and their effect is highly dependent on temperature and weather conditions, height of dissemination, terrain, and the character of built-up areas. Warning devices far more accurate and sensitive than for biological agents. Protective gear and equipment can greatly reduce effects, and sufficiently high numbers of rounds, sorties, and missiles are needed to ease the task of defense. Leave buildings and equipment reusable by the enemy, although persistent agents may require decontamination. Persistent agents may contaminate the ground the attacker wants to cross or occupy and force use of protective measures or decontamination.

Biological Weapons

Destructive Effects: Infectious disease or biochemical poisoning. Contaminating areas, equipment, and protective gear for periods of hours to weeks. Delayed effects and tailoring to produce incapacitation or death, treatable or non-treatable agents, and be infectious on contact only or transmittable. Forcing military units to don highly restrictive protection gear or use incapacitating vaccines antidotes. False alarms and panic. High risk of at least initial misidentification of the agent, or confusion of chemical with biological agents (which may be mixed) leading to failure of defense measures. Military and popular panic and terror effects. Major medical burdens which may lead to mistreatment. Pressure to deploy high cost air and missile defenses. Paralysis or disruption of civil life and economic activity in threatened or attacked areas.

Typical Military Targets: Infantry concentrations, air bases, ships, ports, staging areas, command centers, munitions depots, cities, key oil and electrical facilities, and desalinization plants. Potentially far more effective against military and civil area targets than chemical weapons.

Table 14.1 (continued)

Typical Military Missions: Killing and incapacitation of military and civilian populations. Intimidation. Attack of civilian population or targets. Disruption of military operations by requiring protective measures or decontamination. Area or facility denial. Psychological warfare, production of panic, and terror.

Military Limitations: Most wet agents degrade quickly, although spores, dry encapsulated agents, and some toxins are persistent. Effects usually take some time to develop (although not in the case of some toxins). Effects are unpredictable, and are even more dependent than chemical weapons on temperature and weather conditions, height of dissemination, terrain, and the character of built-up areas. Major risk of contaminating the wrong area. Warning devices uncertain and may misidentify the agent. Protective gear and equipment can reduce effects. Leave buildings and equipment reusable by the enemy, although persistent agents may require decontamination. Persistent agents may contaminate the ground the attacker wants to cross or occupy and force use of protective measures or decontamination. More likely than chemical agents to cross the threshold where nuclear retaliation seems justified.

Nuclear Weapons:

Destructive Effects: Blast, fire, and radiation. Destruction of large areas and production of fallout and contamination--depending on character of weapon and height of burst. Contaminating areas, equipment, and protective gear for periods of hours to days. Forcing military units to don highly restrictive protection gear and use massive amounts of decontamination gear. Military and popular panic and terror effects. Massive medical burdens. Pressure to deploy high cost air and missile defenses. Paralysis or disruption of civil life and economic activity in threatened or attacked areas. High long-term death rates from radiation. Forced dispersal of military forces and evacuation of civilians. Destruction of military and economic centers, and national political leadership and command authority, potentially altering character of attacked nation and creating major recovery problems.

Typical Military Targets: Hardened targets, enemy facilities and weapons of mass destruction, enemy economy, political leadership, and national command authority. Infantry and armored concentrations, air bases, ships, ports, staging areas, command centers, munitions depots, cities, key oil and electrical facilities, and desalinization plants.

Typical Military Missions: Forced dispersal of military forces and evacuation of civilians. Destruction of military and economic centers, and national political leadership and command authority, potentially altering character of attacked nation and creating major recovery problems.

Military Limitations: High cost. Difficulty of acquiring more than a few weapons. Risk of accidents or failures that hit friendly territory. Crosses threshold to level where nuclear retaliation is likely. Destruction or contamination of territory and facilities attacker wants to cross or occupy. High risk of massive collateral damage to civilians (if this is important to attacker).

Source: Adapted by the author from the Office of Technology Assessment, *Proliferation of Weapons of Mass Destruction: Assessing the Risks*, Washington, US Congress OTA-ISC-559, August, 1993, pp. 56–57.

Table 14.2
Comparative Effects of Biological, Chemical, and Nuclear Weapons Delivered Against a Typical Urban Target in the Middle East

<u>Using missile warheads</u>: Assumes one Scud-sized warhead with a maximum payload of 1,000 kilograms. The study assumes that the biological agent would not make maximum use of this payload capability because of design problems. It is uncertain that this assumption is realistic.

	Area Covered in Square Kilometers	Deaths Assuming 3,000–10,000 People per Square Kilometer
<u>Chemical</u>: 300 kilograms of Sarin nerve gas with a density of 70 milligrams per cubic meter	0.22	60–200
<u>Biological</u>: 30 kilograms of Anthrax spores with a density of 0.1 milligram per cubic meter	10.0	30,000–100,000
<u>Nuclear</u>:		
One 12.5 kiloton nuclear device achieving 5 pounds per cubic inch of over-pressure	7.8	23,000–80,000
One 1 megaton hydrogen bomb	190.0	570,000–1,900,000

<u>Using one aircraft delivering 1,000 kilograms of Sarin nerve gas or 100 kilograms of Anthrax spores</u>: Assumes that the aircraft flies in a straight line over the target at optimal altitude and dispenses the agent as an aerosol. The study assumes that the biological agent would not make maximum use of this payload capability because this is inefficient. It is unclear if this is realistic.

	Area Covered in Square Kilometers	Deaths Assuming 3,000–10,000 People per Square Kilometer
<u>Clear, sunny day, light breeze</u>		
Sarin nerve gas	0.74	300–700
Anthrax spores	46.0	130,000–460,000
<u>Overcast day or night, moderate wind</u>		
Sarin nerve gas	0.8	400–800
Anthrax spores	140.0	420,000–1,400,000
<u>Calm, clear night</u>		
Sarin nerve gas	7.8	3,000–8,000
Anthrax spores	300.0	1,000,000–3,000,000

Source: Adapted by Anthony H. Cordesman from the Office of Technology Assessment, *Proliferation of Weapons of Mass Destruction: Assessing the Risks*, Washington, US Congress OTA-ISC-559, August, 1993, pp. 53–54.

status in terms of perceived lethality. At the same time, biological weapons can be as effective—or more effective—than the kind of nuclear weapon Iran is likely to acquire during the next decade. This makes biological weapons a potential substitute for nuclear weapons if Iran cannot obtain fissile material, and creates a strong incentive for Iran to covertly pursue biological weapons as a substitute, as well as for their intrinsic war-fighting capabilities. Indeed, the more effective the United States is in denying Iran nuclear materials, the more Iran is likely to pursue biological weapons as a substitute.

Tables 4.1 and 4.2 do, however, make it clear that biological and nuclear weapons are not interchangeable. They require different employment doctrines, and the military limitations of each type of weapon illustrate why Iran might focus on different types of delivery systems for each weapon, or at least pursue a range of alternative delivery systems until it can be certain of its ability to acquire and deploy such weapons with high lethality. Further, there is no question that most political leaders perceive nuclear weapons as being the most "lethal" form of weapon, and that possession of nuclear weapons confers the most status in terms of how other nations in the region will view Iran. As a result, it is neither prudent nor cost-effective for Iran to make hard choices between its final mix of biological and nuclear weapons and key delivery systems until it knows what it can and cannot acquire and the probable lethality of such weapons.

These are key points that shape much of the following analysis. It is possible to say a great deal about Iran's potential delivery systems. It is possible to say a moderate amount about Iran's chemical weapons efforts, and some useful things about its efforts to acquire biological and nuclear weapons. It is clear that Iran has deployed chemical weapons, and that it has experience with such weapons as a result of the Iran-Iraq War. It is not possible, however, to do more than speculate about the kind of force mix that Iran would like, and it is exceedingly dangerous to try to treat Iran's efforts to acquire biological and nuclear weapons in isolation.

Chapter 15

Iran's Delivery Systems and Long-Range Missile Programs

Many of Iran's potential delivery systems can deliver both conventional high explosive and weapons of mass destruction. Iran had extensive numbers of long-range artillery weapons long before it had any weapons of mass destruction. It acquired long-range strike aircraft under the Shah, and it acquired and used long-range ballistic missiles during the Iran-Iraq War without chemical warheads.

At the same time, Iran's potential capabilities to deliver weapons of mass destruction range from the kind of static devices that might be used for unconventional warfare to very long-range strike systems. Further, Table 15.1 shows that Iran's capabilities are neither limited to—nor focused on—ballistic missiles. This point is of considerable importance to US defense planners who tend to focus on ballistic missiles and ignore or understate the importance of Iran's other capabilities.

IRANIAN ARTILLERY

Iran's conventional artillery weapons and multiple rocket launchers offer a way of delivering very large volumes of fire for ranges up to 20 kilometers, and its tube artillery weapons can deliver precision fire within the limits of Iran's targeting and fire control systems. As the following analysis of chemical weapons shows, Iran already has some experience in using such weapons during the Iran-Iraq War, and it has very extensive experience with their tactical effects as a result of Iraqi chemical attacks on Iran.

Wars rarely repeat themselves, but no Iranian planner or military officer can ignore the possibility that further land/air battles may take place with Iraq that involve chemical weapons. It has been all too clear from UNSCOM's experience in attempting to rid Iraq of such weapons that Iraq continues to lie to the UN,

Table 15.1
Iranian Land-Based Rockets and Missiles Assumed to Be Capable of Delivering Weapons of Mass Destruction

System	Type	Range (Km)	Payload (Km)	CEP (Km)	Solid/Liquid Fuel	Fixed/Mobile Launcher
122 mm CW rockets	rocket	20.5	-	-	solid	mobile
Shahin 2	rocket	20	-	-	solid	mobile
Oghab	rocket	40+	-	-	solid	mobile
Fajr (Fadjr) 3, 5	rocket	40-45	-	-	solid	mobile
HY-2	cruise	80	500	-	liquid	mobile
Mushak (?)	rocket	120-200	-	-	solid	mobile
Iran 130 (Nazeat)	rocket	150+	150	-	solid	mobile
CSS-8 (SA-2)	ballistic	150	-	-	solid	mobile
Iran-200 (?)	rocket	200	-	-	solid	mobile
Scud Model B	ballistic	320	1000	0.7-2.5	liquid	mobile
"Scud C"	ballistic	500-550	500	0.7-1.5	liquid	mobile
Al Fatah (?)	ballistic	950	-	-	-	-
No-Dong (?)	ballistic	1,000	770-1,000	-	liquid	mobile
Zelzal	ballistic	1,500	-	4.0	-	-
SS-4/R-12 Sandal (?)	ballistic	2,000	1,400	0.7-2.0	liquid	fixed

(?)= Systems reported to be in development or possible purchases, but where no real evidence exists regarding acquisition and deployment.
Sources: Adapted from an SAIC working paper dated June 26, 1996; *International Defense Review, Extra*, 2/97, p. 5; and *Jane's Defense Weekly*, November 6, 1996, p. 23.

import feedstocks, and prepare for a break-out capability in weapons of mass destruction once UN sanctions are lifted. This point is particularly important because it provides a further indication that Iran's efforts to acquire weapons of mass destruction are at least partially reactive—rather than driven by ideology and ambition—and may not be regime-dependent.

Unless the Iraqi regime changes radically in character and Iraq becomes open enough to offer a very high probability that it has ceased to proliferate, no Iranian leadership elite will be able to ignore the fact that Iraq made extensive use of artillery to deliver chemical weapons during the Iran and Iraq War, tested artillery rounds with biological agents, and armed medium-range rockets with biological agents. They will have no way to exclude the possibility that Iran might engage in intense land combat using chemical and possibly biological weapons at the tactical level and use them to strike at rear echelons and advancing offensive forces, achieve tactical area denial, panic or paralyze enemy ground forces, and clear lines of advance. They will have no way to exclude the possible need for the use of artillery systems in defensive roles.

There are no unclassified data on exactly how Iran would use artillery to deliver weapons of mass destruction, but Iran made extensive use of massed area fire during the Iran-Iraq War, and its recent exercises show that it retains such tactics while attempting to evolve a better capability for precision fire, targeting at longer ranges, maneuvering artillery, and shifting fires. Iran also has significant assets of long-range tube artillery, with a total of around 2,600 towed and self-propelled weapons.

These weapons include roughly 710 122 mm weapons, 1,000 130 mm weapons, 30 152 mm weapons, 325 155 mm weapons, 30 175 mm weapons, and 50 203 mm weapons. Iraq and the Former Soviet Union (FSU) have demonstrated that 122 mm and 130 mm weapons can be effective in delivering chemical weapons, and the 175 mm and 203 mm weapons have large enough shells to be used for biological weapons. Similarly, Iran has around 900 multiple rocket launchers and 3,500 mortars. These include roughly 160 122 mm and 9 240 mm multiple rocket launchers, and substantial numbers of 4.2" and 120 mm mortars.

These artillery assets could easily support substantial chemical warfare at the corps level, and Iran almost certainly plans to fight such wars. What is less clear is that Iran plans for the large-scale use of artillery weapons to deliver weapons of mass destruction against any enemy other than Iraq, although some such weapons have the range to strike Kuwait and many might be deployed on Iran's coast and islands in the Gulf to deal with any US or other attack as well as Iranian combat ships to attack tankers and coastal targets.

It seems likely that artillery weapons will also be used almost exclusively to deliver chemical weapons. While it is technically possible for Iran to create effective nuclear and biological artillery rounds, it is unlikely to have sufficient assets of nuclear weapons in the near to mid term to use nuclear artillery rounds—even if it can solve the major design problems involved. It also seems unlikely that Iran will use artillery to deliver biological agents, even if it can solve the fusing and dispersal problems in creating such weapons. With the possible exception of toxins, artillery delivery of biological weapons would present serious safety, control, and fratricide problems, and Iran has large numbers of long-range artillery rockets which would offer safer stand-off ranges, and which would be difficult to detect and destroy.

IRANIAN ROCKETS

Iranian rockets present a significant problem for analysis. Iran has extensive experience with such systems and considerable assets. Iraq began to fire FROG-7s at Iranian positions during the first weeks of the Iran-Iraq conflict, and Iran responded by making a major effort to acquire and employ its own long-range unguided rockets. Iran obtained help from the People's Republic of China in manufacturing and assembling copies of Chinese artillery rockets, and it made considerable progress. By the mid-1980s, Iran claimed that it had over 100 factories manufacturing some sort of equipment for missiles and rockets, with major production facilities at Sirjan and Isfahan, facilities at Shahroud, a test monitoring facility at Tabas, and a launch facility at Rafsanjan.

Iran succeeded in producing its own version of a Chinese Type-83 artillery rocket, which it called the Oghab. This rocket is manufactured at Semnan, about 185 kilometers east of Tehran, in a factory built with Chinese help and using Chinese tools, technology, and some Chinese parts. It is fired from Mercedes-Benz LA911B trucks, with three rockets per truck. Iran also used Chinese help to develop an "original" design for a long-range rocket, which it called the Iran-130.[1] The Oghab has only a range of 40 kilometers, and it lacks the range and/or accuracy to hit anything smaller than large area targets like assembly areas and cities. It has a 70–300 kilogram warhead, and its operational CEP may approximate 1,000 meters at maximum range.[2] Further, Iran currently has no way to accurately target the Oghab.[3]

Iran has produced a longer range Iran-130, or Nazeat, since the end of the Iran-Iraq War. The full details of this system remain unclear, but it seems to use commercially available components, a solid fuel rocket, and a simple inertial guidance system to reach ranges of about 90–120 kilometers. It is 355 mm in diameter, 5.9 meters long, weighs 950 kilograms, and has a 150 kilogram warhead.[4] It seems to have poor reliability and accuracy, and its payload only seems to be several hundred kilograms.

Since the end of the Iran-Iraq War, Iran has exhibited another large rocket called the Shahin 2. It too has a 355 mm diameter, but it is only 3.87 meters long and weighs only 580 kilograms. It evidently can be equipped with three types of warheads: a 180 kilogram high explosive warhead, another warhead using high explosive submunitions, and a warhead that uses chemical weapons. Both the Nazeat and Shahin are now in service with the regular Iranian armed forces, in limited numbers.

The practical question is how Iran treats these delivery systems as possible ways of delivering weapons of mass destruction. It is too early to draw any firm conclusions about nuclear warheads, but it seems doubtful that Iran will use such systems for nuclear delivery. They have limited payloads, poor accuracy, uncertain reliability, and limited range. Iran would also have to make a massive breakthrough in nuclear weapons production before it could afford to divert nuclear warheads to such limited systems.

This situation is very different for chemical and biological weapons. Like missile warheads, it is difficult to develop reliable chemical and biological warheads that disperse chemical and biological agents with anything like their potential lethality. Providing the optimal dispersal of a given agent at the right height requires highly advanced engineering and test and evaluation. Past US and Soviet experience indicates that it is all too easy to reduce real-world operational lethalities to levels approaching total ineffectiveness, or to make them completely unpredictable.

At the same time, such rockets are relatively cheap and easy to disperse. They are expendable in terms of potential enemy attacks, and there are many tactical and strategic contingencies where they can be fired in substantial numbers to ensure that they have a significant cumulative effect or where the mere firing of any system with a chemical or biological agent could achieve significant effects in terms of panic, intimidation, or area denial. Further, it is far from clear that Iran's leadership and technical community will have a clear picture of the lethality of such systems, or carry out extensive operational testing. It is at least possible that it might arm such rockets with a weapon of mass destruction without any accurate picture of what the weapon might do in combat. This certainly was the case with many of the Iraqi weapons systems shown in Table 11.1.

Unguided rockets offer Iran a way of striking deep into the rear areas of Iraqi forces or US forces staging land and amphibious operations. They might also be adapted for ship-board launch against islands or coastal targets, and their additional range makes them much safer to use with biological warheads than tube artillery and multiple rocket launchers. They also offer useful trade-offs in terms of cost and attrition. Biological and chemical agents become very cheap when produced in volume, as do artillery rockets and delivery systems. Unlike aircraft and ballistic missiles, unguided rockets offer a cheap way of providing moderate-range tactical strikes, and Iran would have little reason to care if Iraqi, US, or other forces destroyed a large number of such low cost systems. It must be stressed, however, that it is easy to discuss possibilities or to credit such weapons as having chemical and biological warheads, but that no meaningful unclassified data exist to confirm either how Iran intends to employ such weapons or their real-world lethality.

IRANIAN AIRCRAFT

Iran already has chemical bombs, may have biological bombs, and will probably deploy its initial nuclear weapons as bombs. Aircraft offer Iran and other developing nations the ability to deliver high payloads with shapes optimized around weapons design rather than the complex problems involved in ensuring a missile warhead is stable, accurate, and aerodynamic. While new aircraft are more expensive than ballistic missiles, older aircraft are often expendable and can be flown in one-way missions that greatly extend their range or ability to use very low altitude flight and evasive attack patterns.

Iran's air force has suffered badly from the effects of revolution and a cut-off of Western parts and modernization. Nevertheless, Table 15.2 shows both that Iran still has a number of aircraft with significant range-payload capabilities that could be used for a biological, chemical, and nuclear weapons capability, and that it must consider a wide range of combat aircraft in neighboring states as potential threats.

Iran retains some 60 F-4D/Es, has acquired roughly 30 Su-24s, and could easily adapt its F-14s for lob delivery of weapons of mass destruction. It has

Table 15.2
Possible Air Delivery Systems*

Type	Cruise Speed (Km/Hr)		Nominal Range (Kilometers)***		Maximum Payload (Kilograms)
	Low**	High	Low	High	
Possible Iranian Strike Aircraft					
F-4	-	890	-	840	5,900
F-5	-	860	-	310	3,200
F-14	-	980	-	950	4,500
MiG-29	960	890	-	1,150	-
Su-24	930	950	320	1,130	8,000
Other Regional Strike Aircraft					
A-4	-	810	-	1,230	4,500
Alphajet	740	710	170	890	2,800
F-15	-	980	-	1,440	10,700
F-16	-	920	550	930	5,400
F/A-18	-	900	-	740	7,700
Hawk	920	780	-	185	2,950
Jaguar	960	880	-	850	4,750
MiG-21****	880	800	-	480	1,500
MiG-23****	960	950	450	950	3,000
MiG-27	960	890	390	600	4,500
Mirage F-1	980	980	640	-	4,000
Mirage III	970	950	830	-	1,810
Mirage 5/50	970	950	630	-	4,200
Mirage 2000	-	950	-	690	6,300
Q-5/A-5 Fantan	-	-	400	600	2,000
Su-17/20/22	950	950	430	680	4,000
Tornado IDS	-	820	-	1,390	6,800
Tu-16	-	750	-	2,180	9,000
Tu-22 (Blinder)	-	750	-	1,500	10,000
Tu-22M (Backfire)	-	860	-	4,430	12,000

*Excludes modifications of cruise missiles and RPVs/UAVs, or possible developments of such systems. Egypt, Israel, Iran, Iraq, Libya, and Syria have systems with the capability to be modified for the land attack role and/or some development capability to create such systems.
**Low level radar-avoidance approach.
***Low = Lo-Lo-Lo profile, High = Hi-Lo-Hi profile. Excludes refueling and one-way missions with more than double range. Trade-offs can be made between range and payload in most cases. Some air defense fighters are included which could be used for such missions because of exceptional flight performance.
****Performance varies sharply with specific variant.
Sources: Adapted by Anthony H. Cordesman from the Office of the Secretary of Defense, *Proliferation: Threat and Response*, Washington, Department of Defense, April, 1996, and IISS, *Military Balance, 1997–1998*. Data in italics estimated by Anthony H. Cordesman.

significant numbers of F-5s and F-7s that could easily be sacrificed in one-way missions or even converted to drone attacks.[5] Iran would have trouble in massing large numbers of aircraft and sustaining high sortie rates, but it could probably mass 20–30 aircraft every few days to deliver significant numbers of chemical weapons against a force that did not have excellent air cover and ground-based air defense. Iran would have no sustainability and command and control problems in using limited numbers of aircraft more selectively to deliver nuclear or biological weapons against rear area, interdiction, or strategic targets. It is at least possible that Iran might adapt some of its tactical strike fighters to act as dedicated delivery systems to deliver a line-source attack with a biological agent.

Iran might commit such aircraft in one-way low altitude strike profiles with a reasonable probability that they could penetrate all but the best prepared Gulf air defenses. Pop-up attacks across the Gulf against coastal targets provide less than 10 minutes' radar warning in many cases, and only countries with an AWACS or aerostat warning systems could hope to react unless they had advanced fighters patrolling their coast. Iraq had an extremely poor record of detecting and defending against isolated Iranian attacks on Baghdad during the Iran-Iraq War. The Iranian air force also had considerable success in US-Iranian military exercises during the time of the Shah, when it flew extremely low-altitude attack profiles near its Gulf coast and then suddenly broke out of terrain masking to surprise US Navy and Marine Corps forces. These exercises predate the deployment of the AWACS and Aegis, but indicate that Iran might employ such tactics against any US amphibious force operating near its coast.[6]

It is possible that Iran might use helicopters to deliver chemical and biological weapons. Much of its helicopter force is now incapable of high intensity combat operations but might well be employed in limited numbers of chemical and biological attacks using the helicopter as a sprayer or in line-source attacks using dry, storable biological agents. While helicopters are vulnerable and shorter ranged than strike aircraft, they are almost ideal platforms for medium-range biological attacks—particularly if flown in one-way dedicated attacks. Helicopters provide a high degree of mobility and dispersal, can fly nap of the earth profiles at low speeds that make them very difficult to defend against, and line-source attacks using biological agents, toxins, or persistent nerve gases might be delivered against enemy rear areas sufficiently upwind to be outside the detection range of SHORAD radars and anti-aircraft weapons. The Iranian air force has about 50 helicopters that could be used in such missions, and the Iranian army could draw on a pool of roughly 100 AH-1s, 40 CH-47s, 130 Bell 214As, and nearly 200 other helicopters. At least some of these helicopters might be modified for drone delivery on one-way missions.

Once again, there are no unclassified data that provide a clear indication of how Iran intends to employ its aircraft, although there are unclassified news reports that speak in vague terms about Iranian joint exercises involving chemical warfare. It also seems likely that Iran's real-world response would be driven by the nature of a given contingency, and by the state of the art in its air force, its alternative delivery systems, and its biological, chemical, and nuclear weapons programs at the time a contingency occurred.

IRAN'S BALLISTIC MISSILES

Iran began to use surface-to-surface ballistic missile systems during the Iran-Iraq War, and it has already imported a number of long-range systems that are capable of delivering biological, chemical, and nuclear weapons. These systems consist of the Scud B, North Korean variants of the Scud, and the Chinese CSS-8.[7] Iran is now seeking to both import longer-range systems and to manufacture them domestically.[8] It also may be seeking to provide these systems with sheltered bases and facilities, as well as provide a wide range of options for dispersing them and using mobility to reduce their vulnerability. For example, there are unconfirmed reports that Iran is building shelters and tunnels along its Gulf coastline that can be used as missile shelters to reduce vulnerability to air and missile attacks. There is no evidence that Iran has already dispersed its missiles, but these shelters could be used to support operations using Scuds or follow-on systems, and possibly to provide a rapid deployment and launch capability.[9]

Once again, Iran is not alone in this aspect of proliferation, and its efforts to acquire ballistic missiles are at least partially a reaction to the efforts of other neighboring states. Iran only gave long-range missiles high priority after the virtual collapse of its air force early in the Iran-Iraq War. Since that time, it has had to face a wide range of competing efforts by its potential enemies. A comparison of Iran's missiles with the other missile systems in the Middle East is provided in Table 15.3, and the range of Iran's missile systems is shown in Figure 15.1. No Iranian leadership can ignore the Israeli and Saudi programs listed in Table 15.3, or the near certainty that Iraq will attempt to rebuild its missile programs the minute UN sanctions are lifted.

Nevertheless, Iran has made statements clearly designed to intimidate its neighbors. For example, Admiral Mohammed Razi Hadayeq, the commander of Iran's missile forces under the new Khatami government, made a point of stating in October, 1997 that Iran was the "strongest missile power" in the Gulf. He also stated that new missiles like the Qareh had a range of 680 kilometers, which gave Iran the capability to hit targets along the coast of the Southern Gulf.[10]

The Scud B

The Soviet-designed Scud B (17E) guided missile currently forms the core of Iran's ballistic missile forces—largely as a result of the Iran-Iraq War. Iran did not make serious efforts to acquire ballistic missiles under the Shah, but the Khomeini regime saw Iran's air force collapse as an effective fighting force during the first two months of the Iran-Iraq War. While Iran could still fly occasional fighter sorties, its Air Force could do little to resist Iraqi air strikes,

Table 15.3
Possible Missile Delivery Systems*

Type	User Country	Nominal Range (Kilometers)	Maximum Payload (Kilograms)
Shorter-Range			
SS-21 Scarab A	Syria, Yemen	70	480
Ababil-100	Iraq	100-150	?
MGM-52 Lance	Israel (Iran?)	130	450
Iran 130/Mushak 120	Iran	130	190
CSS-8 M78610	Iran, Iraq	150	190
Al Faith	Libya	200	?
Scud B	Afghanistan, Iran, Egypt, Libya, Syria, UAE, (Yemen, Iraq?)	300	985
Project T	Egypt	450	985
Intermediate Range			
Jericho (YA-1)	Israel	500	500
Scud "C" Variant	Iran, Syria (Libya?)	500-550	500
Al Husayn	Iraq	600-650	500
Al Husayn (Short)	Iraq	600-650	?
Al Hijrah	Iraq	600-650	?
Jericho 2 (YA-3)	Israel	1,500	1,000
Badr 2000	(Iraq? Egypt? Libya?)	750-1,000	?
CSS-2 (DF-3)	Saudi Arabia	2,800	2,150

*Excludes modifications of cruise missiles, heavy air-to-surface missiles, anti-ship missiles, other surface-to-air missiles, and RPVs/UAVs, or possible developments of such systems. Egypt, Israel, Iran, Iraq, Libya, and Syria have systems with the capability to be modified for the land attack role and/or some development capability to create such systems.

Sources: Adapted by Anthony H. Cordesman from the Office of the Secretary of Defense, *Proliferation: Threat and Response*, Washington, Department of Defense, April, 1996; *Jane's Defense Weekly*, April 17, 1996, pp. 42–43; and IISS, *Military Balance, 1996–1997*.

and its surface-to-air missile system proved to be largely ineffective except in covering the most heavily defended point targets. A lack of Iranian maintenance capability and Western resupply then led to the steady further attrition of Iran's air and surface-to-air missile capabilities, although Iran retained some capability throughout the Iran-Iraq War.

Iran responded by seeking surface-to-surface missiles from Warsaw Pact countries, Libya, North Korea, and China in an effort to develop the capability to make long-distance strikes on Iraq. It seems to have acquired its initial Scud B missiles from Libya and to have had some support from Syria, and then to have obtained missiles from North Korea and the FSU. These missiles allowed Iran to equip its Revolutionary Guards with their first long-range strike capability, although the Scud B had—and has—important limitations.

Figure 15.1
The Range of Current and Future Iranian Ballistic Missile Systems

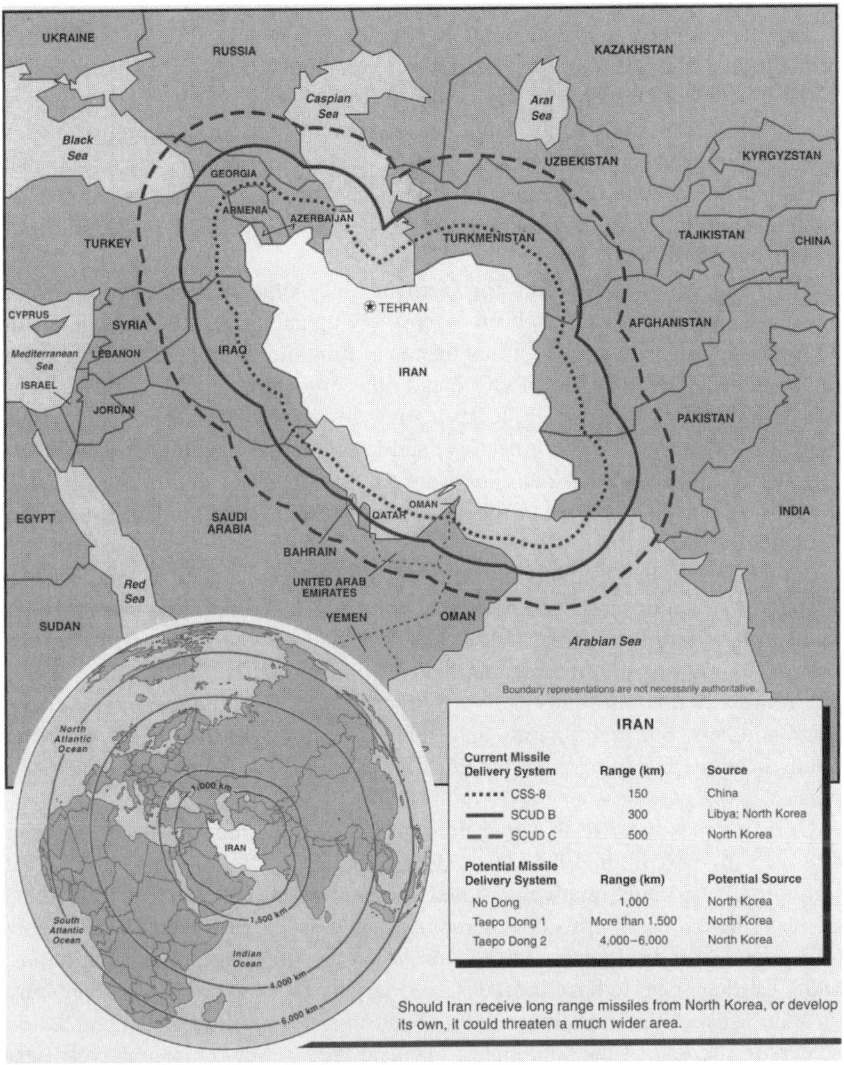

IRAN		
Current Missile Delivery System	Range (km)	Source
CSS-8	150	China
SCUD B	300	Libya; North Korea
SCUD C	500	North Korea
Potential Missile Delivery System	Range (km)	Potential Source
No Dong	1,000	North Korea
Taepo Dong 1	More than 1,500	North Korea
Taepo Dong 2	4,000–6,000	North Korea

Should Iran receive long range missiles from North Korea, or develop its own, it could threaten a much wider area.

Source: Office of the Secretary of Defense, *Proliferation: Threat and Response*, Washington, Department of Defense, April, 1996, p. 17.

The Scud B is a relatively old design which first became operational in 1967. It is a Soviet design, and the Soviet Union designates the system as the R-17E or R-300E. The Scud B has a range of 290–300 kilometers with its normal conventional payload. The export version of the missile is about 11 meters long, 85–90 centimeters in diameter, and weighs 6,300 kilograms. It has a nominal

CEP of 1,000 meters. The Russian versions can be equipped with conventional high explosive, fuel air explosive, runway penetrator, submunition, chemical, and nuclear warheads.[11]

The export version of the Scud B sold to the Middle East comes with a conventional high explosive warhead weighing about 1,000 kilograms, of which 800 kilograms are the high explosive payload and 200 are the warhead structure and fusing system.[12] It has a single-stage storable liquid rocket engine and is usually deployed on the MAZ-543 eight wheel transporter-erector-launcher (TEL). It has a strap-down inertial guidance, using three gyros to correct its ballistic trajectory and internal graphite jet vane steering.[13] The warhead hits at a velocity above Mach 1.5.[14]

The Scud B is derived from the German V-2. Although it uses much more advanced technology and has been extensively updated over the years, it is still an aging design with many serious technical limitations. Nevertheless, it is far more sophisticated than the FROG-7 and other unguided rockets discussed earlier. It is a true guided missile. It has a strap-down inertial guidance using three gyros to correct its ballistic trajectory, and uses internal graphite jet vane steering. It has a warhead that detaches from the missile body during the final fall towards target. This provides added stability and allows the warhead to hit at a velocity above Mach 1.5.

Although Iraq had a monopoly of Scud missiles at the start of the Iran-Iraq War and had deployed a Scud regiment with 9–12 launchers, Iraq did not begin Scud firings until Iran drove Iraq out of Iran and put the Iraqi regime on the defensive. Iraq began to fire regular Scud Bs on October 27, 1982. It now claims that it initially used its Scuds against military targets and fired them in relatively large numbers, but these claims may reflect Iraq's desire to conceal surviving Scuds from the UN by claiming that it fired more missiles than was actually the case.

Other sources indicate that Iraq fired a total of three missiles in 1982, 33 in 1983, 25 in 1984, 82 in 1985, 25 in 1987, and 193 in 1988. It seems likely that Iraq initially had only relatively limited numbers of missiles and was well aware of their limitations in terms of accuracy and lethality. It used the Scud B largely to conduct sporadic "terror attacks" on urban areas or military concentrations, and its strikes seem to have been designed largely to try to put political pressure on Iran. Most of the time, Iraq used its Scud missiles against Iranian population centers to the rear of the battlefield.[15] Typical targets were cities relatively near the border such as Dezful, Ahwaz, Khorramabad, and Borujerd (190 kilometers from the Iran-Iraq border).[16]

Iran only acquired its Scuds in response to Iraq's attacks. It obtained a limited number from Libya and then obtained larger numbers from North Korea. It deployed these units with a special Khatam ol-Anbya force attached to the air element of the Pasdaran. Iran fired its first Scuds in March, 1985. It fired as many as 14 Scuds in 1985, eight in 1986, 18 in 1987, and 77 in 1988. Iran's missile attacks were more effective from the start than Iraq's. This was largely a matter of geography. Many of Iraq's major cities were comparatively close to its border with Iran, but Tehran and most of Iran's major cities that had not already been targets in the war were outside the range of Iraqi Scud attacks. Iran's missiles, in contrast, could hit key Iraqi cities like Baghdad.

However, Iran faced severe war-fighting limitations in exploiting its range advantage, which Iranian leaders must recognize may apply to future Iranian attacks on its neighbors using any type of missiles with conventional warheads. Iran lacked the massive number of missiles needed to sustain frequent attacks and to deliver large amounts of high explosives at a given time, and Iraq had vastly superior air resources it could use as a substitute for or supplement to missile attacks.

Iran also could not exploit its range advantage because of the limited accuracy of the Scud B. If one considers the full error budget, rather than simply the CEP, the technical accuracy of the Scud approaches a kilometer at long range. Its operational accuracy in Iranian hands—taking siting and other factors into account—often proved to be closer to 5 kilometers. Iran rarely hit the major targets it publicly claimed to be attacking, such as the Iraqi Ministry of Defense, although it did score one or two hits that Iraq then denied. Targeting and/or accuracy problems caused most Iranian Scud launches to hit areas outside of Baghdad.[17]

Further, even the missiles that did hit inside the city often hit in open spaces, and even hits on buildings rarely produced high casualties. In fact, the net impact of using Scud missiles against urban targets was roughly similar to randomly lobbing a 2,000 pound bomb into a city every few days or weeks. Scud strikes with conventional warheads usually did little more than produce a loud bang, smash windows, and kill a few innocent civilians. The most lethal attacks on both sides seem to have occurred when missiles hit targets like a school or a large funeral by sheer accident.

This helps explain why the net impact of Iranian and Iraqi missile strikes on the opposite side's public opinion and morale was relatively short lived, and a two-edged sword, until Iraq developed the capability to hit Tehran and far more intensive exchanges began in 1988. The side doing the firing was able to propagandize the firing as lethal retaliation against the enemy. The side receiving the fire, however, experienced only brief periods of panic at worst, and panic often quickly changed into anger and demands for reprisals as the civilians in the target area realized that they could survive the enemy's attacks. Since each Scud missile cost around $500,000–$1,000,000, such attacks were also extremely expensive.

Nevertheless, both Iran and Iraq attempted to improve their ability to use long-range missiles by acquiring much larger numbers or missiles and/or by building their own. Iran tried desperately to obtain large numbers of Scud missiles from Libya, North Korea, and Syria, and to create its own missile manufacturing capabilities. It sought to buy additional Scud Bs, to manufacture them in Iran, to develop its own systems, and to obtain alternative systems like the PRC-made M-9.

As has been discussed earlier, Iran also succeeded in producing its own version of a Chinese Type-83 artillery rocket, which it called the Oghab, and it tried to develop its own long-range rocket called the Iran-130.[18] Iran claimed during the course of 1985–1988 that it had over 100 factories manufacturing some sort of part or equipment for missiles and rockets, with major production facilities at Sirjan and a launch facility at Rafsanjan.

Iran's production efforts were only successful in the case of the Oghab—the weapons systems with the least strategic importance. It started producing this system in 1985, and it immediately began to use it in combat. It seems to have made about 325 Oghab rockets, and to have fired roughly 260–270 rockets out of this total. This allowed Iran to fire nearly 250 in 1988. The Oghabs only have a range of 40 kilometers, however, and they lack the range and/or accuracy to hit more economic or urban targets. They also only have a 70–300 kilogram warhead, and their CEP is in excess of 1,000 meters.[19] Further, Iran had no way to target the Oghab. The most it could do was to launch the Oghabs at the Iraqi cities near the border. These targets included Basra, Abu al-Khasib, Al-Zuybar, Umm-Qasr, Mandali, Khanaqin, and Banmil, but the Oghab strikes generally had far less effect than artillery barrages.[20]

Iran failed to develop and produce the IRAN-130 in any significant numbers. The full details of this system remain unclear, but it seems to have been an attempt to use commercially available components and a simple inertial guidance system to build a missile that could reach ranges of anywhere from 130 to 200 kilometers. In practice, the missile proved unreliable, and it reached a maximum range of about 120 kilometers with very poor reliability and accuracy. Some IRAN 130s were deployed to the regular Pasdaran, however, and the first such missiles were fired against Al-Amarah on March 19, 1988, and four more were fired against the city in April. It is unclear that these strikes hit their targets or had any tactical effect.

Iran never made good on its public claims to be able to produce the Scud during the 1980s, although it could produce all of the missiles except possibly the advanced components of the guidance system and rocket motor by the mid-1990s. The Minister in charge of the Pasdaran, Mohsen Rafiqdust, started making such claims in November, 1987. Iran also claimed in April, 1988 that it was working on a missile with a 320 kilometer range, and claimed that 80% of the Scuds it fired were produced in Iran. In fact, however, this was pure propaganda. Iran never succeeded in firing an Iranian-made Scud missile. Iran did, however, obtain additional Scud missiles from Libya or Syria in 1986, but it was still only able to fire a total of 18–22 missiles in 1987. Iran was more successful in dealing with North Korea. In June, 1987 it obtained agreement to ship 100 more Scuds as part of a $500 million arms package. These missiles were delivered to

Iran in early 1988. Iran also seems to have sought Scuds from the PRC, but was unable to obtain them.

These imports allowed Iran to engage Iraq in a new and more intensive series of missile strikes on population centers. Iran fired at least 77 Scud missiles during a 52-day period in 1988, during what came to be known as the "war of the cities." Sixty-one were fired at Baghdad, nine at Mosul, five at Kirkuk, one at Takrit, and one at Kuwait. Iran fired as many as five missiles on a single day, and once fired three missiles within 30 minutes. This still, however, worked out to an average of only about one missile a day, and Iran was down to only 10–20 Scuds when the war of the cities ended.[21]

It was Iraq, however, that was successful in finding the long-range missiles it needed to strike at Iran's key cities, and which won the "war of the cities," although it took Iraq nearly half a decade to develop this capability. Iraq tried actively from 1982 onward to improve the accuracy of its Scud Bs and to extend their range by allowing them to burn more of their total supply of rocket fuel and using a smaller warhead. Iraq also tried to acquire longer-range missiles. Various Iraqi statements made in early 1983, for example, suggested that the Soviet Union might be willing to supply newer Soviet missiles with longer ranges like the SS-12 to the Iraqis.

Iraq did not demonstrate any improvement in the long-range strike capabilities of its missiles, however, until February 29, 1988. It then began to fire a modified version of the Scud B that burned more of its fuel, and which may also have had additional fuel and used a smaller warhead. This missile gave Iraq the range to attack Iranian cities. It is unclear when Iraq obtained the missiles it modified, but the USSR seems to have delivered up to 300 Scuds to Iraq in 1986.

Iraqi Scuds began striking Tehran and Qom from positions south of Baghdad.[22] Iraq called its new version of the Scud B the Al Husayn.[23] Iraq first announced that it had such a missile—with a range of about 400 miles, or 650 kilometers—in August, 1987. These reports were initially dismissed as propaganda, but they were later confirmed through the observation of five test firings and launches.[24]

Table 15.4 provides an estimate of the resulting interaction between the strategic bombing and missile wars between 1987 and 1988 that then led to the "war of the cities." These estimates are based on Iraqi and Iranian claims, although the details differ significantly according to source. In any case, Table 15.2 is almost certainly valid in indicating the general size of the sudden rise in Iraqi missile attacks and that Iraq's success was the result of both missile and airpower and not simply the total number of missile attacks on Iran's urban targets.[25]

Iraq fired an average of nearly three Scuds a day and backed them with enough air strikes that the cumulative effect of Iraq's missile and air strikes on Iran was far greater in 1988 than in the past. Where the Iranians had previously been able to adapt to the relatively limited and short-lived Iraqi bombing efforts,

Table 15.4
Strikes Reported by Iran and Iraq Affecting the "War of the Cities" in 1987 and 1988

		Residential/Economic Attacks[1]			
Date		Iraq		Iran	
A. 1987		Total Bombing & Missile	Scud[2]	Total Bombing & Missile	Scud[3]
January	1–15	30	-	3	-
	16–31	18	-	15	3
February	1–15	27	-	5	3
	16–28	8	-	5	5
March	1–15	-	-	-	-
	16–31	4	-	-	-
April	1–15	5	-	-	-
	16–30	2	-	-	-
May	1–15	4	-	1	-
	16–31	1	-	1	-
June	1–15	-	-	-	-
	16–30	1	-	-	-
July	1–15	6	-	-	-
	16–31	-	-	-	-
August	1–15	2	-	-	-
	16–31	13	-	7	-
September	1–15	35	-	8	-
	16–30	19	-	3	-
October	1–15	12	-	6	-
	16–31	4	-	8	4
November	1–15	14	-	9	1
	16–30	10	-	2	2
December	1–15	7	-	2	-
	16–31	1	-	-	-
TOTAL IN 1987		223	-	75	18
B. 1988					
January	1–15	1	-	-	-
	16–31	-	-	-	-
February	1–15	3	-	-	-
	16–28	5	-	3	-
March	1–15	215	101	73	31
	16–31	130	36	143	14
April	1–15	78	40	96	11
	16–30	33	26	63	5
May	1–15	2	-	-	-
	16–31	2	-	-	-
June	1–15	-	-	-	-
	16–30	13	-	1	-

Table 15.4 (continued)

		Residential/Economic Attacks[1]			
Date		Iraq		Iran	
B. 1988 (cont.)		Total Bombing & Missile	Scud[2]	Total Bombing & Missile	Scud[3]
July	1–15	3	-	-	-
	16–31	4	-	-	-
August	1–20[4]	5	-	-	-
TOTAL IN 1988		494	203	379	61

1. Bombing and missile attacks as reported in daily war communiqués and other sources.
2. Includes all long-range missiles, but not Oghabs or any Iran-130s that failed to hit economic or civil targets.
3. Includes Scud B missiles fired at Baghdad and other Iranian cities.
4. From beginning of the month to the Iranian acceptance of a cease-fire and UN Resolution 598.

Sources: Adapted from work provided to the author by Gary Sick, and W. Seth Carus and Joseph S. Bermudez, "Iran's Growing Missile Forces," *Jane's Defense Weekly*, July 23, 1988.

the constant pounding of missiles interacted with a growing fear that Iraq might use chemical weapons, and this had a major impact on Iranian morale. So did the rumors and reports that senior Iranian officials—including Khomeini—had left Tehran. According to some reports, nearly a million Iranians had fled Tehran by mid-March, and several million more had fled by late April.[26]

It is important to stress, however, that the Iraqi missile strikes alone would have had relatively little impact on Iran if they had not interacted with the extensive use of airpower and a number of other factors. The Scud strikes were audible over long distances as they neared their target, made a loud bang, and blew out windows over a wide area. Nevertheless, the Scud strikes did not do serious physical damage to any Iranian target, and killed substantially less than an average of two dozen people a missile. The variants of the Scuds that Iraq was using only seem to have had a 130–250 kilogram warhead, and were scarcely "city killers."[27]

What gave the Iraqi missile and barrage a radical new strategic impact was that it occurred in combination with (1) the growing fear of chemical weapons, (2) the impact of Iraq's air raids, (3) the effect on morale of Iran's military casualties during the previous year, (4) growing popular and military exhaustion with the conflict, (5) Iran's inability to retaliate, (6) rumors of internal divisions within Iran's leadership, (7) serious economic hardship and growing prices on the black market, and (8) the knowledge that Iran would no longer be threatened if it halted its offensives.[28] This experience reinforces a lesson from many previous conflicts: The effect of strategic bombardment with conventional weapons on the course of a war is likely to be determined far more by its effect in catalyzing public opinion and in shaping the overall political conditions affecting the war than by the size of the casualties or actual damage that is inflicted by the weapons involved.

These points are important because both Iran's current leaders and its military, and any future Iranian leaders and commanders, are certain to understand their implications. They must realize that any future missile bombardments with conventional warheads are likely to have a limited effect, even if they have improved conventional warheads. They must also understand that such limitations do not simply apply to the Scud B.

Virtually all urban areas, economic targets, and military area targets have large "empty" spaces relative to the lethal area of the most advanced conventional warheads. Unless conventionally armed missiles have highly effective terminal guidance systems—a technology Iran is unlikely to obtain and be able to apply—they will remain "terror" weapons whose political and psychological effects will diminish sharply as populations learn they have relatively limited real-world lethality and usually produce less damage effect than a well-aimed air-to-surface missile or free fall bomb. In fact, the US Army repeatedly found that even advanced terminal guidance systems for Lance and Pershing missiles did not produce useful lethalities with advanced conventional warheads, and only deployed conventional warheads under political pressure.

A conventional missile warhead using high explosives produces different blast effects than a bomb. The missile's added velocity alters the vector of the explosion and creates serious problems in detonating the warhead at precisely the right height to obtain maximum blast effect. As a result, the average missile strike using a conventional warhead is roughly equivalent in lethality to a single sortie on a single target by an F-4 strike-fighter or any other reasonably capable attack aircraft—with the important difference that the warhead of any missile lacking a highly sophisticated terminal guidance system cannot be aimed at a specific target, but only at a relatively broad area. This makes missiles armed with conventional weapons more a political or terror weapon than a method of destroying enemy targets, since it is impractical to launch the volume of missiles necessary to do real damage, even to area targets.

Iran's leaders are also fully aware that Iraq encountered similar problems during its strikes on Israel and Saudi Arabia during the Gulf War, and these lessons do much to explain Iran's efforts to arm its missiles with weapons of mass destruction, to acquire enough Scud Bs to launch substantial survivable volleys against a potential enemy, and to acquire other longer-range, more accurate missiles.

As a result, Iran's Scud Bs may be a more significant threat now than during the Iran-Iraq War. Iran bought an estimated 200–300 Scud Bs from North Korea between 1987 and 1992, and may have continued to buy such missiles after that time. Israeli experts estimate that Iran had at least 250–300 Scud B missiles and at least 8–15 launchers on hand in 1997. US experts also believe that Iran can now manufacture virtually all of the Scud Bs, with the possible exception of the most sophisticated components of its guidance system and rocket motors.

This makes it difficult to estimate how many missiles Iran has in inventory and can produce or acquire over time, as well as to estimate the precise performance characteristics of Iran's missiles, since it can alter the weight of the warhead and adjust the burn time and improve the efficiency of the rocket motors.[29]

It seems nearly certain that Iran's Scud Bs now have chemical warheads, and that they may have experimental biological warheads. However, there are no meaningful unclassified data that indicate the probable design technology and lethality of these warheads or Iran's sophistication and technical support in targeting and employing such weapons.

The low accuracy and high circular error probable (CEP) of the Scud B would force Iran to try to maximize the lethality and dispersal of the agent in a chemical or biological warhead in order to attack any mix of military or civil targets—ranging from an urban area to an air base. However, Iran presently lacks the weather models and remote monitoring equipment necessary to calculate the impact of a chemical or biological warhead on a given target. Iran may also lack the technology to engineer stable warheads, making use of the roughly 1,000 kilogram warhead size necessary to make optimal use of the Scud B as a delivery platform, or can equip these warheads with the mix of stable, easily disseminated lethal agents, fusing systems, and dispersal systems like air bags and cluster bombs necessary to explosively disperse chemical or biological agents with high effectiveness.

These uncertainties are of major importance in war-fighting terms. If one uses Iraq as a standard of comparison, Iraq had only crude, low-lethality chemical and biological missile warheads at the time of the Gulf War. It has, however, been seven years since that time, and it is far from clear that either Iran or Iraq faces the same limitations. Iran may covertly have developed much better warheads and may have had outside technical assistance in doing so. It is possible that it now has binary chemical warheads and effective explosive dissemination technology which is relatively reliable in terms of height of burst. It is less likely but still technologically possible that it possesses similar biological warheads using dry, storable biological agents like Anthrax.

The practical problem in making any estimate of such threats is that obtaining technology per se has never been the issue limiting Third World states; rather, it has been the acute difficulty such states have in managing the effective application of technology. Even if Iran's level of applied technology was known, its level of quality control and reliability would remain major uncertainties. As a result, there is no way to estimate Iran's current and projected level of lethality.

The "Scud C"

Iran has also succeeded in acquiring a longer-range North Korean missile system—often referred to as a "Scud C." Typically, Iran formally denied the fact that it had such systems long after the transfer of these missiles became a reality. Hassan Taherian, an Iranian foreign ministry official, stated in February, 1995, "There is no missile cooperation between Iran and North Korea whatsoever. We deny this."[30]

In fact, a senior North Korean delegation traveled to Tehran to close the deal on November 29, 1990, and met with Mohsen Rezaei, the former commander of the IRGC. Iran either bought the missile then, or placed its order shortly thereafter. North Korea then exported the missile through its Lyongaksan Import Corporation. Iran imported some of these North Korean missile assemblies using its B-747s, and seems to have used ships to import others.[31]

Iran probably had more than 60 of the longer-range North Korean missiles by 1998, although other sources report 100, and one source reports 170.[32] Iran appears to have had 5–10 Scud C launchers, each with several missiles. This total seems likely to include four new North Korean TELs received in 1995.[33] Iran seems to have set a goal of acquiring several hundred Scud C missiles by the late 1990s, and it seems to want a large enough number of launchers to make its missile force highly dispersible.[34] Iran may also have begun to test its new North Korean missiles. There are reports that it has fired them from mobile launchers at a test site near Qom about 310 miles (500 kilometers) to a target area south of Shahroud. There are also reports that units equipped with such missiles have been deployed as part of Iranian exercises like the Saeqer-3 (Thunderbolt 3) in late October, 1993.[35]

The missile is more advanced than the Scud B, although many aspects of its performance are unclear. North Korea seems to have completed development of the missile in 1987, after obtaining technical support from the People's Republic of China. In fact, while it is often called a "Scud C," it seems to differ substantially in detail from the original Soviet Scud B. It appears to be based more on the Chinese-made DF-61 than on a direct copy of the Soviet weapon.

Experts estimate that the North Korean missiles have a range of around 310 miles (500 kilometers), a warhead with a high explosive payload of 700 kilograms, and relatively good accuracy and reliability. While this payload is a bit limited for the effective delivery of chemical agents, Iran might modify the warhead to increase payload at the expense of range and restrict the use of chemical munitions to the most lethal agents, such as persistent nerve gas. It might also concentrate its development efforts on arming its Scud C forces with more lethal biological agents. In any case, such missiles are likely to have enough range-payload to give Iran the ability to strike all targets on the southern coast of the Gulf and all of the populated areas in Iraq, although not the West. Iran could also reach targets in part of eastern Syria, the eastern third of Turkey, and could cover targets in the border area of the former Soviet Union, western Afghanistan, and western Pakistan.[36]

Accuracy and reliability remain major uncertainties, as does operational CEP. Once again, much would also depend on the precise level of technology that Iran deployed in the warhead. Neither Russia nor the People's Republic of China seem to have transferred the warhead technology for biological and chemical weapons to Iran or Iraq when they sold them the Scud B missile and the CSS-8. However, North Korea may have sold Iran such technology as part of the Scud C sale. If it did so, such a technology transfer would save Iran years of development and testing in obtaining highly lethal biological and chemical warheads. In fact, Iran would probably be able to deploy far more effective biological and chemical warheads than Iraq had at the time of the Gulf War.

Iran may be working with Syria in such development efforts, although Middle Eastern nations rarely cooperate fully in such sensitive areas. Iran served as a transshipment point for North Korean missile deliveries during 1992 and 1993. Some of this transshipment took place using the same Iranian B-747s that brought missile parts to Iran. Others moved by sea. For example, a North Korean vessel called the *Des Hung Ho*, bringing missile parts for Syria, docked at Bandar Abbas in May, 1992. Iran then flew these parts to Syria. An Iranian ship coming from North Korea, and a second North Korean ship followed, carrying missiles and machine tools for both Syria and Iran. At least 20 of the North Korean missiles have gone to Syria from Iran, and production equipment seems to have been transferred to Iran and to Syrian plants near Hama and Aleppo. Iran may also be nearing the capability to produce such missiles—possibly in an improved version.

Possible Acquisition of the No-Dong 1 and Tapeo Dong

Some Western experts believe that Iran and Syria—and possibly Pakistan—are cooperating in acquiring and producing some variant of a longer-range North Korean missile called the No-Dong 1. This missile seems to have begun development in 1989, although the program underwent extensive reorganization after failures during 1990–1991. The No-Dong underwent flight tests at ranges of 310 miles (500 kilometers) on May 29, 1993. Some sources indicate that Iranians were present at these tests. Extensive further propulsion tests began in August, 1994, and some reports indicate operational training began for test crews in May, 1995. Missile storage facilities began to be built in July, 1995, and four launch sites were completed in October, 1995.

The missile seemed to be nearing final development in North Korea in early 1997, possibly after aid from military industries in the People's Republic of China. A number of experts believed, however, that the missile could not enter full-scale production in North Korea for two to three more years.[37] It was also unclear whether a North Korea that was in the middle of famine and a major economic crisis had the resources to put the No-Dong into large-scale production. Progress of the program has been slow since 1995, and this may reflect such problems. However, mobile launchers were seen deployed in northeast North Korea on March 24, 1997. According to some reports, a further seven launcher units were seen at a facility about 100 kilometers from Pyongyang.[38]

There also were indications in September, 1998 that North Korea might be preparing for a new round of tests of the No Dong.

The No-Dong 1 is a single-stage liquid-fueled missile with a range of up to 1,000 to 1,300 kilometers (810 miles), although longer ranges may be possible with a reduced warhead and maximum burn. There are also indications that there may be a No-Dong 2, using the same rocket motor, but with an improved fuel supply system that allows the fuel to burn for a longer period.

The missile is about 15.2 meters long—four meters longer than the Scud B— and 1.2 meters in diameter. The warhead is estimated to weigh 770 kilograms (1,200–1,750 pounds), and a warhead manufacturing facility exists near Pyongyang.[39] The No-Dong has an estimated theoretical CEP of 700 meters at maximum range versus 900 meters for the Scud B, although its practical accuracy could be as wide as 3,000–4,000 meters. It has an estimated terminal velocity of Mach 3.5, versus 2.5 for the Scud B, which presents added problems for tactical missile defense. The missile is transportable on a modified copy of the MAZ-543P TEL that has been lengthened with a fifth axle and which is roughly 40 meters long. The added support stand for the vertical launch modes brings the overall length to 60 meters, and some experts question whether a unit this big is practical.[40]

The No-Dong's specifications present a number of operational problems for Iran, which may be the major reason that Iran sought to produce its own version of a liquid fueled missile, and obtained Russian and Chinese aid. The range payload and real-world accuracy of the No-Dong almost certainly present more problems in effectively weaponizing the No-Dong's warhead than is the case with the Scud C. Regardless of the chemical weapon involved, both missiles will probably be limited to large area targets and need the most lethal possible persistent chemical agent to produce significant lethality.

While any warhead can be a terror warhead, the cumulative error budget in such missiles grows steadily with range, as do some of the timing and dispersal problems in warhead design (largely as a result of terminal velocity). A highly lethal biological agent would present fewer problems in terms of operational CEP, but more problems in terms of dispersal technology. A nuclear warhead would present the best solution in terms of lethality and ease of detonation, but both the Scud C and No-Dong would require relatively advanced weapons designs and extensive operational testing with dummy warheads using nuclear devices with non-fissile material to determine operational performance.

While there is a tendency in some US weapons laboratories to underestimate these weaponization problems, past Iranian and Middle Eastern efforts to cope with these design problems and to develop realistic test and evaluation methods indicate that they could be very severe and lead to situations where Iran either relied on aircraft delivery or deployed systems with uncertain and misstated reliability and effectiveness.

Iran also seems interested in two developmental North Korean IRBMs, called the Tapeo Dong-1 or Tapeo Dong-2, which US intelligence detected in early

1994. North Korea also launched a new three-stage on August 31, 1998. North Korea fired the missile over Japan from a military base about 20 miles north of Kimchaek on its northeastern coast.

The first stage of the missile fell into the Sea of Japan, while the second stage splashed down in the Pacific Ocean after crossing over Japan. Parts of the missile landed in the middle of the Sea of Japan, by some accounts in the Russian exclusive economic zone, directly south of the Russian city of Vladivostok. It hit the water about 240 miles from Noto Peninsula, the nearest coast of Japan, or 430 miles northwest of Tokyo and 360 miles northeast of the American military base in Misaw. US experts estimated the booster was large enough to carry large conventional or nuclear warheads.

The launch did not come as a surprise. The Department of Defense had released a report in 1997 that warned that testing of the Taepo Dong-1 "could begin at any time." The Central Intelligence Agency had also been monitoring preparations for the launch for several weeks, as had the Japanese Self Defense Agency and South Korean experts. The test may have been timed for political purposes and to celebrate a North Korean holiday on September 9, 1998, and the promotion of Kim Sung II. However, it came only weeks after American intelligence agents detected work on a secret underground facility that they suspect is part of North Korea's effort to revive its nuclear weapons program.

On September 4, 1998, North Korea claimed that the purpose of the launch of a two-stage rocket was to carry a satellite into orbit, not to test a missile. It denounced Japan and other countries for jumping to the conclusion that it was launching a new class of missile. US, Japanese, and South Korean officials indicated, however, that they had not detected any new satellite.

US intelligence officers were surprised, however, to find that the missile had three, rather than two stages, and that the solid-fueled third stage might have achieved a range as great as 2,408–3,720 miles. They had initially believed that the missile was a test of the Tapeo Dong, and the test was North Korea's first successful launch of a two-stage missile.

It is possible, therefore, that North Korea could have launched the first two stages of the Taepo Dong-1 ballistic missile and tried to use the missile's third stage to place a small satellite into orbit. A US State Department official stated that the launching remained a grave concern for the administration because of the technological advances it demonstrated. "No matter the purpose, it demonstrated the capability to deliver a weapons payload against surface targets at medium ranges." US experts also felt that North Korea had made real progress in its effort to build a longer-range missile with a range of 2,400–3,400 miles. A missile with a 3,400-mile range would give North Korea the ability to strike targets throughout Asia and as far away as Alaska.

Regardless of the recent test, most experts still feel that both Tapeo Dongs are liquid-fueled missiles which have two stages. Unlike the No-Dong, the Tapeo Dongs must be carried to a site in stages and then assembled at a fixed site. The No-Dong transporter may be able to carry both stages of the Tapeo Dong-1, but some experts believe that a special transporter is needed for the first stage of the Tapeo Dong-1, and for both stages of the Tapeo Dong-2.[41] There have been some reports that Iran is seeking full scale manufacturing capability for such systems, although most experts believe that Iran and North Korea have not reached any agreement on the No-Dong program.

These developments may be more important in terms of the transfer of North Korean missile design and production technology than in terms of any new transfers of actual missiles. Even before Iran tested its own missile in July, 1998, there was considerable question as to whether the North Korean–made No-Dong and Tapeo Dong missiles would actually be transferred to Iran. The main argument was that Iran wanted to produce its own missiles and adopt more advanced technology from other countries. The CIA reported in June, 1997 that China and Russia had been Iran's primary source of missile related goods in 1996.[42] However, some experts questioned whether Iran would have the hard currency necessary to pay for major deliveries.[43] There were also Iranian sources that claimed that Iran had ended its interest in the project because it had concluded that any purchase of such systems would end in Israeli preemption.

Iranian-Built Extended-Range Missiles: The Shihab 3 and Shihab 4

It is now clear that virtually all of the technology relating to the design and manufacture of the No-Dong missile has been transferred to Iran, and that Iran is seeking to produce its own missile. Reports indicate that Iran stepped up its cooperation with North Korea in 1996 and 1997, and this had led to a steadily increasing amount of North Korean technology transfer to Iran. Some sources indicate that Iran and Syria are both cooperating with North Korea and helping to push the program forward.

This had led a number of US and Israeli experts to believe Syria and Iran still plan to buy major assembly and production facilities for the No-Dong 1, as well as missiles or missile parts. They also believed that Iran was planning to acquire at least 150 such missiles.[44] At the same time, US and Israeli reports indicated that Iran was using a mix of North Korean, Russian, and Chinese technology to develop two liquid-fueled missiles of its own, called the Shihab-3 and Shihab-4.

Iran has sought the capability to produce its own missiles ever since the first Iraqi Scud strikes on Iran during the Iran-Iraq War. It has bought missile production equipment from a wide range of sources, including Europe, the FSU, Canada, the United States, and Asia. It has obtained extensive support from North Korea and the People's Republic of China, which have supplied new missiles and are helping Iran develop its own missile technology and production capabilities. This is part of a two-track acquisition effort where Iran is acquiring complete missiles from North Korea while it improves its capability to assemble missiles in Iran, and acquires the capability to produce entire liquid and solid-fueled missiles.[45] At the same time, it has made increasing use of Russian technology and technical assistance by bypassing Russian export and security controls.

The exact scale of Iran's current production and assembly efforts is unclear. Iran does, however, have a design center, at least two rocket and missile assembly plants, a missile test range and monitoring complex, and a wide range of smaller design and refit facilities.[46] The design center is said to located at the Defense Technology and Science Research Center, which is a branch of Iran's Defense Industry Organization, and which is located outside Karaj, near Tehran. This center directs a number of other research efforts. Some experts believe it has support from Russian and Chinese scientists.[47]

Iran's largest missile assembly and production plant is said to be a North Korean-built facility near Isfahan, although this plant may use Chinese and Russian equipment and technology. There are no confirmations of these reports, but this region is the center of much of Iran's advanced defense industry, including plants for munitions, tank overhaul, and helicopter and fixed wing aircraft maintenance. Some reports say the local industrial complex can produce liquid fuels and missile parts from a local steel mill.

A second missile plant is said to be located 175 kilometers east of Tehran, near Semnan. Some sources indicate this plant is Chinese-built and began rocket production as early as 1987. It is supposed to be able to build 600–1,000 Oghab rockets per year, if Iran can import key ingredients for solid fuel motors like ammonium perchlorate. The plant is also supposed to produce the Iran-130. Another facility may exist near Bandar Abbas for the assembly of the Seersucker. China is said to have built this facility in 1987, and is believed to be helping the naval branch of the Guards to modify the Seersucker to extend its range to 400 kilometers. It is possible that China is also helping Iran develop solid-fuel rocket motors and produce or assemble missiles like the CS-801 and CS-802. There have, however, been reports that Iran is developing extended-range Scuds with the support of Russian experts, and a missile called the Tondar 68, with a range of 700 kilometers.

Still other reports claim that Iran has split its manufacturing facilities into plants near Pairzan, Seman, Shiraz, Maghdad, and Islaker. These reports indicate that the companies involved in building the Scuds are also involved in Iran's production of poison gas and include Defense Industries, Shahid, Bagheri Industrial Group, and Shahid Hemat Industrial Group.[48]

Iran's main missile test range is said to be further east, near Shahroud, along the Tehran-Mashhad railway. A telemetry station is supposed to be 350 kilometers to the south at Taba, along the Mashhad-Isfahan road. All of these facilities are reportedly under the control of the Islamic Revolutionary Guards Corps.[49]

Since the early 1990s, these design and production activities have led to an increasing number of reports that Iran was developing its own longer-range variants of No-Dong technology for indigenous production with substantial Russian and some Chinese aid. As early as 1992, one such Iranian missile was reported to have a range of 800–930 miles and a 1,650-pound warhead. Reports differ sharply on its size. Jane's estimates a launch weight up to 16,000 kilograms, provided the system is derived from the No-Dong. It could have a launch weight of 15,000 kilograms, a payload of 600 kilograms, and a range of 1,700–1,800 kilometers if it is based on a system similar to the Chinese CSS-5 (DF-21) and CSS-N3 (JL-1). These systems entered service in 1983 and 1987. A longer-range missile was said to have improved guidance components, a range of up to 1,240 miles and a warhead of up to 2,200 pounds. Iran's goals for completing design were then estimated to be 1999–2001.

Iran's programs have been reported to have had continuing support from North Korea and from Russian and Chinese firms and technicians. One such Chinese firm is Great Wall Industries. The Russian firms include the Russian Central Aerohydrodynamic Institute, which has provided Iran's Shahid Hemmat Industrial Group (SHIG) with wind tunnels for missile design, equipment for manufacturing missile models, and the software for testing launch and reentry performance. They may also include Rosvoorouzhenie, a major Russian arms-export agency; NPO Trud, a rocket motor manufacturer; a leading research center called the Bauman Institute, and Polyus (Northstar), a major laser test and manufacturing equipment firm.

The CIA reported in June, 1997 that Iran obtained major new transfers of new long-range missile technology from Russian and Chinese firms during 1996. Since that time, there have been many additional reports of technology transfer from Russia. The reports on Chinese technology transfers involved the least detail. For example, there were reports that Iran placed orders for PRC-made M-9 (CSS-6/DF-15) missiles (280–620 kilometers range, launch weight of 6,000 kilograms). It now seems more likely, however, that PRC firms were giving Iran assistance in developing indigenous missile R&D and production facilities for the production of an Iranian solid-fueled missile.

Some US experts believe that Iran carried out static tests of booster engines in 1997, which were capable of driving a missile range of 1,500 kilometers. US intelligence repeatedly warned from 1994 onwards that Iran was rapidly approaching the point where it will be able to manufacture missiles with much longer ranges than the Scud B. It is less clear when Iran will be able to bring such programs to the final development stage, carry out suitable test firings, develop effective warheads, and deploy actual units.

The first detailed, unclassified description of Iran's actual missile designs came on April 14, 1997, when Eitan Ben Eliyahu—the commander of the Israeli Air Force—reported that Iran had tested a missile capable of reaching Israel. The background briefings to his statement implied that Russia was assisting Iran in developing two missiles with ranges of 620 and 780 miles. Follow-on intelligence briefings that Israel provided in September, 1997 indicated that Russia was helping Iran develop four missiles. US intelligence briefings also indicated that China was helping Iran with some aspects of these missile efforts. Both US and Israeli intelligence sources indicated in early 1998 that Iran had completed the basic transfer of rocket motor technology and production equipment it needed from North Korea, and had already conducted up to nine rocket motor tests with Russian technicians present.

The two missiles that Israeli experts described included the Shihab (also transliterated as Shahab and Shehab and meaning "meteor") missiles, with performance similar to those previously identified with Iranian missiles adapted from North Korean designs. The Israeli reports indicated that the Shihab-3 is a liquid-fueled missile with a range of 810 miles (1,200–1,500 kilometers) and a payload of 1,550 pounds (700 kilograms). Israel claimed the Shihab might be ready for deployment as early as June, 1998. Israel also reported that Iran was developing the Shihab-4, with a range of 1,250 miles (some reports say up to 4,000 kilometers) and a payload in excess of one ton. It indicated that this system could be operational in two to five years. Israel indicated that Iran might have two other missile programs including one longer-range system with a maximum range of up to 4,500–5,500 and another of 10,000 kilometers.[50]

The same officials in the Khatami administration that repeatedly denied that Iran was interested in weapons of mass destruction were much more cautious in their statements about missiles, and some privately indicated that Iran faced continuing threats from Iraq and Israel and that the Pakistani and Indian nuclear tests showed that Iran had a "right" to such missiles.

The reason became clear on July 21, 1998. Iran tested the Shihab-3, claiming that it was a defensive action to deal with potential threats from Israel. The missile flew for a distance of up to 620 miles, before it exploded about 100 seconds after launch. US intelligence sources could not confirm whether the explosion was deliberate, but indicated that the final system might have a range of 800–940 miles (a maximum of 1,240 kilometers), depending on its payload. The test confirmed that the missile was a liquid-fueled system, and some analysts calculated that it meant the Shihab-3 might have a nominal payload of 1,650 pounds. CIA experts indicated that the test came years earlier than would have been possible without the assistance of Russian experts. The CIA also reported that North Korea, Russia, and China had continued to transfer missile technology during 1996–1998. Background briefing also indicated that the Shihab-4 had improved guidance components, a range of up to 1,240 miles and a warhead of up to 2,200 pounds.[51]

General Mohammad Bagher Qalibaf, head of the Islamic Revolutionary Guards Corps' air wing, publicly reported on August 2, 1998 that the Shihab-3 was a 53-foot-long ballistic missile that can travel at 4,300 miles per hour and carry a one-ton warhead at an altitude of nearly 820,000 feet. He claimed that the weapon was guided by an Iranian-made system that gives it great accuracy:

"The final test of every weapon is a real war situation but, given its warhead and size, the Shihab-3 is a very accurate weapon." Other Iranian sources reported that the missile had a range of 800 miles.[52]

On July 27, 1998, President Khatami defended the missile test as demonstrating Iran's right of self-defense. "The defense of the nation is a natural right . . . but the government's policies towards improving relations with various countries, especially our neighbors, has not changed." On August 1, 1998, he stated that Iran was determined to continue to strengthen its armed forces, regardless of international concerns: "Iran will not seek permission from anyone for strengthening its defense capability."[53] Defense Minister Shamkani stated that the missile was "absolutely domestically produced." He stated that it had been developed to defend against Israel, and not Iran's neighbors, and that "At the moment we do not have any plans to produce these missiles, but if we feel the need, would do so."[54]

The test did much to confirm the scale of Iran's efforts, particularly since it was clear that the payload, accuracy, and range of the missile meant that it virtually had to carry a nuclear or biological warhead to be effective. It also raised questions about Iran's longer-range efforts. Martin Indyck, the US Assistant Secretary for Near East Affairs, testified to the Senate Foreign Relations Committee on July 28 that the United States estimated that the system needed further refinement but might be deployed in its initial operational form between September, 1998 and March, 1999. He warned that the Shihab-3 would pose a threat to US forces in the Gulf region, and that the Shihab-4 would be considerably more dangerous.[55]

Iran provided further details on September 26, 1998. Iran displayed its medium-range Shihab-3 missile during a military parade. Defense Minister Ali Shamkhani took the occasion to state: "Certainly we will work on the development of the Shihab-4 and 5, but this does not mean we will start tomorrow." Shamkhani denied that Iran had received help in developing the missiles. He did say, however, that Iran would strike back at Israel if the Jewish state attacked Iran's nuclear plant in Bushehr. "We'll certainly respond firmly to any Israeli attack or aggression in a manner more severe than one can imagine, and we have the capability. The most obvious, but only the minimum, is the Shihab-3." Shamkhani would not say how many missiles Iran possessed, but said that Iran could produce as many as it needed.

The key questions now are the nature of the warheads Iran will use, whether these are designed to carry weapons of mass destruction, and the ultimate range, accuracy, and reliability of each missile. Estimates differ from one to five years for the deployment of finished systems—with much depending on continued access to Russian and Chinese expertise. It seems likely that Iran could arm either missile with a chemical or biological warhead at any point in this time frame. The timing of the availability of a nuclear warhead is much more uncertain.

Iranian Ballistic Missile Production Programs—The Chinese Option

Iran can already assemble sophisticated missiles, and it is seeking the capability to produce its own missiles. Iran has bought missile production equipment from a wide range of sources, including Europe, the former Soviet Union, Canada, the United States, and Asia. It has obtained extensive support from North Korea and the People's Republic of China, which have supplied new missiles and are helping Iran develop its own missile technology and production capabilities. This is part of a two-track acquisition effort where Iran is acquiring complete missiles from North Korea while it improves its capability to assemble missiles in Iran, and acquires the capability to produce entire liquid and solid-fueled missiles.[56]

China has been a major supplier to Iran of arms, missiles, and technology ever since the early years of the Iran-Iraq War. For example, Iran bought 150–200 CSS-8 missiles and 25–30 launchers from the People's Republic of China in 1989. The CSS-8 is a surface-to-surface conversion and upgrade of the Soviet-designed SA-2 surface-to-air missile. It has a range of approximately 150 kilometers (65 miles). The CEP of this missile is so high that it would be nothing more than a terror weapon unless its warhead was equipped with a weapon of mass destruction. There is some uncertainty as to whether such a sale is permitted under the guidelines of the Missile Technology Control Regime (MTCR), to which China has agreed to adhere. The MTCR sets a range limit of 150 kilometers for such sales.[57]

China made these transfers of arms and technology, even though it agreed on October 4, 1994, that it would observe the limits imposed by the Missile Technology Control Regime and would not transfer such missiles or technology to any other state. It has reiterated such pledges on several occasions since that time, almost inevitably after the United States has discovered a new Chinese transfer of technology to a Third World nation.[58]

China seems to have defined compliance in very broad terms. In the case of Iran, for example, China agreed to refrain from selling Iran missile systems which violate the MTCR, but then simultaneously undermined the spirit of the accord by ignoring restrictions on the transfer of components and manufacturing equipment. China has since provided extensive technical support, telemetry systems, specialized computerized tools, and dozens to hundreds of guidance systems—although some of these guidance systems may have been used for relatively simple Iranian rocket systems like the Nazeat—a system somewhat similar to the Russian FROG.[59]

There have been reports that China is actively involved in giving Iran the technology it needs to produce either an extended-range Scud or an M-9 class missile. This technology transfer would be significant because the M-9 is a modern developmental Chinese single-stage solid fueled missile with a range of about 600 kilometers, a 500–600 kilogram warhead, and a CEP of 600–1,000 meters.[60] Other reports indicate that China has provided much of the technology to Iran for its shorter-range M-11 missile program and that Iran is using this technology to develop the Tondar 68 missile. However, US experts see no evidence of Chinese transfer of the M-11 or production technology, believe that the Tondar program is an Iranian attempt to copy the CS-801/CS-802 program, and do not believe these reports have any validity.[61]

The details of such reports are uncertain, and Iran has denied getting help from China.[62] US experts feel, however, that China continues to provide Iran with long-range missile design and production technology—including solid-fuel motors, gyroscopes, accelerometers, maraging steel, specialized X-ray machines for analyzing missile casings and the quality of solid fuel assemblies, and other test equipment. There are reliable reports that Chinese firms like the China Precision Institute New Technology Corporation and Great Wall Industries work closely with Iran, and have provided support to the Shihab programs. There is one report that China is helping Iran develop a solid-fueled missile called the NP-110, with a range of up to 105 miles. This missile is said to use a solid-fueled motor of Chinese design that is 450 millimeters in diameter. Reports also surfaced in May, 1998 that China continued to supply Iran with technology like specialty steels for missile frames and bodies.[63] As has been touched upon earlier, the CIA has identified China and Russia as being Iran's main suppliers of missile technology.[64]

While the Clinton administration indicated in March, 1998 that China might have reduced its support for foreign missiles, US and Israeli experts disagree. Experts indicate that Iran held negotiations with China in April to buy advanced telemetry equipment. They also indicated the Chinese missile technicians continued to visit Iran, Libya, Pakistan, and Syria. Israeli experts also believe that China is provided telemetry for the Shihab-3 and Shihab-4 programs, and sold gyroscopes, test equipment, and accelerometers to Iran's Defense Industries Organization for its long-range missile programs. China may be selling special x-ray equipment to check the status of the solid fuel in missile boosters and look for flaws in missile casings.[65]

Iranian Ballistic Missile Production Programs—The Russian Option

Iranian officers have publicly announced that Iran is building missiles with ranges up to 500 kilometers, and many experts feel that Iran is seeking to acquire the ability to build solid and liquid-fueled missiles with ranges of 2,000 kilometers or more. Both Israeli and US experts feel that Iran has received some technology transfer from China and North Korea for such designs, and that it has obtained the technical details of the Russian SS-4 IRBM and a considerable amount of design information.[66]

Russia agreed in 1994 that it would adhere to the terms of the Missile Technology Control Regime and that it would place suitable limits on the sale or transfer of rocket engines and technology.[67] Nevertheless, the CIA has publicly identified Russia as being a leading source of Iranian missile technology ever since, and the State Department has indicated that President Clinton expressed US concerns over this cooperation to President Yeltsin.[68] This transfer is one reason the president appointed former Ambassador Frank Wisner, and then Robert Galluci, as his special representatives to try to persuade Russia to put a firm halt to aid support of Iran.[69]

The briefings Eitan Ben Eliyahu, the commander of the Israeli Air Force, gave on April 14, 1997, implied that Russia was assisting Iran in developing missiles.[70] Follow-on intelligence briefings that Israel provided in September, 1997 indicated that Russia was helping Iran develop four missiles. These missiles included the Shihab-3, the Shihab-4, and two longer-range systems.[71] The Israeli press reported in August, 1997 that Israel had evidence that Iran was receiving Russian support.[72] In September, 1997 Israel urged the United States to step up its pressure on Iran, and leaked reports indicating that private and state-owned Russian firms had provided gyroscopes, electronic components, wind tunnels, guidance and propulsion systems, and the components needed to build such systems to Iran.

The key Russian firms that US and Israeli experts were then worried about included the Russian Central Aerohydrodynamic Institute, which provided Iran's Shahid Hemmat Industrial Group (SHIG) with wind tunnels for missile design, equipment for manufacturing missile models, and the software for testing launch and reentry performance. They also included Rosvoorouzhenie, a major Russian arms-export agency; NPO Trud, a rocket motor manufacturer; a leading research center called the Bauman Institute; and Polyus (Northstar), a major laser test and manufacturing equipment firm.[73]

In late 1997, President Yeltsin and the Russian Foreign Ministry initially categorically denied that such charges were true. Following a meeting with Vice President Gore, President Yeltsin stated on September 26, 1997, that "We are being accused of supplying Iran with nuclear or ballistic missile technologies. There is nothing further from the truth. I again and again categorically deny such rumors."[74]

Russia had agreed, however, that Ambassador Wisner and Yuri Koptyev, the head of the Russian space program, should jointly examine the US intelligence and draft a report on Russian transfers to Iran. This report reached a very different conclusion from President Yeltsin and concluded that Russia had provided such aid to Iran. Further, on October 1, 1997—roughly a week after Yeltsin issued his denial—the Russian security service issued a statement that it had "thwarted" an Iranian attempt to have parts for liquid fuel rocket motors manufactured in Russia, disguised as gas compressors and pumps.[75]

Since that time, the list of Russian firms helping Iran has grown longer, and includes both the "usual suspects" and several new ones. It includes:[76]

- The Russian Central Aerohydrodynamic Institute which, developed a special wind tunnel; Rosvoorouzhenie, a major Russian arms-export agency. Rosvoorouzhenie and Infor are reported to be involved in deals with the SHIG. These deals are said to include specialized laser equipment, mirrors, tungsten-coat graphite material, and maraging steel for missile development and production;[77]

- Kutznetzov (formerly NPO Trud), a rocket motor manufacturer in Samara;

- The Bauman National Technical University in Moscow, a research center involved in developing rocket propulsion systems;

- The Polyus (Northstar) Research Institute in Moscow, a major laser test and manufacturing equipment firm;

- The Tikhomirov Instrument Building State Research Institute in Moscow, which sent technicians to Iran using false documents indicating that their end destination was Tajikistan;

- The Komintern Plant in Novosibirsk, which sent technicians to Iran using false documents indicating that their end destination was Tajikistan;

- The Tsagi Research Institute, for rocket propulsion development; and

- The Grafit State Scientific Research Institute, which shipped graphite materials to coat missile warheads for reentry to Iran via Austria.

Iranians have been found to be studying rocket engineering at the Baltic State Technical University (also known as the Ustinov Military Mechanical Baltic State Technical University) in St. Petersburg and the Bauman State University.

Russia was also found to have sold Iran high-strength steel and special foil for its long-range missile program, although the Russian government seems to have intercepted some shipments.[78] The Russian Scientific and Production Center Inor concluded an agreement as late as September, 1997 to sell Iran a factory to produce four special metal alloys used in long-range missiles. Inor's director, L. P. Chromova, worked out a deal with A. Asgharzadeh, the director of an Iranian factory, to sell 620 kilograms of a special alloy called 21HKMT, and to provide Iran with the capability to thermally treat the alloy for missile bodies. Iran had previously bought 240 kilograms of the alloy. Inor was also selling alloy foils called 49K2F, CUBE2, and 50N in sheets 0.2–0.4 millimeters thick for the outer body of missiles. The alloy 21HKMT was particularly interesting because North Korea also uses it in missile designs. Inor had previously brokered deals with the Shahid Hemat Industrial Group in Iran to supply maraging steel for missile cases, composite graphite-tungsten material, laser equipment, and special mirrors used in missile tests.[79]

These discoveries led to a new and often tense set of conversations between the United States and Russia in January, 1998. The United States again sent Ambassador Frank Wisner to Moscow, Vice President Gore called Prime Minister Viktor Chernomyrdin, and Secretary of State Madeleine Albright made an indirect threat that the Congress might apply sanctions. Sergi Yastrzhembsky, a

Kremlin spokesman, initially responded by denying that any transfer of technology had taken place.[80]

This denial was too categorical to have much credibility. Russia had previously announced the arrest of an Iranian diplomat on November 14, 1997, that it caught attempting to buy missile technology. The Iranian was seeking to buy blueprints and recruit Russian scientists to go to Iran. Yuri Koptev, the head of the Russian Space Agency, explained this, however, by stating that,

> There have been several cases where some Russian organizations, desperately struggling to make ends meet and lacking responsibility, have embarked on some ambiguous projects ... they were stopped long before they got to the point where any technology got out.[81]

The end result of these talks was an agreement by Gore and Chernomyrdin to strengthen controls over transfer technology, but it was scarcely clear that it put an end to the problem.[82]

Discussions with senior Russian officials from the MVD (Russian Military Intelligence), Foreign Intelligence Service, and diplomatic service in June, 1998 confirmed the fact that Russia was aware that the transfer of missile technology was broader than officially admitted. These discussions also indicated that the Russian officials involved did not feel the central government was strong enough to control the transfer of technology by individual experts and companies, and that some elements of the government deliberately turned a blind eye to such transfers.

Russian technology transfer may involve some very long-range systems, with a range of 3,500 to 6,250 kilometers.[83] Some reports indicate that Iran is using a combination of Russian, Chinese, and North Korean technology to develop a solid-fueled missile known as the Zezal-3, with a range of up to 1,500 kilometers and a CEP in excess of 4 kilometers. According to such reports, both Russian and Chinese experts have provided assistance in this design effort. The China Precision Engineering Institute is also reported to have agreed to sell Iran missile gyroscopes, accelerometers, and test equipment.[84]

It seems clear that Iran has obtained some of the technology and design details of the Russian SS-4. The SS-4 (also known as the R-12 or "Sandal") is an aging Russian liquid-fuel design that first went into service in 1959, and which was supposedly destroyed as part of the IRBM Treaty. It is a very large missile, with technology dating back to the early 1950s, although it was evidently updated at least twice during the period between 1959 and 1980. It has a CEP of 2–4 kilometers and a maximum range of 2,000 kilometers, which means it can only be lethal with a nuclear warhead or a biological weapon with near-nuclear lethality.

At the same time, the SS-4's overall technology is relatively simple, and it has a throwweight of nearly 1,400 kilograms (3,000 pounds). It is one of the few missile designs that a nation with a limited technology base could hope to manufacture or adapt, and its throwweight and range would allow Iran to use a relatively unsophisticated nuclear device or biological warhead. As a result, an updated version of the SS-4 might be a suitable design for a developing country.[85]

There seems little prospect that a divided and economically crippled Russia can bring a firm end to such transfers, even if many elements in the central government would like to do so. There is no honor either among thieves or de facto kleptocracies. In fact, in May, 1998, Nikolai Kovalev, the head of the Russian Federal Security Service (FSB), accused the United States of running sting operations in Russia to trap the sources to such transfers. In passing, he revealed that Russia had stopped at least 12 cases of illegal exports.[86] The Clinton administration has vetoed new sanctions legislation that the Congress targeted against such transfers on the grounds that it would disrupt other useful programs, such as reducing Russia's nuclear stockpile, without doing any good. This may well be true, but it is unclear that further meetings and negotiations are going to solve the problem.

Some sources have indicated that Russian military industries have signed contracts with Iran to help produce liquid-fueled missiles and provide specialized wind tunnels, manufacture model missiles, and develop specialized computer software. For example, these reports indicate that the Russian Central Aerohydrodynamic Institute is cooperating with Iran's Defense Industries Organization (DIO) and the DIO's Shahid Hemmat Industrial Group (SHIG). The Russian State Corporation for Export and Import or Armament and Military Equipment (Rosvoorouzhenie) and Infor are also reported to be involved in deals with the SHIG. These deals are also said to include specialized laser equipment, mirrors, tungsten-coast graphite material, and maraging steel for missile development and production. They could play a major role in helping Iran develop long-range versions of the Scud B and C, and more accurate variations of a missile similar to the No-Dong.[87]

At the same time, the spokesman for the US State Department has stated that Russia has not sold Iran advanced missiles—although he did not totally discount technology transfers or possible negotiations. He also noted that any such transfer of weapons would be a violation of President Yeltsin's pledge to the United States in 1994 to not engage in major new weapons sales to Iran. The United States has never issued such a disclaimer regarding Chinese and North Korean sales and technology transfers to Iran. In fact, it has taken the opposite position.[88]

Iranian Ballistic Missile Production Programs—Other Options

Until it tested the Shihab, Iran reacted to US efforts to deny it missile technology from China and Russia by rejecting the US efforts as "propaganda." It also claimed that the United States was trying to cover up its recent delivery of advanced long-range warplanes to Israel. On January 21, 1998, Foreign Ministry spokesman Mahmoud Mohammadi termed remarks by American officials on Chinese and Russian sales of missiles technology "a propagandistic sensationalism." Tehran radio reported that, "Mohammadi said the unfounded propaganda by America about Iran's cooperation with China and Russia on missiles aimed to cover up Washington's sale of modern F-15 fighters to the Zionist regime (Israel) and its backing of this regime's expansionistic policies in the Middle East region."[89]

This had led some Western sources to ignore or minimize the problem. The most glaring example is a report by the Stockholm Institute of Peace Research Institute that argued that Iran had reversed its policy towards acquiring long-range missiles and is no longer seeking Chinese, North Korean, or Russian missiles. This report argued that Iran had concluded that there was too great a risk of an Israeli preemptive attack, and that Iran had decided to abandon its missile efforts because it cannot defend against such an Israeli strike. While this report is based on interviews in Iran and the statements of Iranian officials, it seems to be little more than a credulous reflection of Iran's long-standing efforts to achieve plausible deniability in every aspect of its efforts to acquire weapons of mass destruction and improved delivery systems.[90]

There is no way to reconcile the different unclassified estimates of Iran's current missile production facilities. It seems clear from discussions with US, British, French, and German experts, however, that Iran's plants already have the ability to assemble large numbers of North Korean and PRC-supplied missile systems. In fact, the German government had traced at least 10 Iranian efforts to buy suitable dual-use or controlled components for missile development and production from German firms during the course of 1996–1997, including gyroscopes and missile targeting systems.[91] There also seems to be a broad consensus among such experts that Iranian denials must be discounted and that Iran is developing the capability to build whole missiles and produce major components.

Such experts feel that such efforts still face important limits, in part because of North Korea's growing economic problems and inability to develop its intermediate range missiles, in part because China has avoided high-profile technology transfers and is having problems in producing its own "M-9" series, and in part because Russian transfer and support remain illegal, inefficient, and limited in scope. At the same time, such experts feel that Iran is slowly acquiring enough technology to eventually design and produce missiles with ranges up to 1,000 kilometers, and it is virtually certain that Iran's efforts are focused on arming such missiles with biological and/or nuclear weapons.

As has been explained earlier, Iran has little, if any, incentive to seek missiles armed with conventional warheads. Many US and European experts feel that Iran now has the capability to equip its existing Scud missiles with Sarin and Lewisite warheads, and possibly biological weapons. They also believe that

Iranian technicians have sufficient expertise to realize that the probable "error budget" limiting the accuracy of an Iranian-produced missile with ranges much in excess of 500 kilometers would be so high that only highly lethal biological and/or nuclear weapons would allow them to inflict high levels of damage, even against such large, vulnerable area targets as cities.

POSSIBLE CRUISE MISSILES

It is possible that Iran may develop a cruise missile that could be armed with weapons of mass destruction, using Chinese and other foreign assistance, although there is no current evidence that it is doing so. Iran has experience with similar systems and fired at least 10 Chinese-made, land-based, anti-ship cruise missiles at targets along the Kuwaiti coast during the period 1987–1988—hitting targets like Kuwait's sea island and a US-flagged oil tanker.

While Iran has no capability to develop and deploy a missile as sophisticated as the Tomahawk (TLAM) missile, US studies indicate that Third World nations like Iran and Iraq may be able to build a cruise missile about half the size of a small fighter aircraft and with a payload of about 500 kilograms by 2000–2005. Such missiles would cost only 10% to 25% as much as ballistic missiles of similar range, and both the HY-2 Seersucker and CS-802 could be modified relatively quickly for land attacks against area targets.

Iran reported in December, 1995 that it had already fired a domestically built anti-ship missile called the Saeqe-4 (Thunderbolt) during exercises in the Strait of Hormuz and Gulf of Oman.[92] Other reports indicate that China is helping Iran build copies of the Chinese CS-801/CS-802 and the Chinese FL-2 or F-7 anti-ship cruise missiles. These missiles have relatively limited range. The range of the CS-801 is 8–40 kilometers, the range of the CS-802 is 15–120 kilometers, the maximum range of the F-7 is 30 kilometers, and the maximum range of the FL-10 is 50 kilometers. Even a range of 120 kilometers would barely cover targets in the Southern Gulf from launch points on Iran's Gulf coast. These missiles also have relatively small high explosive warheads. As a result, Iran may well be seeking anti-ship capabilities rather than platforms for delivering weapons of mass destruction.[93]

A platform like the CS-802 might, however, provide enough design data to develop a scaled-up, longer-range cruise missile for other purposes, and the Gulf is a relatively small area where most urban areas and critical facilities are near the coast. Aircraft or ships could launch cruise missiles with chemical or biological warheads from outside the normal defense perimeter of the Southern Gulf states, and it is at least possible that Iran might modify anti-ship missiles with chemical weapons to attack tankers—ships which are too large for most regular anti-ship missiles to be highly lethal.

Building an entire cruise missile would be more difficult. The technology for fusing CBW and cluster warheads would be within Iran's grasp. Navigation systems and jet engines, however, would still be a major potential problem. Current inertial navigation systems (INS) would introduce errors of at least several kilometers at ranges of 1,000 kilometers and would carry a severe risk of total guidance failure—probably exceeding two-thirds of the missiles fired. A differential global positioning system (GPS) integrated with the INS and a radar altimeter, however, might produce an accuracy of 15 meters. Some existing remotely piloted vehicles (RPVs), such as the South African Skua, claim such performance. Commercial technology is becoming available for differential GPS guidance with accuracies of 2 to 5 meters.

There are commercially available reciprocating and gas turbine engines Iran could adapt for use in a cruise missile, although finding a reliable and an efficient turbofan engine for a specific design application might be difficult. An extremely efficient engine would have to be matched to a specific airframe. It is doubtful that Iran could design and build such an engine, but there are over 20 other countries with the necessary design and manufacturing skills. While airframe-engine-warhead integration and testing would still present a challenge and might be beyond Iran's manufacturing skills, it is inherently easier to integrate and test a cruise missile than a long-range ballistic missile. Further, such developments would be far less detectable than developing a ballistic system if the program used coded or low-altitude directional telemetry. Iran could also bypass much of the problems inherent in developing its own cruise missile by modifying the HY-2 Seersucker for use as a land attack weapon and extending its range beyond 80 kilometers, or by modifying and improving the CS-801 (Ying Jai-1) anti-ship missile. There are reports that the Revolutionary Guards are working on such developments at a facility near Bandar Abbas.[94]

Cruise missiles offer Iran a number of advantages in delivering weapons of mass destruction, particularly chemical and biological weapons. They fly relatively slowly at low-to-medium altitudes and can be developed at virtually any scale from small drones to fighter-sized systems. Most designs are likely to be much cheaper than ballistic missiles, and Gulf and other regional low-altitude air defenses are generally of relatively low quality and readiness. Cruise missiles can be tailored around the desired range-payload, the warhead can be relatively simple, and the missile can deliver a biological or chemical agent slowly in a line-source attack—the optimal manner of delivering biological agents. GPS guidance is more than accurate enough for most biological and chemical attacks, and a larger cruise missile could have precise altitude data. It is also possible that a specially designed cruise missile might be sent into a target area before a biologically or chemically armed missile to develop suitable weather and wind data, or to be modified for target acquisition and battle damage assessment data.

Such cruise missile systems could reach a wide range of targets. A longer-range cruise missile system with a 500 kilometer range—deployed in Iran's border areas—could cover most of Iraq, eastern Turkey, all of Kuwait, the Gulf coast of Saudi Arabia, Bahrain, most of Qatar, the northern UAE, and northern Oman. A system with a 1,200 kilometer range could reach Israel, the eastern two-thirds of Turkey, most of Saudi Arabia, and all of the other Southern Gulf states, including Oman. Such a system could also be programmed to avoid major air defense concentrations at a sacrifice of about 20% of its range. At the same time, the usual cautions apply to Iran's probable success in developing effective systems. It is far easier to postulate technical success than it is to achieve it in the real world, and even large cruise missiles and drones would present major systems integration, manufacturing, and test and evaluation problems.

NOTES

1. The following details of the Iranian missile program are taken from W. Seth Carus and Joseph S. Bermudez, "Iran's Growing Missile Forces," *Jane's Defense Weekly*, July 23, 1988, pp. 126–131.

2. Iran publicly displayed the Oghab at a military show in Libreville in 1989. It is 230 mm in diameter, 4,820 mm long, and weighs 320 kilograms, with a 70 kilogram warhead. Iran also displayed another rocket called the Nazeat, which is 355 mm in diameter, 5,900 mm long, weighs 950 kilograms, and has a 180 kilogram warhead. *Jane's Defense Weekly*, February 11, 1989, p. 219; Lora Lumpe, Lisbeth Gronlund, and David C. Wright, "Third World Missiles Fall Short," *The Bulletin of the Atomic Scientists*, March, 1992, pp. 30–36.

3. *Jane's Defense Weekly*, June 20, 1987, p. 1289; Lora Lumpe, Lisbeth Gronlund, and David C. Wright, "Third World Missiles Fall Short," *The Bulletin of the Atomic Scientists*, March, 1992, pp. 30–36.

4. Some estimates indicate a range of up to 200 kilometers. For background on the system, see *Financial Times*, June 8, 1988, p. 20, and *The Middle East*, April, 1988, pp. 1 and 18.

5. Force estimates are based on the IISS, *Military Balance, 1997–1998*, and Office of the Secretary of Defense, *Proliferation: Threat and Response*, Washington, Department of Defense, April, 1996.

6. The author participated in one such exercise during the time he was stationed at the US embassy in Tehran.

7. Office of the Secretary of Defense, *Proliferation: Threat and Response*, Washington, Department of Defense, April, 1996, pp. 12–16; W. Seth Carus and Joseph S. Bermudez, "Iran's Growing Missile Forces," *Jane's Defense Weekly*, July 23, 1988, pp. 126–131.

8. For additional details, see Anthony H. Cordesman, *Iran and Iraq: The Threat from the Northern Gulf*, Boulder, Westview, 1994; Office of the Secretary of Defense, *Proliferation: Threat and Response*, Washington, Department of Defense, April, 1996, pp. 12–16; and Roger C. Herdman, Director, *Technologies Underlying Weapons of Mass Destruction*, Office of Technology Assessment, US Congress, OTA-BP-ISC-115, December, 1993, Washington, GPO, pp. 197–255.

9. *Jane's Defense Weekly*, May 1, 1996, p. 3, May 8, 1996, p. 4.

10. Associated Press-NY, 10–18–97, 1731 EDT.

11. Defense Intelligence Agency, *The Scud Missile: An Unclassified Overview for Policy Makers*, forwarded under U-3,148/SVI-FOIA, October 22, 1997; Edward L. Korb, ed., *The World's Missile Systems, Seventh Edition*, General Dynamics, Pomona Division, April, 1982, pp. 223–226; *Christian Science Monitor*, December 27, 1993, p. 4; *Washington Times*, February 25, 1994, p. A-15, June 16, 1994, p. A-13. The reader should be aware that all such performance data are nominal, and that various sources report significant differences in given performance characteristics. The Soviet Union is also reported to have had two more advanced versions of the missile which have not been exported. One of these is reported to be a larger missile and has more range. It is 12.2 meters long, 1 meter in diameter, weighs 10,000 kilograms, and has a range of 450 kilometers. The other is the "Scud D" (SS-1e), which is reported to have been designed to deliver submunition busses and is more accurate than previous Scuds. It entered Soviet service in the early 1980s. It has a maximum range of 180–190 miles (290–310 kilometers) with its normal conventional payload, and a maximum flight time of 325 seconds. US experts do not believe such missiles have been deployed, although a Russian Scud B does exist with a longer, specialized warhead. There are no indications that such missiles have been sent to Iran.

12. Office of the Secretary of Defense, *Proliferation: Threat and Response*, Washington, Department of Defense, April, 1996, pp. 12–16; CRS Report for Congress, *Missile Proliferation: Survey of Emerging Missile Forces*, Congressional Research Service, Report 88–642F, February 9, 1989, pp. 52–53.

13. Defense Intelligence Agency, *The Scud Missile: An Unclassified Overview for Policy Makers*, forwarded under U-3,148/SVI-FOIA, October 22, 1997; Edward L. Korb, ed., *The World's Missile Systems, Seventh Edition*, General Dynamics, Pomona Division, April, 1982, pp. 223–226; Office of the Secretary of Defense, *Proliferation: Threat and Response*, Washington, Department of Defense, April, 1996, pp. 12–16.

14. Defense Intelligence Agency, *The Scud Missile: An Unclassified Overview for Policy Makers*, forwarded under U-3,148/SVI-FOIA, October 22, 1997; Edward L. Korb, ed., *The World's Missile Systems, Seventh Edition*, General Dynamics, Pomona Division, April, 1982, pp. 223–226; *Christian Science Monitor*, December 27, 1993, p. 4; *Washington Times*, February 25, 1994, p. A-15, June 16, 1994, p. A-13. The reader should be aware that all such performance data are nominal, and that various sources report significant differences in given performance characteristics. The Soviet Union is also reported to have had two more advanced versions of the missile which have not been exported. One of these is reported to be a larger missile and has more range. It is 12.2 meters long, 1 meter in diameter, weighs 10,000 kilograms, and has a range of 450 kilometers. The other is the "Scud D" (SS-1e), which is reported to have been designed to deliver submunition busses and is more accurate than previous Scuds. It entered Soviet service in the early 1980s. It has a maximum range of 180–190 miles (290–310 kilometers) with its normal conventional payload, and a maximum flight time of 325 seconds. US experts do not believe such missiles have been deployed, although a Russian Scud B does exist with a longer, specialized warhead. There are no indications that such missiles have been sent to Iran.

15. "US Reasserts Aim to Keep Oil Flowing From Persian Gulf," *Washington Times* (February 22, 1984), p. A-1.

16. "Iraqis Fire Missiles on Iranian Cities," *Chicago Tribune* (February 25, 1984), p. 20.

17. Iran had to target an inherently inaccurate missile without the kind of maps, satellite aids, and other targeting systems to correct for the fact that the world is not perfectly round, and the inevitable bias errors in the missile's guidance systems. Beyond visual range targeting in excess of 200 miles is a major problem for nations without extensive test ranges and satellite or other advanced intelligence systems.

18. The following details of the Iranian missile program are taken from W. Seth Carus and Joseph S. Bermudez, "Iran's Growing Missile Forces," *Jane's Defense Weekly*, July 23, 1988, pp. 126–131.

19. Iran publicly displayed the Oghab at a military show in Libreville in 1989. It is 230 mm in diameter, 4,820 mm long, and weighs 320 kilograms, with a 70 kilogram warhead. Iran also displayed another rocket called the Nazeat, which is 355 mm in diameter, 5,900 mm long, weighs 950 kilograms, and has a 180 kilogram warhead. *Jane's Defense Weekly*, February 11, 1989, p. 219.

20. *Jane's Defense Weekly*, June 20, 1987, p. 1289.

21. One source claims that Iran fired 231 Scuds in 1988. This total seems much too high. See Steven Zaloga, "Ballistic Missiles in the Third World," *International Defense Review*, 11/1988, pp. 1423–1437.

22. Baghdad has 23% of Iraq's population and is only 80 miles from the border. Tehran is about 290 miles from the front lines.

23. Iraq was only believed to have about 50 Scud missiles before it began this series of attacks. Rafsanjani claimed Iran had evidence that the missiles were standard Scud Bs which used reduced warhead weight on March 8, 1988. *Washington Times*, March 1, 1988, p. 3, and *Washington Post*, March 9, 1988, p. A-19. *Economist*, March 5, 1988, p. 44; *New York Times*, March 2, 1988, p. A-1, March 4, 1988, p. A-8, March 12, 1988, p. A-3, May 1, 1988, p. 18; *Washington Post*, March 2, 1988, p. A-16; *Baltimore Sun*, March 6, 1988, p. 2-A.

24. Baghdad has 23% of Iraq's population and is only 80 miles from the border. Tehran is about 290 miles from the front lines.

25. Steven Zaloga provides the following estimate of missile firings during the course of the war:

	Iraqi Firings		Iranian Firings	
	FROG-7	Scud	Oghab	Scud
1980	10	-	-	-
1981	54	-	-	-
1982	1	3	-	-
1983		33	-	-
1984	2	25	-	-
1985	-	82	14	-
1986	-	-	8	18
1987	-	25	18	61
1988	-	193	231	104
Total	67	361	271	183

Source: Adapted from Steven Zaloga, "Ballistic Missiles in the Third World," *International Defense Review*, 11/88, pp. 1423–1437. Zaloga seems to have inverted the Iranian Scud and Oghab columns in his original article.

26. Based on discussions with Iranians present in the city at the time, Australian intelligence officers, and Robin Wright.

27. The warhead may have been as small as 130 kilograms. Iraq announced in April, 1988, however, that it had an improved missile called the El-Abbas, with a maximum range of 850 kilometers and a payload of 500–1,000 kilograms at a range of 650 kilometers. *Jane's Defense Weekly*, October 29, 1988, p. 1045.

28. No missiles with chemical warheads were launched during the conflict, although Iraq did make extensive use of bombs, canisters, mortars, and 130 mm and 155 mm artillery shells (UN working paper).

29. These comments as based largely on interviews. Also see Associated Press, July 11, 1996, 0720; *Jane's Defense Weekly*, July 17, 1996, p. 3.

30. These comments as based largely on interviews. Also see *Jane's Defense Weekly*, March 4, 1995, p. 18.

31. Iran allowed a Northern Korean freighter, the Dae Hung Ho, to dock at Bandar Abbas and transshipped to missiles by air. Syria is reported to have allowed Iran to deliver arms to the Hezbollah and Party of God in Lebanon in return. *Defense News*, October 16, 1989, p. 60, January 17, 1994, p. A-1; Office of the Secretary of Defense, *Proliferation: Threat and Response*, Washington, Department of Defense, April, 1996, pp. 12–16; *Washington Times*, June 18, 1990, p. A-1, March 10, 1992, p. A-3; Lora Lumpe, Lisbeth Gronlund, and David C. Wright, "Third World Missiles Fall Short," *The Bulletin of the Atomic Scientists*, March, 1992, pp. 30–36; *Mednews*, Vols. 5, 16, May 18, 1992, pp. 1–5; *Newsweek*, June 22, 1992, pp. 42–44; *Washington Times*, May 24, 1991, p. 5, October 23, 1993, p. A-6, February 24, 1994, p. A-15, June 16, 1994, p. A-13; Gordon Jacobs and Tim McCarthy, "China Missile Sales—Few Changes for the Future," *Jane's Intelligence Review*, December, 1992, pp. 559–563; *Wall Street Journal*, July 19, 1993, p. A-6; *New York Times*, April 8, 1993, p. A-9; *Jane's Defense Weekly*, July 24, 1993, p. 7, January 15, 1994, p. 4, May 7, 1994, p. 1; *Aviation Week*, July 5, 1993, p. 17; Agence France Press, January 4, 1995; *Christian Science Monitor*, December 27, 1993, p. 4.

32. Defense Intelligence Agency, *The Scud Missile: An Unclassified Overview for Policy Makers*, forwarded under U-3,148/SVI-FOIA, October 22, 1997; Associated Press, July 11, 1996, 0720; *Jane's Defense Weekly*, July 17, 1996, p. 3.

33. Some US experts believe that Iran has less than 100 missiles. *Jane's Defense Weekly*, May 13, 1995, p. 5; July 17, 1996, p. 3.

34. Dr. Robert A. Nagler, *Ballistic Missile Proliferation: An Emerging Threat*, Systems Planning Corporation, Arlington, 1992.

35. *Defense and Foreign Affairs*, No. 1, 1994, pp. 4–7; *Baltimore Sun*, March 9, 1989; *New York Times*, March 12, 1992, p. A-12, March 18, 1992, p. A-12; *Washington Post*, February 2, 1992, p. A-1; Lora Lumpe, Lisbeth Gronlund, and David C. Wright, "Third World Missiles Fall Short," *The Bulletin of the Atomic Scientists*, March, 1992, p. 30–36; "North Korea Corners ME Missile Market," *Mednews*, Vols. 5, 16, May 18, 1992, pp. 1–5; *Newsweek*, June 22, 1992, pp. 42–44; Gordon Jacobs and Tim McCarthy, "China Missile Sales—Few Changes for the Future," *Jane's Intelligence Review*, December, 1992, pp. 559–563; *Jerusalem Post*, November 6, 1993, p. 24; Office of the Secretary of Defense, *Proliferation: Threat and Response*, Washington, Department of Defense, April, 1996, pp. 12–16.

36. *Jane's Intelligence Review*, Special Report No. 6, May, 1995, pp. 16–18.
37. *Jane's Intelligence Review*, Special Report No. 6, May, 1995, pp. 16–18; *Washington Times*, October 23, 1993, p. A-6, February 24, 1994, p. A-15, June 16, 1994, p. A-13; Gordon Jacobs and Tim McCarthy, "China Missile Sales—Few Changes for the Future," *Jane's Intelligence Review*, December, 1992, pp. 559–563; *Wall Street Journal*, July 19, 1993, p. A-6; *New York Times*, April 8, 1993, p. A-9; *Jane's Defense Weekly*, July 24, 1993, p. 7, January 15, 1994, p. 4, May 7, 1994, p. 1, April 30, 1997, p. 5; *Aviation Week*, July 5, 1993, p. 17; Agence France Press, January 4, 1995; *Christian Science Monitor*, December 27, 1993, p. 4, December 27, 1993, p. 4.
38. *Jane's Intelligence Review*, Special Report, No. 6, May, 1995, pp. 16–18; *Washington Times*, October 23, 1993, p. A-6, February 24, 1994, p. A-15, June 16, 1994, p. A-13; Gordon Jacobs and Tim McCarthy, "China Missile Sales—Few Changes for the Future," *Jane's Intelligence Review*, December, 1992, pp. 559–563; *Wall Street Journal*, July 19, 1993, p. A-6; *New York Times*, April 8, 1993, p. A-9; *Jane's Defense Weekly*, July 24, 1993, p. 7, January 15, 1994, p. 4, May 7, 1994, p. 1, April 30, 1997, p. 5; *Aviation Week*, July 5, 1993, p. 17; Agence France Press, January 4, 1995; *Christian Science Monitor*, December 27, 1993, p. 4, December 27, 1993, p. 4.
39. Defense Intelligence Agency, *The Scud Missile: An Unclassified Overview for Policy Makers*, forwarded under U-3,148/SVI-FOIA, October 22, 1997; *Jane's Defense Weekly*, May 28, 1997, p. 4.
40. Defense Intelligence Agency, *The Scud Missile: An Unclassified Overview for Policy Makers*, forwarded under U-3,148/SVI-FOIA, October 22, 1997; *Jane's Intelligence Review*, Special Report No. 6, May, 1995, pp. 16–18; *Washington Times*, October 23, 1993, p. A-6, February 24, 1994, p. A-15, June 16, 1994, p. A-13; Gordon Jacobs and Tim McCarthy, "China Missile Sales—Few Changes for the Future," *Jane's Intelligence Review*, December, 1992, pp. 559–563; *Wall Street Journal*, July 19, 1993, p. A-6; *New York Times*, April 8, 1993, p. A-9; *Jane's Defense Weekly*, July 24, 1993, p. 7, January 15, 1994, p. 4, May 7, 1994, p. 1, April 30, 1997, p. 5, May 28, 1997, p. 4; *Aviation Week*, July 5, 1993, p. 17; Agence France Press, January 4, 1995; *Christian Science Monitor*, December 27, 1993, p. 4, December 27, 1993, p. 4.
41. *Jane's Defense Weekly*, March 19, 1994, May 7, 1994, p. 1; January 15, 1994, p. 4, November 11, 1995, p. 16; *Washington Times*, February 25, 1994, p. A-15; *Jane's Intelligence Review*, Special Report, No. 6, May, 1995, pp. 16–18.
42. Director of Central Intelligence, "The Acquisition of Technology Relating to Weapons of Mass Destruction and Advanced Conventional Munitions," Washington, Central Intelligence Agency, June, 1997.
43. Director of Central Intelligence, "The Acquisition of Technology Relating to Weapons of Mass Destruction and Advanced Conventional Munitions," Washington, Central Intelligence Agency, June 1997.
44. *Jane's Intelligence Review*, Special Report, No. 6, May, 1995, pp. 16–18; *Washington Times*, October 23, 1993, p. A-6, February 24, 1994, p. A-15, June 16, 1994, p. A-13; Gordon Jacobs and Tim McCarthy, "China Missile Sales—Few Changes for the Future," *Jane's Intelligence Review*, December, 1992, pp. 559–563; *Wall Street Journal*, July 19, 1993, p. A-6; *New York Times*, April 8, 1993, p. A-9; *Jane's Defense Weekly*, July 24, 1993, p. 7, January 15, 1994, p. 4, May 7, 1994, p. 1, April 30, 1997, p. 5; *Aviation Week*, July 5, 1993, p. 17; Agence France Press, January 4, 1995; *Christian Science Monitor*, December 27, 1993, p. 4, December 27, 1993, p. 4.

45. Kenneth Katzman, "Iran: Arms and Technology Acquisitions," Library of Congress, CRS-97–474F, October 1, 1997; Kenneth Katzman, "Iran: Military Relations With China," Library of Congress, CRS-967–572F, June 26, 1996; Shirley A. Kan, "Chinese Proliferation of Weapons of Mass Destruction, Background and Analysis," Library of Congress, CRS-96–767F, September 13, 1996.

46. See "Iran's Ballistic Missile Program," *Middle East Defense News, Mednews*, December 21, 1992, Vol. 6, No. 6; Office of the Secretary of Defense, *Proliferation: Threat and Response*, Washington, Department of Defense, April, 1996, pp. 12–16; Gordon Jacobs and Tim McCarthy, "China Missile Sales—Few Changes for the Future," *Jane's Intelligence Review*, December, 1992, pp. 559–563; James Wyllie, "Iran—Quest for Security and Influence," *Jane's Intelligence Review*, July 1993, pp. 311–312; and material in Patrick Clawson, *Iran's Challenge to the West, How, When, and Why*, Washington, The Washington Institute Policy Papers, Number Thirty Three, 1993; Dr. Anoushiravan Ehteshami, "The Armed Forces of the Islamic Republic of Iran," *Jane's Intelligence Review*, February 1993, pp. 76–80; *New York Times*, June 22, 1995, p. A-1; *Washington Post*, June 17, 1995, p. A-14; *Jane's Defense Weekly*, July 1, 1995, p. 3.

47. *International Defense Review, Extra*, 2/1997, p. 5.

48. *Insight*, February 27, 1995, p. 13; Agence France Presse, January 4, 1995, 05:22.

49. *Jane's Intelligence Review*, Special Report, No. 6, May, 1995, pp. 16–18.

50. *Defense News*, February 2–8, 1998, p. 8.

51. *Washington Times*, July 23, 1998, p. A-1, July 24, 1998, p. A-1; *New York Times*, July 23, 1998, p. A-1, July 24, 1998, p. A-6; *Jane's Defense Weekly*, July 29, 1998, p. 5, August 12, 1998, p. 18.

52. Associated Press, August 2, 1998, 1614, *The Estimate*, July 31, 1998, p. 4.

53. Reuters, July 27, 1998, 0714.

54. *Washington Post*, July 30, 1998, p. A-22; Associated Press, July 30, 1998, 0827.

55. *Washington Times*, July 29, 1998, p. A-12.

56. Kenneth Katzman, "Iran: Arms and Technology Acquisitions," Library of Congress, CRS-97–474F, October 1, 1997; Kenneth Katzman, "Iran: Military Relations With China," Library of Congress, CRS-967–572F, June 26, 1996; Shirley A. Kan, "Chinese Proliferation of Weapons of Mass Destruction, Background and Analysis," Library of Congress, CRS-96–767F, September 13, 1996.

57. US State Department press release, "Joint US-PRC Statement on Missile Proliferation," Washington, DC, October 4, 1994; Office of the Secretary of Defense, *Proliferation: Threat and Response*, Washington, Department of Defense, April, 1996, pp. 12–16; Robert Shuey and Shirley A. Kan, *Chinese Missile and Nuclear Proliferation*, Congressional Research Service, IB92056, October 4, 1994; *Jane's Intelligence Review*, Special Report No. 6, May, 1995, pp. 16–18.

58. Both the Iranian Foreign Minister, Ali Akbar Velayati, and the Chinese Foreign Minister, Qian Qichen, denied new reports of Chinese transfers of missile technology and the chemicals to produce nerve gas in November, 1996. These reports were based on background briefings by the CIA. *Washington Times*, November 24, 1996, p. A-9.

59. Interviews, *Washington Times*, September 10, 1997, p. A-1.

60. *New York Times*, June 22, 1995, *Baltimore Sun*, June 23, 1995, p. 9-A; *Defense News*, June 19, 1995, p. 1; *Insight*, February 27, 1995, p. 13; *Jane's Intelligence Review*, Special Report No. 6, May, 1995, pp. 16–18.

61. For conflicting reports of leaks of US intelligence reporting on such Chinese actions, see *Washington Times*, December 5, 1994, p. A-14, November 21, 1996, p. A-1; November 23, 1996, p. A-1, November 24, 1996, p. A-9. Also see Joseph S. Bermudez, "Iran's Missile Development," in William C. Potter and Harlan W. Jencks, eds., *The International Missile Bazaar, The New Suppliers' Network*, Boulder, Westview, 1994, pp. 47–74; *Defense News*, March 1, 1993, p. 29, January 17, 1994, p. 29, February 6, 1995, pp. 1, 42, June 19, 1995, pp. 1, 50; *Iran Brief*, January 9, 1995, pp. 8–10; *Jane's Defense Weekly*, April 16, 1997, pp. 25–28; *New York Times*, March 1, 1995, p. A-11; March 23, 1995, p. A-9, June 22, 1995, p. A-1.

62. Associated Press, May 24, 1997; IRNA, May 24, 1997, *New York Times*, May 26, 1997, p. NE11.

63. Reuters, May 29, 1998, 16:57.

64. *International Defense Review, Extra*, 2/1997, p. 5; United Press, September 9, 1996, 1621; Associated Press, July 11, 1996, 0720; Reuters, December 20, 1996, 1051; *Washington Times*, June 17, 1997, p. A-3; Director of Central Intelligence, "The Acquisition of Technology Relating to Weapons of Mass Destruction and Advanced Conventional Munitions," Washington, Central Intelligence Agency, June, 1997.

65. *Washington Times*, March 18, 1998, p. A-1, June 16, 1998, p. A-1.

66. *Defense News*, February 10, 1997, p. A-1; *Los Angeles Times*, February 13, 1997, pp. 1 and 48A; *Rocky Mountain News*, February 13, 1997, p. 48A; *Newsday*, February 13, 1997, p. A-58; *Financial Times*, March 14, 1997, p. 4; *Jerusalem Post*, March 12, 1997; *New York Times*, March 12, 1997; United Press, March 31, 1997, 0636; Reuters, March 4, 1997, 1731, January 16, 1998, 0421 and 0550, January 19, 1998, 2123, January 21, 1998, 2125; Associated Press, February 12, 1997, 0736, January 15, 1998, 1712, January 17, 1998, 1620, January 22, 1998, 1957, January 23, 1998, 2231; *Jane's Defense Weekly*, October 1, 1997, p. 3; *Jane's Intelligence Review and Jane's Sentinel Pointer*, December, 1997, p. 5; *Washington Post*, November 15, 1997, p. A-17.

67. *New York Times*, August 22, 1997, p. A-1.

68. Director of Central Intelligence, "The Acquisition of Technology Relating to Weapons of Mass Destruction and Advanced Conventional Munitions," Washington, Central Intelligence Agency, June, 1997; *Washington Post*, June 6, 1997, p. A-2.

69. Associated Press, August 25, 1997, 1548; *New York Times*, August 22, 1997, p. A-1.

70. Associated Press, March 14, 1997, 1249.

71. *Philadelphia Inquirer*, September 26, 1997, p. A-3; *Washington Post*, September 25, 1997, p. A-31; Associated Press, September 30, 1997, 1821; *Washington Times*, October 16, 1997, p. A-1; *Jane's Defense Weekly*, October 1, 1997, p. 3; *Defense News*, October 6, 1997, pp. 4, 28; *Jane's Intelligence Review and Jane's Sentinel Pointer*, December, 1997, p. 5.

72. Associated Press, August 25, 1997, 0645.

73. *Washington Post*, September 10, 1997, p. A-1; Associated Press, September 10, 1997, 1620.

74. *Washington Post*, September 27, 1997, p. A-16.

75. *Philadelphia Inquirer*, September 26, 1997, p. A-3; *Washington Post*, September 25, 1997, p. A-31, October 3, 1997, p. A-35; Associated Press, September 30, 1997, 1821; *Defense News*, October 27, 1997, p. 4.

76. *Washington Times*, September 10, 1997, p. A-1, October 20, 1997, p. A-1; Associated Press, September 10, 1997, 1620; *Washington Post*, September 25, 1997, p. A-31, October 3, 1997, p. A-35.

77. Director of Central Intelligence, "The Acquisition of Technology Relating to Weapons of Mass Destruction and Advanced Conventional Munitions," Washington, Central Intelligence Agency, June 1997; *Washington Times*, May 22, 1997, p. A-3, June 17, 1997, p. A-3; Victor Mizin, "Russia's Missile Industry and US Non-Proliferation Options," *The Nonproliferation Review*, Spring-Summer, 1998, reprint of article;.

78. Associated Press, April 16, 1998, 0321; Reuters, April 29, 1998, 14:39; *New York Times*, April 25, 1998, p. A-1.

79. *Washington Times*, October 30, 1997, p. A-1.

80. Reuters, March 4, 1997, 1731, January 16, 1998, 0421, and 0550, January 19, 1998, 2123, January 21, 1998, 2125; Associated Press, February 12, 1997, 0736, January 15, 1998, 1712, January 17, 1998, 1620, January 22, 1998, 1957, January 23, 1998, 2231.

81. *Washington Post*, November 15, 1997, p. A-17.

82. Reuters, March 4, 1997, 1731, January 16, 1998, 0421 and 0550, January 19, 1998, 2123, January 21, 1998, 2125; Associated Press, February 12, 1997, 0736, January 15, 1998, 1712, January 17, 1998, 1620, January 22, 1998, 1957, January 23, 1998, 2231.

83. Reuters, December 20, 1996, 1051.

84. *International Defense Review, Extra*, 2/1997, p. 5; United Press, September 9, 1996, 1621; Associated Press, July 11, 1996, 0720; Reuters, December 20, 1996, 1051; *Washington Times*, November 21, 1996, p. A-1.

85. Reuters, December 20, 1996, 1051; Tehran, IRNA, in English, 14:17 GMT, December 26, 1995; FBIS-NES-95–250, December 26, 1995.

86. *Washington Times*, June 23, 1998, p. A-1; *Defense News*, July 27, 1998, pp. 3, 8, and 20.

87. Director of Central Intelligence, "The Acquisition of Technology Relating to Weapons of Mass Destruction and Advanced Conventional Munitions," Washington, Central Intelligence Agency, June, 1997; *Washington Times*, May 22, 1997, p. A-3, June 17, 1997, p. A-3.

88. US State Department, DOSFAN, statement by Nicholas Burns, April 16, 1997; Reuters, April 16, 1997, 1827.

89. Reuters, January 21, 1998, 2125.

90. See the introduction and Chapters 10–13 of Eric Arnett, ed., *Military Capacity and the Risk of War: China, India, Pakistan, and India*, Stockholm, Stockholm Institute of Peace Research Institute, March, 1997; *Jane's Defense Weekly*, April 16, 1997, p. 16.

91. *Jane's Defense Weekly*, October 1, 1997, p. 3.

92. *Jane's Defense Weekly*, May 1, 1996, pp. 19–21; *Jane's Defense Weekly*, December 9, 1995, p. 3.

93. *Jane's Defense Weekly*, July 17, 1996, p. 13.

94. *Jane's Intelligence Review*, Special Report No. 6, May, 1995, pp. 16–18; *Jane's Defense Weekly*, January 30, 1993, pp. 20–21; *Defense Electronics and Computing*, IDR Press, September, 1992, pp. 115–120, *International Defense Review*, May, 1992,

pp. 413–415; *Jane's Remotely Piloted Vehicles, 1991–1992*; Keith Munson, *World Unmanned Aircraft*, London, Jane's 1988; *Air Force Magazine*, March, 1992, pp. 94–99, May, 1992, p. 155; Alan George, "Iran: Cut-Price Cruise Missiles," *International Defense Review*, March, 1993, pp. 15–16.

Chapter 16

Iranian Terrorism, Unconventional Warfare, and Weapons of Mass Destruction

Iran can also conduct major attacks without using any form of dedicated delivery system. The United States almost certainly exaggerates in labeling Iran a "terrorist" nation, but there is no question that Iran trains what it regards as "freedom fighters," encourages radical and extremist groups that use violence, and has developed large-scale capabilities for unconventional warfare. It not only commits acts of state "terrorism," but has the capability to exploit a wide range of potential proxies that either sympathize with Iran or would strike against Iran's enemies for their own reasons.[1]

Iran has not, to date, been proved to have supported mass terrorism or attacks that kill large numbers of civilians, but it has supported movements like the Hezbollah, which have been less than discriminating in their attacks on civilian targets, and has assassinated members of its opposition in a wide range of countries. Its Revolutionary Guards have practiced a variety of unconventional attacks against enemy targets, and unconventional and proxy attacks offer Iran both a way of overcoming many of the limitations in its delivery capabilities and the possibility of achieving plausible deniability or shifting the blame for such attacks to proxy movements.

Once again, there is no way to determine what Iran does or does not plan, and its official attitude toward terrorism is the usual one of denial. Further, Iran's efforts may well be improvised and reactive—with Iran suddenly escalating the scale of its use of unconventional warfare/terrorism in reaction to a given contingency or the failure of its military forces. This makes any effort to characterize Iran's use of such delivery methods purely speculative—whether in terms of warning against such threats or denying their existence.

What is clear is that such attacks are technically feasible, that they could offer Iran significant advantages in a number of scenarios, and that they apply equally to biological, chemical, and nuclear weapons. Table 16.1 illustrates this point. Many of the attacks postulated in this table may seem to borrow from bad spy novels and science fiction, but all of the scenarios are at least technically possible. These scenarios also illustrate the fact that Iran does not need sophisticated military delivery systems, nor highly lethal weapons of mass destruction. Instead, it can use terrorism to pose existential threats, can use complex mixes of weapons of mass destruction, and can mix terrorism with elements of covert action and deniability.

The danger of such scenarios is that they tend to overstate Iran's willingness to adopt extreme forms of terror, the willingness of Iranian agents or proxies to risk dying, and Iran's ability to undetectably execute complex attacks. Recent Saudi statements cast serious doubt on whether Iran had any meaningful ties to events like the bombing of the USAF apartments at Al Khobar towers in Saudi Arabia on June 25, 1996.[2] While Iran and its potential proxies are often portrayed as acting without moral limits and as willing martyrs, little of their real-world behavior conforms with such stereotypes. At the same time, Iran's steady escalation of its support for the Hezbollah and other extremist movements, and the rhetoric and ideology of potential proxies like the Palestine Islamic Jihad and Combatant Partisans of God scarcely rules out mass murder.

Most of the scenarios in Table 16.1 also are not all that difficult to execute, and only a few require large numbers of people and complex technical activity. The actions of Aum Shinrikyo in using nerve gas to attack the Tokyo subway have already shown that it can be extremely difficult to characterize the level of extremism and capability for sophisticated action within a given group until it has committed at least one act of terror. The cell structure used by the violent elements of most Middle Eastern extremist groups also tends to encourage the creation of compartmented groups with different and unpredictable commitments to violence while the loose and informal chain of contacts between extremist movements, known terrorist groups, and radical governments like Iran creates the possibility of random or unpredictable transfers of technology or weapons. Once again, there are many possibilities and no clear probabilities.

NOTES

1. For further discussion, see Anthony H. Cordesman, "Terrorism and the Threat From Weapons of Mass Destruction in the Middle East: The Problem of Paradigm Shift," Washington, CSIS, October 17, 1996; Brad Roberts, *Terrorism With Chemical and Biological Weapons: Calibrating Risks and Responses*, Alexandria, Chemical and Biological Weapons Control Institute, 1997; and Shai Feldman, *Nuclear Weapons and Arms Control in the Middle East*, Cambridge, MIT Press, 1997.

2. Associated Press, April 14, 1997, 1837; *Washington Post*, April 14, 1997, p. A-1; Reuters, April 14, 1997, BC Cycle; *New York Times*, April 14, 1997, p. A-7.

Table 16.1
Possible Iranian Attack Scenarios Using Weapons of Mass Destruction

- A radiological powder is introduced into the air conditioning systems of Saudi high-rise buildings or tourist hotels. Symptoms are only detected over days or weeks, and public warning is given several weeks later. The authorities detect the presence of such a power but cannot estimate its long-term lethality and have no precedents for decontamination. Tourism collapses, and the hotels eventually have to be torn down and rebuilt.

- An Iranian-backed terrorist group smuggles parts for a crude gun-type nuclear device into Israel or bought in the marketplace. The device is built in a medium-sized commercial truck. A physics student reading the US Department of Defense weapons effect manual maps Tel Aviv to maximize fallout effects in an area filled with buildings with heavy metals and waits for a wind maximizing the fallout impact. The bomb explodes with a yield of only 8 kilotons, but with an extremely high level of radiation. Immediate casualties are limited, but the long-term death rate mounts steadily with time. Peace becomes impossible, and security measures become draconian. Immigration halts, and emigration reaches crisis proportions. Israel as such ceases to exist.

- Several workers move drums labeled as cleaning agents into a large shopping mall, large public facility, subway, train station, or airport. They dress as cleaners and are wearing what appear to be commercial dust filters or have taken the antidote for the agent they will use. They mix the feedstocks for a persistent chemical agent at the site during a peak traffic period. Large-scale casualties result, and draconian security measures become necessary on a national level. A series of small attacks using similar "binary" agents virtually paralyze the economy, and detection is impossible except to identify all canisters of liquid.

- Immunized terrorists visit a US carrier or major Marine assault ship during the first hours of visitor's day during a port call in the Middle East. They are carrying Anthrax powder in bags designed to make them appear slightly overweight. They slowly scatter the powder as they walk through the ship visit. The immediate result is 50% casualties among the ship's crew, its Marine complement, and the visitors that follow. The United States finds it has no experience with decontaminating a large ship where Anthrax has entered the air system and is scattered throughout closed areas. After long debates over methods and safety levels, the ship is abandoned.

- An Iranian-backed terrorist group seeking to "cleanse" a nation of its secular regime and corruption introduces a modified type culture of Ebola or a similar virus into an urban area—trusting God to "sort out" the resulting casualties. He scatters infectious cultures in urban areas for which there is no effective treatment. By the time the attack is detected, it has reached epidemic proportions. Medical authorities rush into the infected area without proper protection, causing the collapse of medical facilities and emergency response capabilities. Other nations and regions have no alternative other than to isolate the nation or center under attack, letting the disease take its course.

- An Iranian-backed terrorist group modifies the valves on a Japanese remote-controlled crop spraying helicopter which has been imported legally for agricultural purposes. It uses this system at night or near dawn to spray a chemical or biological agent at altitudes below radar coverage in a line-source configuration. Alternatively, it uses a

Table 16.1 (continued)

large home-built RPV with simple GPS guidance. The device eventually crashes undetected into the sea or in the desert. Delivery of a chemical agent achieves far higher casualties than any conventional military warhead. A biological agent is equally effective, and the first symptoms appear days after the actual attack—by which time treatment is difficult or impossible.

- A truck filled with what appears to be light gravel is driven through the streets of Riyadh, Kuwait City, or Tel Aviv during rush hour or another maximum traffic period. A visible powder does come out through the tarpaulin covering the truck, but the spread of the powder is so light that no attention is paid to it. The driver and his assistant are immunized against the modified form of Anthrax carried in the truck, which is being released from behind the gravel or sand in the truck. The truck slowly quarters key areas of the city. Unsuspected passersby and commuters not only are infected but carry dry spores home and into other areas. By the time the first major symptoms of the attack occur some 3–5 days later, Anthrax pneumonia is epidemic and some septicemic Anthrax has appeared. Some 40–65% of the exposed population dies, and medical facilities collapse, causing serious, lingering secondary effects.

- An Iranian-backed terrorist group scatters high concentrations of a radiological, chemical, or biological agent in various areas in a city and trace elements into the processing intakes to the local water supply. When the symptoms appear, the terrorist group makes its attack known but claims that it has contaminated the local water supply. The authorities are forced to confirm that water is contaminated, and mass panic ensues.

- Immunized terrorists carry small amounts of Anthrax or a similar biological agent onto a passenger aircraft like a B-747, quietly scatter the powder, and deplane at the regularly scheduled stop. No airport detection system or search detects the agent. Some 70–80% of those on the aircraft die as a result of symptoms that only appear days later.

- Several identical nuclear devices are smuggled out of the FSU through Afghanistan or Central Asia. They do not pass directly through governments. One of the devices is disassembled to determine the precise technology and coding system used in the weapon's PAL. This allows users to activate the remaining weapons. The weapon is then disassembled to minimize detection with the fissile core shipped covered in lead. The weapon is successfully smuggled into the periphery of an urban area outside any formal security perimeter. A 100-kiloton ground burst destroys a critical area and blankets the region in fallout.

- The same device is shipped to Israel or a Gulf area in a modified standard shipping container equipped with detection and triggering devices that set it off as a result of local security checks or with a GPS system that sets it off automatically when it reaches the proper coordinates in the port of destination. The direct explosive effect is significant, and "rain out" contaminates a massive additional area.

- Iran equips a freighter or dhow to spread Anthrax along a coastal area in the Gulf. It uses a proxy terrorist group and launches an attack on Kuwait City and Saudi oil facilities and ports. It is several days before the attack is detected, and the attacking group is never fully identified. The form of Anthrax involved is dry and time encapsulated to lead to both massive prompt casualties and force time-consuming decontam-

Table 16.1 (continued)

ination. Iran not only is revenged, but benefits from the resulting massive surge in oil prices.

- An Iranian-backed terrorist group scatters small amounts of a biological or radiological agent in a Jewish area during critical stages of the final settlement talks. Near panic ensures, and a massive anti-Palestinian reaction follows. Israeli security then learns that the terrorist group has scattered small amounts of the same agent in cells in every sensitive Palestinian town and area, and the terrorist group announces that it has also stored some in politically sensitive mosques and shrines. Israeli security is forced to shut down all Palestinian movements and carry out intrusive searches in every politically sensitive area. Palestinian riots and exchanges of gunfire follow. The peace talks break down permanently.

- The Iranian Revolutionary Guards equip dhows to spread Anthrax. The dhows enter the ports of Dubai and Abu Dhabi as commercial vessels—possibly with local or other Southern Gulf registrations and flags. It is several days before the attack is detected, and the resulting casualties include much of the population of Abu Dhabi and government of the United Arab Emirates (UAE). The UAE breaks up as a result, no effective retaliation is possible, and Iran achieves near hegemony over Gulf oil policy.

- An Iranian-backed terrorist group attempting to drive Western influence out of Saudi Arabia smuggles a large nuclear device into Al Hufuf on the edge of the Ghawar oil field. It develops a crude fallout model using local weather data, which it confirms by sending out scouts with cellular phones. It waits for the ideal wind, detonates the devices, shuts down the world's largest exporting oil field, and causes the near collapse of Saudi Arabia.

- Alternatively, the same group takes advantage of the security measures the United States has adopted in Saudi Arabia, and the comparative isolation of US military personnel. It waits for the proper wind pattern and allows the wind to carry a biological agent over a Saudi airfield with a large US presence from an area outside the security perimeter. The United States takes massive casualties and has no ability to predict the next attack. It largely withdraws from Saudi Arabia.

- A freighter carrying fertilizer enters a Middle Eastern port and docks. In fact, the freighter has mixed the fertilizer with a catalyst to create a massive explosion and also carries a large amount of a chemical, radiological, and/or biological agent. The resulting explosion destroys both the immediate target area and scatters the chemical or biological weapon over the area.

- A large terrorist device goes off in a populated, critical economic, or military assembly area—scattering mustard or nerve gas. Emergency teams rush in to deal with the chemical threat, and the residents are evacuated. Only later does it become clear that the device also included a biological agent, and that the response to this "cocktail" killed most emergency response personnel and the evacuation rushed the biological agent to a much wider area.

- An Iranian-sponsored terrorist attack takes place on civilian nuclear reactors, chemical plants, or medical facilities designed to have the effect of using weapons of mass destruction.

Chapter 17

Iranian Delivery Systems and War-Fighting Capabilities Using Weapons of Mass Destruction

Delivery systems are only one part of the problem in assessing Iran's evolving capability to use weapons of mass destruction, and much will be determined by Iran's success in developing biological, chemical, and nuclear weapons and delivery systems. However, it is important to stress that missile capabilities will not determine Iranian war-fighting capability.

Missiles may be the highest technology available, but there are no rules preventing Iran from using artillery, unguided rockets, aircraft, unconventional delivery systems, proxies, or terrorists. Table 15.2 has shown the range-payload capability of typical strike-attack aircraft in the Middle East, and Iran already has F-4s, F-5s, F-14s, Su-24s, and MiG-29s. It is also important to note that the performance of the aircraft in Table 15.2 will be notably greater if they are only flown one way and/or are used in suicide missions. Further, converting an aircraft into a remotely piloted vehicle carrying a weapon of mass destruction and homing in on the target using a GPS and autopilot, with limited command guidance, is well within Iran's technical capabilities.

Furthermore, Iran does not need new ballistic or cruise missile systems to pose a threat. It already has the capability to launch missile attacks against Iraq, to hit coastal area targets in much of the Southern Gulf, and may also be able to use chemical warheads. The volume of such attacks is likely to be very similar to those Iraq launched during the Gulf War, or against Iran during the "war of the cities." The lethality would depend on the warhead, and much depends on the weaponization technology Iran has received from North Korea and/or the People's Republic of China.

Iran is currently limited by its lack of both sophisticated long-range targeting capability and missile systems, whose accuracy is limited to attacking only area targets. Iran can, however, pose a major threat in terms of intimidation and fear by using conventional warheads. It may also be able to use missiles with chemical and biological warheads to destroy or incapacitate military area targets, to paralyze war-fighting capabilities, or even to attack large complexes of particular buildings and facilities. Such missile attacks would be vulnerable to point defense by the improved Patriot, and US air power could probably break up large-scale attacks with strikes against Iran's missile launch facilities. Currently, however, the United States has no way of preventing Iran from confronting it with the same "Scud hunt" problems encountered by the Coalition during the 1991 Gulf War. It would be almost impossible for US air units to hunt out and destroy enough of Iran's missile capabilities to halt all attacks. As a result, the United States might well be forced to deter Iranian missile strikes by escalating its attacks on other high-value Iranian targets.[1]

Iran's acquisition efforts also seem likely to give it a growing capability to launch missile attacks to ranges of over 600 kilometers after the year 2000. By that time, Iran may well have guidance systems accurate enough to use against relatively small area targets like airfields and the assembly areas in ports. It may also have missiles with relatively efficient chemical and biological warheads. Much will depend on the precise level of technology involved, but Iran could easily develop a mobile force with 20–50 launchers and several hundred missiles by the period 2000–2005. Given the level of dual use technology available, it seems possible that Iran could equip such missiles with biological warheads possessing lethalities close to those of small nuclear weapons—which would allow it to launch devastating attacks against cities, critical civil facilities, oil and gas facilities, and military area targets. Iran should also have the capability to deploy shorter range missiles with chemical and biological warheads for use against other military targets, ranging from land force combat formations to large ships, such as carriers.

Depending on how Iran chose to deploy its missiles, it could develop a significant launch-on-warning or launch-under-attack capability which the United States might not be able to preempt, even in a surprise attack. It is doubtful that any "leakproof" defense system could be created to deal with such attacks, although wide area missile defense systems like THAAD or Aegis might have significant capability to degrade such attacks. This would place new emphasis on US ability to deter Iranian missile strikes by escalating its attacks on other high-value Iranian targets, or by threatening the use of US nuclear weapons.

NOTE

1. The technical content of this discussion is adapted in part from the author's discussion of the technical aspects of such weapons in *After the Storm: The Changing Military Balance in the Middle East*, Boulder, Westview, 1993, and *Iran and Iraq: The Threat from the Northern Gulf*, Boulder, Westview, 1994; working material on biological weapons prepared for the United Nations and from the Office of the Secretary of Defense, *Proliferation: Threat and Response*, Washington, Department of Defense, April, 1996,

pp. 12–16; Office of Technology Assessment, *Proliferation of Weapons of Mass Destruction: Assessing the Risks*, United States Congress OTA-ISC-559, Washington, DC, August, 1993; Kenneth R. Timmerman, *Weapons of Mass Destruction: The Cases of Iran, Syria, and Libya*, Los Angeles, Simon Wiesenthal Center, August, 1992; Dr. Robert A. Nagler, *Ballistic Missile Proliferation: An Emerging Threat*, Arlington, Systems Planning Corporation, 1992; and translations of unclassified documents on proliferation by the Russian Foreign Intelligence Bureau provided to the author by the staff of the Government Operations Committee of the US Senate.

Chapter 18

Iranian Chemical Weapons

The ways in which Iran is acquiring weapons of mass destruction also provide important insights into its capabilities and at least some insight into its intentions. Less is known about such efforts than about its potential delivery systems, but it is clear that Iran is pursuing biological, chemical, and nuclear weapons, and that its most advanced and least covert programs involve chemical weapons.[1] The CIA reported in 1996 that Iran's chemical weapons program is "among the largest in the Third World . . . Iran is developing a production capability for more toxic nerve agents and is pushing to reduce its dependence on imported raw materials." It can use artillery, mortars, rockets, bombs, and "possibly even Scud warheads" to deliver such weapons.[2]

Once again, the origins of Iran's chemical weapons programs are largely reactive. Both Iran and Iraq signed the Geneva Protocols of 1925, prohibiting the use of poison gas. Both nations also signed the Biological Warfare Convention of 1972, banning the development, production, and deployment or stockpiling of biological weapons.[3] While this did not prevent Iran from pursuing research into such weapons, Iran does not seem to have planned to go beyond research and development until Iraq began to use chemical weapons against Iranian forces in the early 1980s.

THE IMPACT OF THE IRAN-IRAQ WAR

It is unclear when Iraq first used chemical weapons against Iran, although Table 18.1 provides a summary chronology of Iraq's attacks. There seems to be no evidence of the large-scale use of lethal chemical synthetics and/or biological agents during the initial stages of the Gulf War, but Iran claimed that Iraq used chemical weapons in the Susangerd area during the first six weeks of the war.[4]

Table 18.1
Uses of Chemical Warfare during the Iran-Iraq War

User/Area	Gas	Delivery Means	Effects/Casualties	Date
Iraq Susangerd	CS	Artillery	Limited	June, 1982
Iraq Mandali and Basra	CS/Mustard	Artillery/Mortars	Unclear	July, 1982
Iraq Southern front	Mustard	Unknown	Used against forces massing for human wave attacks. Effect unknown.	December, 1982
Iraq Haj Omran/ Piranshahr/ Mt. Kordeman	Mustard	Aircraft Helicopters	25-100 casualties	August, 1983
Iraq Panjwin	Mustard	Helicopters/ Artillery	Heavy casualties Significant impact on battle	October- November, 1983
Iraq Majnoon Islands	Mustard/CS	Aircraft	Heavy casualties Significant impact on battle	February- March, 1984
Iraq Basrah	Nerve/ Mustard	Artillery	Limited	March, 1984
Iraq Hawizeh Marshes	Nerve/ Mustard	Aircraft/ Artillery	Heavy casualties Significant impact on battle	March, 1985
Iraq Al Faw	Nerve/ Mustard	Aircraft Artillery	Heavy casualties Significant impact on battle	February, 1986
Iraq Khorramshahr	Mustard	Bombs	Disrupt build-up against Basra	January- February, 1987
Iraq and Iran* Basra	Nerve/ Mustard	Aircraft Artillery	Heavy casualties Significant impact on battle	February- April, 1987
Iraq Khorramshahr	Mustard	Bombs	Disrupt build-up against Basra	April, 1987
Iran Mehran	Mustard/ Cyanogen	Artillery	Limited	July, 1987
Iraq Sardasht	Mustard	Bombs	650-3,500 Kurdish civilians	June- July, 1987
Iraq Somar	Mustard	Bombs	disrupt build-up against Basra	October, 1987
Iraq and Iran Halabjah	Mustard Cyanogen	Aircraft Artillery	Up to 5,000 Kurdish civilians	March, 1988
Iraq Al Faw, East of Basra	Nerve/ Mustard	Aircraft Artillery	Heavy casualties Significant impact on battle	April, 1988

Table 18.1 (continued)

User/Area	Gas	Delivery Means	Effects/Casualties	Date
Iraq Mehran	Nerve/ Mustard	Aircraft Artillery	Heavy casualties Significant impact on battle	May, 1988
Iraq Majnoon, Dehloran, Hawizeh	Nerve/ Mustard	Aircraft Artillery	Heavy casualties Significant impact on battle	June- July, 1988
Iraq Kurdistan	Nerve/ Mustard	Aircraft	Terrorize Kurdish rebels and population	August, 1988

*Iran may have used gas artillery shells during this battle.
Sources: Estimate based on various editions of the *SIPRI Yearbook*; Edgar O'Ballance, *The Gulf War*, London, Brassey's, 1988; W. Seth Carus, "Chemical Weapons in the Middle East," *Policy Focus*, Number Nine, December, 1988; JCSS, *Military Balance in the Middle East, 1987–1988*, Boulder, Westview, 1988.

These reports could be either Iranian propaganda or the result of a botched Iraqi attempt to use lethal chemical or biological agents.

Iraq did, however, begin to make significant use of chemical warfare against Iran when Iraq was put on the defensive. Beginning in 1982, Iraq began to use tear gas and nonlethal agents, and a broadcast over Baghdad's Voice of the Masses Radio stated in a reference to the Iranians that there was "a certain insecticide for every kind of insect."[5] In December, 1982, Iraq began to use mustard gas to deal with human wave and night attacks.

Iraq warned Iran that it might make extensive use of poison gas in September, 1983. The Iraqi high command issued a statement that it

> was armed with modern weapons that (will) be used for the first time in war . . . not used in previous attacks for humanitarian reasons . . . if you execute the orders of Khomeini's regime . . . your death will be certain because this time we will use a weapon that will destroy any moving creature on the fronts.[6]

The warning was soon followed by further chemical attacks. Iraq made extensive use of lethal chemical weapons in July (Val Fajr 2) and October, 1983 (Panjwin offensive).[7] Chemical warfare seems to have been used extensively on August 9 near Piranshahr, and then around Panjwin in late October and early November, 1983.[8] Two Iranian soldiers wounded by mustard agents during this campaign were sent to Vienna, where they died. Two members of a second group of wounded soldiers were sent to Stockholm for medical treatment, and they also died.

Further Iranian charges were made that Iraq used chemical weapons during the March, 1984 offensive which led to the Iranian seizure of Majnoon Island.[9] These charges stated that Iraq had killed some 1,700 Iranian troops and used

GD and GB nerve agents, as well as mustard gas. Many of the Iranian allegations about the Iraqi use of lethal synthetic gases during the following months also related directly to the fighting on the islands.[10]

Iran's public response was to try to mobilize world opinion against Iraq. After Iran's initial protests failed to arouse a significant world reaction, Iran flew some of its chemical warfare casualties to London in an effort to force world attention. It had some success in this effort. A UN team then flew to Iran and found several Iraqi bombs for dispersing chemical agents with Spanish markings. These weapons were later found to have contained mustard gas. Other investigations following Iraq's 1984 attacks indicated that there was a high probability that Iraq was using a nerve gas agent called Tabun.[11] These conclusions were validated by a second UN investigation in 1986. It later became apparent that Iraq also had chlorine gas agents, and that Iraq had a major chemical weapons production complex.

These efforts to make a propaganda issue out of Iraq's use of gas may have had some temporary success. Iraq does not seem to have made extensive use of chemical agents between March, 1984 and Iran's Faw offensive in early 1986. It did, however, sporadically use chemical weapons when its forces came under intense military pressure. There are alternative explanations for this pause in Iraq's use of gas. The pause may have been because of the hostile reaction in the West and Third World, but it may also have occurred because Iraq lacked the organization and dispensers to use gas safely. There are indications that unfavorable winds caused Iraqi deaths at Haji Omran in August, 1983, at Majnoon in March, 1984, and near Fish Lake in 1987. Iraq also seems to have become more cautious after the United States formally condemned Iraqi use of chemical weapons in March, 1984.

Changes in the training of the Iraqi Chemical Corps also indicate that Iraq was attempting to become more selective in the use of mustard gas and to attack Iranian rear areas with more care. Further, Iraq was clearly converting its forces to be able to use nonpersistent nerve gases against attacking Iranian troops or in its own attacks on Iranian positions.

In any case, Iraq resumed extensive use of gas warfare in its defense of Faw in 1986, and it made effective use of gas in its defense of Basra in 1987. Iraq also found that mustard and nerve gas were effective in defending against attacking Iranian troops in the north during their attacks on Iraq in 1987 and in the early months of 1988. Chemical weapons offered a potential solution to the problem of mountain or rough terrain warfare, and in many cases, it allowed Iraq to "secure" a mountainous area with relatively few troops. Iraq was particularly ready to use gas against those Iraqi Kurds fighting on the side of Iran, a group which the government regarded as nothing but traitors.

Iraq made massive use of chemical weapons during its recapture of Faw in early 1988, and in its assaults to recover its positions outside of Basra. By April, 1988, Iran claimed that the new round of attacks had raised the total number of casualties from chemical weapons since the start of the war to around 25,600, with some 2,600 dead. These claims may well be legitimate. Although Iran now had extensive defensive equipment, it did not organize or train to use it effectively. Many Iranians died, for example, because they did not shave often enough to allow their gas masks to make a tight seal.[12]

During the final months before the cease-fire, Iraq used chemical weapons in its attacks on Iranian positions in Mehran, the Majnoon Islands, the Hawizeh Marshes, and Dehloran.[13] By the time the war ended in a cease-fire, the Iraqi use of chemical weapons seems to have produced around 45,000 casualties, although there is no way to calculate the seriousness of these casualties or the number dead.

More controversially, anti-Iraqi Kurdish factions charged that Iraq began to make extensive use of gas against noncombatant Kurdish villages and areas early in 1987. According to such reports, there were some 15 such attacks between April 15, 1987, and February 26, 1988. Three of these attacks are claimed to have produced 100 or more casualties: attacks on Arbil, Kanibard, Zeenau, Balookawa, Shaikwassan, the Derasheer mountains, and the Sawseewaken area on April 16, 1987; the Dahok/Amadia area on May 6, 1987; and the Sulaymania/Sergaloo, Yakhsamar, Haledan, and Gweezeela areas on February 25, 1987.[14]

While these charges cannot be confirmed, the worst single use of gas against civilians occurred when both Iraq and Iran used gas during an Iranian attack on the Kurdish town of Halabjah on February 26, 1988. Up to 5,000 Kurdish civilians were killed in the fighting.

After its troops were driven from the area, Iraq seems to have begun chemical attacks by bombing the town with a mustard gas that produced a burning white cloud. Some of the gas victims seem to have fled toward Iraq, rather than Iran, and this may have confused Iraqi forces into thinking they were Iranian troops. Iran seems to have fired hydrogen cyanide gas into the area with artillery shells. The cyanide fired by Iran may have done much of the actual killing, and may have accounted for many of the casualties which Iran blamed on Iraq when it showed the results of the attacks on its state television network.[15]

In spite of the hostile outside reaction to Halabjah, Iraq seems to have begun a major new offensive against its own Kurds on August 25, 1988, and it seems to have made considerable use of gas warfare as part of an effort to depopulate hostile areas. While the exact scale of Iraq's use of gas is uncertain, some 65,000 Kurds fled to Turkey, and many of the refugees gave convincing reports of the use of gas warfare. These attacks only halted after a new wave of US and European protests tended to isolate Iraq from its supporters and resulted in diplomatic pressure on Iraq from the United States.[16]

IRAN RESPONDS BY DEVELOPING ITS OWN PRODUCTION CAPABILITIES

Less publicly, Iran began to produce its own chemical weapons. The Islamic Revolutionary Guards Corps, with support from the Ministry of Defense, was put in charge of developing offensive chemical agents, and Iran launched a crash effort during 1983–1984 to purchase massive stocks of chemical defense gear and to develop its own chemical agents.

The purchase of chemical defensive gear was relatively easy, and Iran purchased large amounts from the mid-1980s onward. Iran also obtained large stocks of nonlethal CS gas, although it quickly found such agents had very limited military impact, since they could only be used effectively in closed areas or in very small open areas. Acquiring poisonous chemical agents was more difficult. Iran did not have any internal capacity to manufacture poisonous chemical agents when Iraq first launched its attacks with such weapons.[17] While Iran seems to have made limited use of chemical mortar and artillery rounds as early as 1985—and possibly as early as 1984—these rounds were almost certainly captured from Iraq.

In order to produce its own weapons, Iran had to covertly obtain outside support, and it took several years to get substantial amounts of production equipment and the necessary feedstocks. Iran sought aid from European firms like Lurgi to produce large "pesticide" plants, and it began to try to obtain the needed precursor chemicals from a wide range of sources, relying heavily on its embassy in Bonn to manage the necessary deals.[18] While Lurgi did not provide the pesticide plant that Iran sought, Iran did obtain substantial support from other European firms and feedstocks from many other Western sources.[19]

By 1986–1987, Iran developed the capability to produce enough lethal agents to load its own weapons.[20] The director of the CIA and informed observers in the Gulf made it clear that Iran could produce blood agents like hydrogen cyanide, phosgene gas, and/or chlorine gas.[21] Iran was also able to weaponize limited quantities of blister (sulfur mustard) and blood (cyanide) agents beginning in 1987.[22] It also had some capability to weaponize phosgene gas and/or chlorine gas.[23] These chemical agents were produced in small batches, and evidently under laboratory scale conditions, which enabled Iran to load small numbers of weapons before any of its new major production plants went into full operation.[24] These gas agents were loaded into bombs and artillery shells and were used sporadically against Iraq in 1987 and 1988.[25]

Iran also seems to have accomplished the completion of a major poison gas plant at Qazvin, about 150 kilometers west of Tehran. This plant is reported to have been completed between November, 1987 and January, 1988. While supposedly a pesticide plant, the facility's true purpose seems to have been poison gas production, using organophosphorous compounds.[26] It is impossible to trace all of the sources of the major components and technology Iran used in its chemical weapons program during this period. Mujahideen sources claim that Iran also set up a chemical bomb and warhead plant operated by the Zakaria Al-Razi chemical company near Mahshar in southern Iran, but it is unclear whether these reports are true. Reports that Iran had chemical weapons plants at Damghan and Parchin that began operation as early as March, 1988, and may have begun to test fire Scuds with chemical warheads as early as 1988–1989, are equally uncertain.

It is interesting to note that debates took place in the Iranian parliament or Majlis in late 1988 over the safety of Pasdaran gas plants located near Iranian towns, and that Rafsanjani described chemical weapons as follows:

Chemical and biological weapons are poor man's atomic bombs and can easily be produced. We should at least consider them for our defense. Although the use of such weapons is inhuman, the war taught us that international laws are only scraps of paper.[27]

US experts believe that Iran was beginning to produce significant mustard gas and nerve gas by the time of the August, 1988 cease-fire in the Iran-Iraq War, although its use of chemical weapons remained limited and had little impact on the fighting.[28] Iranian troops could not be trained and equipped to use chemical weapons effectively, while Iraqi forces already had vastly superior experience and were scoring major victories along the entire front.

They also believe Iran established at least one large research and development center under the control of the Engineering Research Centre of the Construction Crusade (Jahad e-Sazandegi), had established a significant chemical weapons production capability by mid-1989, and was seeking to obtain and/or manufacture surface-to-surface missiles that could be used for both chemical and nuclear strikes.[29] While Iran did not succeed in producing nerve gas during the Iran-Iraq War, it does seem to have developed the capability to start producing nerve agents like Sarin and Tabun in the early 1990s. Its efforts to equip plants to produce V-agent nerve gases seem to have been delayed by US, British, and German efforts to limit technology transfers to Iran, but Iran may have acquired the capability to produce persistent nerve gas during the mid-1990s.

IRANIAN CAPABILITIES IN THE LATE 1990s

By 1995, many outside experts believed that Iran was able to mass-produce Sarin and Tabun nerve gases and persistent nerve gas in the form of V-agents.[30] The CIA also reported in 1996 that Iran had a chemical stockpile of several thousand tons and could produce up to 1,000 tons of chemical weapons annually.[31] In late 1997, the CIA estimated that Iran might have stockpiled up to 2,000 tons of blister, choking, and nerve agents.[32]

Improvements in Production Capability

Iran has obtained precursors from both India, China, and a number of other countries. Ironically, Nahum Manbar, an Israeli businessman, was convicted on June 17, 1998, of selling Iran the material to produce mustard and nerve gas during 1990–1995. He also sold material to produce munitions factories for chemical warheads. Manbar had been based in France since 1985. He was the ideal "third party" to use as a cover for Iranian purchases, and had made some $18 million in profit before his arrest. His defense was interesting: "During that period, no one thought there were any problems with that country.... Another 100 or 200 people should be convicted with me—directors of factories, industry. Why me?"[33]

Iran has probably received substantial Chinese sales of production equipment and technical assistance. CIA sources indicated in late 1996 that China might have supplied Iran with up to 400 tons of chemicals for the production of nerve gas.[34] For example, one report indicated in 1996 that Iran had obtained 400 metric tons of chemicals for use in nerve gas weapons from China—including carbon sulfide. Another report indicated that China supplied Iran with roughly two tons of calcium-hypochlorate in 1996, and loaded another 40,000 barrels in January or February of 1997. Calcium-hypochlorate is used for decontamination in chemical warfare.[35]

Iran also placed several significant orders from China that were not delivered. Razak Industries in Tehran and Chemical and Pharmaceutical Industries in Tabriz ordered 49 metric tons of alkyl dimethylamine, a chemical used in making detergents, and 17 tons of sodium sulfide, a chemical used in making mustard gas. The orders were never delivered, but they were brokered by Iran's International Movalled Industries Corporation (Imaco) and China's North Chemical Industries Co. (Nocinco). Both brokers have been linked to other transactions affecting Iran's chemical weapons program since early 1995, and Nocinco has supplied Iran with several hundred tons of carbon disulfide, a chemical used in nerve gas. Another Chinese firm, only publicly identified as Q. Chen, seems to have supplied glass vessels for chemical weapons.[36]

Such purchases are part of a widespread Iranian purchasing effort. For example, Iran has even sought to obtain impregnated Alumina, which is used to make phosphorous-oxychloride—a major component of VX and GB—from the United States.[37] It has even obtained some of the necessary equipment from Israelis. Nahum Manbar, an Israeli national living in France, was convicted in an Israeli court in May, 1997 for providing Iran with $16 million worth of production equipment for mustard and nerve gas during the period 1990–1995.[38]

While China emphatically denied that it was responsible, the United States imposed sanctions on seven Chinese firms in May, 1997 for selling precursors for nerve gas and equipment for making nerve gas—although the United States made it clear that it had "no evidence that the Chinese government was involved." The Chinese firms were the Nanjing Chemical Industries Group and Jiangsu Yongli Chemical Engineering and Import/Export Corporation. Cheong Yee Ltd., a Hong Kong firm, was also involved. The precursors included tionyl chloride, dimethylamine, and ethylene chlorohydril. The equipment included special glass-lined vessels, and Nanjing Chemical and Industrial Group completed construction of a production plant to manufacture such vessels in Iran in June, 1997.[39] The CIA also reported that "Iran . . . obtained considerable chemical weapons related assistance from China in the form of production equipment and technology," and that Iran obtained additional equipment and feedstocks from India.[40]

A recent report by German intelligence indicates that Iran has made major efforts to acquire the equipment necessary to produce Sarin and Tabun, using the same cover of purchasing equipment for pesticide plants that Iraq used for its Sa'ad 16 plant in the 1980s. German sources note that three Indian companies—Tata Consulting Engineering, Transpek, and Rallis India—have approached German pharmaceutical and engineering concerns for such equipment and technology under conditions where German intelligence was able to trace the end user to Iran.[41]

Possible Stockpiles of Weapons

The question of what use Iran has made of these production capabilities is more uncertain. British, German, and US experts believe that Iran now has stockpiles of between several hundred and 2,000 tons of various lethal chemical agents. They believe that Iran has chemical warheads for its 155 mm artillery shells, 122 mm rockets, bombs, and mines, and may have chemical warheads for some of its longer-range rockets and guided missiles. Furthermore, US experts believe that Iran has at least one chemical warhead assembly plant near Damghan and regularly ships such weapons to other storage sites by rail. A wide variety of experts believe that Iran also has some capabilities to manufacture nerve gas now, and that Iran is seeking to produce its own precursors to avoid dependence on controlled imports. Israeli experts have claimed that Iran is already stockpiling nerve gas weapons.[42]

The lethality of these weapons is impossible to determine because so much depends on the technical details of the design of the weapon carrying chemical agents and the efficiency with which a chemical agent is dispersed. The chemical warheads for Iran's missiles are probably still of limited sophistication; the previous analysis has shown that Iran has had time to develop usable artillery, rocket warheads, and bombs. Iran probably either has storable binary weapons, or can soon introduce them into its inventory, and there are recent indications that Iran is seeking to buy equipment to support its forces in conducting nerve gas warfare.[43]

Table 18.2 shows that this gives Iran a significant potential capability to conduct a chemical war near its borders, to launch limited long-range air raids using chemical bombs, and to use chemical weapons in unconventional warfare.[44] While chemical weapons are the least lethal form of weapons of mass destruction, they are still extremely dangerous. Table 18.3 lists a wide range of agents that Iran may choose to exploit or which it must plan to deal with in planning its defenses against Iraq. Tables 8.1 and 11.1 have already shown that modern nerve gas weapons have serious war-fighting limitations, but can still have a major impact. These capabilities could be important in another Iran-Iraq war,

Table 18.2
Typical War-Fighting Uses of Chemical Weapons

Mission	Quantity
Attack an infantry position: Cover 1.3 square kilometers of territory with a "surprise dosage" attack of Sarin to kill 50% of exposed troops.	216 240-mm rockets (e.g., delivered by 18 12-tube Soviet BM-24 rocket launchers, each carrying 8 kilograms of agent and totaling 1,728 kilograms of agent).
Prevent launch of enemy mobile missiles: Contaminate a 25 square kilometer missile unit operating area with 0.3 tons per square kilometer of a persistent nerve gas like VX.	8 MiG-23 or 4 Su-24 fighters, each delivering 0.9 tons of VX (totaling 7.2 tons).
Immobilize an air base: Contaminate a 2 square kilometer air base with 0.3 tons of VX twice a day for three days.	1 MiG-23 with six sorties or any similar attack aircraft.
Defend a broad front against large-scale attack: Maintain a 300 meter deep strip of VX contamination in front of a position defending a 60 kilometer wide area for three days.	65 metric tons of agent delivered by approximately 13,000 155-mm artillery rounds.
Terrorize population: Kill approximately 125,000 unprotected civilians in a densely populated (10,000 square kilometer) city.	8 MiG-23 or 4 Su-24 fighters, each delivering 0.9 tons of VX (totaling 7.2 tons) under optimum conditions.

Sources: Adapted from Victor A. Utgoff, *The Challenge of Chemical Weapons*, New York, St. Martin's, 1991, pp. 238–242, and the Office of Technology Assessment, *Proliferation of Weapons of Mass Destruction: Assessing the Risks*, US Congress OTA-ISC-559, Washington, August, 1993, pp. 56–57.

although it is important to note that Iran has little practical experience in large-scale chemical operations, while Iraq has a great deal. They also give Iran new capabilities to intimidate the Southern Gulf states and to deter the West.

POTENTIAL WAR-FIGHTING CAPABILITIES

Iranian chemical warfare capabilities will grow steadily with time, and they will not be subject to the limitations that Iraq faces because of UN inspection and sanctions. This potential threat is serious enough to be an important factor behind US efforts to improve its chemical warfare defense capabilities, and US support of the efforts of the UN to create an Organization for the Prohibition of Chemical Weapons to enforce the Chemical Weapons Convention if sanctions on Iraq are lifted.[45]

Further, chemical weapons do not have to be delivered by missiles or aircraft. As is the case with biological and nuclear weapons, devices can be smuggled directly into a target area. Agents can be dispersed by manportable devices or even grenades. They can be used as terrorist or unconventional warfare weapons

Table 18.3
Major Chemical Agents That May Be In Iranian and Iraqi Forces

NERVE AGENTS: Agents that quickly disrupt the nervous system by binding to enzymes critical to nerve functions, causing convulsions and/or paralysis. Must be ingested, inhaled, and absorbed through the skin. Very low doses cause a running nose, contraction of the pupil of the eye, and difficulty in visual coordination. Moderate doses constrict the bronchi and cause a feeling of pressure in the chest, and weaken the skeletal muscles and cause fibrillation. Large doses cause death by respiratory or heart failure. Can be absorbed through inhalation or skin contact. Reaction normally occurs in one to two minutes. Death from lethal doses occurs within minutes, but artificial respiration can help and atropine and oximes act as antidotes. The most toxic nerve agents kill with a dosage of only 10 milligrams per minute per cubic meter, versus 400 for less lethal gases. Recovery is normally quick, if it occurs at all, but permanent brain damage can occur:

Tabun (GA)
Sarin (GB): Nearly as volatile as water and delivered by air. A dose of 5 $mg/min/m^3$ produces casualties, a respiratory dose of 100 $mg/min/m^3$ is lethal. Lethality lasts one to two days.
Soman (GD)
GF
VR-55 (Improved Soman): A thick, oily substance which persists for some time.
VK/VX: A persistent agent roughly as heavy as fuel oil. A dose of 0.5 $mg/min/m^3$ produces casualties, a respiratory dose of 10 $mg/min/m^3$ is lethal. Lethality lasts one to sixteen weeks.

BLISTER AGENTS: Cell poisons that destroy skin and tissue, cause blindness upon contact with the eyes, and which can result in fatal respiratory damage. Can be colorless or black oily droplets. Can be absorbed through inhalation or skin contact. Serious internal damage if inhaled. Penetrates ordinary clothing. Some have delayed and some have immediate action. Actual blistering normally takes hours to days, but effects on the eyes are much more rapid. Mustard gas is a typical blister agent and exposure of concentrations of a few milligrams per meter over several hours generally at least causes blisters and swollen eyes. When the liquid falls onto the skin or eyes it has the effect of second or third degree burns. It can blind and cause damage to the lungs leading to pneumonia. Severe exposure causes general intoxication similar to radiation sickness. HD and HN persist up to 12 hours. L, HL, and CX persist for one to two hours. Short of prevention of exposure, the only treatment is to wash the eyes, decontaminate the skin, and treat the resulting damage like burns:

Sulfur Mustard (H or HD): A dose of 100 $mg/min/m^3$ produces casualties, a dose of 1,500 $mg/min/m^3$ is lethal. Residual lethality lasts up to two to eight weeks.
Distilled Mustard (DM)
Nitrogen Mustard (HN)
Lewisite (L)
Phosgene Oxime (CX)
Mustard Lewisite (HL)

CHOKING AGENTS: Agents that cause the blood vessels in the lungs to hemorrhage and fluid to build up, until the victim chokes or drowns in his or her own fluids (pulmonary edema). Provide quick warning through smell or lung irritation. Can be absorbed through inhalation. Immediate to delayed action. The only treatment is inhalation of oxygen and rest. Symptoms emerge in periods after exposure of seconds up to three hours:

Table 18.3 (continued)

    Phosgene (CG)
    Diphosgene (DP)
    PS Chloropicrin
    Chlorine Gas

BLOOD AGENTS: Kill through inhalation. Provide little warning except for headache, nausea, and vertigo. Interfere with use of oxygen at the cellular level. Cyanogen Chloride (CK) also irritates the lungs and eyes. Rapid action and exposure either kills by inhibiting cell respiration or it does not—casualties will either die within seconds to minutes of exposure or recover in fresh air. Most gas masks have severe problems in providing effective protection against blood agents:

    Hydrogen Cyanide (AC): A dose of 2,000 $mg/min/m^3$ produces casualties, a respiratory dose of 5,000 mg/min/m3 is lethal. Lethality lasts one to four hours.

    Cyanogen Chloride (CK): A dose of 7,000 $mg/min/m^3$ produces casualties, a respiratory dose of 11,000 $mg/min/m^3$ is lethal. Lethality lasts 15 minutes to one hour.

TOXINS: Biological poisons causing neuromuscular paralysis after exposure of hours or days. Formed in food or cultures by the bacterium clostridium botulinum. Produces highly fatal poisoning characterized by general weakness, headache, dizziness, double vision and dilation of the pupils, paralysis of muscles, and problems in speech. Death is usually by respiratory failure. Antitoxin therapy has limited value, but treatment is mainly supportive:

    Botulin toxin (A): Six distinct types, of which four are known to be fatal to man. An oral dose of 0.001 mg is lethal. A respiratory dose of 0.02 $mg/min/m^3$ is also lethal.

DEVELOPMENTAL WEAPONS: A new generation of chemical weapons is under development. The only publicized agent is perfluoroisobutene (PFIB), which is an extremely toxic, odorless, and invisible substance produced when PFIB (Teflon) is subjected to extreme heat under special conditions. It causes pulmonary edema or dry-land drowning when the lungs fill with fluid. Short exposure disables and small concentrations cause delayed death. Activated charcoal and most existing protection equipment offers no defense. Some sources refer to "third" and "fourth" generation nerve gasses, but no technical literature seems to be available.

CONTROL AGENTS: Agents which produce temporary irritating or disabling effects when in contact with the eyes or inhaled. They can cause serious illness or death when used in confined spaces. O-Chlorobenzyl-malononitrile (CS) is the least toxic gas, followed by Chloroacetophenone (CN) and Adamsite (DM). Symptoms can be treated by washing the eyes and/or removal from the area. Exposure to CS, CN, and DM produces immediate symptoms. Staphylococcus produces symptoms in 30 minutes to four hours, and recovery takes 24 to 48 hours. Treatment of Staphylococcus is largely supportive:

    Tear: Causes flow of tears and irritation of upper respiratory tract and skin. Can cause nausea and vomiting:

    Chlororacetophenone (CN)
    O-Chlorobenzyl-malononitrile (CS)

    Vomiting: Causes irritation, coughing, severe headache, tightness in chest, nausea, vomiting:
    Adamsite (DM)
    Staphylococcus

Table 18.3 (continued)

INCAPACITATING AGENTS: Agents which normally cause short-term illness, psychoactive effects (delirium and hallucinations). Can be absorbed through inhalation or skin contact. The psychoactive gases and drugs produce unpredictable effects, particularly in the sick, small children, elderly, and individuals who are already mentally ill. In rare cases they kill. In others, they produce a permanent psychotic condition. Many produce dry skin, irregular heartbeat, urinary retention, constipation, drowsiness, and a rise in body temperature, plus occasional maniacal behavior. A single dose of 0.1 to 0.2 milligrams of LSD-25 will produce profound mental disturbance within a half hour that lasts 10 hours. The lethal dose is 100 to 200 milligrams:

- BZ
- LSD
- LSD-based BZ
- Mescaline
- Psilocybin
- Benzilates

Sources: Adapted from Matthew Meselson and Julian Perry Robinson, "Chemical Warfare and Chemical Disarmament," *Scientific American*, Vol. 242, No. 4, April, 1980, pp 38–47; "Chemical Warfare: Extending the Range of Destruction," *Jane's Defense Weekly*, August 25, 1990, p. 267; Richard Palowski, *Changes in Threat Air Combat Doctrine and Force Structure, 24th Edition*, Fort Worth Division, General Dynamics DWIC-91, February, 1992, pp. II-335 to II-339; US Marine Corps, *Individual Guide For NBC Defense*, Field Manual OH-11-1A, August, 1990; and unpublished testimony to the Special Investigations Subcommittee of the Government Operations Committee, US Senate, by Mr. David Goldberg, Foreign Science and Technology Center, US Army Intelligence Center on February 9, 1989.

for delivery into any building with central air conditioning. A passenger airliner could be used to fly a line and disperse agents as an aerosol. Chemical devices could be smuggled in and detonated in commuter centers, stadiums, or other crowded areas.

Iran does, however, face serious problems in making any attributable offensive use of chemical weapons in a war where US forces are engaged, or where it faces a combination of states with major conventional air-strike capabilities. If Iran uses chemical weapons, it could destabilize and/or escalate a conflict in ways in which it would face massive conventional retaliation. If Iran had any major success in attacking civilian targets or Western forces in the Southern Gulf with chemical weapons, it would at least face the possibility of theater nuclear retaliation.

IRAN AND THE CHEMICAL WEAPONS CONVENTION

Iran has denied that it has chemical weapons. Its representative to the UN stated in May, 1997 that, "The Islamic Republic rejects all allegations of any plan to produce chemical weapons in Iran."[46] The Iranian Majlis passed a bill that would ban the manufacture and deployment of chemical weapons in Iran, and agreed to the Chemical Weapons Convention (CWC) on June 8, 1997. Iran formally ratified the CWC on November 10, 1997.[47]

Iran may have taken this action for several reasons:

- The decision may be a political one, where Iran's political leadership may either not have fully understood the military implications of its actions or may have felt it could conceal the critical elements of its program. It is hard for a nation that has suffered more from the use of chemical weapons than any other nation since World War I to ignore the CWC.
- Agreement to the CWC helps offset charges that Iran was becoming a major proliferator, and puts some pressure on Iraq not to resume its efforts to proliferate once it is free of the sanctions imposed by the UN.
- The CWC gradually phases out chemical imports from nonsignatory countries, and Iran is a major exporter. Once Russia, India, and China had ratified the CWC, enough key customers had ratified the CWC so that Iran was confronted with the possible loss of key markets in Russia, India, China, and western Europe.
- Agreement to the CWC provides access to technology. Nations which ratify the CWC are guaranteed the right to acquire "chemical, equipment, and scientific and technical information relating to the development and application for purposes not prohibited under this convention." A number of experts believe that Iran has used similar provisions in the Nuclear Non-Proliferation Treaty (NPT) to acquire technology and equipment it is using for its nuclear weapons effort.
- It is not clear that Iran has major stockpiles of chemical weapons, and it has little incentive to create a major inventory as long as it is safe from Iraq. As long as Iran does not carry out major production of weapons, it may be able to use the CWC to improve the technology base for its chemical weapons effort and to conceal its efforts from the Organization for the Prohibition of Chemical Weapons (OPCW), which has been established to enforce the CWC.
- Iran may go further and reduce its chemical weapons program to a contingency capability that does not involve holding or producing chemical weapons. As long as the UN Special Commission (UNSCOM) ensures that Iraq cannot rebuild its massive chemical weapons program, it is unclear whether Iran can gain any decisive advantage from an active chemical weapons inventory. Unlike biological and nuclear weapons, chemical weapons do not have the kind of lethality that can decisively intimidate, deter, or alter the war-fighting capabilities in ways which radically change the military balance.

If Iran moves towards moderation, it may also find in time that it no longer needs such a program. At the same time, Iran's acceptance of the CWC is a two-edged sword. The treaty does give Iran time in which to destroy any existing chemical weapons, but it must declare all existing weapons, and the CWC bans any new Iranian development, production, distribution, and stockpiling of such weapons. It also requires Iran to make a formal declaration of its holdings of chemical weapons and production facilities, and allows any nation—including the United States—to require a challenge inspection within 12 hours. Iran may, therefore, face challenges almost as difficult as those UNSCOM poses for Iraq.[48]

NOTES

1. For additional details, see Anthony H. Cordesman, *Iran and Iraq: The Threat from the Northern Gulf*, Boulder, Westview, 1994; Office of the Secretary of Defense, *Proliferation: Threat and Response*, Washington, Department of Defense, April, 1996, pp. 12–16; Office of Technology Assessment, *Technologies Underlying Weapons of Mass Destruction*, US Congress, OTA-BP-ISC-115, December, 1993, Washington, GPO, pp. 15–70; and *Jane's Intelligence Review*, Special Report No. 6, May, 1995, pp. 16–18.

2. *Jane's Defense Weekly*, August 14, 1996, p. 3.

3. General references for this section include "Chemical and Biological Warfare," Hearing Before the Committee on Foreign Relations, US Senate, 91st Congress, April 30, 1969; Department of Political and Security Council Affairs, *Chemical and Bacteriological (Biological) Weapons and the Effects of Their Possible Use*, Report of the Secretary General, United Nations, New York, 1969; unpublished testimony of W. Seth Carus before the Committee on Governmental Affairs, US Senate, February 9, 1989; W. Seth Carus, "Chemical Weapons in the Middle East," *Policy Focus*, Number Nine, Washington Institute for Near East Policy, December, 1988; unpublished testimony of Mr. David Goldberg, Foreign Science and Technology Center, US Army Intelligence Agency, before the Committee on Governmental Affairs, US Senate, February 9, 1989; unpublished testimony of Dr. Barry J. Erlick, Senior Biological Warfare Analyst, US Army, before the Committee on Governmental Affairs, US Senate, February 9, 1989; unpublished testimony of Dr. Robert Mullen Cook-Deegan, Physicians for Human Rights, before the Committee on Governmental Affairs, US Senate, February 9, 1989; Elisa D. Harris, "Chemical Weapons Proliferation in the Developing World," RUSI and Brassey's Defense Yearbook, 1989, London, 1988, pp. 67–88; and "Winds of Death: Iraq's Use of Poison Gas Against Its Kurdish Population," Report of a Medical Mission to Turkish Kurdistan by Physicians for Human Rights, February, 1989.

4. Loren Jenkins, "Iraqis Press Major Battle in Gulf War," *Washington Post* (November 17, 1980), p. 1, and Taylor and Francis, SIPRI Yearbook 1985 (Philadelphia, 1985), pp. 206–219. W. Andrew Terrill, "Chemical Weapons in the Gulf War," *Strategic Review*, Spring, 1986, pp. 51–58.

5. "Iraq's Scare Tactic," *Newsweek*, August 2, 1982.

6. Chubin and Tripp, *Iran and Iraq at War*, p. 59; BBC, ME, April 14, 1983.

7. Loren Jenkins, "Iraqis Press Major Battle in Gulf War," *Washington Post*, November 17, 1980, p. 1; Taylor and Francis, SIPRI Yearbook, 1985, pp. 206–219; W. Andrew Terrill, "Chemical Weapons in the Gulf War," *Strategic Review*, Spring, 1986, pp. 51–58.

8. "In the Pipeline," *The Middle East*, December, 1981, p. 72; "Iraqis Trained for Chemical Warfare," *Washington Post*, November 3, 1980, p. 313. The Iraqis may also have been favorably impressed by the effectiveness of tear gas in instilling panic in Iranian troops. An August, 1982 report in *Newsweek* stated that an entire Iranian division fled in panic when they were exposed to Iraqi tear gas. The Iranians had no idea as to what type of agent they were being exposed to, and had no defenses against any kind of chemical agent.

9. "In the Pipeline," *The Middle East*, December, 1981; "Iraqis Trained for Chemical Warfare," p. 72; *Washington Post*, November 3, 1980.

10. Beginning in 1982, Iraqi agents bought extensive amounts of equipment from a West German manufacturer of equipment to make organophosphate pesticides. The manufacturer, located in Drereich, claims that it had no way to know that the Iraqis were buying extensive feedstock for nerve gas in other countries, including the United States. There may now be five major chemical agent production plants in Iraq. See Gustav Anderson, "Analysis of Two Chemical Weapons Samples from the Iran-Iraq War," *NBC Defense and Technology International*, April, 1986, pp. 62–66; Peter Dunn, "The Chemical War, Journey to Iran," *NBC Defense and Technology International*, pp. 28–37; and "Iran Keeps Chemical Options Open," *NBC Defense and Technology International*, pp. 12–14.

11. "Report of the Specialists Appointed to the Secretary General to Investigate the Allegations of the Islamic Republic of Iran Concerning the Use of Chemical Weapons, United Nations Security Council, Document S 16433, March 26, 1984. Also see the April, 1986 edition of *NBC Defense & Technology International*.

12. W. Seth Carus, "Chemical Weapons in the Middle East," *Policy Focus*, Number Nine, Washington Institute for Near East Policy, December, 1988, p. 7.

13. *Washington Times*, March 23, 1988, p. 1; *Toronto Globe and Mail*, March 24, 1988, p. 1; *Washington Post*, March 24, 1988, p. 1, and April 4, 1988, p. 24.

14. *Congressional Record*, US Senate, September 9, 1988, p. S12135.

15. *Washington Times*, March 23, 1988, p. 1; *Toronto Globe and Mail*, March 24, 1988, p. 1; *Washington Post*, March 24, 1988, p. 1, and April 4, 1988, p. 24; *Wall Street Journal*, September 16, 1988, p. 1.

16. See Peter W. Galbraith and Christopher Van Hollen Jr., "Chemical Weapons Use in Kurdistan: Iraq's Final Offensive," A Staff Report to the Senate Committee on Foreign Relations, September 21, 1988, and Physicians for Human Rights, *Winds of Death: Iraq's Use of Poison Gas Against Its Kurdish Population*, February, 1989.

17. *Washington Times*, October 29, 1986, p. 9-A.

18. Iran was caught trying to buy 430 drums of thiodiglycol feedstock in April, 1988 from a US firm called Alcolac. *Baltimore Sun*, February 11, 1988, p. 6.

19. While rumors surfaced in November, 1986 that Iran had bought nerve gas bombs and warheads from Libya—which had obtained such weapons from the USSR—these reports were almost certainly false. Iran does not seem to have used nerve gas at any time during the conflict.

20. *Washington Times*, October 29, 1986, p. 9-A.

21. Unpublished "Statement of the Honorable William H. Webster, Director, Central Intelligence Agency, Before the Committee on Governmental Affairs, Hearings on Global Spread of Chemical and Biological Weapons," February 9, 1989.

22. Unpublished "Statement of the Honorable William H. Webster, Director, Central Intelligence Agency, Before the Committee on Governmental Affairs, Hearings on Global Spread of Chemical and Biological Weapons," February 9, 1989; Office of the Secretary of Defense, *Proliferation: Threat and Response*, Washington, Department of Defense, April, 1996, p. 15.

23. Unpublished "Statement of the Honorable William H. Webster, Director, Central Intelligence Agency, Before the Committee on Governmental Affairs, Hearings on Global Spread of Chemical and Biological Weapons," February 9, 1989.

24. While rumors surfaced in November, 1986 that Iran had bought nerve gas bombs

and warheads from Libya—which had obtained such weapons from the USSR—these reports were almost certainly false. Iran does not seem to have used nerve gas at any time during the conflict.

25. Unpublished "Statement of the Honorable William H. Webster, Director, Central Intelligence Agency, Before the Committee on Governmental Affairs, Hearings on Global Spread of Chemical and Biological Weapons," February 9, 1989; Office of the Secretary of Defense, *Proliferation: Threat and Response*, Washington, Department of Defense, April, 1996, p. 15.

26. *Baltimore Sun*, February 11, 1988, p. 6; Kenneth R. Timmerman, *Weapons of Mass Destruction: The Cases of Iran, Syria, and Libya*, Los Angeles, Simon Wiesenthal Center, August, 1992, pp. 28–45.

27. IRNA, English, October 19, 1988, as reported in FBIS, *Near East and South Asia*, October 19, 1988, pp. 55–56.

28. Unpublished "Statement of the Honorable William H. Webster, Director, Central Intelligence Agency, Before the Committee on Governmental Affairs, Hearings on Global Spread of Chemical and Biological Weapons," February 9, 1989. For a description of the role of chemical warfare in the Iran-Iraq War, see Anthony H. Cordesman and Abraham R. Wagner, *The Lessons of Modern Warfare, Volume II*, Boulder, Westview, 1988.

29. Iran was caught trying to buy 430 drums of Thiodiglycol feedstock in April, 1988 from a US firm called Alcolac. *Baltimore Sun*, February 11, 1988, p. 6; Kenneth R. Timmerman, *Weapons of Mass Destruction: The Cases of Iran, Syria, and Libya*, Los Angeles, Simon Wiesenthal Center, August, 1992, pp. 28–45; *Jane's Defense Weekly*, April 30, 1997, p. 17; *Christian Science Monitor*, April 28, 1997, p. 3.

30. Based on discussions with various experts, the sources listed earlier, and working papers by Leonard Spector; *Observer*, June 12, 1988; *US News and World Report*, February 12, 1990; *FBIS-NES*, March 23, 1990, p. 57; *Defense and Foreign Affairs*, November 20, 1989, p. 2; *New York Times*, July 1, 1989, May 9, June 27, 1989; *Financial Times*, February 6, 1992, p. 3.

31. *Jane's Defense Weekly*, August 14, 1996, p. 3.

32. *Washington Times*, October 30, 1997, p. A-1.

33. Reuters, June 17, 1998, 1131.

34. *Washington Post*, March 8, 1996, p. A-26; *Washington Times*, November 24, 1996, p. A-9.

35. *Washington Times*, November 21, 1996, p. A-1.

36. *Washington Times*, October 30, 1997, p. A-1.

37. Two men were arrested for attempting to ship the chemicals to Iran via Dubai in January, 1996. *Washington Post*, January, 26, 1997, p. A-10.

38. Reuters, May 5, 1997, 09:16.

39. *Washington Post*, March 8, 1996, p. A-26, May 23, 1997, p. A-1; *New York Times*, May 23, 1997, p. A-1, May 25, 1997, p. NEII; *Washington Times*, October 31, 1997.

40. Director of Central Intelligence, "The Acquisition of Technology Relating to Weapons of Mass Destruction and Advanced Conventional Munitions, Washington, CIA, June, 1997; *Washington Times*, October 31, 1997, p. A-13.

41. *Insight*, February 27, 1995, p. 13; Agence France Presse, January 4, 1995, 05:22.

42. *Jane's Intelligence Review*, Special Report No. 6, May, 1995, pp. 16–18; *Insight*, February 27, 1995, p. 13; Agence France Presse, January 4, 1995, 05:22; *Christian Science Monitor*, April 28, 1997, p. 3.

43. Based on discussions with various experts, the sources listed earlier, Office of the

Secretary of Defense, *Proliferation: Threat and Response*, Washington, Department of Defense, April, 1996, pp. 12–16, and working papers by Leonard Spector; *Observer*, June 12, 1988; *US News and World Report*, February 12, 1990; *FBIS-NES*, March 23, 1990, p. 57; *Defense and Foreign Affairs*, November 20, 1989, p. 2; *New York Times*, July 1, 1989, May 9, 1989, June 27, 1989; *Financial Times*, February 6, 1992, p. 3, *Washington Times*, January 8, 1995, p. A-9; Kenneth Katzman, "Iran: Arms and Technology Acquisitions," Library of Congress, CRS-97–474F, October 1, 1997; Kenneth Katzman, "Iran: Military Relations With China," Library of Congress, CRS-967–572F, June 26, 1996; Shirley A. Kan, "Chinese Proliferation of Weapons of Mass Destruction, Background and Analysis," Library of Congress, CRS-96–767F, September 13, 1996.

44. *Washington Post*, March 8, 1996, p. A-26; *Washington Times*, November 24, 1996, p. A-9.

45. *Jane's Defense Weekly*, May 14, 1997, p. 4, June 4, 1997, pp. 19–27.

46. *New York Times*, May 25, 1997, p. NEII.

47. *Washington Post*, November 10, 1993, p. A-23.

48. *New York Times*, June 9, 1997, p. A-5; *Washington Times*, June 11, 1997, p. A-16; IRNA, June 9, 1997; *Jane's Defense Weekly*, May 14, 1997, p. 4.

Chapter 19

Iranian Biological Weapons

Iran did not seem to have seriously considered developing biological weapons[1] until the Iran-Iraq War. The Shah focused largely on nuclear weapons, and his grandiose nuclear power/weapons programs precluded the need for such a program. While Iran may have conducted defensive biological warfare programs, they were not detected by Western experts and would have had relatively little priority in an environment where most Middle East states were focusing on chemical and nuclear warfare.

Even today there are insufficient unclassified data to characterize the scale of Iran's biological warfare programs, the agents Iran is developing, and their military focus. It is clear, however, that Iran has such programs and that it has good reasons for expanding them and giving them equal priority with its efforts to acquire nuclear weapons. The CIA reported in 1996 that,

We believe that Iran holds some stocks of biological agents and weapons.... Tehran most likely has investigated both toxins and live organisms as biological warfare agents. Iran has the technical infrastructure to support a significant biological weapons program with little foreign assistance.[2]

Iran seems to have begun these efforts to develop biological weapons as early as 1982, once again as a reaction to the Iran-Iraq War. Reports surfaced that Iran had imported type cultures suitable for biological weapons from Europe, and was working on the production of mycotoxins—a relatively simple family of biological agents requiring only limited laboratory facilities for small-scale production.[3]

US intelligence sources reported in August, 1989 that Iran was trying to buy two new strains of fungus from Canada and the Netherlands that can be used to produce mycotoxins. German sources indicated that Iran had successfully purchased such cultures several years earlier.[4] The Imam Reza Medical Center at Mashhad Medical Sciences University and the Iranian Research Organization for Science and Technology were identified as the end users for this purchasing effort, but it is likely that the true end user was an Iranian government agency specializing in biological warfare. Many experts also believe that the Iranian biological weapons effort was placed under the control of the Islamic Revolutionary Guards Corps, which is known to have tried to purchase suitable production equipment for such weapons.

At the same time, it is impossible to determine the level of control the Islamic Revolutionary Guards Corps exerts over the civilian groups that execute the program. Iran also makes extensive use of dummy companies, civilian firms, university research groups, third country imports, third party imports, and other legitimate covers to import the necessary equipment and technology. As is the case with chemical and nuclear weapons, it is extremely difficult to distinguish between real civilian programs, military programs, and programs with dual applications.

Biological weapons are far more controversial, politically sensitive, and provocative than chemical weapons, and Iran has far more reason to deny that it is procuring biological weapons than chemical weapons—at least until its efforts reach the point where declaration and/or demonstration have advanced to the point where they are strategically and politically useful to Iran. It seems likely that such Iranian efforts are highly compartmentalized and classified, and Iranian civilians and officials may or may not know whether a program exists or their program has military applications. This makes it far easier for outside experts and opponents of the regime to make broad charges, and for Iran to issue blanket denials, than to come to grips with the fact that the uncertainties surrounding Iran's biological weapons programs are so great because so little unclassified evidence exists.

What does seem clear is that the Iranian government conducted covert procurement operations linked to biological weapons research and production throughout much of the 1980s and 1990s. It also seems clear that Iran has conducted extensive research on more lethal active agents like Anthrax, hoof and mouth disease, and biotoxins. In addition, Iranian groups have repeatedly approached various European firms for the equipment and technology necessary to work with these diseases and toxins.

Unclassified sources of uncertain reliability have identified a facility at Damghan as working on both biological and chemical weapons research and production, and believe that Iran may be producing biological weapons at a pesticide facility near Tehran.[5] Reports also surfaced in the spring of 1993 that Iran had succeeded in obtaining advanced biological weapons technology in Switzerland and containment equipment and technology from Germany. According to these reports, this led to serious damage to computer facilities in a Swiss biological research facility by unidentified agents. Similar reports indicated that agents had destroyed German biocontainment equipment destined for Iran. More credible reports by US experts indicate that Iran has begun to stockpile Anthrax and botulinum in a facility near Tabriz, can now mass-manufacture such agents, and has them in an aerosol form.[6] None of these reports, however, can be verified.

The CIA has reported that Iran has "sought dual-use biotech equipment from Europe and Asia, ostensibly for civilian use." It also reported in 1996 that Iran might be ready to deploy biological weapons.[7] Beyond this point, little unclassified information exists regarding the details of Iran's effort to "weaponize" and produce biological weapons.

There are reports that Iran has developed effective aerosol weapons and weapons designs with ceramic containers. Such uncertainties make it harder to determine the actual nature of Iran's current and probable future biological war-fighting capabilities than is the case with chemical and nuclear weapons. Iran may encounter continuing difficulties in developing effective ballistic missile warheads using biological agents, but it should be able to meet the technical challenges both in improving its targeting and in finding effective ways to disperse agents from cruise missile warheads and bombs. Iran may already have the technology to disperse agents like Anthrax over a wide area by spreading them from a ship moving along a coast or out of a large container smuggled into a city or an industrial complex. It also seems likely that Iran will be able to create a significant production capability for storable encapsulated biological agents by the year 2000.[8]

As has been discussed earlier, it is impossible to do more than guess at Iran's war-fighting doctrine for using biological weapons. Its leadership and military planners may well go on acquiring such weapons without making specific plans to use them. As for deterrence, Iran would be subject to the same threat of retaliation as with its use of chemical weapons. At the same time, the level of conflict would be more intense, making such retaliation even more likely.

Once again, the perceptual balance may also be as important as Iran's real-world success. Even the possibility that Iran has biological weapons gives it an enhanced capability to deter and intimidate the Southern Gulf and the West. Iran could make overt use of biological weapons in much the same way as chemical weapons, but it has incentives to make covert use of biological weapons because they are particularly well suited to unconventional warfare, or "terrorism."

While biological weapons are fundamentally different in character from both chemical and nuclear weapons, highly effective biological weapons can be as lethal as small nuclear devices. The recent study by the Office of Technology Assessment, summarized in Table 14.2, compared the impact of a 12.5 kiloton nuclear weapon dropped in the center of Washington with the minimum and maximum effect of using a single aircraft to deliver 300 kilograms of Sarin and 30 kilograms of Anthrax spores. The results indicate that the nuclear weapon would cover 7.8 square kilometers and produce the prompt deaths of 23,000–

80,000; the nerve gas would cover 0.22 square kilometers and kill 60 to 200, and the Anthrax spores would cover 10 square kilometers and kill 30,000 to 100,000. Such calculations depend upon the scenario, the time of day, and the weather. They assume a sophisticated bomb or missile warhead. Such data are, however, a warning of the potential risks posed by biological weapons.[9]

Further, biological weapons do not have to be delivered by sophisticated weapons systems; they can be smuggled into a target area. Agents can be dispersed by manportable devices or even grenades, or they can be delivered by the ventilation system of any building with central air conditioning. Unlike chemical weapons, biological agents are lethal enough to be dispersed from the rooftops or heights in urban areas, and wet agents can be placed in reservoirs. A passenger airliner could be used to disperse agents as an aerosol, or spores could be covertly dispersed in commuter centers, stadiums, or crowded areas. Ships moving along the coasts of cities have been found to be ideal platforms for slowly dispersing Anthrax spores in US Army tests.

Iran can also choose from a wide menu of possible biological weapons. While Western experts tend to focus on the most familiar weapons—such as Anthrax— Iraq's acquisition of Aflatoxin has already shown that there is no way to predict which agent a given country will weaponize or what its purposes may be in doing so. Further, many Western studies tend to focus on employment concepts similar to the kind of war fighting projected during the Cold War. There is a tendency to assume that Iran will seek weapons with predictable and controllable lethality, which are designed largely for war-fighting purposes, and to assume that it will use them in scenarios stressing large-scale combat and weapons effects similar to those of theater nuclear weapons. This, however, is "mirror imaging." As the previous analysis has shown, there are many reasons that Iran could pursue different war-fighting concepts.

There is no current arms control treaty that could begin to deprive Iran of biological weapons. Although 136 countries have adhered to the Biological Weapons Convention (BWC) since it was agreed to in 1972, the BWC currently has no enforcement provisions to parallel those of the Chemical Weapons Convention (CWC) and Nuclear Non-Proliferation Treaty (NPT). The United States is actively seeking international agreement on a protocol on a possible enforcement regime, and it indicated that it would have liked to get such an agreement during 1998. It is highly unlikely that the United States will succeed, however, because an enforcement regime would have to be far more complex and intrusive than that now used to enforce the NPT.

Furthermore, even the most intrusive regime might be unworkable. There simply are too many types of dual-use biological research and production facilities that could suddenly be converted to making biological weapons, and there is no way to clearly distinguish between legitimate research and weapons research. A nation like Iran might well be able to develop and produce significant amounts of extremely lethal dry storable agents in small facilities with little chance of detection. It might develop and test biological weapons and warheads using simulated agents—just as the United States did in the 1950s and 1960s. It could also bring a program to the breakout stage, where all research and development was complete and dual-use equipment identified for later use—and not produce such weapons until the need became apparent.

The technology also favors the proliferator, in terms of technology, production, and lethality. Genetic engineering offers major new ways to create such weapons, and Table 19.1 shows that there are many possible weapons. Development brings more and more of the key production technology and equipment to Iran as civil equipment. The development of all types of warhead and bomb technology aids proliferators in solving the problems of dispersing biological weapons, and advanced bioengineering makes it steadily easy to tailor weapons in ways that make vaccines and medical treatment ineffective.[10]

At the same time, it is all too possible to exaggerate Iran's biological threat. The Office of Technology Assessment's calculations are extremely dependent on a particular scenario, time of day, and weather. The missile data assume a very sophisticated missile warhead. US and Israeli experts estimate that neither Iran nor Iraq is likely to be able to acquire such a chemical ballistic missile warhead for 2–4 years, and that they may not be able to acquire such a warhead for a biological weapon for 3–5 years. The air delivered data assume optimal delivery in the form of aircraft dispersing the biological and chemical agents as an aerosol line source, although this would be a vulnerable profile for a manned plane to fly. They also assume a relatively sophisticated level of targeting and weaponization that is probably beyond the capability of either Iran or Iraq for the next five to ten years, which some experts argue is not technically feasible.

NOTES

1. For additional details, see Anthony H. Cordesman, *Iran and Iraq: The Threat from the Northern Gulf*, Boulder, Westview, 1994; Office of the Secretary of Defense, *Proliferation: Threat and Response*, Washington, Department of Defense, April, 1996, pp. 12–16; and Office of Technology Assessment, Director, *Technologies Underlying Weapons of Mass Destruction*, US Congress, OTA-BP-ISC-115, December, 1993, Washington, GPO, pp. 71–118.

2. United Press, August 11, 1996, 0530; *Jane's Defense Weekly*, August 14, 1996, p. 3.

3. Such reports begin in the SIPRI yearbooks in 1982, and occur sporadically throughout the 1988 edition.

4. *New York Times*, August 13, 1989, p. 11; *Jane's Intelligence Review*, Special Report No. 6, May, 1995, pp. 16–18.

5. James Smith, "Biological Weapons Developments," *Jane's Intelligence Review*, November, 1991, pp. 483–487; *New York Times*, August 13, 1989, p. 11; Kenneth R. Timmerman, *Weapons of Mass Destruction: The Cases of Iran, Syria, and Libya*, Los Angeles, Simon Wiesenthal Center, August, 1992, pp. 28–45.

Table 19.1
Key Biological Weapons That May Be in the Middle East

Disease	Infectivity	Transmissibility	Incubation Period	Mortality	Therapy
Viral					
Chikungunya fever	high?	none	2-6 days	very low (-1%)	none
Dengue fever	high	none	2-5 days	very low (-1%)	none
Eastern equine encephalitis	high	none	5-10 days	high (+60%)	developmental
Tick-borne encephalitis	high	none	1-2 weeks	up to 30%	developmental
Venezuelan equine encephalitis	high	none	2-5 days	low (-1%)	developmental
Hepatitis A	-	-	15-40 days	-	-
Hepatitis B	-	-	40-150 days	-	-
Influenza	high	none	1-3 days	usually low	available
Yellow fever	high	none	3-6 days	up to 40%	available
Smallpox (Variola)	high	high	7-16 days	up to 30%	available
Rickettsial					
Coxiella Burneti (Q-fever)	high	negligible	10-21 day	low (-1%)	antibiotic
Mooseri	-	-	6-14 days	-	-
Prowazeki	-	-	6-15 days	-	-
Psittacosis	high	mod-high	4-15 days	mod-high	antibiotic
Rickettsi (Rocky mountain spotted fever)	high	none	3-10 days	up to 80%	antibiotic
Tsutsugamushi	-	-	-	-	-
Epidemic typhus	high	none	6-15 days	up to 70%	antibiotic/vaccine
Bacterial					
Anthrax (pulmonary)	mod-high	negligible	1-5 days	usually fatal	antibiotic/vaccine
Brucellosis	high	none	1-3 days	-25%	antibiotic
Cholera	low	high	1-5 days	up to 80%	antibiotic/vaccine
Glanders	high	none	1-2 days	usually fatal	poor antibiotic
Meloidosis	high	none	1-5 days	usually fatal	mod. antibiotic
Plague (pneumonic)	high	high	2-5 days	usually fatal	antibiotic/vaccine
Tularemia	high	negligible	1-10 days	low to 60%	antibiotic/vaccine
Typhoid fever	mod-high	mod-high	7-21 days	up to 10%	antibiotic/vaccine
Dysentery	high	high	1-4 days	low to high	antibiotic/vaccine
Fungal					
Coccidioidomycosis	high	none	1-3 days	low	none
Coccidiode Immitis	high	none	10-21 days	low	none
Histoplasma Capsulatum	-	-	15-18 days	-	-
Norcardia Asteroides	-	-	-	-	-

Table 19.1 (continued)

Disease	Infectivity	Transmissibility	Incubation Period	Mortality	Therapy
Toxins[a]					
Botulinum toxin	high	none	12-72 hours	high neuromuscular paralysis	vaccine
Mycotoxin	high	none	hours or days	low to high	?
Staphylococcus	moderate	none	24-48 hours	incapacitating	?

[a]Many sources classify as chemical weapons because toxin are chemical poisons.

Sources: Adapted by Anthony H. Cordesman from Report of the Secretary General, Department of Political and Security Affairs, "Chemical and Bacteriological (Biological) Weapons and the Effects of Their Possible Use," New York, United Nations, 1969, pp. 26, 29, 37–52, 116–117; *Jane's NBC Protection Equipment*, 1991–1992; James Smith, "Biological Weapons Developments," *Jane's Intelligence Review*, November, 1991, pp. 483–487.

6. *Sunday Telegraph*, August 10, 1996, on-line edition; *Sunday Times*, August 10, 1996, fax edition; United Press, August 11, 1996, 0530.

7. Director of Central Intelligence, "The Acquisition of Technology Relating to Weapons of Mass Destruction and Advanced Conventional Munitions," Washington, CIA, June, 1997.

8. The technical content of this discussion is adapted in part from the author's discussion of the technical aspects of such weapons in *After the Storm: The Changing Military Balance in the Middle East*, Boulder, Westview, 1993, and *Iran and Iraq: The Threat from the Northern Gulf*, Boulder, Westview, 1994; working material on biological weapons prepared for the United Nations, and from the Office of the Secretary of Defense, *Proliferation: Threat and Response*, Washington, Department of Defense, April, 1996, pp. 12–16; Office of Technology Assessment, *Proliferation of Weapons of Mass Destruction: Assessing the Risks*, United States Congress OTA-ISC-559, Washington, DC, August, 1993; Kenneth R. Timmerman, *Weapons of Mass Destruction: The Cases of Iran, Syria, and Libya*, Los Angeles, Simon Wiesenthal Center, August, 1992; Dr. Robert A. Nagler, *Ballistic Missile Proliferation: An Emerging Threat*, Arlington, Systems Planning Corporation, 1992; and translations of unclassified documents on proliferation by the Russian Foreign Intelligence Bureau provided to the author by the staff of the Government Operations Committee of the US Senate.

9. Office of Technology Assessment, *Proliferation of Weapons of Mass Destruction*, Washington, GPO, August, 1993, especially p. 53.

10. *Christian Science Monitor*, May 21, 1997, p. 3; *Jane's Defense Weekly*, June 25, 1997, p. 6.

Chapter 20

Iranian Nuclear Weapons

The United States has expressed deep and continuing concern regarding Iran's search for nuclear weapons.[1] In early 1995, President Clinton's first Secretary of State, Warren Christopher, stated,

> In terms of its organization, programs, procurement, and covert activities, Iran is pursuing the classic route to nuclear weapons which has been followed by almost all states that have sought a nuclear weapon.... Iran's efforts to acquire nuclear weapons also pose enormous dangers. Every responsible member of the world community has an interest in seeing those efforts fail. There is no room for complacency. Remember Iraq....[2]

Christopher is also quoted as saying that Iran has tried for years to buy heavy water reactors to produce plutonium, is "devoting resources" to enriching uranium to weapons grade levels, and has "scoured" the states of the former Soviet Union for nuclear materials, technology, scientists, and technicians.[3]

President Clinton's new Secretary of State, Madeleine Albright, renewed this warning in her trip to Europe in February, 1997. She expressed particular concern that Europe and Russia cease the supply of dual-use and nuclear weapons-related technology to Iran.[4] Similarly, John Holum, director of the US Arms Control and Disarmament Agency, testified in March 1997 that Iran was actively developing nuclear weapons, although he indicated that the effort was proceeding slowly and that Iran would not have a bomb using Iranian-produced weapons grade material until the period 2005–2007.[5]

The European Union has also expressed concerns of its own. On January 16, 1998, officials of the UAE presented the United States with a list of 15 steps they were taking to prevent Iran from acquiring weapons of mass destruction, and spoke out strongly on the need to oppose Tehran's sponsorship of terrorism.

British Foreign Secretary Robin Cook, whose country just assumed the EU's rotating presidency, and Sir Leon Brittan, vice president of the European Commission, presented US Secretary of State Madeleine Albright with a memo "covering all the things the European countries are doing to halt the equipment and material for weapons of mass destruction from getting into the hands of Iran."[6]

No details were available, but the memo supplemented one given to the United States in 1997. Brittan stated that the memo "shows the continuing resolution and determination of the European Union ... to take vigorous action ... against both the development of weapons of mass destruction and the use of Iran as a terrorist base." Asked if there might be some flexibility in approaching Iran, Cook said,

There must be no room for flexibility in our resolve to halting Iran getting weapons of mass destruction or preventing Iran from acquiring missile capability or stopping Iran from sponsoring state terrorism. . . . On all these fronts we must be quite clear that these are unacceptable dangers based on unacceptable behavior by elements within the government of Iran.[7]

Cook did state, however, that the US effort to isolate the Islamic state would not work. "We must respond to the dangers posed by Iran as well as the opportunities. But isolating Iran is not the right response." Cook condemned the Iran-Libya Sanctions Act, under which Washington punishes foreign companies trying to invest in Iran's oil and gas sectors, saying it was unacceptable to European states and counterproductive.

Isolating Iran won't hit the target we want—economic measures will not have any serious effects on Iran's attempts to acquire weapons of mass destruction. . . . There are the first signs of Glasnost appearing in Iran and we must do what we can to encourage it.[8]

IRANIAN STATEMENTS AND DENIALS REGARDING NUCLEAR WEAPONS

Iran has never confirmed these charges and suspicions. Iran's Deputy President Ayatollah Mohajerani did state in October, 1991 that Iran should work with other Islamic states to create an "Islamic bomb." However, the Iranian government has normally denied that it is seeking nuclear weapons, and it has repeatedly made proposals to create a nuclear-free zone in the Middle East.[9] Iran has countered such charges by repeatedly denying that it has a nuclear weapons program. For example, President Rafsanjani was asked if Iran had a nuclear weapons program in an interview in the CBS program *60 Minutes* in February, 1997. He replied, "Definitely not. I hate this weapon."[10] As has been noted earlier, President Khatami, his foreign minister, and his new head of the Iranian Atomic

Energy Organization have repeated similar denials ever since Khatami became president.

The Iranian media has been equally consistent in making such denials. The Iranian government-run Voice of the Islamic Republic of Iran has described such charges as "baseless," and it has referred to various articles about the transfer of weapons-related technology as "a propaganda ploy by Western media affiliated to the Zionist regime." It has stated that, "Iran's efforts to reach nuclear energy are centered around the axis of the creation of electricity, which is required for the country's developing industry, and using this energy for medical and agricultural objectives," and the IAEA has found that Iran's nuclear programs "respect all the technical and legal aspects of non-proliferation." It has claimed in contrast that, "The Zionist regime has more than 200 nuclear warheads."[11]

The Atomic Energy Organization of Iran (AEOI) issued another denial that it had a nuclear weapons program on August 19, 1997, and that Amrollahi had sought aid from South Africa in obtaining items for its nuclear weapons program during a meeting in March, 1995 with Dr. Waldo Stumpf, the chief executive of South Africa's Atomic Energy Commission.[12] The AEOI also stated that all nuclear activities in Iran were peaceful, that Iran was a signatory to the Non-Proliferation Treaty, the nuclear safety program agreement, and the test ban; that all Iranian activities were under the supervision of the International Atomic Energy Agency (IAEA) and that recent inspection reports showed that Iran fully cooperated; and that the charges against Iran were a Zionist plot. Stumpf issued an equally firm denial, although it was a bit ironic that he indicated that the only Iranian official he had ever met with was Gholamreza Aghazadeh—whom he described as the oil minister, but who was soon to become the new head of Iran's nuclear program.[13]

The timing of these denials is interesting, because they came only days after President Khatami replaced Reza Amrollahi, the head of the Atomic Energy Organization, with Gholamreza Aghazadeh, Iran's former oil minister. The reasons for Gholamreza Aghazadeh's appointment are not clear. Some experts believe that it represented an effort to improve the administration of Iran's nuclear programs (Amrollahi had developed a reputation as an awful administrator and manager). Others felt it might be part of an effort to make Iran's nuclear power program more efficient, and still others felt that it might have been part of an effort to review whether such a program was cost-effective at all, or even a downplaying of Iran's nuclear weapons program.[14]

Iran's new Foreign Minister, Kamal Kharrazi, stated on October 5, 1997, that,

> We are certainly not developing an atomic bomb, because we do not believe in nuclear weapons.... We believe in and promote the idea of the Middle East as a region free of nuclear weapons and other weapons of mass destruction. But why are we interested to develop nuclear technology? We need to diversify our energy sources. In a matter of a few decades, our oil and gas reserves would be finished and therefore, we need access

to other sources of energy.... Furthermore, nuclear technology has many other utilities in medicine and agriculture. The case of the United States in terms of oil reserve is not different from Iran's. The United States also has large oil resources, but at the same time they have nuclear power plants. So there is nothing wrong with having access to nuclear technology if it is for peaceful purposes.[15]

Some Western experts outside of government agree with Iran's claims that it does not have a nuclear weapons program. For example, Eric Arnett of the Stockholm Institute of Peace Research Institute argues that Iran has offered to open any site to IAEA inspection, has agreed to accept improved safeguards for such inspections if they are universally adopted, and has been a strong supporter of regional arms control measures.[16]

In contrast, most Western experts with direct access to their government's intelligence data do believe that Iran has a nuclear weapons program. They base such conclusions largely on human intelligence and on the analysis of the long history of Iranian efforts to acquire nuclear weapons-related technology and dual-use equipment which has little other value to Iran. What they do not believe is that Iran has been able to establish the kind of massive nuclear program that Iraq established.

Most such experts feel that Iran has lacked the funds to establish such a program, and Iran has found it difficult to obtain much of the nuclear technology it desires because of various export control and intelligence efforts. Few Western experts seem to support a report by a former member of the US National Security Council staff that Iran had developed a $10 billion strategy for acquiring nuclear weapons.[17] Iran also does not have anything approaching Iraq's manpower base of several thousand nuclear technicians. Some estimates indicated that Iran had less than 500 nuclear physicists, engineers, and senior technicians in the late 1980s—compared to around 7,500 in Iraq.

Iran's nuclear weapons program seems to be slow and evolutionary. In fact, US estimates of Iran's progress in acquiring nuclear weapons have become more conservative with time. In 1992, the CIA estimated that Iran would have the bomb by 2000. In 1995, John Holum testified that Iran could have the bomb by 2003. In 1997, after two years in which Iran might have made progress, he testified that Iran could have the bomb by 2005–2007.[18] As a result, US experts increasingly refer to Iran's efforts as "creeping proliferation"—*although this description must be carefully caveated as one based on the assumption that Iran cannot buy weapons grade material from any outside source.*

NUCLEAR WEAPONS EFFORTS UNDER THE SHAH

Iran's nuclear effort was much more ambitious when it first began. It began no later than the early 1970s, when the Shah acquired Iran's first nuclear reactor from the United States for the Amirabad Nuclear Research Center (now called the Amirabad Technical College) in Tehran. The 5 megawatt reactor started up in 1967, and it has operated ever since. It is regularly inspected by the IAEA, but it uses a core with 93% enriched uranium, which is suitable for some forms of nuclear weapons.[19]

The Shah established the Atomic Energy Organization of Iran in 1974 and rapidly began to negotiate for nuclear power plants. He concluded an extendible ten-year nuclear fuel contract with the United States in 1974, with Germany in 1976, and with France in 1977. In 1975, he purchased a 10% share in a Eurodif uranium enrichment plant being built at Tricastin in France that was part of a French, Belgian, Spanish, and Italian consortium. Under the agreement the Shah signed, Iran was to have full access to the enrichment technology Eurodif developed, and agreed to buy a quota of enriched uranium from the new plant.[20]

The Shah created an ambitious plan calling for a network of 23 power reactors throughout Iran that was to be operating by the mid-1990s, and he sought to buy nuclear power plants from Germany and France. By the time the Shah fell in January, 1979, he had six reactors under contract and was attempting to purchase a total of 12 nuclear power plants from Germany, France, and the United States. Two 1,300 megawatt German nuclear power plants at Bushehr were already 60% and 75% completed, and site preparation work had begun on the first of two 935 megawatt French plants at Darkhouin that were to be supplied by Framatome.[21] Thousands of Iranians were training in nuclear technology in France, Germany, India, the United Kingdom, and the United States.

Iran signed the Nuclear Non-Proliferation Treaty and followed nuclear safeguard procedures. Nevertheless, US experts believe that the Shah began a low-level nuclear weapons research program, centered at the Amirabad Nuclear Research Center.[22] This research effort included studies of weapons designs and plutonium recovery from spent reactor fuel. It also involved a laser enrichment program which began in 1975, and led to a complex and highly illegal effort to obtain laser separation technology from the United States. This latter effort, which does not seem to have had any success, continued from 1976 until the Shah's fall, and four lasers operating in the critical 16 micron band were shipped to Iran in October, 1978.[23] At the same time, Iran worked on other ways to obtain plutonium, created a secret reprocessing research effort to use enriched uranium, and set up a small nuclear weapons design team.[24]

In 1976, Iran signed a secret contract to buy $700 million worth of yellow cake from South Africa, and it appears to have reached an agreement to buy up to 1,000 metric tons a year.[25] It is unclear how much of this ore South Africa shipped before it agreed to adopt IAEA export restrictions in 1984, and whether South Africa really honored such export restrictions. Some sources indicate that South Africa still made major deliveries as late as the period 1988–1989.[26] Iran also tried to purchase 26.2 kilograms of highly enriched uranium; the application to the United States for this purchase was pending when the Shah fell.

THE REVITALIZATION OF IRAN'S NUCLEAR WEAPONS EFFORT

The new Khomeini government let much of the Shah's nuclear program collapse during the period 1978–1980. It terminated the French and German contracts supporting the program. In March, 1979, Iran refused the request of the Kraftwerke Union (KWU) in Germany to mothball the Bushehr reactor projects, rather than simply turn them immediately over to Iran. As a result, KWU turned the reactor sites over to Iran in late August, 1979, and Iran fully abrogated all past agreements with KWU in late November, 1979. According to one report, the scientific cadre was reduced to only 13 people.[27]

The Iran-Iraq War, however, soon led the Khomeini government to revive Iran's nuclear program and interest in nuclear weapons. The Iranian government provided new funds to the research teams operating the US-supplied reactor at the Amirabad Nuclear Research Center, although it continued to operate the reactor under IAEA safeguards. At least one senior official of the new government, the Ayatollah Mohammed Hussein Beheshti, stated to officials managing the nuclear research effort in 1981 that the mandate of Iran's nuclear program had become the development of a nuclear weapon. Khamenei implied the same thing in a speech to Iran's Atomic Energy Organization of Iran (AEOI) in 1987.

Some experts feel that the IRGC moved experts and equipment from the Amirabad Nuclear Research Center to a new nuclear weapons research facility near Isfahan in the mid-1980s, and formed a new nuclear research center at the University of Isfahan in 1984—with French assistance.[28] Unlike many Iranian facilities, the center at Isfahan was not declared to the IAEA until February, 1992, when the IAEA was allowed to make a cursory inspection of six sites that various reports had claimed were the location of Iran's nuclear weapons efforts.[29]

Further, these Western experts believe that Iran's efforts to acquire nuclear weapons accelerated in the late 1980s—although it is not possible to separate such efforts definitively from efforts to acquire nuclear power generating facilities. Iran's Yazd Province has significant uranium deposits (at least 5,000 tons) in the Shagand region, and Iran announced in 1987 that it had plans to set up a yellow cake plant in the Yazd Province.[30] This facility was under construction by 1989, and Iran may have begun to build a uranium processing or an enrichment facility at Pilcaniyeu.[31]

Iran may also have opened a new uranium ore processing plant close to its Shagand uranium mine in March, 1990, and it seems to have extended its search for uranium ore into three additional areas. Iran may have also begun to exploit stocks of yellow cake that the Shah had obtained from South Africa in the late 1970s while obtaining uranium dioxide from Argentina by purchasing it through Algeria.[32]

Iran began to show a renewed interest in laser isotope separation (LIS) in the mid-1980s, and it held a conference on LIS in September, 1987.[33] On February

7, 1990, the speaker of the Majlis publicly toured the Atomic Energy Organization of Iran and opened the new Jabir Ibn al Hayyan laboratory to train Iranian nuclear technicians.[34] Reports then surfaced that Iran had at least 200 scientists and a workforce of about 2,000 devoted to nuclear research.[35]

Iran opened a new nuclear research center in Isfahan in 1984, located about 4 kilometers outside of the city and between the villages of Shahrida and Fulashans. This facility was built at a scale far beyond the needs of peaceful research, and Iran sought French and Pakistani help for a new research reactor for this center. The Khomeini government may also have obtained several thousand pounds of uranium dioxide from Argentina by purchasing it through Algeria. Uranium dioxide is considerably more refined than yellow cake, and it is much easier to use in irradiating material in a reactor to produce plutonium.[36]

Iran sought foreign support from a range of sources. Pakistan signed a nuclear cooperation agreement with Iran in 1987. Specialists from the Atomic Energy Organization of Iran began to train in Pakistan, and Dr. Abdul Kadr Khan, who has directed much of Pakistan's efforts to develop nuclear weapons material, visited Tehran and Bushehr in February, 1986 and January, 1987.[37]

Iran also strengthened its nuclear research ties to the People's Republic of China. The two countries signed a formal nuclear research cooperation agreement in 1990, although cooperation had begun as early as 1985—after Iran had suffered its first major chemical attacks from Iraq and had started to give its nuclear effort high priority. Iranian nuclear engineers appear to have begun training in China, and China seems to have transferred nuclear research technology for reactor construction and other projects, and possibly some technology for LIS, to an Iranian facility at Isfahan.[38]

While Iran proved unable to get a reactor from France or Pakistan, it had more success with China. It obtained a subcritical research reactor from the People's Republic of China in 1985 and a small Calutron to use in enrichment research in 1987. This Calutron was only a 1 milliamp machine, versus the 600 milliamp machines used by Iraq in its weapons enrichment efforts, and it was so small that it was suitable only for research purposes—specifically to test insulators and liners and to produce stable isotopes of zinc for pharmaceutical purposes.

Iran recruited Iranian nuclear scientists living overseas and tried to renew its power reactor program as a way of getting enriched material. In 1984, the Khomeini government began to restart work at the Bushehr reactor complex. The two 3,765 megawatt reactors were located on the Gulf about 18 kilometers southwest of the city. While most estimates indicate that they were about 60% complete, others indicate that 85% of the construction work and 65% of the electrical and mechanical work were complete.[39]

These Iranian efforts suffered major setbacks, however, when Iraq repeatedly bombed Iran's reactor projects at Bushehr. These Iraqi bombings occurred on March 24, 1984, February 12, 1985, March 4, 1985, July 12, 1986, November

17, 1987, November 19, 1987, and July 19, 1988. At least some foreign technicians died during these bombings, and work on the reactors was often suspended. It is interesting to note that the 1987 and 1988 raids may have been a response to the fact that Iran had begun to move IAEA safeguarded material to the area in February, 1987.[40]

CREEPING PROLIFERATION UNDER RAFSANJANI

The course of the Iranian nuclear program has become harder to trace since the end of the Iran-Iraq War. It has been the source of many unconfirmed rumors which exaggerate the size and progress of Iran's effort—more than a few inspired by untrustworthy extremist opponents of the Iranian regime like the Iraqi-financed Iranian People's Mujahideen.[41]

Most Western experts believe, however, that Iran's program has a far lower scale than Iraq's program before the Gulf War. One key source of such estimates is the character of Iran's imports of dual-use technology and continuing covert Iranian attempts to illegally import controlled technologies from the West. The details of such import efforts are often classified, but Iran's imports follow a pattern that is clearly part of a nuclear weapons program, and Iran's efforts over any given period of time provide a rough picture of its progress.[42]

Those aspects of Iran's program that are visible indicate that Iran has had only uncertain success. Argentina agreed to train Iranian technicians at its Jose Balaseiro Nuclear Institute, and it sold Iran $5.5 million worth of uranium for its small Amirabad Nuclear Research Center reactor in May, 1987. A CENA team visited Iran in late 1987 and early 1988, and it seems to have agreed to sell Iran the technology necessary to operate its reactor with 20% enriched uranium as a substitute for the highly enriched core provided by the United States, and possibly uranium enrichment and plutonium reprocessing technology as well.[43]

Changes in Argentina's government, however, made it much less willing to support proliferation. The Argentine government announced in February, 1992 that it was canceling an $18 million nuclear technology sale to Iran because it had not signed a nuclear safeguards arrangement. Argentine press sources suggested, however, that Argentina was reacting to US pressure.[44]

In February, 1990, a Spanish paper reported that Associated Enterprises of Spain was negotiating the completion of the two nuclear power plants at Bushehr. Another Spanish firm, ENUSA (National Uranium Enterprises), was to provide the fuel, and the KWU would be involved. Later reports indicated that a 10-man delegation from Iran's Ministry of Industry was in Madrid negotiating with the director of Associated Enterprises, Adolofo Garcia Rodriguez.[45] Iran also negotiated with Spain to repair and complete the reactors that the Shah had begun at Bushehr, as well as with Kraftwerke Union and CENA of Germany in the late 1980s and early 1990s. Iran attempted to import reactor parts from

Siemens in Germany and Skoda in Czechoslovakia.[46] None of these efforts solved Iran's problems in rebuilding its reactor program, but all demonstrated the depth of its interest.

Iran took other measures to strengthen its nuclear program during the early 1990s. It installed a cyclotron from Ion Beam Applications in Belgium at a facility in Karzaj in 1991. It signed an agreement with China's Commission on Science, Technology, and Industry for National Defense on January 21, 1991, to build a small 27-kilowatt research reactor at Iran's nuclear weapons research facility at Isfahan. This reactor was evidently to be plutonium fueled, and may have come on-line in 1994.[47] On November 4, 1991, China stated that it had signed commercial cooperation agreements with Iran in 1989 and 1991, and that it would transfer an electromagnetic isotope separator (Calutron) and a smaller nuclear reactor for "peaceful and commercial" purposes.

The Chinese reactor and Calutron were small research-scale systems and had no direct value in producing fissile material. They did, however, give Iran more knowledge of reactor and enrichment technology, and US experts believe that China provided Iran with additional data on chemical separation, other enrichment technology, the design for facilities to convert uranium to uranium hexaflouride to make reactor fuel, and help in processing yellow cake.[48]

Iran conducted experiments in uranium enrichment and centrifuge technology at its Sharif University of Technology in Tehran. Sharif University was also linked to efforts to import cylinders of fluorine suitable for processing enriched material and attempts to import specialized magnets that can be used for centrifuges from Thyssen in Germany in 1991. It is clear from Iran's imports that it has sought centrifuge technology ever since. Although many of Iran's efforts have never been made public, British customs officials seized 110 pounds of maraging steel being shipped to Iran in July, 1996.

Iran seems to have conducted research into plutonium separation, and Iranians published research on uses of tritium that had applications to nuclear weapons boosting. Iran also obtained a wide range of US and other nuclear literature with applications for weapons designs.[49] Italian inspectors seized eight steam condensers bound for Iran that could be used in a covert reactor program in 1993 and high technology ultrasound equipment suitable for reactor testing at the port of Bari in January, 1994.

Other aspects of Iran's nuclear research effort had potential weapons applications. Iran continued to operate an Argentine-fueled 5 megawatt light water highly enriched uranium reactor at the University of Tehran. It is operated by a Chinese-supplied neutron source research reactor and subcritical assemblies with 900 grams of highly enriched uranium at its Isfahan Nuclear Research Center. This center has experimented with a heavy water zero-power reactor, a light water subcritical reactor, and a graphite subcritical reactor. In addition, it may have experimented with some aspects of nuclear weapons design.[50]

Chinese Reactor Deals

After its failures in the West, Iran turned to China and Russia. On September 10, 1992, Rafsanjani made a visit to Beijing, where he is reported to have finished negotiations to purchase one or two 300–330 megawatt reactors from the People's Republic of China. A tentative agreement to sell one such reactor was announced by Iran's Minister of Defense during the visit. Further, the Atomic Energy Organization of Iran seems to have tried to unilaterally transfer the reactor site from Darkovin to less seismically stable sites in Bushehr, and then refused to allow China to fully survey the site or pay for the increased cost of the move.[51] Interestingly enough, this was the same general period in which China joined the Nuclear Non-Proliferation Treaty (it had joined the IAEA in 1988).

This announcement led to immediate US protests to the People's Republic of China.[52] As a result the sale was deferred, and China's willingness to sell to Iran has since fluctuated with the quality of Chinese-US relations. For example, Iran and the PRC announced that they had signed an agreement for the PRC to build a 300-megawatt reactor near Tehran on July 4, 1994.[53] Since that time, Iran has expressed an interest in buying two 300-megawatt pressurized water nuclear reactors from China, similar to the Chinese plant at Qinshan in the Zhejiang Province. At least one of these reactors was evidently to be sited near Esteghial, which is near Bushehr on the Gulf Coast.[54]

Iranian officials indicated in mid-May, 1995 that Iran had already made an $800–$900 million down payment on the deal. Reports also surfaced in September, 1995 that China was helping Iran develop Calutron production facilities at Karaij, about 160 kilometers northeast of Tehran, and the State Department indicated that China was helping Iran develop gas diffusion facilities near Isfahan in April, 1996. Other reports surfaced that China might have revitalized its reactor deal with Iran in November, 1996 and early 1997, and the CIA reported that Iran had made large—but unspecified—nuclear-related purchases from China.[55]

Each of these announcements has been followed, however, by new exchanges between the United States and China that have delayed or blocked Chinese-Iranian deals. For example, discussions with the United States helped lead China to pledge not to provide any assistance to a facility that was not under IAEA safeguards on May 11, 1996. China then issued detailed regulations to implement this pledge on September 11, 1996—after further talks with the United States.[56]

According to US reports, China also agreed not to sell Iran a uranium hexaflouride conversion plant in December, 1996.[57] Similarly, China's Prime Minister, Li Lanqing, is reported to have assured Israel's Prime Minister, Benjamin Netanyahu, that China would not supply Iran with reactor technology or other technology that could be used in a nuclear weapons program during Netanyahu's visit to China in August, 1997.[58] The Chinese Foreign Ministry also issued a statement on October 21, 1997, that "Our peaceful use of nuclear energy with Iran has not been carried out because of some disputes over the contract."[59]

President Clinton gave the issue high priority during President Jiang Zemin's visit to the United States in late October, 1997. In spite of protests by its own National Nuclear Corporation, China agreed to halt nuclear assistance to Iran in return for a US agreement to allow US firms to sell China the technology it needed for nuclear power plants. While China did not agree to join the Nuclear Supplier's Group—because of its nuclear sales to India and Pakistan—it did agree not to provide further nuclear support of any kind to Iran, regardless of whether it was permitted under the terms of the NPT.

The Clinton administration also stated during the visit that China had not provided any assistance to a facility that was not under IAEA safeguards once it had pledged not to do so on May 11, 1996. John Holum, the Acting Under Secretary of State for Arms Control and International Security Affairs, repeated these claims on March 26, 1998, during a visit to China. President Clinton repeated them when he visited China in June.[60]

These statements are interesting because China only seems to have suspended the sale of hundreds of tons of anhydrous hydrogen fluoride (AHF or hydrofluoric acid, a chemical used in enriching uranium) by the China Nuclear Energy Industry to the Isfahan Nuclear Research Center in February, 1998. China only did so three years after US intelligence had first detected the sale, and nearly two years after it had agreed not to make such sales of this kind. The sale was so large that it would have given Iran half a decade's worth of material for an ambitious nuclear program. Furthermore, China was still contracted for the sale, although AHF is also listed as a precursor to nerve gas.[61]

China has limits on what it can sell. Its nuclear industry is still in the developmental stage, and China has had serious problems in bringing some of its reactors on-line and keeping them operating. The Chinese reactor at Qinshan uses a Japanese-made reactor vessel and German primary cooling pumps, and it is not clear if this technology will be exportable to Iran.[62] When these uncertainties are coupled with Iran's financial problems, they make any major Chinese deal with Iran a continuing uncertainty, particularly if China does become a major importer of nuclear technology from the United States.[63]

Nevertheless, Iran may still be getting nuclear technology from China. Iran denied that China had halted nuclear cooperation on March 15, 1998, and called US claims "unsubstantiated propaganda." There are some indications that China also continues to supply maraging steel to Iran and components that can be used for centrifuges.[64]

Russian Reactor Deals

Iran first began to seek nuclear reactors from Russia in the mid-1980s, and it has conducted negotiations with Russia ever since. Reports surfaced in the late

1980s that Russia had signed a contract to sell two nuclear reactors to Iran—although the existence of any such contracts was not made public, and no tangible steps seemed to follow. Reporting by the Atomic Energy Organization of Iran indicates that the deal may have broken down because Iran proposed a site at Gorgan that was not properly stable and then attempted to move the site back to Bushehr without proper coordination.[65]

Iran's negotiations with Russia resumed, however, and had more success. On November 20, 1994, Iran announced that Russia had agreed to a $780 million deal to complete a reactor at Bushehr that German companies had begun during the time of the Shah.[66] Iran signed this agreement with Russia on January 8, 1995, by which time its cost had escalated to $850 million.[67] The nuclear facility at Bushehr is about 730 miles south of Tehran and 15 miles from the city of Bushehr. It is the site of the two incomplete 1,200-megawatt reactors that Siemens had begun to construct in 1976.

Although work stopped at the site in 1979, after the fall of the Shah, Iran kept the facility active, and some 300–400 Iranians normally lived on the site and maintained it during the period before Russia agreed to sell Iran a reactor. Iran had invested about $6 billion in the facility by the time the Shah fell. Construction of the main buildings and steel containment vessel for one of the reactors at Bushehr had reached 85% of completion at the time of the Shah's fall, and construction for the other was partially finished.[68] Facilities existed to house some 2,000 workers at the site, with a capacity to support up to 2,000 more. As a result, Russia was able to quickly deploy some 150 technicians to the reactor site once it signed an agreement with Iran. It began shipment of material in 1995 and announced that it planned to deploy up to 2,000 Russian workers and train some 500 Iranian technicians.[69]

The deal originally called for Russia to complete work on the first reactor by 2000.[70] The completion date and the cost of the contract depend, however, on whether Russia will be able to make the desired use of the existing facilities at the site, and whether Russia can tailor its VVER-1000 reactor design to fit these facilities.[71]

Both reactor facilities were damaged during the Iran-Iraq War, and the Russian VVER-1000 is physically different from a Siemens 1,300-megawatt reactor. Further, Siemens had not yet installed the reactors themselves and the steam generators which produce steam for the turbines.[72] Russian technicians and experts inspected the site in September, 1994 and concluded that corrosion was extensive, that their work would be hampered by the absence of the German technical documentation, and that it would be necessary to modify the outdated 1970s' design and redesign the buildings to take a Russian water-moderated, water-cooled reactor with a capacity of 1,000 megawatts, the VVER-1000.[73]

As a result, Russia is at best able to use some of the remaining buildings and control facilities, and bringing the reactor fully on-line will probably lag until at least 2005, although Reza Amrollahi, the head of the Atomic Energy Organization of Iran, still claimed in July, 1997 that it would come on-line during

2000.[74] Past efforts to export reactor designs have led to significant delays and cost escalation—without the complications inherent in Russia's attempt to make use of facilities designed for Germany's very different reactors.

There are reports of other problems and delays. Iran is reported to have objected to the fact that some of the Russians in the bank financing the project were Jewish. There seem to be unanticipated problems with vulnerability to earthquakes that could delay progress by a year, and it is far from clear whether Iran and Russia have established an efficient method of transferring payments and measuring progress. There is also considerable friction between the Iranian and Russian workers at Bushehr, and the Russians experience problems in getting visas and decent living and working conditions for the Russian workers at the reactor site.[75]

The United States has created other problems by persuading the Ukraine to keep its state-owned AOA Turboatom from supplying the turbines for Bushehr. On March 6, 1998, the United States and the Ukraine initialed an accord allowing US firms to bid on work on Ukrainian nuclear power plants, after the Ukraine promised not to supply nuclear technology to Iran. This agreement meant that the Ukraine had to give up a $45 million contract for the turbines, but it also allowed it to obtain US bids on badly needed work to revitalize the Soviet-supplied nuclear power plants in the Ukraine, work worth some $1.2 billion.[76]

Iran did, however, convert many of its subcontracts to "turnkey" Russian projects on February 2, 1998. It did so in an effort to eliminate consistent delays and quality control problems in the work done by Iranian subcontractors, and to give the Russian team greater control over the entire project effort and systems integration. Iranians were originally supposed to build the reactor hall, and the resulting delays were so serious that the project had only accomplished five months of work over a 25-month period, putting the project some 20 months behind.

In making this deal, Iran also agreed to buy the turbines from a Russian factory in St. Petersburg and increased the cost of its contracts with Russia by a significant, although unstated, amount above the $850 million contracts that had previously been agreed to. Russian sources report that Iran also improved the flow of its payments. As a result, Iran seems deeply committed to completing the project in spite of growing problems with low oil revenues.[77]

Longer-Term Reactor Programs

The purchase of Russian support may also prove to be the first step in a far more ambitious Iranian effort. Iran has shown an interest in purchasing another VVER-1000 reactor for use at Bushehr. Various sources also indicate that Iran is seeking to purchase two V-213 VVER 440 power reactors and another large research reactor, or that it is seeking to purchase a total of five large 1,300 megawatt reactors.[78]

At least one speech by Reza Amrollahi indicated that Iran eventually expected to build up to 20 nuclear power plants, although he later stated that his views had been misinterpreted and that Iran also expected to get 5% of its electricity from nuclear power plants by the year 2000.[79] Georgi Kaurov, a spokesman for the Russian Atomic Energy Ministry, confirmed in a public statement on March 6, 1998, that Russia was willing to sell such reactors in spite of US pressure not to do so.[80]

US experts believe that Iran is now seeking to buy four to five light water reactors from Russia, including two 1,000 megawatt reactors and two 463 megawatt reactors (at a cost in excess of $5 billion) that can be used to produce substantial amounts of fissile material for nuclear weapons. They also believe that Iran has aggressively sought to buy highly enriched and/or fissile material from the former Soviet Union, as well as the services of Soviet nuclear weapons designers.[81]

These conclusions have been supported by recent developments in Iran. Shortly after President Khatami replaced Reza Amrollahi, the head of the Atomic Energy Organization of Iran, with Gholamreza Aghazadeh, Aghazadeh reaffirmed Iran's commitment to a massive nuclear power program. On October 3, 1997, Amrollahi indicated during a meeting with Hans Blix, the head of the International Atomic Energy Agency (IAEA), that Iran planned to eventually produce 20% of Iran's electric power needs from nuclear units. This meant adding a second 1,000 megawatt generating unit to its existing efforts to build a 1,000 megawatt unit in Bushehr. He indicated that Iran had approached Russia to buy two more 440 megawatt reactors and was seeking an eventual total of six, and that it was still seeking two 300 megawatt nuclear reactors from China.[82]

Reactors and Proliferation

It is not clear that Iran's reactor purchases are meant to be an integrated part of Iran's nuclear weapons effort, as distinguished from a way of acquiring the necessary nuclear technology and creating a mid-to long-term contingency capability. Iran has justified its reactor program by claiming that it needs to provide electric power from nuclear generators to reduce its use of exportable oil and gas. There are some experts who argue that Iran is seriously seeking to pursue this goal, that power reactors are an extremely inefficient way to obtain fissile material, and that Iran is more likely to support its weapons programs with specially designed smaller reactors, purchases of fissile material from the FSU, or other methods of enrichment.

Nevertheless, Iran's claims relating to its need for nuclear power present serious economic credibility problems that are the subject of debate within Iran as well as within the West. One Iranian newspaper, for example, referred to the efforts of the Atomic Energy Organization of Iran in September, 1997 by stating that, "the construction of a nuclear power plant in Iran is more like a joke."[83]

Reactors that cost billions of dollars in hard currency seem to make limited economic sense in a country with vast supplies of natural gas that can be used to generate electricity at 25% to 33% of the cost of nuclear electricity at market price conditions. This is particularly true since Iran faces a major problem in terms of spending hard currency, and will have to pay at least twice per installed kilowatt than what it would have to pay for the capital cost of a gas-fired power plant. US intelligence studies have found that Iran has little hope of ever breaking even on an investment in nuclear power relative to the consumption of domestic natural gas, and that it makes limited economic sense for Iran to concentrate all of the reactors in one area so far away from Iran's cities and industrial facilities in the north.[84]

The credibility of such claims is further undermined by the long history of problems with the nuclear weapons programs in other countries, by Iran's policy of underpricing oil and gas to the point where the increase in domestic consumption is cutting into its export capacity, and by Iran's acute hard currency problems. For example, President Rafsanjani undercut the argument that Iran needed nuclear power to allow gas to be exported by announcing that Iran had "endless" gas reserves and over 150 years of oil reserves in a speech to the Majlis on June 1, 1996. Rafsanjani announced the discovery of a new gas field of at least 9 trillion cubic feet and estimated Iran's oil reserves at 93 billion barrels.[85] US and European studies confirm these estimates and indicate that Iran's gas reserves are probably substantially larger.

Some experts argue that Iran does not plan in economic terms and that Russia has priced its initial contracts so far below the normal world market price for such reactors that they might be economical, even for a nation with Iran's gas resources. Such experts also argue that Iran has little experience with the real-world life cycle cost of nuclear reactors and may be reacting to price quotes that give it a false impression of the economics involved.

Russia is selling light water reactors which are less suited to producing plutonium than the heavy water reactors Iran sought initially. Russia has repeatedly denied that it will give Iran any assistance in developing nuclear weapons, has repeatedly indicated that it will take back the plutonium-bearing spent fuel in the reactor, and has announced that Iran has signed a $30 million deal with Russia to provide fuel for the reactors and reprocess spent fuel in Russia.[86]

These Russian denials, however, need to be put into context. The United States put intense pressure on Russia immediately after its deal with Iran when the United States received strong indications that Russia had agreed to provide centrifuge and other enrichment technology as part of the deal. The United States claimed that Victor Mikhaliov, the head of Russia's Atomic Energy Ministry, had proposed the sale of a centrifuge plant in April, 1995. The United States also indicated that it had persuaded Russia not to sell Iran centrifuge technology as part of the reactor deal during the summit meeting between Presidents Clinton and Yeltsin in May, 1995. According to some reports, Russia was to reprocess the fuel at its Mayak plant near Chelyabinsk in the Urals, and could store it at an existing facility, at Krasnoyarsk-26 in southern Siberia.[87]

It was only after US pressure that Russia publicly stated that it never planned to sell centrifuge and advanced enrichment technology to Iran, and Iran denied that it had ever been interested in such technology.[88] For example, the statement of Mohammed Sadegh Ayatollahi, Iran's representative to the IAEA, revealed that, "We've had contracts before for the Bushehr plant in which we agreed that the spent fuel would go back to the supplier. For our contract with the Russians and Chinese, it is the same."[89]

Iran may have given up little by making overt agreements not to reprocess plutonium. Moving forward with the reactor deal means that Iran will end up with enough technology transfer to build reactors on its own. While the Russian reactor design is scarcely ideally suited to producing plutonium, it is a large facility that can be used to produce plutonium if Iran changes its mind. Once the reactor is in operation, it is far from clear what the world would do about any Iranian violation of the IAEA. Plutonium reprocessing technology is not particularly challenging, and no country that has so far attempted such reprocessing has failed. Iran can also go on with an overt reactor program while it pursues low-level or covert efforts to acquire uranium enrichment capabilities.

There are still major uncertainties as to how many scientists and technicians from the former Soviet Union may be supporting Iran. Few US intelligence experts seem to believe the recurrent press reports of a large presence of FSU technical experts in Iran. At the same time, US, British, French, and Israeli experts do indicate that Iran has sought to buy nuclear technology on the black market in a number of FSU countries, and attempted to buy stocks of fissile material from one. There also are reports that some FSU nuclear scientists and technicians are working in Iran in areas that have nothing to do with its Russian-supported nuclear power program. There are also serious questions as to whether Russian scientists might work with Iranian experts to use the reactor at Busher to covertly produce plutonium isotopes, if the reactor begins operation.[90]

Furthermore, private and state-owned Russian firms may not be fully honoring the agreements of the Russian government. The CIA indicates that Russia provided important transfers of nuclear technology to Iran in 1996. The Clinton administration quietly complained to President Yeltsin about such transfers in July, 1997. It expressed concern that Russia had broadened its technology transfers and might not be limiting its aid to Iran in setting up a plutonium reprocessing capability.[91]

These problems and uncertainties led Israel to claim in early 1997 that Russia was providing Iran with nuclear weapons technology. Israeli Prime Minister Benjamin Netanyahu raised the issue during a March 10–12 visit to Moscow. He received assurances from President Yeltsin that, "The nuclear cooperation [with Iran] was at a very rudimentary level and that [cooperation on] ballistic missiles, he said, was not taking place and will not take place." Israel and Russia also reported to have reached an agreement to cooperate in countering the illegal traffic in such technology on March 12, 1997.[92]

Russia still has vast stocks of nuclear weapons, fissile material, and highly enriched material. The United States officially stated that it "has no evidence whatsoever'' of any transfer of Russian nuclear weapons to Iran with the *Jerusalem Post* reported that it had documents showing that Iran had smuggled in two weapons from Russia in the early 1990s. (The documents implicated Brigadier General Rahim Safavi, then Deputy Commander of the IRGC, and Reza Amrollahi, then head of the Iranian Atomic Energy Organization.)[93]

The article did, however, raise an important problem. Iran has consistently sought enriched and weapons grade material from the former Soviet republics since 1990, and has been implicated in nuclear smuggling efforts. In July, 1998, Turkish police seized 25 tubes of nuclear material in a raid in Turkey's border area with Iran and arrested six men, including an Iranian. The arrests came only after prior smuggling incidents had been successful.[94] There is a serious risk that Iran will be successful in getting fissile material, highly enriched material, or actual weapons at some point in the future.

Interestingly enough, Russian officials are privately ambiguous about the character of the Russian effort to block nuclear transfers. Discussions with senior Russian officials from the MVD, Foreign Intelligence Service, and diplomatic service in June, 1998 indicated that the officials involved felt that the Russian reactor would have little direct value in helping Iran build a bomb. At the same time, Russian intelligence officers stated that Iran had sought other nuclear technology in Russia that seemed to be part of a nuclear weapons program, and that Russia had arrested Russian citizens involved in the transfer of such technology. They also stated that Russia had only dropped Iran from its public list of proliferators after the reactor sale, and that this was only done as the result of political direction.

PROLIFERATION AND THE NUCLEAR NON-PROLIFERATION TREATY

Iran has firmly and repeatedly denied that it is seeking nuclear weapons. Some of these Iranian denials have been cited earlier, but there are many others. For example, Khamenei stated on July 13, 1992, that charges that Iran was proliferating were the result of "American and Zionist loudspeakers . . . obviously false. . . . They know it is a lie. . . . You are mistaken if you think that the Islamic Republic's strength lies in the obtaining or domestic manufacture of an atomic bomb . . . the power of faith will foil all the conspiracies and ploys of the enemy."

Reza Amrollahi, the former head of the Atomic Energy Organization of Iran, has said that, "Our nuclear program is peaceful. . . . My country has signed the NPT and has repeatedly expressed its willingness to honor it. . . . Also, we are an active member of the IAEA."[95] The Iranian official news agency declared on January 8, 1995, that, "Iran simply does not have the ambition to become a nuclear weapons state. Iran does not, and will not, in light of its own interest, engage in a nuclear weapons program."[96] President Rafsanjani answered a question relating to Iran's desire to proliferate in an interview on the program

Figure 20.1
The Location of Iranian Nuclear Facilities and Major Transshipment Centers

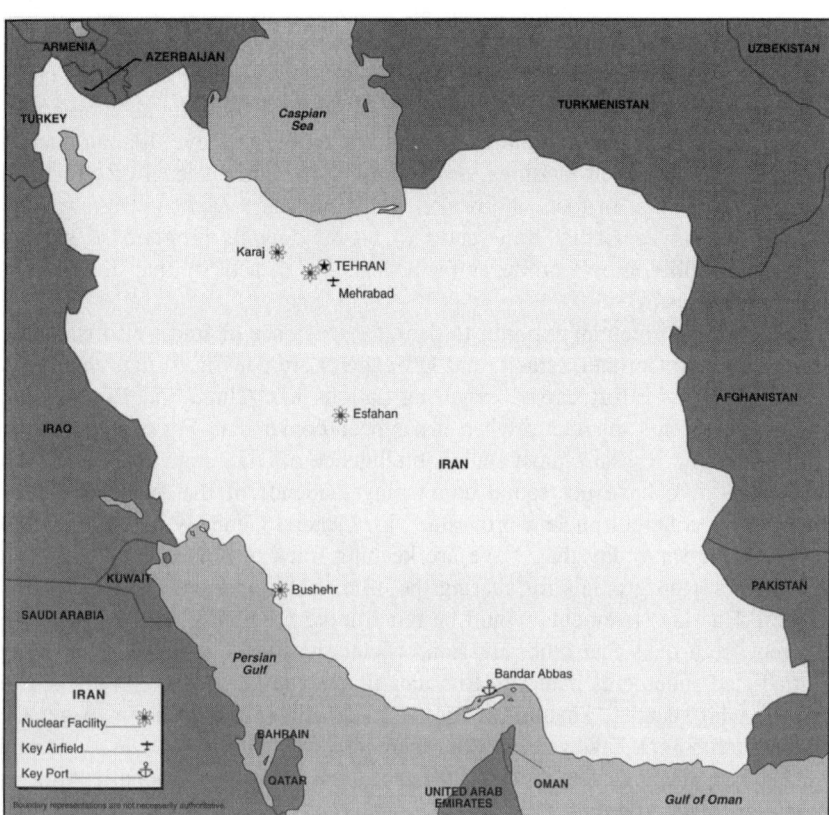

Source: Office of the Secretary of Defense, *Proliferation: Threat and Response*, Washington, Department of Defense, April, 1996, p. 15.

60 Minutes in April, 1997 in which he stated, "Definitely not. I hate this weapon."[97]

The problem with such statements is that they often seem to be contradicted by Iran's purchase and acquisition programs, and are tied to the assumption that proliferation can be tracked by identifying key facilities and using the IAEA to inspect them.

Iranian Nuclear Weapons Facilities

It is far easier to know that a nation is proliferating than it is to know specifically where it is proliferating. The location of several key declared Iranian nuclear facilities and known nuclear transshipment centers is shown in Figure 20.1. However, little credible data is available on the exact size and nature of

Iran's nuclear weapons effort, the specific facilities involved, or the exact nature of Iran's imports of nuclear weapons-related and dual-use technology.

Iran has demonstrated that it is capable of copying the sheltering and satellite deception techniques used by Iraq before the Gulf War, and a small, well-dispersed nuclear weapons program is very difficult to detect and characterize without on-site inspection and continuous monitoring.[98] Without such an effort, there is no way to publicly validate the existence of a low-level Iranian nuclear weapons effort at given facilities, or to describe the current level of effort and its probable results. In fact, one reason Iran's nuclear weapons program is so difficult to analyze is that Iran seems to be building its program so slowly. "Creeping proliferation" produces far fewer signs of activity than Iraq's massive investments.[99]

This allows a potential exporter to deny the existence of Iran's efforts. While British, French, German, Israeli, and US experts are convinced that an Iranian nuclear weapons effort exists, exporting nations like China and Russia have effectively rejected this claim when it has been convenient. For example, Yevgeny Primakov, Russia's most senior intelligence official, stated on March 23, 1995, that "We have not found convincing evidence of the existence in the country of a coherent nuclear program." Lt. General Gennady Yevstafiyev declared on the same day that, "We are keeping track of developments.... But so far, we see no grounds for sharing the official US position."

These Russian statements would be much more credible if they were not so different from ones that other Russian officials had made a year earlier. They contradicted statements made by Russians like Alexei Yablokov, an advisor to Yeltsin, who stated, "Thanks to Russia, Iran will be in a position to get the nuclear bomb in a few years.... By signing this contract, Russia is arming Iran." They do, however, illustrate the fact there is no international consensus regarding Iran's activities.[100]

Scare Reports and Deliberate Misinformation

The situation has not been helped by scare reports and deliberate misinformation. For example, Israeli sources have claimed that Iran sought to buy the nuclear enrichment facilities that South Africa developed for its nuclear weapons program, although there is little evidence to support these reports.[101] Similarly, the People's Mujahideen, a violent anti-regime group, has made a long series of detailed claims. At various times, the People's Mujahideen has reported that:

- Iran's facilities include a weapons site called Ma'allem Kelayah, near Qazvin on the Caspian. This is said to be an IRGC-run facility established in 1987, which has involved an Iranian investment of $300 million. Supposedly the site was to house the 10-megawatt reactor Iran tried to buy from India.
- Two Soviet reactors were to be installed at a large site at Gorgan on the Caspian, under the direction of Russian physicists.

- The People's Republic of China provided uranium enrichment equipment and technicians for the site at Darkhouin, where Iran once planned to build a French reactor.
- A nuclear reactor was being constructed at Karaj; and another nuclear weapons facility exists in the south central part of Iran, near the Iraqi border.
- The ammonia and urea plant that the British firm M. W. Kellog was building at Borujerd in the Khorassan Province, near the border with Turkestan, might be adapted to produce heavy water.
- The Amir Kabar Technical University, the Atomic Energy Organization of Iran (AEOI) (also known as the Organization for Atomic Energy of Iran, or AEOI), Dor Argham Ltd., the Education and Research Institute, GAM Iranian Communications, Ghoods Research Center, Iran Argham Co., Iran Electronic Industries, Iranian Research Organization, Ministry of Sepah, Research and Development Group, Sezemane Sanaye Defa, the Sharif University of Technology, Taradis Iran Computer Company, and Zakaria Al-Razi Chemical Company are all participants in the Iranian nuclear weapons effort.[102]

Other sources based on opposition data have listed the Atomic Energy Organization of Iran, the Laser Research Center and Ibn-e Heysam Research and Laboratory Complex, the Bonab Atomic Energy Research Center (East Azerbaijan), the Imam Hussein University of the Revolutionary Guards, the Jabit bin al-Hayyan Laboratory, the Khoshomi uranium mine (Yazd), a possible site at Moallem Kalayeh, the Nuclear Research Center at Tehran University, the Nuclear Research Center for Agriculture and Medicine (Karaj), the Nuclear Research Center of Technology (Isfahan), the Saghand Uranium mine (Yazd), and the Sharif University (Tehran) and its Physics Research Center.[103]

The problem with such lists of weapons facilities is that they have never been confirmed as being accurate and end in discrediting more cautious and balanced reports. They also tend to include virtually all of the major publicly known research centers in Iran, and to ignore the fact that much of Iran's effort may take place in facilities that do not have a name relating to nuclear research or consist of purchasing efforts made through Iran's vast network of cutouts and purchasing officers abroad.

Iran's present purchasing network is the product of more than 15 years of covert efforts to end-run Western and other foreign controls, and Iran has systematically lied about its activities ever since it set this network up following the beginning of the Iran hostage crisis. It is almost impossible to track all of the various fronts and covers Iran uses, but the German Ministry of Economics has circulated a wide list of such Iranian fronts which are known to have imported or attempted to import controlled items. These fronts include the

- Bonyad e-Mostazafan;
- Defense Industries Organization (Sazemane Sanaye Defa);
- Pars Garma Company, the Sadadja Industrial Group (Sadadja Sanaye Daryaee);
- Iran Telecommunications Industry (Sanaye Mokhaberet Iran);

- Shahid Hemat Industrial Group, the State Purchasing Organization, Education Research Institute (ERI);
- Iran Aircraft Manufacturing Industries (IAI);
- Iran Fair Deal Company, Iran Group of Surveyors;
- Iran Helicopter Support and Renewal Industries (IHI);
- Iran Navy Technical Supply Center;
- Iran Tehran Kohakd Daftar Nezarat, Industrial Development Group; and the
- Ministry of Defense (Vezerate Defa).[104]

There is no question that Iran has a large enough research and industrial base to hide a nuclear weapons effort of moderate size and a highly sophisticated purchasing network. The problem is to determine exactly what organizations and facilities are or are not "guilty."

The NPT, IAEA Inspections, and Deniability

Unfortunately, the Treaty on the Non-Proliferation of Nuclear Weapons (NPT) and the International Atomic Energy Agency (IAEA) are currently both a partial solution to this problem and a way of making it worse. The NPT and IAEA provide a set of controls and an inspection capability that has significant value, but they also legitimize the import of "peaceful" nuclear technology that can be used to develop a weapons program, and can be exploited to provide a cover for proliferation.

Under Article V of the NPT, nations are entitled to import nuclear reactors and substantial amounts of nuclear technology, as long as they allow IAEA inspection of the reactors in their declared facilities. This transfer of "peaceful" nuclear technology is giving Iran a steadily improving nuclear technology base which, in turn, improves Iran's capability to build covert reactor facilities, centrifuge facilities, and/or chemical separation facilities.

While the IAEA can and does regularly inspect Iran's declared nuclear facilities, this does not necessarily provide guarantees against proliferation. The IAEA only fully inspects declared Iranian facilities which have reactors or declared nuclear material. Any visits to other Iranian facilities do not involve the kind of intrusive inspection that can differentiate between a legitimate nuclear facility and one dedicated to a covert weapons program. As a result, IAEA efforts to date can neither confirm nor deny the existence of an Iranian nuclear weapons program. This is demonstrated by the fact that the IAEA repeatedly certified that Iraq was in compliance with the NPT before the Gulf War—a certification which was meaningless because the IAEA only inspected the facilities Iraq declared.

Even those Iranian facilities that are subject to IAEA inspection can present risks. As North Korea has demonstrated, a country could fully comply with all of the safeguards affecting reactor sales and then could reject IAEA safeguards once the reactor or reactors are complete. It can then process the used reactor rods for plutonium, and a nation like Iran will be able to refuel its reactors with locally made uranium rods. The types of reactors Iran is buying scarcely seem to be optimal designs for either plutonium irradiation or massive "cannibalization" of the reactor fuel, but Iran cannot buy other kinds of reactors. No one is selling the kind of research reactors France offered to Iraq at the time of the Osriaq deal, and Iraq showed at the time of the Gulf War that a nation would take drastic steps to create a nuclear weapon, even if its reactors were unsuitable designs.[105]

The IAEA can also be used to confuse or obfuscate a nation's activities. For example, the IAEA has made two special visits. It conducted a limited, prearranged visit to six of 10 suspected sites in February, 1992 and found no sign of weapons activity at any of these sites. It found that the uranium mining site at Saghand was at least five years away from production and had no uranium concentration plant. It also found the facility at Ma'allem Kelayah, which was said to be a nuclear weapons research center, to be little more than a motel-sized training and conference center. Further, the People's Republic of China-supplied Calutron at Shiraz was found to be so small that it could only be used to produce isotopes for medical research.[106]

Some sources charged that the IAEA only conducted a "familiarization tour" during its 1992 visit. They also charged that the IAEA may have been led to a decoy site, when it thought it was investigating a facility called Ma'allem Kelayah. IAEA spokesman David Kydd vehemently denied such reports that the IAEA was led to the wrong site, and this denial seems accurate. At the same time, the IAEA scarcely conducted a comprehensive inspection, did not carry out highly detailed examinations of the site, and did not inspect every activity.[107]

Iran let a new team from the IAEA visit during October–November, 1993.[108] This IAEA team had been given detailed briefings by the United States and other Western countries and was allowed to visit suspected buildings at three main nuclear research complexes near Tehran, Isfahan, and Karaj. Like the previous IAEA mission, however, it was a visit, not a full or special inspection mission. The IAEA was not equipped or organized to find covert Iranian activities or examine all of the activities in the research facilities it was allowed to visit. Further, the IAEA team did not have adequate access to soil and particle samples in the facilities it was allowed to visit.[109] Meaningful enforcement of the Nuclear Non-Proliferation Treaty would require all Iranian facilities to be subject to IAEA challenge inspection, and the IAEA would have to be supported by extensive national intelligence efforts to "target" suspected undeclared facilities.

Even then, there could be serious problems in determining what Iranian activities were and were not part of a weapons effort. Nuclear weapons research and development efforts are becoming steadily smaller in scale and easier to hide and disperse. Much of the data is now public. Computer simulation and pilot-scale testing can now be substituted for the large-scale efforts of the past, and can permit much smaller efforts than those of Israel, India, Pakistan, and South Africa. It would require continuing IAEA inspection of all mining, processing, and enrichment related research efforts and the analysis of weapons system delivery programs to firmly determine whether Iran's programs proved it was acquiring nuclear weapons.

At present, Iran can use the NPT and the IAEA to pursue a policy of deliberate ambiguity. It also can compartmentalize its efforts so the researchers involved may not know the real purpose of the effort, or to achieve "deniability." For example, Austrian scientists were discovered in 1997 to have spent a year working on a cyclotron at Iran's Karaj nuclear research center that some experts felt might be used as a prototype for processing uranium, and which other experts felt might be legitimate medical research. Only on-site inspection could hope to resolve such issues, provided that the ultimate intent of the program was clear from the physical evidence, its records, or interviews.[110]

Similarly, British customs officials seized 50 kilograms (110 pounds) of maraging steel in June, 1996. Maraging steel is a controlled export that can be used for some conventional weapons, including ballistic missiles, although its most likely use is the manufacture of centrifuges. The smuggler was identified as Ali Asghar Manzarpouri, a British citizen of Iranian origin living in Brighton. Manzarpouri was charged in a Brighton court on July 31, 1996. The Iranian effort to import maraging steel could not be linked to a specific end-user facility, and only intrusive challenge inspection could have hoped to identify the true end use of the material—provided that sufficient intelligence existed to identify the precise facility in Iran.[111] These same problems arose much earlier when Iran bought extensive amounts of nuclear centrifuge technology from Germany—although it denied doing so—and other specialized equipment that could be used to design and manufacture nuclear weapons and simulate nuclear tests.[112]

This situation may change. Governors of the IAEA took up a proposal in May, 1997 that would allow the IAEA to cover any facility in an NPT country, whether it was declared or not. The proposal would also allow routine environmental monitoring to detect the small amounts of isotopes that are likely to escape from any industrial scale plant or process and use spectrometry to identify the isotopic ratio of a sample containing a billionth of a gram of material. This would detect any unusual ratio of U-235 to U-238 and the presence of any element involved in plutonium processing in unusual amounts, as well as the products of nuclear fission like radioactive iodine and krypton isotopes. Small samples from the surface of walls and equipment, along with soil, water, air, and vegetation samples, might reveal a great deal.[113]

At the same time, the NPT does not currently provide the kind of intrusive inspection regime that would be needed, and it is unclear that the new rules proposed to strengthen the NPT in May, 1997 will make a critical difference in preventing proliferation by a determined, closed society conducting small-scale, well-dispersed covert programs. Certainly, Iran would have to fully comply with every aspect of the new NPT inspection regime for there to be any hope that the IAEA could prevent a significant effort.[114]

Meaningful enforcement of a non-proliferation inspection effort would also require better international cooperation in reporting the export of dual-use technology, and arrangements that allowed the IAEA to directly interrogate countries as to the purpose of such exports and their end user, and to then inspect the resulting supplier facilities. This is particularly true of China and Russia. Only a few countries really cooperate in pooling sensitive export data, and none allow foreign inspection of possible suppliers. Most countries also carefully compartmentalize their efforts to control nuclear proliferation so that only a few officials know the full details.

Furthermore, fully effective cooperation would be dependent on the existence of some kind of secure forum for exchanging data that prevented the leakage of sensitive intelligence material. It has become clear to US intelligence professionals that there are severe limits on how much detail on Iran's efforts can be briefed to other states. Classified briefings to nations in the Gulf, some European countries, and Japan have led to extensive leaks, because the foreign ministries of export-oriented countries tend to ignore the advice on their own national intelligence services. At present, nations like the United States run a major risk that providing data to the IAEA and to a number of key supplier countries may simply result in leaks to Iran which allow it to conceal or move its efforts. The end result is that US intelligence and targeting data are compromised without any benefits in limiting Iran's capabilities.

In summary, limited IAEA visits and Iranian denials scarcely mean that Iran does not have a clandestine nuclear program. Many Western experts believe that the fact that Iran has clandestinely sought the material needed for a nuclear weapons effort for more than a decade is more important than the ability to target given facilities.

POSSIBLE DATES FOR IRAN'S ACQUISITION OF NUCLEAR WEAPONS

There is no way to estimate when Iran will get nuclear weapons or to be certain that Iran will push its nuclear programs forward to the point where it has actual weapons. As has been noted earlier, President Khatami replaced Reza Amrollahi—the long-serving head of the Atomic Energy Organization of Iran— in early September, 1997. He replaced Amrollahi with Iran's former Oil Minister, Gholamreza Aghazadeh, who was also appointed a vice president and a member of the Expediency Council. Such an appointment could mean that Khatami was emphasizing the effective management of Iran's nuclear power program, seeking new direction for its nuclear weapons effort, or simply being part of the normal process of bureaucratic rotation and change.[115]

If Iran does push forward with nuclear weapons, it seems unlikely that it will acquire them in the near term, unless it can somehow buy fissile material from an outside source. As Lt. General Binford Peay, the former commander of USCENTCOM, stated in June, 1997,

> I would predict to you that it would be some time at the turn of the next century . . . I wouldn't want to put a date on it. I don't know if it's 2010, 2007, 2003. I am just saying it's coming closer. Your instincts tell you that that's the kind of speed they are moving at.[116]

Some sources have indicated in the past that Iran may be able to build a weapon relatively quickly, but they have proved to be pessimistic. Robert Gates, then Director of Central Intelligence, testified to Congress in February, 1992 that Iran was "building up its special weapons capability as part of a massive . . . effort to develop its military and defense capability."[117] In 1992 press reports by the US Central Intelligence Agency (CIA), National Intelligence Estimates (NIE) on this subject indicated that the CIA estimated that Iran could have a nuclear weapon by the year 2000. Reports coming out of Israel in January, 1995 also claimed that the United States and Israel estimated that Iran could have a nuclear weapon in five years.[118]

Other sources believe it may take Iran substantially longer to obtain nuclear weapons. US intelligence sources denied the reports coming out of Israel and estimated that it might take seven to fifteen years for Iran to acquire a nuclear weapon.[119] As has been mentioned earlier, John Holum testified to Congress in 1995 that Iran could have the bomb by 2003. In 1997, he testified that Iran could have the bomb by 2005–2007.[120] Although two years had passed in which Iran might have made substantial progress, the US estimate of the earliest date at which Iran could make its own bomb slipped by two to four years.

Such estimates are inherently uncertain. US Secretary of Defense William Perry stated on January 9, 1995, that "We believe that Iran is trying to develop a nuclear program. We believe it will be many, many years until they achieve such a capability. There are some things they might be able to do to short-cut that time."[121] In referring to "short cuts," Secretary Perry was concerned with the risk that Iran could obtain fissile material and weapons technology from the former Soviet Union or some other nation capable of producing fissile material. This risk creates another serious uncertainty affecting Iran's future nuclear capabilities. Reports during 1992 and 1993 that Iran had hired large numbers of Soviet nuclear scientists have proven to be unreliable.[122] Similarly, far more dramatic reports that Iran had succeeded in buying weapons-grade material from the former Soviet Union or nuclear armed missiles from Kazakhstan are unsubstantiated.

Martin Indyck, the Assistant Secretary of State for Near East Affairs, testified to the Senate Foreign Relations Committee on July 28, 1998, that Iran's Shihab-3 and Shihab-4 programs were clearly linked to its efforts to acquire nuclear weapons. He made it clear that the missiles would give Iran the range to hit targets in Israel, Turkey, and Saudi Arabia. In regard to Iran's nuclear program, Indyck stated that Iran had a "clandestine nuclear weapons program. People tend to say that a nuclear weapons capability is many years off. Our assessments vary. I would want to be a bit cautious about that because I believe there are large gaps in our knowledge of what is going on there because it's a clandestine program."[123]

At present, most experts feel that Iran has all of the basic technology to build a bomb, but lacks any rapid route to getting fissile uranium and plutonium. They also believe that Iran is increasingly worried about preemptive strikes by Israel or the United States. As a result, Iran deliberately has lowered the profile of its activities and only conducts a low-to-moderate level weapons design and development effort.[124] No serious expert has claimed that a major weapons grade production effort has yet been detected. As a result, many feel that Iran is at least five to seven years away from acquiring a nuclear device using its own enriched material, and six to nine years away from acquiring the ability to design a nuclear weapon that can be fitted into the warhead of a long-range missile system.

The "wild card" in all of these estimates is that the deadlines would change so radically if Iran could buy fissile material from another nation or source—such as the 500 kilograms of fissile material the United States airlifted out of Kazakhstan in 1994. This was enough material to make up to 25 nuclear weapons, and the United States acted primarily because Iran was actively seeking to buy such material.[125] If Iran could obtain weapons grade material, a number of experts believe that it could probably develop a gun or simple implosion nuclear weapon in nine to 36 months.

The risk of such a transfer of fissile material is significant. US experts believe that all of the weapons and fissile material remaining in the former Soviet Union are now stored in Russian facilities. The security of these facilities is still erratic, however, and there is a black market in nuclear material. While the radioactive material sold on the black market by the CIS and Central European citizens to date has consisted largely of plutonium 240, low-grade enriched uranium, or isotopes of material which have little value in a nuclear weapons program, this is no guarantee for the future. There are also no guarantees that Iran will not be able to purchase major transfers of nuclear weapons components and nuclear ballistic missile warhead technology.

IRAN'S NUCLEAR WAR-FIGHTING DOCTRINE AND CAPABILITIES

It is possible to speculate at vast length on what Iran would do with nuclear weapons. However, it is impossible to determine how aggressively Iran would exploit such a capability in terms of threatening or intimidating its neighbors, or putting pressure on the West. Trying to guess at Iran's nuclear war-fighting doctrine and actions is as speculative as guesses about how it would use biological weapons. It is quite possible that Iran has not yet looked far enough beyond its nuclear weapons acquisition efforts to work out detailed plans for possession. There is no way to know if Iran would choose a relatively stable model of deterrence or aggressively exploit its possession politically. It is equally difficult to guess whether Iran would develop an aggressive doctrine for use, consider developing a launch on warning/launch under attack capability, or reserve the use of such a weapon as a last resort.[126]

What is clear is that if Iran acquired a working nuclear device, this would suddenly and radically change perceptions of the military balance in the region. Iran is likely to acquire such weapons at about the same time it acquires Medium Range Ballistic Missiles (MRBMs), and this would be a volatile combination. Iran could destroy any hardened target, area target, or city within the range of its delivery systems. Iran's Southern Gulf neighbors are extremely vulnerable to attacks on a few cities, and even one successful nuclear attack might force a fundamental restructuring of their politics and/or economy. They are effectively "one bomb" countries.

Iranian nuclear capabilities would raise major mid-term and long-term challenges to the Southern Gulf states and to the West in terms of deterrence, defense, retaliation, and arms control. It would almost certainly accelerate efforts to deploy theater missile defenses—although such systems seem more likely to be "confidence builders" than leak-proof. It would almost certainly lead the United States to consider counterproliferation strikes on Iran, and to work with its Southern Gulf allies in developing an adequate deterrent. Given the US rejection of biological and chemical weapons, this raises the possibility of creating a major US theater nuclear deterrent, although such a deterrent could be sea and air based and deployed outside of the Gulf.

If the United States failed to provide such a deterrent, it seems likely that the Southern Gulf states would be forced to accommodate Iran or to seek weapons of mass destruction of their own. Further, such Iranian possession would almost certainly trigger a major new Iraqi effort to acquire such weapons and make any efforts at arms control meaningless for some years to come.

It is also impossible to dismiss the possibility that Iran or Iraq would choose to develop and use a "radiological weapon." Such a weapon could take three forms—all of which would interact with its potential use of chemical and biological weapons.

- *The first would be a "dirty weapon"* using fissile material with contaminated or low enrichment levels that would have limited heat and blast effects, but still produce yields of 3 to 5 kilotons, and which would effectively poison a city if detonated near the ground. Such a device would reduce some of the manufacturing and design problems inherent in creating clean or efficient nuclear weapons.
- *The second would be to use a weapon that had not been tested, which was felt to be unreliable, or which was on an inaccurate missile* and detonate it near the ground so that radiation effects compensate for a failure to reach design efficiency or accuracy of the delivery system.

- *The third would be to use radioactive material in micropowder or liquid form as a terror or an unconventional weapon.* It would be very difficult to get substantial lethality from the use of radioactive material, and such a weapon would be less efficient than biological weapons in terms of weight and lethality. It would, however, have the capacity to contaminate a key area and to create panic.

While the United States and Russia have rejected radiological weapons because they have the ability to precisely control the yield from their nuclear weapons, such options might be attractive to Iran or Iraq. As is the case with chemical and biological weapons, even the prospect of Iran's acquiring any such nuclear weapons has increased its ability to intimidate its neighbors.

As for war-fighting capability, the actual yield and effects of any Iranian nuclear weapon are probably not key issues. Any working nuclear device that Iran is likely to develop will be sufficient to destroy any hardened target, area target, or city in the Middle East. Nuclear weapons do, however, differ sharply in their effect as they grow in size. It is not possible to quantify these effects in terms of fallout, and the data on prompt radiation are controversial in terms of their lethal effect.

Iran's nuclear programs will also be heavily interactive with its biological and chemical programs and its efforts to improve its delivery capabilities. By the time Iran has significant nuclear capability, it also should have significant missile, cruise missile, and long-range strike aircraft capability—although it may not have cruise missiles capable of carrying a nuclear weapon. It should have rebuilt much of its conventional capabilities to the point where it has significant war-fighting capabilities, and it will pose a major threat to other nations in the region—possibly as far away as Israel.

NOTES

1. For additional details, see Anthony H. Cordesman, *Iran and Iraq: The Threat from the Northern Gulf*, Boulder, Westview, 1994; Office of the Secretary of Defense, *Proliferation: Threat and Response*, Washington, Department of Defense, April, 1996, pp. 12–16; and Roger C. Herdman, Director, *Technologies Underlying Weapons of Mass Destruction*, Office of Technology Assessment, US Congress, OTA-BP-ISC-115, December, 1993, Washington, GPO, pp. 119–196.
2. *Washington Post*, April 17, 1995, p. A-12; *New York Times*, May 2, 1995, p. A-6.
3. *Washington Post*, April 17, 1995, p. A-12; *New York Times*, May 2, 1995, p. A-6.
4. *Washington Times*, February 24, 1997, p. A-1; *Sunday Telegraph*, February 23, 1997, p. 1.
5. Associated Press, May 5, 1997, 01:26.
6. Reuters, January 16, 1998, 0551.
7. Reuters, January 16, 1998, 0551.
8. Reuters, January 16, 1998, 0551.
9. Congressional Research Service, Issue Briefs 92076, 92056, and 93033; *Washington Times*, December 19, 1994, p. A-18.
10. Associated Press, May 5, 1997, 01:26.

11. United Press, August 14, 1996, 1041. These statements are typical of the comments of Iranian officials and media found in a review of the FBIS-NES during the period 1995–1997. For example, see FBIS-NES-97-233, August 21, 1997, and *Tehran Jomhuri-ye-Eslmai*, August 21, 1997.

12. IRNA, August 17, 1997, 2041; BBC Summary of World Broadcasts, August 19, 1997.

13. IRNA, August 17, 1997, 2041; BBC Summary of World Broadcasts, August 19, 1997, August 28, 1997, September 12, 1997; Agence France Presse, August 16, 1997, 15:22; *London Times*, August 16, 1997; SAPA, September 11, 1997, 0946; Xinhua, September 11, 1997, 0911305.

14. David Kyd, a spokesman for the IAEA, stated on August 19, 1997, that the IAEA had no evidence that Iran was trying to obtain nuclear weapons components from South Africa. See IRNA, August 17, 1997 (FBIS-TAC-97-229, August 17, 1997), 2041; BBC Summary of World Broadcasts, August 19, 1997, August 28, 1997, September 12, 1997; Agence France Presse, August 16, 1997, 15:22; *London Times*, August 16, 1997; SAPA, September 11, 1997, 0946; Xinhua, September 11, 1997, 0911305.

15. *Washington Post*, October 5, 1997, p. C-4.

16. See Eric Arnett, "Iran, Threat Perception and Military Confidence-Building Measures," www. sipri, se/projects/technology/Iran-CBM.html, accessed April 17, 1997; the introduction and chapters 10–13 of Eric Arnett, ed., *Military Capacity and the Risk of War: China, Pakistan, and India*, Stockholm, Stockholm Institute of Peace Research Institute, March, 1997; *Jane's Defense Weekly*, April 16, 1997, p. 16.

17. According to one report by Zalmay Khalizad in *Survival*, Pakistan was deeply involved in this $10 billion effort, as was China. US experts do not confirm these reports. *Washington Post*, May 17, 1995, p. A-23.

18. Associated Press, May 5, 1997, 01:26.

19. For a detailed history and list of suppliers, see the author's *Weapons of Mass Destruction in the Middle East*, London, Brassey's, 1991, and *After the Storm: The Changing Military Balance in the Middle East*, Boulder, Westview, 1993.

20. Working papers by Leonard Spector, Daniel Poneman, *Nuclear Power in the Developing World*, London, Allen, and Unwin, 1982, Chapter 5; "Iran's Nuclear Weapons Program," *Mednews*, Vol. 5, 17/18, June 8, 1992, pp. 1–7.

21. Some reports indicate that one reactor at Bushehr was 80% complete.

22. Much of this analysis is based on research by Leonard Spector of the Carnegie Endowment.

23. The lasers were exported by a firm headed by Dr. Jeffrey Earkens, who had worked on classified laser enrichment technology. They seem to have been exported filled with gases that did not produce the optimal wavelength for nuclear enrichment, but could be refilled with the gases necessary to produce the required wavelength.

24. *Los Angeles Times*, August 22, 1979; Leonard Spector, *Going Nuclear*, Cambridge, Ballinger, 1987, pp. 47–53; Shyam Bhatia, *Nuclear Rivals in the Middle East*, London, Routledge, 1988, p. 85; JPRS-NTD, December 23, 1989.

25. *Observer*, May 17, 1987.

26. Yellow cake is not subject to IAEA inspection. Kenneth R. Timmerman, *Weapons of Mass Destruction: The Cases of Iran, Syria, and Libya*, Los Angeles, Simon Wiesenthal Center, August, 1992, pp. 28–45.

27. See Atomic Energy Organization of Iran, *The Performance of the Atomic Energy Organization of Iran, Tehran*, AEOI, August, 1997; *Tehran Salam*, August 21, 1997,

and August 27, 1997; FBIS/NES, September 5, 1997, 09031007000318; September 8, 1997, NC0809092597.

28. *Jane's Intelligence Review*, Special Report No. 6, May, 1995, p. 14.

29. Working papers by Leonard Spector and *Washington Post*, April 12, 1987.

30. The agreement made under the Shah was to have given Iran about 250–300 metric tons of Uranium enriched to 3%. During the period 1980–1990, Iran refused to accept the material or to pay for it. When Iran did ask for the material in 1991, France used the fact that Iran's option to obtain enriched material for its investment had expired to deny Iran shipment of the material guaranteed under the original terms of the Iranian investment. *Washington Times*, November 15, 1991, p. F-4; David Albright and Mark Hibbs, "Spotlight Shifts to Iran," *Bulletin of the Atomic Scientists*, March, 1992, pp. 9–12.

31. *Washington Post*, April 12, 1987, p. D-1; James Bruce, "Iraq and Iran: Running the Nuclear Technology Race," *Jane's Defense Weekly*, December 5, 1988, p. 1307; working papers by Leonard Spector; JPRS-TND, October 6, 1989, p. 19.

32. *El Independent*, Madrid, February 5 and 6, 1990; *FBIS-Middle East*, December 1, 1988; *Jane's Intelligence Review*, Special Report No. 6, May, 1995, p. 14.

33. *Jane's Intelligence Review*, Special Report No. 6, May, 1995, p. 14.

34. *El Independent*, Madrid, February 5 and 6, 1990; *FBIS-Middle East*, December 1, 1988.

35. *El Independent*, Madrid, February 5 and 6, 1990; *FBIS-Middle East*, December 1, 1988.

36. Uranium dioxide is normally subject to IAEA safeguards and inspection, but Argentine compliance is uncertain. Argentina sold at least three metric tons to Algeria in January, 1986. *Nucleonics Week*, May 7, 1987, p. 6.

37. Working papers by Leonard Spector; *Observer*, June 12, 1988; Office of the Secretary of Defense, *Proliferation: Threat and Response*, Washington, Department of Defense, April, 1996, pp. 12–16; *US News and World Report*, February 12, 1990; *FBIS-NES*, March 23, 1990, p. 57; *FBIS-EAS*, December 9, 1989, December 11, 1989; *Defense and Foreign Affairs*, November 20, 1989, p. 2; *New York Times*, May 8, 1989, June 27, 1989.

38. *Nucleonics Week*, May 2, 1991; Robert Shuey and Shirley A. Kan, *Chinese Missile and Nuclear Proliferation*, Congressional Research Service, IB92056, October 4, 1994, pp. 6–7; *Jane's Intelligence Review*, Special Report No. 6, May, 1995, p. 14.

39. *Washington Times*, April 22, 1987, page 6; *Economist*, "Foreign Report," April 2, 1987, p. 7; "Iran's Nuclear Weapons Program," *Mednews*, Vol. 5, 17/18, June 8, 1992, pp. 1–7.

40. Many of the details on these aspects of the Iranian effort are drawn from working papers provided by Leonard Spector of the Carnegie Endowment and Warren Donnelly of the Congressional Research Service. Also see *Nucleonics Week*, November 19, 1987, p. 1; November 26, 1987, p. 5; March 3, 1988, p. 7; July 28, 1988, p. 15.

41. For further background on recent developments, see Director of Central Intelligence, "The Acquisition of Technology Relating to Weapons of Mass Destruction and Advanced Conventional Munitions," Washington, CIA, June, 1997; Leonard Spector, Mark G. McDonough, and Evan S. Medeiros, *Tracking Nuclear Proliferation*, Washington, Carnegie Endowment, 1995; Russian Foreign Intelligence Service, *Treaty on the Non-Proliferation of Nuclear Weapons: Problems for Its Prolongation*, Moscow, 1995; Greg Gerardi and Maryam Ahrinijad, "An Assessment of Iran's Nuclear Facilities,"

Nonproliferation Review, Spring-Summer, 1995, pp. 209–215; David A. Schwarzbach, "Iran's Nuclear Puzzle," *Scientific American*, June, 1997, pp. 62–65; David A. Schwarzbach, *Iran's Nuclear Program: Energy or Weapons*? Natural Resources Defense Council, Nuclear Weapons data book series, 1995; Shahram Chubin, "Does Iran Want Nuclear Weapons? *Survival*, Vol. 37, No. 1, Spring, 1995, pp. 86–104.

42. There is a broad consensus among Western intelligence experts and governments that quiet discussions with potential supplier nations and corporations and criminal prosecution of violators in the West works better than open efforts to embarrass given suppliers. Suppliers are more cooperative and have less fear of media attacks that have often been launched against companies who have not actually made the reported transfers. More important, it is possible to keep the nature of such tracking efforts secret, and to avoid providing a model of what to buy to other proliferators. As a result, most Iranian purchasing efforts do not become public. Western governments and intelligence organizations do occasionally deliberately embarrass uncooperative governments and companies with "leaks," but these are usually deliberately vague enough to preserve security. Similarly, briefings to outside governments and experts are usually very carefully limited. Intelligence experts have found that even classified briefings to friendly governments almost inevitably leak in detail to the media or to hostile sources.

43. The United States had supplied 11 pounds of 93% enriched uranium in the mid-1970s, but this was largely depleted and could not keep the reactor running continuously. Based upon work by Leonard Spector; *Nucleonics Week*, May 14, 1989, p. 2; *Observer*, March 6, 1988.

44. Reuters, February 7, 1992, AM Cycle, and *Rio Negro*, February 7, 1992; *Washington Post*, November 17, 1992, pp. A-1 to A-30.

45. *Nuclear Engineering International*, March, 1990, p. 3.

46. *Jane's Intelligence Review*, Special Report No. 6, May, 1995, p. 14.

47. Robert Shuey and Shirley A. Kan, *Chinese Missile and Nuclear Profileration*, Congressional Research Service, IB92056, October 4, 1994; *Washington Times*, October 31, 1991, November 6, 1991, p. F-4, November 1, 1991, p. 7; *Los Angeles Times*, October 31, 1991, p. B-4, March 17, 1992, p. 1; David Albright and Mark Hibbs, "Spotlight Shifts to Iran," *Bulletin of the Atomic Scientists*, March, 1992, pp. 9–12; *Washington Post*, October 31, 1991, p. 1, January 12, 1992, p. C-7, February 2, 1992, p. A-1, September 12, 1992, p. A-13, June 26, 1991, October 30, 1991; "Iran's Nuclear Weapons Program," *Mednews*, Vol. 5, 17/18, June 8, 1992, pp. 1–7; *New York Times*, September 11, 1992, p. A-6, May 27, 1993; *Nucleonics Week*, May 2, 1991, September 24, 1992, October 1, 1992; *Los Angeles Times*, January 18, 1993, p. A-1, March 17, 1992, p. A-1; *Jane's Intelligence Review*, Special Report No. 6, May, 1995, p. 14.

48. Robert Shuey and Shirley A. Kan, *Chinese Missile and Nuclear Proliferation*, Congressional Research Service, IB92056, October 4, 1994, pp. 6–7; *Washington Post*, April 17, 1995, p. A-1, April 18, 1995, p. A-13.

49. *New York Times*, May 16, 1995, p. A-1; United Press, August 14, 1996, 1041; Leonard S. Spector, Mark G. McDonough, and Evan S. Medeiros, *Tracking Nuclear Proliferation*, Washington, Carnegie Endowment, 1995, pp. 119–123; *Washington Times*, May 17, 1995, p. A-15.

50. Office of the Secretary of Defense, *Proliferation: Threat and Response*, Washington, Department of Defense, April, 1996, pp. 12–16; Leonard S. Spector, Mark G. McDonough, and Evan S. Medeiros, *Tracking Nuclear Proliferation*, Washington, Carnegie Endowment, 1995, pp. 119–123; *Washington Times*, May 17, 1995, p. A-15.

51. See Atomic Energy Organization of Iran, *The Performance of the Atomic Energy Organization of Iran, Tehran,* AEOI, August, 1997; *Tehran Salam,* August 21, 1997, and August 27, 1997; FBIS/NES, September 5, 1997, 09031007000318; September 8, 1997, NC0809092597; Kenneth Katzman, "Iran: Arms and Technology Acquisitions," Library of Congress, CRS-97-474F, October 1, 1997; Kenneth Katzman, "Iran: Military Relations With China," Library of Congress, CRS-967-572F, June 26, 1996; Shirley A. Kan, "Chinese Proliferation of Weapons of Mass Destruction, Background and Analysis," Library of Congress, CRS-96-767F, September 13, 1996.

52. *Washington Post,* November 17, 1992, p. A-1, April 18, 1995, p. A-13; *Wall Street Journal,* May 11, 1993, p. 14; Robert Shuey and Shirley A. Kan, *Chinese Missile and Nuclear Proliferation,* Congressional Research Service, IB92056, October 4, 1994, pp. 6–7; *Nucleonics Week,* September 24, 1992, October 1, 1992; *New York Times,* May 27, 1993; *The Middle East,* July/August, 1994, pp. 9–10.

53. *Washington Post,* November 17, 1992, p. A-1, April 18, 1995, p. A-13; *Wall Street Journal,* May 11, 1993, p. 14; Robert Shuey and Shirley A. Kan, *Chinese Missile and Nuclear Proliferation,* Congressional Research Service, IB92056, October 4, 1994, pp. 6–7; *Nucleonics Week,* September 24, 1992, October 1, 1992; *New York Times,* May 27, 1993; *The Middle East,* July/August, 1994, pp. 9–10.

54. *New York Times,* February 23, 1995, May 16, 1995, p. A-1, May 18, 1995, p. A-11; *Washington Post,* April 18, 1995, p. A-13, May 8, 1995, p. A-22, May 18, 1995, p. A-22; *Nucleonics Week,* February 13, 1992, p. 12, October 14, 1993, p. 9, December 16, 1993, p. 11, September 22, 1994, p. 1, October 6, 1994, p. 11; *Washington Post,* February 14, 1992, February 12, 1995; *Nuclear Fuel,* March 14, 1994, p. 9, March 28, 1994, p. 10; *Nuclear Engineering,* April, 1992, p. 67, November, 1994, pp. 4, 10, United Press, November 21, 1994, Reuters, November 20, 1994.

55. *Washington Times,* April 18, 1996, p. A-7.

56. *Washington Times,* October 14, 1997, p. A-1; October 15, 1997, p. A-3; *Washington Post,* October 25, 1997, p. A-1; October 30, 1997, p. A-15; *New York Times,* on-line news service, October 31, 1997.

57. *Christian Science Monitor,* December 19, 1996, p. 1; Associated Press, May 5, 1997, 01:26; Director of Central Intelligence, "The Acquisition of Technology Relating to Weapons of Mass Destruction and Advanced Conventional Munitions," Washington, CIA, June, 1997; Leonard Spector, Mark G. McDonough, and Evan Medeiros, *Tracking Nuclear Proliferation,* Washington, Carnegie Endowment, 1995, p. 123; *Treaty on the Non-Proliferation of Nuclear Weapons: Problems for Its Prolongation,* Moscow, Russian Foreign Intelligence Service, 1995, pp. 56–59; Greg Gerardi and Maryam Ahrinijad, "An Assessment of Iran's Nuclear Facilities," *Nonproliferation Review,* Spring–Summer, 1995, pp. 209–215.

58. Associated Press, August 24, 1997, 2216.

59. *Washington Times,* October 22, 1997, p. A-12.

60. *Washington Times,* October 14, 1997, p. A-1, October 15, 1997, p. A-3; *Washington Post,* October 30, 1997, p. A-15; *New York Times,* on-line news service, October 31, 1997; Reuters, March 15, 1998, 1312, March 26, 1998, 0743; *Washington Post,* March 13, 1998, p. A-1.

61. *Washington Post,* March 13, 1998, p. A-1.

62. *New York Times,* February 23, 1995, May 18, 1995, p. A-11; *Washington Post,* April 18, 1995, p. A-13, May 8, 1995, p. A-22, May 18, 1995, p. A-22; *Nucleonics Week,* February 13, 1992, p. 12, October 14, 1993, p. 9, December 16, 1993, p. 11, September

22, 1994, p. 1, October 6, 1994, p. 11; *Washington Post,* February 14, 1992, February 12, 1995; *Nuclear Fuel,* March 14, 1994, p. 9, March 28, 1994, p. 10; *Nuclear Engineering,* April, 1992, p. 67, November, 1994, pp. 4, 10, United Press, November 21, 1994, Reuters, November 20, 1994.

63. Executive News Service, September 23, 1993, 1730, September 28, 1995, 1647; *Washington Times,* September 25, 1995, p. A-1; *Washington Post,* September 28, 1995, p. A-22; *New York Times,* September 30, 1995, p. A-4.

64. Reuters, March 15, 1998, 1312.

65. See Atomic Energy Organization of Iran, *The Performance of the Atomic Energy Organization of Iran, Tehran,* AEOI, August, 1997; *Tehran Salam,* August 21, 1997, and August 27, 1997; FBIS/NES, September 5, 1997, 09031007000318; September 8, 1997, NC0809092597.

66. *Chalk Times,* January 11, 1995, p. 1; *New York Times,* January 5, 1995, p. A-10.

67. *New York Times,* January 8, 1995, p. A-8, February 23, 1995, p. A-8; *Washington Post,* January 7, 1995, p. A-17, February 11, 1995, p. A-11, March 3, 1995, p. A-32, April 17, 1995, p. A-13; *Washington Times,* February 21, 1995, p. A-13; *Jane's Intelligence Review,* "Iran's Weapons of Mass Destruction," Special Report No. 6, May, 1995, pp. 4–14; Gerald White, *The Risk Report,* Vol. 1, No. 7, September, 1995; *Jane's Intelligence Review,* October, 1995, p. 452.

68. *New York Times,* February 23, 1995, May 18, 1995, p. A-11; *Washington Post,* May 8, 1995, p. A-22; *Nucleonics Week,* February 13, 1992, p. 12, October 14, 1993, p. 9, December 16, 1993, p. 11, September 22, 1994, p. 1, October 6, 1994, p. 11; *Washington Post,* February 14, 1992, February 12, 1995; *Nuclear Fuel,* March 14, 1994, p. 9, March 28, 1994, p. 10; *Nuclear Engineering,* April, 1992, p. 67, November, 1994, pp. 4, 10, United Press, November 21, 1994, Reuters, November 20, 1994; *Los Angeles Times,* March 10, 1995, p. A-3.

69. *New York Times,* February 23, 1995, May 18, 1995, p. A-11; *Washington Post,* May 8, 1995, p. A-22; *Nucleonics Week,* February 13, 1992, p. 12, October 14, 1993, p. 9, December 16, 1993, p. 11, September 22, 1994, p. 1, October 6, 1994, p. 11; *Washington Post,* February 14, 1992, February 12, 1995; *Nuclear Fuel,* March 14, 1994, p. 9, March 28, 1994, p. 10; *Nuclear Engineering,* April, 1992, p. 67, November, 1994, pp. 4, 10, United Press, November 21, 1994, Reuters, November 20, 1994; *Los Angeles Times,* March 10, 1995, p. A-3; *Jane's Intelligence Review,* "Iran's Weapons of Mass Destruction," Special Report No. 6, May, 1995, pp., 4–14; Gerald White, *The Risk Report,* Vol. 1, No. 7, September, 1995; *Jane's Intelligence Review,* October, 1995, p. 452.

70. Reuters, November 6, 1996, 0909; ECU Country Reports, *Iran,* August 2, 1996; ECU Views Wire, January 17, 1997, January 20, 1997; Leonard S. Spector, Mark G. McDonough, and Evan S. Medeiros, *Tracking Nuclear Proliferation,* Washington, Carnegie Endowment, 1995, pp. 119–123; *Washington Post,* March 3, 1995, p. A-32; *Journal of Commerce,* January 8, 1997, p. 6B; *Times-Picayune,* February 8, 1997, p. B-6; *Financial Times,* March 14, 1997, p. 4.

71. *New York Times,* February 23, 1995, May 18, 1995, p. A-11; *Washington Post,* May 8, 1995, p. A-22; *Nucleonics Week,* February 13, 1992, p. 12, October 14, 1993, p. 9, December 16, 1993, p. 11, September 22, 1994, p. 1, October 6, 1994, p. 11; *Washington Post,* February 14, 1992, February 12, 1995; *Nuclear Fuel,* March 14, 1994, p. 9, March 28, 1994, p. 10; *Nuclear Engineering,* April, 1992, p. 67, November, 1994, pp. 4, 10, United Press, November 21, 1994, Reuters, November 20, 1994; *Los Angeles Times,* March 10, 1995, p. A-3.

72. FBIS-SO, July 21, 1995, p. 1.
73. FBIS-SO, June 29, 1995, pp. 5–7; *Washington Times*, May 5, 1997, p. A-13.
74. Reuters, July 3, 1997, 0640.
75. *Washington Post*, April 17, 1995, p. A-12, May 17, 1995, p. A-23; *New York Times*, May 19, 1995, p. A-1, May 22, 1995, p. A-1; Leonard S. Spector, Mark G. McDonough, and Evan S. Medeiros, *Tracking Nuclear Proliferation*, Washington, Carnegie Endowment, 1995, pp. 119–123.
76. Reuters, March 6, 1998, 1452, March 11, 1998, 0947; *Washington Post*, March 7, 1998, p. 4–15.
77. ITAR-TASS, FBIS-SOV-98–050; Reuters, March 6, 1998, 1242; *New York Times*, March 7, 1998, p. A-3; *Washington Times*, March 7, 1998, p. A-6.
78. *New York Times*, February 23, 1995, May 18, 1995, p. A-11; *Washington Post*, May 8, 1995, p. A-22; *Nucleonics Week*, February 13, 1992, p. 12, October 14, 1993, p. 9, December 16, 1993, p. 11, September 22, 1994, p. 1, October 6, 1994, p. 11; *Washington Post*, February 14, 1992, February 12, 1995; *Nuclear Fuel*, March 14, 1994, p. 9, March 28, 1994, p. 10; *Nuclear Engineering*, April, 1992, p. 67, November, 1994, pp. 4, 10, United Press, November 21, 1994, Reuters, November 20, 1994; *Los Angeles Times*, March 10, 1995, p. A-3.
79. Reuters, November 6, 1996, 0909; ECU Country Reports, *Iran*, August 2, 1996; ECU Views Wire, January 17, 1997, January 20, 1997.
80. *New York Times*, March 7, 1998, p. A-3; *Washington Times*, March 7, 1998, p. A-6.
81. *Chalk Times*, January 11, 1995, p. 1; *New York Times*, January 5, 1995, p. A-10.
82. *Middle East Economic Digest*, October 17, 1997, p. 10.
83. Not always politely. See Atomic Energy Organization of Iran, *The Performance of the Atomic Energy Organization of Iran*, Tehran, AEOI, August, 1997; *Tehran Salam*, August 21, 1997, and August 27, 1997; FBIS/NES, September 5, 1997, 09031007000318; September 8, 1997, NC0809092597.
84. For further details, see David A. Schwarzbach, "Iran's Nuclear Puzzle," *Scientific American*, June, 1997, pp. 62–65; David A. Schwarzbach, *Iran's Nuclear Program: Energy or Weapons?* Natural Resources Defense Council, Nuclear Weapons data book series, 1995.
85. Associated Press, June 2, 1996.
86. Leonard S. Spector, Mark G. McDonough, and Evan S. Medeiros, *Tracking Nuclear Proliferation*, Washington, Carnegie Endowment, 1995, pp. 119–123; *Washington Post*, March 3, 1995, p. A-32, April 4, 1995, p. A-19, May 4, 1995, p. A-17, May 5, 1995, p. A-29; *Washington Times*, February 21, 1995, p. A-13, August 8, 1995, p. A-9; *Iran Business Monitor*, Vol. IV, No. 6, June, 1995, p. 1; *Newsweek*, May 15, 1995, p. 36; *New York Times*, May 5, 1995, p. A-8; Executive News Service, October 6, 1995, 1640; October 10, 1995, 1522, October 12, 1995, 1045.
87. Leonard S. Spector, Mark G. McDonough, and Evan S. Medeiros, *Tracking Nuclear Proliferation*, Washington, Carnegie Endowment, 1995, pp. 119–123; Office of the Secretary of Defense, *Proliferation: Threat and Response*, Washington, Department of Defense, April, 1996, pp. 12–16; *Washington Post*, March 3, 1995, p. A-32, April 4, 1995, p. A-19, May 4, 1995, p. A-17, May 5, 1995, p. A-29; *Washington Times*, February 21, 1995, p. A-13, August 8, 1995, p. A-9; *Iran Business Monitor*, Vol. IV, No. 6, June, 1995, p. 1; *Newsweek*, May 15, 1995, p. 36; *New York Times*, May 5, 1995, p. A-8; Executive News Service, October 6, 1995, 1640; October 10, 1995, 1522, October 12,

1995, 1045; *Journal of Commerce*, January 8, 1997, p. 6B; *Times-Picayune*, February 8, 1997, p. B-6; *Financial Times*, March 14, 1997, p. 4.

88. Leonard S. Spector, Mark G. McDonough, and Evan S. Medeiros, *Tracking Nuclear Proliferation*, Washington, Carnegie Endowment, 1995, pp. 119–123; *Washington Post*, March 3, 1995, p. A-32, April 4, 1995, p. A-19, May 4, 1995, p. A-17, May 5, 1995, p. A-29; *Washington Times*, February 21, 1995, p. A-13; *Iran Business Monitor*, Vol. IV, No. 6, June, 1995, p. 1; *Newsweek*, May 15, 1995, p. 36; *New York Times*, May 5, 1995, p. 8; *Jane's Intelligence Review*, "Iran's Weapons of Mass Destruction," Special Report No. 6, May, 1995, pp. 4–14; Gerald White, *The Risk Report*, Vol. 1, No. 7, September, 1995; *Jane's Intelligence Review*, October, 1995, p. 452.

89. Leonard S. Spector, Mark G. McDonough, and Evan S. Medeiros, *Tracking Nuclear Proliferation*, Washington, Carnegie Endowment, 1995, pp. 119–123; Office of the Secretary of Defense, *Proliferation: Threat and Response*, Washington, Department of Defense, April, 1996, pp. 12–16; *Washington Post*, March 3, 1995, p. A-32, April 4, 1995, p. A-19, May 4, 1995, p. A-17, May 5, 1995, p. A-29; *Washington Times*, February 21, 1995, p. A-13, August 8, 1995, p. A-9; *Iran Business Monitor*, Vol. IV, No. 6, June, 1995, p. 1; *Newsweek*, May 15, 1995, p. 36; *New York Times*, May 5, 1995, p. A-8; Executive News Service, October 6, 1995, 1640; October 10, 1995, 1522, October 12, 1995, 1045; *Journal of Commerce*, January 8, 1997, p. 6B; *Times-Picayune*, February 8, 1997, p. B-6; *Financial Times*, March 14, 1997, p. 4.

90. For typical press reporting on such issues, see *International Defense Review*, 2/1997, pp. 21–23, and *Washington Times*, September 23, 1997, p. A-13; extensive separate analysis has been done by the CSIS.

91. *Washington Post*, July 3, 1997, p. A-7; Director of Central Intelligence, "The Acquisition of Technology Relating to Weapons of Mass Destruction and Advanced Conventional Munitions," Washington, CIA, June, 1997; Reuters, July 3, 1997, 0640.

92. *Jane's Defense Weekly*, March 19, 1997, p. 3.

93. *Jerusalem Post*, March 19, 1997, p. 3.

94. *Washington Post*, July 5, 1998, p. A-10.

95. *Washington Post*, November 17, 1992, p. A-30. *Wall Street Journal*, May 11, 1993, p. A-14; *Christian Science Monitor*, February 18, 1993, p. 7.

96. *Chalk Times*, January 9, 1995, p. 6; *New York Times*, January 5, 1995, p. A-10, January 8, 1995, p. A-8, January 10, 1995, p. A-3; *Washington Times*, December 19, 1994, p. A-18, January 6, 1995, p. A-15; *Washington Post*, January 7, 1995, p. A-17.

97. *Washington Times*, May 5, 1997, p. A-13.

98. Leonard S. Spector, Mark G. McDonough, and Evan S. Medeiros, *Tracking Nuclear Proliferation*, Washington, Carnegie Endowment, 1995, pp. 119–123; *New York Times*, April 3, 1995, p. A-1.

99. For a range of typical reporting on Iran, see *Nucleonics Week*, February 13, 1992, p. 12, March 26, 1992, p. 7, May 28, 1992, p. 3, August 6, 1992, p. 13, August 20, 1992, p. 7, September 24, 1992, p. 2; *Nuclear Fuel*, July 6, 1992, p. 17, December 7, 1992, p. 5; *Nuclear News*, April, 1992, p. 67; *Los Angeles Times*, January 29, 1992, p. A-4, March 21, 1992, p. A-1; *Washington Post*, October 18, 1992, p. C-5.

100. Office of the Secretary of Defense, *Proliferation: Threat and Response*, Washington, Department of Defense, April, 1996, pp. 12–16; *Washington Post*, March 24, 1995, p. A-28, April 29, 1995, p. A-8, May 5, 1995, p. A-29; *New York Times*, April 3, 1995, p. A-1, April 29, 1995, p. A-6; *Philadelphia Inquirer*, May 3, 1995, p. A-3; February 27, 1995, p. 27; *Jane's Intelligence Review*, "Iran's Weapons of Mass Destruc-

tion," Special Report No. 6, May, 1995, pp. 4–14; Gerald White, *The Risk Report*, Vol. 1, No. 7, September, 1995; *Jane's Intelligence Review*, October, 1995, p. 452.

101. Associated Press, December 24, 1997, 1305.

102. *Washington Times*, November 15, 1991, p. F-4; *Washington Post*, February 7, 1992, p. A-18, February 15, 1992, p. A-29; Associated Press, PM Cycle, February 6, 1992; "Iran's Nuclear Weapons Program," *Mednews*, Vol. 5, 17/18, June 8, 1992, pp. 1–7.

103. Gerald White, *The Risk Report*, Vol. 1, No. 7, September, 1995.

104. Gerald White, *The Risk Report*, Vol. 1, No. 7, September, 1995.

105. It may also be possible to cheat an IAEA inspection. At least one effort was detected in Iraq to create reactor design which concealed an irradiation chamber in the reactor for producing plutonium. Israel permitted US inspection of its facilities in Dimona in one point in its nuclear weapons program where it provided a false control panel and records simulating a different operational cycle and smaller reactor capacity than was actually the case. The technology now available to the IAEA makes it unlikely that such efforts could succeed, but such success is at least possible.

106. Robert Shuey and Shirley A. Kan, *Chinese Missile and Nuclear Proliferation*, Congressional Research Service, IB92056, October 4, 1994, pp. 6–7; *Jane's Intelligence Review*, "Iran's Weapons of Mass Destruction," Special Report No. 6, May, 1995, pp. 4–14; Gerald White, *The Risk Report*, Vol. 1, No. 7, September, 1995; *Jane's Intelligence Review*, October, 1995, p. 452.

107. Patrick Clawson, *Iran's Challenge to the West: How, When, and Why*? Washington, The Washington Institute Policy Papers, Number Thirty-Three, 1993, pp. 60–61; *Financial Times*, February 6, 1992; *Washington Post*, February 15, 1992, pp. A-29-A-30, November 17, 1992, p. A-30; *Los Angeles Times*, March 17, 1992, p. 1; Associated Press, AM cycle, February 12, 1992; Agence France Presse, February 12, 1992; *Christian Science Monitor*, February 18, 1993, p. 7; *Wall Street Journal*, May 11, 1993, p. A-14; *Middle East Economic Digest*, March 17, 1995, p. 7.

108. The major uncertainty in such matters is whether Iran has a significant centrifuge effort in a secret or underground location. A few experts feel that there is some risk that Iran might also have a secret reactor to produce plutonium, but this seems unlikely. *Washington Post*, November 20, 1993, p. A-13.

109. *Washington Post*, November 20, 1993, p. A-13.

110. *Sunday Telegraph*, February 24, 1997, p. 1; *Washington Times*, February 24, 1997, p. A-1.

111. United Press, August 14, 1996, 1041; *Sunday Telegraph*, August 12, 1996.

112. For more background, see the author's *Weapons of Mass Destruction in the Middle East*, London, Brassey's, 1992, and *Iran and Iraq: The Threat From the Northern Gulf*, Boulder, Westview, 1994. Also see the Office of the Secretary of Defense, *Proliferation: Threat and Response*, Washington, Department of Defense, April, 1996, pp. 12–16; *US News*, November 14, 1994, pp. 87–88; and *New York Times*, December 27, 1994, p. A-17.

113. David A. Schwarzbach, "Iran's Nuclear Puzzle," *Scientific American*, June, 1997, p. 62.

114. White House "Fact Sheet," May 14, 1997; *Washington Post*, May 15, 1997, p. A-24. Also see the discussion of monitoring and country activity in Director of Central Intelligence, "The Acquisition of Technology Relating to Weapons of Mass Destruction and Advanced Conventional Munitions, July–December, 1996," Washington, CIA, June,

1997, and Shai Feldman, *Nuclear Weapons and Arms Control in the Middle East*, Cambridge, MIT Press, 1997.

115. Reuters, September 3, 1997, 0150.

116. Speech at the annual USCENTCOM conference, June 26, 1997.

117. *Los Angeles Times*, March 17, 1992, p. 1.

118. *New York Times*, November 30, 1992, pp. A-1 and A-6, January 5, 1995, p. A-10; *Washington Times*, January 6, 1995, p. A-15.

119. *New York Times*, January 10, 1995, p. A-3; *Jane's Intelligence Review*, "Iran's Weapons of Mass Destruction," Special Report No. 6, May, 1995, pp. 4–14; Gerald White, *The Risk Report*, Vol. 1, No. 7, September, 1995; *Jane's Intelligence Review*, October, 1995, p. 452.

120. Associated Press, May 5, 1997, 01:26.

121. *Chalk Times*, January 10, 1995, p. 31; *Washington Times*, January 19, 1995, p. A-18.

122. Although the possibility is a real one. *Financial Times*, January 30, 1992, p. 4; Agence France Presse, January 26, 1992; *Sunday Times*, January 26, 1992; *Der Spiegel*, July 20, 1992, p. 117; Patrick Clawson, *Iran's Challenge to the West: How, When, and Why*? Washington, The Washington Institute Policy Papers, Number Thirty-Three, 1993, pp. 63–65; *United States News and World Report*, November 14, 1994, p. 88; *Jane's Intelligence Review*, "Iran's Weapons of Mass Destruction," Special Report No. 6, May, 1995, pp. 4–14; Gerald White, *The Risk Report*, Vol. 1, No. 7, September, 1995; *Jane's Intelligence Review*, October, 1995, p. 452.

123. *Washington Times*, July 29, 1988, p. A-12.

124. *Washington Times*, May 17, 1995, p. A-15; Office of the Secretary of Defense, *Proliferation: Threat and Response*, Washington, Department of Defense, April, 1996, pp. 12–16.

125. *New York Times*, May 14, 1995; *Washington Post*, November 5, 1997, p. A-1.

126. For interesting insights into possible scenarios and their implications, see Anthony H. Cordesman, "Terrorism and the Threat From Weapons of Mass Destruction in the Middle East: The Problem of Paradigm Shift," Washington, CSIS, October 17, 1996; Brad Roberts, *Terrorism with Chemical and Biological Weapons: Calibrating Risks and Responses*, Alexandria, Chemical and Biological Weapons Control Institute, 1997; Shai Feldman, *Nuclear Weapons and Arms Control in the Middle East*, Cambridge, MIT Press, 1997.

Chapter 21

The Uncertain Implications of Iran's Weapons of Mass Destruction

The most important single conclusion of the preceding analysis is that Iran's uncertain and evolving process of "creeping proliferation" creates far more possibilities than it does probabilities. Iran's weapons developments, force plans, strategy, doctrine, and war plans are in a state of flux where the end result is more likely to be determined largely by Iran's internal political developments, external contingencies, and ability to obtain foreign technology and supplies.

While it is clear that Iran is making significant efforts to acquire chemical, biological, and nuclear weapons, it is not yet clear whether Iran is engaged in efforts that will succeed in making it a major proliferator that can join the "nuclear club" or use biological weapons as a substitute. Iran's efforts are evolving relatively slowly, and Iran is not involved in the kind of grandiose effort that Iraq indulged in before the Gulf War. Iran's changing political climate may also reduce the level of its efforts, or even end them.

At the same time, Iran's acquisition of highly lethal biological weapons, or nuclear weapons, offers a potential guarantee against Iraq's efforts to proliferate, and is the one action Iran could take to threaten the present balance of deterrence in the Gulf. Biological and/or nuclear weapons would allow Iran to offset at least some aspects of the conventional military superiority of US power projection forces and to present a potential threat to the flow of oil exports out of the Gulf on a long-term basis. It would also have a major impact on US power projection planning and planning for two near-simultaneous major regional contingencies.

If Iran does push ahead with proliferation, it is not clear whether its regime will try to use weapons of mass destruction to create the relatively stable balance of mutual assured destruction and highly structured deterrence that gave a great deal of stability to the nuclear arms race during the Cold War. Iran seems to have a tactical doctrine for using chemical weapons in some contingencies, but it may well fail to articulate detailed war plans and employment doctrine in other areas. It may not go beyond exploiting the prestige of acquiring such weapons, broad threats, and efforts to intimidate its neighbors and the West.

Like many other developing nations, Iran is unlikely to develop a strategy or doctrine for using any type of weapon of mass destruction which fits Western norms and expectations regarding the value of arms control. Even if Iran appears to articulate a strategy of deterrence or employment, this strategy may often consist more of words than detailed war-fighting capabilities, and its crisis behavior may be very different. Iran is also nearly certain to engage in concealment, denial, and compartmentalization, and to focus more on the acquisition and development of weapons of mass destruction than on planning for their employment. This is likely to limit the development of Iran's targeting plans, test and evaluation methods, and understanding of weapons lethality.

There is also a strong possibility that the Iranian leadership may turn many of the details of Iran's efforts over to the Revolutionary Guards, and keep them covert and separate from other Iranian military forces. This could place Iran's biological, chemical, and nuclear weapons under the direct control of ruling elites with little real military experience. It could create separate lines of C^4I/BM, which report directly to the leadership. It could lead to storage methods that make weapons retrieval difficult or which do not permit the kind of accounting and security measures that ensure that Iran's leadership can control each weapon. Alternatively, a divided command could prevent effective training for the employment of weapons under realistic wartime conditions and place the control of Iran's weapons in units that are chosen more for loyalty than capability.

Little about Iran's recent history would indicate that its employment of biological, chemical, and nuclear weapons is likely to be irrational or reckless, but Iran's restraint in attacking civilian targets or mass employment against armed forces may be more limited than that of the United States or Western powers. Iran may make carefully structured threats before or during a crisis, but any actual Iranian employment of such weapons is likely to be crisis driven and altered to meet the demands of the immediate situation. Iran's utilization and escalation may well be more a product of the attitudes and decisions of the ruling political elite in power at a given moment than of strategic analysis or the recommendations of any part of the military command chain. Iran's level of risk taking will almost inevitably be leader-specific and based on perceptions of a crisis shaped more by internal political attitudes than an objective understanding of the military situation. An Iranian regime might even take existential risks in escalating if it feels it is likely to lose power or be defeated.

Iran does, however, pay keen attention to the actions of its neighbors and the United States. As a result, it can be expected to pay detailed attention to US counterproliferation and Anti-Tactical Ballistic Missile (ATBM) efforts at the technical level, and to outside discussions of the possible use of weapons of mass destruction and the lessons of previous wars. Iran has already shown that it will seek to steadily improve its concealment, denial, and countermeasures. Its past actions also strongly indicate that it will consider the use of unconventional means to deliver weapons of mass destruction, and it may seek to use proxies and unconventional delivery means with little or no warning.

In summary, there are many possible ways Iran can employ weapons of mass destruction, but no examination of Iranian war-fighting capabilities can ignore the following issues relating to unconventional warfare or terrorism:

- Existing and projected detection and control technologies, arms control proposals, and concepts for missile defense assume that the primary threats are organized states and that relatively large weapons efforts must be used.
- Conventional structures of deterrence assume identifiable and limited sets of opponents and similar values in dealing with issues like mutual destruction. Terrorist movements may be willing to take catastrophic risks, as may leaders who identify themselves with the state and/or see martyrdom as a valid alternative to victory.
- War may not be fought between states or for limited strategic objectives. It may be a war of proxies or terrorists. It may be fought to destroy peoples or with minimal regard for collateral damage and risks.
- The target of unconventional uses of weapons of mass destruction may not be military in the normal sense of the term. It may be a peace process, US commitment to the defense of a given region, a peacekeeping force, a ruling elite, or growing cooperation between formerly hostile groups.
- Terrorist organizations have already attempted to use crude chemical weapons. The development and use of chemical and biological weapons is well within the capability of many extremist and terrorist movements, and states can transfer weapons or aid such movements indirectly or with some degree of plausible deniability, although such efforts would require the cover of some new relationship or splinter group in case of long-established relationships between Iran and terrorist organizations.
- Covert or unconventional delivery means may be preferable to both states and nonstate organizations. Cargo ships, passenger aircraft, commercial vehicles, dhows, or commercial cargo shipments can all be used and routed through multiple destinations. A well-established series of covert transport and smuggling networks exists throughout the region. Biological weapons can be manufactured in situ.
- The Marine Corps barracks incident has shown the potential value of "mass terrorism," as was demonstrated by the media impact of the Oklahoma City bombing and disruptive effect of far more limited events like the suicide bombings by Hamas, the assassination of Yitzhak Rabin, and the National Guard Headquarters and Al Khobar Towers bombings in Saudi Arabia.
- Biological and chemical weapons present special problems because they can be used in so many ways. Chemical poisons were once used to contaminate the Israeli fruit crop. Infectious biological agents could be used to mirror image local diseases or with long incubation times. Persistent nerve agents could be used in subways, large buildings, or shopping malls/bazaars to create both immediate casualties and long-term risks.

- Mixes of biological and chemical agents could be used to defeat detection, protection gear, or vaccines.
- Arms control efforts assume large state efforts with detectable manufacturing and weaponization programs in peacetime. The development of a capability to suddenly manufacture several hundred biological and chemical weapons with little or no warning is well within the state of the art using nothing but commercial supplies and equipment, and much of the R&D effort could be conducted as civil or defensive research.
- Unconventional and terrorist uses of weapons can involve the employment of extremely high risk biological agents transmitted by human carriers, commercial cargoes, and similar carriers.
- The incentives for the unconventional use of weapons of mass destruction increase in proportion to the lack of parity in conventional weapons, the feelings of hopelessness by alienated or extremist groups, or the prospect of catastrophic defeat.
- Similarly, the incentive for the unconventional use of weapons of mass destruction will increase in direct proportion to the perceived effectiveness of theater missile and other regular military defense systems.
- Rogue operations will be a constant temptation for state intelligence groups, militant wings of extremist groups, and revolutionary forces.

Two other points are important. The previous analysis has shown that Iran may regard arms control as an extension of conflict and rivalry by other means and not as a valid security option. Unless Iran can be convinced that a comprehensive regional arms control regime will disarm the Iraqi and Israeli efforts, shown in Table 11.1, in ways that benefit Iran in terms of the resulting overall military balance, including conventional and nuclear weapons, Iran may only pay lip service to arms control agreements, will seek to exploit them for whatever technology it can obtain for "peaceful" and "dual-use" purposes, and may lie or cheat as it feels necessary to achieve its national objectives.

Iran may also attempt to exploit the arms control process to maintain plausible deniability in terms of its broader diplomatic and economic relations with other nations, to embarrass rivals like Iraq and Israel, or to limit the proliferation efforts of other states. Fundamental and currently unforeseen changes must take place in the regimes of Iran, Iraq, and Israel—and possibly in neighboring regimes like Egypt, India, Libya, Pakistan, Saudi Arabia, and Syria—before Iran will see arms control as anything other than an extension of rivalry and war by other means.

Further, Iran's process of creeping proliferation is unlikely to be regime-specific as long as other Middle Eastern states continue to proliferate. The regime of President Khatami may or may not prove to be more moderate than that of President Rafsanjani. Iran may or may not improve its overall relations with its neighbors and the West. The fact remains, however, that Iran cannot trust its neighbors not to proliferate or to pose a future strategic threat, and Iran's neighbors cannot trust Iran.

This creates a climate of mistrust that could only be resolved by the most intrusive possible inspection procedures—simultaneously affecting all types of weapons of mass destruction and major delivery systems on a region-wide basis. There is no near to mid-term basis for trust on anyone's part. Even if the character and actions of Iran's future regime could be predicted, and a new regime was extraordinarily moderate, the United States and Iran's neighbors could not avoid planning for the risk that Iranian behavior might change suddenly in the course of some coup or revolution, or as the result of a catastrophic miscalculation in the course of a crisis.

These uncertainties make a strong case for efforts that restrict transfers of weapons and technology to Iran as much as possible. While the case for the political and economic containment of Iran seems dubious, the case for military containment seems much stronger. It is difficult to argue whether Iran has any serious need for the most threatening dual-use technologies, especially those involving the chemical and biological weapons technologies most needed for weapons purposes and for similar aspects of nuclear and missile technology.

Iran has no domestic economic need for the kind of chemical production facilities needed to eliminate or reduce its dependence on imported precursors and production equipment. While it does have a legitimate need for medical research facilities, it has no near to mid-term priority for most of the kinds of research and production facilities suited for biological weapons—all of which can be obtained far more cost-effectively from other countries. Iran has no need for a major nuclear research program, and no need for a space program.

There will also be a need for deterrence. Until it is clear that decisive and lasting changes have taken place in Iran's regime, the West and Iran's neighbors must have the military strength to convince Iran that the threat to use such weapons will be ineffective and that it has nothing to gain from using them. As a result, the limits to Iran's willingness to use chemical and biological weapons will be heavily dependent on the military capabilities of its neighbors to deter through retaliation and on strong US counterproliferation efforts.

These steps do not rule out a parallel effort to agree on regional arms control measures or the full enforcement of new inspection regimes for treaties like the Nuclear Non-Proliferation Treaty, Chemical Weapons Convention, and Biological Weapons Convention. Arms control and mutual "transparency" among all of the Gulf states and proliferators in the region may eventually replace containment and confrontation with mutual confidence. While such measures may be difficult and time consuming to develop, negotiate, and implement and still never eliminate some risks, the difficulties and risks in regional proliferation are far greater and far more threatening.

At the same time, no combination of arms control efforts and controls on the transfer of technology to Iran can provide regional stability without a much broader easing of tensions, and fundamental changes in the regimes of both Iran and Iraq. Even the most moderate Iranian leadership will need evidence that Iran does not need to proliferate, and containment and deterrence are not enough to bring lasting regional stability. Neither the West nor Iran's neighbors can afford to forget that Iran has legitimate national interests, that it continues to face a serious mid- to long-term threat from Iraq, and that Iran has been the leading victim of proliferation as well as one of its causes.

In the interim, all of the powers involved need to understand that this is not a game that any nation can "win." Iran should have no illusions about the risks it runs in proliferating and the catastrophes that might ensue if proliferation turns into actual war fighting. The United States, other Western nations, and Iran's regional allies need to understand that military containment and deterrence do not mean hostility, and that every effort to broaden trust and political and economic relations that benefits both sides will help make the balance most stable. The goal must be to make the same progress that took place during the Cold War, and move from containment to peaceful coexistence, and then to cooperation. In the long run, proliferation can only be dealt with through the creation of a regional security structure that both meets the needs of all regional states and ensures the free and stable flow of the energy exports needed to fuel the global economy.

Chapter 22

Iran's Military Future and the Proper Response

It is tempting to deal with Iran's military future by focusing on its intentions, its capacity to carry out a major build-up, or its capability to conduct a major regional war with the United States and some combination of the coalition of Gulf states. In practice, however, there are serious limits to the value of such an approach. It is impossible to predict Iran's present and future intentions to the point where they can be described in terms of well-defined plans for a military build-up or plans for specific kinds of war fighting.

It is easy to declare that Iran is seeking to be a hegemon or trying to dominate the Gulf, but it is anything but clear that this is true. Iran faces powerful limits in its ability to import arms, develop its weapons of mass destruction, and create effective military forces. Iran also cannot easily change this situation, since every hostile or threatening act it takes is likely to provoke a reaction from the United States, Southern Gulf states, and Iraq.

Similarly, it is too early to declare that Iran is "moderate." President Khatami's election marks an important shift in this direction, but many elements of Iran's regime and revolution still seem hostile to the West and Iran's neighbors in many ways, but this hostility is not being expressed in terms of aggression or a major military build-up, and it scarcely involves any stated willingness to start a major conflict. Iran's revolutionary rhetoric is increasingly mixed with statements describing its good intentions, and its threats increasingly seem to move towards defensiveness.

THE LIMITS TO SCENARIO-DRIVEN ANALYSIS

No one can see into the minds of Iran's present leadership, and it is not clear that such a mind-reading exercise would provide an accurate prediction of the future. Neither the future course of Iran's revolution nor its leadership is predictable. The election of President Khatami is an important signal of political change, and many revolutions have moved toward moderation long before they moderated all of their actions and words.

Many of Iran's leaders—including the Ayatollah Khamenei, President Khatami and many members of his cabinet, and Iran's senior military commanders—have bitter experience with the costs of war, and there are few indications that Iran's leaders are indifferent to risk. They have sometimes been "risk takers" in dealing with terrorism and unconventional warfare, but they have been cautious in dealing with serious military contingencies.

Iran seems to be a rational player in the game of nations. It has set reasonably consistent military goals, and its exercises and military literature are increasingly well thought out and reveal a realistic perception of the risks that Iran faces. Iran's leaders clearly perceive the risks of escalating any military actions, and even hard-liners like Rezaei have made reference to the risk of fighting a two-front war against the United States and Iraq.

At the same time, history shows that today's "moderation" and "pragmatism" may sometimes be tomorrow's extremism. Iran's revolution may be losing its aggressive edge as well as its popular fervor, but the election of moderates and/or the loss of revolutionary fervor proceeded the rise of aggressive regimes in "played out" revolutions in post-Bourbon France, a Stalinist Soviet Union, and Nazi Germany.

Iran's behavior is also likely to be highly contingency-driven. Iran is so weak that it must deal with major crises and contingencies on a reactive basis. Iran cannot predict its access to foreign arms, and Iran has little prospect of obtaining enough access to arms and money to conduct a systematic and an orderly military build-up technology, and its forces are in a constant state of turbulence and conversion. It lacks the military cohesion to develop and implement a well-defined mix of strategy and tactics, and it does not have clearly articulated war plans, force plans, and modernization plans by Western standards.

Much of Iran's experience with war is the wrong kind of experience: experience in using a different generation of revolutionary and popular army forces against an Iraq which may have better technology but which was slow moving and often inept. Iran's leaders may have studied the Gulf War, but they did not experience it.

Iran's recent military exercises have a negative side, as well as a positive one. They reflect a number of improvements that seem to be building on a realistic perception of the lessons of the Gulf War. At the same time, there is often more propaganda than realism in the scenarios Iran chose and the tactics it practices. Its exercise maneuvers also do not seem sophisticated enough to indicate that Iran's top leadership has any basis for fully understanding Iran's strengths and weaknesses in dealing with a US military threat. As a result, Iran's real-world military actions and willingness to escalate may be contingency-driven and improvised on a case-by-case basis.

There is also a vast range of scenarios that can occur between a successful containment of Iran and a major regional conflict. In fact, some "wild card" scenario involving an unpredictable mix of different elements of Iran's force structure in a low-to-mid-intensity conflict seems more likely than any Iranian version of the Gulf War, or a deliberate Iranian decision to use weapons of mass destruction. As a result, the details of Iran's strategy, tactics, and escalatory behavior in any given crisis may be as unpredictable to Iran's top leadership as to Iran's neighbors and the West.[1]

IRAN'S UNCERTAIN FORCE DEVELOPMENT

Another factor that will contribute to this unpredictability is the fact that Iran's military future is so uncertain. Even if Iran does have ambitious goals and plans, it currently is unable to carry out a major military build-up, at least in any coherent sense of the term. Unless Iran can obtain free access to advanced arms and technology from a nation like Russia, it will have to modernize on an erratic and a partial basis, achieving far less capability than it desires.

As a result, worst case analyses of Iran's conventional military build-up are more likely to be useful in justifying the military budgets and force plans of opposing nations than they are to reflect what Iran will actually do. Focusing on Iran's capability to fight a large regional war does little to explain the complex trends in Iran's military forces. In fact, such efforts are likely to do more to disguise the range of issues and possibilities that need to be analyzed than provide a meaningful way of summarizing Iran's military capabilities.

The real questions shaping Iran's military build-up are likely to be:

- the rate of the military build-up and proliferation in other regional states;
- the money and resources Iran can afford to devote to the military, both in financial and political terms. Those are factors which will be heavily driven by world oil prices and Iran's success in economic reform;
- the rate of domestic arms production, and the level of sophistication Iran's military industries can achieve;
- the willingness of foreigners to sell and the rate at which Iran can obtain partial deliveries of the conventional weapons and technology it needs the most;
- how dependent Iran will become on weapons of mass destruction;
- Iran's ability to carry out a more limited and carefully focused military build-up that can threaten tanker and other ship movements through the Gulf; and
- the improvements that Iran makes in its capacity to carry out unconventional warfare.

This means that Iran's military future will be heavily shaped by external factors and will continue to be contingency-driven. Key external factors include US and British willingness to remain in the Gulf and retain major power projection capabilities, Iraq's ability to put an end to sanctions and its future military build-up, and the progress the Southern Gulf states make in strengthening their military forces.

Nothing Iran does will take place in a power vacuum. In fact, the more Iran does to improve its military forces, the more likely it is to provoke a Western and regional response. Iran may be able to sustain the regional arms race, but there is little present reason to assume it can "win" it. The Gulf is an interactive system, and any analysis that assumes that any nation can conduct a military build-up without a response is inherently unrealistic.

PREDICTING THE "UNPREDICTABLE"

The fact that Iran's military future is not predictable in the narrow sense of the word does not mean that it is an exercise in "chaos theory." The previous analysis has shown that many broad trends in its military behavior and capabilities are highly predictable, at least in the near term. While it is impossible to dismiss a long list of "wild card" events and changes, it is possible to summarize the most probable trends in Iran's military future by looking at a range of the most likely contingencies and Iran's present and future capabilities in each such contingency.

Confrontation in the Gulf

Iran cannot win a naval-air battle against US forces in the Gulf, and it has no prospect of doing so in the foreseeable future. It would have to rebuild and modernize both its regular navy and air force at levels of strength and capability it simply cannot hope to achieve in the next decade. Alternatively, it would need to develop its capabilities to deliver weapons of mass destruction to the point where it could back its conventional military capabilities with a threat that might seriously inhibit US military action and/or the willingness of Southern Gulf states to support the United States and to provide air and naval facilities.

Until Iran makes such massive force improvements, the United States could probably sink every major surface ship in the Iranian navy in a matter of days and suppress its air force and anti-ship missile capabilities within a week. Similarly, the United States could quickly defeat Iran's regular navy in any lesser contingency, defeat Iranian amphibious operations, and halt Iranian attacks on offshore facilities. The United States can also use its air and missile power to inflict enough strategic damage on Iran to create a massive deterrent to any Iranian escalation to chemical or biological weapons, and back these capabilities with the ultimate threat of US theater nuclear escalation.

This does not mean that Iran could not score some gains from a well-planned raid, or that such a conflict would not involve US losses. Iran could not succeed in any significant way, however, in the face of US opposition. If anything, Iranian escalation is likely to end in increasing the grossly asymmetric damage that the United States can inflict on Iran in return. Iran can make things worse, but there is no near-term prospect that it can win a major confrontation in the Gulf simply by escalating the level of force involved.

The "wild cards" in such contingencies are the US determination to act, the size of the US presence in the Gulf, and US power projection capabilities at the time of a given crisis, Southern Gulf support for the United States and willingness to provide the United States with suitable facilities, and the political liabilities the United States would face—if any—in terms of the response from nations outside of the region. Far more is involved in a confrontation in the Gulf than military capability, and Iran would have far more contingency capability if the United States could not respond for political or budgetary reasons.

Confrontation or Conflict With Iraq

Iran has a rough overall military parity with Iraq, although it could not sustain a massive land offensive against Iraq's military forces. Iran has long had the naval and air capabilities to defeat Iraq's negligible naval strength and deny Iraq naval and commercial access to the Gulf. Iran is slowly increasing the capabilities of its land and air forces relative to those of Iraq and its ability to use chemical warfare in another Iran-Iraq conflict. Iran is now a much stronger defensive power than it was in 1988, both because of Iran's force improvements and because of Iraq's defeat and the sanctions that have followed.

It is highly unlikely, however, that Iran will acquire enough of an "edge" over Iraq to win a major conflict, decisively defeat Iraq's military forces, and avoid a repetition of the grinding war of attrition that took place during the Iran-Iraq War. In spite of Saddam Hussein, the Iraqi army seems more likely to unite in a defensive conflict than to divide, and Iraq still has nearly twice Iran's tank strength, and Iraq still has a significant air force.

The "wild cards" in any contingencies involving a conflict between Iran and Iraq are the possibility of internal unrest and divisions in Iraq that are serious enough to split the Iraqi armed forces, and/or lead to a new Shi'ite uprising. Similarly, a major Kurdish uprising would greatly complicate Iraq's ability to concentrate its forces to defend against an Iranian attack on Iraq's center and south. At the same time, any Iranian victory over Iraq might prove to be more apparent than real. It is far from clear that the United States or the Southern Gulf states would tolerate an Iranian victory that did more than depose the present Iraqi regime. Further, the split between Persian, Arab, and Kurd seems likely to remain so great that Iraqi independence would rapidly reassert itself if Iran attempted to occupy or dominate a substantial part of Iraq.

Adventures in the Southern Gulf

There is little present prospect that Iran will develop enough power projection capability—and supporting power from its navy, air force, and weapons of mass destruction—to win any conflict in the Southern Gulf, or to force its way in support of a coup or uprising. This contingency is also the one most likely to unite the United States and the Southern Gulf states and to ensure European and other support for a strong US-Southern Gulf response.

At the same time, there are three important "wild cards" affecting any Iranian military involvement in the Southern Gulf:

- Nothing can prevent Iran from exploiting the fracture lines within and between the Southern Gulf states. This is particularly true of the Shi'ite in Bahrain and Saudi Arabia, but it might also prove true of future confrontations between Bahrain and Qatar and Saudi Arabia and Yemen.
- The United States would face serious problems in responding to any change of government in a Southern Gulf state that resulted in a pro-Iranian regime and which sought Iranian military advice or an Iranian military presence. The United States cannot save a Gulf regime from its own people or (openly) endorse such action by other Southern Gulf countries.
- Iran's process of creeping proliferation is making enough progress so that the United States and the Southern Gulf states must reach some degree of agreement on taking suitable counterproliferation measures. A power vacuum in which Iran proliferates, the Southern Gulf states growing steadily more vulnerable, and US resolve seems progressively more questionable and could give Iran far more capability to directly or indirectly intervene in Southern Gulf affairs.

Proxy Wars Against Israel and Other States

Iran has already demonstrated that it is steadily improving its ability to conduct "proxy wars" by training, arming, and funding movements like the Hezbollah. The IRGC and the Quds Force are likely to continue to exploit such methods as long as they are directed to do so by the Iranian regime, and there is little that can be done to force Iran to stop.

Iran's success in such "proxy wars" will depend on its ability to train and arm such movements. In many cases, Iran will need bases, training centers, staging facilities, and at least the tacit political support of third nations like the Sudan and Syria, which are close to the scene of such proxy conflicts. Similarly, proxy wars can only be fought against vulnerable governments. They will have little impact on a successful Arab-Israeli peace settlement, or in sustaining civil conflict in the face of a government that demonstrates it has the capacity to govern and deal with its social problems.

At the same time, the failure of the peace process and of secular regimes may make Iran's use of proxy wars more successful in the future. Iran has shown in Lebanon that it has a growing ability to transfer advanced weapons and technology to proxy movements and to give them the capability to challenge modern counterterrorist and counterinsurgency forces. It is impossible to dismiss the possibility that Iran might directly or indirectly provide its proxies with weapons of mass destruction. As a result, proxy wars are an area where Iran will have considerable leverage in spite of its overall military weakness.

Unconventional Offensive Conflicts

Iran has steadily improving capabilities for unconventional warfare, including the potential use of chemical and biological weapons. The practical problem Iran faces is finding a place and contingency where it can exploit such capabilities that offer more return than using proxies and which allow Iran to act at an acceptable risk.

In broad terms, there do not seem to be many contingencies where Iran can currently achieve major gains by using Iranian unconventional military forces in offensive warfare. However, there are many ongoing and potential conflicts in the region where Iran might be able to tip the balance by sending in such Iranian reinforcements and cadres. These include exploiting ethnic conflicts like the Kurds, aiding Azerbaijan, supporting internal conflicts in the Central Asian republics, deploying military cadres to Yemen, and a wide range of similar possibilities. Iran could deploy such forces with the direct overt support of the regime, or as "volunteers."

The key "wild cards" affecting this set of contingencies are Iran's willingness to take the risk of using such forces and alienating other states, the uncertain value of such adventures to Iran, and the willingness of other states and non-Persian movements to accept such Iranian support and the probable political price tag. So far, Iran's leaders have limited themselves to proxy interventions, but this might change if:

- an armed Shi'ite movement could establish itself in an organized form in Saudi Arabia or Bahrain;
- Iran could send volunteers to Lebanon and Syria under circumstances where such conflicts have broad enough Arab support to avoid further isolating Iran, and Israel was sufficiently preoccupied with other threats so that it could not retaliate;
- actively supporting the Kurds and/or Shi'ite opposition in a post-sanctions Iraq appeared to be a safe way of limiting the Iraqi threat or ending Iraqi support for anti-Iranian movements;
- supporting an alienated Yemen offered Iran a low-cost way of using unconventional forces to threaten or put pressure on Saudi Arabia;
- Iranian support of the PKK in Turkey helped constrain or pressure a hostile Turkish regime; and
- Iranian support of Shi'ite elements in Afghanistan prevented a challenge from a hostile Islamic movement like the Taliban or it was necessary to put pressure on the Afghan regime.

None of these contingencies are risk-free. At the same time, the risks of Iran using its unconventional warfare capabilities should not be discounted. If nothing else, Iran might act in a "spoiler role," attempting to deny some other nation's influence even if Iran could not make clear strategic gains on its own.

Weapons of Mass Destruction

The previous analysis has shown that chemical, biological, and nuclear weapons do not define a narrow set of contingencies, but rather are tools to an end. It is also clear that weapons of mass destruction do not necessarily make radical changes in Iran's contingency capabilities. At the same time, such weapons do give Iran a post-Gulf War edge over Iraq. They also inevitably affect US, British, Israeli and Southern Gulf perceptions of the risks inherent in attacking Iran. Much depends on these perceptions of the risk in engaging Iran, refusing its demands, and dealing with Iranian escalation and/or retaliation.

It seems unlikely that Iran's "creeping proliferation" will reach the point in the near term where Iran's capabilities are great enough to change US, British, Israeli and/or Southern Gulf perceptions of risk to the point where they would limit or paralyze outside military action. Further, it seems unlikely that Iran can continue to build up its capabilities without provoking even stronger US counterproliferation programs, including retaliatory strike capabilities. The same is true of a response by Iraq and the Southern Gulf states. As a result, Iran's weapons of mass destruction may end simply in provoking a "creeping arms race" in response to "creeping proliferation."

Arms races do not, however, always bring deterrence and stability. Further, four "wild cards" deserve special attention:

- One such wild card is a successful Iranian attempt to buy significant amounts of weapons grade material. This could allow Iran to achieve a nuclear breakout capability in less than a year. Both the United States and the region would find it much harder to adjust to such an Iranian effort than the slow development of nuclear weapons by creating fissile material in Iran. It seems likely that the United States could deal with the situation by extending a nuclear umbrella over the Gulf, but even so, the Southern Gulf states might be far more responsive to Iranian pressure and intimidation. Most, after all, are so small that they are virtually "one-bomb states."

- Another wild card is a change in the US and regional perception of biological weapons. Biological weapons are now perceived largely as unproven systems of uncertain lethality. Regardless of their technical capabilities, they have little of the political impact of nuclear weapons. Iran might, however, conduct live animal tests to demonstrate that its biological weapons have near-nuclear lethality or some power might demonstrate their effectiveness in another conflict. The successful mass testing or use of biological weapons might produce a rapid "paradigm shift" in the perceived importance of such weapons and of Iran's biological warfare programs.

- Iraq might break out of UN sanctions and reveal a substantial breakout capability of its own. Paradoxically, such an Iraqi capability would help legitimize Iran's programs and the escalation to the use of such weapons. Alternatively, massive conventional air and missile strikes on Iran could be seen in Iran, and in much of the Third World, as justifying Iran's acquisition and use of such weapons.

- Iran might use such weapons through proxies or in covert attacks with some degree of plausible deniability. Terrorism and unconventional warfare would be far more intimidating if they made use of weapons of mass destruction.

The Defense of Iran

The previous contingencies assume that Iran will take offensive action. If it does, it may well be confronted with a US-led attack on Iran. If this attack is confined to naval and coastal targets, particularly those Iranian military capabilities that potentially threaten Gulf shipping, there is little Iran can do other than try to ride out the attack by dispersing and hiding its smaller boats, antiship missiles, and so on.

If a US-led attack includes strategic conventional missile strikes and bombings, there is little Iran can do in immediate response other than escalate by using weapons of mass destruction in ways that are more likely to end in increasing the risk and damage to Iran than deter or damage US forces. Iran can, however, respond over time with terrorism, unconventional warfare, and proxy wars. It is much easier for air and missile power to inflict major damage on Iran than it is to predict or control the political and military aftermath. The resulting casualties and damage will be extremely difficult to translate into an "end game."

US amphibious and land attacks would be considerably more difficult. Iran can probably mount a relatively effective guerrilla and unconventional defense against amphibious and air attacks on its coastline and islands. Most high value target areas in Iran now have a substantial IRGC presence that can dig in and which does not rely solely on static major weapons that can be identified and attacked from the air. It is unclear that Iran could defend its islands for more than a few days, but it could still probably inflict politically meaningful casualties.

Attacks on the Iranian mainland that went beyond a punitive raid would be much more costly. A US-led coalition could defeat Iran's regular forces, but would have to be at least corps level in size, and occupying Iran would be impractical without massive land forces of several entire corps. Even limited amphibious and land attacks on the mainland would expose the invading forces to a much higher risk of low intensity and guerrilla combat with Iranian forces that constantly received reinforcement and resupply. Further, Iran's use of terrorism and weapons of mass destruction would be politically easier to justify in a defensive conflict than in an offensive one. Such attacks would probably end in futility, and in creating a revanchist Iran.

Exploiting "Wars of Intimidation"

The previous contingencies assume that Iran's strength will be determined largely by the war-fighting capabilities of its military forces. Iran may, however, be able to achieve some of its objectives though intimidation and direct and indirect threats. Its ability to provide such threats will improve steadily in the near to mid term, in spite of its military weakness. In many cases, its neighbors may be willing to accommodate Iran to some degree. This is particularly true of those states whose gas and oil resources are most exposed—such as Qatar—or those that see Iraq as a more serious threat—such as Kuwait.

Much will depend on regional perceptions of the long-term resolve of the United States, the ability of the Southern Gulf states to avoid major divisions, and the willingness of the Southern Gulf states to show that they will support a firm US response to Iran, even at some risk. Much will also depend on the ability of Iran's leadership to set achievable demands and avoid open confrontation. In broad terms, it seems likely that Iran's ability to intimidate will slowly improve over time, but there is no way to predict how quickly or how much.

THE VALUE OF CONTAINMENT AND DETERRENCE

Time scarcely heals all wounds, but time may well be easing the problems that the West and the Southern Gulf states face with Iran. Iran's regime is in the process of change that may well produce a government that is more moderate and pragmatic, and which is focused on Iran's security interests and need for national development rather than exporting revolution and achieving regional dominance.

Time, however, may only be valuable to the degree to which Iran's access to arms and technology is limited. Regardless of whether Iran ultimately deserves to be "sanctified" or "demonized," there are good reasons to keep Iran's proliferation down to the "creeping" level. At least in the near to mid term, regional stability is also likely to be dependent on Iranian perceptions that the US and Southern Gulf states are not vulnerable to intimidation and attacks. They are also likely to be dependent on Iraq's ability to preserve defensive military parity, and on the continued presence of US and British forces in the region.

There is nothing new about this situation. A similar mix of containment and deterrence was critical to creating "peaceful coexistence" during the Cold War, to leading to the meaningful arms control agreements between East and West, and to ensuring that the collapse of the Soviet empire did not involve military adventures. Further, there is more consensus in pursuing such an approach than some analysts realize. It is easy to forget that the debate over "dual containment" and "critical dialogue" is largely a nondebate in the West and the Southern Gulf when it comes to limiting arms transfers, the sale of dual-use technologies, and the need for at least an "over-the-horizon" US military presence in the Gulf. There is also a tendency to ignore the fact that many of these aspects of containment have already been proven successful.

Iran has major near-term vulnerabilities in *all* scenarios, and Iran's leaders seem to recognize this. It should be possible to use the limits of Iranian military capabilities to ride out the present hostility of Iran's leaders and reach a stable modus vivendi without a major regional war. In spite of the comments of extremists like Rezaei, the election of leaders such as Rafsanjani and Khatami indicates that conflict is probably avoidable if the US and Southern Gulf show the proper amount of determination and resolve.

At the same time, it is important to understand that military containment and deterrence is not a "two person-zero sum game," and that there are ways to buy time until Iran's regime evolves and better political and diplomatic relations can be established. Containment and deterrence are forms of insurance and do not mean that Iran must be treated as a military enemy. The search for military security is no reason to give up on dialogue, to cut off trade and investment that does not contribute to Iran's military build-up, or to fail to reach out to the Iranian people. Iran may have significant and growing military capabilities in *some* scenarios, but it has yet to demonstrate the intention to use them. The election of President Khatami may prove to be a major step in Iran's evolution towards a more positive political and strategic posture.

Difficult as the goal may seem today, the end game is to replace containment and deterrence with arms control efforts that limit or end proliferation and this threat to all of the nations in the region. It is to move from containment to peaceful coexistence and then to cooperation, and to create a regional security structure that both meets the needs of all regional states and ensures the free and stable flow of the energy exports needed to fuel the global economy. This may take decades, but decades of patient effort are infinitely preferable to paroxysms of war.

Sources and Methods

This book is the product of extensive and iterative research over a period of several decades. The author served in Iran during the early 1970s and has been involved in the analysis of Iran ever since. The author has talked extensively to Iranian officials and exiles outside of Iran since the Iranian revolution. He visited Iran in 1998 and spoke of many of the issues discussed in the text with both Iranian officials and foreign diplomats. He also has visited a number of other Gulf countries and has discussed the material involved in depth with European and US experts and officials.

This text has been distributed for comment to a number of experts and officials in the United States and other countries, to officials in several international agencies and institutions, and to various private experts. The author has drawn heavily on the input of such reviewers throughout the text. It was agreed upon with each reviewer, however, that no individual or agency should be attributed at any point in the text except by specific request, and that all data used be attributed to sources that are openly available to the public. The reader should be aware of this in reviewing the notes. The data contained in the analysis have often been extensively modified to reflect expert comment which cannot be referenced.

Data from open sources are deliberately drawn from a wide range of sources. Virtually all of these sources are at least in partial conflict. There is no consensus over demographic data, budget data, military expenditures and arms transfers, force numbers, unit designations, or weapons types.

While the use of computer databases allowed some cross-correlation and checking of such sources, the reporting on factors like force strengths, unit types and identities, and tactics often could not be reconciled. Citing multiple sources for each case is not possible and involves many detailed judgments by the authors in reconciling different reports and data.

The Internet and several on-line services were used extensively. Since such databases are dynamic and change or are deleted over time, there is no clear way to document much of this material. Recent press sources are generally cited, but are often only part of the material consulted.

In many cases, the author adjusted the figures and data used in the analysis on a "best guess" basis, drawing on some thirty years of experience in the field. In some other cases, the original data provided by a given source were used without adjustment to ensure comparability, even though this leads to some conflicts in dates, place names, force strengths, and so on within the material presented—particularly between summary tables surveying a number of countries and the best estimates for a specific country in the text. In such cases, it seemed best to provide contradictory estimates to give the reader some idea of the range of uncertainty involved.

Extensive use is made of graphics to allow the reader to easily interpret complex statistical tables and see long-term trends. The graphic program used was deliberately standardized and kept relatively simple to allow the material portrayed to be as comparable as possible. Such graphics have a drawback, however, in that they often disguise differences in scale and exaggerate or minimize key trends. The reader should carefully examine the scale used in the left-hand axis of each graph.

Most of the value judgments regarding military effectiveness were made by Anthony H. Cordesman on the basis of American military experience and standards. Although the author has lived in the Middle East and worked as a US advisor to several Middle Eastern governments, he feels that any attempt to create some Middle Eastern standard of reference is likely to be far more arbitrary than basing such judgments on his own military background.

Mapping and location names presented a major problem. The author used US Army and US Air Force detailed maps, commercial maps, and in some cases commercial satellite photos. In many cases, however, the place names and terrain descriptions used in different sources presented major contradictions that could not be resolved from available maps. No standardization emerged as to the spelling of place names. Sharp differences emerged in the geographic data published by various governments, and in the conflicting methods of transliterating Arabic and Farsi place names into English.

The same problem applied to reconciling the names of organizations and individuals—particularly those being transliterated from Arabic and Farsi. It became painfully obvious that little progress is being made in reconciling the conflicting methods of transliterating such names into English. A limited effort has been made to standardize the spellings used in this text, but many different spellings are tied to the relational database used in preparing the analysis, and the preservation of the original spelling is necessary to identify the source and tie it to the transcript of related interviews.

NOTE

1. For interesting insights into possible scenarios and their implications, see Zalmay M. Khalilzad, David A. Shalpak, and Daniel L. Byman, *The Implications of the Possible End of the Arab-Israeli Conflict for Gulf Security*, Santa Monica, RAND, 1997; Shai Feldman, *Nuclear Weapons and Arms Control in the Middle East*, Cambridge, MIT Press, 1997; Andrew Rathmell, *The Changing Military Balance in the Gulf*, London, Royal United Services Institute, Whitehall Papers 38, 1996; and Geoffery Kemp and Robert E. Harkavy, *Strategic Geography and the Changing Middle East*, Washington, Carnegie/Brookings Endowment, 1997.

Selected Bibliography

Albright, David, and Mark Hibbs, "Spotlight Shifts to Iran," *Bulletin of the Atomic Scientists*, March, 1992, pp. 9–12.
Amuzegar, Jahangir, "The Iranian Economy Before and After the Revolution," *The Middle East Journal*, Vol. 46, No. 3, Summer, 1992, pp. 413–425.
———. "Islamic Fundamentalism in Action: The Case of Iran," *Middle East Policy*, September, 1995, pp. 22–23.
Anderson, Gustav, "Analysis of Two Chemical Weapons Samples from the Iran-Iraq War," *NBC Defense and Technology International*, April, 1986, pp. 62–66.
Arms Control and Disarmament Agency (ACDA), *World Military Expenditures and Arms Transfers*, Washington, GPO, various editions.
Arnett, Eric, ed., *Military Capacity and the Risk of War: China, India, Pakistan, and India*, Stockholm, Stockholm Institute of Peace Research Institute, March, 1997.
Atkenson, Edward B., *The Powder Keg*, Falls Church, NOVA Publications, 1996.
Belyakov, Rostislav, and Nikolai Buntin, "The MiG 29M Light Multirole Fighter," *Military Technology*, 8/1994, pp. 41–44.
Ben-Meir, Alon, "The Dual Containment Strategy Is No Longer Viable," *Middle East Policy*, Vol. IV, No. 3, 1996, pp. 50–57.
Bermudez, Joseph S., "Iran's Missile Development," in William C. Potter and Harlan W. Jencks, eds., *The International Missile Bazaar: The New Suppliers' Network*, Boulder, Westview, 1994, pp. 47–74.
Bhatia, Shyam, *Nuclear Rivals in the Middle East*, London, Routledge, 1988.
Bill, James, "The United States and Iran: Mutual Myths," *Middle East Policy*, Vol. II, No. 3, 1993, pp. 98–107.
Caldwell, Dan, "Flashpoints in the Gulf: Abu Musa and the Tunb Islands," *Middle East Policy*, Vol. IV, No. 3, 1996, pp. 50–57.
Carus, W. Seth, "Chemical Weapons in the Middle East," *Policy Focus*, Number Nine, Washington Institute for Near East Policy, December, 1988.

Carus, W. Seth, and Joseph S. Bermudez, "Iran's Growing Missile Forces," *Jane's Defense Weekly*, July 23, 1988, pp. 126–131.
Chubin, Shahram, "Does Iran Want Nuclear Weapons?" *Survival*, Vol. 37, No. 1, Spring, 1995, pp. 86–104.
Chubin, Shahram, and Charles Tripp, *Iran-Saudi Arabia: Relations and Regional Order*, Adelphi Paper 304, Oxford, IISS, 1996.
CIA, *World Factbook*, Washington, GPO, various editions.
Clawson, Patrick, *Iran's Challenge to the West: How, When, and Why?* Washington, The Washington Institute Policy Papers, Number Thirty Three, 1993.
―――, *Iran's Strategic Intentions and Capabilities*, Washington, National Defense University, GPO, 1994.
Cordesman, Anthony H., *After the Storm: The Changing Military Balance in the Middle East*, Boulder, Westview, 1993.
―――, *The Gulf and the Search for Strategic Stability*, Boulder, Westview, 1984.
―――, *Iran and Iraq: The Threat from the Northern Gulf*, Boulder, Westview, 1994.
―――, *Iran and Weapons of Mass Destruction*, Washington, CSIS, 1997.
―――, "Terrorism and the Threat From Weapons of Mass Destruction in the Middle East: The Problem of Paradigm Shift," Washington, CSIS, October 17, 1996.
―――, *Weapons of Mass Destruction in the Middle East*, London, Brassey's, 1991.
Cordesman, Anthony H., and Ahmed S. Hashim, *Iran: Dilemmas of Dual Containment*, Boulder, Westview, 1997.
Cordesman, Anthony H., and Abraham R. Wagner, *The Lessons of Modern Warfare, Volume II, The Iran-Iraq War*, Boulder, Westview, 1988.
Cottam, Richard W., *Iran and the United States*, Pittsburgh, University of Pittsburgh Press, 1988.
Defense News, various editions.
Director of Central Intelligence, "The Acquisition of Technology Relating to Weapons of Mass Destruction and Advanced Conventional Munitions, July–December, 1996," Washington, CIA, June, 1997.
Dunn, Peter, "The Chemical War, Journey to Iran," *NBC Defense and Technology International*, pp. 28–37.
―――, "Iran Keeps Chemical Options Open," *NBC Defense and Technology International*, pp. 12–14.
Ehteshami, Anoushiravan, "The Armed Forces of the Islamic Republic of Iran," *Jane's Intelligence Review*, February, 1993, pp. 76–79.
―――, "Iran Strives to Regain Military Might," *International Defense Review*, 7/1996, pp. 22–26.
―――, "Iran Boosts Domestic Arms Industry," *International Defense Review*, 4/1994, pp. 72–73.
―――, "Iran's National Strategy," *International Defense Review*, 4/1994, pp. 29–37.
Eisenstadt, Michael, *Iranian Military Power, Capabilities, and Intentions*, Washington, Washington Institute, 1996.
Erlick, Dr. Barry J., Senior Biological Warfare Analyst, US Army, testimony before the Committee on Governmental Affairs, US Senate, February 9, 1989.
Feldman, Shai, *Nuclear Weapons and Arms Control in the Middle East*, Cambridge, MIT Press, 1997.
Fromkin, David, *A Peace to End All Peace*, New York, Henry Holt, 1989.

Fuller, Graham E., *The Center of the Universe: The Geopolitics of Iran*, Boulder, Westview, 1991.
Galbraith, Peter W., and Christopher Van Hollen, Jr., "Chemical Weapons Use in Kurdistan: Iraq's Final Offensive," A Staff Report to the Senate Committee on Foreign Relations, September 21, 1988.
George, Alan, "Iran: Cut-Price Cruise Missiles," *International Defense Review*, March, 1993, pp. 15–16.
Gerardi, Greg, and Maryam Ahrinijad, "An Assessment of Iran's Nuclear Facilities," *Nonproliferation Review*, Spring–Summer, 1995, pp. 209–215.
Gerges, Fawaz, "Washington's Misguided Iran Policy," *Survival*, Winter, 1996–1997, pp. 154–158.
Goldberg, David, Foreign Science and Technology Center, US Army Intelligence Agency, testimony before the Committee on Governmental Affairs, US Senate, February 9, 1989.
Grimmett, Richard F., *Conventional Arms Transfers to the Third World*, Washington, Congressional Research Service, various editions.
Harris, Elisa D., "Chemical Weapons Proliferation in the Developing World," *RUSI and Brassey's Defense Yearbook, 1989*, London, 1988, pp. 67–88.
Hashim, Ahmed, "The Crisis of the Iranian State," Adelphi Paper 296, London, IISS, Oxford, July, 1995.
Herdman, Roger C., Director, *Technologies Underlying Weapons of Mass Destruction*, Office of Technology Assessment, US Congress, OTA-BP-ISC-115, Washington, GPO, December, 1993.
Hopkirk, Peter, *The Great Game*, New York, Kodansha Press, 1991.
Indyk, Martin, Graham Fuller, Anthony Cordesman, Phoebe Marr, "US Policy Towards Iran and Iraq," *Middle East Policy*, Vol. III, No. 4, 1994, pp. 1–27.
International Defense Review, various editions.
International Institute for Strategic Studies (IISS), *Military Balance*, various editions.
Iranian Journal of International Affairs, various editions.
Jacobs, Gordon, and Tim McCarthy, "China Missile Sales—Few Changes for the Future," *Jane's Intelligence Review*, December, 1992, pp. 559–563.
Jane's Defense Weekly, various editions.
Jane's Information Group, *Jane's Air-Launched Weapons*, London, Jane's Publishing, various editions.
———, *Jane's Aircraft Upgrades*, London, Jane's Publishing, various editions.
———, *Jane's All the World's Aircraft*, London, Jane's Publishing, various editions.
———, *Jane's All the World's Armies*, London, Jane's Publishing, various editions.
———, *Jane's Armor and Artillery*, London, Jane's Publishing, various editions.
———, *Jane's Avionics*, London, Jane's Publishing, various editions.
———, *Jane's C⁴I Systems*, London, Jane's Publishing, various editions.
———, *Jane's Fighting Ships*, London, Jane's Publishing, various editions.
———, *Jane's Helicopter Markets and Systems*, London, Jane's Publishing, various editions.
———, *Jane's Intelligence Review*, "Iran's Weapons of Mass Destruction," Special Report Number 6, May, 1995.
———, *Jane's Land-Based Air Defense*, London, Jane's Publishing, various editions.
———, *Jane's Military Communications*, London, Jane's Publishing, various editions.

———, *Jane's Military Vehicles and Logistics*, London, Jane's Publishing, various editions.
———, *Jane's Naval Weapons Systems*, London, Jane's Publishing, various editions.
———, *Jane's Radar and Electronic Warfare Systems*, London, Jane's Publishing, various editions.
———, *Jane's Sentinel: The Gulf States, 1997*, London, Jane's Publishing, various editions.
———, *Jane's Underwater Technology*, London, Jane's Publishing, various editions.
———, *Jane's Underwater Warfare Systems*, London, Jane's Publishing, various editions.
———, *Jane's Unmanned Aerial Vehicles and Targets*, London, Jane's Publishing, various editions.
———, *Jane's World Air Forces*, London, Jane's Publishing, various editions.
Jenkins, Loren, "Iraqis Press Major Battle in Gulf War," *Washington Post*, November 17, 1980.
Jordan, John, "The Iranian Navy," *Jane's Intelligence Review*, May, 1992, pp. 213–216.
Kan, Shirley A., "Chinese Proliferation of Weapons of Mass Destruction, Background and Analysis," Library of Congress, CRS-96-767F, September 13, 1996.
Katzman, Kenneth, "Iran: Arms and Technology Acquisitions," Library of Congress, CRS-97-474F, October 1, 1997.
———, "Iran: Current Developments and US Policy," Congressional Research Service, IB93033, September 9, 1994.
———, "Iran: Military Relations With China," Library of Congress, CRS-967-572F, June 26, 1996.
———, "Iran's Regional Strategy," DIA Symposium, August, 27, 1996.
———, *The Warriors of Islam: Iran's Revolutionary Guard*, Boulder, Westview, 1993.
Katzman, Kenneth, and Scott Modell, "Terrorism: Middle Eastern Groups and State Sponsors, 1997," Library of Congress, CRS-97-6924F, July 10, 1997.
Kemp, Geoffery, and Robert E. Harkavy, *Strategic Geography and the Changing Middle East*, Washington, Carnegie Endowment/Brookings, 1997.
Khalilzad, Zalmay M., David A. Shalpak, and Daniel L. Byman, *The Implications of the Possible End of the Arab-Israeli Conflict for Gulf Security*, Santa Monica, RAND, 1997.
Korb, Edward L., ed., *The World's Missile Systems, Seventh Edition*, General Dynamics, Pomona Division, April, 1982, pp. 223–226.
Kramer, Martin, "The Real Islamic Threat," *Survival*, Winter, 1996–1997, pp. 5–21.
Lenczowski, George, "Iran: The Big Debate," *Middle East Policy*, Vol. 2, No. 3, 1994, pp. 52–62.
Lumpe, Lora, Lisbeth Gronlund, and David C. Wright, "Third World Missiles Fall Short," *The Bulletin of the Atomic Scientists*, March, 1992, pp. 30–36.
Markov, David, "More Details Surface of Rubin's 'Kilo' Plans," *Jane's Intelligence Review*, May, 1997, pp. 209–215.
McCarthy, Tim, "China Missile Sales—Few Changes for the Future," *Jane's Intelligence Review*, December, 1992, pp. 559–563.
Middle East Economic Digest, various editions.
Milani, Mohsen M., *The Making of Iran's Islamic Revolution*, Boulder, Westview, 1994.
Miller, David, "Submarines in the Gulf," *Military Technology*, 6/1993, pp. 42–45.

Mullen Cook-Deegan, Dr. Robert, Physicians for Human Rights, testimony before the Committee on Governmental Affairs, US Senate, February 9, 1989.
Munson, Keith, *World Unmanned Aircraft*, London, Jane's Publishing, 1988.
Nagler, Dr. Robert A., *Ballistic Missile Proliferation: An Emerging Threat*, Arlington, Systems Planning Corporation, 1992.
Noorbaksh, Mehdi, "Political Islam, the Special Case of Iran," *Middle East Policy*, Vol. II, No. 3, 1993, pp. 78–97.
Office of the Assistant Secretary of Defense for International Security Affairs (Middle East and African Affairs), "United States Security Strategy for the Middle East," Washington, Department of Defense, May, 1995.
Office of Naval Intelligence, *Worldwide Challenges to Naval Strike Warfare*, Washington, Department of the Navy, January, 1996, p. 31.
Office of the Secretary of Defense, *Proliferation: Threat and Response*, Washington, Department of Defense, April, 1996.
Pawloski, Richard, *Changes in Threat Air Combat Doctrine and Force Structure, 24th Edition*, General Dynamics DWIC-91, Fort Worth Division, February, 1992, pp. I-85–I-117.
Physicians for Human Rights, "Winds of Death: Iraq's Use of Poison Gas Against Its Kurdish Population," Report of a Medical Mission to Turkish Kurdistan by Physicians for Human Rights, February, 1989.
Ramazani, R. K., "Iran's Foreign Policy: Both North and South," *The Middle East Journal*, Vol. 46, No. 3, Summer, 1992, pp. 393–413.
Rathmell, Dr. Andrew, *The Changing Military Balance in the Gulf*, London, Royal United Services Institute, Whitehall Papers 38, 1996.
———, "Iran's Rearmament: How Great a Threat?" *Jane's Intelligence Review*, July, 1994, pp. 317–322.
Roberts, Brad, *Terrorism With Chemical and Biological Weapons: Calibrating Risks and Responses*, Alexandria, Chemical and Biological Weapons Control Institute, 1997.
Roberts, Mark J., *Khomeini's Incorporation of the Iranian Military*, Washington, Institute for National Security Studies, National Defense University, January, 1996.
Russian Foreign Intelligence Service, *Treaty on the Non-Proliferation of Nuclear Weapons: Problems for Its Prolongation*, Moscow, Russian Foreign Intelligence Service, 1995.
Schwarzbach, David A., *Iran's Nuclear Program: Energy or Weapons?* Natural Resources Defense Council, Nuclear Weapons data book series, 1995.
———, "Iran's Nuclear Puzzle," *Scientific American*, June, 1997, pp. 62–65.
Shuey, Robert, and Shirley A. Kan, *Chinese Missile and Nuclear Proliferation*, Congressional Research Service, IB92056, October 4, 1994.
Smith, James, "Biological Weapons Developments," *Jane's Intelligence Review*, November, 1991, pp. 483–487.
Spector, Leonard S., Mark G. McDonough, and Evan S. Medeiros, *Tracking Nuclear Proliferation*, Washington, Carnegie Endowment, 1995.
Terrill, W. Andrew, "Chemical Weapons in the Gulf War," *Strategic Review*, Spring, 1986, pp. 51–58.
Timmerman, Kenneth R., *Weapons of Mass Destruction: The Cases of Iran, Syria, and Libya*, Los Angeles, Simon Wiesenthal Center, August, 1992, pp. 28–45.
United Nations Security Council, "Report of the Specialists Appointed to the Secretary General to Investigate the Allegations of the Islamic Republic of Iran Concerning

the Use of Chemical Weapons," United Nations Security Council, Document S 16433, March 26, 1984.

US Naval Institute, *The Naval Institute Guide to the Combat Fleets of the World, 1993: Their Ships, Aircraft, and Armament*, Annapolis, Naval Institute, various editions.

US State Department, *Country Reports on Human Rights Practices*, Annual Report to the US Senate Committee on Foreign Relations, February, various editions.

US State Department press release, "Joint US-PRC Statement on Missile Proliferation," Washington, October 4, 1994.

USCENTCOM, *Atlas, 1996*, MacDill Air Force Base, USCENTCOM, 1997.

Viorst, Milton, "Iran's Aging Revolution," *Foreign Affairs*, November–December, 1995, pp. 63–76.

Webster, William H., "Statement of the Honorable William H. Webster, Director, Central Intelligence Agency, Before the Committee on Governmental Affairs, Hearings on Global Spread of Chemical and Biological Weapons," February 9, 1989.

White, Gerald, *The Risk Report*, Vol. 1, No. 7, September, 1995.

Wootten, James P., "Terrorism: US Policy Options," Congressional Research Service, IB92074, October 6, 1994.

Wyllie, James, "Iran—Quest for Security and Influence," *Jane's Intelligence Review*, July, 1993, pp. 311–312.

Zaloga, Steven, "Ballistic Missiles in the Third World," *International Defense Review*, 11/1988, pp. 1423–1437.

Index

Abdullah, Crown Prince, 26
Abu Musa, 26
Afghanistan, 27; Taliban movement in, 28
Aflatoxin, 252, 254
Afshar, Alireza, 36
Aghazadeh, Gholamreza, 10
Aging weapons, 69–73
Ahmadian, Ali Akbar, 9, 208
Air/air defense, 76–77
Aircraft, 77, 79
Air defenses, ground-based, 176–83
Air force, 151–72, 288–91; command structure of, 151–52; modernization of, 163–67; readiness and quality of, 161–63; strength and organization of, 152–60; war-fighting capabilities of, 167–72
Air-to-air missiles, 164
Air-to ship missiles, 63, 72, 75, 77, 160, 167
Air-to-surface missiles, 165
Albright, Madeleine, 38, 231, 362
Amirabad Nuclear Research Center, 365, 367
Amphibious warfare, 141–43, 198–99, 209, 408
Amrollahi, Reza, 378

Anthrax, 236–37, 252, 357–58
Anti-aircraft weapons, 63, 77, 123–24
Anti-armored weapons, 113–14
Anti-ship missiles, 63, 72, 75, 77, 160, 191, 199–202
Anti-tank weapons, 76
Arab-Israeli peace process, 24
Armored forces, 99–114
Arms Control and Disarmament Agency, 41–42
Arms race, 26
Arms transfers: new agreements, 62–63; quality of, 63–69; quantity of, 55–61
Artillery, 66, 78, 114–23, 284–86; battlefield rocket launchers, 122–23; beyond visual range targeting capability of, 118; doctrine and proficiency, 123; mortars, 121; multiple rocket launchers, 121–22; self-propelled, 120–21; towed, 120–21
Atomic Energy Organization of Iran, 237, 364
Aviation industry, 79
Avionics, 69
AWACS airborne control system, 162
Azarazkhsh (Lightning) fighter, 77, 79, 167
Azerbaijan, 171

Bandar Abbas, 191
Bani Sadr, Abol Hassan, 34–35
Baqai, Habib, 151
Baqer-Zolqadr, Mohammed, 36
Basij (Population Mobilization Army), 92, 135–36
Battlefield rocket launchers, 122–23
Battle management, 126
Biological weapons, 4, 236–37, 252–56, 263, 280–83, 355–59
Biological Weapons Convention, 358
Black and gray markets, 72
Border guards, 137
Botulinum, 237, 252, 357
Britain, 21–22

Calutrons, 368
Centrifuge technology, 241, 256, 258
Chemical weapons, 4, 233–36, 248–51, 259, 262–63, 280, 337–51; possible stockpiles of, 345–46
Chemical Weapons Convention, 349–51
Chernomyrdin, Viktor, 67, 231
Chieftain tanks, 16
China, 227–28, 311–12; and nuclear technology, 73, 371–72; purchases from, 55, 63, 72; US dialogue with, 6
China Nuclear Energy Corporation, 243
Chinese aircraft, 163–64
Christopher, Warren, 362
Clinton, William Jefferson, 5–6, 67
Cockpit display, 164
Cohen, William, 14
Command structure, 275–77; competence and cohesion of, 39–40; internal security, 38–39; partial reform of, 35–36
Communications, 126
Computers, 69
CONOCO, 2
Conservatives, 1
Containment and deterrence, 414–15
Conventional arms, 55–80
Conventional war-fighting options, 217–19
Cook, Robin, 363
Corvettes, 193–94
Council of Guardians, 4

Creeping proliferation, 243, 264, 365, 369–78, 412
Cruise missiles, 232, 318–20

Defense Industries Organization, 74
Dehqan, Hussein, 36–37
Delivery systems, 223–33, 245–48, 258–59, 261–62, 272, 284–320, 334–35
Demonization, 2, 16–18
Destroyers, 192–93
"Devil's bargain," 25
Divisions, armored, 94
Dual-use biotech equipment, 357, 359

Eastern Europe, 55
Electronic warfare, 79, 124, 165, 168, 176, 180, 210
Ethnic division, 86–87, 137
European Union, 27, 362–63
Expediency Council, 3

Fighter planes, 77
Fire control systems, 115, 118
Firouzabadi, Hassan, 36
Fissile material, 387
Force development, 407–8
Frigates, 193

Gas and oil reserves, 376
General Command, 32
General Staff of the Armed Forces, 35–36
Genetic engineering, 359
Genocide, 28
"Glitter factor," 169
Global positioning system, 232, 319
Gore, Al, 67, 230–31
Grachev, Pavel, 68
The "Great Game," 21
Ground-based air defenses, 176–83
Ground crew training, 162
Gulf Cooperation Council, 24
Gulf forces: air force and air defense manpower of, 156; attack helicopters of, 159; combat aircraft of, 155, 157–58; confrontations, 408–10; ships of, 190

Gulf of Oman, 197; submarines in, 206
Gulf War, 1, 23

Hadayeq, Mohammed Razi, 14, 291
Hamas, 132
Hansani-Sadi, Hussein, 35–36
Hazaras, 28
Helicopter and army aviation forces, 124–26, 159
Hezbollah, 3, 7, 12–13, 27, 38–39, 132
Holum, John, 362, 365, 372, 386
Hormuz, Strait of, 16, 20, 168, 186, 200–201; channels of, 206
Hovercraft and coastal patrol craft, 195–96
Human wave attacks, 220

Indyck, Martin, 386
Internal Security, 38–39, 134–37
International Atomic Energy Agency, 10, 364, 382–85
International Institute of Strategic Studies, 42
International Monetary Fund, 42
Interoperability, 72, 140
Iran: aging weapons of, 69–73; air force of, 151–72; armored forces of, 99–114; artillery of, 114–23, 284–86; biological weapons of, 355–59; chemical weapons of, 337–51; conventional arms of, 55–80; defense of, 413; delivery systems of, 284–320; demonization of, 2, 16–18; expediency council of, 3; foreign intelligence operations of, 39; gas and oil reserve of, 376; ground-based air defenses of, 176–83; internal security of, 127, 129; land forces of, 93–143; military expenditures of, 40–52; military future of, 405–15; military industries of, 73–79; military leadership of, 31–52; military manpower of, 85–92; national security policy of, 7; naval forces of, 186–211; nuclear power program of, 10; nuclear war-fighting capabilities of, 387–89; nuclear weapons of, 362–89; oil boom of, 22–23; plans of, 271–77; ports of, 27; pragmatists of, 1; reasons for pursuing weapons of mass destruction, 265–70; repatriation of POWs of, 15–16; special forces of, 4; strategic goals of, 1; strategic perspective of, 20–29; strengths and weaknesses of, 79–80; threatening actions of, 2–4; war-fighting options of, 217–21, 346–49; and weapons of mass destruction, 222–64, 399–404
Iranian intelligence, 6–7
Iran-Iraq War, 1; defeat, 32; impact of, 337–41; and the tanker war, 3, 23; "war of the cities," 297
Iraq, 17; biological weapons of, 252–56; chemical weapons of, 248–51, 339–41; delivery systems of, 245–48; nuclear weapons of, 256–58
"Islamic bomb," 239, 363
Islamic Revolutionary Guards Corps (IRGC), 8, 32–38, 74, 126–35, 275–77; air elements of, 160; anti-ship missile systems of, 200; and biological weapons, 356; and chemical weapons, 341–42; naval branch of, 207–8; Quds (Qods) forces, 130–33; strength and combat units of, 128–30
Israel, 8; chemical weapons of, 259–60; delivery systems of, 258–59; intelligence systems of, 261; missile defenses of, 260–61; proxy wars against, 410–11

Jalali, Hosein, 37
Jannati, Ayatollah Mohammad, 12

Karbaschi, Gholamhoession, 11–12, 16
Khamenei, Ayatollah, 3, 5–6, 13, 33, 180
Kharrazi, Kamal, 8, 15, 28, 266–67; on nuclear weapons, 364–65
Khatami, Mohammad, 1–3, 16–17, 24–25, 310; and change, 4–13; defeats and victories of, 11–13, 40; election of, 405–6; national security appointments of, 9–11; on nuclear weapons, 363–64
Khomeini, Ayatollah, 26, 32–33
Kilo-class submarines, 203–6
Kraftwerke Union, 367, 369
Kurdish groups, 27, 38, 341
Kuwait, invasion of, 23

Land forces, 93–143; anti-aircraft weapons, 123–24; anti-armored weapons, 113–14; armored, 111–12; command structure and deployments, 99; communications and battle management, 126; contingency capabilities of, 141–43; helicopter and army aviation forces, 124–26; main battle tanks, 103–11; major combat formations, 94–99; major weapons and equipment, 133; need for improvements, 141; war-fighting capabilities of, 137–43
Laser isotope separation, 367
Law Enforcement Forces of the Islamic Republic, 38
Light tanks, 111
Linguistic divisions, 86–87
Long-range missile programs, 284–320
Long-range reconnaissance assets, 277
Look-down/shoot-down capabilities, 164
Low-intensity combat, 142

Main battle tanks, 103–11
Maintenance, 72
Majlis (Consultative Assembly), 3, 7–8
Major combat formations, 94–99
Manpower management, 91–92
Marine units, 187
Martyrdom, 32
Midget submarines, 203
MIG-29s, 164, 166
MIG-27s, 16
Military electronics, 79, 124, 165, 168
Military exercises, 28–29
Military expenditures, 40–52
Military forces, control and leadership of, 31–52
Military industries, 73–79
Military manpower, 85–92
Mine warfare, 4, 196–98, 205
Ministry of Intelligence and Security, 34
Missile patrol boats, 194–95
Missiles, 4, 78, 246–48; air-to-air, 164; air-to-surface, 165; anti-aircraft, 63, 176–83, 233; anti-ship, 63, 72, 75, 77, 160, 167, 191, 199–202, 231–32; anti-tank, 112; Chinese option, 311–12; defenses, 260–61; Hawk, 16; Iranian production programs, 317–20; long-range, 284–320; manportable, 124; Phoenix, 161; purchased from China, 63; Russian option, 312–16; surface-to-surface, 152, 223–31, 291–317
Missile Technology Control Regime, 308, 312–13
Moderates, 1
Mohajerani, Ataollah, 8
Mohtaj, Abbas, 9, 14
Mortars, 121
Multiple rocket launchers, 121–22
Mussadiq, Mohammed, 22
Mycotoxins, 236, 355–56

Narcotics, 28
Naval forces, 186–211; air capabilities, 199; amphibious warfare, 198–99; anti-ship missiles, 199–202; capabilities of, 208–11; corvettes, 193–94; destroyers, 192–93; frigates, 193; hovercraft and coastal patrol craft, 195–96; IRGC branch of, 207–8; manpower, 189; mine warfare, 196–98, 205; missile patrol boats, 194–95; patrol and fast attack craft, 195, 207–8; ships, 188; submarines, 16, 66, 202–6
Nerve gas, 233–36, 248–51, 259, 262–63, 280
No-Dong 1, 303–4
North Korea, 4, 55, 302–6
Nouri, Abdoullah, 8, 12
Nuclear Non-Proliferation Treaty, 268, 366, 378–85
Nuclear technology, 73
Nuclear weapons, 237–45, 256–58, 260, 263–64, 272, 281–83, 362–89; possible dates for acquisition of, 385–87
Nye, Joseph S., 40, 222

Oghabae'i, Abdollah, 135
Oil, 22–23; revenues, 51–52
Opposition movements, 127
Organization of Islamic Countries Conference, 2, 13

Pakistan, nuclear tests of, 266
Palestinian Islamic Jihad, 27, 132

Paramilitary forces, 135–37
Patriot missiles, 260
Peay, Binford, 386
People's Mujahideen, 5, 14, 25, 27, 171, 380
Perry, William, 386
Phoenix missiles, 161
Pilot quality, 162
Pipelines, 27
Plutonium separation, 241, 368, 370
Ports, 27
Power projection, 209
Pragmatists, 1
Primakov, Yevgeny, 132
Prisoners of war, 24
Professionalism, 21, 94
Proliferation: creeping, 243, 246, 365, 369–78, 412; denial of, 267–68; Iran's reasons for, 268–70; and the Nuclear Non-Proliferation Treaty, 378–85; and regional security, 404
Proxy wars, 410–11

Qalibaf, Mohammad Bagher, 309
Quds (Qods) forces, 130–33

Radar, 69
Radiological weapons, 257, 388–89
Rafsanjani, Ali Akbar Hashemi, 1, 3, 26; creeping proliferation under, 369–78; and the General Command, 32–36; and military expenditures, 51; on nuclear weapons, 363
Reactive armor, 75
Reactor deals: Chinese, 371–72; Russian, 372–74
Reconnaissance aircraft, 160; stealth drones, 187
Redd, John Scott, 201
Reflagging, 23
Religious differences, 28, 86–87
Remotely piloted reconnaissance system, 14
Rezaei, Moshen, 20, 24, 134, 301
Reza Shah, 21
Riots, 135–36
Rocker launchers, 121–23, 286–88
Russia, 21–22, 230; and ground-based air defense, 181–83; and missile development, 308–9, 312–16; reactor deals, 372–78; as a supplier, 63–68, 164–65, 172, 227

Safavi, Yahya Rahim, 10–11, 37, 134
Sanctification, 16–18
Sarin, 357
Satellites, 305; deception techniques, 380
Sattari, Mansour, 35, 151, 161
Saudi Arabia, 26, 152; mechanized forces of, 102
Scenario-driven analysis, 405–7
Scorpion tanks, 16
Scud B missile, 291–301
Scud C missile, 301–2
Self-propelled guns, 76, 120–21
Shahdid Industrial Complex, 75
Shah Mohammad Reza Pahlavi, 2, 21; after Mussadiq, 22–23
Shahroud, 307
Shamkani, Ali, 9
Shatt al-Arab, 23
Shihab missiles, 306, 309–10
Shi'ite sect, 24
Short range air defense systems (SHORADS), 140
Siemens, 373
South Africa, 366
Special forces, 4
Special Operations Council, 34
Standardization, 66–67, 72, 140
Stealth reconnaissance drones, 187
Strait of Hormuz, 16, 20, 168, 186, 200–201; channels of, 206
Submarines, 16, 66, 202–6; in the Gulf of Oman, 206
Sukhoi 24 fighters, 16
Supreme Council for Military Policy, 36
Supreme Council for National Security, 7, 34
Surface navy, 187–96
Su-24s, 165–66
Syria: biological weapons of, 263; chemical weapons of, 262–63; delivery systems of, 261–63; nuclear program of, 263–64

Table of organization and equipment, of an armored division, 94
Taliban movement, 28–29
Tanker war, 3; and reflagging, 23–24
Tanks: Chieftain, 16, 113; main battle, 103–11; Scorpion, 16, 111; for unconventional warfare, 78; Zulfiqar, 75
Tapeo Dong missiles, 304–6
Targeting capability, 118, 277
Terrorism, 3–5, 27, 35, 127, 131–32, 219, 329–30, 401
Torkan, Akbar, 34, 161–62
Towed artillery, 120–21
Training, 140; advanced, 169; ground crew, 162; joint, 138–39; lack of, 72, 87–88; of terrorist forces, 143
Transport jets, 77
Tritium, 370
Tube artillery, 120–21

UN Coalition, 41
Unconventional war-fighting options, 219, 401–4, 411–12
United Arab Emirates, 23
United States, 22, 24; Central Command, 91; military forces, 21; and Russian arms sales, 67
Uranium deposits, 367
Uranium dioxide, 368
Urban warfare, 134

War-fighting options, 273–74, 279
War games, 14
Wars of intimidation, 413–14
Weaponization problems, 304
Weapons of mass destruction, 222–64, 329–30; biological, 4, 236–37; chemical, 4, 233–36, 248–51, 259, 262–63, 280, 337–51; delivery systems, 223–33, 245–48, 258–59, 261–62, 284–320, 334–35; future of, 412–13; Iranian reasons for pursuing, 265–70; Iraq's search for, 245–58; uncertain implications of, 399. *See also* Nerve gas; Nuclear weapons

Yellow cake, 366–67
Yeltsin, Boris, 67, 230, 313

Zulfiqar tank, 75–76, 110

About the Author

ANTHONY H. CORDESMAN is Senior Fellow and Co-director of the Middle East Program at the Center for Strategic and International Studies, and a special consultant on military affairs for ABC News. The author of numerous books on Middle Eastern security issues, he has served in senior positions for the secretary of defense, NATO, and the United States Senate.